D1431948

The Late Tang

Chinese Poetry of the Mid-Ninth Century

(827–860)

Harvard East Asian Monographs 264

The Late Tang

Chinese Poetry of the Mid-Ninth Century

(827–860)

Stephen Owen

Published by the Harvard University Asia Center
Distributed by Harvard University Press
Cambridge (Massachusetts) and London 2006

Printed in the United States of America

The Harvard University Asia Center publishes a monograph series and, in coordination with the Fairbank Center for East Asian Research, the Korea Institute, the Reischauer Institute of Japanese Studies, and other faculties and institutes, administers research projects designed to further scholarly understanding of China, Japan, Vietnam, Korea, and other Asian countries. The Center also sponsors projects addressing multidisciplinary and regional issues in Asia.

Library of Congress Cataloging-in-Publication Data

Owen, Stephen, 1946–

The late Tang : Chinese poetry of the mid-ninth century (827-860) / Stephen Owen.

p. cm. -- (Harvard East Asian monographs ; 264)

Includes bibliographical references and index.

ISBN 0-674-02137-1 (alk. paper)

1. Chinese poetry--Tang dynasty, 618-907--History and criticism.

I. Title. II. Title: Chinese poetry of the mid-ninth century (827-860)

PL2321.094135 2006

895.1'148--dc22

2006024793

Index by Christopher J. Dankin

♾ Printed on acid-free paper

Last figure below indicates year of this printing

16 15 14 13 12 11 10 09 08 07 06

for

Tian Xiaofei,

beloved wife and companion in poetry

Acknowledgments

No matter how solitary one is in working, "acknowledgements" are a way of remembering the degree to which academic books, like the poems discussed in this book, grow out of a social fabric. Some chapters of this book made their first appearance at talks and conferences, at "New Perspectives on the Tang" held at Princeton in spring of 2002 and in a Hsiang Lecture at McGill in the fall of the same year. Other chapters took shape through a seminar on Li Shangyin. To all those who offered comments I owe a dept of thanks. I want to thank my student Wangling Jinghua for proofreading the Chinese texts and Chris Dakin of the University of Washington for making the index, both with meticulous care. Finally I would like to thank my wife, Tian Xiaofei, whose learning and sense of poetry has been a constant joy throughout the process of writing, in scholarship as in life.

S.O.

Contents

The Late Tang

Chinese Poetry of the Mid-Ninth Century

(827–860)

Introduction

Latecomers

杜牧, 齊安郡晚秋
Du Mu, Late Autumn in the District Offices at Qi'an[1]

柳岸風來影漸疏	Winds come to willow-lined shores, the reflections grow gradually sparser,
使君家似野人居	the governor's home is like where someone lives in the wilds.
雲容水態還堪賞	I can still enjoy the look of the clouds and charm of the waters,
嘯志歌懷亦自如	I whistle my aims, sing my cares, and do as I please.
雨暗殘燈棋欲散	Rains darken the dying lamp, soon the chess pieces will be removed,
酒醒孤枕雁來初	I sober up on my pillow alone, the geese begin to come.
可憐赤壁爭雄渡	I am moved how at Red Cliff, the crossing where heroes contended,
唯有簑翁坐釣魚	there is only an old man in a raincoat, sitting and fishing.

In the spring of 842 the forty-year-old Du Mu went to take up his new post as governor of Huangzhou, sometimes known as Qi'an, on the northern bank of the Yangzi River in modern Hubei. The prefecture was believed to include the famous site of the Battle of Red Cliff. The story of that battle was well known. It was recounted in the *Account of the Three Kingdoms* 三國志, the standard history of the period, and was

---

1. 28153; Feng 208.

probably already part of popular storytelling traditions. It was to Red Cliff that Cao Cao brought his great northern army, preparing to cross the Yangzi and invade the southern kingdom of Wu. He had an invasion fleet readied there, secured with iron chains against the winds and currents.

Young Zhou Yu, the admiral of Wu's Yangzi River fleet, was charged with stopping the invasion. Knowing that Cao Cao was awaiting a grain shipment, Zhou Yu gathered fire boats and disguised them as grain transport vessels, screening his own war fleet. The whole plan depended on an east wind, and the wind did indeed blow from the east that day. When the "grain ships" came in close, they were set ablaze and the fire quickly spread through Cao Cao's chained fleet. With his fleet gone, Cao Cao had no choice but to retreat north again, leaving Wu sovereign in the Southland.

In the mid-ninth century Huangzhou was a small, poor prefecture—certainly not the worst of prefectural assignments, but far from the best. Du Mu once described it with ironic affection as "the place where I got enough sleep," and that captures the spirit of the first part of the poem, with the wind blowing the leaves off the willow trees along the shore, gradually opening vistas but creating a mess in the governor's residence. With a characteristic mellowness, the poet can enjoy both the scenery and his life here.

What Du Mu gives us in the penultimate line is by no means new in Late Tang poetry, but it is a poetic trope that appears so often in this period that it seems to have had a special resonance for the age. This is a scene of absence invoked in saying it is no longer there. In this case the scene of absence is one of battle and burning war galleys, which becomes a ghostly backdrop on which the present figure of an old fisherman is superimposed. Absorbed in his fishing, the old fisherman clearly shares the mood of the world with the governor, our poet. The difference is, of course, that only the poet sees in his mind's eye the ancient fleet in flames at the same time as he sees the old fisherman.

Such juxtapositions create relationships that are significant: in the old fisherman we see diminution, a tiny figure in a large landscape, in comparison to the great battle involving fleets and flames; we see aging, an old man in late autumn; we see vanished glory and in its place a quiet tranquility. This figure of the old fisherman is not just anyone: he has his own cultural and poetic history. Although he is anonymous, he made his appearance many times before Du Mu's poem: he was Taigong the fisherman, recognized by King Wen of the Zhou and made his minister and architect of the Zhou conquest of the Shang; he was the fisherman whom Qu Yuan later encountered and who advised Qu Yuan not to worry about his misunderstood virtue but rather to go with the times. He had signified too many things to refer to only one thing here: he may be poetically ambiguous, but he is definitely "poetic." A few decades earlier he made a winter appearance in Liu Zongyuan's 柳宗元 most famous poem, entitled "River Snow" 江雪:[2]

千山鳥飛絕	A thousand mountains, flights of birds are gone,
萬徑人蹤滅	ten thousand paths, the tracks of people vanished.
孤舟簑笠翁	In a lone boat an old man in rain hat and raincoat
獨釣寒江雪	fishes alone in the snow of the cold river.

The old fisherman was a quintessentially poetic figure, evocative and overdetermined. He is the figure here defined by a distance of perspective, a figure replacing a scene of violence in Du Mu's poem. The perspective he lends to the past battle is anticipated in the image of the chess pieces removed from the board, literally "scattered." In this we have both an aftermath of conflict and its formal displacement into a game. The figurative "storm" of an age of warfare becomes a literal rainstorm whose shadowy clouds darken the chessboard. This is the "work" of poetry: taking turbulence and transforming it into beautiful patterns and images, reconfiguring it.

Du Mu's contemporary Wen Tingyun used exactly the same trope of superimposition in a song about Han emperor Wu's naval maneuvers on Kunming Lake, near Chang'an, where through symbolic intimidation and sympathetic magic Emperor Wu overwhelms the enemy kingdom of Tianchi (in the far southwest). The Han emperor is the descendent of the Crimson Dragon, first appearing as a rippling reddish reflection, followed by his galleys and warriors.

溫庭筠, 昆明治水戰詞
Wen Tingyun, Lyrics for the Naval Maneuvers on Lake Kunming[3]

汪汪積水光連空	A vast flood of massed waters, light stretching off to the sky,

---

2. 18520; Wang Guo'an 268.
3. 31900; Zeng 32.

重疊細紋交澈紅	fine patterns in endless folds, crisscrossing ripples red.
赤帝龍孫鱗甲怒	The Crimson Emperor's dragon-spawn, scaled armor in rage,
臨流一晒生陰風	glares out on flowing waters, giving off shadowy wind.
鼉鼓三聲報天子	Three sounds from the lizard-skin drum announce the Son of Heaven,
雕旗獸艦凌波起	eagle banners and beast-headed galleys rise up over the waves.
雷吼濤驚白若山	Thunder roars out, breakers surge, white as mountains,
石鯨眼裂蟠蛟死	the eyes of the Stone Leviathan split, coiling krakens die.
滇池海浦俱喧豗	On Tianchi's seashore all is howling and shrieking,
青翰畫鷁相次來	green-winged painted cormorant prows come in succession.
箭羽槍纓三百萬	Fletched arrows and spear tassels, three million strong,
踏翻西海生塵埃	trample over the Western Sea until dust rises from it.

Then, in the last stanza, Wen Tingyun turns back to the present:

茂陵僊去菱花老	The immortal of Maoling has gone away, water-chestnut blooms grow old,
唼唼游魚近煙島	swimming fish make bubbles in water near to misty isles.
渺莽殘陽釣艇歸	In a vast expanse of fading sunlight a fishing skiff turns home,
綠頭江鴨眠沙草	and green-headed river ducks sleep among sandy grasses.

Maoling was Emperor Wu's tomb, and no one would miss the irony of calling him the "immortal of Maoling," especially considering Emperor Wu's passionate quest for immortality. The past invoked in the first stanzas of the poem does not involve actual violence but rather a theatrical display of martial prowess. It has its own poetic beauty, invoked only to be replaced by a different kind of poetic beauty found in the present. That expanse of water is again still; the bird-headed prows of ancient war galleys are replaced by green-headed ducks asleep; and there, in the fading sunlight, is the fishing boat with the poetic old fisherman.

The poetry of the Late Tang often looked backward, and many poets of the period distinguished themselves by the intensity of their retrospective gaze. Beguiling moments of the past, both historical and poetic, caught their attention and haunted their present. Chinese poets, like their premodern European counterparts, had always looked backward to some degree, but for many Late Tang poets the echoes and traces of the past had a singular aura. In this sense the "Late Tang" deserves to be called "late." Our study ends around 860, so one cannot say that these poets felt the approaching end of the dynasty—though they were certainly aware that the polity was in serious trouble. Their "lateness" was primarily a sense of cultural belatedness, standing in the shadow of past masters of poetry and past glory.

The reign of Xuanzong 玄宗 (beginning in the second decade of the eighth century and lasting until the An Lushan Rebellion of 755) was already a legendary period of splendor by the mid-ninth century. Poets active after the An Lushan Rebellion, who were later associated with the Dali 大曆 Reign (766–779), were the model of classical grace and formal restraint for the craftsmen of regulated verse. Next came the Mid-Tang poets, who were associated with the Yuanhe 元和 Reign (806–820); these poets left a rich heritage of invention, mapping out new directions for poetry, a heritage against which many younger poets reacted but which loomed large in the recent past. By the time our study begins in the mid-820s, there was already a century of memorable poetry in the immediate past.

Accounts of Late Tang poetry inevitably must address the question of how the period term is being used. Originally the term "Late Tang" was applied to the entire century and a half following the An Lushan Rebellion of 755; in other words, it encompassed the entire second half of the dynasty. This was obviously useless in defining a period, not only in the context of literature but in all areas of historical study. Gao Bing's 高棅 (1350–1423) *Tangshi pinhui* 唐詩品彙 of 1393 helped to institutionalize the idea of a "Mid-Tang," which ended with the Yuanhe generation. Roughly the last seventy-five years of the dynasty thus became the "Late Tang." The invention of a "Mid-Tang" helped to account for the very striking differences between the famous poets of the Yuanhe generation and those that followed, differences about which poets active in the second quarter of the century were intensely conscious. Many centuries of critical discourse on the history of Tang poetry have made these makeshift periods seem true and self-evident. The actual record, however, complicates the easy periodization.

Literary historians like to characterize periods in general terms. In part because of the amount of Late Tang poetry that has survived and also because of the social and geographical dispersal of poetic production, we find that poetry was going in various directions during this period, developing a diversity that defies simple characterization. We can see groups of poets that share common interests, new fashions emerging, particular locales as centers of poetic production, and specific individuals following their own singular paths irrespective of contemporary poetic fashions. In other words, when we look closely, there is no coherent "Late Tang" except as a span of years.

Even considered as a mere span of years the idea of the Late Tang presents problems when we look for its boundaries in literary culture. Considering the "Tang" part of the term, the Late Tang should conclude with the formal end of the dynasty in 907—even though the dynasty had been no more than a shadow court for several decades, with many poets working in the provinces and regional courts that would become the Five Dynasties. If, however, we look for a major change in literary culture and the world of poetry, we do not find it until the emergence of the group of poets around Ouyang Xiu 歐陽修 in the second quarter of the eleventh century. If we do not worry too much about the "Tang" part of our period term, we could easily see Late Tang poetry as lasting two centuries, not unlike the span of the late Southern Dynasties poetic style, which also crossed a period of transition and the establishment of a new, stable regime.

When poetry finally underwent a major change in the second quarter of the eleventh century, Ouyang Xiu quite consciously modeled his literary group on that of Han Yu, returning to the Yuanhe generation at the beginning of the ninth century. The deaths of the major figures of the Yuanhe generation and the marked rejection of their poetic styles should give us a clear beginning for the Late Tang (though, as we will see, Bai Juyi and Liu Yuxi lived on for decades). That moment of reaction and redirection of poetic interests does indeed mark a period change.

We will begin our study in that period of change in the mid-820s and carry it through to roughly 860. This latter date is one of convenience rather than the mark of a moment of change. During this interval spanning roughly thirty-five years, a group of old men—holdovers of the Yuanhe generation—were still writing prolifically; Jia Dao perfected a craft of regulated verse that brought him a century and a half of devoted followers; and the three poets who have come to define Late Tang poetry—Du Mu, Li Shangyin, and Wen Tingyun—composed almost all their poems. Of those three Li Shangyin and Wen Tingyun went largely unrecognized as poets in their own lifetimes; and Du Mu, though prominent, shared the stage with many other poets whose names have largely been forgotten.

During this period the Tang did not seem in danger of imminent collapse, though toward the end of the period local rebellions had begun to break out. The process of dynastic disintegration had started and would accelerate in succeeding decades. After Huang Chao occupied Chang'an early in 881, the Tang was only a regional power, though it retained a nostalgic aura that still brought young men from far places seeking the prestige of the empty bureaucratic titles that the dynasty still had the power to confer. There is much poetry after 860 that is worthy of consideration. It is easy to read the poetry of this later period with an eye to the momentous events that were occurring, but the vast majority of poems composed during this period simply carry on the kinds of poetry created in the period encompassed by our study. It was a poetry that may have been traumatically ossified. If we wish to uncover the relation between the history of poetry and the larger sense of "history," we may find it not in changes in poetry but in poetry's refusal to change, in its fine couplets, its absorption in pleasures both poetic and sensual.

Chang'an, the great city, was doomed. We know virtually nothing about the monk called Zilan 子蘭 except that he was writing at the end. The first couplet of the following poem could have been written at any time, whereas the second evokes a moment like no other in Chang'an.

子蘭, 長安早秋
Zilan, Early Autumn in Chang'an[4]

風舞槐花落御溝	The wind sets the ash flowers dancing, they fall in the royal moat,
終南山色入城秋	the colors of Zhongnan Mountain enter the city autumnal.

---

4. 44998.

閭閭走馬徵兵急	Horses gallop past every gate urgently calling up troops,
公子笙歌醉玉樓	while the songs and pipes of young nobles make marble mansions drunk.

The last line echoes a famous line by Li Bai, composed in happier times but now containing a dark irony. We cannot date with any certainty the following poem in relation to the preceding one, but it is hard not to read it in seasonal sequence. We know that when Huang Chao's army entered Chang'an in 881, he was at first welcomed. During the sack of the city and the subsequent battles over possession of the city between loyalist forces and Huang Chao's army, the citizens of Chang'an were as terrible as any army.

子蘭, 長安傷春

Zilan, Pain at Spring in Chang'an[5]

霜隕中春花半無	Frost descends in mid-spring, half the flowers are gone
狂遊恣飲盡兇徒	running amok, drinking wildly, the mob rages everywhere.
年年賞玩公卿輩	Lords and grandees who year after year enjoyed this season
今委溝塍骨漸枯	are now left to lie in ditches and fields, bones gradually stripped bare.

We see here vividly depicted the death of Chang'an. Yet the poems written at those parties before the fall—while the horses were galloping outside conscripting men for the defense of the city—were probably very much like the ones we will read here. This same poetry may have continued mimetically in the provinces during the Five Dynasties; but the society in which the poetry was first created was dead, bodies left rotting in the ditches and fields.

Although the diversity of the poetry between the mid-820s and 860 permits no single overall characterization, we do see new values and interests emerging. In most cases we can trace the roots of these new phenomena to an earlier period, and all continue through the ninth century into the tenth. We have already commented on the backward gaze

---

5. 45002.

of Late Tang poets and their fascination with the poetic and cultural past. Poets had a particular fascination with the later Southern Dynasties; it is tempting to see in this a sense of doom hanging over the dynasty, but this was probably true only indirectly. They were fascinated with absorption in various modes, and the image of heedless absorption in poetry and pleasure presented by the Southern Dynasties provoked an ambivalence that both attracted them and demanded censure.

Absorption was a way of excluding the larger world, of looking inward and isolating a particular object or domain. Figures of absorption play an important role in the representations of poets and poetry during this period. We witness a growing sense of poetry as a separate sphere of activity, demanding absolute commitment, with the "poet" as a distinct type. Poetry continued to flourish as a shared practice among a wide cross-section of the Tang elite, but we find groups who celebrated their devotion to poetry as a vocation, matched by a growing contempt for "poets" by some in court circles.[6] As poetry became a separate sphere of commitment, like the vocation of a Buddhist monk, poets began to think of their poetry in terms of an accumulation, a "legacy," based on the model of amassing land and goods or the "merit" accumulated over a lifetime of official service or Buddhist practice. Few poets are as different as Bai Juyi and Jia Dao, but in both we find scenes involving contemplation of their own accumulated poetic production in the form of physical manuscripts. Already in the 810s Yuan Zhen was working on preparing versions of his literary collection, followed by Bai Juyi, who produced multiple manuscript copies with ongoing updated editions and supplements. By mid-century editing one's own poetry had become widespread, along with the production of subcollections of poems on special topics that might not be included in an author's main collection.

One form of absorption in poetry was devotion to the craft of the perfect parallel couplet and a celebration of the effort and concentration it demanded. As we will see, such carefully crafted couplets are usually framed by more discursive, straightforward couplets, sometimes

---

6. The Southern Song critic Yan Yu strongly disapproved of Late Tang poetry, but by his age the changes that had occurred in the period had been so deeply assimilated that they were taken for granted. Thus, Yan Yu insists that poetry should be *danghang* 當行, probably as close as classical Chinese comes to "professional."

showing an influence from the vernacular (the latter element was often even more salient in the last part of the ninth century). We see a growing divergence and tension between registers, along with disapproving comments on the low register that was championed by Bai Juyi. In this opposition of registers we first glimpse a sense of the "poetic" or "classical," which would have profound consequences in later literary culture, whether the "classical" was held up as a standard to be followed or condemned as artificial. Earlier there had simply been "poetry" with a wide range of registers, one of which was usually used consistently in a poem; mixed-register poetry heightened the contrast between "high" and "low."

We begin by "Setting the Stage" (Chapter 1), supplying the political historical background, introducing the poets, and addressing how the literary record of the period was shaped by the preservation of texts. We then turn to "The Old Men" (Chapter 2), the elderly members of the Yuanhe generation, of whom Bai Juyi was the most prominent, who continued to write prolifically into the 840s. Bai Juyi's militant casualness was a transformation of Yuanhe poetic values that helped articulate opposing values among the craftsmen of "Regulated Verse in the Short Line" (Chapter 3). In this chapter we first address some of the larger issues in this conservative tradition and then discuss individual poets in the circle around Yao He and Jia Dao in "The Craftsmen of Poetry" (Chapter 4).

In "The Legacy of Li He" (Chapter 5) we look at the impact of the recovery and dissemination of Li He's poetry in the early 830s. In "Regulated Verse in the Long Line" (Chapter 6) we examine the way in which the "personality" and history of a poetic genre shaped poetic production, using the Late Tang "meditation on the past," *huaigu* 懷古, as an illustrative example. Here we can clearly see how later poets borrowed from and transformed the work of their predecessors. In "Poets of the Long Line" (Chapter 7) we look at some poets who were known for their work in regulated verse in the long line, which enjoyed renewed popularity after the middle of the 830s. During the late 830s and 840s these poets all exchanged poems with Du Mu, whose work is the subject of the following chapter (Chapter 8).

In "Daoism: The Case of Cao Tang" (Chapter 9) we examine some of the works of this Daoist poet, presenting an eroticized and romanticized poetry on the immortals, which sets the stage for the succeeding chapters on the poetry of Li Shangyin (Chapters 10–14). After an introductory section on the problems of interpretation in Li Shangyin's poetry, we discuss his hermetic poetry, "poems on history," "poems on things," and those occasional poems that can be dated. In these chapters we try to situate his poetry in the discursive context of his age. Our final chapter takes up the poetry of Wen Tingyun (Chapter 15) and the division of poetry into specialized "types," which may have had significant consequences for what was preserved in the literary record for other poets.

Rather than making generalizations about the period as a whole, I have tried to be as historically specific as possible, always paying attention to the way the Tang poetic legacy was textually preserved.

This book is deeply indebted to Chinese scholarship of the past quarter century, and most of all to the work of Fu Xuancong, whose extensive work on biography and dating of Tang poets and poetry is the groundwork that made a study like this one possible. We know far more now than we did thirty years ago when I was working on the Early Tang and High Tang.

At the same time, this book is essentially different from the kind of work that has been done by Chinese scholars. Although these differences will no doubt be attributed to a "Western" viewpoint, part of my intention is to reconcile a division within Chinese scholarship itself, between the precise work on the lives and dates of poets and poems, on the one hand, and, on the other, the kinds of generalizations that are made about this very long period, which has, through a complex historical accident, been labeled as a single entity, namely, the "Late Tang." The richness of the record and the efforts of scholars (of whom there are many) like Fu Xuancong now make it possible to look at a delimited period in greater detail. Thanks to this process, we can see clearly the shortcomings of the received categories according to which the literary history of the period has been written.

To take just one example, instead of using a general term like "schools," *pai* 派, to describe associations of poets, we see a variety of quite distinct cultural phenomena: groups of friends of roughly the same age (such as the circle around Bai Juyi); younger poets seeking and finding the approbation of established older poets (such as the circle around Yao He and Jia Dao); a dead poet's works entering circulation and exerting an influence (Li He); and the reevaluation and resurgent influence of a poet largely rejected by the previous generation (as in Pi Rixiu's admiration for Bai Juyi). These are all distinct literary historical phenomena and not simply "schools." We see poets who write essentially one kind of poetry, and those who write in all the styles then available. Instead of "schools" we can now see more clearly the dynamics of literary historical interaction among poets.

This study also addresses issues that do not follow directly from recent Chinese scholarship. Although excellent in tracing the lineage of printed editions, Chinese scholarship has been less interested in issues of manuscript culture and, in particular, the question of how the manuscript legacy emerged in the Northern Song and the way in which particular sources mediate our image of what survives. If our study often turns to these issues of early manuscript transmission, it is because this is an essential part of literary history that has too often been ignored. If a poet like Li Kuo 李廓 was known to be an associate of Jia Dao and Yao He yet his extant poems are all *fengliu* 風流 (an untranslatable term that combines sensuality, melancholy, and swashbuckling panache), the reason may simply be the focus of the particular anthology where those poems were preserved. If we have a poet whose extant works are primarily quatrains, it may have nothing to do with a predilection for quatrains but rather simply be the consequence of Hong Mai having had a more comprehensive edition than that which now survives and having copied all the quatrains into his large anthology of Tang quatrains. We also have many tantalizing surviving texts that remind us—by their very limitations—of a larger and more diverse world of poetic production in the Late Tang, material that has largely been lost.

Perhaps the most difficult problem in engaging Chinese scholarship on Late Tang poetry is the case of Li Shangyin, where there is more scholarship and a longer history than all the other poets combined. "Li Shangyin studies" is a field unto itself and deals with questions that have arisen through centuries of research. I have tried to learn the field well enough to engage it when it is relevant to my purposes, while at the same time maintaining enough of a distance that I do not find myself attempting to answer questions that cannot be answered or recapitulating the arguments of others in such attempts. Rather than seeking answers to old questions, I want to focus attention on how the poems themselves generate such questions and, at the same time, refuse the possibility of an answer. I would also like to situate Li Shangyin's poetry in the context of contemporary poetry and the problems of manuscript culture. We owe our Li Shangyin to one man, Yang Yi, who was often maligned as a writer by the generation that followed him. His singular devotion to reconstituting Li Shangyin's poetry—given force by a social network that could ferret out manuscripts in far-flung places—stands as an example of what might have been the case with other poets if they had had such an editor.

There are other ways the present book could have been written. Had this book already been available to me, or had I understood the period in the way I came to understand it through the process of writing the book, I probably would have preferred to write it differently. However, before one can follow such interesting alternative approaches in an informed way, it is necessary to sort out the poets, the generations, the changing values and fashions, and the mediation of manuscript transmission. Without such a process of elementary sorting, critical work on Late Tang poetry is trapped in anachronisms, such as not paying attention to who was writing when or not distinguishing between our own sense of a poet's importance and the way the world of poetry looked at the time. Anecdotes from the end of the ninth and tenth centuries (especially when incorporated into standard historical sources) cannot be taken as mid-ninth-century fact.

Despite the length of this book, there are many additional chapters that I feel I ought to have written. There are other poets I should have discussed, such as the much maligned Xu Ning 徐凝. There are also a large number of poets whose careers began in the period under study but who lived on to be very productive in the 860s, 870s, and even beyond. A certain amount of triage was necessary. The two great women poets of the ninth century, Xue Tao 薛濤 and Yu Xuanji 魚玄機, fall outside this period, one earlier and the other later. The temptation to include Yu Xuanji was particularly strong, but to do so would have brought me into Yizong's reign and forced me to include a large number of contemporaries who could easily have doubled the size of the present book.

Among the other directions this book might have taken, types and situations of poetry would have been fruitful to pursue. Poetry on music and the *jinü* 妓女 ("entertainers" and often bonded courtesans) is particularly rich during this period. A chapter on "teasing" poems, *chao* 嘲, would have been useful, though I treat them briefly in the first part of the chapter on Wen Tingyun. There is much more to be done, and I can only hope this book will serve as a useful starting point.

Over the years I have abandoned and returned to literary history many times. Each time I have come back to it, literary history has seemed different, though with some constancy of questions that bring me back to it and allow me to call it by the same name. The differences are in part a consequence of changes in the scholar who comes back to literary history and in part a function of the changing interests in the broader community of literary scholars. We all know that historical representations are a function of the period in which they are written; that is a commonplace. There is, however, another and more profound element in these differences: we must acknowledge the degree to which literary history, as an enterprise, is a function of the particularities of the period it represents. This is a truth as interesting as it is uncomfortable. To admit as much is to say that literary history—and, by extension, all history—is not a unified discipline that focuses on different "objects" but rather is always reconfigured by the objects it pretends to describe. If that is true, then bad history is universalizing history, which, by being grounded in one period, misreads others, always looking for what is not there.

When we read within a given period, we are inevitably guided by the interests of that period. Later we will examine the role of poetry's formal genres. It is easy to discuss Mid-Tang poetry without stressing the fact that the Mid-Tang poets we now consider important all did their best work in "old style" verse. That generic choice, with its particular liberties, changes the very way we think about the period. If Late Tang poets predominantly worked in regulated forms, such a choice is not only part of history but shapes the very notion of history.

It is fair to say, as we have stated above, that the Late Tang begins in the 820s in reaction to the now famous poets of the Yuanhe generation. The fuller literary historical reality—particularly when viewed through the eyes of the craftsmen of regulated verse—is more complicated. Where we look for change, they saw continuity. The poetic conservatism of regulated verse challenges the way we read for literary history.

We might return to the Dali poets mentioned above. These poets, including a number of poet-monks whose works survive only in small numbers, perfected a highly refined craft of regulated verse in the short line (the five-syllable line). The now famous poets of the Yuanhe generation preferred "old style" verse and rejected this polished craft. Even though these poets—Han Yu, Meng Jiao, Li He, Bai Juyi, Yuan Zhen, among others—dominated the Yuanhe era, the old conservative craft of regulated verse continued both in popular and elite circles.

The surviving poetry anthologies tell a story very different from standard literary historical accounts. Let us begin with the representative anthology of the Dali era. When Gao Zhongwu 高仲武 compiled his poetry anthology entitled *The Superior Talents of the Restoration, Zhongxing xianqi ji* 中興閒氣集, in 785 or shortly thereafter, he restricted himself to recent regulated poems composed between 756 and 779. Probably between the ninth and twelfth year of the Yuanhe Reign (814–817) Linghu Chu 令狐楚 compiled his *Poems for Imperial Perusal, Yulan shi* 御覽詩.[7] The poems that Linghu Chu was offering for Xianzong's reading pleasure were primarily by the same poets anthologized by Gao Zhongwu thirty years earlier.[8] Like Gao Zhongwu's anthology, *Poems for Imperial Perusal* primarily consists of quatrains and regulated verse in the short line. Absent are all the contemporary poets whom we now recognize as major figures of the Yuanhe. Given that those famous Yuanhe poets often set themselves against the contemporary literary establishment, Linghu Chu, representing that very literary establishment, ignored them in turn. Linghu Chu lived on, rising to political eminence and eventually becoming a close friend of Liu Yuxi and Bai Juyi as well as Li Shangyin's first patron. As a patron of poets, he became a considerable force in poetry of the second quarter of the ninth century.

The continuity of conservative taste becomes even clearer when we look at the poetry anthology *Supreme Mystery, Jixuan ji* 極玄集, compiled by Yao He 姚合 around 837, about two decades after *Poems for Imperial Perusal.* Yao He emerged as one of the leading poets in the decades following the Yuanhe and was recognized as a master of regulated verse in the short line. In his anthology we again see a focus on regulated verse in the short line and the predominance of the same poets from the Dali era, along with some Yuanhe poets in that conservative tradition. Perhaps the most significant change in Yao He's anthology was to begin with the "High Tang" poet Wang Wei, giving the conservative writers of regulated verse a High Tang ancestor.

From one perspective, rather than "Mid-Tang" and "Late Tang," we have here three generations: the Dali generation, the Yuanhe generation,

7. Fu (1996) 363.

8. There are some surprises (e.g., ten poems from the Daoist eccentric Gu Kuang 顧況), but the only inclusion of a now well-known Mid-Tang poet is one quatrain by Zhang Ji 張籍.

and the generation of the second quarter of the ninth century. From another perspective, there was one continuous "poetry," with the "Yuanhe style" as a fascinating and often disapproved aberration produced by a narrow community of writers. This latter perspective seems closest to the way the regulated-verse masters of the second quarter of the ninth century conceived the poetic past. For them the preceding century was not a "history" of poetry. They identified only one period style, the "Yuanhe style"; aside from that there was an enduring classical style.

The conservative craftsmen of regulated verse represent only one view among many. In the Late Tang our very notion of the history of poetry begins to change. Poets had always drawn on past poetry, but in the Late Tang the poetic past was beginning to assume the form it would possess in China for the next millennium: it was becoming a repertoire of available choices—styles, genres, and the voices of past poets. As we will see, Li Shangyin, the most famous poet of the Late Tang, could assume many roles and many voices. On different occasions he writes like Du Fu, Han Yu, and Li He. One of his many voices—entirely his own creation—came to define him for later readers; but no one reading his collected poems can limit him to that voice. His antitheses are Meng Jiao and Li He, the poet he greatly admired. Meng Jiao's and Li He's poems are so indelibly stamped by their singular poetic personalities that despite many variations it would be hard not to immediately identify any poem of theirs. No Late Tang poet is so distinctive—except for Li Shangyin—and that distinctive voice represents only one segment of his work. Other poets chose one poetic style widely practiced by others or tried their hand at many different styles. Although there are real historical differences later on, such a repertoire, as it crystallized in the Late Tang, would endure.

As has been my practice in earlier books, I have used the numbers assigned to poems in the *Quan Tang shi* in Hiraoka Takeo 平岡武夫, Ichihara Kōkichi 市原亨吉, and Imai Kiyoshi's 今井清 *Tōdai no shihen* 唐代の詩篇. This is simply a way to locate poems in *Quan Tang shi* and to see their easily identifiable sources. Where available, I have also included a source in a modern critical or annotated edition. In general, I have followed the latter, noting where I make a particular textual decision at variance with that of a critical edition.

In the matter of dating and biography, I have generally been conservative, avoiding some of the less secure precisions in Chinese scholarship concerning various poets. In these matters I have relied on Fu (1987—plus the important corrections in supplementary volume 5, published in 1990) and Fu (1998), as well as studies of individual poets.

Over the years I have struggled to find a graceful way to refer to Chinese line length in English. I used to prefer "pentasyllabic" and "heptasyllabic," then changed to the more straightforward "five-syllable line" and "seven-syllable line." The poets of this period commonly refer to these as the "short line," *duanju* 短句, and "long line," *changju* 長句; and I have adopted that usage here.

The attentive reader will note some overlap in texts and issues addressed in my book *The End of the Chinese "Middle Ages": Essays in Mid-Tang Literary Culture* (1998). This is unavoidable since the present book grew out of that one, as the Late Tang emerged from the Mid-Tang. The present book, however, takes those texts and issues in new directions and places them in new contexts. The earlier book consists of a set of essays on interrelated issues, whereas the present book, like its predecessors on the Early Tang and High Tang, is a literary history.

ONE

Setting the Stage

Emperors

During the night of January 9, 827, the eighteen-year-old Tang emperor returned from a nocturnal hunt and was holding his usual late revels with his favorite guards and eunuchs. He went to relieve himself. When he returned, the lamps were suddenly extinguished—as was the emperor himself shortly thereafter. The plotters, led by the eunuch Liu Keming, planned to put the emperor's uncle Li Wu on the throne. Another eunuch, palace secretary Wang Shoucheng, led a swift counter-coup, executing Liu Keming and fortuitously eliminating Li Wu in the process. In Li Wu's stead, the late emperor's brother Li Han 李涵 was placed on the throne on January 13, having immediately changed his name to the more august Li Ang 李昂.

Li Ang thus became the fourth emperor on the Tang throne in seven years. Early in 820 the activist Xianzong, the Yuanhe emperor (r. 806–820), had died suddenly of unknown causes at the age of forty-three: although poison was suspected, elixirs to promote longevity were probably the more likely cause. Xianzong had inherited a well-stocked treasury and a troubled polity from his cautious grandfather Dezong. In the wake of the An Lushan Rebellion of the mid-eighth century, regional militarization had forced the court to concede virtual autonomy to many areas, especially in the northeast. Certain armies were highly unreliable and would periodically rise up against their court-appointed officers. Many prefectures in the northwest with predominantly Chinese populations had fallen under Tibetan rule. Xianzong's fifteen-year reign saw a major reassertion of dynastic power. Although the loss of dynastic authority continued in the northeast and northwest, the regional armies were under somewhat firmer central control and the core tax-producing provinces were even more secure.

On his death Xianzong was succeeded by his twenty-six-year-old son, the Changqing emperor, best remembered for his love of acrobatic troupes and dressing his favorite court ladies in filmy silk inscribed with lewd verses. Perhaps like his father, the Changqing emperor inadvertently poisoned himself with Daoist elixirs a few years after taking the throne. On his death in 824 he received the temple name Muzong. Sexual activity began early for Tang princes, so that eldest sons were sometimes the fruit of the emperor's early teens. Muzong, dying in his late twenties, was succeeded by his sixteen-year-old son, the Baoli emperor, whose wild youth came to the unfortunate end described above. On his death he received the temple name Jingzong. Li Ang, who was the same age as his foolish brother, was to rule much longer, but he, too, died at the early age of thirty-three, receiving the temple name Wenzong. According to custom, in 827 (the year following the death of his brother) Wenzong proclaimed a new reign title, the Taihe 大和, "Great Peace."

In dealing with unruly generals and sometimes equally unruly armies, Tang emperors and their advisers had to weigh expense against the political and symbolic (and occasionally economic) importance of maintaining central government control. As was previously mentioned, Xianzong's activism had been founded, in part, on the treasury built up by Dezong. A string of military revolts during Muzong's and Jingzong's reigns were largely tolerated, whether through fiscal prudence, fear of military humiliation, or sheer pusillanimity. Wenzong tended to favor a more active response, with the burden ultimately borne by the rich lower Yangzi prefectures, which were already slowly heading toward the economic collapse that would eventually spell the end of the dynasty.

Wenzong's best-known physical trait was a large, curly beard. He was ostentatiously frugal and studious, determined to be a good emperor.[1] Had he acquired the throne in more stable times, he probably would have been an excellent emperor whose reign would have been

---

1. Zha Pingqiu makes the interesting point that Wenzong, Wuzong, and Xuānzong had never been crown princes and therefore had never received the stylized education of the crown prince's establishment and had probably received broader exposure to the intellectual currents of the day. Zha Pingqiu 查屏球, *Tangxue yu Tangshi: Zhong Wan Tang shifeng de yizhong wenhua kaocha* 唐學與唐詩: 中晚唐詩風的一種文化考察 (Beijing: Shangwu yinshuguan, 2000), 242–43.

remembered by Confucian historians with great admiration. As was often said of talented young men who failed in political life, Wenzong "did not meet the right time," *bu yu shi* 不遇時. The times probably required an emperor who was ruthless and canny rather than one who tried to live up to classical ideals of moral governance. In the last years of his reign he became profoundly troubled about his future reputation. In a famous incident that occurred on November 16, 839 (only a few months before his death), Wenzong asked to see what had been written about him in the Court Diary. He was refused permission by the Diarist, who insisted that the credibility of the Diary was guaranteed by the principle that the emperor would not have access to it. Wenzong's great ancestor Taizong had gone to great lengths to appear to yield when his councilors rebuked him on the basis of Confucian principles. What was for Taizong political theater was for Wenzong incapacity. Wenzong's suspicions were correct: history was not kind to him, both in terms of his fortunes during his lifetime and his reputation following his death. At best he was accorded a certain pathos.

The grim fate of his brother must have always been on Wenzong's mind; he was surrounded by powerful eunuch factions of the inner court that controlled not only his physical person but also the palace army, the *Shence* Army, which was the military force in the capital and surrounding areas. In the outer court he faced feuding factions of officials who were constantly speaking ill of their enemies. The main factions were centered around two men, Niu Sengru 牛僧孺 (779–847) and Li Deyu 李德裕 (787–850), whose enmity could be traced back to the examinations of 821, when Li Deyu, along with Yuan Zhen and Li Shen, complained that the examinations had been unfair and demanded a retest under the poet Bai Juyi and the famous *fu* writer Wang Qi 王起.

Outside the court were the emperor's restive armies, whose leaders had defied the court on a number of occasions during earlier reigns. If sufficiently angered by a court-appointed commander, some armies had been known to eat the offending official. This sometimes made the appointment of a replacement difficult. In one case, when an army ate the new commander's aide, who had been sent ahead, the incumbent, Li Ting, decided that he was too sick to take up the appointment.[2] On the frontiers there were always troubles. The Tibetans, major adversaries in

---

2. *Zizhi tongjian* 7879.

the eighth century, were fortunately preoccupied with their own internal difficulties. Early in 830, however, the Nanzhao kingdom to the southwest invaded Sichuan and plundered the provincial capital, Chengdu. These were not easy times to be emperor, though they were not all that different from the preceding reigns and far better than the situation the dynasty faced in the second half of the century.

Breaking the power of the eunuchs was Wenzong's chief concern in the first part of his reign. There were some earlier abortive plans, but the most significant event—indeed, the defining one of his reign—was the Sweet Dew Incident 甘露之變 of late 835. Largely masterminded by the courtier-physician Zheng Zhu 鄭注 and the former Academician Li Xun 李訓, a plot had been laid to kill all the eunuchs. Armed men had gathered, hidden in a section of the palace where it was reported auspicious "sweet dew" had appeared. When the emperor sent his eunuchs to witness the happy omen, a breeze is said to have blown aside the curtain, revealing the armed men. Seizing the emperor, the eunuchs retreated into the inner palace and barred the doors. They then unleashed the *Shence* Army. A bloodbath ensued in the capital, in which many distinguished officials and their families were killed. Under torture, one of the plotters "confessed" that if the coup had been successful, Wenzong was to have been deposed and Zheng Zhu placed on the throne. Wenzong at least pretended to believe this—he had little choice—and sanctioned the purge of the plotters. Zheng Zhu, a doctor by background, had been particularly despised in official circles; and while there was great sympathy for individuals who had been killed among the plotters, the "public opinion" of officialdom seems to have truly condemned the actions of Zheng Zhu.

In the aftermath a new reign name, the Kaicheng 開成, was declared. *Kai* is used in the sense of "beginning," while *cheng* means "completion." *Cheng*, however, is a problematic term since in some contexts "completion" also implies "ending." Although it is not at all the meaning intended by the court ritualists who devised it, it is not entirely perverse to interpret the new reign title in retrospect as the "Beginning of the End."

It is stated in many sources that after the Sweet Dew Incident Wenzong became increasingly despondent, paying less attention to governing and the pleasures of being emperor. He did seem to have developed a growing interest in poetry, one resisted at every turn by his court officials. In many ways Wenzong was as much their prisoner as he was the prisoner of the eunuchs. He died early in 840 and was replaced by his far more incompetent younger brother, Li Yan 李炎, whom history would remember as Wuzong, the Huichang emperor. Wuzong temporarily settled the factional struggles by making Li Deyu his minister and keeping him in the post. Wuzong's brief reign is memorable primarily for his obsession with Daoism and, under the influence of his Daoist advisers, for issuing a series of edicts against Buddhism, culminating in the edict of 845, which ordered the closing of most of the temples throughout China and the forced laicization of the clergy. By the spring of 846 Wuzong was dead from an overdose of Daoist elixir, no doubt to the unexpressed relief of many officials.

Wuzong was replaced by a more mature emperor, a thirty-seven-year-old son of Xianzong, now known by his temple name of Xuānzong 宣宗 (not to be confused with the more famous Xuanzong 玄宗 of the High Tang). Xuānzong, the Dazhong emperor (846–859), was a bitter, dour man who had done his best to stay out of court politics during the preceding reigns, when so many members of the imperial family lost their lives. With Xuānzong's ascension to the throne, Li Deyu was sent off to Hainan Island, where he eventually died. His death was followed by that of Niu Sengru in 847, thus bringing to a close the most famous age of court factionalism. The new chief minister was Linghu Tao, who was the son of Linghu Chu, the grand old statesman and patron of poets. Increasingly, however, the politics of Chang'an was becoming irrelevant. Although Xuānzong kept tight control over his court and ruled as best be could, a number of revolts during the last years of his reign clearly show that the polity was beginning to disintegrate. We must, to some degree, discount descriptions of the excesses of his successors Yizong 懿宗 and Xizong 僖宗 (who took the throne at twelve) as "bad late emperors." Nevertheless, anecdotal sources contribute to the impression of a court that had lost all hope of managing the polity and was out of touch with political reality. The Tang was always a theatrical dynasty whose power was, in part, maintained by a canny use of political spectacle. This impulse grew more pronounced in Yizong's reign, though the spectacle had become hollow and consumed too much of the dynasty's diminished resources. The history of the Tang in the second half of the ninth century increasingly became that of a court that held power over ever-shrinking territory. After Huang Chao's devastating rebellion and occupation of Chang'an in 880, it literally became merely a court, sometimes residing in the ruined capital and sometimes fleeing from place to place.

Wenzong and Poetry

In the ninth century poetry was more widely practiced than ever before, and its significance within the culture was changing. Scholars tend to generalize about Tang attitudes toward poetry—or perhaps Late Tang attitudes toward poetry. In any given period there were, in fact, diverse attitudes toward poetry varying by both groups and individuals. In the ninth century the wide range of sources permits us to glimpse something of this variety and the relations among positions. We have a singularly prominent lover of poetry in the person of Wenzong; we have a number of prominent court officials who, for various reasons, disapproved of poets and poetry as a qualification procedure in the *jinshi* examination; and we have some poets who were beginning to think of poetry as a vocation in its own right rather than as a social skill and an adjunct of a life whose ultimate purpose was serving the state. There is clearly a connection between the disapproval of poets on the part of high court officials and the sense of poetry as a vocation separate from public service. What we cannot know is which was the cause and which the effect. More likely, the two phenomena evolved in tandem.

Although contempt for poets was not unknown in earlier periods, and although many well-placed officials were still known for their poetry in our period, the general distrust of poets and poetry seems to have increased in the second quarter of the ninth century. Li Deyu had managed to get poetry and poetic expositions (*fu*) removed from the 833 examination for *jinshi*, though it was reinstated the following year.[3] Li Deyu, who had come to office through *yin* privilege, offered what was essentially a rationalization of the *yin* privilege—one that was not entirely unpersuasive.[4] Young men who grew up in the households of high officials had more understanding of the real demands of public

---

3. The *jinshi* was an examination on literary composition and policy that qualified men for the Selection (*Xuan*), by which they might be awarded civil office in the central bureaucracy.

4. The *yin* privilege, granted to officials of the third rank and higher, allowed them to designate male relatives—usually sons—for selection to office without taking the examination.

office than someone who could compose a rhetorically well crafted poem and a poetic exposition on a set theme. Indeed, examination verse was not what we would now consider true "poetry." Nevertheless, in the popular imagination poetic talent in the usual sense seemed to imply the capacity to write examination verse. Many talented poets discovered the fallacy of this assumption empirically.

To admire poetry, moreover, might be looked upon as a dangerous diversion from serious pursuits. In May 836, the year after the Sweet Dew Incident, Wenzong was strolling about with his grand councilor Zheng Tan 鄭覃, with whom he wished to discuss questions of poetic skill. As so often happened, Wenzong's unguarded expression of interest earned him the following sermon:

> As for skill in poetry, nothing can compare to the three hundred poems of the *Classic of Poetry*. All were written by people of the domains to praise or criticize the government of the times; rulers selected them only in order to observe the state of customs. One does not hear of the rulers themselves writing poems. The poems of later literary men are mere flower without the fruit, and do not help governing. The Last Emperor of Chen and Sui Yangdi were both skilled in poetry, and they inevitably destroyed their own dynasties. What is there for Your Majesty to derive from such things!?[5]

The *Zizhi tongjian* goes on to say that the emperor had great respect for Zheng Tan as a scholar of the classics. Like Li Deyu, Zheng Tan had come to office through *yin* privilege and was reputed to have had no skill in literary composition; he was just another of several powerful figures in the 830s who opposed the use of poetry and poetic expositions in the *jinshi* examination as a useless criterion for judgment. The emperor was not entirely dissuaded from revealing his poetic interests. On another occasion it is said that he showed one of his poems to Zheng Tan, who told him to focus instead on the long-range interests of the dynasty. Fortunately for the imperial ego, there were other courtiers willing to express their admiration with an approving sigh.

In 838 Wenzong took it in mind to establish seventy-two Academicians of Poetry in the Hanlin Academy and asked for recommendations. Suggestions were offered up. However, when Yang Sifu (who had once sighed in approval at Wenzong's poetry) suggested that Liu Yuxi was the best poet of his day, Wenzong signified his imperial disapproval

---

5. *Zizhi tongjian* 7925.

through silence. The emperor's proposal soon led to another sermon, this time in a memorial from Li Jue 李珏:

> To establish Academicians of Poetry would look rather bad at the present moment. Poets, moreover, are generally poor and unreliable men, ignorant of the nature of office-holding. Our current Hanlin Academicians are all men well versed in letters; it is quite proper that Your Majesty peruses past and present writers and finds amusement therein. If you have questions, it is quite proper that you consult with your regular Academicians. Some time ago Your Majesty commanded Wang Qi and Xu Kangzuo to serve as attendant lecturers, and all the world felt that Your Majesty loved antiquity and honored scholars, that you were devoted to and encouraged simplicity and depth. I understand that Xianzong [the Yuanhe Emperor] wrote poetry, and that his style matched that of the ancients. But back then, certain frivolous fellows displayed their rhetorical gifts and decorated lines, and with a grandiose, tortuous, and obscure style they satirized current events. Thereafter their reputations were bruited about, and they called it the "Yuanhe Style." It was certainly not the case that imperial preferences then were for things like this. If Your Majesty now goes on to establish Academicians of Poetry, I worry very much that frivolous and inferior men will try to outdo one another in verses of ridicule, giving their attention to clouds, mountains, plants, and trees. And might this not get called the "Kaicheng style"? Such a blemish on the imperial civilizing mission would indeed be no small matter.[6]

The assumptions behind this diatribe show that something important had happened in the understanding of poetry. When Li Jue spoke of "poets," he did not simply mean those who wrote poetry but rather someone who was somehow defined by that activity. He would see such a person in, say, the post of Drafter [of edicts] as "a poet serving as a Drafter" rather than a "Drafter who writes poetry." "Being a poet" was the primary definition of such a person, and any office that person might hold was secondary. In effect, poetry had become a separate sphere, a vocation in its own right, and thus potentially distinct from office-holding, which was seen as a different vocation and capacity. Li Jue's assumption is close to the premise for Li Deyu's argument against the use of poetry in the *jinshi* examination.

------

6. *Tang yulin* 149. The current reign was the Kaicheng Reign. If we read Bai Juyi's "Feeling Bad About Spring: Presented to Administrator Li [Jue]" 惜春贈李尹 (24180) of the preceding year (837), we can get some sense of how Li Jue developed his opinions about poets.

There is an original note that accompanies this section on the emperor's wish for Academicians of Poetry in the *Tang yulin* (and probably in the unknown source Wang Dang 王讜, the author of *Tang yulin*, used). After stating that when the emperor wanted to establish Academicians of Poetry, some of the existing Academicians suggested names, the note adds: "At that time the poet Li Kuo 李廓 was very famous." The anecdote about the emperor's silence at Yang Sifu's recommendation of Liu Yuxi immediately follows the note and strongly suggests that Li Kuo was among those names suggested that met with approval.

Posterity has given us a great many poets of greater or lesser fame active in 838—and Li Kuo is someone of decidedly lesser fame. Nineteen of his poems have been preserved.[7] Two points are worth mentioning. First, Li Kuo was closely associated with the poets Jia Dao and Yao He, who were indeed very famous at the time and were master stylists of regulated verse in the short line.[8] Second, Li Kuo was the son of the minister Li Cheng.

When we consider Li Kuo's family background together with Li Jue's objections, we encounter one of the issues surrounding poetry in the 830s. Liu Yuxi, whose name was met with silence, came from a family of lower-to-middle officialdom.[9] Poetic fame, combined with the use of poetry in the examination, was a means of social mobility (restricted, of course, to local elites); and there were many high court officials who strongly disapproved of scholars from "poor families" (*hanmen* 寒門, not necessarily poor at all) rising in the bureaucracy and entering the inner circle surrounding the emperor. Military commissioners (*jiedushi*) and surveillance commissioners (*guanchashi*) had at their disposal an array of posts that could be awarded based on their personal choice—quite unlike the complex processes involved in the assignment of central government offices. Many of these commissioners had a fondness for talented young literary men. It proved an attractive route for young men to gather the necessary connections and recommendations before taking the examination as well as after passing

---

7. Eighteen in *Quan Tang shi* and one in *Quan Tang shi buyi*.

8. Fu (1987), vol. 3, 132. Few of Li Kuo's extant poems show this affiliation, but that is probably a function of how few survive and their particular sources.

9. In *Tang yulin* (150) Zhou Xunchu mentions a speculative comment by Hu Yinglin in the *Shisou* that this was because Liu Yuxi had been a member of the Wang Shuwen faction in 805. We will suggest some other reasons.

the examination. Unlike scholarship based on the classics or achievement in the military or civil government, poetry was particularly problematic because poetic "fame" derived from some invisible barometer of "public opinion."[10] Moreover, if prestige was a significant currency of power in the Tang, praise and the company of well-known poets could increase the recipient's prestige.[11] We might observe here that Li Jue's anxiety that poets might criticize current policy was certainly more a memory of the Yuanhe Reign than a judgment of the current poetic practice of the 830s. More troubling was the thought of an uncontrolled pool of young men gaining *ming* 名, "name" or "fame," beyond the reach of bureaucratic oversight that allotted degrees of *ming* through the usual channels. Hanlin Academicians of Poetry would have been the worst-case scenario; such men would have been appointed outside bureaucratic channels and would have had direct access to this poetry-loving emperor, earning his protection and favor.[12]

Something of Wenzong's passion for poetry can be discerned in an anecdote from the last year of his life. Early in 839 the seventy-five-year-old Pei Du 裴度, one of the grand statesmen of the preceding third of the century, was called back to the capital and given the largely ceremonial post of Director of the Secretariat. The old man's health was clearly failing. On April 21 of that same year Wenzong held a party for his court officials at Winding River Park 曲江, in the southeastern corner of Chang'an. Poems were composed, as they always were on such occasions. Because of illness, Pei Du was unable to attend, so the emperor sent one of his eunuch attendants with a quatrain and a note to Pei.

注想待元老	My thoughts are fixed, awaiting our elder statesman,
識君恨不早	I regret I did not get to know you earlier.

---

10. "Public opinion" is here restricted to officialdom; many were troubled by the more general popularity of Bai Juyi, which was believed to extend into the masses of the population.

11. An apt example here is the anecdote in *Tangshi jishi* about Zhang Hu and Wang Zhixing 王智興. See p. 238.

12. Moreover, a Hanlin appointment was an imperial prerogative, circumventing the usual channels of advancement in the bureaucracy.

我家柱石衰	The pillar-stone of my family decays,
憂來學丘禱	in care, I imitate praying for Confucius's recovery.[13]

And His Majesty added a note which read:

> We have wanted to see an exchange poem with you in Our own poetry collection, so We have ordered that you be shown this. Right now you have not recovered from your illness and, of course, you don't have the strength to do so. But in some future day, present something to Us. It is the common belief that springtime is the hardest season for protecting one's health. Try your best to take care of yourself, and you will very quickly be back to normal. Our thoughts are very much with you, but We won't go on any longer. If you need anything in the way of medicine, don't be afraid to send Us a request.

By the time the emperor's note had reached Pei Du's home, Pei had already passed away."[14]

Wenzong was never able to add Pei Du's answering poem to his poetry collection.

We might consider the emperor's note to the dying Pei Du. The interest in Pei Du's health and the offer of medicine are touching and were no doubt sincere, but the note linked imperial kindness to another motive, namely, the hope that Pei Du would get better so that he could add an exchange poem from Pei Du to "Our own poetry collection," *zhen shiji* 朕詩集 (using the imperial pronoun). As we will see, the emperor here shares a new tendency to think not simply of his poems but of his collected works; exchange poems, in particular, were prized as a record of one's connections—evidently even for the emperor.

The System

Although we have spoken of poetry emerging as a "separate sphere" of activity, the moods and movements of poets were situated primarily within the context of the Tang bureaucracy in its ninth-century version. Ruling such a large empire, even ineffectively, required a large

---

13. *Analects*, 7, 34: "The Master was gravely ill. Zilu asked permission to pray for him 子疾病, 子路請禱. The Master said, 'Is this done?' Zilu answered, 'It is. A eulogy speaks of "Praying for you to the gods of earth and air."' Confucius said, 'I have been praying long.'"

14. *Jiu Tang shu* 4433.

bureaucracy, though probably not a bureaucracy nearly as large as that of the Tang. Perhaps the best way to think of the Tang bureaucracy was as a way to occupy surplus males of the elite through a complex structure consisting of goals, rewards, and punishments. Part of the bureaucracy was staffed by those who had passed the regional and national examinations, the latter being the examination for *jinshi* 進士, "presented scholars." Although the examination was theoretically based on merit, being allowed to take it and passing it depended on the support of powerful patrons; the position one received after the examination depended even more on family and patronage. Far more young men took the examination than passed, and many took the examination a number of times. Just enough young men passed to keep the system alive to maintain hope.

Every post in the bureaucracy had a grade ranging from nine (lowest) to one (highest), with each grade having two steps. The prestige of a post was based on two factors: its grade and its proximity to the capital and, within the capital, its proximity to the emperor. A lower-grade post involving close contact with the emperor might be more desirable than a higher-grade post in the far-flung provinces. Officials were moved frequently, particularly higher officials, and they were often preoccupied with the changing gradations of prestige and power.

One of the most common humble posts was that of "district defender" (*wei* 尉), essentially a county sheriff. The county magistrate was a bit better. We often see mid-level officials (and demoted officials) as governors of prefectures (*zhou* 州), of which there were a great many, each containing a number of counties. On a higher level were the circuits (*dao* 道), each of which had a military commissioner (*jiedushi* 節度使) with an army, and his civilian counterpart, the surveillance commissioner (*guanchashi* 觀察使). In Tang history one most often hears of those military commissioners who were virtually autonomous, defying court commands or kept tenuously loyal by means of deft political skills. In many cases it was not the military commissioner himself who was autonomous but rather his army, which proposed and deposed commanders at will. The loyal regions of the empire, however, also had circuits and commissioners, both military and civil, and these are more important for our purposes here. High-ranking capital-based officials who had fallen from favor were often given such posts; for those rising through the ranks, appointment as a commissioner would bring a mid-level official into the upper ranks.

One feature of the system of military and surveillance commissioners was of particular importance for the social background of literature in the Mid- and Late Tang. While prefectural and county appointments were theoretically under central government control, military and surveillance commissioners could appoint their own staffs. As a result, the commissioners often kept a large entourage of promising young men who either had not yet passed the examination or who had not yet received posts. This was a patronage investment. Even more striking, we often see young men who, after passing the examination, gave up good, junior capital posts to go off to the provinces with a commissioner. The reasons for doing so are not always clear, but we can be sure that such posts must somehow have seemed more promising for their careers.[15] It is hard not to associate this phenomenon with growing regional power that eventually led to regional states at the end of the century. Resources seem to have been increasingly retained or commandeered by regions rather than being sent to the capital; the poet-retainers of regional commissioners rarely complained of their poverty.

The government system also had a large number of sinecures that entailed no duties. The best place for sinecures was Luoyang, the Eastern Capital; we will see a number of eminent figures holding posts in the establishment of the Heir Apparent, "Luoyang Assignment." These were wonderfully untroubled posts occupied by the empire's elderly poets.

There were, of course, also the posts in the central government in Chang'an itself, of which there were a great many. At the top was the ceremonial post of Chief Minister or Councilor-in-Chief, *chengxiang* 丞相, who was nominally in charge of both the Secretariat and the Chancellery. Hardly any of our poets attained that level.

The Literary Scene

Younger men rose to prominence and older men died, but the world of letters in 827, the first year of the Taihe Reign, looked much the same for the next two decades. Perhaps the best way to sort out the many

---

15. In some cases the nominal capital posts given to those serving with commissioners were a step above the capital post currently occupied, so that the decision might be viewed as a promotion. However, we sometimes see those who served with the military commissioners coming back to capital posts equal to or lower than those they left.

names and overlapping relationships is to provide a general overview of the successive generations.

As we remarked above, the Yuanhe Reign had been a period of great diversity and poetic invention.[16] The sharp criticism of that era—particularly of Bai Juyi—which we begin to find in the 830s had not yet begun, but poetic taste was changing—or perhaps returning to a conservative, regulated verse norm that had continued beneath the surface of Yuanhe invention. Meng Jiao, Li He, and Han Yu were dead, but many other less distinctive Yuanhe poets lived on. Wang Jian 王建 (766?–ca. 830) and Zhang Ji 張籍 (766?–ca. 830)—famous for their earlier *yuefu* (and Wang Jian for his "Palace Lyrics" 宮詞, perhaps composed around 820)—lived on into the beginning of the Taihe Reign. Zhang Ji, in particular, welcomed contact with younger poets in the 820s; while he is best known for his *yuefu* of social commentary, which were probably composed in the Yuanhe Reign, he was known in our period as a poet of regulated verse.

Three men—Bai Juyi 白居易 (772–846), Liu Yuxi 劉禹錫 (772–842), and Li Shen 李紳 (772–846)—who were all aged fifty-seven at the start of the Taihe Reign, lived on for many years, forming their own circle and exchanging poems with the leading political figures of the

---

16. No small part of the literary scene of 827 was its background, the poetry of the Yuanhe generation. From our current perspective the poetry of the Yuanhe period itself admits no single characterization: it encompassed the simple, rambling poetry of Bai Juyi, the stridency of Meng Jiao, the fantastic imagination of Li He, and the archaism of Han Yu, to name just a few of its poetic trends. If there is a unity in this diversity, it was in poetic experiment that went beyond earlier poetic norms, whether favoring simplicity or difficulty, the quotidian or the visionary. As we noted in the introduction, a more restrained, conservative type of poetry was also being written. Although much poetry of this period was distinctive, we would not be justified in identifying any particular poetic trend as the "Yuanhe Style" were it not for the fact that Chinese writers from the Yuanhe on referred to the "Yuanhe Style" 元和體. We have already seen Li Jue make reference to this in his memorial to Wenzong, where it is seen as an unfortunate yet current term referring to a small group of poets who hijacked the reign title and did not represent the true cultural spirit of Xianzong, the Yuanhe emperor. Here and in general the term "Yuanhe Style" refers to certain works of Bai Juyi, Yuan Zhen, and the poets of their circle. It can also refer to the very different poetry of Meng Jiao and others. It is best to understand the term as one of shifting valence, while always acknowledging the powerful presence of the Yuanhe poets in the Late Tang imagination.

day.[17] Bai Juyi's ballads of social criticism and long sentimental narratives belonged to the preceding era, but he continued to write prolifically in the last two decades of his life. His voluminous poetic exchanges with Liu Yuxi brought the two poets close together in style. We know that Li Shen, who was yet to become an important political figure, had been active poetically in the Yuanhe; but most of his extant poems are contained in a collection completed in 837 or 838. Another somewhat younger figure, Yuan Zhen 元稹 (779–831), also belonged to this group and was a very prominent politician. We might also mention the sixty-eight-year-old Wang Qi 王起 (760–847). Although we know that he participated in poetic exchanges with members of the circle, relatively few of his poems survive. He was, however, the most prominent writer of "regulated poetic expositions" (*lüfu* 律賦), most of which are undatable but were probably composed in an earlier era.

Two somewhat younger poets, Jia Dao 賈島 (779–843) and Yao He 姚合 (ca. 779–ca. 849), probably both the same age as Yuan Zhen, had come to exercise a strong influence in the world of poetry. Even by 827 "popularity" and "fame" were becoming a function of different circles and often of different locales. Nevertheless, in Chang'an Jia Dao and Yao He were arguably the most popular poets of the day. Masters of regulated verse in the five-syllable line, they cultivated the acquaintance of many younger poets who made their appearance in Chang'an. Though they remained friends, Yao He had passed the examination in 816 and was on a slow upward career path. Jia Dao, by contrast, never passed the examination and became the very image of the "pure" poet. Jia Dao had originally been a monk; another member of their circle was his younger cousin, the monk Wuke 無可.

The next group we might identify consists of poets in their thirties. It should be noted that these men belong to roughly the same generation as Li He 李賀 (790–816), the brilliant and daring young poet of the Yuanhe era. We do not know when Shen Yazhi 沈亞之 was born, but he first came to Chang'an in 810 and made friends with Li He. More than any poet, he carried on one version of the Yuanhe style, albeit muted, into this new era. Zhang Hu 張祜 (ca. 792–ca. 854) had

---

17. Not knowing birthdays, it is impossible accurately to describe a person's age in contemporary Western terms. I will follow the Chinese practice: a person is "one year old" (*sui* 歲) when born and becomes "two" the following New Year.

addressed a poem to Han Yu between 809 and 811, and we may take this as his debut on the poetic scene. Although he was often recommended for office, he remained unsuccessful, wandering from place to place and living off his poetic reputation. We find him as Du Mu's aging poetic companion in 845, writing poems in a style very much like Du Mu's own. Xu Hun's 許渾 (ca. 788?–ca. 854?) earliest poems date from the Yuanhe. He seems to have been in the capital in 827, or perhaps even earlier, but he was not as visible as Zhang Hu. He passed the *jinshi* examination in 832. While Zhang Hu was one of the most famous poets of his own day but was largely forgotten later on, Xu Hun had only modest fame during his lifetime but was much admired by the end of the century and in the Song.

Although there was some contact, neither Zhang Hu nor Xu Hun were closely identified with the circle of poets around Jia Dao and Yao He. In that circle Gu Feixiong 顧非熊 (ca. 796–ca. 854), son of the eccentric Daoist poet Gu Kuang 顧況, was very prominent. Gu Feixiong seems to have wandered from patron to patron, though he did finally pass the *jinshi* examination in 845. Like his father, he spent much of his life at Maoshan, the center of an important Daoist sect. Another figure in the circle was Zhu Qingyu 朱慶餘 (ca. 796–ca. 837), who had recently passed the *jinshi* examination in 826 when Wenzong first assumed the throne. Like many poets in this circle, we know nothing of his family background, which in Tang terms generally meant that he came from provincial gentry without a history of posts in the capital. When they passed the examination, such men usually received low-level posts. We know that Zhu became an editor in the Imperial Library, a post close to the bottom of the bureaucratic ladder (which, however, was equal to the first posts held by Du Mu and Li Shangyin). Zhang Xiaobiao 章孝標 passed the *jinshi* examination in 819 and figures prominently in exchange poems of the group.

There were also many younger poets in their twenties and teens. Whether due to their proximity to the age of printing, their popularity, or a combination of both, we begin to find many more poetry collections surviving from writers active in this period. These collections are admittedly often incomplete and contain many problematic attributions; but unlike most poetry collections by minor poets dating from the first half of the eighth century, the works of these ninth-century poets have survived independently and were not re-compiled from anthology sources.

Among the regulated-verse writers centered around Jia Dao and Yao He, Yong Tao 雍陶 was already active in the 820s; after several unsuccessful attempts, he finally passed the *jinshi* examination in 834. Yong Tao was one of the few poets of the period from Sichuan and was there when the Nanzhao Kingdom invaded and pillaged Chengdu in early 830. Ma Dai 馬戴 was also active in this circle in the 820s, though he did not pass the *jinshi* examination until the early 840s.

Young poets continued to appear in Chang'an and joined the circle. Xiang Si 項斯 (ca. 802–847) appears in poetic exchanges in the early 830s, as does Liu Deren 劉得仁. We are not at all certain of the dates of the monk Qingse 清塞, who, it is said, was persuaded to return to the laity by Yao He when he was governor of Hangzhou (834–36). At this point Qingse reverted to his secular name of Zhou He 周賀, by which he is now most commonly known. All these poets specialized in regulated verse composed in the five-syllable line. Among the last poets to enter the circle was Yu Fu 喻凫, who passed the *jinshi* examination in 840 and died around 850. When he left the capital in 841, Yao He, Wuke, and Gu Feixiong were there to see him off, as they had done earlier for so many young poets. Another such poet was Li Pin 李頻, who came to Chang'an in 839 hoping to study poetry with Yao He, who—as teachers sometimes did with their disciples—married his daughter to him. Li Pin carried the regulated-verse tradition into the next generation, finally passing the *jinshi* examination in 854 and dying in the mid-870s.

Although the circle around Jia Dao and Yao He probably represented the most active group of younger poets at the time, not all poets were associated with them. Li Yuan 李遠 was in the capital in the late 820s and early 830s (he passed the *jinshi* examination in 831), but he did not participate in the poetic occasions of the group. Zhao Gu's 趙嘏 (ca. 806–852) earliest poem can be dated to the late 820s, but at the beginning of the 830s he found his patron in the military commissioner Shen Chuanshi, whose headquarters were in Xuanzhou. Du Mu was also there in Shen Chuanshi's service and the two became friends. Zhao thus belongs to the new generation of poets appearing in the 830s. Another talented young poet who earned Du Mu's admiration in the late 830s was Li Qunyu 李群玉 (ca. 813–861).

The generation of these younger poets also included three individuals now considered to be the representative poets of the Late Tang: Du Mu 杜牧 (803–853), Li Shangyin 李商隱 (812–858), and Wen Tingyun

溫庭筠 (ca. 801?–866).[18] With the exception of Du Mu, however, none of the three seemed like rising poetic stars in the second quarter of the ninth century. Du Mu had large political and cultural ambitions; his image as a poet was, to some degree, antithetical to those aspirations. Li Shangyin, certainly the most gifted and eventually the most famous of Late Tang poets, seems to have been known as a poet only in limited circles during his lifetime (though he was clearly better known as a writer of parallel prose), but he gradually gained prominence in the last part of the century. Wen Tingyun composed some justly celebrated regulated poems, but his fame as a *shi* writer was later to become a by-product of his later prominence as the first important writer of song lyrics (*ci* 詞). In his *yuefu*, however, he is the most prominent representative of the legacy of Li He.

There were, of course, other new faces that appeared in the 840s. However, during the second quarter of the ninth century we can identify three rough groupings: the senior poets associated with Bai Juyi; the poets who had close relations with Jia Dao and Yao He; and later poets who had contact with Du Mu. Others, like Wen Tingyun and Li Shangyin, worked largely outside these circles.

Survivals

It would be a great error to believe we are in possession of "Late Tang poetry." Rather, we have pieces of it, each of which carries its own unique history of interests and accidents. When Song Taizong instituted his great book search in 984, it was for works from the 731 catalogue done for Xuanzong; Taizong was evidently satisfied with his Late Tang holdings.[19] The uneven but intense scholarly interest in recovering Mid- and Late Tang material that began around the turn of the eleventh century produced extensive but no less uneven results that provide clues concerning the ways in which relatively popular "recent" manuscripts circulated.

What we would most desire, of course, would be to have a copy of a poet's works in his own hand. In one case we have essentially that: the

---

18. Wen's dates are pure supposition; here I follow Fu Xuancong's guess. I will return to this question in the chapter on Wen Tingyun.

19. See Glen Dudbridge, *Lost Books of Medieval China* (London: British Library, 2000), 2–4.

Southern Song scholar Yue Ke 岳珂 made a facsimile of an incomplete manuscript containing 171 poems of Xu Hun's *Black-silk Line Poems*, *Wusilan shi* 烏絲欄詩, dated precisely to the third month of the fourth year of the Dazhong Reign (850).[20] Yue Ke preserved this not as a literary scholar would do for the works of a poet but as an example of Xu Hun's fine calligraphic hand. Because it is preserved for the calligraphy rather than the text, we have greater confidence that this is an exact reproduction of the manuscript.[21] Collation of this text with the received texts and variants is a good illustration of the fluidity of manuscript culture.

The next best thing to the author's own manuscript would be to have Tang manuscripts, which is what we do have in the case of Bai Juyi, preserved in Japan and in Dunhuang fragments. In this case we are more confident that we have the poet's "complete works" roughly as he intended, with differences in some measure a function of the poet's own versions of his oeuvre. If some additional poems are not included in the early versions of the collection, we can often assume that they were omitted. In this case, however, we have already entered the world of manuscript circulation, and we have a substantial number of variants in the manuscripts and early printed versions—though fewer than we find in most popular poets.

In most cases, however, what survives of a poet's works is a consequence of accidents of preservation, some of which we can clearly see while others of which we can only guess at. Xu Ning 徐凝 achieved some fame as a result of having been chosen by Bai Juyi for *jinshi* candidacy over Zhang Hu. Contempt for Xu Ning's poetry from that famous comparative misjudgment was compounded by Xu Ning's poem on the Cascade at Lu Mountain, immortalized as an exemplary bad poem by Su Shi in the Song. However, if we wish to judge Xu Ning's works for ourselves, we find that his surviving poems consist almost entirely of quatrains. The reason is not Xu Ning's preference for the quatrain form. The only edition of Xu Ning's poems known in the Song was in the possession of Hong Mai 洪邁 (1123–1202). The latter

---

20. We also have a reprint of a smaller collection by Li Ying 李郢, supposedly in his own hand, collected in the Song and preserved in the Qing palace collection but now evidently lost.

21. For further discussion of this point, see Luo 12.

also compiled a massive anthology of Tang quatrains, *Wanshou Tangren jueju* 萬首唐人絕句, into which he clearly copied virtually every Tang quatrain he could find. We should therefore not be surprised to find that the primary source for virtually all Xu Ning's quatrains is *Wanshou Tangren jueju*.[22] If we consider the usual proportion of quatrains to poetry in other genres, this gives us some indication of the extent to which Xu Ning's poetry has been lost.

We have already encountered Li Kuo as the poet whose name apparently met with imperial approval in the proposal for Academicians of Poetry. Considering his affiliations with the Jia Dao circle and the poems written to him, we would expect him to be writing graceful and polished regulated verses in the short line. When we look at his small corpus of extant poems, however, we find seven "Ballads of Youth in Chang'an," on the wild behavior of rich young men; a song of a woman longing for her husband, who is at the frontier; a lyric concerning a magic mirror; and a ballad about a fierce man-at-arms. There are a few others, but these poems represent the majority. We can be reasonably certain that topics like these were not what Wenzong had in mind for his Academicians of Poetry. Again, the explanation is the particular venue of preservation. It turns out that the primary source for virtually all Li Kuo's surviving poems was the mid-tenth-century anthology *Caidiao ji* 才調集, which reflected a strong predilection for poems about women, warriors, wonders, and extravagant young gallants.

These are particularly obvious examples of how the record is shaped by accidents of preservation. When Du Mu compiled his collected poems, he culled his verse radically. Many of his poems, particularly his quatrains, were popular and were preserved, eventually being gathered in supplements to his collection in the Song. Modern scholarship has demonstrated that those supplements contain a large number of poems attributed to others on better authority; they also contain poems attributed to others that were almost certainly by Du Mu. The majority of the poems in the supplements are uncontested, but the fact that an attribution is uncontested does not mean it is reliable. It is reasonable to

---

22. Another case is Shi Jianwu 施肩吾, of whose nearly two hundred poems only twelve are not quatrains. We might add that Hong Mai would often extract a quatrain from a regulated verse; since a fair number of Shi Jianwu's quatrains in the long line rhyme ABCB, we cannot tell whether Shi preferred that less common rhyme form or if Hong Mai took sections from longer poems.

suspect that these uncontested poems in the supplements can also be divided into poems written by others and attributed to Du Mu and poems actually by Du Mu.

We have the case of Yin Yaofan 殷堯藩, fairly well known in the second quarter of the ninth century and prominent in the circle around Yao He and Jia Dao. A short collection of his poems existed in the Song, and his works were republished in the Ming, supposedly based on a rare Song edition. It turns out, however, that many of the poems in the collection were written by Yuan and Ming poets; we can rely on only eighteen pieces attested to in early anthologies. The Ming editor clearly thought it was a shame that Yin Yaofan's poems were lost and decided to provide him with a collection.[23]

Although in his later years Bai Juyi seems to have preserved most if not all of his poems, an author's "collected poems" were rarely complete. Furthermore, poems commonly circulated in abbreviated collections (*xiaoji* 小集, what we would call "anthologies" of a poet's work).[24] It is only in the eleventh century that we see a concerted scholarly effort to gather all a poet's literary remains, and by that time the literary remains of most poets were incomplete in varying degrees. Song editorial notices often speak of manuscript collections with distinct but overlapping contents, which were combined to produce fuller versions.

The particular nature of Song print culture—many titles were issued in relatively small print runs—made accident an important factor in the survival of particular works. Far more Song editions were preserved in the Ming and Qing, and they were often reprinted. The acquisition of a Song edition had immense cultural cachet; forgeries often claimed to be a reprint of an otherwise unknown, unique Song edition, as was the case with Yin Yaofan's collection, mentioned above. Genuine Song editions have nevertheless continued to resurface; the fairly recent rediscovery of a Sichuan printing of Zhang Hu's poetry has greatly expanded our corpus of that poet's works. The additional poems—numbering over a hundred—are not scattered throughout the collection but instead constitute a consecutive standard sequence in a

---

23. See note by Chen Min 陳敏 in Fu (1987), vol. 5, 283.

24. In contrast to Du Fu's *xiaoji*, which seems to have been what we would call an "edition" of Du Fu's selected works, its seems likely that many of these *xiaoji* were simply poems that an interested reader fancied and copied from a larger edition.

collection organized by genre: regulated verses in the long line and *pailü*. This provides us with yet another type of loss and survival. It is clear from this that all the standard versions of Zhang Hu's poetry before the discovery of the Song Sichuan edition were based on a unique printed copy from which one *ce* (volume) or part of one *ce* was lost (a vulnerability of traditional string-bound books).

A considerable corpus of Late Tang poetry has survived. In the ninth century as a whole, the record is rich enough to look at literary history in detail, something that is simply not possible earlier. Still, it is important to remember that the record is skewed in odd ways by vagaries of taste and accident.

TWO

The Old Men

Longevity is an inconvenience for literary history. Poets can live on past their most creative years characterized by poetic innovation and achievement. Secure in their fame, such senior poets often remain untouched by the new directions taken by younger poets. These old poets can join with other figures of cultural power to become a literary establishment, an enclosed world of often complacent celebrity. This more or less describes the circle of aging poets and political figures around Bai Juyi. In the case of Bai Juyi and his friends, it was a literary establishment situated in a retirement community, realized in sinecures in Luoyang, far from the hopes and perils of political life in Chang'an or the wanderings of younger poets looking for preferment. Bai Juyi enjoyed such semi-retirement, never forgetting that he was now out of public life. He had removed himself from more active public life by choice, but he celebrated his decision so frequently that it is hard not to feel that he "protested too much."

There is a genuine charm in many of the poems Bai Juyi wrote as an old man in Luoyang, but it is a charm that can be sustained only by limiting one's reading to a few poems. In large doses these poems become repetitive, facile, and self-absorbed—and the aging Bai Juyi wrote very many poems indeed. Bai Juyi's spontaneity and ease were a cultivated style, but in poetry these are precarious virtues. One can admire such poems, while at the same time understanding why younger poets seem to have reacted against the style.

Poets were always coming and going in Chang'an, where in the 830s the dominant fashion seems to have been the finely crafted regulated verse, centered around figures like Yao He and Jia Dao. The other major center of poetic activity was Luoyang. The latter was the Eastern Capital, with dilapidated palaces and a substantial bureaucracy that had very little to do. No emperor had visited Luoyang for as long as anyone could remember; this fact became something of a theme in the city's poetry. Since the succession was far from certain, positions in the crown prince's establishment, the "Regency Office," were already at some remove from the exercise of power, either in the present or in the anticipated future. However, positions in the "Luoyang assignment" of the crown prince's establishment were sinecures in the fullest sense; their incumbents were secure in the thought that a real crown prince would never call upon their services.

In the spring of 827, at the beginning of Wenzong's reign, Bai Juyi completed his term as governor of Suzhou. The poet was called to the capital to serve as Director of the Imperial Library. In the spring of 828 he moved up a step to Vice Minister of Justice. Up to this point in his career, Bai Juyi had been very much a part of the political world. However, in the spring of the following year, at his own request, Bai was transferred to the post of Adviser to the Heir Apparent, "Luoyang assignment."

The older as well as some of the younger holdovers of the Yuanhe generation were passing away. Around 827 Li Yi, a grand old man of letters and already a well-known poet in the last quarter of the eighth century, passed away; and around 830 Wang Jian and Zhang Ji died. More unexpectedly, on September 2, 831, Bai Juyi's dearest friend Yuan Zhen passed away at the relatively young age of fifty-three. Yuan Zhen had been considered, together with Bai, one of the leading poets of the Yuanhe generation, though in his later years he became increasingly preoccupied with political life and had become a powerful figure. By that point Bai had moved to the post of Metropolitan Governor (*yin* 尹) of Luoyang, a post that required some administrative involvement.

Late in 831 or early 832 Liu Yuxi, another survivor of the generation and a fellow poet and close friend, stopped over in Luoyang on his way to assume his new post as governor of Suzhou, the post Bai himself had held just five years earlier. Liu Yuxi was to fill the void left by Yuan Zhen's death, becoming Bai Juyi's closest poetic correspondent. In the following year Bai, complaining of "illness," resigned as Metropolitan Governor and resumed his old post as Adviser to the Heir Apparent. Liu Yuxi served out his term in Suzhou, and after passing through other short stints as a prefectural governor, he arrived in Luoyang to take up Bai Juyi's post as Adviser to the Heir Apparent. Bai Juyi was elevated to the distinguished title of Junior Mentor (*shaofu* 少傅) to the Crown Prince, no less a sinecure. That same year Li Shen, another well-known poet and friend, came to Luoyang to take Bai's earlier post as Metropolitan Governor. Li Shen was to move on to other distinguished political posts, but Bai Juyi and Liu Yuxi would remain in Luoyang until their deaths, Liu dying in 842 and Bai in 846.

These were all men in their late fifties, sixties, and (for Bai Juyi) seventies. All were famous and highly connected. Luoyang was on the most popular travel route from Chang'an, and through it passed the eminent statesmen of the day, including the very senior Pei Du, Linghu Chu, and the dominant younger figures of current political life, including Niu Sengru and Li Deyu (though Li Deyu was reputed to have disliked Bai Juyi and was much closer to Liu Yuxi). Such figures would stop by on their way to take up new posts, banqueting and exchanging poems with the Luoyang poets; sometimes they would occupy Luoyang posts, which were effectively vacations or rustications from their still active political careers. Bai's and Liu's companion pieces to poems by these eminent statesmen show that they were much more active poetically than their surviving poems often seem to indicate. Despite the fierce political feuds of the day, they represented a unified cultural community. Moreover, with the exception of Linghu Chu, who always had an eye for younger talent, they did not exchange many poems with the aspiring younger poets of the age. These younger poets sometimes came through Luoyang as well and would address poems to the senior statesmen or Bai Juyi (less often to Liu Yuxi); sometimes their poems were acknowledged, but more often they were ignored.

Social and poetic relationships play a large role in Bai Juyi's poetry dating from this period. This is true not only in poetry intended for social occasions or explicitly sent to friends; ostensibly solitary poetry, always concerned with the poet's self-representation, was also widely distributed in his circle (and always carefully copied into the ever-growing manuscripts Bai was preparing). Liu Yuxi's poetry composed during this period is overwhelmingly social, and his relationships with Bai and Linghu Chu stand at the center of his poetic network.[1] Other poets of the day speak of culling their poems—often radically—for the poetry collections that would preserve their work for posterity. Particularly in

---

1. The case of Li Shen is more complex because we do not have the full range of his social poems. What we have is *Recollecting Past Travels* 追昔遊 in three *juan* with a preface dated 838; I discuss this later.

his later years, Bai Juyi seems to have included in his collection most of what he wrote. We do find companion pieces (primarily by Liu Yuxi) to Bai Juyi's poems that no longer survive; considering the quality of some of Bai Juyi's pieces that do survive, it is hard to believe that the exclusions were based on aesthetic grounds.

When we read Bai Juyi's easygoing poems written in Luoyang in the early 830s—poems that not infrequently concerned concubines and singing girls—we should remember that in Luoyang during this very same period Du Mu wrote his famous ballad for Zhang Haohao (see pp. 272–74) and the young Li Shangyin wrote his densely difficult "Yan Terrace" poems (see pp. 180–81). Although Du Mu's ballad for Zhang Haohao derives in part from Bai Juyi's younger work in the narrative ballad, Du Mu and Li Shangyin represented very different worlds of poetry from that of Bai Juyi. Moreover, these distinct poetic communities, located in the same city and active at the same time, never seem to have crossed paths (apart from a few courteous exchange poems). In other words, although the characteristic poetry of the Late Tang was taking shape nearby in the same city, Bai Juyi seems to have been completely unaware of it. Li Shangyin did meet Bai Juyi in Luoyang (probably in 829–30), but Bai does not mention it.[2]

It is difficult to imagine what Bai Juyi would have made of Li Shangyin's "Yen Terrace" poems—though they seem to have lit a fire under the Luoyang demimondaine whom Li generically called "Willow Branch." It is not hard to imagine the existence of a community of young people in Luoyang who probably knew of Bai Juyi but had very different tastes in poetry. Du Mu seems to have shared something of his friend Li Kan's deep dislike of Bai Juyi's poetry (see p. 277). In his famous "Epistle on Presenting My Poems" he implicitly but clearly distinguished his poetic aims from the "familiar and common" style (*xisu* 習俗) that would have instantly been associated with Bai.[3] Li Shangyin did not personally comment on Bai's poetry. Li paid his tribute to Du

---

2. On this point see Liu Xuekai 劉學鍇 and Yu Shucheng 余恕誠, *Li Shangyin wen biannian jiaozhu* 李商隱文編年校注 (Beijing: Zhonghua shuju, 2002), vol. 4, p. 1801; see also Xie Siwei 謝思煒, "Bai Juyi yu Li Shangyin" 白居易與李商隱, in Wang Meng 730–34. We must dismiss the later legend that Bai Juyi much admired Li Shangyin's poetry and prose; see Liu Xuekai et al. (2001) 25.

3. *Fanchuan wenji* 242. That everyone could recognize Bai Juyi behind the "familiar and common" style was, of course, tacit recognition of Bai's fame.

Fu, Han Yu, and Li He, but he never tried his hand at the distinctive style of Bai Juyi. We may presume that it was for Li Shangyin's mastery of parallel prose that Bai Juyi's adopted heir called on him to write the tomb inscription, which mentions Bai's literary fame in other countries and the size of his collection but provides no details about his achievements as a poet. Yao He was old enough, sufficiently politically elevated, and poetically bland enough to enter the orbit of the group surrounding Bai Juyi. But, apart from Yao He, it is striking how completely divorced the older Bai Juyi and his friends were from other poets working at the time.

Although the poems of Liu Yuxi and Li Shen have enough in common with Bai Juyi to warrant their inclusion in the same chapter (commonalities that in no small measure reflect Bai Juyi's influence), Bai Juyi was clearly the major poet. His poetry is unified by a set of recurrent concerns that in the aggregate lend a degree of depth to poems that can sometimes seem trivial on the surface.

Bai Juyi

Any critical survey of Bai Juyi's poetry will disclose a sharp divide between those who considered him one of the greatest of all poets and those who were openly hostile to his poetry. Such a division was already apparent in the ninth century. We have already mentioned Li Kan's criticism (and will return to it); in Du Mu's account Li Kan wished for absolute political power simply to expunge Bai Juyi's insidiously popular poetry from the empire. Later in the ninth century Sikong Tu 司空圖 (837–908) described Bai and Yuan Zhen as "overbearing in force, yet feeble in [natural] energy [*qi*], like domineering merchants in the marketplace."[4] Tang writers tended to be relatively restrained in their criticism of other poets, so these are strong words indeed. In later criticism Bai Juyi was often used as a minatory case of the style the careless poet can fall into. Pi Rixiu 皮日休 (ca. 834–883), no less eminent than Sikong Tu, had only the highest praise for Bai. Zhang Wei's 張為 *Schematic of Masters and Followers Among the Poets* 詩人主

---

4. Chen Youqin 陳友琴, *Bai Juyi shi pingshu huibian* 白居易詩評述匯編 (Beijing: Kexue chubanshe, 1958), 10. Although Bai's name is conventionally paired with that of Yuan Zhen, it was Bai Juyi who was primarily praised or condemned.

客圖 places Bai Juyi at the head ("master") of his first category: "exten-sive and grand civilizing power" 廣大教化. What we see here is no or-dinary disagreement about the quality of a poet but rather extreme posi-tions on either side. No other Tang poet divided critics so sharply. Such a split was a consequence of different understandings of what poetry was and should be.

These general assessments of Bai Juyi's work were directed primarily at that body of his poetry written in the Yuanhe Reign and immediately thereafter, particularly the "New *Yuefu*" and the two famous ballads. However, we can see from passages cited by critics from the Song on-ward that Bai Juyi's later poems were indeed read. The term that was applied to Bai Juyi's poetry was *su* 俗, meaning "common," "vulgar," appealing to popular taste. In Bai Juyi's case this meant many things, from the actual popularity of his famous narrative ballads (which were easy to understand but not particularly vernacular), to the rambling clar-ity of his longer personal poems in "old style" verse, to some of the poems of his old age that were aggressively *su* in many ways.

Roughly half of Bai Juyi's immense poetic oeuvre dates from the reigns of Wenzong and Wuzong; that is, from 827 onward.[5] In 827, the first year of the Taihe Reign, Bai Juyi, aged fifty-six, was already estab-lished as a poet. To put this in perspective, Han Yu died at fifty-six, while Liu Zongyuan, Yuan Zhen, Du Mu, and Li Shangyin (not to mention Li He) all died at a younger age. It is fair to say that had Bai Juyi died at fifty-six, not only would his literary collection have been far smaller, but his reputation and contribution to Chinese poetry would have remained unchanged. We speak here only in literary-historical terms; in his later work Bai Juyi effectively invented a new poetry of old age and wrote some wonderful poems. At the same time, he preserved too many poems, which collectively give the impression of carelessness and repetitiousness.[6] In part his style reflects a studied casualness; when he writes lines that are pure vernacular, there can be little doubt that it is a conscious gesture.[7] Rather, this "carelessness" was the result of his

---

5. Only a small number of poems from the last years of his life have survived.

6. Not only do we find repetition among the later poems, but Bai would also redo earlier poems. For example, compare "Too Lazy to Be Able To" 慵不能 (23237; Zhu 1505) of 830 with "On Laziness" 詠慵 (21999) of 814.

7. See, e.g., the last line of "A Question for the Young Man" 問少年 (24056; Zhu 2188), which is explicitly framed as speech: 作个狂夫得了無.

habit of writing so many poems over so many years that certain patterns of verse seem to have come to him automatically. Other poets wrote as succinctly as possible, whereas Bai Juyi did not hesitate to use unnecessary words and to add a second line when the point had already been made in the first line.

Bai Juyi's facile style was a topic in Song critical discourse, but it was understood as a conscious choice. This was implied by the famous (and certainly apocryphal) anecdote that whenever Bai composed a poem, he would recite it to an old woman and change whatever she did not understand. In *Shiren xuxie* this anecdote is coupled with a report by Zhang Lei 張耒 (1054–1114) that he had seen the drafts of several poems by Bai, and that these had been extensively revised.[8] Facility was obviously a self-conscious value in much, though not all, of Bai Juyi's poetry throughout his career, and it is easy to believe that many of his earlier poems were carefully revised to achieve the fluent transparency that has made them memorable. However, a large number of the later poems have a roughness and redundancy that suggest a first draft. These poems were rarely anthologized or noted in "remarks on poetry" *shihua* 詩話. Such apparent haste goes hand in hand with Bai's growing interest in the quantity of his poetry.

The poetry of the last seventeen years of Bai Juyi's life, written during his residence in Luoyang, was the result of a decision that was, in its own way, every bit as radical as Tao Qian's decision to withdraw from public life. As was the case with Tao Qian, justifying and celebrating that decision became a recurrent, almost obsessive topic in Bai Juyi's subsequent poetry. Bai Juyi could have played the role of Tao Qian, whom he greatly admired, were it not for one striking difference of which Bai was intensely aware. When Tao Qian decided to withdraw, he had to farm for himself; he had to constantly worry about his survival, and he sometimes faced near starvation. Tao Qian's decision was a radical one whose consequences were always a source of anxiety.

Bai Juyi effectively sought retirement in the "Luoyang assignment" as a court official with a 3a rank, that is, he was a Regency official in the top echelons of the imperial bureaucracy, wore the "gold and purple,"

---

8. Wei Qingzhi 魏慶之, *Shiren yuxie* 詩人玉屑 (Shanghai: Gudian wenxue chubanshe, 1958), 175. The anecdote and Zhang Lei's note are given with a comment by Hu Zi, which I have not been able to locate in *Tiaoxi yuyin conghua*.

and was on intimate terms with ministers and senior statesmen. He didn't wind up on a ramshackle farm, worrying about how his bean crop was doing. He retired to a modest urban estate (with garden and pool) in the empire's second city, with sufficient savings, a considerable salary, and a domestic establishment that included singing girls. He no longer rode the political roller-coaster of Chang'an, but he was not Tao Qian. He had to establish a new poetic position for himself and his situation. He did so by means of a humorous twist on the old distinction between "greater" and "lesser" hermits: he was the "hermit in between" 中隱.

白居易, 中隱

Bai Juyi, The Hermit in Between[9]

大隱住朝市	The greater hermits stay in court and market,
小隱入丘樊	the lesser hermits enter the cage of the hills.[10]
丘樊太冷落	The cage of the hills is too cold and dreary,
朝市太囂諠	court and market are too noisy.[11]
不如作中隱	It's better to be a hermit in between,
隱在留司官	hermit in an auxiliary post.
似出復似處	It resembles service as well as retirement,
非忙亦非閑	not too busy, not idle either.
不勞心與力	Without taxing mind or energy,
又免飢與寒	I can also avoid hunger and cold.
終歲無公事	No public duties all year long,
隨月有俸錢	but I get my salary every month.
君若好登臨	If you like to go climbing for the view,
城南有秋山	there are autumn mountains south of the city.
君若愛遊蕩	If you love wild excursions,
城東有春園	there are spring gardens to the east.
君若欲一醉	If you want to get drunk,
時出赴賓筵	you can go out often to parties.
洛中多君子	With the many good gentlemen of Luoyang
可以恣歡言	you can talk merrily, as much as you please.
君若欲高臥	And if you want to rest in solitude,

---

9. 23223; Zhu 1493. See the discussion of this poem in Xiaoshan Yang's *Metamorphosis of the Private Sphere: Gardens and Objects in Tang-Song Poetry* (Cambridge, Mass.: Harvard University Asia Center, 2003), 38–39.

10. The "cage of the hills" or "fenced-in area in the hills" was a Southern Dynasties term for the place to which a recluse would withdraw.

11. As an example of repetition, see 24416; Zhu 2483.

但自深掩關	just hide deep behind barred gates.
亦無車馬客	There are also no visitors in fine coaches
造次到門前	unexpectedly showing up at your door.
人生處一世	A person lives only one life,
其道難兩全	and you can't have the best of both worlds.
賤即苦凍餒	If poor, you suffer from cold and want,
貴則多憂患	when rich, you have many troubles and cares.
唯此中隱士	Only such an in-between hermit
致身吉且安	can bring himself peace and good luck.
窮通與豐約	Failure and success, opulence and straits—
正在四者間	he is right in between these four.

Although old-style poems such as this one generally have more logically lucid expositions than regulated poems, Bai Juyi can be particularly pellucid. He is trying to make a space for himself between equally uncomfortable alternatives—and the issue is indeed his personal comfort, put forward in explicit terms that have few precedents in the tradition. This was one of the problems of scholars from "poor families" entering the bureaucracy: they depended on their salaries for a comfortable life and could not, like officials from wealthier backgrounds, go into high-minded withdrawal from public life without jeopardizing not only their own livelihood but that of the often considerable domestic establishments they had acquired. No Tang poet talks about his salary and his domestic establishment as much as Bai Juyi. No doubt many others were equally preoccupied with this subject, but Bai Juyi immortalized it in his verse and prose.

As Bai Juyi well knew, court service was unstable. Apart from the aftermath of the Sweet Dew Incident of 835, few lost their lives; but for a poet in his late fifties and sixties—one who liked his creature comforts—the prospect of being sent off to some remote prefecture in the far south because a friend or marriage relation fell from power was not an attractive one. The "Luoyang assignment" was thus ideal. It was an escape that Bai had himself chosen; and he can be forgiven some gentle gloating when those who mocked his choice were later packed off to the pestilential south in advanced old age. The following couplet probably refers to Li Zongmin's exile to Chaozhou in 835:[12]

---

12. 24042; Zhu 2176.

今日憐君嶺南去	Today I pity you,
	going off south of the Alps,
當時笑我洛中來	back then you laughed at me
	for coming to Luoyang.

To enjoy such unencumbered economic security and leisure was one thing; to write about it was another. The recurrent discourse of personal comforts and money was perhaps one aspect of his work that divided Bai Juyi's readers. This was, according to one view, the very essence of vulgarity (recall Sikong Tu's image of Bai as a "domineering merchant in the marketplace," suggesting someone with power and money). Bai Juyi's somewhat uncomfortable poetic genius derived from a certain social blindness: he stood at the center of his universe; poetically he often stepped back a few paces to contemplate and admire himself, to comment on his great good fortune. If, in old age as in youth, he occasionally experienced embarrassment when encountering the sufferings of people of lower social status, there was something peculiarly egotistical and self-congratulatory about it, not unlike the whiff of envy we catch when he writes of those who are wealthier.[13] As the "hermit in between," he is always measuring where he is and comparing himself to others, either real people or speculative models.

As many critics have observed since the Song, Bai Juyi likes to count things: he counts his age; how many years are left to him; how many years between the present and some moment in the past; how many things he has; or, implicitly in the poem above, the advantages of his position.[14] He compares himself to those who are better and worse off. The changing world is quantifiable, so that one knows one's gains and losses. It is important always to take stock.

The Tang imperial system of bureaucratic and social rank was intended to control the "place" of the elite by claiming a monopoly on social value. For such a system to function through the agency of the

---

13. In "A Poem I Wrote on Being Stirred by a Newly Finished Fine Silk Padded Jacket" 新製綾襖成感而有詠 (23826; Zhu 1986) Bai does express the wish, in very conscious imitation of Du Fu, to have a great cape to cover all Luoyang; but in Bai Juyi's case, in striking contrast to Du Fu, it follows a vivid celebration of his personal comfort. See also "Year's End" 歲暮 (23863; Zhu 2016).

14. See Hong Mai's 洪邁 (1123–1202) *Rongzhai suibi* 容齋隨筆 for a dramatic list of lines on his age. See also Chen Youqin 陳友琴, *Bai Juyi shi pingshu huibian* 白居易詩評述匯編 (Beijing: Kexue chubanshe, 1958), 118.

government—rather than social value inhering in a person through birth—the government had to continually exercise its power over individual members of the elite to add and subtract social value. The imperial government invested a great deal of wealth and energy in conferring rank and title and in constantly moving members of the bureaucracy, both between positions and geographically (far more frequently in this part of the ninth century than in earlier eras). Members of the bureaucracy, in turn, sought to move "up," and when they were demoted "down," they sought to move back up. It was a system predicated on mobility, realized through a currency of prestige that was a government monopoly. And since income was a function of rank, rank-prestige could be linked to financial security for those who had no independent source of family wealth.

A system of social mobility through quantifiable value, even on a restricted social scale, clearly has formal counterparts in early modern Europe. In the Song—particularly in the Southern Song—a commercial culture would develop in competition with and woven into the rank-salary structure of value that remained a government monopoly. In the Tang, however, the restriction of merchants and the contempt in which they were held was perhaps a function of the recognition that this represented a structure of value that might compete with the very basis of the central government's social power.

Although we can see in prose, in anecdotes, and in history that relations of social "value" and mobility were central concerns of the Tang elite, this was generally hidden in poetry or expressed through sanctioned tropes, such as the desire for someone (of higher standing and power) to recognize one's worth or the plea for preferment. The "poetic" world generally involved a circumscribed range of sentiments and a physical world made up of things possessing a poetic aura. Such a version of the "poetic" had its own social function as an alternative to the hierarchy of social value that was so much a visible part of the Tang world. Circles of poets often ignored differences in social hierarchy.

Although he had withdrawn from the precarious mobility of high officialdom, of all Tang poets Bai Juyi most fully internalized that social structure of value and brought it to the surface—in the sense of always tallying up what he possessed and comparing that with what others had. Like Tao Qian before him, he claimed to be satisfied with what he had. Yet he "had" so much more of everything—rank, years, friends, poems, salary, and possessions—that his claims of satisfaction take on a very different tone.

Bai Juyi often celebrates both utilitarian and ornamental domestic objects that were not part of the usual repertoire of "poetic" things treated by other poets. The way in which he poetically figures his relation to these things is often of considerable interest.

白居易, 別氈帳火爐

Bai Juyi, Parting from My Felt Curtain and Brazier[15]

憶昨臘月天	I recall recently in late winter weather
北風三尺雪	the north wind and three feet of snow.
年老不禁寒	Getting old, I couldn't stop feeling cold,
夜長安可徹	how was I to get through the long nights?
賴有青氈帳	Luckily I had a green felt curtain,
風前自張設	I hung it up against the wind.
復此紅火爐	Also there was this red brazier
雪中相暖熱	that warmed me up in the snow.
如魚入淵水	I was like a fish diving into deep water,
似兔藏深穴	like a rabbit hiding deep in his hole.
婉軟蟄鱗蘇	Tender and gentle, the wintering scales revive,
溫燉凍肌活	poached in warmth, frozen flesh revitalized.
方安陰慘夕	But then those dark and gloomy evenings
遽變陽和節	changed instantly to a time of balmy light.
無奈時候遷	It's the seasons moving inevitably on—
豈是恩情絕	of course my affection has not ceased.
毳簾逐日卷	The frizzy curtain is rolled up with the days,
香爐隨灰滅	the ashes die in the fragrant brazier.
離恨屬三春	Parting's pain belongs to springtime,
佳期在十月	our tryst will be in the tenth month.
但令此身健	If only this body stays healthy,
不作多時別	we will not be parted for long.

Hidden behind this ninth-century poem is the famous fan poem attributed to Lady Ban, in which the fan—figured as or a figure for the harem favorite—worries about being "put away" when the cool autumn wind comes, when passion slackens. Bai Juyi's domestic objects protect him from the cold but likewise suffer rejection, in this case when warm weather comes.

---

15. 23189; Zhu 1455.

In this now domestic drama between a person and his objects, Bai Juyi has placed himself at the center as the speaker and the person with the power to give or withhold favor, which is value. He humanizes his objects, giving them eyes to look at him with desire: they want to be used and valued. His drama of ownership is one in which his own pleasure in use and possession is displaced into inanimate things that look upon him with a desire to be possessed and cared for. He does, however, want to be benevolent.

He begins in personal discomfort, and his comfort is provided for. (Recall the rhetoric of imperial "anxiety," the sovereign's discomfort that sends armies out to conquer places and restore the imperial sense of well-being.) However, in contrast to the fan poem, in which gratitude is desired but not expected by the fan, Bai Juyi is generously grateful. When the season comes to put away the instruments of his comfort, he assures them that they are not being rejected; they will only experience a brief period of separation, after which they will be received again with equal love. Bai Juyi's enduring concern for his body and health returns as a final qualification of his reassurances: if the object-as-lover wants to be reunited with the beloved Bai, it must hope for Bai's continuing good health. From shivering helplessness Bai has humorously empowered himself.

The figure addressed in Lady Ban's poem, the person who has the power to give or withhold favor, is the emperor. The poet has written himself into this imperial role among his household possessions. They are his harem or his officials, who gain or lose value through his favor and his need.

We have here an economics of variable value granted by favor of a central authority in recognition of utility. To this a second system of value should be added, a system of capital that touches on the first system in various ways. *Ye* 業 is perhaps best translated as "capital" in a broad sense—whether financial, scholarly, cultural, or karmic. It is something one can inherit, accumulate, and pass on. Property, bureaucratic and religious merit, and learning can be understood this way.

At the beginning of Wenzong's reign Bai had been called to the capital to become Director of the Imperial Library (rank 3b). For the first time in his life he received the "gold [seal] and purple [sash]," the mark of a high court officer. This was, as the poet wrote, "glory in this age." If he had had sons who had lived, they could have inherited office by *yin* privilege, a fact about which he remarked elsewhere. But the capital of "name" that might have gone to his descendents in the male line was wasted. Later, when a son died in infancy, here is how he ended a poem to Yuan Zhen and Cui Xuanliang:[16]

| 文章十帙官三品 | Ten cases of writings, an office of the third rank— |
| 身後傳誰庇廕誰 | to whom will I pass the one on after my death, who will get the yin privilege? |

The *yin* privilege, his capital accumulated through long service in the bureaucracy, was wasted. His writings, as a quantifiable legacy, would go somewhere and bear his name, even if not to a descendent in the male line. If he wrote—or saved—too many poems it was his *chanye* 產業, the "capital produced," the "inheritance" for the future. A more conventional *chanye* would be quantifiable; his poetic production became that. In his numerous prefaces and letters from this period he is always counting how many poems he has produced and how many have been added to the current store. It is as if instead of working at accumulating capital of goods and prestige for his descendents (who would bear his "name after his death"), he is accumulating poems for that "name."

白居易, 初授秘監并賜金紫閒吟小酌偶寫所懷

Bai Juyi, On First Being Appointed Director of the Palace Library and on Being Granted the "Gold and Purple," a Leisurely Verse on Drinking a Little, at Which I Chance to Describe What Is on My Mind[17]

紫袍新秘監	A purple gown, new Library Director,
白首舊書生	white-haired, a former student.
鬢雪人間壽	Snow at my temples, old age among mortals,
腰金世上榮	gold at my waist, glory in this age.
子孫無可念	Nothing to brood on about descendents,
產業不能營	no busying myself with providing inheritance.
酒引眼前興	Ale brings elation to my eyes,
詩留身後名	poems will preserve my name after my death.
閒傾三數酌	Idly I pour myself a few cups
醉詠十餘聲	and drunk sing out a dozen lines.
便是羲皇代	Even if it is the age of a sage-king,
先從心太平	one should first set the heart at peace.

---

16. 23816; Zhu 1978.
17. 23471; Zhu 1711.

A few years later he "set his heart at peace" in the "Luoyang assignment," but he retained a strong sense of his literary oeuvre as a physical and quantifiable capital that would be passed on. His bookcase resembled nothing so much as a miser's chest.

白居易, 題文集櫃

Bai Juyi, On the Cabinet for My Literary Collection[18]

破柏作書櫃	I broke up cypress to make a book cabinet,
櫃牢柏復堅	the cabinet sturdy and the cypress strong.
收貯誰家集	Whose collection is stored there?—
題云白樂天	the heading says "Bai Letian."
我生業文字	My lifetime's capital is in writing
自幼及老年	from childhood on to old age.
前後七十卷	Seventy scrolls from beginning to end,
小大三千篇	in size, three thousand pieces.
誠知終散失	I know well that at last they will be scattered,
未忍遽棄捐	but I cannot bear to rashly throw them away.
自開自鎖閉	I open it up, I lock it tight,
置在書帷前	placing it by my study curtain.
身是鄧伯道	I am childless Deng You,
世無王仲宣	and there is no Wang Can in this age.[19]
只應分付女	I can only entrust it to my daughter
留與外孫傳	to keep and pass on to my grandchild.

Though translated as a noun, the "capital" of the fifth line, *ye*, is used as a verb here, loosely translated as "to build capital" or "to build a legacy." It is literally inscribed with his "name." It is quantified and—most interesting—is locked up when the poet is not using it. The fatalistic recognition that it will be scattered someday could temporarily be countered by a son who would inherit both the accumulated cultural capital and the name. In Bai Juyi's case this capital will have to go "out," *wai* (the untranslatable qualifier of the grandchild in the final line, who is on the "distaff" side, "outside" the main line of the family as a result of having a different surname).

---

18. 23915; Zhu 2072. See the discussion in Christopher Nugent, "The Circulation of Poetry in Tang Dynasty China" (Ph.D. diss., Harvard University, 2004), 254–55.

19. This probably refers to the anecdote of the famous literary man Cao Yong 蔡邕 meeting the adolescent Wang Can; Cao was so impressed with Wang Can's talent that he immediately thought he should give the young man all his books. *Sanguo zhi* 597.

Bai Juyi's passion for counting and measuring overflows his spiritual economy of value: it becomes a form of representing the world and goes hand in hand with his poetic loquacity. The true Bai Juyi of the 830s and 840s does not appear fully in the handful of poems commonly anthologized or translated but rather in the sea of verse in which these better-known poems float.

白居易, 答崔賓客晦叔十二月四日見寄 (來篇云, 共相呼喚醉歸來)
Bai Juyi, Answering the Poem Sent by Tutor Cui Huishu [Xuanliang] on the
Fourth Day of the Twelfth Month (The poem he sent had the line:
"Let us call to each other to go back drunk")[20]

今歲日餘二十六	The days that remain in the present year are twenty-six,
來歲年登六十二	next year's rich harvest— the age of sixty-two.
尚不能憂眼下身	Still I cannot worry about this body that I see,
因何更算人間事	why should I calculate any more affairs in the mortal world?
居士忘筌默默坐	This recluse has forgotten the fish-trap and sits silently,[21]
先生枕麴昏昏睡	you, sir, pillow your head on mash and sleep in a stupor.
早晚相從歸醉鄉	Sooner or later we will go together back to the Land of Drunkenness—
醉鄉去此無多地	from here to the Land of Drunkenness is not very far.

Some of the points mentioned earlier should be apparent here: an eight-line poem performs three calculations (ll. 1, 2, 8), and in the fourth line the poet invokes calculation by refusing to "calculate." Bai Juyi is always reckoning his years and time; probably only he would have noticed the inverse symmetry of 26 and 62.

The loquaciousness of the above poem—despite the poet's claims to have "forgotten the fish-trap" of language—is of a very special sort. The apocryphal anecdote in which Bai revised his poetry to make it understood by an old woman undoubtedly grew out of the recognition

---

20. 23193; Zhu 1461.

21. Recall Zhuangzi's parable of language: when you get the fish, you forget the fish-trap; when you get the meaning, you forget words.

that Bai Juyi's poetry was widely comprehensible aurally. This comment requires some nuance. Middle Chinese of the Tang had many more phonemes than modern Mandarin; thus, there was less potential ambiguity in recognizing both individual words and compounds. If we recognize "poetic Chinese" as a special idiolect with its own habitual situations, grammatical patterns, and lexicon, then most Tang poetry was comprehensible aurally by those fully familiar with the idiolect. Although Bai Juyi kept the formal constraints of "poetic Chinese," he preferred a low-register lexicon that made it accessible to a wider audience. If standard poetic Chinese preferred *hua hong* 花紅, "the red of flowers," Bai Juyi would write *hong hua* 紅花, "red flowers." Apart from a few compounds that involve allusions (ironically including "forgetting the fish-trap"), Bai Juyi's entire poem above is made up of very simple compounds and compound phrases. This worked best in the long line (which remained the dominant form of oral popular poetry from the Tang through the twentieth century).

Bai Juyi was quite capable of writing complex, erudite verse—though he had difficulty sustaining the "high style" throughout a poem. He was predisposed to write the kind of poem cited above, of which he was fully conscious. The poem *is* careless, but it is self-consciously so; it is a style "marked" as *su* 俗 (the "common," the "low," the "popular," the "vernacular").[22] In his old age he wrote far less about the art of poetry than he did in his earlier poetry (although he continually spoke of composing poems). We have some texts reflecting on the *changhe* 唱和 form, in which poets "matched" poems by friends. But perhaps the most significant piece for his later view on poetics can be found in an 828 poem and preface for the monk Daozong, whose Buddhist poetry is written for the salvation of souls rather than "for the sake of poetry" 不爲詩而作.[23] He praises Daozong's poetry for its formal perfection and clarity of exposition: "No error in a single tone, / four lines in organized sequence" 一音無差別, 四句有詮次. He praises how Daozong "lets his words go freely in a relaxed manner, / drifting off and leaving [the art of] the written word" 從容恣語言, 縹緲離文字. The

22. Here one might contrast Du Fu, famous for his use of vernacular phrases in poetry. In Du Fu's works the vernacular and high "poetic" are easily integrated rather than articulated against one another.

23. 23180; Zhu 1445.

description perfectly describes Bai Juyi's own poetry—though without Daozong's religious purpose.

Bai Juyi further favorably contrasts Daozong's kind of Buddhist poetry with the works of the poet-monks of the late eighth century, masters of regulated verse in the short line, who did indeed write "for the sake of poetry." Bai Juyi was in Chang'an when he composed this poem, and he can hardly have been unaware of the popularity of regulated-verse masters such as Jia Dao and Yao He, poets who clearly much admired those very poet-monks who wrote "for the sake of poetry."

What we see here in the second quarter of the ninth century is the first stirring of an opposition of high and low registers as a type of stylistic choice.[24] The poetics of the "low style," *su*, had profound consequences in Chinese poetry. By foregrounding ease and immediacy in composition, the poetics of the "low style" contributed negatively to the "high style," which increasingly celebrated the traces of effort and time spent in composition. As we shall see in the next chapter, this was the poetics of "bitter chanting" or "painstaking composition," *kuyin* 苦吟.

The dynamics of register set in motion went far beyond two groups of poets with different values. *Kuyin* in regulated verse was very much the art of the parallel couplet, and these poets would often frame their "high style" couplets with a closing couplet (and occasionally an opening couplet) in a "low" register, often very vernacular and reminiscent of Bai Juyi. Such interplay between high and low register passages became an essential part of the poetics of song lyric (*ci* 詞). In embryonic form the emergence of a "low" or vernacular aesthetic led to the opposition between it and the "classical" or "poetic" that was to play such an important role in later literary culture.

Bai Juyi's adoption and cultivation of a low poetic register was not a neutral act but rather a stylistic instantiation of a set of values that are thematically reiterated throughout his poetry, especially his later poetry. As the poet often says, he is doing what suits him and following his

---

24. Earlier poets had sometimes engaged in individual play on register. Beginning in the late eighth century there was a publicly recognized opposition between registers associated with the "ancient," *gu* 古, and the "modern." The "ancient" style, however, claimed an aura of ethical value, lacking in Bai Juyi's "low" style. The "poetic" or "high" style was very much in the lineage of the "modern" in the opposition between "ancient" and "modern."

nature. He acts on whim and responds to situations spontaneously. In short, in Bai Juyi the low register is part of the claim of the "natural," and it remained part of various versions of such a claim later in the tradition.

A claim about behaving "naturally" or composing poetry "naturally" is very different from simply "being natural." From a broad perspective it would be hard to argue that a human being is ever capable of not being "natural." A claim about behaving naturally is based on an idea of what the "natural" is; for such a person the "natural" has certain attributes; it is a value and thus something to be desired. It is negatively defined against some state or behavior—usually social—conceived as somehow "unnatural," constraining or violating the self. In its essential negativity the "natural" must break out of constraint; it must appear against something else. It is confirmed only in being seen from the outside. (After all, how can one know one is "behaving naturally" without recognizing it from the perspective of an imagined alternative?)

Bai Juyi and many poets that followed in his lineage had a genius in picturing themselves. The poet sees himself as he must look. Indeed, from his earlier poetry Bai Juyi possessed a remarkable ability to picture and imagine himself as the object of the perception of others. The following poem, from the Luoyang period, captures one of Bai Juyi's characteristically humorous domestic moments, ending with the poet's witty observation, which is also an observation of self.

白居易, 偶眠

Bai Juyi, Falling Asleep by Chance[25]

放盃書桉上	I set down my cup on the desk,
枕臂火爐前	rest my head on my arm before the burning stove.
老愛尋思事	Old, I am fond of thinking back on things,
慵多取次眠	lazy, I often fall asleep at random times.
妻教卸烏帽	My wife makes me take off my black cap,
婢與展青氊	the maid spreads a green blanket on me.
便是屏風樣	Exactly the pose you see on a screen!—
何勞畫古賢	why bother to paint ancient worthies?

To write a poem about nodding off, you have to be awake. Apparently the poet's wakefulness is the result of his loving but officious household—his wife making him remove his hat (or removing it herself) and

---

25. 23487; Zhu 1725.

the maid covering him with a blanket. To fall asleep this way is indeed "natural," but clearly from another perspective, provided by the women of the household, it is all too natural and needs to be done the "right" way. What is, of course, striking about the poem is that once the person dozing is properly attired (or unattired), he is no longer the sleeper but the outer eyes seeing himself as a sleeper. In precise terms it is a *yang* 樣, translated as "pose," but also a "fashion" or "manner." He sees himself as a figure in a screen painting, and in this pose he obviates the need for actual paintings.

The representation of being seen occurs often in Bai Juyi's poems, particularly in the closing section. In some cases it is less seen than listened to.

白居易, 偶吟

Bai Juyi, Chanting by Chance[26]

里巷多通水	Much water is passing through the ward lanes,
林園盡不扃	none of the groves and gardens are barred.
松身爲外戶	The pine tree is my outer door,
池面是中庭	my courtyard is the surface of a pool.
元氏詩三帙	Three cases of Yuan Zhen's poems,
陳家酒一瓶	a bottle of Mr. Chen's ale.
醉來狂發詠	When I get drunk, I sing out wildly,
鄰女映籬聽	a neighbor girl listens, half hidden by the hedge.

Bai Juyi gives us a flooded city, in which everyone is apparently isolated and the poet is kept at home and barred from his usual excursions. What remain to him are the two things most commonly put in parallel positions (as here) in party poems: "poems" and "ale" (conveniently, a level tone balancing a deflected tone). Inaccessible friends in Luoyang are replaced by the poems of a more remote friend, Yuan Zhen. Left to his own devices, the poet recites the poems "wildly," *kuang* 狂, heedless of normal restraint. His heedlessness is, however, heeded and he heeds the person heeding his heedlessness. There is a characteristic satisfaction in noting the neighbor girl "half hidden by the hedge," listening to him and no doubt thinking: "what a crazy old man!"

Kuang is used often in Bai Juyi's poetry to describe the poet's recitation or behavior. It is an interesting term in that it already incorporates an outside perspective. Perfectly "natural" and spontaneous behavior

---

26. 23674; Zhu 1887.

would have no outside from which to recognize itself: the poet who knows he is *kuang* is already picturing himself in relation to some other standard.

To picture oneself is one thing; to be pictured by another is quite another. One of Bai Juyi's finest poems, written in 810 when he was at the height of his poetic powers, consists of a playful contemplation of his own portrait.

白居易, 自題寫真 (時爲翰林學士)
Bai Juyi, On My Portrait (at the time
I was a Hanlin Academician)[27]

我貌不自識	I didn't recognize my own face,
李放寫我眞	Li Fang painted my portrait true.
靜觀神與骨	Calmly I observe the spirit and the bone structure:
合是山中人	this must be some man of the mountains.
蒲柳質易朽	Willow wood and rushes easily rot away,
麋鹿心難馴	the heart of a deer is not to be tamed.
何事赤墀上	Why then in the court's red pavements
五年爲侍臣	have I served in attendance for five years?
況多剛狷性	Worse still, this nature so hard and blunt
難與世同塵	cannot share the dirt of the world.
不惟非貴相	Not only not a face with signs of nobility,
但恐生禍因	I fear only it will be the cause of misfortune.
宜當早罷去	Best then to quit and go as soon as I can,
收取雲泉身	to take away this body of clouds and streams.

Here Bai Juyi wittily plays the role of the physiognomist, reading his nature in his portrait. He pretends to discover his "real," "natural" self in the process, a self that does not belong in the court role in which he is represented. We know that this is play, that his "discovery" is what he already knows about himself; and yet the poetic move he makes is a significant one, seeing himself from the outside in order to discover what is "true" or "genuine," *zhen* 眞, the term for portraiture, *xiezhen* 寫真, "depicting the true."

In 829, when still Vice Director of the Board of Punishments in Chang'an, Bai Juyi saw that same portrait again—and perhaps remembered his old poem.

---

27. 21968; Zhu 311.

白居易, 感舊寫眞
Bai Juyi, Moved by an Old Portrait[28]

李放寫我眞	Li Fang painted my portrait true,
寫來二十載	since he painted it, twenty years have gone by,
莫問眞何如	Don't ask how the true original looks,
畫亦銷光彩	the painting has also lost its gloss.
朱顏與玄鬢	Rosy complexion and dark locks of hair
日夜改復改	change and keep changing day and night.
無嗟貌遽非	Sigh not that the face is suddenly not what it was—
且喜身猶在	just be glad that the body is still here.

Bai Juyi begins with an exact quotation from his earlier poem, but the "true" quality of the portrait has become complicated. In place of physiognomy that reads unchanging nature, the poet now reads aging. Even though he tells us not to ask about the "true [original]," *zhen*, the use of "also" lets us know that the "true" has changed, like the portrait itself. Still, the painting and its original have parted company: the painting may have lost its gloss, but it still has traces of the "rosy complexion and dark locks of hair" that are gone from the original—an original that had not yet taken the playful advice of 810 to get out of office.

Although here the once-legible body has simply become the surviving body, Bai Juyi's fascination with stepping outside himself and taking a snapshot of himself exerted a profound influence on the tradition; from the Southern Song on, there is a familiar type of quatrain in which the poet pictures himself in the last line. Here is Bai Juyi in a quatrain from 838.

白居易, 東城晚歸
Bai Juyi, Returning Late in the Day
in the East of the City[29]

一條邛杖懸龜榼	A single staff of Qiong bamboo, a tortoiseshell mug suspended,
雙角吳童控馬銜	a Wu servant lad with a pair of tufts leads the horse's bit.
晚入東城誰識我	Late I enter the east of the city, who recognizes me?—

---

28. 23219; Zhu 1491.
29. 24255; Zhu 2359.

短靴低帽白蕉衫   short boots, a low hat,
         a tunic of white plantain fiber.

It is a gaffer's fashion show, and we know this gaffer is a bibulous poet from his outfit. It is, in effect, iconography inviting painting, legible even when portraiture that captures the "true" appearance fails to account for a changing body. Such a vignette of self-portrayal, involving not the features of the face but visible markers of a "type," would itself become a poetic "type" later in the tradition.

白居易, 自詠
Bai Juyi, On Myself[30]

鬢白面微紅   Whiskers white, the face faintly red,
醺醺半醉中   in a tipsy, half-drunken state.
百年隨手過   Life's hundred years pass in a snap,
萬事轉頭空   ten thousand cares gone in the nod of a head.
臥疾瘦居士   Lying sick, a gaunt man in retirement,
行歌狂老翁   going singing, a wild old man.
仍聞好事者   And I heard that some who are interested
將我畫屏風   have painted me on screens.

Bai Juyi's theatrical "naturalness" is, to his credit, only one aspect of his later poetry—though a very large one. He could also be unctuously polite, celebrate the austerities of Chan, and lament family and friends. In addition, he could also laugh at himself.

Bai Juyi was immensely fond of his Luoyang home, his Taihu rock, his cranes, his garden, his comfortable clothes and blankets, his small pleasures. Sometimes he let things go, always celebrating his act of renunciation in a poem. One of his favorite things was the skiff he had transported to Luoyang from Suzhou, after he finished his term as governor there. It served him well on his little pond. Bai was usually cheerful—or tried to be—when facing old age, though the topic recurs with such frequency that we can see it was always on his mind. In 839 he had a stroke that left him partially paralyzed in one leg. As any householder knows, constant vigilance is necessary; otherwise things break down. After he became somewhat mobile again, he went out into his garden and surveyed the scene:

---

30. 24259; Zhu 2362.

白居易, 感蘇州舊舫
Bai Juyi, Stirred by My Old Skiff from Suzhou[31]

畫梁朽折紅窗破	My painted beams have decayed and snapped, the red window is broken,
獨立池邊盡日看	I stand alone beside my pool looking all day long.
守得蘇州船舫爛	The skiff that I kept from Suzhou is rotten,
此身爭合不衰殘	then how should not this body of mine be wasting away?

Like his portrait and his body, his "things" also deteriorate. His attachment to Buddhism was sincere and seems to have deepened in his later years. We might leave Bai Juyi by recalling a poem of 845, the year before his death. The old sensualist clings to attachments and calls back pleasures in memory, even as he claims to let them go.

白居易, 齋居春久感事遣懷
Bai Juyi, Living in Abstention Spring Lasts Long; Stirred,
I Get Things off My Chest[32]

齋戒坐三旬	I have stayed in abstention for thirty days
笙歌發四鄰	as song and piping emerge from all the neighborhood.
月明停酒夜	Moon bright on nights I have quit drinking,
眼闇看花人	the eyes dim of the one who looked at flowers.
賴學空爲觀	Luckily I study Void for my viewpoint,
深知念是塵	and well understand that Thought is dust.
猶思閒語笑	Still I think of idle chatter and laughter
未忘舊交親	and have never forgotten my old friends.
久作龍門主	Long I was master at Dragongate,[33]
多爲兔苑賓	and often have been a guest in Rabbit Park.[34]
水嬉歌盡日	Sporting on the water, song lasted all day;
雪宴燭通晨	feasting in snow, candles burned until dawn.
事事皆過分	In everything I exceeded the measure,

---

31. 24310; Zhu 2399.

32. 24506; Zhu 2561.

33. Dragongate was the western side of Fragrant Mountain, Xiangshan, near whose temple Bai had a retreat.

34. This was the park of the Prince of Liang, in the Western Han, and stands for a patron of poets.

時時自問身   again and again I ask myself why.
風光拋得也   All spring's glory has been cast away
七十四年春   in this spring of my seventy-fourth year.

Interlude

To single out the distinctive concerns of a poet like Bai Juyi is to overlook a significant amount of purely social verse, which was rarely read even though it was the currency of the network in which someone with a reputation as a poet maintained his social connections. For example, any notable public event in the life of a highly placed friend or acquaintance called for a poem—just as we might write a note or send a card in modern times. Each common social situation had a set of topics that should or could be addressed with poetic grace, but an established poet would be expected to provide at least one fine couplet to display his skill. Without delving too deeply into this mode, we might consider just one poem.

In the spring of 832 Linghu Chu was transferred from a command in the east to become Regent, Metropolitan Governor, and military commissioner in Taiyuan, the Northern Capital. We might recall that it was this same spring that Li Ting, a general with a long history of distinguished service—and one humiliating defeat—was given command of the Wuning army, headquartered in Xuzhou, and declined the appointment on the grounds of ill health, after the Wuning army ate one of his subordinates.[35] The army at Taiyuan was less troublesome, and Linghu Chu had a special affection for this city where his father had served as administrator. It is said that the locals had a reciprocal affection for Linghu Chu.

When someone of Linghu Chu's stature was given such a post, congratulations, usually in the form of poems, would come from his friends in the official world. From Suzhou Liu Yuxi sent "Lord Minister Linghu Transfers His Command from Tianping to Taiyuan: Extending My Congratulations in a Poem" 令狐相公自天平移鎮太原以詩申賀, concluding grandly with a comparison of Linghu Chu to Wang Shang of the Han:[36]

---

35. *Zizhi tongjian* 7879.

36. 19029. After Wang Shang's bearing intimidated the Shanyu of the Xiongnu, the emperor exclaimed that he was a "true Minister of the Han."

夷落遙知眞漢相	Far away the barbarian tribes 　　know a true Minister of the Han
爭來屈膝看儀形	and compete to come on bended knee 　　to behold his deportment.

Bai Juyi, Linghu Chu's counterpart as Regent in the Eastern Capital, sent his own congratulations in the form of a parting poem.

白居易, 送令狐相公赴太原
Bai Juyi, Seeing Off Lord Minister Linghu,
Who Is Setting Off for Taiyuan[37]

六纛雙旌萬鐵衣	Six pennants, paired banners 　　ten thousand suits of armor,
並汾舊路滿光輝	the former road of Bing and Fen 　　fills with radiance.
青衫書記何年去	A clerk in blue student gown, 　　what year did you leave?
紅旆將軍昨日歸	now a general with red streamers 　　you recently returned.
詩作馬蹄隨筆走	In poems you make the horse's hooves 　　speed along with the brush;
獵酣鷹翅伴觥飛	hunting, you intoxicate the hawk's wings, 　　flying together with drinking horns.
北都莫作多時計	Do not make long-term plans 　　to stay in the Northern Capital—
再爲蒼生入紫微	for the sake of the people once again 　　enter the Purple Precincts.

Such poems possess a distinct quality of social ritual: they contain a series of topics that must be mentioned in a roughly predetermined order. The particulars of the situation and Linghu Chu's stature map most of Bai Juyi's poem for him. He needs an opening couplet on the entourage to represent Linghu Chu's prestige in transit. Voyaging to take up an important provincial post was political theater: the incumbent would travel with banners, insignia, an entourage, and troops commensurate with the importance and nature of the post. Since Taiyuan was where Linghu Chu started out as a much-admired young graduate, Bai could not resist the couplet contrasting the young student with the mature Regent. Finally, a parting poem begs for a conclusion expressing the hope

---

37. 23627; Zhu 1864.

that the person leaving will return soon. Bai Juyi nicely twists that convention into a gracious compliment, asking that, "for the sake of the people," Linghu Chu return soon to Chang'an and the imperial palace.[38]

This leaves Bai Juyi only one couplet (the third) to demonstrate his prowess as one of the empire's best-known senior poets. Generals entertain themselves by galloping in the hunt; literary men (and civil officials) entertain themselves by writing poetry and drinking. Linghu Chu combines the virtues of a military man (a military commissioner) and a literarily inclined civil servant. When someone with poetic talent writes, his brush "speeds," as do his horse's hooves. At a drinking party the goblets are said to "fly," as does the hunting hawk, metaphorically intoxicated by the hunt. In its peculiar way the third couplet combines all these elements while maintaining perfect parallelism. The ingenuity, however, fills one of the requirements of such poems: it must somehow refer to the post (or, in this case, the multiple posts) that the incumbent is to assume.

Linghu Chu would have written back to both Bai and Liu, either separately or jointly. Linghu Chu's response does not survive, though we do have a poem from Linghu Chu to both Bai and Liu, responding to poems they wrote earlier when he assumed command of the Xuanwu army.[39]

Liu Yuxi

劉禹錫, 寓興
Liu Yuxi, Figurative (second of two)[40]

世途多禮數	The world's ways have many different customs:
鵬鷃各逍遙	peng bird and sparrow each roam free.
何事陶彭澤	Why, then, did Tao Qian of Pengze
拋官爲折腰	drop his post because he had to bow low?

Although Liu Yuxi has, in the past half century, become known and approved for his imitations of Southern folksongs (and for his youthful political affiliation with the Wang Shuwen government of 805), these

---

38. The choice of words often has a weight of association that borders on allusion but does not rise to explicit allusion. To choose the phrase *cangsheng* 蒼生 for "the people" recalls *Shishuo xinyu* XXV.26 where Gao Song hopes the great statesman Xie An will give up retirement and come to the capital for the sake of "the people" (*cangsheng*).

39. 17712.

40. 19176; Qu (1989) 560.

hardly represent his poetic oeuvre as a whole and do not capture the poet in his later years. Like Bai Juyi, a chronological overview of his works reveals that about half his poems were composed beginning in Wenzong's reign. Yet the numerous modern anthologies of Liu's poetry tend to represent that prolific period of his career with only a few poems, often seemingly chosen out of a sense of embarrassment about leaving his last years in silence. Far more than for Bai Juyi, Liu Yuxi's later poetry was produced in response to his extensive social network. More often than not, Liu is responding to the poems of others; when not responding, he is sending a poem hoping for a response. This is not necessarily a bad thing, but Liu was often corresponding with men who were both politically powerful and poetically mediocre. Many of his poems are responses to those of senior statesmen, such as Pei Du and Linghu Chu, and somewhat younger men at the height of their power, such as Li Deyu and Niu Sengru; the surviving poems of Pei Du and Linghu Chu set a level of banality that Liu Yuxi matches, with an added touch of servility. Liu was obviously prominent—even more so than Bai—as an exchange poet, but one can only sympathize with Wenzong's silence at the prospect of Liu Yuxi as one of his speculative Academicians of Poetry.

Liu Yuxi has a few justly famous poems, but the same is true of many other contemporary poets who were less fortunate in the eyes of literary history. He was more fortunate than he deserved, as Zhang Hu, the striking counterexample, was less fortunate.

A significant proportion of Tang poetry was sent to friends or in answer to poems sent by friends. In this period we begin to find many collections of such poetry, called "Song and Response Collections" (*changhe ji* 唱和集), circulating independently in the groups of senior poets around Bai Juyi. Liu Yuxi participated with three men in such collections: the *Pengyang Song and Response Collection* 彭陽唱和集 with Linghu Chu; a collection with Li Deyu; and collections with Bai Juyi. Only a modest number of Linghu Chu's poems survive. Judging both from those extant poems and the poems Liu Yuxi wrote in response to Linghu Chu, this was no great loss to Tang poetry. In the poems exchanged between Bai Juyi and Liu Yuxi, however, most of the sets are still extant. Along with the poems exchanged between Bai Juyi and Yuan Zhen, these are our best examples of how exchange poetry worked.

Bai Juyi's greatest poetic gift was invention, and even if Bai's inventive powers declined somewhat in his old age, his poems still provided interesting topics on which Liu could base his responses. Even when Liu writes first, Bai Juyi overwhelms him. Bai is always himself: he can be spiritually "vernacular" in strict form.

白居易, 南園試小樂

Bai Juyi, Putting on a Small Musical Performance
in My South Garden[41]

小園班駁花初發	A riot of color in my small garden, the flowers begin to bloom,
新樂鏗鏦教欲成	the clang and blare of new music almost fully learned.
紅蕚紫房皆手植	The red stamens and purple calyces all planted by my own hand,
蒼頭碧玉盡家生	my servant "Sapphires,"[42] all born in my own household.
高調管色吹銀字	The colors of the pipes tuned high, they blow the "silver word";[43]
慢拽歌詞唱渭城	song lyrics slowly drawn out as they sing "Wei City."
不飲一杯聽一曲	If you don't drink a cup with me and listen to a tune,
將何安慰老心情	how will this old man's feelings ever be consoled?

Bai Juyi claims to control his domestic spectacle in a peculiar conjunction of disorderly display and ownership. It is the theater of domestically circumscribed excess. Everything that he wants to show is "his." This is Tang social display in a new key, and it seeks someone to recognize it. Liu Yuxi gives Bai what he wants.

---

41. 23592; Zhu 1821.

42. Sapphire was a famous singer (plural in the text because Bai boasts a number in his service). Thus, Bai Juyi's household musicians are the children of older bond-servants.

43. This is a pipe with an inscription in silver inlay.

劉禹錫, 和樂天南園試小樂

Liu Yuxi, A Companion Piece for Letian's "Putting on a
Small Musical Performance in My South Garden"[44]

閒步南園煙雨晴	Walking calmly in the southern garden the misty rain clears,
遙聞絲竹出牆聲	from afar I hear the strings and piping come out over the walls.
欲抛丹筆三川去	About to give up the red brush and go off to Three Rivers,[45]
先教清商一部成	he first has a performance learned in the clear Shang mode.
花木手栽偏有興	Flowering trees planted by his hand are particularly inspiring,
歌詞自作別生情	song lyrics he wrote himself have a distinct mood.
多才遇景皆能詠	When one of great talent encounters a scene he can always make a verse,
當日人傳滿鳳城	and this very day people will pass it all through Phoenix City.[46]

The third line dates the poem to the spring of 829, just before Bai Juyi left Chang'an to take up his Luoyang post. The poem is, in effect, an extended compliment, praising various elements raised in Bai's poem. The music passing over the walls recapitulates from an outside perspective Bai's description of the musicians practicing in his garden. He mentions Bai Juyi's new office, the "Luoyang assignment." He praises the effects of Bai as gardener and lyricist. Finally, he praises Bai's poem itself, whose quality is such that it will be repeated and passed throughout the capital in the course of the day.

In his old age Bai Juyi was often a poet of the senses. In the preceding poem he could see the analogy between the riotous display of colors in the flowers and music being practiced for his little performance. No earlier poet wrote so affectionately of his comfortable, soft clothes

---

44. 18998; Qu (1989) 1086.

45. Bai Juyi is about to give up the "red brush" for drafting convictions in his post on the Board of Punishments and to take up a post as Adviser to the Heir Apparent in Luoyang.

46. Chang'an.

and blankets. He appreciated the warmth where the sunlight touched his body or the developing bouquet of steeping tea.

白居易, 閒臥寄劉同州
Bai Juyi, Resting at Leisure: to Liu of Tongzhou[47]

軟褥短屏風	A soft quilt, a short folding screen,
昏昏醉臥翁	an old man lying in a drunken daze.
鼻香茶熟後	After tea is steeped, sweet smell in the nose,
腰暖日陽中	in the sunlight my midsection warm.
伴老琴長在	Old age's companion, a zither ever here,
迎春酒不空	to welcome spring, the ale is not drunk up.
可憐閒氣味	Yet too bad, for the flavor of leisure
唯欠與君同	lacks only being together with you.

The poem essentially celebrates how good the poet feels. In order to fully enjoy his pleasures, Bai likes to display them to others. He therefore sends the poem to his friend, here as elsewhere tacking on a polite note in the last couplet, saying, in effect: "I just wish you were here."

In contrast to Bai Juyi's celebration of what lies close at hand, in his answering poem Liu Yuxi thinks of effects: the tea serves a purpose; ale is not simply meant to "welcome spring" but to work together with herbal medicine. The third couplet is a "poetic" one, not unlike those of the contemporary regulated-verse masters; Liu Yuxi could easily have written it at some other time and dropped it in here to show off.

劉禹錫, 酬樂天閒臥見寄
Liu Yuxi, Answering Letian's "Resting At Leisure"[48]

散誕向陽眠	Blissfully content, you lie facing the sun,
將閒敵地仙	in leisure rivaling an immortal on earth.
詩情茶助爽	Tea aids the briskness of poetic feelings,
藥力酒能宣	ale can bring out the effect of medicines.
風碎竹間日	Wind shatters the sunlight amid bamboo,
露明池底天	dew brightens the skies at the pool's bottom.
同年未同隱	Alike in age, but not alike in retirement
緣欠買山錢	all because I lack money to "buy a mountain."

Bai Juyi is the self-proclaimed "hermit in between" who still draws a comfortable salary. Liu has chosen to read Bai Juyi's polite "I wish you

47. 24121; Zhu 2242.
48. 18870; Qu (1989) 1215.

were here" at least semiseriously. The desire to "buy a mountain," satirizing a certain attitude toward retirement in its original *Shishuo xinyu* context, had become in the Tang simply a way to refer to the savings needed to retire in comfort. Liu, the prefectural governor with serious duties, seems to be reminding his friend that not everyone can enjoy such leisure.

Liu Yuxi was indeed the same age as Bai Juyi, but he seemed always to be following the more famous poet: Bai had been governor of Suzhou, and Liu was given the same position; later Liu received Bai Juyi's post as Adviser to the Heir Apparent, Luoyang assignment, as Bai was moved up to Junior Mentor. The coincidence in offices was somehow appropriate for Liu, who was "following" Bai Juyi's poetic lead in other ways.

The impulse to write a "companion piece," in which a prior poem provides some direction, is nicely demonstrated in the following poem, sent from the capital to Bai Juyi in Luoyang and Yuan Zhen in Zhedong.

劉禹錫, 月夜憶樂天兼寄微之
Liu Yuxi, Moonlit Night, Recalling Letian and Sent to Weizhi As Well[49]

今宵帝城月	The moon tonight in the imperial city,
一望雪相似	in my gaze it is like the snow.
遙想洛陽城	I imagine far off there in Luoyang
清光正如此	its clear rays are exactly like this.
知君當此夕	And I know that you, Weizhi, this evening
亦望鏡湖水	are also gazing into Mirror Lake's waters.
展轉相憶心	This heart, recalling you, tosses and turns,
月明千萬里	the moon is bright for thousands of leagues.

This is, of course, a hidden "companion piece" to another poem of the same title from a different era.

杜甫, 月夜
Du Fu, Moonlit Night[50]

今夜鄜州月	The moon tonight in Fuzhou
閨中只獨看	she just watches alone in her chamber.

---

49. 18648; Qu (1989) 1111.

50. 10974; Qiu 309.

遙憐小兒女	I am moved by my children far off there
未解憶長安	who don't yet know to recall Chang'an.
香霧雲鬟濕	Fragrant fog, her coils of hair damp,
清輝玉臂寒	its clear glow, her jade-white arms are cold.
何時倚虛幌	When will we lean at the empty window,
雙照淚痕乾	doubly lit, the tracks of our tears dry?

The epigone's poem stands with some embarrassment beside the original. Du Fu's domestic imagination is redeployed to Liu's circle of friends, with Liu placing himself in Du Fu's part in Chang'an. All three are at this moment gazing at the moonlight, which is either figured as snow or reflected in Mirror Lake's waters. In place of Du Fu's children, who are too young to be troubled by memories of Chang'an and their father, Liu Yuxi gives us Luoyang in moonlight in the second couplet. Significantly, he does not indicate that Bai Juyi there is gazing at the moon. In place of Du Fu's gazing wife in the moonlight, in the third couplet Liu puts Yuan Zhen, who *is* gazing. Absent is Du Fu's vision of a future reunion; there is only Liu's longing and the moonlight that spans the distances of separation.

Bai Juyi lived on after his greatest poetic achievements and their era had passed. Only rarely, however, do we catch him looking down upon the present generation and longing for the good old days. Liu Yuxi, by contrast, was often nostalgic. Nostalgia for the "old music" was something of a poetic commonplace, one that seems to have appealed to Liu.

劉禹錫, 與歌者米嘉榮

Liu Yuxi, For the Singer Mi Jiarong[51]

唱得涼州意外聲	For singing the unbelievable notes of Liangzhou
舊人唯數米嘉榮	of former people only Mi Jiarong is worth considering.
近來時世輕先輩	Recently our age belittles the previous generation—
好染髭鬚事後生	best to dye your whiskers to serve younger men.

---

51. 19270; Qu (1989) 783. This quatrain has many variants. I have followed the text given in Qu. I have treated Mi as if it were a surname; the name is clearly Central Asian and may be the aural representation of a single name.

This piece is probably from 828, which is somewhat earlier than the period in which we begin to find attacks on the Yuanhe style. Mi Jiarong's skill in singing "Liangzhou" (one of the then-lost border prefectures, whose music would evoke lost Tang glory in 828) is certainly not the Yuanhe style, but Liu's comment in the third line of the quatrain is a broader judgment than mere musical taste. The numerous variants of this poem suggest its popularity, and this is the kind of poem that might easily have made its way into the palace and perhaps reached the ears or eyes of the twenty-year-old, heavily bearded emperor. To search for the precise reasons for Wenzong's apparent dislike of Liu Yuxi as a poet is futile, but Liu Yuxi generously supplies several possibilities.

As a young man, Liu Yuxi had participated in the Wang Shuwen government during the brief reign of Shunzong in 805. Whether this was a reform movement, a virtual coup d'etat, or a little of both, members of that government were sent off into long-term exile when Xianzong assumed the throne at the end of 805. In 815 Liu was briefly back in the capital, only to be sent off to the distant provinces again. Only in the early years of Wenzong's reign did he serve again in the capital. Apart from the short period in 815, Liu Yuxi had been away from Chang'an for well over two decades. In 805, aged thirty-four, he had been a bright young star on an upward career path; back in Chang'an in 828, aged fifty-seven, he had little hope of reaching the highest echelons of government. Some nostalgia was understandable, and hearing the old musicians obviously touched him deeply.

劉禹錫, 與歌者何戡

Liu Yuxi, For the Singer He Kan[52]

二十餘年別帝京	Parted from the emperor's capital for more than twenty years,
重聞天樂不勝情	hearing again Heaven's music is emotion I cannot bear.
舊人唯有何戡在	Of those I once knew only He Kan remains
更與殷勤唱渭城	and once again he does his best to sing "Wei City" for me.

We cannot date this poem with precision, but "Wei City" was a parting song, and it is tempting to place this late in 831, when Liu Yuxi was

---

52. 19283; Qu (1989) 786.

again sent out to be a prefectural governor—though this time of Suzhou, one of the most desirable prefectures. The pain at hearing the old music performed by one of the old singers also suggests that this might have occurred not long after his return to the capital.

The old music conjured up the end of the long Zhenyuan Reign, when Liu was a successful young man with a promising career.

劉禹錫, 聽舊宮中樂人穆氏唱歌

Liu Yuxi, Listening to the Former Palace
Musician Mu Sing a Song[53]

曾隨織女渡天河	You used to accompany the Weaver Woman fording the River of Stars,
記得雲間第一歌	and recall the finest song of all from up there in the clouds.
休唱貞元供奉曲	Sing no more those songs for the Emperor of the Zhenyuan Reign—
當時朝士已無多	the court officials of those times are not many anymore.

One of Liu's most famous poems touches on such a sense of a life somehow missed, a life that could have been fully realized only in Chang'an. Liu Yuxi is only the recurrent visitor.

劉禹錫, 再遊玄都觀 (幷引)

Liu Yuxi, Again Visiting Xuandu Lodge (with preface)[54]

余貞元二十一年爲屯田員外郎, 時此觀未有花. 是歲出牧連州, 尋貶朗州司馬. 居十年, 召至京師, 人人皆言, 有道士手植仙桃, 滿觀如紅霞, 遂有前篇以志一時之事. 旋又出牧, 今十有四年, 復爲主客郎中. 重遊玄都觀, 蕩然無復一樹, 唯兔葵燕麥動搖於春風耳. 因再題二十八字, 以俟後遊, 時大和二年三月.

In the twenty-first year of the Zhenyuan Reign (805), I was Vice Director of the State Farms Bureau. At that time there were as yet no flowers at the Lodge. That year I went out to govern Lianzhou and soon was banished to the post of Assistant in Langzhou. After staying there ten years, I was summoned to the capital. Everyone said that a Daoist master had planted immortal peaches that filled the lodge like red clouds. In consequence I wrote a piece to commemorate the moment. Soon I was once again sent out to govern a prefecture; and now, fourteen years later, I am back as Director of the Bureau of Receptions.

---

53. 19272; Qu (1989) 784.
54. 19269; Qu (1989) 703.

Again I visited Xuandu Lodge, and it was swept bare, without a single tree left. There was nothing but rabbit mallow and wild wheat waving in the spring breeze. Thus I wrote another poem of twenty-eight syllables in anticipation of some later visit. At the present it is the third month of the second year of the Taihe Reign.

百畝中庭半是苔	In the hundred-acre courtyard half is moss,
桃花淨盡菜花開	peach blossoms have been cleansed away, wild vegetables are blooming.
種桃道士歸何處	The Daoist master who planted the peaches, where has he gone?—
前度劉郎今又來	young master Liu of the previous times today comes once again.

Lang 郎, "young master," was not quite appropriate for the vice director of a bureau in his mid-thirties in 805; it has a comic dissonance for the aging poet in the Taihe Reign. The ironic poetic game Liu Yuxi is playing is that he has not changed, but the "immortal" world of the magic peaches has come and gone.[55]

Not insignificantly, the moment of splendor that came and vanished during Liu Yuxi's long absences from the capital was in the Yuanhe Reign of Xianzong, witnessed by Liu only for a few months in 815. It was a glory seen only in passing; and behind the wit and pathos, there is nostalgia. One phrase, usually unnoticed, mitigates the nostalgia: the quatrain is written "in anticipation of some later visit." The poet anticipates being sent out to the provinces again—as indeed he was—and returning. Young master Liu will check to see if the peach blossoms have returned. We have no record that they did return.

Li Shen and "Recollecting Past Travels"

Li Shen was an exact contemporary of Bai Juyi and Liu Yuxi, dying in 846, the same year as Bai Juyi. He passed the *jinshi* examination in 806, the first year of the Yuanhe Reign, and belonged to that generation of poets. Little remains of his work from the Yuanhe era, though he does

---

55. The poem also plays on the well-known story of Liu Chen and Ruan Zhao, who met two goddesses on Mount Tiantai among the peach blossoms, stayed with them awhile, and then left. When they returned, they could not find the grotto of peach blossoms again.

make an appearance at a very important moment. At the end of "Ying-ying's Story" 鶯鶯傳 by Yuan Zhen, the speaker "Zhang" approached Li Shen, who then wrote a companion piece entitled "Yingying's Song" 鶯鶯歌 to go with the prose story. This was clearly a narrative-ballad version, like Bai Juyi's "Song of Lasting Bitterness" 長恨歌. Li Shen's ballad does not survive intact, but pieces were preserved, some in the Jin "Account of the Western Chamber in All Modes" 西廂記諸宮調, by Scholar Dong 董解元. A few of his other poems that have been preserved suggest that Li Shen was once very much a poet of the Yuanhe generation.

Li Shen's modest place in the history of Tang poetry is due to a peculiar and unprecedented collection of poems that did survive, with a preface dated to 838. This collection was entitled *Recollecting Past Travels* 追昔遊 in three *juan*. Some of the poems were composed on the occasions they describe, but most were written retrospectively in 838 or slightly earlier, covering his life between 820 and 836.[56] In the preface Li Shen gives a succinct account of his life and career. The poems, arranged chronologically, are supplied with copious internal notes explaining whatever circumstances might be obscure to a later reader. The preface ends: "There are things that concern me in the phrases, and the inspiration arose from resentment; thus, the words are not all of the same order, sometimes obscure and sometimes obvious; they are nothing more than hope for someone who truly understands (*zhiyin*) in some future time" 詞有所懷, 興生於怨, 故或隱或顯, 不常其言, 冀知音於異時而已.[57]

Yuan Zhen seems to have been the first to actively compile his own collected works, with explanatory materials (in the form of prefaces or

---

56. A few of the poems in this collection have prefaces explicitly stating that they were composed on the occasion they describe and that the author has included ("compiled" *bian* 編) them in the collection. In the preface to the series entitled "On the Day I Finished My Term at Shouyang" 壽陽罷郡日, he justifies such inclusion by saying that the poems are "no different from recollection" 與追懷不殊 (Wang Xuanbo 37). Many poems are explicitly or implicitly marked as memory; the explicit notation that a poem was composed on the occasion represented suggests that the majority of the remaining poems are also retrospective, though not marked as such. The poems in the last part of the collection, closer in time to the compilation of the collection, were most likely compiled close to the occasions they describe.

57. Wang Xuanbo 157.

letters), at a relatively young age in the 810s.[58] Bai Juyi (along with others in his circle) continued and extended the practice, writing his own prefaces for the ever expanding versions. As Bai Juyi's collection grew in his later years, the poems added were arranged more or less chronologically, though they were sometimes divided between regulated and nonregulated groups.[59] In short, Bai's collection was the prototype of the poetic diary. Li Shen's *Recollecting Past Travels* is, by comparison, the prototype of poetic autobiography. We do not know how much Li Shen wrote in the years covered by *Recollecting Past Travels*, but it seems likely that, in contrast to Bai Juyi, his efforts in poetic composition were sporadic. He could not simply arrange existing poems in chronological order; when he had a past poem representing some significant moment, he included it. Rather, Li Shen is supplementing an apparently sketchy poetic record of his life since 820 with the poems that he "should have" written. Indeed, *Recollecting Past Travels* looks very much like an attempt to retrospectively construct a "poetic life," a chronological oeuvre that looked like Bai Juyi's oeuvre.

The use of poetry to chronologically "document" a life was an important new way of thinking about poetry. We see here the ancestor of a long tradition of scholarship that painstakingly tries to date every poem in a poet's work and arrange each chronologically within a collection. In the Song Dynasty Du Fu became the central figure whose poetic oeuvre was read this way, but that form of reading can be traced back to the group around Bai Juyi.

Li Shen's unique act is part of a larger interest in making poetry collections to publicize, preserve, and document. In many ways the spread of exchange collections marks a shift in attitude from considering such poems as ephemera that might be preserved in a poet's literary remains to the publicized documentation of a long-term literary relationship.

---

58. Since we know that various versions of certain authors' works (as opposed to individual pieces or small "samplings") circulated during their lifetime even in the eighth century, the practice was, on some level, older. What generally distinguishes the ninth-century practice is the care and publicity given to the act of self-editing. There are, of course, exceptions, such as Yuan Jie's 元結 collection, with its 767 preface.

59. Most collections of Tang poetry have been lost, and those that have survived probably do not reflect their original form. Poems may have circulated in rough chronological sequence within generic divisions before Bai Juyi, but from what survives Bai represents the strongest model of chronology as a principle of organization.

Exchange collections between Bai Juyi and Yuan Zhen and between Bai and Liu Yuxi were already in circulation in 833 when Liu Yuxi received the following letter from Linghu Chu:

Mr. Bai, the governor of Three Rivers [Luoyang] compiled the poems sent and answers received between you and him. He wrapped this in a bag of pale blue silk and gave them to me. Mr. Bai wrote some prefatory words at the beginning and called it the *Liu and Bai Collection.* Long I pondered over how the pieces I have written with you also fill trunks and wrappers—why not put them in order to silence mockery from Three Rivers [i.e., Bai Juyi]?[60]

Linghu Chu was a very literary senior statesman who had first entered public service because of his writing. Although Linghu Chu is speaking playfully, there is something competitive here, the desire to publicize a poetic relationship which we assume had been carried on for many years for the sheer pleasure it provided. In response to Linghu Chu's request, Liu Yuxi compiled the *Song and Response Collection with Pengyang* 彭陽唱和集.[61] Later in 835 Linghu Chu would compile his exchange poems with Li Fengji 李逢吉, the canny and somewhat ruthless former minister who had died that year.[62] We see the same desire to publicly document a relationship through poetry in the anecdote, quoted earlier, in which Wenzong had hoped to add a poem from the dying Pei Du to his own poetry collection.

Documentation of a life or relationship in poetry might be undertaken with an eye to current prestige, but it was clearly directed outward, to readers who might not know the particulars that could be assumed between old friends exchanging poems for the pleasure of it. The author's note explaining the circumstances behind a line is the clearest indication of such a general audience. Earlier we mentioned Linghu Chu's poem answering Bai Juyi and Liu Yuxi after assuming command of the Xuanwu army in 828. The opening line reads:

蓬萊仙監樂天客曹郎劉爲主客

Penglai's librarian immortal (Letian), the Reception's Director [Liu was in the Bureau of Receptions]

---

60. Qu (1989) 1496.

61. Liu also compiled a later version of this collection, as well as a collection of poems exchanged with Li Deyu.

62. Fu (1998), vol. 3, 114.

It seems likely that this was originally preserved through the *Song and Response Collection with Pengyang*; and although the identifying notes may have been added later, it seems to suggest that the collection circulated with explanatory notes.

No group of poems at this time was provided with such rich explanatory notes as *Recollecting Past Travels*, and few were as explicit as Li Shen in stating that his collection was intended for future readers. The idea, however, was implicit in Bai Juyi's editorial efforts. We have seen how Bai conceptualized his literary collection as "capital"; and the multiple copies of his collection that he had made and deposited in various temples (as Sima Qian planned to deposit the *Shiji* at some "famous mountain" to await future readers) suggests just such an eye to future readers. Indeed, Bai offers what was perhaps the most singular and interesting anticipation of future readership in the preface to his *Luoyang Collection* 洛中集, to be deposited at the Xiangshan Temple: "How do I know that I won't revisit this temple in some future life and, looking at these writings again, recapture memory of this past life?"[63]

Li Shen was not a major poet, but he deserves more credit than he is generally given. One reason we might willingly believe that he compiled *Recollecting Past Travels* in the shadow of Bai Juyi's model is that Li Shen so often wrote with prior poetry in mind. Older poets were in his head, and he sometimes cites poems and lines of past Tang poets associated with sites he visits. Old poems were the occasion for new poems.

Transferred from exile in the far south to a better position as prefect of Chuzhou, Li Shen was visited by an unnamed pipa player; in the musician's style Li Shen detected the legacy of the court musician Maestro Cao, who together with Mu (mentioned above in Liu Yuxi's poem) were the stars of the court musical establishment at the beginning of the ninth century. Any lover of Tang poetry knows what to expect from Li Shen on this occasion: a ballad in the long line in which Bai Juyi's "Ballad of the Pipa" meets Du Fu's "On Seeing a Student of Mistress Gongsun Dance the 'Sword Dance.'"[64] Like Du Fu, Li Shen recognizes the teacher in the disciple, provides a long section on hearing Maestro Cao earlier in his life, tells of his own exile, the death of

---

63. Zhu 3806.
64. 10818; Qiu 1815.

Maestro Cao, and the present performance. The requisite description of pipa playing, however, derives from Bai Juyi.

李紳, 悲善才

Li Shen, Lament for the Maestro[65]

余守郡日, 有客遊者, 善彈琵琶. 問其所傳, 乃善才所授. 頃在內庭日, 別承恩顧, 賜宴曲江, 敕善才等二十人備樂. 自余經播遷, 善才已歿. 因追感前事, 爲悲善才.

When I was governing the district [Chuzhou], a visitor came through who was good at the pipa. Asking where he learned the style in which he played, it turned out that he had learned it from the Maestro. During the time I was in the Inner Court, I was shown particular favor; an imperial banquet was given in Twisting River Park, in which the Maestro and some twenty other musicians were appointed to provide the music. During the period of my exile the Maestro passed away. Thereupon I recollected and was moved by those past experiences and wrote a lament for the Maestro.

穆王夜幸蓬池曲	By night King Mu paid a visit to the bends of Penglai Pool,[66]
金鑾殿開高秉燭	the Hall of Golden Bells was opened, candles were held high.
東頭弟子曹善才	The eastern ensemble's Maestro Cao
琵琶請進新翻曲	begged to present a newly composed tune for the pipa.
翠蛾列坐層城女	Lined in seats with kingfisher brows girls from Tiered Walls,[67]
笙笛參差齊笑語	pipes and flutes of different lengths, equal to laughing chatter.
天顏靜聽朱絲彈	His Majesty's visage calmly listened to vermillion strings plucked,
眾樂寂然無敢舉	the other musicians were silent and did not dare to play.
銜花金鳳當承撥	A golden phoenix, flowers in beak, was there where the plectrum was plied,

---

65. 25586; Wang Xuanbo 30.
66. Muzong, figured as King Mu of Zhou.
67. Tiered Walls was the dwelling of the immortals in the Kunlun Mountains.

轉腕攏弦促揮抹	with arching wrist he gathers the strings, to speed the "sweep" and "rub."[68]
花翻鳳嘯天上來	Flowers floated, the phoenix shrilled coming from Heaven,
徘徊滿殿飛春雪	and lingering there, filling the hall, spring snow flew.
抽弦度曲新聲發	He pulled the strings composing a melody, and the newest music emerged,
金鈴玉佩相磋切	golden bells and jade pendants clinking against each other.
流鶯子母飛上林	Fluent orioles, mother and chicks, flew through the Imperial Grove,
仙鶴雌雄唳明月	immortal cranes, hen and mate, shrill to the bright moon.
此時奉詔侍金鑾	At this time I received a summons to wait on the golden-belled palanquin,
別殿承恩許召彈	in the detached palace I received grace and was permitted to call him to play.
三月曲江春草綠	In the third month at the Twisting River the springtime grasses were green,
九霄天樂下雲端	from nine-tiered wisps heaven's music came down from the edge of clouds.
紫髯供奉前屈膝	The purple-whiskered imperial servant came forward and knelt,
盡彈妙曲當春日	he played all the most wondrous melodies during the spring day.
寒泉注射隴水開	Cold fountains gushed out, Longtou's waters began,[69]
胡雁翻飛向天沒	Turkish geese winged in flight and sank away in the sky.
日曛塵暗車馬散	The sunlight faded, dust muffled the light, horses and carriages scattered,
爲惜新聲有餘歎	and because I cherished that new music, I heaved continuing sighs.

---

68. "Gathering," *long* (or *rong*) 攏, "sweeping," *hui* 揮, and "rubbing," *mo* 抹, were all technical terms for fingering techniques: *long* is a left-hand technique; *hui* and *mo* are right-hand techniques.

69. This line both describes the music and an old *yuefu* about Longtou's waters.

明年冠劍閉橋山	The following year his cap and sword were enclosed in Bridge Mountain,[70]
萬里孤臣投海畔	ten thousand leagues away this lone official lodged by the oceanside.
離禽鍛羽強迴飛	The isolated bird's ruined plumage struggled to turn in flight,
白首生從五嶺歸	and white-haired I returned from over the Five Alps.
聞道善才成朽骨	I heard then that the Maestro had become rotting bones,
空餘弟子奉音徽	and there only remained his disciple to inherit those dulcet tones.
南譙寂寞三春晚	Southern Jiao is still and lonely late in the third month of spring,
有客彈弦獨淒怨	there was a visitor plucking the strings, uniquely sharp and bitter.
靜聽深奏楚月光	Calmly I listened as deeply he played in the light of the moon in Chu,
憶昔初聞曲江宴	and recalled long ago when first I heard it at a Twisting River banquet.
心悲不覺淚闌干	The heart was touched and unawares my tears were streaming,
更為調弦反覆彈	then he tuned the strings once more for me and played it over again.
秋吹動搖神女佩	Autumn gusts sets swaying the goddess's pendants,
月珠敲擊水晶盤	bright moon pearls strike upon a plate of crystal.
自憐淮海同泥滓	I pity myself, this Huaihai region sharing its muck and mud,
恨魄凝心未能死	my angry soul fixes the thought that I have not been able to die.

---

70. That is, Muzong passed away. The reference is to Han Wudi's question as to why, if the Yellow Emperor became an immortal and rose to Heaven, he had a tomb at Bridge Mountain. The answer was that only his cap and sword were buried in the tomb.

| 惆悵追懷萬事空 | Depressed in these thoughts of the past, everything is gone, |
| 雍門琴感徒爲爾 | being stirred by the zither of Yongmen was all for nothing.[71] |

One could point out the correspondences in detail: as Bai complained about the rusticity of Xunyang in "Ballad of the Pipa," Li Shen complains about the Huaihai region. One small point of correspondence, however, deserves particular attention. Toward the end of Bai Juyi's "Ballad of the Pipa," he asks the woman to play one more time:

| 莫辭更坐彈一曲 | Don't refuse to sit once more and play a melody, |
| 爲君翻作琵琶行 | and I will compose for you a "Ballad of the Pipa." |

Here, too, we have the motif of the encore:

| 心悲不覺淚闌干 | The heart was touched and unawares my tears were streaming, |
| 更爲調弦反覆彈 | then he tuned the strings once more for me and played it over again. |

This encore of the encore is interesting in that while Bai Juyi specifically asks for it, the musician here seems to offer the encore spontaneously. We do not want to give too much weight to the representational accuracy of the line, but it suggests a significant possibility. It may not be simply Li Shen who is poetically reenacting Du Fu's and Bai Juyi's poem: the unnamed pipa player may also know the poems, and may be playing his role according to the old poetic "script." Earlier poetry (and particularly "Ballad of the Pipa") was becoming part of a general cultural legacy in which later poets participated along with others.

Buddhism was clearly an important force in Li Shen's life, and *Recollecting Past Travels* tells of vows made in youth and fulfilled. Bai Juyi characteristically enjoyed the intellectual consolation of Buddhism, the company of monks, and the perversely sensuous pleasures of austerities. Li Shen sometimes seems more truly religious. One of his finest poems is

---

71. A reference to the Lord of Mengchang's response to hearing Yongmen Zizhou play the zither; it seemed to the Lord of Mengchang as if Yongmen Zizhou were someone whose kingdom and home city had fallen.

based on a famous Suzhou singer who, according to her abiding wish (*zhi*), was buried in the precincts of a Buddhist temple. It was a topic that invited the confrontation of values and worlds, with the Sanskrit chanting of sutras enduring as the singer's voice faded into nothingness.

李紳, 眞娘墓
Li Shen, The Tomb of the Pure Miss[72]

吳之妓人, 歌舞有名者. 死葬於吳武丘寺前, 吳中少年從其志也. 墓多花草, 以滿其上, 嘉興縣前亦有吳妓人蘇小小墓. 風雨之夕, 或聞其上有歌吹之音.

She was a singing girl of Wu and famous for her singing and dancing. When she died, she was buried in front of the Wuqiu Temple in Wu. The young men of Wu honored her abiding wish to be buried there. Many flowers grow on her tomb, covering the whole top. In Jiaxing County there is also the tomb of the Wu singing girl Su Xiaoxiao. On evenings when there are rainstorms, the notes on song and piping are sometimes heard from upon it.

一株繁艷春城盡	A trunk of thick and voluptuous color the springtime city is gone,
雙樹慈門忍草生	the "paired trees" Gate of Compassion[73] suffers the flowers to grow.
愁態自隨風燭滅	Her melancholy charm was extinguished with a candle in the wind,
愛心難逐雨花輕	a passionate heart can never be so light as Heaven's rain of flowers.[74]
黛消波月空蟾影	Moonbeam glances have melted from brows, there is only the light of the moon,
歌息梁塵有梵聲	her songs let the dust on the beams rest, but there are sounds of Sanskrit chanting.
還似錢塘蘇小小	She is like Su Xiaoxiao of Qiantang—
祇應回首是卿卿	but one should only look back on this little darling.

The poem is built around a series of contrasts: the "Pure Miss" (her virginal name clearly at odds with her profession, but perhaps related to

---

72. 25649; Wang Xuanbo 100. For another poem on this theme, see Zhang Hu, 27282; Yan Shoucheng 16.

73. It was under a pair of śāla trees that the Buddha entered nirvana.

74. The flowers that fell from Heaven when the Buddha preached.

her wish to be buried in the temple grounds) is a flowering tree set against the śāla trees under which Buddha achieved enlightenment, a compassion that allows flowers to keep growing on her tomb. The weight of sensuality of a "passionate heart" melts away in each particular, her flowers replaced by the rain of flowers from Heaven, her "wave-like" glances replaced by the moonbeams from a brow-like crescent moon, her songs fading into the chanting of sutras. The last couplet compares her to another courtesan with a famous tomb, but the latter lacks the enduring commitment to the truth of Buddhism that distinguished the "Pure Miss."[75]

The retrospective stance of Li Shen's collection as a whole invited not only the "meditations on the past," *huaigu*, so popular in the ninth century, and reminiscences of his youth; it also disposed him to see himself from the outside, as Bai Juyi so often did, only in a different key. We do not know if the following was one of the poems actually composed on the occasion described, but the title suggests that this is the Li Shen of 838, recalling passing his native region (modern Wuxi) in 833 on his way to his post as surveillance commissioner of Zhedong, at that time recalling his youth spent studying at Hui Mountain Temple.

李紳, 憶題惠山寺書堂

Li Shen, Recalling My Study Hall in the
Hui Muntain Temple[76]

故山一別光陰改	Once I left the mountains of home, 　　time passed,
秋露清風歲月多	autumn dew and clear breeze, 　　the years and months grew many.
松下壯心年少去	A bold heart under the pines, 　　the young man went away,
池邊衰影老人過	a wasted reflection in the pool, 　　an old man passing by.
白雲生滅依巖岫	White clouds appear and vanish 　　beside the cliffs and crags,
青桂榮枯託薜蘿	green cassia flourish and wither, 　　the hanging moss still on them.

---

75. The sense of the last line is very uncertain.
76. 25609; Wang Xuanbo 57.

惟有此身長是客   There is only this body of mine,
                                             ever a traveler,
又驅旌斾寄煙波   hurrying on with banners raised
                                             into the misty waves.

Lines like the opening couplet are so dreadful that it is hard to read on. Yet when we do, the poem redeems itself in its multiple retrospective visions from both 833 and 838. *Zhuangxin* 壯心, "bold heart" or "heart of someone in his prime," is disembodied in memory: it belonged to the young man who did not look at himself but only thought to go off to Chang'an and enter public life long ago—indeed, to become the very high official who traveled in 833 "with banners raised."

The young man went away; an older man returned, remembering the young man and seeing his own aging reflection in the pool. He is, however, only "passing by," bound to the constant changes in post to which the young man, who stayed here long in study, aspired. We can view the white clouds as constant change, the ultimate emptiness of this life, or perhaps even as the figure of riches and honor, which were to Confucius "as drifting clouds." The cassia tree, which is usually flourishing in poetry and whose boughs are figuratively plucked by the successful examination candidate, is here clearly withered. Nevertheless, it must remain standing, providing support for the dependent hanging moss that still lives by clinging to it. The successful official acquires his "family," going far beyond the "nuclear family" and even the genetic family proper, and their dependency in turn holds him in place, whether "flourishing" or "withered." To provide the necessary income, he is always a traveler, in the constantly shifting posts of Tang bureaucratic life.

In the end he (whether the "he" of 833 or 838) sees himself leaving the site of youth, the new surveillance commissioner with banners flying, fading off into the river mist. This was his home; but once left, he became "always a traveler"—though the eyes that view the scene at the end remain at home to see himself fade away.

None of the younger generation—the poets we think of as belonging to the "Late Tang"—achieved anything like the public distinction of these aging poets of the Yuanhe generation. Their relative success and continuous engagement in the mid-to-upper echelons of political life made them unique among Tang poets. In many ways this was the true end of an era in which poetry could still have a place in public life. The man who in his intemperate youth wrote "Yingying's Story" and was likely its protagonist, Yuan Zhen, became a minister. The man who wrote the ballad for Yingying sailed off with banners flying as a surveillance commissioner. The man who satirized social abuses in the Yuanhe, Bai Juyi, ended up in a well-paid sinecure, enjoying a salary that ultimately derived from Southland peasants—though he sometimes still felt guilty over the fact that his quilts provided warmth while the common folk were freezing.

THREE

Regulated Verse in the Short Line

Masters of Eagle Shooting

Even in his earlier years Bai Juyi delighted in representing himself as an eccentric, unconstrained by convention. In one of his best-known poems dating from 818, Bai celebrated his self-image as the wild poet.

白居易, 山中獨吟
Bai Juyi, Chanting Poems Alone in the Mountains[1]

人各有一癖	Each person has some one addiction,
我癖在章句	my addiction is to writing:
萬緣皆已銷	All worldly attachments have melted away,
此病獨未去	I am left with this sole affliction.
每逢美風景	Whenever I chance on a lovely scene,
或對好親故	or face some dear friend or family,
高聲詠一篇	I sing a poem out in a loud voice,
怳若與神遇	in a daze as if touched by some god.
自爲江上客	Since I sojourned here by the River,
半在山中住	I spend half my time in the hills.
有時新詩成	There are times when a new poem is finished,
獨上東巖路	and I go alone up the east cliff road,
身倚白石崖	I lean against scarps of white stone,
手攀青桂樹	with my hand I pull the green cassia.

---

1. 22069; Zhu 407. This translation, with modifications, appears in my study entitled *The End of the Chinese "Middle Ages": Essays in Mid-Tang Literary Culture* (Stanford: Stanford University Press, 1998), 105.

狂吟驚林壑	Mad chanting alarms the wooded ravines,
猿鳥皆窺覷	birds and gibbons turn all eyes on me.
恐爲世所嗤	I'm afraid I'll be mocked by the times,
故就無人處	so I come to this place where no man is.

In addition to "mad chanting," *kuangyin* 狂吟, Bai also favored the term "drunken chanting," *zuiyin* 醉吟, and was even named "The Master Who Chants Drunkenly," *Zuiyin xiansheng* 醉吟先生, in a tomb inscription he supposedly wrote for himself.[2] We noted earlier his fondness for self-description as *kuang*, "wild" or "mad." He often represented himself as writing however he pleased, the very antithesis of the craftsman.[3] Jia Dao may not be referring to Bai Juyi specifically in the opening lines of "Presented to a Friend" 贈友人, but Jia's praise of a very different kind of poet is suggestive:[4]

五字詩成卷	Your five-syllable poems now make a scroll
清新韻具偕	clear and fresh, their rhymes all match.
不同狂客醉	Not sharing the drunkenness of those mad fellows,
自伴律僧齋	your company is vegetarian monks bound by rules.

The "rules," *lü* 律, are the *vinaya* of the monastic community, one of which requires avoidance of drink. "Rules" are also the "regulation" of poetry, appropriate for this unnamed poet, who, as is clear from the second line, strictly obeys the regulations for tonal euphony and strict rhyme.[5]

Jia Dao celebrates austerity here, in which the discipline of poetry—not accidentally linked to regulated poetry in the five-syllable line—is associated with religious discipline. That linkage was to be developed into a much deeper affinity between poetry and the religious discipline

---

2. Zhu 3815. The authenticity of this inscription has been questioned. Since it should date from the very end of his life, it is not at all impossible that it was not included in the collections Bai himself so carefully prepared.

3. It was probably the contemporary fascination with the craft of regulated verse—"bitter chanting" or "taking pains on poetry," *kuyin* 苦吟—that led Bai Juyi to claim (in 827) that he was that kind of poet when younger. See "Idle Singing" 閑詠, 23470, Zhu 1710. Note that Yao He speaks of Jia Dao as "madly bringing forth chanting like weeping" 狂發吟如哭, though the matching line puts Jia in Chan meditation: "when melancholy, you sit as if in Chan" 愁來坐似禪 (26419; Liu Yan 29).

4. 31649; Qi 268.

5. Although *lü* did not come into general use for poetic "regulation" until the Song, there are Tang precedents for this usage.

of Buddhism in the last part of the century.[6] Jia Dao himself had been a monk, and there was behind him a tradition of poet-monks working at the end of the eighth and the beginning of the ninth centuries in the Southland. Even more than the secular Dali poets, those poet-monks specialized in regulated verse in the five-syllable line.

In 832 Liu Yuxi was governor of Suzhou. It was probably in this year that a monk named Xiufeng 秀峰 approached him and requested a preface for the collected poems of his master, the celebrated poet-monk Lingche 靈澈 (749–816). Xiufeng had selected three hundred of Lingche's two thousand poems in his later years and an additional three hundred exchange poems (another contribution to the mania for collections of exchange poems). After reviewing Lingche's career and the occasion to write the preface, Liu Yuxi offered the following judgment:

The poet-monks that are spoken of in the world have mostly come from the Southland. Lingyi was the fountainhead; Huguo followed in his footsteps; Qingjiang stirred the waves; and Fazhen followed after him. Like the lone resonance from a single string, these enter the ear but for an instant; they are not the notes of a great orchestra. Only Jiaoran of Wuxing was able to comprehend the full range of various forms, and after Jiaoran, Lingche carried this on.[7]

The praise of Lingche and Jiaoran comes at the expense of a tradition of poetry by Buddhist monks that, in Liu Yuxi's eyes, failed as a result of its limitation, a failure to "comprehend the full range of various forms." Theirs is a one-stringed instrument rather than an orchestra. What this actually means is that these poet-monks specialized in regulated verse in the short line, focusing on perfectly formed couplets constructed of a limited range of images and vocabulary—exactly the kind of poetry practiced by Jia Dao and Yao He.

Around 837, five years after Liu Yuxi's preface, Yao He compiled his anthology of poetry entitled *The Supreme Mystery, Jixuan ji* 極玄集. Yao He's anthology included primarily regulated poetry in the short line. In

---

6. Toward the end of the ninth and throughout the tenth century we find a recurrent pairing of poetry and the [Buddhist] Way or Chan ("meditation"). Poetry is sometimes treated as a supplement to Chan, sometimes the competitor, and at other times another form of Chan. We are not speaking here of the influence on poetry of Buddhism as a religion but rather of Buddhism as the model for poetry as an austere lay "discipline," demanding complete commitment and setting the practitioner apart from ordinary people.

7. Qu (1989) 520.

a relatively restricted selection of poets, Yao He included Lingyi, Fazhen, and Qingjiang, three of the four poet-monks that Liu Yuxi dismissed for their narrow scope. Yao He did include four poems by Jiaoran, but, significantly, these were all regulated verses in the short line.

Another line of attack against the poet-monks is suggested by Bai Juyi in 827, in the poem and preface, cited earlier, praising the poetry of the monk Daozong 道宗, whose poetry was written for the sake of the dharma and salvation and "not written for the sake of poetry" 不爲詩 而作也. Others, not knowing Daozong, will talk of "Huguo, Fazhen, Lingyi, and Jiaoran."[8] Although Bai Juyi was not writing poetry to save souls, his subsequent description of Daozong's poetry obviously articulates his own poetic values as well. "Writing for the sake of poetry" precisely describes the work of Jia Dao, Yao He, and the circle around them.

This was not an open feud—Yao He was on good terms with Bai Juyi and Liu Yuxi—but it was a quiet conflict of generations and poetic taste. Some younger poets of the day seem to have written regulated verse in the short line almost exclusively.[9] The perfect couplet in the short line was true "poetry" in one sense; the cleverness of the "Yuanhe style" and "mad chanting" were not for them.

When we read the poets of Jia Dao's and Yao He's circle, Liu Yuxi's critique of the limited range of the poet-monks strikes a resonant chord. In addition to limitation, we have the impression of anonymity: it often seems that however fine a poem might be, it could just as easily have been written by another poet in the group. It was, by and large, a shared craft. At this point we might reflect on a basic contradiction that underlies such a poetic enterprise. Most of these young men and their mentors sought success in the examinations, commonly referred to as *ming* 名, both "name" and "fame." Poetic success was also *ming*. The opposite impulse was embodied in the *sangha*, the Buddhist monastic community, whose members "renounced home (and family)," *chu jia* 出家, giving up their secular, family "name" for a religious name. They dressed alike, ate together, and carried out the rule-bound activities of

---

8. 23180; Zhu 1445. See pp. 57–58.

9. We say "seem to" because of the uncertainties and vagaries of preservation; it may be that the regulated verse of such poets was disproportionately preserved.

the monastic day. Their perfection was to disappear as individuals in the practice of a discipline.[10] In the same way the poetic craft of regulated verse was anonymous; it was not the celebration of personality (so strong in Bai Juyi's poetry) but the masterful practice of a shared art. Ironically, the greater their achievements in this essentially anonymous craft, the greater were their "names"/"fame."

Wine, women, song, and "mad chanting" offer a conventional scene of pleasure; but there can also be a pleasure in asceticism and restriction. One of the best indications of the changing conception of poetic craft is the transformation of the term *kuyin* 苦吟 during the 820s and 830s from "bitter chanting" (in which the poem is the expression of the poet's bitterness resulting from life's circumstances) to "painstaking composition" (which poets speak of as a pleasure).[11] Although the weight of the term changed, it still remained "chanting" of the oral and noisy sort sure to annoy the neighbors. Liu Deren, a younger poet of the Jia Dao and Yao He circle, does it all night, hating the coming of dawn—an activity not only sought but one he does not want to give up.

劉得仁, 夏日即事

Liu Deren, "What Happened on a Summer's Day"[12]

到曉改詩句	I revise lines of poems until it is dawn,
四鄰嫌苦吟	my neighbors detest my bitter chanting/ painstaking composition.
中宵橫北斗	Midnight, the Dipper stretches across the sky,
夏木隱棲禽	and summer trees hide roosting birds.
天地先秋肅	Heaven and Earth shrivel up before autumn,
軒窗映月深	railing and window are deep, catching moonlight.
幽庭多此景	My secluded yard has many such scenes,
惟恐曙光侵	and I fear only morning's light creeping in.

---

10. Poetry was still on the secular side of the opposition between the secular and religious, as illustrated in the following couplet, in which Yao He sees off the monk Wuke: "You renounced family, but still take care of your mother, / you maintain the rules, but also are good at poetry" 出家還養母, / 持律復能詩 (26345).

11. For a fuller discussion of this transformation, see Stephen Owen, "Spending Time on Poetry: The Poetics of Taking Pains," in Olga Lomová, ed., *Recarving the Dragon: Understanding Chinese Poetics* (Prague: Charles University in Prague, 2003), 167–92.

12. 29824.

Although the poetics of the regulated-verse craftsmen and Bai Juyi were in some ways opposed, opposites share a common ground to articulate difference. Both Bai Juyi and Jia Dao speak of poetry as a compulsion; however, unlike "mad chanting," "bitter chanting" is a compulsion to labor and effort, a pleasurable pain.

賈島, 戲贈友人

Jia Dao, Playfully Presented to a Friend[13]

一日不作詩	One day I didn't write poetry,
心源如廢井	mind's wellhead was like a dried-up well.
筆硯爲轆轤	Brush and ink-stone were the well pulley,
吟詠作縻綆	chanting served as the hempen rope.
朝來重汲引	With dawn I drew from it again,
依舊得清泠	as before I found what was clear and fresh.
書贈同懷人	I write it to give to one who feels as I do,
詞中多苦辛	in the words are much bitter pains.

The "bitter pains" of which Jia Dao speaks at the end are the counterpart of the new sense of "bitter chanting," not the hardships of life outside poetry but the pains taken in composition. The ideal reader, "the one who feels as I do," will not discover a personality in the words; he will perceive and appreciate the labor of the poem's making.

The Jia Dao "Legend"

From his later years and, increasingly, following his death, Jia Dao became the very image of "the poet" as much as the author of particular poems. His death was lamented, his grave was frequently visited, and his poems were imitated and echoed. In one of the most suggestive, probably apocryphal anecdotes, the later poet Li Dong 李洞 (who died ca. 897) was supposed to have had a bronze statue of Jia Dao made.[14] Although the *Tang zhiyan* version says that he "worshiped it like a god" 事之如神, the association is primarily Buddhist: the *Beimeng suoyan* version says that Li Dong "always invoked Jia Dao's name as the Buddha" 常念賈島佛. Here again we see clearly the association between the

---

13. 31515; Li Jiayan 17; Qi 71.

14. Zhou Xunchu 1464–65. See Xu Zong 許總, *Tangshi tipailun* 唐詩體派論 (Taibei: Wenjin chubanshe, 1994), 608, who compares the number of Late Tang poets writing on Jia Dao with poems based on now more famous Tang poets.

kind of poetry Jia Dao represented and Buddhist religious forms: not the "content" of Buddhism but the idea of an esoteric knowledge, linked to austere discipline, that can be passed down from master to disciple. It seems unlikely that Jia Dao composed the *Secret Instruction of the Two Nan, Ernan mizhi* 二南密旨, a poetry manual dating from the ninth or tenth centuries, but it implies the transmission of knowledge to a select individual or group.[15]

According to another legend, every New Year's Eve Jia Dao took out the poems he had written the preceding year and placed them on a table; then he poured a libation of ale, bowed, and offered a devotional invocation: "These are what I have suffered over during this whole year."[16]

We must be careful to distinguish Jia Dao in his own work and age from the Jia Dao legend that was taking shape in his later years and grew following his death. As we will see, anecdotes about him are strongly shaped by a new vision of what a "poet" should be. Nevertheless, we can see in his poetry—including the poem quoted above— motifs that supported and doubtlessly contributed to the image.[17]

Although many of Jia Dao's poems cannot be dated, we possess poems from the Yuanhe era (when he was associated with Han Yu and Meng Jiao) through his years of exile from 837 until his death in 843. From the datable poems, however, it seems that he was most active during the 820s and the first part of the 830s, when he was part of a circle of poets in Chang'an. Jia Dao was already prominent and older than most in that circle of regulated-verse writers, but there he was essentially one poet among many. Indeed, his combination of relative seniority with lack of status seems to have contributed to the ease with which he mixed with younger poets and the absence of deference (far, indeed, from being in-

---

15. *Mizhi* 密旨 is primarily the "secret instruction" of an emperor to a subordinate, as befits a work that superficially adopts a "Confucian" approach to poetry. The form, of both the title and the contents, belies the ideological persuasion. Such exclusive knowledge more perfectly fits the select transmission of a Buddhist master's knowledge to a single disciple or group of disciples.

16. Cited in *Tang caizi zhuan*; Fu (1987), vol. 3, 332–33.

17. Wen Yiduo called the entire age the "age of Jia Dao." Wen's remarkably acute judgment is supported by texts throughout the ninth century. If modern critics point out other poets who more perfectly "reflect" the condition of the times, that is a function of the interests of modern critics rather than the way contemporaries viewed their poetry. See Tian Gengyu 田耕宇, *Tangyin yuyun: wan Tang shi yanjiu* 唐音餘韻: 晚唐詩研究 (Chengdu: Ba Shu shushe, 2001), 53–55.

voked as a poet-Buddha). These poets continually celebrated one an-
other's comings, goings, failures, successes, and important occasions.
Yao He, who was the same age as Jia Dao, did possess political status,
but he was just as active in this community of poets. In their own time Jia
Dao and Yao He seem to have shared a roughly equal reputation. Jia
Dao, however, was transformed into something far greater, and it is
worthwhile to consider the components of his transformation.

Yao He achieved a relatively high degree of political success. Jia Dao
never passed the examination, had no hope of success, and ended his
years in "administrative exile" in the provinces as Assistant Magistrate
of Changjiang and Administrator of Granaries at Puzhou. Whether by
inference or knowledge, it was suggested that he received the Chang-
jiang posting because he offended someone.[18] This soon became an an-
ecdote in which the offended party was none other than the emperor.

If part of Jia Dao's appeal was that of a politically unsuccessful, soli-
tary figure (despite his very large network of friends) who died in pro-
vincial "exile," those qualities were transformed into an absorption in
poetic craft that led him to disregard authority. The compulsion to
compose poetry was given social significance as an enterprise whose
claims were greater than respecting one's place in a hierarchical world;
in both cases the transgression is forgiven—in one case immediately.
Two of the most famous anecdotes are variations on the same story,
each variation appearing in slightly different versions.

Whether walking or sitting, eating or lying with his eyes closed, he never
stopped chanting and savoring the words. Once he was astride his mule with
an umbrella over his head, cutting across a main thoroughfare in the capital. At
the moment the autumn wind was at its most severe, and the yellow leaves
could be swept up. Jia Dao suddenly chanted: "Falling leaves fill Chang'an." In
his mind he was quite pleased with what had come to his lips so spontaneously,
and he was trying to find another line to make a couplet. Lost in his inability to
find the matching line, he was unaware of where he was going. In this manner
he bumped into Liu Qichu, the Metropolitan Governor of the capital. He
spent an evening in chains, and then Liu released him.[19]

---

18. From another point of view we might note that Jia—who never passed the *jinshi*
examination and had neither *yin* privilege nor powerful connections—was indeed given
a post, however humble.

19. Zhou Xunchu 1111. Based on *Tang zhiyan*.

The most famous version of the second anecdote is found in He Guangyuan's 何光遠 *Jianjie lu* 鑒戒錄 from the Five Dynasties.

忽一日於驢上吟得 "鳥宿池中樹, 僧敲月下門" 初欲著推字, 或欲著敲字, 煉之未定, 遂于驢上作推字手勢, 又作敲字手勢. 不覺行半坊. 觀者訝之, 島似不見. 時韓吏部愈權京尹, 意氣清嚴, 威振紫陌. 經第三隊呵唱, 島但手勢未已. 俄爲官者推下驢, 擁至尹前, 島方覺悟. 顧問欲責之. 島具對 "偶得一聯, 吟安一字未定, 神游詩府, 致衝大官, 非敢取尤, 希垂至鑒." 韓立馬良久, 思之, 謂島曰 "作敲字佳矣."

One day, while riding on his mule, he suddenly came up with the verse: "The bird spends the night in the tree by the pool, / the monk knocks at the gate under the moonlight." At first he wanted to use the word "shove"; then he wanted to use the word "knock." Not having settled on the best usage, he rode along on his mule, first drawing the character "shove" with his hand, then drawing the character "knock." Without realizing it, he passed through half a city ward in this fashion. Those who observed him were astonished, but Jia Dao seemed not to see them. At the time Han Yu was serving as provisional Metropolitan Governor of the capital. Han had a stern and punctilious disposition, and his awesome presence at that moment made itself felt on the great avenue. Passing the third avenue, the criers were clearing the way, but Jia Dao just went on writing characters with his hand. Only when he was suddenly pushed down from his mule by officials and dragged before the Metropolitan Governor did Jia Dao realize the situation. The advisers wanted to have him reprimanded, but Jia Dao responded, "I just happened now to come up with a couplet, but I haven't been able to get a particular word right. My spirit was wandering in the realm of poetry, and this is what led me to run into Your Excellency. I do not dare call your wrath down upon me, but I hope you might be kind enough to give this some consideration." Han Yu halted his horse, thought about it for a while, and said to Jia Dao, "'Knock' is finer."[20]

These are obviously essentially the same story, with the couplet and the offended high official changed. The poet is so absorbed in the practice of his art that he violates the proper deference to hierarchy, institutionalized in the law, which states that a commoner must make way for a high official. In the first case he is arrested for a night but soon forgiven; in the second his engagement in poetry is immediately appreciated by the particular official in question. Both Liu Qichu and Han Yu were Jia Dao's friends in real life, which adds force to the anecdote. Behind this story is the image of Li He riding his donkey and coming

---

20. Zhou Xunchu 1111–12.

up with lines of poetry, which we will discuss at length at a later point. The new elements in the Jia Dao anecdotes are the concomitant disregard for hierarchy and authority and the social leveling that can occur through engagement with poetry.

The third anecdote occurs in versions with three different emperors (including Xuānzong, who assumed the throne only after Jia Dao's death). Here the emperor, passing by, hears someone chanting poetry in an upper storey. He goes upstairs and finds Jia Dao. The emperor picks up the scroll to read the poem. Jia Dao, not recognizing him, grabs his arm and angrily snatches back the paper. The emperor, mortified, goes back downstairs; and Jia Dao is later sent into exile.[21] This is a very similar parable of poetic absorption, though one touching on a level in the social hierarchy that cannot be lightly transgressed. Nevertheless, even though he must be punished, the poet symbolically remains in a separate realm that does not "recognize" even the emperor.

Nowhere is that declaration of a separate realm of poetry so perfectly invoked as in a joking couplet attributed to the poet Zhou Pu 周朴 (d. 879), famous for his devotion to the craft of poetry. He is addressing the Chan monk Dawei:[22]

禪是大溈詩是朴   For Chan it is Dawei,
                                  for poetry it is Zhou Pu,
大唐天子只三人   with the Great Tang Son of Heaven—
                                  just three people.

Buddhism is the original "separate realm," operating within the secular empire but transcending it, with a hierarchy that, by virtue of its separateness from the entire secular hierarchy, is on a par with it. Zhou Pu makes poetry the third realm, claiming sovereignty for himself. The only three people that matter are the three "rulers," of whom the Great Tang Son of Heaven is only one.

We can situate these stories about Jia Dao in a long and rich tradition of anecdotes in which an exceptional person shows disregard for the usual social hierarchy. The anecdotal tradition surrounding Li Bai was very much a part of this tradition. There is, however, a profound difference in these Jia Dao anecdotes: Li Bai disregarded authority and

---

21. See Fu (1987), vol. 2, 328.
22. *Quan Tang shi*, 7704.

convention because of his personality, whereas Jia Dao disregards it because he is absorbed in the craft of poetry. Poetry is his end, not the means by which he shows his disregard.

In both of the first two anecdotes Jia Dao is working on a couplet, not a whole poem. Both of those couplets now appear in occasional poems referring to situations other than riding a donkey through the capital. Especially in the famous "knock"/"shove" anecdote in which Jia Dao encounters Han Yu, the time of composing the couplet is different from the time it ostensibly represents. It has become an "art" in the Western sense, disjoined from lived experience. Whether composed beforehand or revised afterward, the couplet is like a jewel, to be "set" within a poem.

Marking Poetic Craft

When we say that regulated verse in the short line represents "craft," it creates two opposing values in the form. One value is the poem that flows naturally and hides the strict rules that inform it; the second value is the poem that celebrates and foregrounds craft, which means the craft of the couplet. To appear, craft must stand out against less ostentatiously "poetic" language. Thus, in the second value there is an inherent disposition to play one or both of the middle parallel couplets off against the plainer diction of the opening and closing couplets.

As an example of the first value, in which the formal rules disappear in apparently artless utterance, let us consider a regulated verse by Zhang Ji, believed to have been written in 793 in the poet's youth.[23]

張籍, 薊北旅思

Zhang Ji, Traveler's Thoughts in Jibei[24]

日日望鄉國	Every day I gaze toward my homeland,
空歌白紵詞	singing in vain the "White Linen" song.
長因送人處	And always when I send someone off,
憶得別家時	I recall the time that I left home.
失意還獨語	Losing heart, I often talk to myself,
多愁祇自知	the degree of my sorrow known to myself alone.

---

23. I have chosen this example because Fang Hui has described it as the best poem in Zhang Ji's collection. Fang Hui 1270.

24. 20186; Li Dongsheng 88. Although *Yingkui lüsui* and critics have treated this as regulated verse, it contains strong tonal violations in the fourth positions of the third and fifth lines.

客亭門外柳	Willows outside the pavilion gate
折盡向南枝	have all their southward branches broken.

Each line and couplet in this poem follows in some easily recognizable way from the preceding line or couplet. The second couplet is parallel, but the first line is a dependent clause, and the two lines together form a single sentence (in the terms of Chinese poetics, "two lines with a single sense"). Even the third couplet, with two distinct predicates characteristic of parallel couplets, develops a single thought. In terms of later poetics, both middle couplets are *qingyu* 情語, the "discourse of feeling," rather than *jingyu* 景語, the "discourse of scene."[25] Only the final couplet turns to things that belong to the scene, rather than the poet's feelings; and the willows are purely evidence of partings, branches snapped exclusively by those traveling southward.

We might set Zhang Ji's poem against a regulated verse of uncertain date by Jia Dao.

賈島, 旅遊

Jia Dao, Journeying[26]

此心非一事	This state of mind has more than one concern,
書札若爲傳	how can a letter convey it?
舊國別多日	From homeland parted for many days,
故人無少年	among old friends, no youths.
空巢霜葉落	An empty nest where frosty leaves have fallen,
疏牖水螢穿	through lattice's wide gaps pierce river fireflies.
留得林僧宿	A woodland monk got me to spend the night—
中宵坐默然	at midnight we sit in utter silence.

This is a very different aesthetic. The opening couplet represents the kind of discursive diction we find throughout Zhang Ji's poem: the paraphrase would be the single sentence "how can a letter convey the various things on my mind?" The second couplet, composed of two independent predicates, clarifies the situation referred to in the first couplet. This is, in fact, the most famous couplet in the poem, and the poet and critic Zha Shenxing 查慎行 (1650–1727) specifically notes that it is "very

---

25. In the Southern Song *Tang santi shi* 唐三體詩, this would be "middle couplets empty" 四虛.

26. 31532; Li Jiayan 22; Qi 94.

much like Zhang Ji" 頗似張司業.[27] The third couplet, however, is something else: its relation to the preceding couplets is oblique at best, though it is supposed to be related somehow. Its disjunction from the obvious discourse of "journeying" to seemingly unrelated scenes in the natural world is one marker of "craft." It could easily have been composed independently of the poem's occasion and "used" here; such couplets are often cited in isolation and are sometimes represented as being "worked on." These finely crafted couplets often appear in context as disjunctive, with the poet turning his attention to the scene around him; the best of these couplets notice patterns that return to the context of the poem as a whole and enrich it.

The thirteenth-century critic Fang Hui interprets the fifth line as leaves falling into the nest, but it could also be that the fallen leaves reveal the nest. Clearly the "empty nest" is a figure that reminds the poet of home. Chinese critics note that the scene contributes to the bleak mood of the poem, but the visual pattern is striking. The tightly woven twigs of the nest are articulated against the more widely meshed interstices of the window. The leaves, shining with frost, are caught in the nest; the smaller fireflies, bright in the darkness, penetrate the window lattice. As is often the case in parallel couplets, there is a conceptual pair (conceptual terms in Chinese often being antithetical) with some resonance in the situation. The leaves in the nest are "blocked" while the fireflies "get through": we have *tongse* 通塞, "blockage" and "getting through," a conceptual pair to describe enterprises, particularly the course of political life and "journeying."

Many things in the poem are "blocked," not only the poet's career but also his attempt to communicate what is on his mind (communication was also conceptualized as *tong*, "getting through," in the sense of "getting through to someone"). The fireflies' entry into the window quietly anticipates his own lodging for the night, but what he finds is not communication but silence, sitting face to face with his host in silence.

Jia Dao's couplet may lie behind one of Yong Tao's most beautiful couplets also on "blockage and getting through." The leaves are now butterflies, trapped in the widely meshed but sticky spider's web. The fireflies get through, entering the empty nest from which the swallows

---

27. Fang Hui 1273. The poem Zha Shenxing is thinking of is probably Zhang Ji's "Meeting an Old Friend" 逢故人 (20449).

have departed. The couplet is found in a poem entitled "In Sickness Dwelling in Autumn" (秋居病中).

| 荒簷數蝶懸蛛綱 | By leaf-strewn eaves several butterflies hang in a spider's web; |
| 空屋孤螢入燕巢 | in the empty room a lone firefly enters the nest of swallows. |

Yong Tao's couplet and poem deserve consideration quite apart from the transformation of Jia Dao's couplet, but reworking the fine lines of predecessors is continuous with the process of an individual reworking his own lines. The poetics of spontaneity implies perfection in the immediacy of the relation between thought and words; in the poetics of craft the words are always being changed and recast.

Eagle Shooting

A fragment of Yao He's preface to his anthology *The Supreme Mystery* has survived; there he compares the poets he selects to "masters of eagle shooting," *shediao shou* 射雕手, a phrase from the *History of the Northern Qi*, in which Hulü Guang 斛律光, on a hunt with the emperor, looked up, shot, and brought down an eagle.[28] Yao He was the first to transfer this figure of consummate skill in archery to skill in poetry. It is indeed an image of mastery, only of a particular sort.

It was the earlier Yuanhe generation that raised Li Bai and Du Fu to represent the height of Tang poetry. One of the most striking images of poetry from that era can be found in Han Yu's "Teasing Zhang Ji" 調張籍, in which Han compares the acts of poetic creation by those earlier poets to Great Yu carving up the landscape of China to drain the flood.[29] Comparison of Li Bai and Du Fu to Great Yu was a grand

---

28. *Bei Qi shu* (*History of the Northern Qi*) 222. Shooting eagles can ultimately be traced back to a story in the "Biography of Li Guang" in the *Shiji*. A court eunuch was sent out to the great Han general Li Guang when he was on campaign. With a party of a few dozen men, the eunuch was out on the steppes when he encountered a group of three Xiongnu. The vastly superior Chinese party attacked the Xiongnu, who proceeded to ride around the Chinese party, shooting until everyone, including the court eunuch, was wounded. When the outraged eunuch reported the incident back to Li Guang, the general commented that the three Xiongnu must have been out eagle shooting. He sent a detachment after the Xiongnu and captured them, and they were indeed out to shoot eagles.

29. 17922; Qian Zhonglian 989.

image of the poet as demiurge. It is ultimately a craft metaphor, troping on an earlier image of poetry as "carving"; but this is "carving" on the grandest level. Analogies between the poet and cosmic "fashioning," *zaohua* 造化, were common among the Yuanhe poets (and continued through the ninth century).[30] We may contrast such an image of writing poetry with a mastery of eagle shooting, both involving skill and precision in hitting a difficult mark just right.

If Han Yu looked back to Li Bai and Du Fu, it is not surprising to find Yao He beginning his anthology with Wang Wei, another High Tang poet.[31] Following the eagle-shooting figure of the preface, it is perhaps no accident that one of the Wang Wei poems he selects is the following:

王維, 觀獵
Wang Wei, Watching the Hunt[32]

風勁角弓鳴	The wind is strong, the horn-bow sings,
將軍獵渭城	the general is hunting east of Wei City.
草枯鷹眼疾	The plants are sere, the hawk's eye keen,
雪盡馬蹄輕	snow is gone, horses' hooves move easily.
忽過新豐市	Suddenly they are past Xinfeng market,
還歸細柳營	then back around to Thinwillow Camp.
回看射雕處	Turn and look where the eagle was shot—
千里暮雲平	a thousand leagues of evening clouds flat.

This is one version of the High Tang at its best. The images present the evidence of the senses: the sound of a bow twanging in the wind, which is sensory evidence of the hunt. The fact that the leaves are dried and have fallen from the plants gives the hawk a better view, and the absence of snow (either in patches on the ground or falling) lets the horses move more easily. The poem ends beautifully with a vision of absence, a vast skyscape in the distance in which there was an eagle—a small bird to shoot, and smaller still from a distance—that is now not there. Wang Wei's poem illustrates one possibility for regulated verse, in which great energy is represented as being under formal control, a precise skill that masters dangerous force, represented by "eagle shooting." It is probably

30. See Shang Wei, "The Prisoner and the Creator: The Self-Image of the Poet in Han Yu and Meng Chiao," *CLEAR* 16 (December 1994): 19–40.

31. Yao He did, however, acknowledge Li Bai's greatness as a poet; see 26384.

32. 05978; Chen Tiemin 609.

the strongest poem in Yao He's anthology and an allegory of the poetic craft of "eagle shooters."

Most of Yao He's eagle-shooting masters belong to his past, from a century to a quarter century before the anthology was compiled. To have Yao He's own day represented, we have to look to a future anthology, indeed, one that explicitly presents itself as the successor of Yao He's anthology of poetry. This is Wei Zhuang's 韋莊 *Further Mystery, Youxuan ji* 又玄集, dating from 900. Yao He's anthology represents the continuity of conservative poetic taste among elite circles for a half century; *Further Mystery* opens with Du Fu, Li Bai, and Wang Wei joined together, reconciling the values of the conservatives and the Yuanhe radicals into something that begins to look like the canon of Tang poetry we now know. What had occurred in between *Supreme Mystery* in 837 and *Further Mystery* at the end of the century was the complete destruction of the social world dominated by the conservative elite, the repeated sack of Chang-an, and the reduction of the Tang Dynasty to a handful of courtiers and palace guards surviving at the whim of various warlords.

Since Wei Zhuang's anthology is the sequel to Yao He's, it includes a sequel to Wang Wei's "Watching the Hunt," a poem probably composed in 820, right after the end of the Yuanhe Reign.

張祜, 觀魏博[何]相公獵

Zhang Hu, Watching His Excellency Li of Weibo in the Hunt[33]

曉出郡城東	At dawn he goes out east of the district walls,[34]
分圍淺草中	dividing, encircling among the low grasses.[35]
紅旗開向日	Red banners unfurl toward the sun;
白馬驟迎風	white horses dash into the wind.
背手抽金鏃	Hand at his back, he draws the metal barb,
翻身控角弓	bending, he pulls the horn-bow.
萬人齊指處	Where ten thousand people point together,
一雁落寒空	a single goose falls from the cold sky.

---

33. 27241; Yan Shoucheng 1. The title is given in Chinese, which is how it appears in *Further Mystery*; in the collected poems the title is given as "Watching Li Minister of Works of Xuzhou on the Hunt" 觀徐州李司空獵. The title in *Further Mystery* is probably erroneous and should be Li rather than He. This is most likely Li Su 李愬 and the year was probably 820 (Fu, vol. 2, 808).

34. That is, the seat of government and headquarters for the Weibo military region.

35. Hunts used beaters to cover an area and drive animals in toward the center, where they could easily be killed.

Zhang Hu's poem has its own beauty, but it is an intensely theatrical poem, with Wang Wei's control but without his restraint. From encirclement we have the theatrical advance of red banners and white horses, focusing at last on the body of military commissioner Li as he notches an arrow and draws his bow. The flight of that arrow is marked by ten thousand people pointing; the object of the arrow, the gaze, and ten thousand fingers is a wild goose falling from the sky. Shooting wild geese is not easy, but it is a considerably less demanding skill than shooting eagles: wild geese are larger, fly lower, and travel more slowly.

We should note that Yao He, our anthologist—who would later compare earlier poets to "masters of eagle shooting"—was also at Weibo at roughly the same time and may have witnessed both the wild-goose hunt and Zhang Hu's little poem.[36]

What had occurred between Wang Wei's masterful eagle shooting and Zhang Hu's easier and splendidly staged wild-goose hunt was the Mid-Tang, which can be summed up in another hunting scene involving a much gaudier bird. The poem is not regulated verse at all but rather an old-style poem by Han Yu in the seven-syllable line, probably written around 799.

韓愈, 雉帶箭

Han Yu, The Pheasant Takes a Hit[37]

原頭火燒靜兀兀	On the plain the fire has burned, now calm and utterly still,
野雉畏鷹出復沒	a wild pheasant, dreading the hawk, rises then sinks back down.
將軍欲以巧伏人	The general wants, by his skill, to humble others—
盤馬彎弓惜不發	he wheels his horse, bends his bow, holds back, not shooting.
地形漸窄觀者多	The space gradually narrows, the watchers grow many,
雉驚弓滿勁箭加	the pheasant springs, the bow full drawn, the sturdy arrow notched.
衝人決起百餘尺	Dashing toward people, it rises up sharply over a hundred feet,

---

36. Jia Dao may also have been there.

37. 17848; Qian Zhonglian III.

紅翎白鏃隨傾斜	the red fletches and silver barb arc after it.
將軍仰笑軍吏賀	The general looks up smiling, his subalterns congratulate him
五色離披馬前墜	as the many colors, rent asunder, plummet before his horse.

Here we can see the more recent ancestor of Zhang Hu's poem, with an even more explicitly staged scene of mastery, in which the landscape has been burned bare of everything but bird, performer, audience, and arrow. Like most of Han Yu's poetry of the time, it is "old-style" verse, allowing greater liberty. What distinguishes Han Yu's poem from those of the earlier and later poet-craftsmen, Wang Wei and Zhang Hu, is the self-conscious and explicit pride in mastery: "the general wants, by his skill, to humble others." At the successful shot the general smiles; he is aware not only of his own skill but of the clapping audience. The prey ends up as a brightly colored trophy, pierced by the arrow, lying on the ground at his feet. If one wanted to translate such a staged act of skill into the form of regulated verse, the most obvious solution would be the parallel couplet, "marked" as a triumph of craft.

One version of the Yuanhe generation's poetry was the impression of naturalness that we saw in the Zhang Ji poem and the stylized spontaneity of Bai Juyi; its opposite was the mannered daring of poets like Meng Jiao, Han Yu, and Li He. When Jia Dao first came to Luoyang from the northwest in 810, he became part of the Han Yu group, and some of his most famous poems show the translation of the poetics of the Han Yu group into regulated verse.

In January 816, the last lunar month of the tenth year of the Yuanhe Reign, the Chan monk Baiyan ("Cypress Cliff") passed away. On hearing the news Jia Dao composed a regulated verse, one of whose couplets became famous because Ouyang Xiu made it an exemplary case of the potential misreading of poetry.

賈島, 哭柏巖和尚

Jia Dao, Lamenting the Monk Baiyan[38]

苔覆石牀新	The moss covering your stone couch is fresh,
師曾占幾春	how many springs did the Master occupy it?

---

38. 31529; Li Jiayan 21; Qi 89.

寫留行道影	They traced and kept his silhouette, practicing the Way,
焚卻坐禪身	burned away the body that sat in meditation.
塔院關松雪	The pagoda garden bars snow on pines within;
經房鎖隙塵	the sutra chamber locks in dust in the cracks.
自嫌雙淚下	I despise that this pair of tears streams down,
不是解空人	I am not one who understands the Emptiness of things.

The famous couplet here is the second one, imitated within a few decades, anthologized in Wei Zhuang's *Further Mystery* in 900, and taken up again in the eleventh century in Ouyang Xiu's *Remarks on Poetry* (*Shihua*, entry XVIII), where it comes up in a discussion of how a poem can fail to communicate some meaning in an elementary sense. Ouyang Xiu cites the couplet:

| 寫留行道影 | They traced and kept his silhouette, practicing the Way, |
| 焚卻坐禪身 | burned away the body that sat in meditation. |

Then he comments that some readers thought that they had burned a living monk. Ouyang Xiu cites the case as a joke; in a nice twist, he turns from poetry failing to make sense to the foolish failure of readers to make sense of poetry. There is something here about reading poetry and paying attention to traces.

The figuration in the second couplet exists only in a language without tense markers; it necessarily disappears in English translation. Chinese poetry, especially on the level of a single line, generally assumes a unity of time; and that assumption produces the potentially comic effect that Ouyang Xiu mentions: if there is "sitting in meditation" and "burning," one would normally take these as contiguous moments. The good reader, however, would recognize that the play between different moments in time was already announced in the third line, where the time of "practicing the Way" and the continued presence of the image are contrasted. To repeat that antithesis between present and past in the fourth line is a small triumph of parallelism. Such a conflation of moments—the body in meditation and its cremation—is significant as well as poetically striking. The body in meditation is the vessel of a mind that is empty in being aware of the emptiness of appearances; it is that same body, empty of mind and soul, that is later cremated, literally "burned away."

In many ways this poem represents the shared craft of regulated verse in the short line at its best, with a characteristically Yuanhe inflection in the second couplet. The balance of level and deflected tones is perfect, the parallelism is technically skillful, and the rhyme-words are commonplace in the extreme. In some ways it is a comfortable and easy craft, within which the poet can sometimes achieve a remarkable beauty of pattern, which can be significant. Every poetic form has its particular gift for poets. In regulated verse we often see a particular pattern or relationship recurring in various versions; as with metaphor, such homologies of pattern invite us to consider seemingly very different phenomena as in some way alike.

There is covering and ground, surface and depth. The covering is "appearance," in Buddhist terms, *se* 色, *rupa*, the sensuous surface of things. The surface changes; beneath is emptiness. Even the monk's name repeats this figure, "Cypress Cliff," the stone ground covered with the green of cypress, which in miniature reappears in the stone couch covered by moss. The moss replaces the monk, whose meditating presence kept the moss away. Moss and monk are both "coverings" and "overlays" of sorts, the loss of one being the gain of the other. Every spring that the monk sat on that bench—the enumeration of years that the second line invokes—was a spring when the moss could not grow. But moss was always awaiting regeneration, like the tears that the poet sheds at the end.

The absent body is preserved as a "silhouette," "outline," "reflection," or "shadow," *ying* 影, the merest of appearances preserved in a representation, just another "image" in the "doctrine of images," *xiang-jiao* 象教, that teaches us through images the emptiness of the world beneath the images. The shadow is preserved while the body that cast the shadow is gone—an early-eighth-century anticipation of the pathos of the old photograph, enriched by the fact that the "reflection" or "shadow" is of the monk "practicing the way," learning within that surface of appearances the truth that all within is empty. The "body sat in meditation," became aware of Emptiness; and when that enlightened body died, it was cremated and became smoke.

The ashes of the body go to the pagoda, in whose winter garden the pines have a covering of snow, pines being the standard figure for that which endures through change. As the body's ashes go to the pagoda, the painting of the body goes to the library, where we have another covering of surfaces, a covering of dust, much like a covering of snow.

But "dust" has strong Buddhist overtones of the "six dusts," the delusions of the senses, the attachment to images as surfaces rather than as self-consuming indices of the emptiness beneath the surface.

Through the habitual poetics of regulated verse, Jia Dao is "parsing" surface and depth in various versions: moss, body, snow, and dust. And at the end we have the tears, both as a response and as a cleansing. Something comes forth from within the body that should be emptied, the trace of mind not as impartial mirror but as the sentimental heart. Failure to understand Emptiness is the claim of the secular man, who feels the loss of the person—even though he knows that any particular incarnation is only a moment in a continuous process of reincarnation, terminated only by Enlightenment. Poetically he says he despises the fact that he weeps. He knows better. He does understand the emptiness of things, but he does not accept it.

It is difficult not to read a contradiction of poetics here as well: the Yuanhe poet, with his showy daring, is working in a poetic discipline and representing the truth of a religious discipline that teaches austerity and the emptiness and extinction of self.

Before considering the direction that Jia Dao's poetry was later to take, we might consider an imitation by the younger poet Zhou He (perhaps at this time still a monk, Qingse). The poem cannot be dated precisely, but judging from Zhou He's career, it probably postdates Jia Dao's poem by at least a decade.

周賀, 哭閑霄上人

Zhou He, Lamenting the Monk Xianxiao[39]

林徑西風急	On the forests paths the west wind blows hard,
松枝講鈔餘	pine boughs after reading sutra and sermon.
凍髭亡夜剃	His icy whiskers were shaved the night he died,
遺偈病時書	the remaining gatha, written when he was sick.
地燥焚身後	The ground was scorched after they cremated the body;
堂空著影初	the hall was empty when his silhouette was first revealed.

---

39. 26896. This is entitled a lament for Baiyan in *Tangshi jishi*, but that is probably too early for Zhou He.

弔來頻落淚　　　　　　Lamenting him, tears often fall,
曾憶到吾廬　　　　　　and I recall that he came to my cottage.

In the third couplet of this poem Zhou He is obviously imitating Jia Dao's second couplet, but the epigone tropes on his predecessor in less obvious ways as well. Jia Dao opened his poem with the image of a stone bench covered with moss, a visual trace of absence. In the categories of parallel matching, Jia Dao's is a couplet of "seeing" (*jian* 見). Zhou He gives the proper answering category of "hearing" (*wen* 聞) for his trace of absence: the sound of the wind in the pines that marks the disappearance of Xianxiao's sutra chanting and discourses.

The second couplet continues the motif of remainders, now the whiskers and the gatha, the devotional verse. We assume that the corpse is shaved (hence "icy" whiskers). In the third couplet Zhou He takes up Jia Dao's earlier couplet; in this case it would be hard to argue that the mannered and daring images of the Mid-Tang disappeared entirely in the Late Tang. Here the epigone poet carries the image of the predecessor to new extremes. *Ying* 影 is "silhouettes," "shadow," and "reflection." The term was used for religious representations; hence the "hall of reflections," *yingtang* 影堂, was where religious paintings were displayed. Zhou He keeps the explicit reference to the portrait, but he adds another kind of grotesque "shadow" of the monk in the scorch marks on the ground left from the cremation of the corpse.

As Jia Dao had wept, so Zhou He must also weep the tears of the secular man—or of the poet-monk, sinking into the spiritual error of the laity for the sake of poetic effect. Zhou He, however, is not offering a grand opposition of his tears in contrast to those who understand the emptiness of things. Zhou He weeps as a result of a memory of a visit, a remembered presence in the face of Xianxiao's absence.

Jia Dao's famous couplet represents the "strong line" in a Mid-Tang sense of the term, just as Zhou He's imitation shows how easily such lines can slip into almost comic grotesqueness. It was a style that Jia Dao was abandoning for a very different kind of "strong line" that characterizes the Late Tang. Already in 812 Han Yu had remarked that Jia Dao would turn away from mannered daring to a more "bland and even," *pingdan* 平淡, style.[40] The "bland and even" style better charac-

---

40. *Song Wuben shi gui Fanyang* 送無本師歸范陽. Qian Zhonglian 820.

terizes Yao He's selection of earlier regulated verse in *Supreme Mystery*. However, as Jia Dao matured as a poet, he found a new kind of poetic beauty in more subdued versions of the strong line.

The following poem is also regulated verse in the five-syllable line and likewise intended for a Buddhist monk. This poem can probably be dated to the Taihe Reign (827–835). According to conventional periodization, it belongs to the "Late Tang," just as the lament for Baiyan belongs to the "Mid-Tang." There is something a bit absurd in giving different period names to two poems written by the same poet in the same form, both in a Buddhist social context, separated by one or two decades. Yet the contrast between the two poems seems to bear out the notion that a change in poetic sensibility had occurred in the interim.

The later poem lacks the modestly figurative couplet that caught Ouyang Xiu's attention, which was to become one of the touchstones of Jia Dao's craft. The poem also lacks the repeated patterns that function like metaphor.

賈島, 寄白閣默公

Jia Dao, Sent to Reverend Mo of White Tower Mountain[41]

已知歸白閣	I know you have gone back to White Tower,
山遠晚晴看	I watch that hill far in the clear evening sky.
石室人心靜	In stone chambers man's mind grows still,
冰潭月影殘	on an icy pond moonbeams barely remain.
微雲分片滅	Wispy clouds melt, dividing in puffs,
古木落薪乾	ancient trees dry, shedding kindling.
後夜誰聞磬	Who hears chimes in the last part of night?—
西峰絕頂寒	cold is the highest summit of the western peak.

Reverend Mo is literally "Reverend Silence," and except for the peculiar question in the seventh line—asking who hears chimes—the poem is one of silence.

Like the lament for Baiyan, the poem begins with an image of absence as the poet stares toward the distant mountain to which Reverend Mo has gone. The images in the middle couplets all belong to that imagined distance. The stillness, *jing* 靜, is both the silence of the place and the serenity of mind, an enclosure of stone that contains a mind rather than a body. In the capping line of the couplet Jia Dao flattens

---

41. 31541; Li Jiayan 25; Qi 110.

the space of containment into a two-dimensional surface, playing on the Buddhist figure of the mind as a mirror, which in turn is the figure of the calm pool reflecting the moonlight. Moreover, the light is fading in that mirroring pool. The distance of speculation opens a space for images of nature and the person to merge. Self is obliterated here more effectively than in the lament for Baiyan.

In many ways this is a more beautiful and subtle poem than "Lamenting the Monk Baiyan." The fading daylight that opens the poem becomes fading moonlight in a pool that is the figure of the dispassionate mind. The third couplet continues the image of dissolution, first with light clouds breaking into pieces and disappearing (*mie* 滅 of course being the term for "extinction" in Nirvana), then in the trees shedding pieces of dry wood—specifically "kindling," the material for fire that will consume itself and the material body in a brief light. In the end we have an unheard sound in the darkness, which is once again the image of the immateriality of existence until at last there is only cold.

Such regulated verse in the five-syllable line has a restrictive lexicon, and poems on monks have their own favorite images and terms. There is nothing daring about Jia Dao's poem; it is, in some ways, highly conventional in terms of the poetic practice of the age. Yet the images are deployed with a mastery of the craft that is as self-effacing as it is perfect.

Zhang Ji

Jia Dao became the epitome of the poet-craftsman; the visible craft of the couplet stands out even in the relatively understated poem above. However, no account of regulated verse in the second quarter of the ninth century can be complete without considering very different values that were no less strong. The Chinese critical tradition has often associated these values with the regulated verse of Zhang Ji.

Zhang Ji was very much a poet of the Yuanhe era, famous for his *yuefu*, for mannered archaism in old-style verse, and as an admirer of Du Fu. Moving between the groups of poets around Han Yu and Bai Juyi, Zhang Ji demonstrated remarkable stylistic diversity in an era that valued personality recognizable in a single, distinct poetic "manner." Zhang Ji's Yuanhe contemporaries celebrated him for the values of the era. His Southern Tang editor Zhang Jih 張洎 adds to those Yuanhe virtues a claim about his importance in the history of regulated verse and its Late Tang traditions.⁴² In a preface dating from 949 or shortly thereafter Zhang Jih writes:

又長於今體律詩. 貞元已前. 作者間出. 大抵互相祖尚. 拘於常態.迨公一變. 而章句之妙. 冠於流品矣.

He also excelled at recent-style regulated verses. Prior to the Zhenyuan Reign [785–804] writers [in this form] did appear intermittently; but they pretty much followed in one another's footsteps and were confined to a commonplace manner. Then the transformation wrought by Zhang Ji came about, and the excellence of his style crowned the types in circulation.⁴³

In his preface to Xiang Si's collection Zhang Jih goes on to treat Zhang Ji's influence:

吳中張水部爲律格詩. 尤工於匠物. 字清意遠. 不涉舊體. 天下莫能窺其奧. 唯朱慶餘一人親授其旨. 沿流而下. 則有任蕃陳標章孝標倪勝司空圖等. 咸及門焉. 寶歷開成之際. 君聲價籍甚. 時特爲水部之所知賞. 故其詩格頗與水部相類. 詞清妙而句美麗奇絶. 蓋得於意表. 迨非常情所及.

In his regulated poetry Zhang Ji of the Bureau of Waterways was exceptionally skilled in fashioning the representation of things. His words were lucid, and his concepts far-reaching. He did not slip into the prior style. No one in the world could get close enough to glimpse the profundity of his work. Zhu Qingyu alone personally received his instruction. As the tradition continued, Ren Fan, Chen Piao,⁴⁴ Zhang Xiaobiao, Ni Sheng, Sikong Tu, and others all became secondary disciples. At the juncture between the Baoli and Kaicheng Xiang Si's reputation was quite widespread, and at that time he was particularly appreciated by Zhang of the Bureau of Waterways. Thus, the formal style of his poetry came to very much resemble that of Zhang Ji. The diction is lucid and wondrous, and the lines are lovely and most remarkable. Indeed, he achieved this beyond definite concept; it is hardly something ordinary sentiments could achieve.⁴⁵

We do not know if Zhang Jih is basing these comments on some tradition of judgment or, in his unbounded admiration for Zhang Ji, simply extrapolating from some of Zhang's exchange poems. We should be reluctant to dismiss such a precise account of regulated-verse traditions

---

42. Here I romanize Zhang Ji 張洎 as Zhang Jih to avoid confusion between the tenth-century preface writer and the poet he is writing about.

43. QTw 9123.

44. I have chosen the reading *piao* 標 rather than the more common *biao*.

45. QTw 10906 (*Tang wen shiyi*).

from the mid-tenth century, though Zhang Jih's claims are excessive and he elides the long Taihe Reign between the Baoli and Kaicheng (Zhang Ji died in the Taihe, half a decade before the Kaicheng).[46] Zhang Ji wrote a laudatory poem to Xiang Si (who must have been rather young at the time); and as editor of Zhang Ji's collected poems, Zhang Jih knew this and may have based his comments on it. Unlike many of the more senior poets, Zhang Ji did patronize younger poets in his later years, and there may be some truth to Zhang Jih's claim of his influence.

At the very least, Zhang Ji well represents values in regulated verse that were an alternative to focusing on the craft of the couplet. Bai Juyi was not particularly talented in regulated verse—though he wrote a great many. In Bai Juyi the form disappears behind the poet. Zhang Ji achieved ease and fluency through perfect form; at Zhang Ji's best the requisite parallelism of the middle couplets half disappears. Only very rarely do we see the striking couplets so marked in Jia Dao's poetry. As the Song critic Zhang Jie 張戒 observed: "Although Zhang Ji's regulated poems have a flavor, they lack literary flash" 籍律詩雖有味而少文.[47]

This kind of poetic value exists in many traditions and is the hardest to translate. It is also a value that wears thin with repetition and easily slips into banality. Whether or not the poets of the second decade of the ninth century associated it with Zhang Ji, it was a value in the regulated verse of the period, existing side by side with—and sometimes trying to incorporate the poetics of—the glorious couplet.

We might here cite one of Zhang Ji's most anthologized regulated verses in the short line, which can serve as a touchstone of his success and his limitations in the form. It has the pleasing quality of *dan* 淡, "limpidity" or "blandness."

---

46. Such a high estimate of Zhang Ji was not universal at the time. Zhang Wei's *Shiren zhuke tu*, admittedly eccentric in its classifications, places Zhang Ji in the second order of the category "Clear and strange, classical and upright" 清奇雅正, whose "master" was Li Yi 李益.

47. Chen Yingluan 陳應鸞, *Suihantang shihua jiaojian* 歲寒堂詩話校箋 (Chengdu: Ba Shu shushe, 2000), 72. "Flash" is perhaps too flippant a translation for *wen*, but it does convey something of this sense of appeal through a finesse of wording.

張籍, 夜到漁家
Zhang Ji, Coming to a Fisherman's Home by Night[48]

漁家在江口	The fisherman's home is at the river's mouth,
潮水入柴扉	the high tides come into his wicker gate.
行客欲投宿	The traveler wants to stay overnight,
主人猶未歸	but the owner has still not returned.
竹深村路遠	Deep in bamboo the village road lies afar,
月出釣船稀	the moon comes out, fishing boats grow fewer.
遙見尋沙岸	Afar I see movement along the sandy shore,
春風動草衣	the spring breeze stirring a coat of straw.

The parallelism of the third couplet here is more salient in the Chinese than in the translation:

Bamboo	deep	village	road	far
moon	comes out	fishing	boat(s)	few

There is, however, nothing striking in the relation of the parallel elements; rather, they are complementary, as the speaker looks to the road and the river for the return of the fisherman, at whose home he wants to stay. In the last couplet he sees the fisherman, identifiable by his straw coat, strolling along the sandy shore.

In contrast to Bai Juyi's stylized "wildness," *kuang* 狂, or Jia Dao's "strangeness," *qi* 奇, "blandness," *dan*, is an elusive quality. If Bai Juyi's "wildness" is a theatrical display of personality and Jia Dao's "strangeness" is a display of painstaking craft (in which personality disappears in the craftsman), then "blandness" is the ultimate askesis of regulated verse, in which both salient personality and craftsmanship disappear in a polished ease realized in familiar poetic form.

---

48. 20203; Li Dongsheng 98.

FOUR

The Craftsmen of Poetry

When writing about poets who were active almost twelve centuries ago, we are at the mercy of our sources. Apart from those rare poets like Bai Juyi, with full biographies and careful documentation of their lives within their works, we often have only fragments of biographical information. Some of these fragments come from cursory biographies in official histories, themselves often based on uncertain sources; sometimes we have a note attached to a bibliographical entry; often we have anecdotes of highly dubious veracity. In many cases biographical information is painstakingly pieced together from references in poem titles and poems.[1] Apart from the problematic anecdotes, much of what we learn involves office rank and/or location at a given time. The nature of such information easily reduces the "lives" of poets to a sequence of titles and posts, marking upward or downward movement in public prestige, presumed to make the poet proportionately happier or less happy. In the process, this same poet is often also moving back and forth across the map of China. When we come to poets who never had a public career or began their official careers late in life (like poor Xiang Si, who received his first post in middle age and died a year or so later in that same post), we have only the poems.

Given the fact that this is the kind of information we possess, we are doomed to repeat it when talking about individual poets. We should, however, not forget the things we do not know. We rarely know what

---

1. Here there are new uncertainties involving questions of attribution and the fact that poems titles, on which much depends, were the most textually variable part of the poem. An additional problem is that if the addressee of a poem was currently holding a post lower in rank than one previously held, the poet would commonly refer to him by his higher, former title.

earlier poets they read and admired in their youth. Unless their fathers were officeholders or their mothers had important family relations, we know next to nothing about their families. Unless they held office, we don't know how they supported themselves—often over the course of decades. We know little of the practice of their art: we don't see the drafts, the revisions, and usually don't know which poems were discarded. One reason Bai Juyi is attractive is that in his poetry and prose he does give us information about such matters.

Their reticence about some details of their lives is largely a function of the thematic restriction of their art. The poet Yong Tao seems to have witnessed the Nanzhao invasion of Sichuan in 829–30, in which his beloved Chengdu was sacked and a large percentage of its population carried off to death or slavery. He does have poems about the captives, but they are strangely disappointing. He personally escaped somehow, but we would like to know what happened. Had he been writing in the seventeenth century, he would certainly have left us a more dramatic and detailed record, either in poetry or prose. As we will see, Yong Tao does give us another vivid moment involving staying for the night in a temple with Tibetan monks in the contested frontier regions of Sichuan. Although such a poem does provide us with the singular particulars of experience, we must bear in mind that spending the night at a temple was a "proper" topic for a poem.

As we discuss these poets below, we will briefly comment on their public careers—if indeed they had public careers, since many did not. It is enough to roughly situate them in the social world of which they were a part. We will try to position them poetically among the other regulated-verse craftsmen. Although askesis was a shared virtue—in contrast to the strong personalities of the Yuanhe era—the poetics of regulated verse had its own internal issues and differences. Once we have outlined those issues and differences, however, we will be forced to conclude that much of their poetry is alike; they write beautiful and memorable poems, most of which could easily have been written by half a dozen other poets. (Variant attributions, moreover, are not uncommon.) In a later tradition that increasingly prized a biographical frame of reference and a distinct poetic personality, these poets were ultimately doomed to the status of "minor poets."

These poets, however, became fully "minor" in a process of canon formation that only assumed its mature shape in the sixteenth century, became increasingly codified in the Qing, and was institutionalized, with modifications, in the Republican and PRC school systems. Prior to that era, most of these poets had their passionate advocates, and many were singled out—by perceptive critics—as the best poets of the century.

"Names" of poets remain the way we organize the surviving poetic corpus. In the case of the masters of regulated verse, we can question the usefulness of this old habit. Nevertheless, we will follow tradition and touch on the names in brief sketches. It is hard to decide where to stop: we will look primarily at two generations, leaving off with those poets a great part of whose work lasted past 860.

Yao He 姚合

Like many of the regulated-verse craftsmen and despite his considerable reputation[2] and relatively extensive public career, Yao He's dates are uncertain: Fu Xuancong places his birth around 779 and his death around 849. We know that he passed the *jinshi* examination in 816, the same year that Li He, ten years his junior, died. Yao He was roughly the same age as Yuan Zhen, and he could easily have belonged to the Yuanhe generation; but his period of greatest poetic activity did not begin until the 820s.

Yao He claimed the family glory of relatively distant ancestry, in this case descent from Yao Chong 姚崇 (650–721), a famous and much-admired minister early in Xuanzong's reign. The Tang had, by this point, a long enough history that a substantial percentage of the gentry could claim descent from someone famous. Yao He's father, however, had only been a county magistrate (though his mother's family was better connected).

Yao He had a remarkably smooth public career, beginning with a series of low-level posts as "district defender" (county sheriff). Under the reign of Wenzong, he held several mid-level posts in the central government, later accepting prefectural governorships in Jinzhou and the

---

2. Yao He's collection was continuous from the Song. There are almost 540 poems extant by him. In addition to an anthology entitled *The Supreme Mystery, Jixuan ji* 極玄集, he is also credited with a collection of exemplary couplets, the *Shi li* 詩例, which is no longer extant.

plum prefecture of Hangzhou. Provincial posts are often associated with loss of favor in the capital; in some cases this is unquestionably true, but the consistency with which prefectural governorships appear at a certain stage in one's career suggests that this is something more routine than the consequence of factional shifts in power.[3] Following his term in Hangzhou, Yao He returned to the capital, advancing steadily, including a stint as surveillance commissioner in 839. (During this time he reinstated Li Shangyin in his post of district defender after the latter had been dismissed for countermanding a criminal sentence made by Yao's predecessor.) He ultimately attained the post of Director of the Imperial Library, which had previously been held by various distinguished literary men, including Bai Juyi.

As was mentioned earlier, Yao He had a wide range of acquaintances among younger poets in Chang'an, most of whom had not passed the *jinshi* examination and some of whom belonged to obscure provincial families with no history of officeholding. When addressed by his official titles in poems, some deference is shown, though far less than was the norm. In this group we find a remarkable degree of social leveling around a shared love of poetry. Yao He was also the only regulated-verse master to penetrate the margins of the Bai Juyi circle (perhaps because he was politically successful in Bai Juyi's lifetime). Above all, Yao He was a close associate of Jia Dao, with whose name his is always paired. As such, Yao He's poetry is considered more "bland and even," *pingdan* 平淡, compared to Jia's more striking couplets.[4] Both praise and criticism of his work employ many of the same terms used to describe the regulated verse of Zhang Ji. Yao seems to have been well aware of the "blandness" of his work, as we can see in the following poem of self-deprecation realized in a remarkably barbed compliment.

---

3. Although Yao He's provincial posts are not generally interpreted as the result of factional dissatisfaction, the scholarly conviction that provincial posts meant disfavor (sometimes supported by the dissatisfactions of incumbents in such posts) overlooks the simple fact that the empire had many prefectures and counties that needed administrators.

4. "Bland and even" is a relative quality. See pp. 110–11, where Han Yu observes that Jia Dao was turning to a "bland and even" style in the Yuanhe Reign.

姚合, 寄李干
"Yao He, To Li Gan[5]

尋常自怪詩無味	I ordinarily fault myself,
	that my poems lack any flavor;
雖被人吟不喜聞	although they are recited by others,
	I don't delight in hearing them.
見說與君同一格	But when I was told that I shared
	the same style with you:
數篇到火卻休焚	I stopped burning those several pieces
	I had put into the fire.

The relation between "blandness," *dan*, and "lacking flavor," *wuwei* 無味, is an interesting one. The two terms are very close in meaning; if they seem different, it is because "bland" is often a positive term, whereas here "lacking flavor" is pejorative.

One difference from Zhang Ji in Yao He's work is the growing sense of poetry as a vocation and the pleasure of craftsmanship. The poem may seem steady and artless, but he tells us that he devotes himself to carefully "choosing words," *xuan zi* 選字.

姚合, 閑居晚夏
Yao He, Dwelling in Calm in Late Summer[6]

閑居無事擾	Dwelling in calm, nothing to disturb me,
舊病亦多瘥	my former illness also largely cured.
選字詩中老	Choosing words, I grow old in poetry,
看山屋外眠	looking at the hills, I lie down outside.
片霞侵落日	A rosy cloud intrudes on the setting sun,
繁葉咽鳴蟬	thick leaves choke with cicadas singing.
對此心還樂	Facing this, the heart is again joyous,
誰知乏酒錢	who notices lacking money for ale?

The poet who "grows old in poetry" is declaring poetry as a way of life. We are not too thematically distant from Bai Juyi, who often declares in his Luoyang semiretirement that all he needs are poetry and ale. The phrasing of the third line, however, is more radical, not only defining poetry as craft, as "choosing words," but also poetically spatializing the art as something one can grow old "in." Bai Juyi grew old "in" Luoyang, enjoying "poetry and ale." "Ale," *jiu* 酒, was the term most commonly

---

5. 26476; Liu Yan 44.
6. 26560; Liu Yan 68.

conjoined with "poetry," *shi* 詩, whether as a compound or placed in parallel positions in a couplet. Significantly, poems and the scenes for poems are joys in their own right, making him forget about drinking (though remembering that he has forgotten it). This new sense of poetry is a self-sufficient world; it is no longer, along with ale, an adjunct of entertainment. Again we may here contrast Bai Juyi's self-conscious poetic "wildness," which is often linked to drinking.

The third couplet is the "poetic scene," marked by craft and demonstrating that this is indeed a poet who "chooses words." It is not particularly striking or daring. However, given as the scene perceived when the poet "lies down outside" in the fourth line, it is remarkable in recapitulating the situation of the perceiver. Both are scenes of occlusion, with the cloud covering the sun, producing the "hiddenness," *yin* 隱, of the poet in seclusion, a poet growing old, just as the sun is sinking. From another space of hiding (leaves and clouds) comes the sound of cicadas, a sound closely associated with poets who engage in *kuyin*, "bitter chanting" or "painstaking craft" (like "choosing words").

One of Yao He's most famous couplets is contained in the first of a series of thirty poems he wrote while assistant magistrate of Wugong county in the late Yuanhe Reign:

姚合, 武功縣作三十首
Yao He, Written in Wugong County[7]

縣去帝城遠	The county lies far from the Emperor's city,
爲官與隱齊	holding office here is equal to reclusion.
馬隨山鹿放	My horse, left to graze with the mountain deer,
雞雜野禽棲	my chickens roost among wild fowl.
繞舍唯藤架	Around my cottage are only vine trellises,
侵階是藥畦	rising up on my steps is the herb garden.
更師嵇叔夜	Beyond this I will make Xi Kang my teacher:
不擬作書題	I do not plan to write the letters I should.[8]

The second couplet is the one remembered, with the animals that accompany civilized humanity reverting to nature or merging seamlessly with it. Fang Hui complains about the third couplet, saying "it resembles

---

7. 26526; Liu Yan 59.

8. In his letter on breaking off his friendship with Shan Tao, Xi Kang, the famous Wei eccentric, complained about having to write letters.

Zhang Ji, yet is too facile" 似張司業而太易.[9] However, we might here note the first couplet, so close in sentiment to Bai Juyi's famous "hermit in between" written later. We see the poet looking on his official post as a "job" with a salary, the less onerous the better; certainly many officeholders felt the same, but poets were beginning to celebrate such paid leisure publicly. We can do no better here than to again cite Li Jue's memorial of 838: "Poets, moreover, are generally poor and unreliable men, ignorant of the nature of officeholding." Li Jue is perhaps judging from experience or basing himself on report. However, it is quite possible that this opinion, seemingly widespread in court circles, derived from the self-description of poets in office.

If public office is a "job," a space is opened for poetry as the true vocation. This can be true of monks as well, as Yao He writes to Jia Dao's cousin, the poet-monk Wuke.

姚合, 送無可上人遊越

Yao He, Seeing Off the Monk Wuke Traveling to Yue[10]

清晨相訪立門前	In the clear morning I visit you, and stand before your gate—
麻履方袍一少年	in hemp sandals and cassock a single young man.
懶讀經文求作佛	Too lazy to recite the sutras to seek to become a Buddha,
願攻詩句覓昇仙	you willingly polish lines of poems, aspiring to join the Immortals.
芳春山影花連寺	Shadows of hills in sweet-smelling spring, flowers stretch to the temple,
觸夜潮聲月滿船	the sound of the tide braving the night, moonlight filling your boat.
今日送行偏惜別	Today I send you on your way, especially regretting to part:
共師文字有因緣	as we both are disciples of the art of words, there must be a karmic affinity.

The second couplet is a theme one sees with increasing frequency throughout the ninth century: poetry is the true object of devotion, and

---

9. Fang Hui 244.

10. 26365; Liu Yan 13. We know that Wuke was younger than Jia Dao, though we do not know how much younger. To describe him as a "young man" suggests that this poem dates from the late 810s or 820s.

the poet escapes his other duties and commitments into poetry. Yao He describes himself and Wuke as "disciples of the art of words." In the choice of the "art of words," *wenzi* 文字 (specifically the written word), we can begin to glimpse the terms of a contemporary dispute. In praising the verse of the monk Daozong, Bai Juyi used *wenzi* pejoratively, as the type of poetry that Daozong transcended.[11]

Jia Dao 賈島 (779–843)

Chinese poets are often grouped in pairs. Jia Dao[12] is unusual in that he is a member of two such pairings: he is linked with the gloomy and rugged Mid-Tang poet Meng Jiao and with Yao He. Such a double pairing is interesting in that one could never imagine Meng Jiao and Yao He themselves as a pair. This suggests that in the critical imagination Jia Dao's art somehow mediated between Mid-Tang poetic daring and the "bland," conservative craft of Yao He.

The critical catchphrase in pairing Meng Jiao and Jia Dao was "Jiao cold, Dao lean" 郊寒島瘦. Meng Jiao wrote almost exclusively in old-style verse, and some of Jia Dao's poems in that form clearly show Meng's influence. Regulated verse, however, was Jia Dao's preferred form, the one for which he was best known and the form that sustained his later image as a poetic craftsman. In terms of poetic activity, the two poets overlapped for only seven years, at the end of Meng Jiao's career and the beginning of Jia Dao's; in fact, most of Jia Dao's poetry was written after Meng Jiao's death in 817. There is, however, one way in which these two rather different poets—the "cold" and the "lean"—occupied a similar poetic sphere in the ninth- and tenth-century imagination. Both poets were associated with suffering, ambiguously located in their personal lives and in artistic askesis resulting from their devotion to poetry. Such ambiguity is precisely realized in the changing sense of *kuyin*, from "bitter chanting" (or chanting from personal bitterness) to "painstaking composition."

By the turn of the tenth century the changes set in motion in the second quarter of the ninth century had developed into a notion of

---

11. See pp. 57–58.

12. Jia Dao's poems survive in a collection with a tradition that can be traced back to the Song. About four hundred poems are attributed to him, though these include a number of dubious authenticity.

"poetry" as an almost mystical entity and secular devotional practice, commonly paired with Chan. If Jia Dao was poetry's Buddha, his name religiously repeated by poets, Meng Jiao was also considered a founding patriarch of this austere art. The prolific poet-monk Guanxiu 貫休 begins "On Reading Meng Jiao's Collected Poems" 讀孟郊集 with a remarkable statement that would have been unimaginable a century earlier:[13]

東野子何之	Where did the master Dongye go?—
詩人始見詩	among poets we first see poetry.
清刳霜雪髓	His purity scraped out frost and snow's marrow,
吟動鬼神司	his chanting stirred officers of spirits and gods.
舉世言多媚	His whole age, filled with beguiling words,
無人師此師	no one took this master as his master.[14]
因知吾道後	Thus I know that after my Way is over,
冷淡亦如斯	I too will be like this in cold limpidity.[15]

The second line is open to various interpretations, all leading to the notion that we first find real "poetry" in Meng Jiao. Guanxiu would not have denied the greatness of Li Bai, Du Fu, or other important poets before Meng Jiao. Rather, he seems to be invoking some notion of "pure poetry" (or, to adopt another interpretation of the line, the poetry of a true "poet"), poetry that is not an adjunct of life but an end of life to which the poet sacrifices everything else and suffers. While Bai Juyi shares many themes with such "poets," his garrulous good cheer and complacent pleasure in his creature comforts radically exclude him from this notion of "poetry."

While both Meng Jiao and Jia Dao do speak of absorption in poetry, they lived lives of relative poverty since they were both political failures. After failing several times, Meng Jiao finally did pass the *jinshi* examination. However, when he was at last given a minor provincial post, he had to be relieved of responsibility because of neglect of duty. Jia Dao

---

13. 45247.

14. I understand this as referring to Meng Jiao's own age, in that rejection by others was a constant theme in his poetry; it could, however, refer to Guanxiu's own age. Note that *shi* 師, "master" or "teacher," was also commonly used in the Buddhist spiritual hierarchy.

15. Note that "limpidity" is *dan*, "blandness," discussed above. This was not a quality usually associated with Meng Jiao's poetry.

never passed the *jinshi* examination.[16] Considering Jia Dao's background, this is not surprising. Not only did he come from a family without officeholders—if there were any, we would know about them since there is a short biography in the *New Tang History* and a *muzhiming*—but he had a monastic education, apparently in his native Fanyang or somewhere nearby, far from the culturally developed parts of the empire. Fanyang, near modern Beijing in the northeast, had been the center of An Lushan's rebellion, and it had never completely passed back into central government control. It was clearly not a place known to nurture poets.

One can only imagine the kind of verse Jia Dao, then a thirty-one-year-old Buddhist monk with the religious name Wuben 無本, was writing when he came to Luoyang and Chang'an in 810 and met Meng Jiao and Han Yu. Both poets prized roughness as a mark of the "ancient," and we may reasonably suspect that a native of Fanyang with a monastic education was a "diamond in the rough." The pieces that we can reasonably date to 810 are not distinguished. Over the next three decades, however, Jia Dao became the very image of the polished craftsman, though his craft often had rough edges that had been filed smooth, which distinguished his art from poets like Yao He, for whom "blandness" came easily. We cannot believe the literal truth of the legends about him, but for someone of his background to have made such a place for himself in the culture of ninth-century Chang'an, he must have been a figure of singular passion and drive. It is unlikely that a man with such an education could have written a successful examination essay, *fu*, or poem. Nowhere in his poetry do we see the elaborate and florid "high style," nor does he often use allusion. Indeed, there is no indication in his work that he had much learning. Perhaps the only arena left for his energies was his own kind of poetry—and in that sense it is possible that he became the figure of the "poet."

Although we can place Jia Dao in Chang'an and various other places at particular times, we know almost nothing of his life during the more than quarter century between his arrival in Chang'an in 810 and his posting to Changjiang as assistant magistrate in 837. We know that he

---

16. One might note here Wei Zhuang's memorial to posthumously pass all the famous Mid- and Late Tang poets who never passed the *jinshi* examination. (Wei mistakenly includes a few who actually did pass.) See *Tang zhiyan* 116–19.

renounced his Buddhist vows in the Yuanhe and took the *jinshi* examination a number of times, but we have no idea how he supported himself. (We do know that Linghu Chu helped him out with gifts when he was serving in Changjiang.) His claims of extreme poverty were probably justified. Although his Changjiang posting provided a salary, it seems to have been an unwelcome post and was considered an "exile." Around 840, after his term at Changjiang was up, he was made prefectural administrator of granaries in Puzhou, where he died in 843. Poets often served in lowly positions, but a prefectural administrator of granaries, however essential to the well-being of the empire, fell below the horizon of positions contemplated by the literary elite of the capital.

There is a striking difference between Jia Dao's regulated verse and his old-style poems, which have the strong accent of Meng Jiao and the Yuanhe. It is tempting to think of these old-style poems as somehow earlier, but the majority cannot be dated. The following lament for Lu Tong, one of the most mannered of the Yuanhe stylists, was probably composed around 812–13, although there was a popular story, long in circulation, that Lu was killed in the Sweet Dew Incident of 835.[17] Such a poem could just as easily have been written by Meng Jiao.

賈島, 哭盧仝

Jia Dao, Lamenting Lu Tong[18]

賢人無官死	A worthy man has died without office,
不親者亦悲	even those not close to him feel sad.
空令古鬼哭	Older ghosts are made to weep helplessly
更得新鄰比	on getting another new neighbor.
平生四十年	Throughout the forty years of his life
惟著白布衣	he wore only plain commoner's clothes.
天子未辟召	The Son of Heaven never summoned him,
地府誰來追	who from the Underworld came seeking him out?
長安有交友	He has friends in Chang'an to whom
託孤遽棄移	he entrusted his orphans, absconding suddenly.
塚側誌石短	The memorial stone by his tomb is short,
文字行參差	the lines of the characters are not even.
無錢買松栽	There was no money to buy a pine,
自生蒿草枝	but sprigs of artemisia grow there naturally.

---

17. See Fu (1987), vol. 2, 270–71.
18. 31472; Qi 8.

在日贈我文	The writings you gave me when alive,
淚流把讀時	I take them in hand to read, and my tears flow.
從茲加敬重	From now on I will revere them even more,
深藏恐失遺	hide them deep away for fear of losing them.

Although Jia Dao's most famous regulated verses are very different from the above poem, we can still see a continuity not only in the images of poverty and cold but also in the diction of lines that frame the fine couplets that display regulated-verse craft.

賈島, 冬夜

Jia Dao, Winter Night[19]

羈旅復經冬	I pass through winter again in travels,
瓢空盎亦空	the ladle empty, the pot empty as well.
淚流寒枕上	Tears stream upon a cold pillow,
跡絕舊山中	my tracks are gone in my former hills.
凌結浮萍水	Ice forms in waters with drifting duckweed,
雪和衰柳風	snow blends with the wind in ruined willows.
曙光雞未報	The cock does not announce dawn's light,
嘹唳兩三鴻	but a few wild swans are screeching.

Jia Dao often gives us legible traces to read: an empty ladle and pot; tracks of tears in parallel to vanished tracks in his native mountains. From that he provides a striking, descriptive parallel couplet marked by careful craft. Often, as here, its relation to what has gone before is suggestive yet hard to read as an obvious "trace." Duckweed, floating unrooted on the surface of the water, was a common figure for a traveler, and there is an analogy between this winter traveler and the duckweed in the waters icing up from the shore. The anticipated freezing of the whole stream (or pond) trapping the duckweed is picked up in the snow blowing through the willows, though here the white, icy element has become fluid. Finally the dawn arrives, with the traveler listening for the rooster's call but hearing instead the sharp cries of migratory swans, travelers like himself.

The poem is entitled "Winter Night" and poets were supposed to stick to their "topic" (*ti* 題, also "title")—in this case the passage from night to dawn. The third couplet, however, is not something easily visible at night, particularly when the poet is clearly—and, considering

---

19. 31594; Qi 188.

the weather, wisely—inside. The stylistic disjunction of the couplet—carefully crafted yet set amid less artful lines—is matched by its disjunction from the immediate scene at hand. The line is a poetic construct: he could have remembered these scenes or imagined these images on a "winter night," or he could have written the couplet at some other time and fit it into the poem. Tang poets were very aware of "sticking to the topic," and the frequent appearance of such couplets tends to separate at least one kind of "poetry" from older assumptions of the representation of immediate experience. The disjunction of the "poetic couplet" from the poem was implicit in the anecdotes about Jia Dao in which he deliberates on the choice of words while wandering in Chang'an—far from the sites and occasions of the poems in which those couplets were set, sites and occasions that constitute the "title"/"topic."

The following verse simultaneously embodies the beauties of Jia Dao's poetry and the tensions they stirred in the mainstream of Chinese poetics.

賈島, 泥陽館

Jia Dao, The Inn at Niyang[20]

客愁何併起	Why do sorrows of travel all rise together?—
暮送故人迴	at twilight I send my old friends back.
廢館秋螢出	Autumn fireflies emerge from the abandoned inn,
空城寒雨來	cold rains come to the deserted city.
夕陽飄白露	Evening sunlight tosses white dew in wind,
樹影掃青苔	the shadows of trees sweep green moss.
獨坐離容慘	I sit alone, the brooding look of someone apart
孤燈照不開	the solitary lamp does not dispel with its light.

The scene is apparently one in which the poet's friends have accompanied the poet as far as Niyang and then turned back, leaving the poet alone to begin his travels. The scenes of the middle couplets are beautiful examples of couplet craft, particularly in the play of light and shadow in the third couplet. However, the reader expecting not "poetry" but the representation of experience is inevitably going to be profoundly troubled: we have the twilight departure of his friends; we have fireflies (night); we have rain. This is a possible sequence. Then we have evening sunlight and white dew (associated with the end of night and early morning) in the wind. The sunlight literally "tosses"

---

20. 31634; Qi 240.

white dew (the translator has added "wind," since this "tossing" usually implies it). We might take the third couplet as a movement back in time to the evening scene; but in terms of natural phenomena this is a very busy poem. We might take the "abandoned" inn as Jia Dao's subjective mood, following the departure of his friends; but the word here should mean completely abandoned, falling into ruins. Then we have, in parallel, a "deserted city": the modern commentator Qi Wenbang assures us that in the Mid-Tang the "ancient city" (or "ancient walls") of Niyang still survived, but we are hard put to discover what historical "[walled] city" that was.

We raise these points because they would easily have troubled—indeed, did trouble—late imperial readers. (Even the modern Qi Wenbang feels he must account for the presence of a "deserted city" in a small Tang county.) The Qing critic Ji Yun 紀昀 (1724–1805) begins by offering an emendation and then throws up his hands in dismay. For the "white dew" he says: "I suspect this should be 'white egrets'; still, while 'white dew' does make sense, 'white egrets' is not very good."[21] He concludes: "When you have 'fireflies emerge' and 'rains come' together with 'sit alone,' you should not also have 'evening sunlight' and 'shadows of trees.' This poem is a complete jumble and beyond explanation."[22] Not all readers of poetry were bothered by this, but Ji Yun represents a strain of referential reading that was very deeply ingrained in the later tradition. The images work beautifully together as a construct of art, a play of pattern and mood; moreover, there is no indication that Tang readers demanded referential consistency. However, such transgressions of referential consistency had consequences in the later reading of Jia Dao's poetry and often brought the poet under attack.

In the following poem dating from 826 we are moving away from Mid-Tang themes and manner toward the polite verse expected on certain occasions. The poet Zhu Qingyu (Zhu Kejiu) had passed the *jinshi* examination and was making the routine trip home to formally announce the news to his parents. At the end Jia Dao politely assured Zhu that he would not be home long because he would be summoned to take up an office in some bureau—in other words, a desirable capital post.

---

21. Qi 241. "Dew," *lu* 露, was homophonous with "egret" 鷺.
22. Qi 241.

賈島, 送朱可久歸越中
Jia Dao, Seeing Zhu Kejiu Off on His Return to Yue[23]

石頭城下泊	You will moor by the Fortress on the Rock,[24]
北固暝鐘初	as the bell in darkness from Beigu begins.[25]
汀鷺潮衝起	Beach egrets rise, dashing against high tides,
舟窗月過虛	the boat window empty as the moon passes.
吳山侵越眾	Wu's mountains get numerous entering Yue,
隋柳入唐疏	Sui willows grow sparser, coming into Tang.
日欲躬調膳	You would personally prepare fine food daily,[26]
辟來何府書	but a summons will come from some bureau.

Jia Dao here follows one of the standard models for parting poetry, en-
visioning the traveler on the journey ahead.[27] He begins with a scene of
Jiankang (in Wu), then moves from Wu into Zhu's native Yue. When
he reaches home, he will soon be called back to Chang'an.[28] Critics of-
ten remark on the clever parallelism of the third couplet, balancing in-
crease and decrease yet also setting historical change against movement
through space.

The "poetic" couplet, however, is clearly the second. The couplet is
not one of Jia Dao's best or most famous, but it represents the finely
crafted "scene" set in an occasional poem. It is appropriate for a Yangzi
River scene, but it is generic. There is no sense that it is necessary to
the structure of poem, though one could interpret the flight of the egret
as a consequence of the bell ringing. Rather than contributing to a
whole, the couplet is framed by the whole, which serves to bring Zhu
Qingyu to the speculative site of the couplet and carries him on when
the couplet is done. We have white egrets (or a white egret) rising from
the whitish sands of a beach, moving against the direction of the

---

23. 31543; Qi 113.

24. In Jiankang (Jinling).

25. Beigu Mountain: downstream from Jiankang on the Yangzi River, near Zhen-
jiang. The reference is to the bell at Ganlu Temple on Beigu Mountain.

26. Preparing food for one's parents was a standard marker of filial devotion.

27. It would, of course, be plausible, based on the poem itself, to take the opening
scene as present at the time of parting, thus placing the poet around Jinling (Nanjing).
The poem, however, uses the same rhyme as a poem by Yao He on the same occasion,
and we can place both Yao He and Jia Dao in Chang'an in 826.

28. Cf. the closing of "Seeing Proofreader Dong Off to Enquire After His Parents
in Changzhou" 送董正字常州覲省. 31545; Qi 116.

incoming waves of the river tide. This day scene is matched by a night scene depicting the white moon passing the window.[29] The large scene of the first line is matched by a framed scene of another white shape in slow passage. As we said, the scene is "local" in the sense of being appropriate for a certain point in Zhu Qingyu's itinerary—it raises none of the referential problems of "The Inn at Niyang"—but that is immaterial to Jia Dao's art. The couplet is not about a Yangzi River scene but about pattern: a play of light, color, and motion.

Zhu Qingyu 朱慶餘

We know very little about Zhu Qingyu[30] apart from the date he passed the *jinshi* examination (826) and his poetic friendships, which included Zhang Ji, Jia Dao, and Yao He. He was referred to as editor, *jiaoshu [lang]* 校書郎, which was a common first post for graduates distinguished by their literary abilities. He seems to have risen no further. Laments for his death refer to him as belonging to the imperial musical establishment (*xielü* 協律), though this may have been an honorary title, as it often was. We can guess that he returned to Chang'an, held an entry-level post as editor, rose no further, and returned to Wu—perhaps in 829 or in the following years, for we find him passing through Xuanzhou when Shen Chuanshi was surveillance commissioner. (Du Mu and Zhao Gu were also there at the time.) He seems to have passed away sometime in the late 830s in his native Yue.

Zhu Qingyu is best known for an anecdote with a figurative quatrain sent to Zhang Ji in which a new bride worries about how she looks, understood as looking for Zhang Ji's support in the examination (the last line understood as: "is my poetry the kind that will pass the examination?").

---

29. I have taken *xu* in its obvious sense here, but in conjunction with moonlight it often has the sense of something plastic or without definite form, referring to a space of moon glow. Cf. Du Fu, "The Middle of Night" 中宵: "setting moonlight formless, stirring on stands" 落月動沙虛 (11635). In this sense we would understand the window as filling with moonlight as the moon passes rather than with the shape of the moon.

30. Zhu Qingyu's slim collection of about 175 poems in one *juan* comes from a Song edition rather than being reconstituted from anthologies. However, a number of additional pieces preserved in *Wenyuan yinghua* suggest that the Song edition was an anthology (*xiaoji* 小集) of his poems.

朱慶餘, 閨意
Zhu Qingyu, Boudoir Theme[31]

洞房昨夜停紅燭	Last night in the bedchamber the red candles were put out,
待曉堂前拜舅姑	she waits for dawn to pay respects to her parents-in-law in the hall.
妝罷低聲問夫壻	Having finished her makeup, in a soft voice she asks her husband:
畫眉深淺入時無	"Is the way I have painted my brows in fashion or not?"

Zhang Ji is supposed to have replied with approval. I cite this not because it is part of the history of poetry but because it shows how anecdotes became attached to poets. Zhu Qinyu may have written the poem and given it to Zhang Ji with the purpose ascribed in the anecdote. The historical truth cannot be known, but the anecdote had its own life, defining Zhu Qingyu and representing him in a long line of poetry anthologies. Based on this anecdote critics have focused exclusively on Zhu's relation to Zhang Ji and have interpreted his poetry as following Zhang Ji's style.

Zhu Qingyu was clearly indebted to Zhang Ji for support, as we can see in the following poem, a remarkably direct expression of gratitude to a patron.

朱慶餘, 上張水部
Zhu Qingyu, Presented to Zhang Ji,
of the Bureau of Waterways[32]

出入門闌久	I have long frequented your home,
兒童亦有情	even your boy has a friendly familiarity.
不忘將姓字	You never forget to mention my name
常説向公卿	whenever you speak to great lords.
每許連牀坐	You often let me sit bench to bench with you,
仍容並馬行	and further allowed me to ride side by side.
恩深轉無語	The deeper your kindness, the less I can say,
懷抱甚分明	but the feeling is utterly clear.

This poem does resemble Zhang Ji in that the parallel couplets effectively disappear in a continuous discursive line. However, emulation of

---

31. 27804.
32. 27661.

a patron in addressing the latter is probably less of a large influence on a poet's works than a community. In the following poem we have such a community, with Jia Dao and Yao He, in a gathering that probably took place in the autumn of 823.[33]

朱慶餘, 與賈島顧非熊無可上人宿萬年姚少府宅

Zhu Qingyu, Spending the Night at the House of District Defender Yao He of Wannian Together with Jia Dao, Gu Feixiong, and the Monk Wuke[34]

莫厭通宵坐	None weary sitting through the night,
貧中會聚難	gatherings are hard when one is poor.
堂虛雪氣入	The hall empty, snowy air enters,
燈在漏聲殘	the lamp remains, the water clock sound fades.
役思因生病	Thoughts on public duties bring sickness,
當禪豈覺寒	in meditation one never feels the cold.
開門各有事	The gate opens, each has matters to attend to—
非不惜餘歡	not that we fail to cherish the lingering pleasure.

Here is the lingering trace of celebrating the poet in poverty, cold, and sickness—or, in this case, a community of poor poets. Like the parallel couplet within the poem, this is the poet's interval, set within a larger sequence of concerns. The second couplet is the "poetic" one, though not labored or clever. The snowy air blowing in is matched by the fading sound of the water clock, indicating that morning is approaching. The lamp that continues to burn marks the fact that the poets have stayed up all night. The poem constantly returns to the fact that this occasion of community and poetry is only a brief interval: it is hard to meet; there are thoughts on public duties to come, and the departing poet holds on to the mood of the night. We have every reason to suspect that these men are not really sitting in Chan meditation but composing poetry, yet the sixth line suggests a Chan-like absorption that keeps out the cold.

Like many others, Zhu Qingyu seems to have been happier away from Chang'an, as suggested by the following poem:

---

33. This is the date given in Fu (1998).
34. 27670.

朱慶餘, 泛溪
Zhu Qingyu, Sailing on a Creek[35]

曲渚迴花舫	Past winding isles turns my flowered boat,
生衣臥向風	in summer clothes I lie, facing the wind.
鳥飛溪色裏	Birds fly in the colors of the creek,
人語棹聲中	people speak amid the sound of oars.
餘卉纔分影	Of remaining growth I now discern reflections,
新蒲自作叢	new reeds form clumps on their own.
前灣更幽絕	The bay ahead is even more quiet and secluded—
雖淺去猶通	though shallow, I can still get through.

Here is the regulated-verse poet in all his glory, lying down, transforming the world around him into beautiful couplets. The title is, as we said, a "topic"—indeed, a common one often treated by others. As a common poetic topic, it raises the question of whether the poet writes a poem because he has been "sailing on a creek," goes sailing on a creek in order to write a poem on that "poetic" topic, or whether he is simply writing on a standard topic without ever getting into a boat. The relation between experience and writing poetry becomes explicit in a poem (with the same title) by Xiang Si, another member of the group.

項斯, 泛溪
Xiang Si, Sailing on a Creek[36]

溪船泛渺瀰	Boat on a creek, sailing a far-reaching flood,
漸覺滅炎輝	I gradually sense the fiery glow disappearing.
動水花連影	Stirring water, flowers reach to their reflections,
逢人鳥背飛	birds fly away when they meet a person.
深猶見白石	Though deep, one can still see white stones,
涼好換生衣	so cool it's best to change summer clothes.[37]
未得多詩句	Not having gotten many lines for poems,
終須隔宿歸	I'll have to stay overnight before returning.

----

35. 27647.
36. 30458.

37. This plays on the double sense of *shengyi* 生衣 as both "summer clothes" and plants or algae growing on the surface of the water. In effect, the air is so cool that the creek should "change clothes."

Experience here seems to demand a certain quota of "lines for poems," and the poet playfully uses the failure to fill his quota as an excuse for staying. We are not far from the image of Li He going riding every day to "get" lines of poetry, one we will take up in the next chapter.

Gu Feixiong 顧非熊 *(ca. 795–ca. 854)*
and Wuke 無可

Among other poets in the circle active before 827, including Zhang Xiaobiao 章孝標 and Li Kuo, we might mention Gu Feixiong[38] and Wuke,[39] both of whom were present at the gathering in Yao He's house in 823. Gu Feixiong was the late-born son of the more famous poet Gu Kuang 顧況 (born ca. 727). By some accounts Gu Feixiong spent three decades in Chang'an trying to pass the *jinshi* examination, finally succeeding in 845, around the age of fifty. After taking a minor provincial post as district defender, he seems to have given it up and withdrawn, like his father, to Maoshan, the site of an important Daoist cult. We see his name frequently passing in and out of occasional poetry from the early 820s to the mid 840s.

The following, though not a distinguished poem, gives some sense of the young (and not so young) men who had come to Chang'an. The "poet" is already a type apart.

顧非熊, 落第後贈同居友人
Gu Feixiong, After Failing the Examination,
Given to a Friend Who Lives With Me[40]

有情天地內	Of all who have feeling in this world,
多感是詩人	those moved most of all are the poets.
見月長憐夜	Seeing the moon, they ever love the night,
看花又惜春	looking at flowers, they also cherish spring.
愁爲終日客	Sad to be a sojourner all through my days,
閑過少年身	passing in idleness, this young man's body.

---

38. A small collection of Gu Feixiong's poems—probably an anthology—has survived independently. Seventy-nine of his poems are extant.

39. Wuke's collection was recompiled from anthology sources, probably in the Ming, with about 10 clearly spurious attributions among the 101 items preserved under his name in the *Complete Tang Poems*.

40. 27186.

寂寞正相對	In somber stillness we face one another,
笙歌滿四鄰	song and piping fill neighbors' homes all around.

This poem is uncharacteristic in being purely discursive; the hallmark of these poets is the descriptive parallel couplet, often popping up incongruously in poems that are otherwise routinely delivering their social message. A friend is leaving, and Gu Feixiong doesn't make it in time for the leave-taking, necessitating an apology:

顧非熊, 下第後送友人不及

Gu Feixiong, After Failing the Examination, I Fail to
Make It in Time to Send Off a Friend[41]

失意經寒食	Despondent, I passed through the Cold Food Festival,
情偏感別離	my mood particularly stirred by partings.
來逢人已去	When I came to meet him, he was already gone,
坐見柳空垂	and I saw the willows hanging there in vain.
細雨飛黃鳥	The fine rain had yellow birds flying in it,
新蒲長綠池	new rushes grew tall in the green pond.
自傾相送酒	I poured the cup of farewell ale for myself,
終不展愁眉	but my sad brows never relaxed in a smile.

The willows are "hanging there in vain"; had he made it in time, he would have snapped a branch at parting. The lovely scene of the third couplet is perhaps what the poet saw upon arriving at the location after his friend had already gone, but it is a poetic snapshot that contributes little to the social "business" of the poem.

Wuke was the only monk in the circle in the early years. He was Jia Dao's younger cousin and had probably followed Jia Dao to the capital. Wuke appears frequently at poetic occasions alongside members of the group. We know virtually nothing about his life except that he did outlive Jia Dao.

The regulated-verse craftsmen figure prominently in the various lists of "illustrative couplets," *jutu* 句圖, from the Five Dynasties and Song, and their works are often remembered for particular couplets. The

---

41. 27175.

poems in which the couplets are set are often undistinguished, as in the following piece (it exists in several versions), which is filled with variants that change the sense.

無可, 秋寄從兄賈島
Wuke, Autumn, Sent to My Cousin Jia Dao[42]

暝蟲喧暮色	Insects in darkness, noisy in twilight's colors,
默思坐西林	brooding in silence I sit in the western grove.
聽雨寒更徹	Listening to rain to the end of the coldest hours,
開門落葉深	I open the gate, the fallen leaves are deep.
昔因京邑病	Long ago, because we were sick in the capital
併起洞庭心	in both of us rose the mood for Lake Dongting,
亦是吾兄事	But then it is because of my cousin's affairs
遲回共至今	that we have both lingered on until now.

The second couplet here became a favorite illustration of what was called "a line beyond image" 象外句 in Song poetics. This simply meant that the "sound of rain" turned out, on opening the gate, to be falling leaves—this might be called a "metaphor of mistake." Once this interpretation was attached to the couplet, it became the natural way in which it was read. The Qing critics He Zhuo 何焯 (1661–1722) and Ji Yun pointed out—the latter with endless good sense that is sometimes blind but often refreshing—that while the standard interpretation was possible, there was nothing unusual about having rain at night and then discovering fallen leaves in the morning.[43]

Ma Dai 馬戴

Ma Dai[44] appears at a parting banquet with Jia Dao, Yao He, Zhu Qingyu, and Wuke in the winter of 823–24. He must have been a rather young man in his early twenties. He did not pass the *jinshi* examination until 844. According to Fu Xuancong's speculations, he died around

---

42. 44349.

43. Fang Hui 436.

44. Ma Dai has about 170 extant poems, the numbers varying with editions and resulting from dubious attributions. The collection has survived independently, rather than having been put together from anthology sources, and appears to have been an anthology of his poetry.

869. Like many other poets in the group, we can place him at various datable gatherings and know that he held certain offices without, however, being able to date them. A fair amount of information about him exists, none of which coheres into anything like a biography. However, according to the Southern Song critic Yan Yu 嚴羽—perhaps the single most influential judge of poetry in the late imperial period—Ma Dai was the best poet of the Late Tang (allowing that Yan Yu profoundly disliked Late Tang poetry). The quality of Ma Dai's poems praised by later critics was associated with the High Tang: the poems had a "natural coherence" (a lame rendering of *huncheng* 渾成), in contrast to the Late Tang tendency to foreground perfect parallelism and effort in the couplet.

When we read Ma Dai's poetry, we can understand why later critics made this judgment—particularly concerning the poems included in anthologies. At the same time, we can see why these High Tang virtues did not necessarily make Ma Dai a better poet. Jia Dao's poems are indeed constructs of self-conscious "art" that reveals itself. At their best Jia Dao's poems work through complex reiterations of pattern. Ma Dai's poems are more truly descriptive, invoking a complete scene. The parallelism is just as obvious, but because it is less complicated and demanding, it disappears into the whole, which creates a greater sense of unity and continuous flow.

馬戴, 江行留別
Ma Dai, Traveling on the River, Detained at Parting[45]

吳楚半秋色	Wu and Chu, mid-autumn colors,
渡江逢葦花	crossing the river, I encounter reed flowers.
雲侵帆影盡	Clouds encroach, the outlines of sails are gone,
風逼雁行斜	the wind presses the wild geese lines aslant.
返照開嵐翠	Sunlight cast back opens blue mountain haze,
寒潮蕩浦沙	cold tides sweep over the sands of the shore.
余將何所往	Where am I going to go now?—
海嶠擬營家	I plan to build a home on high peaks in the sea.

---

45. 30526; Yang Jun 2.

This is a grand and beautiful Yangzi River scene that somehow inspires in the poet the desire to sail off to the world of the immortals. It does seem to be the gift of the moment (recalling how Jia Dao's couplets sometimes signal their separate existence as constructs of craft by not fitting the situation announced in the title). On some deeper level, however, Ma Dai remains very much the Late Tang poet. In many of his best poems we find that characteristic attention to the single poetic moment, whether in a line or a couplet, which becomes the focus and center of the poem. In the following poem memory creates a single beautiful scene that stands for and hides the monk's presence: climbing the mountain in the night rain, at last coming to a lamp burning before an image of Buddha.

馬戴, 寄終南眞空禪師

Ma Dai, Sent to the Chan Master Zhenkong
on Mount Zhongnan[46]

閑想白雲外	Idly I fancy you beyond white clouds,
了然清靜僧	perfected, a monk who is utterly serene and pure.
松門山半寺	Gate among pines, temple half up the mountain,
夜雨佛前燈	night rain, a lamp before Buddha.
此境可長住	In such a realm one might stay forever,
浮生自不能	in this life adrift I myself am not able.
一從林下別	Since we parted then in the woods,
瀑布幾成冰	the cascade has almost turned to ice.

The scene of memory or fancy in the second couplet is a single fixed image of permanence in a "life adrift," one that carries the poet on and away. It is in many ways the experiential counterpart of the Late Tang poetic craft, in which the particular point, the finely phrased couplet, is the poetic moment that holds the whole poem together around it. Such an art reflected a discipline of attention, both in the process of polishing that perfected it and in reading. It is an art distinct from the poetry of the High Tang.

---

46. 30536; Yang Jun 9.

Yong Tao 雍陶

Yong Tao[47] makes his first appearance in 822, writing to Bai Juyi after twice failing to pass the *jinshi* examination. We have no evidence that Bai wrote back. This young poet who was to achieve some prominence in poetic circles of the capital was invisible to Bai. We don't see Yong Tao with the circle around Jia Dao and Yao He until 825. From this point on he was very much part of the group. Yong Tao was a native of Sichuan (though Fu Xuancong argues for Yun'an 雲安 in Kuizhou, eastern Sichuan, rather than Chengdu). He passed the *jinshi* examination in 834 but seems to have had no official career until about two decades later, when, in 852, he was an Erudite teaching the *Mao Shi* in the imperial academy. In 854 be became governor of a prefecture, but he seems to have gone no further.

Yong Tao was a poet of considerable talent. The surviving accounts claim that he was well aware of such talent and was somewhat arrogant. More than most of his contemporaries, he could integrate the craft of the couplet into a poem.

雍陶, 寒食夜池上對月懷友

Yong Tao, On the Night of the Cold Food Festival Facing the
Moon by a Pool and Thinking of Friends[48]

人間多別離	Among mortals partings come often,
處處是相思	there is longing wherever you go.
海內無煙夜	In this sea-girt world, a night without mist,
天涯有月時	at earth's edge, a time of moonlight.
跳魚翻荇葉	The leaping fish turns over watercress leaves,
驚鵲出花枝	startled magpies emerge from flowering boughs.

---

47. Yong Tao has slightly over 130 extant poems, a large proportion of which are quatrains recovered from *Wanshou Tangren jueju*. Although there are a number of other poems preserved in *Tangyin tongjian*, more than half of Yong Tao's poems other than quatrains are from anthology sources. Early bibliographical notices describe a collection in five or ten *juan*. Taken together, this suggests that Hong Mai had access to a much larger version of the collection, but what we now have is a Ming recompilation from anthology sources plus perhaps a small selection of Yong Tao's work.

48. 27889; Zhou Xiaotian 16.

親友皆千里	Kin and friends, all a thousand leagues away,
三更獨繞池	at midnight I circle the pool alone.

The beauty of this poem lies in its construction of space, with the poet circling a reflecting pool. Outside that circle is far space, leading off to remote distances where his friends are. Inside the circle is the pool, close at hand but mirroring the larger world thanks to the good luck of the weather and the moon. He begins with one of those lovely generalities: the constant meeting, parting, and longing that is the fate of human beings. The poet seems always in motion, *chuchu*, "wherever you go." The present scene is one of those places in "wherever you go," but it is a lucky one—a night with moonlight and no mist. The reflected moon, by poetic convention, makes one think of those others who are also looking at the moon, though far away—as Liu Deren wrote in the simple and beautiful opening of a poem to Yong Tao:[49]

圓明寒魄上	Round and bright, the cold moon rises,
天地一光中	Heaven and Earth in a single light.

Returning to Yong Tao's poem, suddenly a fish leaps in that mirror that turns the poet's thoughts outward and disturbs the reflecting surface. Next, above, a bird—perhaps startled by the sound of the fish—takes flight, moving away from the reflecting pool. The poet's thoughts also move outward to those dear to him. The poem then moves back from the distant world outside to the immediate space inside his circling. Thoughts are directed outward, and yet in the end he keeps circling the pool, looking inward at the reflecting surface. Such an inward gaze toward the immediate particular as a reflection of the outer is almost an allegory of Late Tang poetics. The pattern is almost legible.

Yong Tao's Sichuan was something of a contested frontier. Earlier we mentioned the Nanzhao invasion of 829–30. Tibet was no longer the warlike, expansionist kingdom it had been, but many areas in Tibet and the western part of the empire were culturally mixed and militarily contested zones. Perhaps we can discover the key to the preceding poem and something of Yong Tao's poetics in the following piece:

---

49. 29857.

雍陶, 塞上宿野寺

Yong Tao, Staying Overnight at a Temple
in the Wilds on the Frontier[50]

塞上蕃僧老	On the frontier the Tibetan monks grow old,
天寒疾上關	when weather turns cold, they lock gates quickly.
遠煙平似水	The distant mist is as level as water,
高樹暗如山	the tall trees darkened like mountains.
去馬朝常急	Horses leaving at dawn are always hurried,
行人夜始閒	only at night can the traveler be at rest.
更深聽刁斗	The hour is late, I listen to the watch-kettles,[51]
時到磬聲間	often coming amid the sounds of chimes.

In the preceding poem on circling the pool, the third couplet shifted suddenly to attention to the beautiful particulars of pattern, ostensibly turning away from thoughts about distant friends but leading back to them. Here we see the same movement in the descriptive second couplet. We are on the frontier; although we don't know quite where, the presence of Tibetan monks suggests some part of Sichuan. It is a world of cold and ubiquitous danger. Autumn is the season of warfare, and the Tibetan monks bar their gates early. The temple is a safe haven. Those who must travel onward set out early and with haste. Armies lie nearby—the sound of the kettles beaten for the watch combines with the chimes of the temple. In the second couplet, however, we have the aesthetic counterpart of the temple: the descriptive parallel couplet in which the dangerous darkness of trees and mist become poetic pattern.

In these examples the shift from the discursive to the finely crafted parallel couplet is not incongruous, as it was in the Gu Feixiong poem, cited above; rather, the enclosed world of the parallel couplet mirrors or carries on the larger theme of the poem. The following piece, one of Yong Tao's finest, includes the couplet discussed earlier.

---

50. 27888; Zhou Xiaotian 15.
51. "Watch-kettles" were kettles struck at night in army camps.

雍陶, 秋居病中
Yong Tao, In Sickness Dwelling in Autumn[52]

幽居悄悄何人到	In the utter silence of my secluded dwelling no one comes,
落日清涼滿樹梢	the clear cool of the setting sun fills the tips of the trees.
新句有時愁裏得	From time to time new lines are found in melancholy,
古方無效病來抛	old remedies have no effect, in sickness I've given them up.
荒簷數蝶懸蛛綱	By leaf-strewn eaves several butterflies hang in a spider's web;
空屋孤螢入燕巢	in the empty room a lone firefly enters the nest of swallows.
獨臥南窗秋色晚	I lie alone by the south window in the lateness of autumn colors,
一庭紅葉掩衡茅	a yardful of red leaves closes barred door and thatched cottage.

Although the poet could easily have been sick in his younger years, it is tempting to take this as one of his later poems, particularly in the context of the renewed interest in regulated verse in the long line that began in the mid-830s. If we compare this to regulated verses in the long line by poets like Xu Hun or Du Mu, we can see the degree to which Yong Tao is simply translating the craft of the short line into the long line.

One touchstone of regulated verse in the long line is to read the first and final couplets together, which combine to form a formally perfect regulated quatrain in the long line. In cases where the first and last couplet do not make sense as a poem or are not a short version of the poem in question, the middle couplets were "active" and necessary to the poem. In many cases (like Yong Tao's poem above) this same "trick" shows the degree to which the middle couplets are fine gems set in a frame.

幽居悄悄何人到	In the utter silence of my secluded dwelling no one comes,
落日清涼滿樹梢	the clear cool of the setting sun fills the tips of the trees.

---

52. 27902; Zhou Xiaitian 29.

獨臥南窗秋色晚	I lie alone by the south window in the lateness of autumn colors,
一庭紅葉掩衡茅	a yardful of red leaves closes barred door and thatched cottage.

This could easily have been preserved as a quatrain under the same title without any sense of incongruity.

If the first and last couplets are a formal "container" for the parallel middle couplets, they also concern containment: the poet is enclosed in his home and is sick, with the middle couplets describing what he does and sees. Indeed, what he "does" and "sees" are the same: his actions involve "getting" new couplets for poems, which parallels abandoning old remedies for his sickness.

Often, when a poet speaks of finding poetic lines in the second couplet, the third couplet will possess a polished perfection that suggests that it is the sort of poetic lines found.[53] The third couplet here is the poetic gem, contained by the first and last couplets. The poetic gem, of course, becomes the enigmatic reflection of its container, picking up motifs of "blockage" and "getting through," discussed earlier. The butterflies are trapped and awaiting their end; the dying sunlight outside is replaced by the tiny light of the firefly, moving from day to night and into the interior of the house, to the empty nest from which the swallows have departed (by late autumn). The poem is constructed to focus on that couplet; the latter bears the weight of attention by the suggestiveness of its associations and, in this case, by the intricacy of its patterns.

We have only the partial remains of Yong Tao's poems. Perhaps the best representation of his full range can be seen in his quatrains, richly preserved by Hong Mai in *Tangren wanshou jueju*.

雍陶, 宿大徹禪師故院
Yong Tao, Spending the Night in the Old
Quarters of the Chan Master Dache[54]

竹房誰繼生前事	In the bamboo hut who carries on what he did while he was alive?—
松月空懸過去心	in vain the moon hangs in the pines, heart of a former life.

---

53. Compare Yao He, pp. 120–21.
54. 27959; Zhou Xiaotian 65.

秋磬數聲天欲曉　　Several notes of autumn chimes,
　　　　　　　　　　the sky about to brighten:
影堂斜掩一燈深　　the image chamber ajar hides
　　　　　　　　　　a single lamp deep within.

We will return to the beautiful closing image here later, but in this context we can see Yong Tao's singular gift in packing an image with resonance. We have the "lamp," a loaded image of the transmission of the dharma in Chan Buddhism, in the "image chamber," which, as we have seen, contains the portraits of deceased monks. The lamp burns through the night, picking up the image of the moon as the "heart of a former life," and is envisaged here just before dawn breaks.

The poets mentioned above were figures already meeting and writing poems together in the first part of the 820s. In 827, with Wenzong on the throne, new poets began to appear in the circle. This younger generation grew up reading the poems of the older members of the circle. Congratulating Gu Feixiong on passing the *jinshi* examination in 845, Liu Deren begins:[55]

愚爲童稚時　　　　When I was just a little boy
已解念君詩　　　　I already knew how to recite your poems.

This conservative art of regulated verse in the short line, in its characteristic Late Tang inflection, was passed down to another generation. If the passing on of the lamp was the Chan image of transmitting the dharma, the image of the lamp burning in the temple by night was passed down from one generation to the next.

Zhou He 周賀 *(Buddhist name: Qingse* 清塞*)*

We have seen Zhou He[56] earlier in "Lamenting the Monk Xianxiao," a very deliberate imitation of Jia Dao's lament for the monk Baiyan (see pp. 106–7). A couplet from this poem is central to the best-known

---

55. 29844.
56. Zhou He has about 90 poems extant. Although his collection is supposed to have been copied from the Buddhist *Hongxiu ji*, most of the selections can be found in Song anthologies like *Wyyh* and *Tangshi jishi*. This suggests that the collection was actually compiled from those sources.

anecdote about Zhou He. The lament for Xianxiao was supposedly presented to Yao He, who particularly admired the following couplet:

| 凍髭亡夜剃 | His icy whiskers were shaved the night he died, |
| 遺偈病時書 | the remaining gatha, written when he was sick. |

Indeed, Yao He admired the poem so much that he persuaded Zhou He to renounce his Buddhist vows and revert to his secular name.

Although the anecdote is clearly apocryphal, like many such stories it contains a deeper figurative truth. Just as Zhou He's poem imitates Jia Dao, the anecdote re-enacts the story of Jia Dao, who gave up his Buddhist vows at the urging of Han Yu. Zhou He appears here as the epigone; as is often the case with epigones, Zhou He's poems are more like the ideal Jia Dao than Jia Dao himself. When Zhou He made his first datable appearance—writing a poem to Zhu Qingyu in 827 or 828—he was clearly a younger person joining a group of famous poets. We know almost nothing about his life, except that he spent much time in the vicinity of Lu Mountain and remained a monk throughout most of the 830s. He appeared frequently at poetic occasions involving members of the group and seems to have been particularly close to Yao He.

As Ma Dai was Yan Yu's choice for the best poet of the age, Zhou He was the choice of the Qing poet and critic Weng Fanggang 翁方綱 (1733–1818). Weng considered him the best regulated-verse poet of the "late Mid- and early Late Tang."[57] Despite the somewhat comic restriction of dating, this is exactly the period we are considering. Zhou He was indeed a master of the couplet.

周賀, 題何氏池亭
Zhou He, On He's Pool Pavilion[58]

信是虛閒地	This is truly a place of leisure and calm,
亭高亦有苔	the pavilion, high-set, with moss as well.
繞池逢石坐	Circling the pool, when I find a rock, I sit,
穿竹引山回	going through bamboo, I turn, led by the mountain.
果落纖萍散	When a fruit falls, the tiny duckweeds scatter;
龜行細草開	where a turtle moves, slender plants open.

---

57. Weng Fanggang 翁方綱, *Shizhou shihua* 石州詩話 (Beijing: Renmin wenxue chuanshe, 1981), 68.

58. 26857.

主人偏好事	My host has unusual discrimination,
終不厭頻來	and I will never weary of coming often.

Here we can clearly see the marked stylistic difference between the parallel middle couplets and the banal framing couplets. Indeed, Zhou He could have kept the first and last couplets as a generic setting to praise anyone's pavilion. There is nothing that binds the middle couplets to this particular frame, but they are, in themselves, striking. The second couplet involves contours, both of the pool and the mountain, that shape the poet's motion, which progresses from the open space of the pool to the bamboo thicket. The poet's motions are circumscribed even though he cannot see the whole shape that guides him.

That same pattern recurs in miniature in the third couplet, where solid things, shaping other things by their contours, first appear falling into the water and then surfacing from beneath. Attention is guided first by the sudden "plop" of the falling fruit; looking toward something that can no longer be seen (the fruit has sunk under the water), the eyes detect the subtler motion of plants, which mark the presence of the turtle.

Zhou He seems to have had a particular fondness for traces hidden and half hidden:

周賀，入靜隱寺途中作
Zhou He, Written on the Road into Jingyin Temple[59]

亂雲迷遠寺	Tangled cloud hides the distant temple,
入路認青松	I recognize the green pines of the road thither.
鳥道緣巢影	The course of birds follows the nest's shadow,
僧鞋印雪蹤	a monk's shoes print tracks in the snow.
草煙連野燒	Smoke over plants stretches to a wilderness fire,
溪霧隔霜鐘	fog on the creek blocks the frosty bell.
更遇樵人問	Then I meet a woodsman and ask the way:
猶言過數峰	he says I still must cross several peaks.

Here is the hopeful traveler reading the signs: the pines; the prints left by a monk's shoes; the temple bell. Only at the end does he find that he is still far from the temple.

Although Jia Dao and other older members of the group did write regulated verse in the long line, somewhat younger poets like Zhou He

---

59. 26891.

and Yong Tao more successfully translated the Late Tang couplet into the long line.

周賀, 送忍禪師歸盧嶽

Zhou He, Seeing Off Chan Master Ren on
His Return to Mount Lu[60]

浪匝湓城嶽壁青	Where the waves encircle Pencheng the mountain's cliff is green,
白頭僧去掃禪扃	the white-haired monk goes off to sweep his Chan gate.
龕燈度雪補殘衲	Lamp in a niche crossed by snow, he mends his tattered cassock;
山日上軒看舊經	when the mountain sun rises by the railing he reads the former sutras.
泉水帶冰寒溜澀	The stream's water bears ice along, the cold rivulets rough;
薜蘿新雨曙煙腥	ivy after a recent rain, the morning mist reeks.
已知身事非吾道	I have learned that that the things I do are not my Way,
甘臥荒齋竹滿庭	I would gladly lie in a tumbledown chapel with bamboo filling the yard.

Even in this modest selection of roughly contemporary poems, the attentive reader may recognize the same images recurring and being reconfigured into new phrasing. Earlier in Ma Dai's "Sent to the Chan Master Zhenkong on Mount Zhongnan" we called attention to the line:

夜雨佛前燈	night rain, a lamp before the Buddha.

In "Spending the Night in the Old Quarters of the Chan Master Dache," Yong Tao closes his quatrain with a similar image:

影堂斜掩一燈深	the image chamber ajar hides a single lamp deep within.

Here in Zhou He we have the monk actually appearing:

龕燈度雪補殘衲	Lamp in the niche crossed by snow, he mends his tattered cassock . . .

---

60. 26930.

Often when we find an image that seems striking and original in this poetry, further reading shows us similar images in various other poets. This was the nature of their art: their achievement usually lay not in finding new images but rather in the phrasing, placement, and integration of the line into a larger pattern. Ma Dai's burning lamp was a focus of memory; Yong Tao's lamp was the focus of many things; in Zhou He it is the small light placed in parallel to the morning sun rising over the mountains and streaming in to illuminate the monk's reading. The image itself is a suggestive one, with its own associations, but its force continually changes as it is reused in new contexts.

Liu Deren 劉得仁

With the exception of Yao He, the poets who gathered and wrote poems to and with each other either were unsuccessful *jinshi* examination aspirants or had passed but had poor-to-mediocre job prospects in the bureaucracy. By the 830s many of them were far from young. A shared love of poetry brought together men whose backgrounds could not have been more diverse. Coming from very different geographical regions, they included monks, a number of men with apparently no family history of government service, and the son of a minister (Li Kuo, the name mentioned in conjunction with Wenzong's proposal for Academicians of Poetry).

Liu Deren[61] was a member of the imperial family, probably the grandson (on the distaff side) of an imperial prince.[62] Liu Deren begins to appear at poetic gatherings and exchanges in the mid-830s. Considering the level of "affirmative action" for members of the imperial family— especially in Wenzong's reign—and the success of his brothers, Liu's political failure was striking. An oft-quoted poem by the monk Qibai 棲白 lamenting his death (a poem with many variants) begins:

忍苦爲詩身到此	Enduring suffering to write poems his body came to this,
冰魂雪魄已難招	his soul of ice and snow cannot be called back.

---

61. About 140 poems by Liu Deren survive, most of which are in *Wyyh*, suggesting a collection that was recompiled at some point.

62. See Fu (1987), vol. 5, 321.

Liu Deren often speaks of his efforts at writing poetry. An attentive reading of his surviving poems suggests that those efforts paid off. We see this in his fine couplets, which are characteristic of the age, as in the following example:[63]

| 岸浸如天水 | The shore is soaked by waters like the heavens, |
| 林含似雨風 | the woods are filled with wind resembling rain. |

The art of choosing words becomes increasingly obvious, as in the following couplet, in which the somewhat humorous parallel is enriched by the verb *wo* 握, to "clutch," which is usually applied to humans but is here transferred to the oblivious but precarious birds:[64]

| 吟身坐霜石 | My chanting body sits on a frosty rock, |
| 眠鳥握風枝 | sleeping birds clutch the wind-blown branches. |

Although Liu Deren uses the standard images of regulated verse, he often deploys them in ways that create moments of strangeness, as in the following example:[65]

| 石溪盤鶴外 | A rocky creek circles beyond the cranes, |
| 岳室閉猿前 | house on the mount, shut in front of the gibbons. |

Since *pan* 盤, translated as "circles," can also describe the wheeling flight of birds, we might want to take the first line as "a rocky creek beyond the circling crane." However, the parallel line presses us to make the translation given above. In the same way, we can dispel some of the strangeness by taking the second line as "before the gibbons [begin to cry out]." However, the parallelism will dispose the reader to take the line spatially. Such an art of the parallel couplet is pressing toward a world of words that cannot be stabilized by imagining a referential scene.

---

63. 29812.
64. 29874.
65. 29827.

Xiang Si 項斯

After passing the *jinshi* examination and then deciding not to pursue an official career but to devote himself to Daoist studies, the poet Shi Ji-anwu 施肩吾 wrote his most famous couplet to the Vice Director of the Board of Rites:[66]

九重城裏無親識	In the city of ninefold walls, no kin or acquaintances;
八百人中獨姓施	among eight hundred men, the only one named Shi.

In short, Shi Jianwu knew no one in Chang'an and was the only person taking the examination with the surname Shi. The couplet reminds us not only what a tight-knit circle the Tang elite comprised but how much a newcomer to that world might feel himself an outsider. The community of poets was one venue where one's surname seemed to matter less. Shi Jianwu joined that circle, but it apparently was not enough.

Shi Jianwu may have felt self-conscious about his surname, but it was merely uncommon among the Tang elite. Xiang Si[67] was another case altogether. If Liu Deren represented the aristocracy in our circle of poets, Xiang Si represented what must have been rural gentry, with no history of officeholding. Although he shares a surname with the great Xiang Yu of antiquity, others with that surname are very rare throughout the entire Tang.[68] Poetry was one of the primary means to make the connections that might lead from such obscure origins to officeholder, and it does seem that he was known as a poet from early childhood.[69]

---

66. 26117.

67. Xiang Si has somewhat less than a hundred poems in a collection that seems to have survived independently. The collected poems include a number of items with multiple attributions.

68. Fu Xuancong, Zhang Chenshi 張忱石, and Xu Yimin 許逸民's *Tang Wudai renwu zhuanji ziliao zonghe suoyin* (Beijing: Zhonghua shuju, 1982) lists only four Xiangs: our poet, two painters, and a representative for the *Yuanhe xingzuan* 元和姓纂, the compendium of surnames.

69. Cf. the following: "My poetic fame from childhood remains" 自小詩名在 (30446).

Zhang Jih 張洎, the enthusiastic Southern Tang editor of both Zhang Ji's and Xiang Si's poetry, makes much of Zhang Ji's appreciation of Xiang Si and the similarity of their respective poetry. One poem addressed to Zhang Ji suggests that the latter knew him in the early 820s.[70] Xiang Si begins to appear at poetic occasions in the Jia Dao and Yao He circle in 832. He seems to have traveled widely—no doubt in search of patrons—and both his poetry and his person were widely admired. After failing the *jinshi* examination several times, he finally passed it in 844. Finally entering the bureaucracy (probably in 845), he was assigned the lowly position of district defender in Dangtu County in Runzhou (where the poet Xu Hun had been posted as magistrate about half a decade earlier). His success did not last long. We can infer that he died between 845 and 847 while still in office; Fu Xuancong's conclusion that he was born around 802 is based on a very shaky conjecture.[71]

Xiang Si is a rather bland poet in whose works one rarely finds the striking couplets of figures like Jia Dao, Yong Tao, Zhou He, or Liu Deren. We can perhaps see something of Zhang Ji's discursive handling of regulated verse in the following:

項斯, 中秋夜懷

Xiang Si, Thoughts at Night in Mid-Autumn[72]

趨馳早晚休	Sooner or later my scurrying ceases,
一歲又殘秋	once again in a year, the last of autumn.
若只如今日	But if it were as it is this day,
何難至白頭	what problem going on thus till my hair is white?
滄波歸處遠	Gray waves go off to far places,
旅食尚邊愁	dining on travels, still the grief of the frontier.
賴見前賢說	At least I see what former wise men said:
窮通不自由	success or failure does not come freely from oneself.

---

70. 30439. The poem in Zhang Ji's collection to Xiang Si is probably by Wang Jian; see Tong Peiji 267.

71. See Fu (1987), vol. 3, 330.

72. 30479.

Yu Fu 喻鳧

With Yu Fu,[73] one of the last to join the now aging group of poets around Yao He and Wuke, we are entering a new generation of poets, one in which Yu Fu and others maintained the old style. Yu Fu passed the *jinshi* examination in 840, after having been in the capital for about a decade; and we have poems exchanged among members of the group dating from the early 840s.[74] He also knew Li Shangyin. Like Xiang Si, he died while holding an early post as a county magistrate. Fu Xuancong offers the speculative dates of 810–850.

Tangshi jishi cites the *Beimeng suoyan* as saying that Yu Fu took Jia Dao as his model. Although this is obvious from his poetry, like several of the younger poets who entered the group, his descriptive couplets are often more theatrical and less restrained than Jia Dao's.

喻鳧, 浴馬

Yu Fu, Bathing a Horse[75]

解控復收鞭	Take off the reins and put the whip away,
長津動細漣	it stirs tiny ripples in the long ford.
空蹄沈綠玉	The green jade of its bare hooves sinks,
閣臆沒連錢	the linked patches of its broad chest go under.
沫漩橋聲下	Its froth swirls beneath sounds of a bridge;
嘶盤柳影邊	its neighing lingers beside willows' reflections.
常聞稟龍性	I have always heard that, endowed with a dragon nature,
固與白波便	it is truly at home among white waves.[76]

This is, of course, a descriptive poem and not fully comparable to occasional poems; but the marked couplet of craft can be seen in the following, with the poet's horse hesitating before turbulent waters matched by a hawk diving into the clouds.

---

73. A short collection of just over 60 poems survives independently.

74. Yu Fu's surname is as obscure as Xiang Si's, and we may make similar inferences about his family background.

75. 29744.

76. 便 here is *pian*: "to be at rest in," translated as "be at home."

喻鳧，晚次臨涇
Yu Fu, Coming to Linjing in the Evening[77]

路入犬羊群	My path enters flocks of sheep and dogs,
城寒雉堞曛	the walls cold, battlements catch evening's glow.
居人祇尚武	The inhabitants value only martial skills,
過客謾投文	the passing traveler offers poems in vain.
馬怯奔渾水	My horse dreads the rushing, turbid waters,
雕沈莽蒼雲	a falcon sinks into a riotous waste of clouds.
沙田積蒿艾	In the sandy fields weeds accumulate,
竟夕見燒焚	and all evening long I see fires burning.

Yu Fu often has a visual brilliance, with the opening glow of sunset on the walls echoed in the nightlong fires burning at the end. The poem also provides us with one of those small details that help us to understand the lives of these poets: the traveler offers a poem in hopes of some reward—no doubt food and lodging. Here, near the frontier, poems are not appreciated. Elsewhere, we infer, this is not the case. We have come very close to the poet as a wandering professional, living off his art and moving on.

Although, as we will see, regulated verse in the long line became increasingly popular in the late 830s and 840s, a later generation carried the craft of the short line into the second half of the ninth century. There was young Li Pin 李頻, who so admired Yao He that he went off to study poetry with him and eventually became his son-in-law; his relatively large collection, which survived independently, mainly consists of regulated verse in the short line. There was Fang Gan 方干, who joined the group in the 830s and continued writing well into the latter half of the century. Nor should we forget the arch-epigone Li Dong 李洞, writing toward the end of the century, who was reciting Jia Dao's name as a Buddha before the statue of the master.

The passionate devotion to craft became a commonplace, leading to claims that, in an earlier era, would have been very strange indeed. Poets seem to have forgotten that their art was once supposed to have been a demonstration of "talent" that could be of use to the state. Li Jue's complaint about the uselessness of poets in government is turned on its head, as Du Xunhe 杜荀鶴 (846–904) boasts of his indifference

---

77. 29748.

to anything but poetry in order to persuade a potential patron to recommend him to the capital:

杜荀鶴, 投李大夫

Du Xunhe, Respectfully Presented to Grand Master Li[78]

自小僻於詩	I have been obsessed with poetry since childhood,
篇篇恨不奇	I hate if any piece is less than remarkable.
苦吟無暇日	I take pains composing without a day of respite,
華髮有多時	my hair flecked with white for a very long time.
進取門難見	I work hard to advance, but the way through is hard to see;
升沈命未知	my fate, to rise or sink, is not yet known.
秋風夜來急	Last night the autumn wind blew hard,
還恐到京遲	yet I still fear it will be slow to get to the capital.

Here the obsessed poet is, at the same time, the quasi-professional obviously advertising his wares in hopes of a recommendation that will be the "wind" that blows him to Chang'an. Du Xunhe claims a continuous and absolute devotion to the craft, which doesn't leave him any free time at all. Poetry had once been an adjunct of a young man's well-rounded education, one who might serve as imperial adviser, provincial administrator, or even military planner. Here it is the product of a "poet," his sole "work"—and the poet needs a job.

---

78. 38492.

FIVE

The Legacy of Li He

In 816, in the eleventh year of the Yuanhe Reign, Li He died at the age of twenty-six (twenty-seven according to Chinese reckoning).[1] Given his brief poetic career, his surviving poetic output of over two hundred poems is considerable. Li He's was a singular and distinctive style, sharing qualities with some of his Yuanhe contemporaries, like Lu Tong 盧仝, and more generally enabled by the remarkable spirit of poetic daring and inventiveness in the last decade of the eighth century and first two decades of the ninth. By 820 the Yuanhe Reign was over. The inventiveness of the era had been exhausted, with poetry taking a decidedly conservative turn.

Li He died without poetic issue, as he died childless in the more literal sense. These two forms of progeny are not entirely unrelated: preparing a poet's "literary remains" (which is what Tang literary collections generally were before the second quarter of the ninth century) was a task that often fell to a writer's son. Writers would sometimes entrust their collected works to friends, particularly if their children were not especially literary and lacked the connections to ensure the dissemination of the collection. This is what Li Bai had done. Li He seems to have done the same, presenting a manuscript of his poems to his then-young friend Shen Shushi 沈述師.[2]

Li He's choice was not a wise one—except in the odd way that things sometimes work out for the best in the long run. Shen Shushi kept the manuscript and soon forgot about it. It apparently accompanied his

---

1. Li Shangyin erroneously says that he died at twenty-four *sui*, a number frequently cited in earlier Chinese commentaries.

2. It is possible that other copies of the manuscript were given to others. It is likely that some of the poems circulated independently.

personal baggage for about fifteen years. One night in November or early December 831, while staying at his brother's post in Xuanzhou, Shen had been drinking and could not fall asleep. While rummaging through his trunks, he found Li He's poems. Obviously sentimental from his drinking, Shen felt guilt over his neglect, having failed to fulfill the most obvious responsibility of any editor of literary remains, namely, to supply the collection with a preface by a known literary figure. A friend came to mind, a promising young writer of twenty-nine, also in the employ of his brother. Deciding to act while the matter was still on his mind, Shen took the rather unusual step of sending a midnight messenger over to Du Mu's lodgings to ask him to write a preface.

Du Mu, understandably startled by this late-night request, refused. Shen continued to press him until Du Mu finally agreed, producing what is certainly the strangest preface in Tang literature. Prefaces often included accounts of how the writer was petitioned to undertake his task, so it is not entirely surprising that Du Mu gave an account of the story of the manuscript—though it was an unusual one. What sets Du Mu's preface apart from virtually all others is the fact that he clearly disapproved of Li He's poetry. Du Mu concludes:

These are indeed the remote descendents of the Sao; and although they are not its equal in the order of things (*li* 理), they go beyond it in diction. The Sao is stirred to resentment and makes furious jabs; its words touch on order (*li* 理) and disorder in the relation between prince and minister, sometimes provoking thoughts in the reader. In what Li He wrote, however, there is none of this. Li He was skilled at digging out past events; thus his deep sighs expressed bitterness at what no one had ever spoken of in present or past times. In pieces like "The Bronze Immortals Take Leave of Han" or "Supplying the Missing 'Palace-Style Ballad' of Yu Jianwu of the Liang" he sought to capture the quality and manner [of the moment]; yet he departed so far from the usual paths of letters that one scarcely knows of them. Li He died in the twenty-seventh year of his age. People of the time all said, "Had Li He not died and improved somewhat in his sense of the order of things, he might have commanded the Sao as a servant."[3]

The last sentence is left purposely ambiguous as to who is the servant. Even if we read this passage in its most generous sense, the praise is

---

3. *Fanchuan wenji* 149.

not intended for the Li He that Du Mu was reading but rather for the Li He that might have been. *Li* 理, translated as the "order of things" and "order" (as "good government," a standard Tang usage), is roughly what a modern reader of literature would call "significance."[4] In this passage Li He's poetry depends upon gorgeous diction and fresh ideas, only without the engagement in the social and political world that produced one kind of depth in a Tang context of values. In the comparative case of the "Sao," generally referring to the works attributed to Qu Yuan, such engagement arouses a depth of feeling in the reader, one that gives a work its force. In effect, Du Mu is saying that Li He's poetry rings hollow.

Young Du Mu was very "serious" in the conventional Tang sense, and he brought his sense of seriousness to bear on Li He, who was something else altogether. The most telling passage in Du Mu's preface immediately precedes the passage quoted above. It can be read as expressing either admiration or irony; but in the context of the changing values of poetry in the 830s it is somehow fateful.

A continuous stream of clouds and mist has not such a manner as his [lit. "are not adequate to make his manner"]; waters stretching off far into the distance have not such a mood as his; all spring's flowering glory has not his gentleness; autumn's bright purity has not his strictness of form; masts driven by the wind and horses in the battle line have not his daring; tile sarcophagi and tripods with seal-script have not his antiquity; the season's flowers and fair women have not his sensuality; walls run to weeds and ruined palaces and tomb mounds overgrown with brush have not his resentment and mournfulness; the leviathan's gaping maw and the leaping sea turtle, the bull demon and the snake god, have not his sense of fantasy and illusion.[5]

This is a wonderful passage, essentially claiming that the qualities in Li He's poetry surpass those same qualities in the world [or in the realm of the spirits, adjunct to the easily accessible empirical world]. The qualities found in Li He are thus more perfectly embodied in poetry than in the world. The "serious" Du Mu had to reject Li He's poetic world precisely because it was not "serious" in Du Mu's Tang sense: it offered no moral

---

4. Here we should pay close attention to the contemporary weight of the word. For a contrary view, see Chen Zijian 陳子建, "Du Mu 'Li Changji geshi xu' 'li' yibian" 杜牧李長吉歌詩序理義辯, *Shehui kexue yanjiu* 6 (1988).

5. *Fanchuan wenji* 149.

and political lessons, no deep feeling arising from the poet's engagement with these issues. It was a different kind of poetry altogether. Yet anyone who reads Du Mu's poetry through the 830s can see the impact of his reading of Li He. Unlike some other poets of his day, Du Mu never overtly emulated Li He's poetry; but he clearly was caught by his own description of the latter, creating markedly "poetic" worlds that were more real than any possible empirical experience. Moreover, Du Mu admitted being seduced by these "poetic" scenes, which lacked the conventional "seriousness" of response to the political "order of things."

Poems engaged with the "order of things" often have titles or prefaces that enable us to link the poem to a specific historical moment, and from there to a particular circumstance. Li He's most famous and characteristic poems lack such markers. The same is generally true of poems that emulate him. It is therefore hard to know exactly when the influence of Li He's poetry began to make an impact. We can see it in Li Shangyin's poems, which can be dated to the 830s, and in poems by Wen Tingyun, which probably cannot be earlier than the 830s and may be much later. Several other minor poets in which we see this influence were acquaintances or friends of Du Mu. We cannot be certain, but it is tempting to conclude that Li He's collection, with Du Mu's preface, entered general circulation in the early 830s and made an impact. Du Mu's judgment may have been negative, but it was the kind of judgment that attracted attention and pointed to possible values in poetry that had their attraction, values distinct from but close to those of the regulated-verse craftsmen.

Li Shangyin's "Short Biography of Li He," *Li He xiaozhuan* 李賀小傳, was composed sometime between 832 and 835.[6] It is no less unusual than the preface. Inspired by Du Mu's preface, Li Shangyin began by setting out to find the person behind the poems. Unlike most biographies, Li Shangyin proceeded empirically by interviewing Li He's sister. He discovered that the "person behind the poems" was not a Qu Yuan, tormented by his personal lack of success or political and social ills. Rather, he discovered what he was perhaps seeking: the image of a

---

6. Li Shangyin refers to Du Mu only as "Du Mu of the Capital," which would have been proper only before Du Mu took up a post as Investigating Censor in 835. Since Li Shangyin saw Du Mu's preface, the biography cannot be earlier than 832.

"poet," utterly absorbed in his art. Although this image has obvious parallels with the image of poetry as practiced by the craftsmen of regulated poetry, the poetics of "taking pains," *kuyin* 苦吟, it is far stranger and more extreme.

Du Mu of the capital wrote a preface for Li Changji's literary collection and described Changji's strangeness most thoroughly. It is now in general circulation. The younger sister of Changji, who married into the Wang family, has given a particularly thorough oral account of Changji. Changji was delicate and thin, his eyebrows met, and he had long fingernails; he was good at painstaking composition (*kuyin*) and writing swiftly. Han Yu of Changli was the very first person to understand him. Among those of his acquaintance, he was closest to Wang Canyuan, Yang Jingzhi, Quan Qu, and Cui Zhi. Every day at dawn he would go on excursions with various gentlemen; but whenever he wrote a poem on some assigned topic, he never brooded over it or forced things to work together or worried about a time limit.[7]

He would always go off riding a donkey, followed by a young Xi slave. On his back he carried an old, tattered brocade bag. If he happened to get something [i.e., come up with lines of poetry], he would write it down at once and throw it in the bag. When he went back in the evening, his mother had a serving girl take the bag and empty its contents; when she saw how much he had written, his mother burst out with: "This boy won't stop until he has spit out his heart." Then she lit the lamps and gave him his dinner. Li He next had the serving girl get what he had written; then, grinding ink and folding paper, he would complete them, at which point he would throw them into another bag. He usually acted like this unless he was very drunk or in mourning. When he finished he didn't look at the poems ever again. Now and then people like Wang and Yang would come, seek them out, and copy them. Changji would always ride alone back and forth to Luoyang.[8] Sometimes when he came to a place he would write something, then throw it away. It was for this reason that there were only four *juan* left in Shen Shushi's possession.

When Changji was about to die, he suddenly saw, in broad daylight, a man in scarlet robes riding a red dragon. He was holding a tablet whose writing was like the seal-script of high antiquity or thunder-stone script. He said that it was to summon Changji. Changji tried but could not read it. He suddenly got out of bed, touched his head to the ground, and said: "My mom is old and sick—I don't want to go." The man in scarlet robes laughed and said: "The Emperor

---

7. The grammar of this long sentence is troublesome and admits of various interpretations.

8. He was most likely traveling between his home in Changgu and Luoyang.

has completed his tower of white jade and immediately summons you to write him an account of it. The joys you are given in Heaven are such that you won't suffer." Changji was alone there weeping; everyone beside him saw it. After a while Changji's breath stopped. In the window of the room where Changji always stayed there was a swelling vapor and one could hear the sound of a carriage and pipes playing. His mother immediately stopped the others from weeping and, waiting the brief time it takes to cook five pints of millet, Changji at last died. His sister in the Wang family would not have been able to fabricate such claims about Changji; this was what she really saw.

Heaven is high and blue-gray. Is there indeed an Emperor there? And does that Emperor indeed have things to enjoy, like parks, palaces, and pavilions? If this is to be believed, then, considering the remote heights of Heaven and the majesty of its Emperor, then it would also be fitting that he have personages and literary talents exceeding comparison with those in our world. Why, then, was he so singularly fond of Changji and why did he prevent him from living a long life? How could it be that those in our world who are considered rare and talented are not only few on Earth but also not many in Heaven? Changji lived twenty-four years, and his post never went further than that of a ritual participant in the Court of Imperial Ceremonies. Moreover, many of his contemporaries spoke ill of him and did him harm. How could it be that the Emperor in Heaven alone values the rare and talented, while mortals, on the contrary, do not value them? How could mortal understanding surpass the Emperor's?[9]

Behind the *chuanqi* atmosphere of Li Shangyin's "biography" we recognize the image of the poet in Han Yu's "Teasing Zhang Ji," *Tiao Zhang Ji* 調張籍.[10] There a ruthless Heaven sends Li Bai and Du Fu to Earth to suffer so that they will write beautiful poems. The god then sends down his minions to gather up the poems and bring them back to Heaven. The differences, however, in Li Shangyin's version are telling. Li Bai and Du Fu write beautiful poems because of their sufferings in life, sufferings caused by the god. Li He is not appreciated by mortals, but Li Shangyin suggests neither that this causes him suffering nor that his experiences in political life are the context for his poems. Li He is completely absorbed in his work; and if he suffers, "spitting out his heart," it is a result of the effort expended in writing poetry.

---

9. Ye (1959) 358–59.
10. 17922; Qian Zhonglian 989.

It is important to keep in mind that the "Short Biography" reflects the values of the 830s, retrospectively invested in Li He and realized through his image. Unlike Han Yu's Li Bai and Du Fu, and unlike the dominant earlier notion of poetry, here poetry is not a consequence of experience of the world—specifically the social and political world. Li He "is" a poet regardless of his experiences in social and political life. Indeed, he is more a poet when simply left to write poetry. If he works at poetry, it is not the social poetry that is the norm. Li He (in the reading of the passage I have adopted) does compose social poems, but he writes them without effort or thought. The poetry that he truly works at is of an altogether different kind: lines found alone when traveling around with his Xi servant, lines worked over at night.

Li He was indeed a poet of *kuyin* 苦吟, "taking pains in composition." However, this was also the claim of Yao He and Jia Dao, the most celebrated poets of the 830s, almost all of whose work was social poetry. Li Shangyin's Li He shares some elements with them: the poem "takes time"; it is something made and not simply the inspiration of the moment. It is something the poet does every day, like a profession.[11] Li He differs from the regulated-verse craftsmen in one other essential detail: once the poem is completed, he is no longer interested. Sometimes the poems lie around for others to copy; sometimes he simply throws them away. This is an art practiced out of passion, for its own sake, and not for the mere product, the poem. This is the very antithesis of Bai Juyi's vision of his poetry as quantitatively cumulative "capital," to be stored in a special bookcase with Bai's name visibly written on it. In "Teasing Zhang Ji" Li Bai's and Du Fu's poetic production is also "capital," to be collected by Heaven, envisaged as something like an absentee landlord. One of the many anecdotes about Jia Dao reveals a sense of poetic production much closer to that of Bai Juyi than to Li He: every New Year's Day Jia Dao was said to spread out all the poems he had composed during the year, to which he would offer up a sacrifice of meat and wine to them as the things that had consumed his spirit in the course of the preceding year.[12] The aggregate of these

---

11. Cf. also the presumption of the need to compose poems every day in Jia Dao's "Playfully Presented to a Friend," p. 94.

12. Zhou Xunchu 1114.

various anecdotes and references in poems vividly demonstrates a set of issues surrounding poetry and its composition that truly belong to the ninth century and that were almost entirely absent in eighth-century discourse on poetic composition.

Li 理, the "order of things," was an important word in Chinese thought, although it had an easy, conventional sense of "political order" during the Tang. Du Mu claimed that the differing qualities of representations in Li He's poetry were more perfect than what was ordinarily experienced in the world, yet Li He's poetry was lacking in *li*, the "order of things." Du Mu was not concerned with nice philosophical questions here: he might simply have meant that Li He's verbal skills overshadowed his other qualities. And yet Du Mu's description of Li He's poetry was, at the very least, the seed of a profound contradiction, suggesting that there might be an "order of things" possible in poetry that was different from what was commonplace in Tang moral and political culture.

If one sets aside the *Chu ci*, which on the surface is as fragmentary and elusive as Li He's work, Du Mu's charge that Li He's poetry lacked *li* has some substance. Tang poetry tended to parataxis, with each line a distinct predicate; but expectations usually made it easy to bring those pieces into a coherent whole (as Wang Yi's interlinear commentary tried to do with *Chu ci*). Such coherence was *li*, the "order of things." If, for example, a poet feels miserable in exile, and his representations of the world around him support such a state of mind, the poem has a subjective, experiential coherence that was satisfying to Tang readers. Li He's parataxis was more extreme: there was more distance between the lines, creating the effect of verbal fragments that only partially cohered. There was often also no presumed subject—either the historical poet or a conventional persona—to easily account for these images as percepts, feelings, and thoughts in a unifying consciousness. The effect of Li He's poetry was sometimes dreamlike; such partial coherence of fragmentary images was clearly part of Li He's attraction. At the same time, such a poetics could not but have been troubling to the young Du Mu: he could not see the "point" of the poems, the lesson or the person who held the images together.

We might consider one of Li He's easier poems on the theme of frontier warfare:

李賀, 雁門太守行
Li He, Song for the Governor of
Wild Goose Gate[13]

黑雲壓城城欲摧	Black clouds press down on walls, the walls seem about to collapse;[14]
甲光向日金鱗開	glint of armor faces the sun, golden scales appear.
角聲滿天秋色裏	Sounds of trumpets fill the heavens within the colors of autumn,
塞土燕脂凝夜紫	borderland soil is tinted rouge that hardens to night's purple.[15]
半捲紅旗臨易水	Our red banners stand half-furled beside the river Yi;
霜重鼓寒聲不起	the frost is heavy, the drums cold, their sounds do not stir.
報君黃金臺上意	We will pay back the honor shown by our lord on the Terrace of Gold[16]
提攜玉龍爲君死	and take in hand the jade dragon-swords, to die for our lord.[17]

A *xing* 行, here translated as "song," is a *yuefu* and thus does not require the presumption of a historical poet at a particular site, yet a reader of the early ninth century would still look for signs of a commonplace empirical order to unify the poem. For example, the reader would look for weather signs, yet here we begin with a cover of black clouds, followed by light glinting on armor. That sunlight marks daytime, but in the fourth line we have night. The frost should be late night or early morning. The half-furled banners can be seen as an unexpected and

---

13. 20661; Ye (1959) 23. This is a *yuefu* title with precedents in the Southern Dynasties.

14. The Qing commentator Wang Qi cites the *Jin shu* as follows: "Whenever there are black clouds like a roof over a strong fortress, they are called the 'essence of the army.'" The rather ominous quality of the image here makes it uncertain whether this sign of martial valor is intended.

15. This refers to the explanation in the *Gujin zhu* 古今注 that frontier walls were made of an earth that gave them a purplish color.

16. The Terrace of Gold 黃金臺 was erected by King Zhao of Yan to receive scholars and knights (both *shi* 士) and was emblematic of a prince's generosity and appreciation of the talents of those who served him.

17. *Yulong* 玉龍 (lit. "jade dragon") must be taken as a kenning for a fine sword.

inauspicious image (particularly before a battle), as are the muted sounds of the drums, which are supposed to stir the valor of the troops. In this context the vow to "die for our lord" is distinctly fatalistic, as if troops are going forth to fight a battle they cannot win. It is a scene built up of vivid fragments that do not cohere empirically (without considerable commentarial ingenuity), but which give the impression of doomed battle more perfectly than any ordinary *yuefu*.

This poem clearly made a strong impression. In the anecdotal tradition Li He presented this poem when he first went to pay his respects to Han Yu in Luoyang. Upon reading the opening lines, Han Yu was so impressed that he had Li He summoned.[18] Wei Zhuang included the piece in his anthology *Further Mystery* at the end of the ninth century. As we will see, it also inspired imitation. Significantly, the "sun" in the second line is sometimes quoted as "moon"—suggesting how the Tang sense of the "order of things" influenced textual reproduction to produce a scene more easily reconciled with "night" in the fourth line—overlooking the less obvious fact that one needs a daytime scene to have the "colors of autumn."

We cannot date Zhang Hu's version of "Song for the Governor of Wild Goose Gate." Zhang's dates are far from certain: he was roughly Li He's contemporary (born within a decade of Li He), but he lived on into the first part of the 850s. Significantly, he was a friend of Du Mu. It is not impossible that Zhang Hu's version dates from the Yuanhe, but echoes of other Li He poems clearly show that it both postdates Li He's poetry and is aware of it. Most likely the poem dates from the 830s or 840s, when Li He's full collection was in circulation.

張祜, 雁門太守行
Zhang Hu, Song for the Governor of Wild Goose Gate[19]

城頭月沒霜如水	Atop the wall the moon sinks away, the frost is like water,
趑趄踏沙人似鬼	with swishing sounds they march on sands, the men like ghosts.

---

18. Zhou Xunchu 1071.

19. 27237; Yan Shoucheng 201. This seems to have entered the standard version of Zhang Hu's collection from *Yuefu shiji*; it is not included in the recently recovered *Zhang Chengji wenji*.

燈前拭淚試香裘	In the lamplight he wipes away tears,
	tries on the scented cape,
長引一聲殘漏子	one note of a long melody
	the last of the water-clock's dripping.
駝囊瀉酒酒一杯	The camel-skin sack spills forth ale,
	a single cup of ale,
前頭滴血心不回	the front lines are weeping blood,
	their hearts do not waver.
閨中年少妻莫哀	Youth in the woman's boudoir,
	wife do not weep,
魚金虎竹天上來	the metal fish and tiger bamboo
	come from Heaven.[20]
雁門山邊骨成灰	Beside Goose Gate Mountain
	their bones become ash.

Zhang Hu uses Li He's technique of paratactic lines, but the scenes have a greater coherence. There is no problem with the time sequence here: as night comes to an end, a soldier (or, more likely, an officer) prepares for battle. A long tradition of frontier poetry invites reference to the soldier's wife, which is here answered with the commitment to serve the emperor, as in Li He's poem. Li He's closure on the point of battle (the last moment in which the doomed soldier would have a "viewpoint") was probably too radical, and Zhang Hu offers a more conventionally satisfying last line—from an external perspective seen over a long span of time—in which the soldiers' bones turn to dust. In short, Zhang Hu effectively domesticates Li He.

We know next to nothing about Zhuang Nanjie 莊南傑 except that he was supposed to have been a rough contemporary of Jia Dao (who had a very long poetic career) and very much a Li He epigone, to judge from the surviving poems.[21]

---

20. These are the tallies of military authority from the emperor (Heaven).

21. The claim that Zhuang was a contemporary of Jia Dao is based entirely on a note to that effect in *Zhizhai shulu jieti*. Fu Xuancong speculates that Zhuang is somewhat younger than Jia Dao. See Fu (1987), vol. 2, 336. Although such notes involving dating in Song bibliographies represent precious evidence, they are sometimes wrong.

莊南傑, 雁門太守行
Zhuang Nanjie, Song for the Governor of Wild Goose Gate[22]

旌旗閃閃搖天末	Flags and banners flashing, waving at Heaven's edge,
長笛橫吹虜塵闊	the long fifes and horizontal flutes, an expanse of nomad dust.
跨下嘶風白練獰	Between his legs the white silk that neighs at the wind is fierce;
腰間切玉青蛇活	at the waist the green snake that cuts into jade is lively.[23]
擊革撾金熸牛尾	Beating leather, striking metal, we ignite the oxtails,[24]
犬羊兵敗如山死	troops of dog and sheep barbarians defeated, dying in heaps like hills.
九泉寂寞葬秋蟲	The Nine Springs are lonely and still, autumn's insects are interred,[25]
濕雲荒草啼秋思	damp clouds and wild grasses weep autumn longings.

Despite Zhuang Nanjie's striking images, which are clearly modeled on Li He, this is a far more conservative poem, developing from a Chinese attack on the "barbarians," their defeat, and a silent aftermath.

Li He's is the earliest extant Tang version of "Song for the Governor of Wild Goose Gate." There are, however, pre-Tang examples. There is an anonymous *yuefu* in the "Treatise on Music" of the *Song shu*, but that seems to have provided no inspiration for Li He. Li He's precursor here was clearly Xiao Gang 蕭綱, Emperor Jianwen of the Liang, who wrote two poems under this title, which were also highly imagistic treatments of the frontier theme. Li He was clearly fascinated with the poetry of the sixth century, the Liang and Chen, which provided a model for a compelling poetry that escaped the oppressive Tang sense of "seriousness." Just as Li He's poetry was criticized for lacking

---

22. 24969.

23. This couplet refers to the soldier's white horse and sword.

24. "Beating leather, striking metal" refers to beating drums and gongs. The last part refers to a stratagem by which the Qi general Tian Dan tied firewood to the tails of oxen, then ignited it, causing the oxen to overrun his enemies.

25. The Nine Springs refer to the underworld.

engagement with the "order of things," so Liang poetry too was conventionally criticized for lacking seriousness.

Li He was clearly fascinated with the unique poetry of the Liang and later Southern Dynasties. It was probably in part thanks to the poetry of Li He that we find a sustained interest in the culture of the later Southern Dynasties in the middle of the ninth century, particularly in the poetry of Li Shangyin and Wen Tingyun. This interest always mixed fascination and critical judgment. On the one hand, there was the absorption in a sensual world of images; this can be traced to the poetry of the Liang and Chen itself, but it was very much mediated by Li He's creation of a separate poetic realm. On the other hand, there was the conviction that the poetic failure to engage the political "order of things" on the part of poet-emperors and their poet-courtiers was an indulgence that resulted in the fall of dynasties.

"Historical contextualization" in scholarship on Chinese literature is often done in very broad strokes. We must know when a poem was written, when it was read, the community for which it was written, and the temper of the particular age. It is true that the later Southern Dynasties evoked absorption in aesthetic pleasure shadowed by impending doom. Li He was writing in the first part of the reign of Xianzong, a period of great optimism and confidence in the resurgence of Tang dynastic power. Despite Liu Fen's intemperate prediction of dynastic ruin in the late 820s (see p. 512), the first part of Wenzong's reign seems to have generally been a period of guarded optimism. A poet writing of the later Southern Dynasties during these periods was probably thinking of the cultural past aesthetically rather than politically. Such texts, if written or read in the wake of the Sweet Dew Incident, would most likely have had a much stronger contemporary political resonance. Li He's remarkably short career historically contextualizes all his poems. More often than not, however, we do not know when poems invoking past styles or moments in history were written. Although this is unfortunate, the principle remains the same: periods like the later Southern Dynasties may be fascinating in their own right or they may inescapably echo a sense of the present moment. It all depends on when one is reading or writing.

In many ways Li He is reminiscent of Li Bai in his fascination with old songs and anecdotes. Both poets were less at home in the contemporary social world of poetry than in imaginary worlds based on their reading. From the Southern Dynasties came the ghostly song of the famous Hangzhou singer Su Xiaoxiao.

蘇小小歌

Su Xiaoxiao's Song[26]

妾乘油壁車	I ride a coach with oiled sides,
郎騎青驄馬	he rides a blue dapple.
何處結同心	Where will we tie a true love knot?—
西陵松柏下	on West Mount, under the cypress and pine.

Her tomb was famous, but Li He never went there. He didn't need to—though he had perhaps heard the story that sometimes, when there was wind and rain, passers-by could hear the sounds of song and music coming from it.

李賀, 蘇小小墓

Li He, The Tomb of Little Su[27]

幽蘭露	Dew on the hidden orchid.
如啼眼	like crying eyes.
無物結同心	Nothing ties a love knot,
煙花不堪剪	flowers in mist I cannot bear to cut.
草如茵	Grass like the carriage cushion,
松如蓋	pines like the carriage roof,
風爲裳	the wind is her skirt,
水爲珮	the waters, her pendants.
油壁車	A carriage with oiled sides
夕相待	awaits in the evening.
冷翠燭	Cold azure candle
勞光彩	struggles to give light.
西陵下	At the foot of West Mound
風吹雨	wind blows the rain.

This is a ghost-song, a scene of the mind realized in poetry. The old singer half materializes, scattered in the scene around her tomb, then in the coach of the old song, and finally as a flickering ghost-light, waiting still—until a gust of wind-blown rain puts out the candle and ends the poem.

---

26. Lu Qinli 1480.
27. 20664; Ye (1959) 27.

There is little question that Zhang Hu knew Li He's poem, though the form of his title and his many years of travel in the Southland suggest that he wrote the following poem while visiting the tomb in person.

張祜, 題蘇小小墓
Zhang Hu, On the Tomb of Su Xiaoxiao[28]

漠漠窮塵地	Billowing, a place of poor dust,
蕭蕭古樹林	whistling in the wind, grove of ancient trees.
臉濃花自發	Cheeks' luster, flowers come out on their own,
眉恨柳長深	brows' reproach, willows ever deep.
夜月人何待	Why does one wait under the night moon?—
春風鳥自吟	in spring breeze birds chant by themselves.
不知誰共穴	I know not if any shares the grave with you:
徒願結同心	in vain you wished to tie a true love knot.

Zhang Hu's poem seems uncomfortably bad only because we have Li He's original. It does, however, embody the weaker side of Li He's influence in the Late Tang. Zhang Hu was clearly attracted by the ghostly aura of Li He's poem and sought to reproduce it. However, while the form of Li He's poem was a creative way of representing a vision, Zhang Hu was trapped by the formal order of exposition of regulated verse in the short line. Many of the pieces of Li He's song are still present, but they have been organized in an all-too-familiar way: the first couplet sets the scene; the second couplet sees reminders of the woman in natural phenomena; the third couplet is a scene of hopeless waiting; in the fourth couplet the poet offers a comment from his own perspective.

No individual so perfectly embodied the potential conflict between the political (the Tang "order of things," *li* 理) and the apolitical gratification of personal will as Qin Shihuang, the First Emperor. According to Legalist thought, the First Emperor was to be the core of a true political "machine," the invisible center of an absolutist structure that functioned with the impersonal precision of nature. Unfortunately, the historical center of that machine, the First Emperor, had a human will that set itself against ordinary Nature: he wanted to dominate the universe and live forever. His foolish ventures, his megalomania, the very mortal political machinations that followed his death, and the stunningly swift collapse of his empire after his death were favorite Tang topics.

---

28. 27276; Yan Shoucheng 14.

In the following poem Li He first presents himself as epigone, re-
sponding directly to the opening lines of Li Bai's third "Old Style"
古風, but doing so in such a brilliant and daring way that the epigone's
lines are more memorable than the original that they recast. First let us
cite Li Bai:[29]

秦皇掃六合	Qin's emperor swept the six directions bare,
虎視何雄哉	how manly his tiger's gaze was!
揮劍決浮雲	His sword, brandished, cut drifting clouds,
諸侯盡西來	and the Lords of the Domains all came west.

Li He's First Emperor is even more flamboyant.

李賀, 秦王飲酒
Li He, The King of Qin Drinks Wine[30]

秦王騎虎遊八極	Qin's king is riding a tiger, he roams to the Eight Extremes,
劍光照空天自碧	his sword-light shines in the emptiness, the heavens turn sapphire.
羲和敲日玻璃聲	Xihe strikes the sun with her whip, the sound of glass,
劫灰飛盡古今平	kalpa ashes have all flown away, past and present pacified.
龍頭瀉酒邀酒星	The dragon's head trickles ale, he invites the Alestar,
金槽琵琶夜棖棖	pipas with golden bridges twang in the night;
洞庭雨腳來吹笙	raindrops on Lake Dongting come to the blowing reed organs,
酒酣喝月使倒行	tipsy with ale he hoots at the moon and makes it go backward;
銀雲櫛櫛瑤殿明	silver clouds like comb's teeth, alabaster palaces brighten.
宮門掌事報一更	At the palace gate the Watchman announces the first watch of night:
花樓玉鳳聲嬌獰	in flowering towers the phoenix of jade has a voice both feral and sweet,

---

29. Zhan Ying 詹鍈, *Li Bai quanji jiaozhu huishi jiping* 李白全集校注彙釋集評
(Tianjin: Baihua wenyi chubanshe, 1996), 37.

30. 20685; Ye (1959) 53.

海綃紅文香淺清	mermen's silk with red patterns
	has a fragrance faint and clear,
黃娥跌舞千年觥	yellow beauties stumble dancing,
	a flagon for a thousand-year toast.
仙人燭樹蠟煙輕	From the immortals' candelabra
	the waxy smoke is light,
清琴醉眼淚泓泓	at the clear zither, drunken eyes
	shed tears in floods.[31]

This was something unprecedented in Chinese poetry. The fragmentary discontinuity of brilliant lines effectively embodies a state of dreaming, drunkenness, and madness in which the First Emperor seeks to dominate the universe and time. Space does not permit a detailed discussion of Li He's poem, but it is not difficult to see why Li He's poetry had such an impact when it resurfaced in the early 830s.

It is understandable that such a poem might invite Du Mu's critique of Li He's work, but there are ways in which it does not deserve the critique—as adumbrated by Du Mu's own comments. Unlike Du Mu's First Emperor, implicit in his "Poetic Exposition on Apang Palace" (see pp. 259–60), the images do not cohere in any expected way, and Li He offers no "lesson," either direct or implied. The poem cannot be read as a reiteration of the proper "order of things." At the same time, as Du Mu said, Li He's poetry embodies qualities more perfectly than we find in the world: "The King of Qin Drinks Wine" is therefore more mad than even the First Emperor. Li He brings us into a strange world, reserving judgment on that world to our more sober moments.

What we might call the "lesson of Li He" was absorbed by the poets of the 830s in two ways. On the simplest level Li He's brilliant diction was reabsorbed into a fundamentally more conventional poetry based on the Tang sense of the "order of things," both structurally and in terms of moral lessons. The more complicated aspect of the "lesson" was perhaps fully grasped only by Li Shangyin: by disrupting conventional poetic order, poetry can be used to enact states of disorientation rather than simply refer to them.

---

31. Here I follow the received text rather than the variant adopted from *Wenyuan yinghua*: Qingqin 青琴, "Blue Zither," the name of a goddess. This source itself reads the text as above but cites "Blue Zither" as one of two variants.

The middle of the ninth century has many poems about the First Emperor, and although none of these sound like Li He's poem, we can clearly see his influence in the first and simpler level. Wei Chulao 韋楚老 (803–841), an acquaintance of Du Mu, was very much under Li He's spell. In a poem on the First Emperor entitled "Ancestor Dragon," he begins with an unmistakable echo of Li He's "Ballad of the Governor of Wild Goose Gate": "Black clouds weigh on the walls, the walls are about to collapse" 黑雲壓城城欲摧:

韋楚老, 祖龍行
Wei Chulao, The Ballad of Ancestor Dragon[32]

黑雲兵氣射天裂	In black clouds the vapor of troops shoots to Heaven and splits it,
壯士朝眠夢冤結	bold warriors sleeping at dawn, their grievances congealed in dream.
祖龍一夜死沙丘	One night Ancestor Dragon died at Sanddune,[33]
胡亥空隨鮑魚轍	Huhai in vain followed the wagon tracks of abalone.[34]
腐肉偷生三千里	The rotting flesh pretended life for three thousand leagues,
偽書先賜扶蘇死	a false rescript first granted death to Fusu.[35]
墓接驪山土未乾	His tomb touched Mount Li, but before the earth was dry,[36]

---

32. 27145; Wang Zhongyong 1543. "Ancestor Dragon" is Qin Shihuang. The "Annals of Qin Shihuang" in the *Shiji* relates how one night an envoy was passing Huayang when a man holding a jade disk stopped him and told him to give the disk to the "Lord of Hao Pool," adding, "This year Ancestor Dragon will die."

33. The location in Hebei where Qin Shihuang died.

34. Huhai was the prince that the eunuch Zhao Gao set on the throne as the Second Emperor of Qin. When Qin Shihuang died, Zhao Gao and the minister Li Si wanted to keep this secret, so they put the corpse in a wagon together with a load of abalone to disguise the smell.

35. Qin Shihuang had wanted to have Prince Fusu succeed him, but Li Si drafted a false edict putting Huhai on the throne and condemning Fusu to death.

36. Qin Shihuang's tomb lies just east of Mount Li, near Chang'an.

瑞光已向芒碭起	auspicious light had already risen from Mounts Mang and Dang.[37]
陳勝城中鼓三下	In Chen Sheng's[38] city the drums rolled thrice,
秦家天地如崩瓦	and the universe of the House of Qin was like crumbling tiles.
龍蛇撩亂入咸陽	In a tumult dragons and serpents entered Xianyang,[39]
少帝空隨漢家馬	and Emperor Shao in vain followed the horses of the Han.[40]

This is not a memorable poem in its own right, though the serial allusions recall Li Shangyin. Nevertheless Wei Chulao's "Ballad of Ancestor Dragon" shows the link between Li He and the "poem on history" of the mid-ninth century. As so often in Li He's poetry, each line or couplet offers a separate image (the radical parataxis that lies behind the anecdote of Li He emptying his bag in the evening and stitching lines together into a poem); but in Wei Chulao these isolated images are arranged in perfect chronological order, corresponding to the account of the fall of Qin in the *Shi ji*. What appeared to be poetically discontinuous was, in fact, unified by a prior narrative known to contemporary readers. Though the ethical lesson about Qin's fall is not stated explicitly, it is nonetheless obvious to all in the end, with the last Qin emperor following the horses of Han. Such a poem would have happily satisfied Du Mu's concern for the poetic presentation of the "order of things."

Both Li He and Wei Chulao were writing songs in the long line (*gexing* 歌行). If we translate Wei Chulao's more "orderly" historical song into the aesthetics of regulated verse, we find the "poem on history" in its characteristically Late Tang inflection.

---

37. This was where Liu Bang lived in obscurity before rising in rebellion against Qin and founding the Han.

38. One of the leaders of the rebellions against Qin's authority.

39. The "dragons and serpents" refer to Liu Bang and Xiang Yu, both of whom entered the Qin capital at Xianyang.

40. Emperor Shao was Qin Shihuang's grandson, placed on the throne after the assassination of his uncle, Huhai, the "Second Emperor."

杜牧, 過驪山作
Du Mu, Written on Passing Mount Li[41]

始皇東游出周鼎	When the First Emperor roamed east to bring forth Zhou's tripods,[42]
劉項縱觀皆引頸	Liu Bang and Xiang Yu watched their fill, both craning their necks.[43]
削平天下實辛勤	Conquering and pacifying all the world was hard work indeed,
卻爲道旁窮百姓	but thereby he drove to desperation those peasants by the roadside.
黔首不愚爾益愚	The common folk were not the fools; you were more foolish still;
千里函關囚獨夫	the thousand leagues of Hangu Pass imprisoned the autocrat.
牧童火入九泉底	Then a herd boy's fire made its way to the Nine Springs below,
燒作灰時猶未枯	and when you were burned to ashes, your bones were not yet bare.[44]

Although Du Mu's poem may seem fragmented and elliptical, like Wei Chulao's poem it is supported by a narrative with which all educated contemporary readers would have been familiar. By contrast, Li He's poem does allude to stories about the First Emperor, but there is no real grounding in historical narrative.

Figures like Zhuang Nanjie and Wei Chulao were clearly Li He admirers, but their dates are uncertain and very few of their poems survive.

---

41. 28054; Feng 87. Although this is usually treated as a single poem, its rhyme structure (AABA CCDC) is identical to that of two quatrains. Mount Li was next to the burial mound of Qin Shihuang.

42. On a journey east in 219 B.C. Qin Shihuang passed by the site where the Zhou tripods—symbols of legitimate kingship—were supposed to have been lost underwater. He sent people to try to recover them but was unsuccessful.

43. This alludes to separate accounts in the *Shi ji*, in the *Annals* of Han Gaozu and Xiang Yu, on seeing the First Emperor of Qin during his journeys. Liu Bang's comment was: "That's how a great man should be!" 大丈夫當如此也. Xiang Yu's comment was: "He can be replaced" 彼可取而代也.

44. Using a torch to find a lost sheep that had escaped into the First Emperor's great underground tomb complex on Mount Li, a herd boy accidentally caused a fire that consumed the tomb and its contents.

Among major poets with extensive collections, Li He's most ardent Late Tang admirers were Li Shangyin and Wen Tingyun. Wen Tingyun's dates are still a matter of conjecture, but Li Shangyin turned twenty in the early 830s, around the time when Li He's collection entered circulation. Wen Tingyun's relation to Li He has been extensively discussed by Paul Rouzer, and we will defer our own consideration of Wen's *yuefu* to a later chapter.[45] Since Wen used the kind of song forms Li He preferred and the paratactic style that Rouzer calls "montage," the debt is obvious in this case. Li Shangyin did write a number of obscure stanzaic songs, such as "Heyang," 河陽詩, in which the debt to Li He is no less obvious—not to mention the fact that Li He wrote a song to the same title (see pp. 369–70). However, Li Shangyin generally preferred regulated forms, where Li He's influence appears in themes, diction, and parataxis. Du Mu noted that Li He particularly liked to write poems based on stories that "no one had ever spoken of in present or past times." One example is a poem on Feng Xiaolian 馮小憐 ("Little Love"), the favorite of the last Northern Qi emperor.[46] One should not be surprised to find "Little Love" appearing again in Li Shangyin, in two quatrains entitled "The Northern Qi" 北齊 (see pp. 425–27). Memories of Li He's poetry reappear, albeit transformed, throughout Li Shangyin's works.

One of the two poems that particularly caught Du Mu's attention was the piece he called "Supplying the Missing 'Palace-Style Ballad' of Yu Jianwu of the Liang" 補梁庾肩吾宮體謠. This is clearly the piece now entitled "Song on the Return from Kuaiji" 還自會稽歌.[47] In the Jin Dynasty lyrics were "supplied," *bu* 補, for *Shijing* poems preserved only as titles. However, what Li He did here was truly unprecedented: he assumed the voice of an earlier poet and wrote the poem that the earlier poet "should have written." Certainly no small part of Li He's influence was his singular re-creation of the mid-sixth-century style, the "palace style," distinguished more by its daring sensuousness and imagery than by its attention to women (though that was a possibility within it). Far more radical was to place himself in the position of a historical poet known for writing in the palace style. Wen Tingyun caught

---

45. Rouzer 43–60.
46. 20784.
47. 20647; Ye (1959) 6–7.

one dimension of Li He's poetry by often writing lyrics that "should have been written" in the past; but he does not take the more radical step of impersonating an earlier poet. We find that more radical move in only one case where one would not normally find Li He's influence, namely, where Li Shangyin writes as Du Fu in Chengdu (see p. 444). In general, Li Shangyin showed a fondness for the persona poem, particularly in exchange dialogues, and some of these used historical figures.[48]

Only a relatively small proportion of Li He's surviving poems could properly be classed as "boudoir poems," which focused on women and their surroundings. Nevertheless, later poets appear to have associated such themes with his work. We cannot tell whether this impression derived from specific "boudoir poems" by Li He or from a general sensuality in his verse and his interest in Liang and Chen poetry. When Li Shangyin writes a poem expressly "Imitating Changji [Li He]" 效長吉, the theme involves a palace woman waiting in vain for the ruler's visit.

李商隱, 效長吉

Li Shangyin, Imitating Li He[49]

長長漢殿眉	Long, long are the brows in the halls of Han,
窄窄楚宮衣	tight-fitting, the gown in the palace of Chu.
鏡好鸞空舞	The mirror fine, the simurgh dances in vain,[50]
簾疏燕誤飛	curtains wide-meshed, swallows in error fly in.
君王不可問	She may not ask of the ruler's affection—
昨夜約黃歸	last night she returned, having applied forehead yellow.

One can, indeed, find a handful of poems like this in Li He's collection, but it is far more an imitation of what the Tang saw as the palace style of the sixth century than of Li He. In some ways we can see the explicit imitation here as Li Shangyin's attempt to "contain" the appearance of Li He's influence in his work, with a poem whose triviality implies that of its source.

Li He's poems on women and romance did indeed influence Li Shangyin's more famous poems on these themes. Among Li He's

---

48. Take, for example, the personal exchange between a performer and the Lechang Princess of Chen, 29450–51 (*Jijie* 1044; Ye 389–90).

49. 29589; *Jijie* 1841; Ye 519.

50. This refers to a famous story in which the solitary simurgh (a kind of phoenix), longing for a mate, saw its own reflection in a mirror and danced.

poems we find several social poems for Luoyang beauties and a fine piece on a woman combing her hair. The strangest and most ambitious Li He poem of the boudoir type is "Tormentor," *Nao gong* 惱公, a veritable inventory of images from the tradition of boudoir poetry pressed into strange new shapes.[51]

Since they generally lack specific occasional reference, it is virtually impossible to accurately date Li Shangyin's poems about women. In one case, however, we can date a single set of Li Shangyin's most famous poems to the years just after Li He's collection entered circulation. These are Li Shangyin's four "Yan Terrace" poems 燕臺四首, which must have been written in 835 or a few years earlier.[52] Like many of Li He's poems, these are in four-line stanzas, and they have the fragmentary density associated with Li He's work. Moreover, they circulated and were probably written in Luoyang, where Li He had been writing only two decades earlier and where he still may have been remembered. If we read the first of these poems, entitled "Spring," against Li He's "Pearl, the Fair Maid of Luoyang" 洛姝眞珠, we find something like a frame for understanding Li Shangyin's impossible obscurity.[53]

Earlier we discussed the kind of poetry Bai Juyi was writing during this same period in Luoyang. Bai Juyi's poetic world never intersected with those of Li Shangyin or Du Mu, who came to the city in 835, having just been appointed Investigating Censor with a "Luoyang Assignment." Considering that the Sweet Dew Incident was to occur in the winter of that year, it was a fortunate time not to be posted in Chang'an.

Although Du Mu disapproved of Li He, the latter's poetry clung to him. At a bar in Luoyang in 835 Du Mu encountered by chance the singing girl Zhang Haohao, whom he had known earlier at the headquarters of his patron, Shen Chuanshi. He wrote a long ballad for her, which recounts her debut at age thirteen before Shen Chuanshi and how she later became the concubine of Shen Shushi (Du Mu's friend and the man who had kept Li He's poems over the years). At this point

---

51. 20751; Ye (1959) 138. The interpretation of the title is uncertain. Ye, for example, takes it as "teasing myself."

52. We can date these poems because Li Shangyin refers to them in a preface to a datable group of poems. See Stephen Owen, "What Did Liuzhi Hear? The 'Yan Terrace Poems' and the Culture of Romance," *T'ang Studies* 13 (1995): 81–118.

53. 20686; Ye (1959) 56. This is discussed in my article "What Did Liuzhi Hear?"

Shen Chuanshi had died and Shen Shushi had evidently abandoned her. Very much a ballad in the Yuanhe style, it is sentimental and adopts a clear narrative line. Although Du Mu chooses the short line, Bai Juyi's famous "Ballad of the Pipa," *Pipa xing* 琵琶行, in the long line, is clearly in the background. We will defer discussion of this ballad for a later chapter, but in the context of our present discussion we might cite the brief passage where Zhang Haohao becomes Shen Shushi's concubine:

聘之碧瑤佩	As engagement gift he gave sapphire pendants,
載以紫雲車	he carried you off in a coach of lavender cloud.
洞閉水聲遠	The deep chamber closed, the sound of waters far,
月高蟾影孤	the moon was high, its Toad-light, lonely.[54]

The image of the *sound* of waters being far (or growing farther away) is not a common one. Lightly in the background here is the closing of Li He's "A Song of the Bronze Immortal Taking Leave of Han" 金銅 仙人辭漢歌.[55] Here the bronze immortal cast by Emperor Wu of the Han is carried off east to Luoyang by Cao Rui, the Wei emperor.

攜盤獨出月荒涼	Holding the pan I go forth alone, the moon chill and desolate,
渭城已遠波聲小	the city by the Wei is already far, the sound of the waves grows faint.

The "city by the Wei" refers to Chang'an in a general sense. The context is the bronze immortal's sense of loss at his growing distance from Chang'an, forcibly taken from his old master (Emperor Wu, long dead) to serve a new master. If we are being conservative, this is merely a verbal echo, with solitude in the moonlight matching the familiar sound of waters that are now far away.[56] Yet it is tempting to interpret the associations of the Li He passage in a stronger sense, suggesting Zhang Haohao's own feeling of loss at having been taken from Shen Chuanshi in watery Xuanzhou or her later abandonment by Shen Shushi. Du

---

54. Chinese viewers saw the figure of a toad in the moon; as a moon-dweller, the toad became a common synecdoche for the moon.

55. 20703; Ye (1959) 77.

56. In *Du Mu xuanji* Zhu Bilian takes this as a reference to Liu Chen and Ruan Zhao encountering immortal maidens and staying with them. He thus takes the line as positive, with Zhang Haohao entering an immortal realm. This does not fit the tone of the line or its companion line.

Mu never imitated Li He, but fragments of striking passages in Li He's poetry come back to him now and then, sometimes carrying strong associations from the source text.

Li Shangyin's "Yan Terrace Poems" dating from about the same time are something else. Like Li He's set on the twelve months, Li Shangyin's four poems represent the four seasons. Beginning in the mid-seventeenth century, Li Shangyin's commentators all duly explicate these poems, sometimes offering paraphrases and at other times inventing scenarios. It is important to recognize the motive here for paraphrase and scenario: the poems offer a sequence of fragmentary images that have hazy links, and their attraction, like the attraction of Li He's "Tormentor," is precisely a realm of ambiguity and half-comprehension. These are not poems intended to "make sense" in the way that Du Mu's poem on Zhang Haohao does. The images are immensely resonant in the poetic tradition, but Li Shangyin uses these poetic codes of concealed reference to tease the reader on by constantly deferring understanding. In some ways this is indeed youthful poetic mystification, though it is carried out in the hands of a poet of genius.

李商隱, 燕臺詩四首: 秋
Li Shangyin, Yan Terrace: Autumn[57]

月浪衡天天宇溼	Moon-waves stretch across heaven, the vault of heaven is wet,[58]
涼蟾落盡疏星入	the cool Toad has sunk away, the sparse stars go down.[59]
雲屏不動掩孤嚬	The mica screen does not stir hiding her solitary frown,
西樓一夜風箏急	all night long in the western tower the wind chimes ring furiously.
欲織相思花寄遠	She wants to weave of longing flowers to send afar,
終日相思卻相怨	all the day through she longs for him, but then resents him.
但聞北斗聲迴環	She hears only the Northern Dipper's sound turning in its rounds,

---

57. 29635; *Jijie* 79; Ye 571; Zhou 63.
58. Ye prefers the variant *chong* 衝, waves "dash against" heaven.
59. The Toad is the moon.

不見長河水清淺 — she does not see the clear and shallow waters
of the Long River of stars.[60]

金魚鎖斷紅桂春 — The golden fish-lock has locked her off
from the springtime of red cassia,

古時塵滿鴛鴦茵 — dust of olden times fills
the mandarin duck sleeping mat.

堪悲小苑作長道 — Worthy of sorrow that the small garden
becomes the distant road,

玉樹未憐亡國人 — the jade trees feel no pity for
the person whose kingdom has fallen.[61]

瑤瑟愔愔藏楚弄 — The jade zither's sounds are gentle,
concealing the lays of Chu,

越羅冷薄金泥重 — Yue gauze is cold and thin,
its metal appliqué heavy.

簾鉤鸚鵡夜驚霜 — The parrot on the curtain hook
by night is alarmed at the frost,

喚起南雲繞雲夢 — summoning up southern clouds
circling Yunmeng Park.[62]

雙瑞丁丁聯尺素 — A pair of earrings tinkling,
attached to a letter,

內記湘川相識處 — therein is noted the place they met
on the River Xiang.

歌脣一世銜雨看 — Singing lips for a whole lifetime
watched, holding back rain,[63]

可惜馨香手中故 — a pity that the fragrance
grows old upon the hand.

---

60. Echoing "Nineteen Old Poems" X, in which the Weaver Woman gazes toward her beloved Oxherd across the Milky Way: "The River of Stars is shallow and clear" 河漢清且淺.

61. The Last Emperor of Chen composed a famous song lyric entitled "On Jade Tree Flowers in the Rear Courtyard" 玉樹後庭花. Those who heard it recognized it as the "notes of a falling kingdom."

62. Yunmeng Park is associated with the erotic dream of the king of Chu in which the goddess of Wu Mountain visited him.

63. Rain here refers to tears. Some commentators have interpreted this line as the woman singer looking at the letter, whose fragrance grows old in the hand. This has the advantage of tying the stanza together but requires making "lips" the subject of "look at."

The Qing commentator He Zhuo appropriately comments on the series: "These four poems are truly works of the utmost strangeness, in no way less than Li He."

This poem, like others in the set, touches all the resonant chords of the tradition of Chinese "erotic" poetry, including the woman longing for the absent beloved, the love message, and the goddess of Wu Mountain. It closes with a strange and memorable image of a lifetime spent with eyes focused on singing lips, suspended in time, even while the fragrance—a trace of the beloved—fades away on the hand. Even more successfully than "Tormentor," this is a gestural poetics rather than a referential one: it plays chords that evoke fragments of a conventional love narrative, but there is no real concealed narrative apart from those invented by readers and commentators who want to link the poem to some version of the "order of things."

SIX

Regulated Verse in the Long Line
The "Meditation on the Past"

The Question of Genre

Structures that organize literary material in critical discussions and anthologies are historical formations that enforce certain priorities in the contextual identity of texts. The two dominant organizational structures in China have been chronology and genre, with thematic subcategories sometimes added in larger anthologies.[1] Although chronology and genre are not irreconcilable, they have long competed for primacy. Modern anthologies of poetry ("poetry" itself remains a broad organizing category) generally arrange poets in chronological order, then follow the standard sequence of genres to organize their selections. (In some cases, such as that of Du Fu, the chronology of a poet's works sometimes overrides generic distinctions.) By contrast, premodern anthologies are generally organized according to a sequence of poetic genres, with poets arranged chronologically within the genres. This is a significant difference—not unlike asking someone whether he or she understands individual identity primarily as a member of a family or in the context of other contemporaries belonging to the same generation.

The surviving Tang anthologies, all of which are relatively short, have a certain attraction in sometimes chaotically mixing genres and chronology. After the Tang it is only in generically structured

---

1. Since authorship is a principle of grouping texts common to both chronological and generic anthologies, we need not discuss it here. It is, however, worth keeping in mind that authorship as a primary organizational principle has not been universally the case in poetry anthologies outside China.

anthologies, such as *Tang santi shi* 唐三體詩 or *Tangshi guchui* 唐詩 鼓吹, that we find the principle of chronological sequence of authors violated—though violation of chronological sequence remains the exception rather than the rule and generally characterizes anthologies with less cultural status.

Chronological organization is, of course, the precondition of literary history. In premodern times genre remained the system of organization that resisted unifying claims of literary historical period. For example, the Ming critic Hu Yinglin's 胡應麟 extensive study of poetry, the *Shi sou* 詩藪, is divided into a section treating authors and works chronologically and a section on individual poetic genres. This was the only way Hu Yinglin could offer generalizations about authors and periods across genres; at the same time, he had to leave room for issues specific to each genre. Genre was not understood ahistorically. Rather, it was the rough equivalent of a genealogy or local history, which conceived of itself within a larger whole but affirmed its own distinctiveness and internal dynamics.

Modern as well as some premodern notions of literary history presume a certain degree of homology among works of a given period that transcends generic difference.[2] The final victory of chronology as the predominant form of organization in the twentieth century was in many ways the consequence and counterpart of the creation of an institutionalized "national" culture.[3] It seeks unified cultural narratives rather than the differing histories of subsets. That victory has been so complete that it now requires a compensatory act of historical imagination to see in genre alternative versions of the history of poetry.

It is a fact of some significance that none of the poets who have come to define the Mid-Tang are represented in any significant way by

---

2. The older Chinese notion of literary history unified works of a particular period through a presumed contingency on political history (e.g., "the tones of a fallen kingdom" 亡國之音, the sense of imminent dynastic collapse); such historical unities transcend generic difference.

3. This same uneasy balance between history and genre can be seen in earlier European literature. Any reader of poetry knows that a sixteenth-century pastoral poem will resemble the pastoral poems of Virgil far more than the love sonnets by that same author. Not only has a more totalizing version of literary history also come to dominate genre in Western literary studies, but it has tended to prefer periods (such as the early seventeenth century) in which period characteristics are dominant despite generic distinctions.

regulated verse—with the partial exception of the younger Jia Dao.[4] Regulated verse was certainly no less common in the Mid-Tang than in the periods before and after, but it was largely rejected by some poets (Meng Jiao, Li He), comprised only a minor part of the work of others (Han Yu), and involved the lesser-known work of some others (for example, Bai Juyi before 820). Such a turn away from regulated verse was a self-conscious move on the part of most of these poets and a rejection of a still very active conservative poetic establishment. These poets of old-style verse ventured to claim the period as their own—and by and large they succeeded. However, were we to write a "history of Tang poetry" with regulated verse as the constant center, it would be quite a different history between 790 and 820 and would foreground very different poets.

Regulated verse in the seven-syllable line—what was called the "long line" (*changju* 長句) in the ninth century—acquired a distinctive tone or, better, a range of tones. "Tone" is a patently elusive term, yet when one is dealing with a genre that is formally defined, it is an integral of syntactic and lexical norms, thematic affinities, and norms of "mood," an equally elusive term. After repeated reading in a form, a reader learns to recognize a tone—indeed, it is often the first and primary thing a reader recognizes. It is, of course, the quality most difficult to capture in translation.

Regulated verse in the long line was positioned in a generic system with a network of affinities and distinctions. The seven-character line began as a song line, and it never entirely lost that association. In the Tang it was the line length of popular narrative poetry. It had close affinities with literary ballads and stanzaic "song" in the long line (which was probably not sung) and with quatrains in the long line (which were often sung). At its best, regulated verse in the long line often balanced the easy, popular quality of the line against the formal rules of regulated verse. As the Ming critic Hu Yinglin recognized, regulated verse in the long line had an expansiveness that could get out of hand and fail in regard to the careful craftsmanship that regulated

---

4. The poetry of Liu Zongyuan is an interesting case. It was much admired and often anthologized as regulated verse, but it does not play an important role in accounts of Mid-Tang poetry.

verse required.[5] This "popular" aspect of the long line was only one prominent element in a wider range of associations. For example, regulated verse in the long line had long associations with sumptuous court poetry; this made it particularly appropriate for congratulating officials on high-level appointments.

The five-syllable line, known as the "short line," had a very different range of associations: in old-style verse: it could evoke archaic dignity, ethical engagement, or directness of emotion. Regulated verse in the short line, whether tending to blandness or to the craftsmanship of the couplet, also had a markedly different character from regulated verse in the long line. The motifs of craftsmanship discussed earlier—ascetic discipline analogous to Buddhism or *kuyin*, "painstaking composition"— were largely restricted to regulated verse in the short line. As the brevity of the short line came to be associated with an aesthetic asceticism and self-control, the long line became associated with "letting loose" either in emotion or behavior.

The "Meditation on the Past"

One way to present the "local history" represented by genre is to consider a group of regulated verses in the long line on a specific topic. Thematic continuities can provide a basis from which to view other kinds of continuity—in tone, style, and exposition. The "meditation on the past," *huaigu* 懷古, was usually occasioned by a visit to a historical site and was very popular in the Late Tang. We can see some of the thematic issues surrounding the topic in Fang Hui's 方回 (1227–1307) anthology of regulated verse entitled *Yingkui lüsui* 瀛奎律髓. The latter is divided into subgenres (theme and occasion), with each subgenre further divided between regulated verse in the short line and the long line. Under those divisions poems are arranged chronologically (with some striking errors). Fang Hui's brief note on the subgenre describes the tension between sympathy and moral judgment that runs through such poems:

"Meditations on the past" involve seeing past sites and brooding on people of the past; they concern only rise and fall [of the state] and virtue or folly therein.

---

5. Hu Yinglin, *Shi sou* 詩藪 (Shanghai: Shanghai guji chubanshe, 1979), 81.

One may take some cases as a model, yet people have not taken them as a model; one may take other cases as a warning, yet people have not been warned. And this is what grieves those born still later. To consider Peng Zu's long life as equal to an early death or to forget ethical judgment in reference to sage-king Yao and tyrant Jie is heterodox discourse. A person with a kindly heart must think in terms of the moral condition of his own age and thus cannot remain silent with regard to these matters.[6]

Fang Hui's demand for ethical judgment in such poems counters the tendency for pathos to overwhelm judgment, but the resistance to moral judgment often gives such poems much of their attraction.

Fang Hui opens his selection of regulated verse in the long line with four poems by Liu Yuxi, one of which became very famous. The same poems were also included in the somewhat later anthology *Tangshi guchui*. Both anthologies were popular, with the *Tangshi guchui* becoming extremely popular. We present three of the Liu Yuxi poems here. The first can be dated to 805 (the year before the Yuanhe Reign), the second to 814, and the third and most famous one to 824, when poetic taste was already beginning to turn against the "Yuanhe style." If there is a progression here, it is one of increasing mastery rather than any real change of period style or sensibility. Indeed, as we will see, the poems must be viewed within a longer history of works in the same form rather than being forced into the standard literary historical narrative of their respective periods.

劉禹錫, 荆州道懷古

Liu Yuxi, Meditation on the Past on the Jingzhou Road[7]

南國山川舊帝畿	A Southern realm's mountains and rivers, an emperor's former domain,
宋臺梁館尚依稀	A terrace of Song, a lodge from Liang can still be faintly discerned.
馬嘶古樹行人歇	A horse neighs among ancient trees, travelers cease to pass,

---

6. Fang Hui 78.

7. 18935; Qu (1989) 678; Jiang 29. Jingmen or Jingzhou 荆州, also known as Jiangling 江陵, was briefly the capital of the Liang under Yuandi, following the deaths of his father Wudi and his brother Jianwendi, when the rebel Hou Jing held the traditional capital at Jiankang.

麥秀空城澤雉飛	wheat rises high in the empty city, marsh pheasants are flying.[8]
風吹落葉填宮井	Wind blows the falling leaves filling the palace well,
火入荒陵化寶衣	fire enters the weed-grown mound, transforming the burial suit.[9]
徒使詞臣庾開府	In vain the poet, Commander Yu, was made
咸陽終日苦思歸	to spend whole days in Xianyang longing terribly to return.[10]

In these poems it is sometimes hard to see the clear moral judgment the anthologist Fang Hui demanded and presumably made his criterion for selection. Certainly Liang Yuandi (ruled 552–554) was far from an exemplary ruler, and the echo of the *Shijing* in the fourth line can be taken as implying the ruler's failures, leading to the loss of the dynasty. To speak of the "mountains and rivers" (here *shanchuan* 山川 rather than the more common *shanhe* 山河 or *jiangshan* 江山) is both a general term for the landscape and for dynastic territory. All that remains are a few edifices to recall that past age, edifices that are gradually sinking underground; further underground is the lavish imperial tomb, reduced to ashes. However, insofar as the poem refers to history, it is "poetic history," with the poet Yu Xin, "Commander Yu," as a positive figure of pathos; forgotten is the fact that he fled from his post at a crucial bridge in the defense of Jiankang against Hou Jing.

---

8. This echoes the Mao interpretation of *Shi* 65, in which an officer of the Eastern Zhou passes the site of the Western Zhou capital covered in millet. Such scenes are also associated with the song attributed to the Shang prince Jizi, who, following the Zhou conquest, passes by the ruins of the old Shang capital.

9. This echoes the story of a herd boy, who, when looking for a sheep, accidentally started a fire in the tomb mound of the First Emperor. The "burial suit" is literally the "precious-stone clothes," probably referring to the kinds of jade burial coverings discovered by archeologists.

10. The Liang poet-courtier Yu Xin was sent north on a mission and detained; he ended up in Northern Zhou Chang'an (poetically Xianyang, the nearby Qin capital) serving the Northern Zhou. His most famous work is "Alas for the Southland" 哀江南賦, a long poetic exposition telling of the destruction of Jiankang during the Hou Jing Rebellion.

劉禹錫, 漢壽城春望 古荆州刺史治亭, 其下有子胥廟兼楚王故墳

Liu Yuxi, Spring View at Hanshou City (the old administrative
pavilion for the Governor of Jingzhou; below is a temple to
Wu Zixu and an old tomb of the King of Chu)[11]

漢壽城邊野草春	By the city walls of Hanshou 　　wilderness grass turns spring,
荒祠古墓對荆榛	tumbledown shrine and ancient tomb 　　face thickets of thorns.
田中牧豎燒芻狗	Out in the fields a herd boy 　　is burning straw dogs,[12]
陌上行人看石麟	while passersby on the lanes 　　look at the stone unicorn.
華表半空經霹靂	An inscribed pillar half bare, 　　has been through lightning,
碑文纔見滿埃塵	a stele inscription barely visible, 　　covered with dirt and grime.
不知何日東瀛變	I know not in what future day 　　there will be a great sea change,
此地還成要路津	and this place will again become 　　a crucial concourse.

Not all poems considered "meditations on the past" need have the
term *huaigu* in the title (though a variant title for this poem replaces
"spring view" with "meditation on the past"). Hanshou was not a usual
site for "meditations on the past," and the place has no particularly
strong historical associations. The poet does not comment on the irony
of a shrine to Wu Zixu in close proximity to a Chu royal tomb. (Wu
Zixu, in his passion for revenge against the king of Chu, dug up and
flogged the corpse of his former Chu ruler.) At least three lines of the
poem are devoted to surviving artifacts—"ruins"—a prominent feature
of these ninth-century "meditations on the past." The stone unicorn is a
funerary beast and forms part of the royal tomb complex (as the herd
boy burning the straw dogs presumably relates to the Wu Zixu shrine).
The inscribed texts that might fully historicize these remains are either
damaged or covered over. Indeed, the entire locale is being covered over,
part of the process that may someday lead to a sea change (literally

---

11. 18934; Qu (1989) 674; Jiang 146.

12. Straw dogs were used in popular ritual. As Zhuangzi described it, they were
treated with great reverence during the ceremony, then trampled afterward.

the "Eastern Sea changing [with land]"), after which the locale may become important again.

These rather ordinary "meditations on the past" set the stage for one of Liu Yuxi's most famous poems, composed about ten years after the poem at Hanshou.

劉禹錫, 西塞山懷古

Liu Yuxi, Meditation on the Past at Xisai Mountain[13]

西晉樓船下益州	The Western Jin's towered galleys descended from Yizhou,
金陵王氣漠然收	the royal aura around Jinling spread out and withdrew.
千尋鐵鎖沈江底	The thousand-yard iron chain sank to the river bottom,[14]
一片降幡出石頭	and a single flag of surrender came forth from the Rock.[15]
人世幾回傷往事	In human generations how many times have men felt pain at what was past?—
山形依舊枕寒流	the form of the mountain as before is pillowed on the cold stream.
今逢四海爲家日	Now we come upon a time when all the seagirt world is one,[16]
故壘蕭蕭蘆荻秋	winds moan over the ancient fort, and the reeds turn autumn.

Not only is this one of Liu Yuxi's most famous poems; it is one of the most famous of all Tang "meditations on the past." The poem's most significant difference from the two preceding examples is the series of imagined scenes from the past, a sequence of events that led to the fall of the Wu capital and the brief reunification of China under the Western Jin. Once the war galleys set out from Sichuan, the "royal aura" said to hover over Jinling (Jiankang, modern Nanjing) dissipated; the

---

13. 18977; Qu (1989) 669; Jiang 301. Xisai Mountain, near Wuchang, was the first line of Yangzi River defenses protecting the capital at Jiankang (Tang Jinling). The poem refers to the Western Jin campaign under Wang Jun 王濬, launched from Sichuan (Yizhou) against the city, then Jianye, when it was the capital of Wu.

14. The chain was part of the Wu river defense. Wang Jun was said to have melted it with fire boats.

15. The Rock was the fortress defending the approaches to Jiankang.

16. That is, the unification of China in the Tang.

supposedly impregnable defenses of the city melted before the Jin advance. The fourth line, often alluded to in later poetry, contrasts the magnitude of the enterprise—both the assault and the defense—with the tiny banner that marks its end.

The third couplet—in traditional poetics the "turn," *zhuan* 轉—shifts from the past to the present. If the fifth line is phrased in a general way, it is perhaps because Liu Yuxi is not actually at Jinling, the place he is largely writing about. Rather, he is upstream at one of the great city's defenses. It is clear, however, that he has Jinling in mind. In the following line he turns back to Xisai Mountain, invoking perhaps the most durable commonplace in "meditations on the past": the continuity of nature and the landscape versus the impermanence of human beings and their works. Finally Liu Yuxi sums up past and present in the scene before his eyes, the ancient fortress in the autumn wind, below which are the white reeds of autumn.

"Meditation on the Past at Xisai Mountain" and Its Family

There are many contexts in which we might situate "Meditation on the Past at Xisai Mountain." Perhaps the least interesting of such contexts would be "literary history" in the broad sense, locating the poem between the Mid-Tang, as defined by its now-famous poets, and the Late Tang. It is, however, very much part of a smaller "family" history of poems that precedes it by a century and a half. Looking at other members of the family, both before and after "Meditation on the Past at Xisai Mountain," can teach us something about intertextuality and poetic form. The moment the reader reads the title, recognizes the form, and notices the rhyme-word in the first line, Liu Yuxi's poem becomes part of a network of past poems. Many of these poems were—and still are—among the most famous works written in the dynasty.[17]

---

17. Here and elsewhere, when considering intertextual echoes in this study, we are confronted with the vexed question of whether the later poet actually had access to the earlier poem. In some cases—such as Cui Hao knowing the Wang Bo poem or Li Bai knowing Cui Hao's poem—we are somewhat confident that the later poet did know the particular poem by his predecessor. However, considering the unsystematic circulation of poetry in the Tang, with far more variants than have been preserved, in most cases there can be no certainty that a later poet actually read (or heard about) his predecessor's text, which we are suggesting as a possible source. We can nevertheless assume

Rhymes—particularly the easiest and most familiar rhyme-words—can draw together certain objects, actions, situations, and sentiments. They become familiar points that define a familiar configuration. Liu Yuxi's poem is in the *ou* rhyme, with some of the less and most common words in that rhyme: *zhou* 州, "prefecture" (Yizhou); *shou* 收, "withdraw"; *tou* 頭, "head" (here a nominal suffix in *Shitou* 石頭, the "Rock," Jinling's fortress); *liu* 流, "flow" or "stream"; and *qiu* 秋, "autumn." In the Yangzi, even around Jinling, there are "[low] isles," *zhou* 洲, often with river "gulls," *ou* 鷗; above there are "towers" or multistoried buildings, *lou* 樓, sometimes "mounds," *qiu* 丘. In such places, either walking or in a "boat," *zhou* 舟, one can "roam," *you* 遊, in "seclusion," *you* 幽. Facing ancient sites and vistas under skies that seem to go "on and on," *youyou* 悠悠, one may feel "cares," *you* 憂, or simply "sad," *chou* 愁. Poets do use other *ou* rhymes, but the commonplace rhyme-words set norms of a certain kind of poetic experience whose elements have a powerful inertia in composition.

The earliest poem in this set is not a regulated verse but rather an eight-line poem that changes rhyme midway. The second half of the poem is, however, perfectly regulated and uses the *ou* rhyme, setting the tone for a long lineage of later poems. In 676 Wang Bo 王勃 was on a journey south and visited the tower built by Li Yuanying 李元嬰, the Prince of Teng—twenty-second son of Gaozu, the Tang founder—when he was commander of Hongzhou 洪州 (modern Nanchang in Jiangxi). For convenience we will italicize the rhyme-words in translation.

王勃, 滕王閣
Wang Bo (650–676), The Tower of the Prince of Teng[18]

滕王高閣臨江渚   The Prince of Teng's high tower
                              looks down on river isles,
珮玉鳴鸞罷歌舞   pendant jades, ringing phoenix bells,
                              they ended dance and song.

---

the existence of a family of such texts far larger than the poems that have been preserved, and our intertextual echoes should be understood in that sense, allowing for other variation and intermediaries. If Li He's poetry represents a distinctive author whose collection entered circulation at a certain moment in history, the material in poems like the ones cited is constantly being borrowed and reworked across the centuries.

18. 03444; He Lintian 何林天, *Chongding xinjiao Wang Zi'an ji* 重訂新校王子安集 (Taiyuan: Shanxi renmin chubanshe, 1990), 38.

畫棟朝飛南浦雲	Its painted rafters at dawn send flying clouds of the southern shore,
朱簾暮捲西山雨	its red curtains at twilight roll up rain on the western hills.[19]
閑雲潭影日悠悠	Calm clouds, reflections in pools go *on and on* each day,
物換星移幾度秋	things are changed, stars shift on, how many *autumns* passed?
閣中帝子今何在	The prince in the tower, where is he today?—
檻外長江空自流	beyond the railing the long river just keeps *flowing* on.

Wang Bo's famous poem is indeed a "meditation on the past," though a none-too-distant past. As is often the case in later meditations on the past, the place that inspires the meditation is seen as a site of former pleasures. The sexuality of the vanished dancers returns in the natural scene from the tower: the "dawn clouds" and "evening rain" of the goddess of Wu Mountain. Precisely when the scene of the second couplet occurs is uncertain, but the sensual clouds of the third line are picked up at the beginning of the second half (the new "stanza") in the calm and aloof clouds that continued between past and present. Finally, the poet invokes the Prince of Teng, simultaneously locating him "in the tower" and asking where he is today. It is a rhetorical question that offers him the closing image of the river, like the clouds, continuously passing.

The rhyme, the tone, and the building named for someone or something no longer present reappear more than half a century later in a very famous poem by Cui Hao. The poem is mostly regulated, and the site was Yellow Crane Tower in Wuchang (Wuhan). The poem was clearly very popular and was included in several of the extant poetry anthologies compiled in the Tang. There are various etiological stories behind Yellow Crane Jetty and its tower, all of which involved an immortal riding off to Heaven on the back of a crane.

---

19. The curtains "roll up" the rain in the sense that when they are rolled up, they reveal the rain. From its early use in the "River Earl" 河伯 of the "Nine Songs" the "southern shore" 南浦 became associated with parting. Embedded in this couplet are the "clouds of dawn" 朝雲 and "twilight rain" 暮雨, which were the two avatars of the goddess of Wu Mountain.

崔顥, 黃鶴樓

Cui Hao (ca. 704–754), Yellow Crane Tower[20]

昔人已乘白雲去	Someone long ago already rode the white clouds away,
此地空餘黃鶴樓	leaving on in this place only Yellow Crane *Tower*.
黃鶴一去不復返	Once the yellow crane went away, it never again returned,
白雲千載空悠悠	for a thousand years the white clouds just go *on and on*.
晴川歷歷漢陽樹	On the sunlit river are clearly seen the trees of Hanyang,
芳草萋萋鸚鵡洲	and flowering plants grow in profusion on Parrot *Isle*.
日暮鄉關何處是	At sundown where is it?— the pass that leads toward home,
煙波江上使人愁	misty waves on the river make a person *sad*.

Although this is indeed an "ancient site," there is nothing here to call forth the moral judgment that Fang Hui felt was necessary for a proper "meditation on the past." There is only the pathos of the vanished immortal, leaving an "empty name," a site named "Yellow Crane" without the yellow crane, like the Prince of Teng's Tower without the Prince of Teng. Again we have the scene of nature that endures, but now it is imbued with an absence. That sense of loss seems to stir a sense of isolation in the poet that makes his heart turn homeward at the end.

As we will discover, intertextuality appears in many guises in these poems. Here we see a line with words in the same positions:

Wang Bo

閑雲潭影日悠悠	Calm clouds, reflections in pools go *on and on* each day

Cui Hao

白雲千載空悠悠	for a thousand years the white clouds just go *on and on*.

---

20. 06244; Wan Jingjun 萬競君, *Cui Hao shi zhu* 崔顥詩注 (Shanghai: Shanghai guji chubanshe, 1982), 42.

We can also see how the later line builds on the earlier one: Wang Bo's line is simply a scene of time passing as the reflections of clouds pass over the pool; Cui Hao's line has us looking up into those "same" clouds, knowing that the crane disappeared into them and would return through them—though it does not return. In other words, Cui Hao has taken the implications of passing time in Wang Bo's line, made it explicit in "for a thousand years" (serving the function of Wang Bo's *ri* 日, "each day"), and added a new level in the absence of the crane (both implicit in the context of the preceding line and implied in *kong* 空, "just," also "empty").

Another poet subsequently visited Yellow Crane Tower and supposedly wrote a couplet expressing his frustration at not being able to outdo Cui Hao's famous poem.[21] Later, while visiting Jinling in 761 (or 747), that same poet wrote a perfectly regulated poem emulating and perhaps competing with Cui Hao's famous poem. He was successful in that the poem has become at least as famous as its model.

李白, 登金陵鳳凰臺
Li Bai, Climbing Phoenix Terrace in Jinling[22]

鳳凰臺上鳳凰游
On the Terrace of the Phoenix
once the phoenix *roamed,*

鳳去臺空江自流
the phoenix went, the terrace bare,
the river *flows* off on its own.

---

21. Shang Wei has discussed the relationship between Li Bai's poem and Cui Hao's extensively in an unpublished paper.

22. 08569; Qu (1980) 1234; Zhan Ying 詹鍈, *Li Bai quanji jiaozhu huishi jiping* 李白全集校注彙釋集評 (Tianjin: Baihua wenyi chubanshe, 1996), 3010; Yu Xianhao 郁賢皓, *Li Bai xuanji* 李白選集 (Shanghai: Shanghai guji, 1990), 252. Yu Xianhao opts for the date 747; Zhang Ying prefers 761. Phoenix Terrace was located in Jinling and received its name in the Liu-Song, when three birds of remarkable plumage alighted on the terrace. One might translate "phoenix" in the plural above; however, phoenixes are not birds often thought of in flocks, and it seems likely that Li Bai would have imagined one phoenix. Hu Zi 胡仔 (*Tiaoxi yuyin conghua* 苕溪漁隱叢話 [Beijing: Renmin wenxue chubanshe, 1962], 30) cites *Gaiwen lu* 該聞錄 to the effect that on visiting Yellow Crane Tower, Li Bai despaired of writing a poem himself, offering instead the doggerel couplet: "There is a scene before my eyes, I cannot speak— / the poem that Cui Hao wrote stands preeminent" 眼前有景道不得, 崔顥題詩在上頭. Then, when he reached Jinling, he composed the poem on Phoenix Terrace in imitation. The historical veracity of this anecdote is questionable, but there seems little doubt that this poem was clearly written with Cui Hao's poem in mind.

吳宮花草埋幽徑	Flowering plants of the palace of Wu bury secluded paths,
晉代衣冠成古丘	caps and gowns of the Jin reigns have now formed ancient *mounds*.[23]
三山半落青天外	Triple Mountain sinks halfway out beyond blue sky,[24]
一水中分白鷺洲	a single stream divided midpoint by White Egret *Isle*.[25]
總爲浮雲能蔽日	All because the drifting clouds can block out the sun,[26]
長安不見使人愁	Chang'an is not seen, makes a person *sad*.

In the two preceding poems there was little occasion for the ethical judgment that Fang Hui considered essential to the "meditation on the past." Here in Jinling the poet could easily find matter for judgment, yet there is no hint of the failings that brought down the Three Kingdoms state of Wu or the Eastern Jin and other Southern Dynasties. The auspicious bird (or birds) vanished above the clouds long ago, like Cui Hao's yellow crane. The traces of mortals have vanished below the soil, leaving liminal traces in "buried" paths (the term "bury," *mai* 埋, is a strong usage in this period, though it does not suggest funerary "burial") and mounds. The "caps and gowns" of officials are the primary association of *wenwu* 文物, a difficult term to translate that we will simply call "finery"; it is a term we will see recurring in similar lines later.

Li Bai imitates Cui Hao's poem not only in the form of specific lines, as in the opening couplet, but also in the *taxis* of the poem, the sequence of topics treated, what later writers on Chinese poetics would call *zhangfa* 章法. Thus, the third couplet takes up the permanent features of the landscape that remain. The landscape, however, is not represented as "pure nature"; it is described with place names that resonate from the past, names that also linger on, as did Phoenix Terrace and

---

23. Jinling had been the capital of the Three Kingdoms state of Wu and of the Jin following its loss of North China.

24. Triple Mountain is located on the Yangzi, southwest of Jinling.

25. White Egret Isle was located in the Yangzi, just west of Jinling.

26. Not only is this an empirical image of the sun blocking the poet's vision, but clouds blocking the sun was a conventional image for slanderers blocking someone from the ruler's favor.

Yellow Crane Tower. The landscape is on its way to its characteristic form in ninth-century poetry: it is no longer nature itself but rather nature marked by an absence.

The image of the passing clouds had occupied a prominent place in Wang Bo's and Cui Hao's poems. In Li Bai's version the clouds return in the seventh line, here no longer markers of passing time and absence but presumably an empirical presence that immediately becomes figurative. Clouds to the northwest block the sunlight and the poet's steady gaze toward Chang'an, becoming those who prevent him from basking in the glow of imperial favor. Like Cui Hao, Li Bai ends by gazing toward that which he cannot see, longing to go off to the hidden destination of his gaze. Both are poems of displacement: mythical birds that have flown off, past grandeurs below the soil, and a blocked destination for the poet's lateral gaze.

Although Li Bai's poem was the most famous response to Cui Hao's piece, he was not the only High Tang poet to take up the challenge of an old tower by the river in long-line regulated verse using the rhyme *ou*. Although many elements in the poem are determined by the usual rhyme-words, we see how the form is acquiring a melancholy mood of vanished glories.[27]

王昌齡, 萬歲樓
Wang Changling, The Tower of Ten Thousand Years[28]

江上巍巍萬歲樓	Looming over the river, *Tower* of Ten Thousand Years,
不知經歷幾千秋	I do not know through how many thousand *autumns* it has passed.

---

27. Here we may contrast Meng Haoran's "Climbing the Wall Tower at Anyang," a poem of uncertain date but almost certainly earlier than either Wang Changling's or Li Bai's poems. Although this is another tower-climbing regulated verse in the long line using the rhyme *ou*, it is remarkably cheerful. Once this "type" had acquired its associations from a famous set of poems, such a cheerful tone was difficult to sustain.

28. 06759; Li Yunyi 李雲逸, *Wang Changling shizhu* 王昌齡詩注 (Shanghai: Shanghai guji chubanshe, 1984), 112; Li Guosheng 李國勝, *Wang Changling shi jiaozhu* 王昌齡詩校注 (Taibei: Wenshizhe chubanshe, 1973), 125; Hu Wentao 胡問濤 and Luo Qin 羅琴, *Wang Changling ji biannian jiaozhu* 王昌齡集編年校注 (Chengdu: Ba Shu shushe, 2000), 146. The Tower of Ten Thousand Years was a Wu building, rebuilt in the Jin, in Runzhou (Zhenjiang).

年年喜見山長在	Year after year it rejoices to see the mountains ever there,
日日悲看水濁流	day after day it sadly watches the water's murky *flow*.
猿狄何曾離暮嶺	When have gibbons and apes ever left the twilight peaks?
鸕鷀空自泛寒洲	cormorants just by themselves bob beside cold *isles*.
誰堪登望雲煙里	Who can bear to climb and gaze into the clouds and mist?—
向晚茫茫發旅愁	as evening comes the vast expanse brings forth the *sadness* of travel.

We might note that the particular rhyme-words in the second half of
the poem are identical with those used by Cui Hao and Li Bai (though
we do not know whether this poem or Li Bai's came first). Critical
opinion is strongly divided regarding this poem. The Ming critic Hu
Yinglin calls it "laughably clumsy and flaccid" 拙弱可笑, an indication
that regulated verse in the long line was not Wang Changling's strength.
However, the famous critic Jin Shengtan 金聖嘆 (1608–1661) provides
a detailed, enthusiastic discussion of the poem. The taxis remains virtu-
ally identical to Cui Hao's poem: the first couplet makes reference to
the tower, the second refers to the passage of time, the third describes
the landscape, and the poem concludes with an obstructed gaze.

The genius of Li Bai was to rewrite Cui Hao's poem as well as or
better than Cui Hao's original. The genius of Du Fu was his virtual in-
ability to write like anyone else. Du Fu has two regulated poems in the
long line that follow the usual rhymes; neither are among his better-
known works. One has nothing to do with the family we are describing,
while the other transforms the melancholy vista, though with no hint of
"meditation on the past." To follow the lineage of Cui Hao closely, we
need to look at more conventional poets, such as Zhang Ji,[29] another
mid-eighth-century figure. Whereas the famous precedents had all been
set along the Yangzi River or in the mountainous south, inspiration
came to Zhang Ji in Shandong, with its less dramatic landscape.

---

29. This Zhang Ji is not the famous Mid-Tang poet discussed earlier.

張繼, 秋日道中
Zhang Ji, On the Road on an Autumn Day[30]

齊魯西風草樹秋	The west wind in Qi and Lu, the plants and trees in *autumn*,
川原高下過東州	high and low over rivers and plains I pass the eastern *prefectures.*
道邊白鶴來華表	At the roadside a white crane comes to a stone pillar,[31]
陌上蒼麟臥古丘	by the path a gray unicorn reclines by an ancient *mound.*
九曲半應非禹跡	Of the River's nine bends half are surely not traces of Yu's work;[32]
三山何處是仙洲	Three Mountains, where are they, those immortal *isles?*[33]
逕行俯仰成今古	Passing through, with the nod of a head, there is past and present,
卻憶當年賦遠遊	and I recall back in those days how he wrote "Far *Roaming.*"[34]

Although outwardly Zhang Ji's poem does not seem to share many traits in common with those of the three preceding poems, if we look more closely we can see the resemblances. The first couplet announces the place—in this case a general region rather than a particular

---

30. 12659; Zhou Yigan 周義敢, *Zhang Ji shizhu* 張繼詩注 (Shanghai: Shanghai guji chubanshe, 1987), 32.

31. Cranes are associated with immortality. Zhou Yigan 周義敢 links this line specifically with the story of Ding Ling Wei 丁令威, as recounted in the *Soushen houji* 搜神後記. After achieving immortality, Ding Ling Wei was transformed into a crane and flew back to his home in Liaodong, where he alighted on a pillar (*huabiao*) by the city gate. When young boys took shots at him, he recited a doggerel verse in which he declared that, returning after a thousand years, the city looked the same but the people were not.

32. The Yellow River was supposed to have nine distinct stretches, the *jiuqu* 九曲. However, Yu was supposed to have cut the Yellow River's course, at least to the present Shandong region. Zhang Ji's point here is uncertain.

33. These are the three islands of the immortals in the Eastern Ocean.

34. Qu Yuan was supposed to have composed the "Far Roaming," which begins with revulsion at the corruption and confinement of the human world and goes on to roam the universe in a quest for the immortals and immortality.

edifice—though such an opening was a normative possibility in poetic exposition. In the second couplet we see that Zhang Jì has Li Bai in mind, as Wang Changling had Cui Hao in mind:

晉代衣冠成<u>古丘</u>   caps and gowns of the Jin reigns
                      have now formed ancient mounds.

and:

陌上蒼麟臥<u>古丘</u>   by the path a gray unicorn
                      reclines by an ancient mound.

Not only are the last two characters identical, but the grammar of the line is the same. Li Bai tells us what is beneath the soil, while Zhang Jì tells us what is above. If Li Bai's phoenix flew away, never to return, the white crane on the stone pillar recalls the story of Ding Ling Wei, the immortal who returned to his home as a white crane, only to discover that all those he had known were long dead.

The third couplet is concerned with landscape, opposing "mountains" and "waters." Li Bai's "Triple Mountain," *sanshan* 三山, visible from near Jinling, reappears as the "Three Mountains," the immortal isles in the Eastern Ocean, and continues the motif of the mortal world of change set against the world of the immortals elsewhere. Just as Cui Hao ended with a speculative journey home and Li Bai ended by gazing toward Chang'an (with a desire to go there), so Zhang Jì closes with the memory of Qu Yuan's journey to the realm of the immortals, implying his own desire to do the same.

The regulated verse poets of the second half of the eighth century used the *ou* rhyme and the common rhyme-words in their poems in the long line. Although most of these are not "meditations on the past," they invoke scenes (in part because of the rhyme-words) with the same kind of melancholy vistas. It seems that the famous precedent texts had already established a certain mood when this rhyme was used. We will give one example by Han Hong, whose poem describes a visit to a Daoist temple. Such a poem was supposed to praise the temple and the Daoist enterprise. Han Hong accomplishes what is expected of him, but the weight of the form with this particular rhyme produces lines whose mood acts as a counterpoint to the upbeat tone required by the occasion.

韓翃, 同題仙游觀

Han Hong, Jointly Composed at the Lodge of Roaming Immortals[35]

仙臺下見五城樓	Below the immortals' terrace one sees the *towers* of the Five Cities,[36]
風物凄凄宿雨收	things in the scene are dreary, the nightlong rain *withdraws*.
山色遙連秦樹晚	The colors of hills stretch far to reach evening in the trees of Qin,
砧聲近報漢宮秋	fulling blocks' nearby sounds tell of *autumn* in the Han palace.
疏松影落空壇靜	Shadows of a sparse pine fall on the calm of the empty altar,
細草香開小洞幽	scent of tiny plants opens into the *seclusion* of a small grotto.
何用別尋方外去	What use to seek out elsewhere, go off "beyond the norms"?—
人間亦自有丹丘	in the world of mortals also there is a Cinnabar *Mound*.[37]

Han Hong begins politely, praising the temple in terms of buildings of the immortals, but immediately thereafter he turns to the melancholy landscape following the rain, one consistent with the mood of the earlier poems. There may be no particular ancient site, but the sound of the fulling blocks (used both for washing and to soften clothes for cold weather) marks not only "autumn," the rhyme-word, but "autumn in the Han palace." In the second half of the poem the proper tone of the occasion takes over, with Han Hong praising the seclusion of the site and comparing it to Cinnabar Mound, the dwelling of the immortals.

As we move into the ninth century, we encounter Liu Yuxi's famous poem, which links the melancholy of mutability with the "meditation on the past," with some site of human history and without reference to vanished immortals. It is at this point Fang Hui considers such poems

---

35. 12787; Chen Wanghe 陳王和, *Han Hong shiji jiaozhu* 韓翃詩集校注 (Taibei: Wenshizhe chubanshe, 1973), 332. The publication date is taken from the preface.

36. This refers to the "Five Cities and Twelve Towers" 五城十二樓 supposedly constructed for the immortals during the reign of the Yellow Emperor.

37. This was purportedly the place where the immortals lived. This final line is a gracious compliment to the Daoist lodge.

true "meditations on the past" and opens his anthology section on "meditation on the past" in the long line. Fang Hui does include the following poem by Xu Hun, most probably written after Liu Yuxi's famous poem of 824. Han Hong had a good phrase which Xu Hun plundered. Xianyang, from whose walls Xu Hun gazes, was the site of the old capital of Qin north across the Wei River from Chang'an.

許渾, 咸陽城西樓晚眺

Xu Hun, Gazing at Evening from the West Wall Tower of Xianyang [38]

一上高城萬里愁	Once I climbed this high wall I felt *sadness* at thousands of miles,
蒹葭楊柳似汀洲	the reeds and rushes and willows resemble beaches and *isles.*
溪雲初起日沈閣	Clouds first rise from the creek, the sun sinks past a kiosk,
山雨欲來風滿樓	rain from the hills is about to come, wind fills the *tower.*
鳥下綠蕪秦苑夕	Birds alight on green weeds in the evening of Qin's parks,
蟬鳴黃葉漢宮秋	cicadas sing among yellow leaves, *autumn* in the Han palace.
行人莫問前朝事	Let the traveler not ask of what happened in a former dynasty—
故國東來渭水流	going eastward toward my homeland, the Wei's waters *flow.*

In the famous eighth-century examples and Liu Yuxi's version the scene before the poet's eyes is an index of something missing: the vanished immortal; the poet's home; a significant moment in the past; or those dead under the soil. The visible world thus achieves pathos by simultaneously invoking something else and denying access to it. Eventually this quality comes to inhere in the scene itself, without specifying what, precisely, is absent (as Cui Hao specified the absence of the yellow crane and Li Bai the absence of the phoenix, as well as the Wu and Jin past). We can see such implicit pathos emerging in Han Hong's poem, where it is repressed by the demands of the occasion to offer praise. Liu Yuxi invokes scenes of history so that he can present such a

---

38. 28798; Jiang Congping 5; Luo 137. Xianyang was a favorite site for subsequent "meditations on the past."

landscape of absence in his last line: "winds moan over the ancient fort, and the reeds turn autumn." The ruined fortress certainly suggests absence, but the autumnal scene itself seems to convey the mood in its own right. We should note that while this mood is in no way restricted to regulated verse in the long line rhyming *ou*, such poems are predisposed to this kind of pathos because of the growing history of famous poems in the form with the same rhyme.

When Xu Hun climbs a wall tower at Xianyang, he does not need to specify absences: they are already immanent in both the form and the locale. Indeed, the first line tells us quite explicitly that it is the conventional circumstance (in the familiar form and rhyme) that invokes both sadness, *chou* 愁, and the rhyme-determined scenes that will follow. There is nothing inherently sad about the autumnally pale rushes and willow leaves, which resemble beaches and sandy isles. We read pathos into such a scene, and from that we infer that they remind the poet of his home in the Southland. If birds descend to the "green weeds" of Qin's parks, we think of them as untended and running wild, marking the ruin of Qin. Critics and commentators immediately associated this with *Shi* 65, in which an official of the Eastern Zhou passes the site of the Western Zhou capital and sees the grain growing over the ruins. "Autumn in the Han palace," marked by a sound (washing blocks in Han Hong and cicadas here), is more a poetic mood than a specific scene, the pathos of vanished glories immanent in the autumn scene. Finally, the poet explicitly invokes the two expected absences: the vanished glory of a former dynasty and his home, unified by the Wei River, which marks both the passage of time (as in Wang Bo's poem) and the movement east toward the poet's home.

This is one of Xu Hun's most famous poems, with a rich accumulation of critical comment. Although the critics are finely attuned to the mood of the poem, they generally refrain from commenting on the degree to which the quality of the poem depends upon a history of earlier poems on similar topics in the same form using the same rhyme. We can perhaps identify one aspect of Late Tang poetry here: an established body of earlier poetry had invested certain topics, images, forms, and even certain rhymes with powerful associations of mood. The response to conjunctions of these elements was a poetically "conditioned response." Although this could be used very successfully, as in Xu Hun's poem cited above, it was a particularly problematic poetics, inviting endless repetition and easy satisfactions. Perhaps one reason so many Late Tang poems have become unreadable is because these conditioned moods were invoked too often.

One finds poems belonging to this family continuously reproduced through the ninth century; some are explicit "meditations on the past," while others are occasional poems infected by the mood. We here offer two epigones: Wei Zhuang writing at the end of the ninth century and Liu Cang writing toward the middle of the ninth century.

韋莊, 咸陽懷古

Wei Zhuang, Meditation on the Past at Xianyang[39]

城邊人倚夕陽樓	By the wall a person leans from a *tower* in evening sunshine,
城上雲凝萬古愁	over the wall clouds mass into *sadness* for all eternity.
山色不知秦苑廢	The mountains' colors do not know that Qin's parks lie abandoned,
水聲空傍漢宮流	the sound of waters in vain *flows* on beside the palace of Han.
李斯不向倉中悟	Li Si was not enlightened in the granary;[40]
徐福應無物外遊	Xu Fu should never have *roamed* beyond the ordinary world.[41]
莫怪楚吟偏斷骨	Marvel not that the chants of Chu especially break the heart—[42]
野煙蹤跡似東周	the traces in the wilderness mist are just like the Eastern *Zhou*.[43]

---

39. 39073; Jiang Congping 江聰平, *Wei Duanji shi jiaozhu* 韋端己詩校注 (Taibei: Taiwan Zhonghua shuju, 1969), 227; Li Yi 李誼, *Wei Zhuang ji jiaozhu* 韋莊集校注 (Chengdu: Sichuan sheng shehui kexueyuan chubanshe, 1986), 427.

40. Li Si—later Qin Shihuang's minister, subsequently executed—served as a clerk in his youth. In the privy next to his office he saw rats eating filth, while people and dogs would chase them away. In the public granaries he saw rats eating the grain, with no dogs or people chasing them away.

41. Xu Fu was sent off by the First Emperor together with a group of young men and women of Qin, to find the immortal isles in the Eastern Ocean. He never returned.

42. This probably refers to the "Lament for Ying" 哀郢 in the *Jiuzhang* of the *Chuci*, a lament for the fall of the Chu capital.

43. *Shi* 65, on the Eastern Zhou officer seeing the site of the Western Zhou capital.

Wei Zhuang writes very much as the epigone, standing where other poets have stood and seeing a scene not unlike what they saw. There is little doubt that Xu Hun's poem is in the background, with "Qin's parks" set in parallel to the "Han palace" in the fifth and sixth positions of the lines in the second couplet. The direct historical allusions in the third couplet have not been part of the poems previously discussed, but that was common in the taxis of regulated verse.

The surviving poems of Liu Cang are almost entirely regulated verse in the long line. Here he writes on the supposed site where Nongyu 弄玉, daughter of the duke of Qin, was carried off to heaven on a phoenix together with her husband Xiaoshi 簫史.

劉滄, 題秦女樓

Liu Cang, On the Tower of Qin's Royal Daughter[44]

珠翠香銷鴛瓦墮	Scent melts from pearls and kingfisher, the duck tiles *fall*,
神仙曾向此中遊	yet immortals at one time *roamed* here.
青樓月色桂花冷	In the blue tower the color of moonlight, the cassia blossoms cold,[45]
碧落簫聲雲葉愁	the sound of pipes from the Sapphire Net,[46] wisps of cloud are *sad*.
杳杳蓬萊人不見	Far away is Penglai, those persons are not seen;
蒼蒼苔蘚路空留	gray-green are the mosses, for nothing the road *remains*.
一從鳳去千年後	Once the phoenix went away a thousand years ago,
迢遞岐山水石秋	remote lies Mount Qi, its waters and stones in *autumn*.

The long line was looser and more fluid than the five-syllable line. Here we can see the padded lines, which were always a problem in the form, especially in the second line. The poetic moves are familiar and are performed rather thoughtlessly.

---

44. 32391.

45. This refers to the cassia in the moon, whose light is cold.

46. This is a literal rendering of a compound of uncertain derivation, referring to the heavens inhabited by the immortals.

Occasionally the Late Tang "mood poem" could be handled with a certain genius. Though less famous than Xu Hun's piece, Li Qunyu's view from the tower may represent this kind of poetry at its best.

李群玉, 江樓閑望懷關中親故

Li Qunyu, Gazing Calmly from a Tower by the River and
Thinking of My Old Friends in Guanzhong[47]

搖落江天欲盡秋	River sky of falling leaves, 　　*autumn* almost done,
遠鴻高送一行愁	distant swans on high bring on 　　a single line of *sadness*.[48]
音書寂絶秦雲外	All news is utterly silent 　　beyond the clouds of Qin,
身世蹉跎楚水頭	self and the world—stumbling here 　　*beside* the waters of Chu.
年貌暗隨黃葉去	Unnoticed, the years in my face 　　go off with the yellow leaves,
時情深付碧波流	I give over feelings for the times 　　to sapphire waves' deep *flow*.
風淒日冷江湖晚	The wind is biting, the sun is cold, 　　the lakes and river turn evening,
駐目寒空獨倚樓	my eyes rest on the cold empty sky 　　as I lean here alone on the *tower*.

Although this is not formally a "meditation on the past," its overall tone is so similar that we scarcely notice the absence of an ancient site. Many of the poems in this family combine the *huaigu* motif of absence with the poet gazing toward and longing for home. Longing for absent friends in the capital region (Guanzhong) becomes the central topic here.

In 838 the young Li Shangyin was serving in Anding (modern Gansu) under the military governor Wang Maoyuan. He climbed the wall tower, as Xu Hun had climbed the wall tower of Xianyang, and fell into the expected form and rhyme. Li Shangyin used the same phrases in the beginning, but once the tone was set, he took off in an entirely new direction.

---

47. 31346; Yang Chunqiu 51.

48. The "single line" of wild geese is the character *yi* 一, "one," reminding the poet that he is alone.

李商隱, 安定城樓
Li Shangyin, The Wall Tower of Anding[49]

迢遞高城百尺樓	Reaching far above, the high wall's hundred-foot *tower*,
綠楊枝外盡汀洲	beyond the branches of green willows, everywhere beaches and *isles*.
賈生年少虛垂涕	When Jia Yi as a young man shed his tears in vain;[50]
王粲春來更遠遊	Wang Can, when spring came, *roamed* on farther still.[51]
永憶江湖歸白髮	Ever I think on rivers and lakes where I'll go with white hair;
欲迴天地入扁舟	I want to turn Heaven and Earth, then get into a tiny *boat*.[52]
不知腐鼠成滋味	I do not think a rotten rat tastes very good—
猜意鵷雛竟未休	yet suspicions of the yuanju bird never *cease*.[53]

---

49. 29386; *Jijie* 264; Ye (1985) 330; Zhou 89.

50. Full of ambition, the young Han intellectual Jia Yi laid his plans for reform before Han Wendi and was deeply discouraged when they were ignored. In his memorial to the throne he spoke of "one matter to make one weep painfully, two matters to make one shed tears, and six matters to make one sigh." He thus became the exemplary figure of the disappointed young talent.

51. This refers to Wang Can's poetic exposition "Climbing the Tower" 登樓賦. Hoping to find a prince who would appreciate his talents, Wang Can soon thereafter left his patron Liu Biao and entered the service of Cao Cao.

52. The desire to "turn Heaven and Earth" reflects the desire to achieve great deeds. To go off in a tiny boat afterward (i.e., to become a recluse) was the decision of Fan Li 范蠡, the minister of Gou Jian, the king of Yue. After helping Gou Jian accomplish his act of revenge and destroy the state of Wu, Fan Li set off in a small boat on the five lakes.

53. This refers to the famous story in the "Autumn Floods" 秋水 chapter of the *Zhuangzi*. Zhuang Zhou's friend Hui Shi was minister of Liang, and Zhuang Zhou planned to visit him while passing through Liang. One of Hui Shi's friends told him that Zhuang Zhou wanted to replace him as minister. To counteract this suspicion, Zhuang Zhou told Hui Shi the parable of the yuanju bird. While flying from the Southern Ocean to the Northern Ocean, it would only roost on the tung tree and would only eat the fruits of the bamboo. An owl had gotten hold of a rotting rat carcass, and as the yuanju bird flew high overhead, the owl looked up and said, "Shoo!" Zhuang Zhou thus suggested that Hui Shi was trying to shoo him away from the state of Liang. In its

Although we do not know the date of Xu Hun's poem, it is still valuable to remember his first line:

一上<u>高城</u>萬里愁   Once I climbed this high wall I felt
                          sadness at thousands of miles

We may set this against Li Shangyin's line:

迢遞<u>高城</u>百尺樓   Reaching far above, the high wall's
                          hundred-foot *tower*

Intertextual reference does not always use the same phrase in the same position in a line, but when we find it, it is worth noting—especially when we have measures of distance ("thousands of miles" to "hundred-foot") in another parallel position. In this period it is very unlikely that Xu Hun would be echoing Li Shangyin. The relationship between Li Shangyin's and Xu Hun's poems continues in the second line.

Xu Hun

蒹葭<u>楊柳</u>似<u>汀洲</u>   the reeds and rushes and willows
                          resemble beaches and *isles*.

Li Shangyin

綠<u>楊</u>枝外盡<u>汀洲</u>   beyond the branches of green willows,
                          everywhere beaches and *isles*.

Given constant climatic changes and the existence of microclimates, it is hard to dismiss the empirical possibility of such a view from Anding in dry, modern Gansu. Still, we cannot but recognize that Li Shangyin is seeing Anding as a view from Xianyang, one that is actually realized only in Xu Hun's imaginings of the lower Yangzi River region.

Although there can be no doubt that Li Shangyin is building on a well-known form based on recent and earlier poems, he turns it in a different direction, namely, to a statement of his personal ambitions, with ancient parallels. Thus, the intertextual associations of the opening couplet function like the traditional *xing* 興, the "affective image" in the *Shijing*, setting a tone that frames the reference to human affairs in the remainder of the poem.

---

present application, Li Shangyin suggests that he has no personal desire for power (and will retire, like Fan Li, once his great deeds are accomplished). Nevertheless, there are those who still doubt him.

Other elements of the preceding poems return as well, albeit redirected. As Cui Hao and Xu Hun had longed to go home (the latter to the land of rivers and lakes), so Li Shangyin longs to go there as well—but only when his hair has turned white—after he has achieved great deeds. Yellow cranes and phoenixes may have vanished from Cui Hao's and Li Bai's landscapes, but Li Shangyin closes with another kind of phoenix as a figure of the self, flying high and away. Li Shangyin's "meditation on the past" is not a response to a site. Rather, it gestures to thoughts of talented young men of the past who were unappreciated by their rulers (Jia Yi) and patrons (Wang Can) while seeking to put their talents to good use. The third couplet jumps ahead to the aftermath following great deeds, such as Fan Li's giving up reward and retiring. The last couplet affirms a distaste for office and takes a jab at those who view his desire to serve the state as motivated by mere ambition.

The Late Tang "Meditation on the Past"

"Meditations on the past"—and historical topics in general—were very popular in poetic expositions (*fu*) and all genres of poetry during the ninth century. Nor were "meditations on the past" in regulated verse in the long line new in the ninth century—later readers would immediately think of Du Fu's "Singing My Cares at Ancient Sites" 詠懷古跡—but they became much more common during that period. Failed dynasties and reigns in particular—such as the Qin (Xianyang), the Southern Dynasties (Jinling), Sui Yangdi (Guangling, Jiangdu, Yangzhou), and Xuanzong's fall—appealed to a taste for historical pathos. Given the fact that the Tang itself began to disintegrate during the second half of the ninth century, it is tempting to link such an interest with the contemporary political situation. However, the taste for such themes was established much earlier, when the dynasty was still relatively healthy.

The conventions of the form become immediately apparent. The most durable is the one referred to above, what we will call the "scene of absence," in which the natural world evokes the absence of the significant events that previously occurred in that place. Chinese critics often speak of the "mountains and rivers surviving," echoing Du Fu's famous line. Nature does persist, but it is no longer merely nature: it is Nature, which, by continuing, has replaced the past. The poets often name what is gone or what happened in that particular place. Sometimes they declare that some form in nature recalls past human presences. Sometimes there are residual traces: ruins, tomb mounds, tiles. Sometimes the poet passes the kind of ethical judgment that Fang Hui called for. When a poem devotes much of its space to imagining the past, the "meditation on the past" merges with the "historical poem," in which the poet does not have to declare his presence either at a particular site or merely thinking of it (though Fang Hui includes a number of such poems by Li Shangyin).

Jinling (sometimes referred to by its old names of Jianye and Jiankang, by the Qin designation Moling, or by the Tang county Shangyuan) was the former capital of the Southern Dynasties and was always a favorite topic in different poetic genres. By way of contrast to the version in the long line, we might look at a regulated verse in the short line by Zhou He. One does not always have to be physically present at a site to write a "meditation on the past," and this poem is technically a parting poem. However, Fang Hui includes it as a "meditation on the past."[54]

周賀, 送康紹歸建業

Zhou He, Seeing Kang Shao Off on His Return to Jianye[55]

南朝秋色滿	The Southern Dynasties, autumn colors full,
君去意如何	what is on your mind now, as you go off?
帝業空城在	Of an imperial legacy an empty city survives,
民田壞塚多	in commoners' fields are many ruined tombs.
月圓臺獨上	The moon round, you will climb terraces alone,
栗綻寺頻過	chestnuts form seams, often stop by temples.
籬下西江闊	Below the hedge, Westriver is broad,
相思見白波	longing, you will see white waves.

Although one can learn to appreciate these Late Tang regulated verses in the short line, they sometimes seem stiff in comparison with the long line. While both forms were written continuously, in the latter half of the 830s we see younger poets writing more extensively in the long line. (The mid-century poet Liu Cang has only two extant poems that are not regulated verse in the long line.)

Xu Hun clearly exerted the strongest influence on "meditations on the past" in regulated verse in the long line. These were repeatedly

---

54. Ji Yun objects that the poem does not really belong in the category; but Fang Hui seems to have had difficulty finding good examples of the topic in regulated verse in the short line: many involve stopping by dwellings of individuals.

55. 26859.

echoed throughout the second half of the century. Xu Hun's Jinling poem draws on earlier poems on the same topic, as well as giving it a canonical treatment that inspired his immediate successors. As was the case with the *ou* rhyme, Xu Hun's choice of the *iung* rhyme here, with its obvious rhyme-words, became part of the poetry of Jinling, though, as we will see, we will have a few more pieces in the *ou* rhyme.

許渾, 金陵懷古
Xu Hun, Meditation on the Past at Jinling[56]

玉樹歌殘王氣終	The song of jade trees died away, the royal aura was gone,[57]
景陽兵合戍樓空	troops converged on Jingyang, the guard towers were bare.[58]
松楸遠近千官塚	Pines and catalpas far and near, tombs of a thousand officials;
禾黍高低六代宮	millet growing high and low, palaces of six dynasties.[59]
石燕拂雲晴亦雨	Stone swallows brush the clouds, rain even in clear skies,[60]
江豚吹浪夜還風	river porpoises puff waves, wind again by night.[61]
英雄一去豪華盡	Once bold heroes departed, the power and glory were gone,
唯有青山似洛中	all that remains are the green mountains, just like in Luoyang.[62]

---

56. 28794; Luo 129; Jiang Congping 147.

57. "On Jade Trees Flowers in the Rear Courtyard" 玉樹後庭花, a song composed by the Last Emperor of the Chen, was taken as a sign of the imminent fall of the dynasty. In the time of Qin Shihuang the appearance of a "royal aura" around Jinling foretold that it would become the capital.

58. Jingyang Palace was part of the palace compound. When Sui troops entered the city, the Last Emperor hid in the Jingyang well with his two favorite consorts.

59. This echoes *Shi* 65; see note 8. This is probably a purely literary reference since the Nanjing area was not a millet-growing region.

60. The legendary stone swallows of Lingling Mountain would turn into living birds when it rained and would return to stone when the rain stopped.

61. The Yangzi River porpoises were supposed to bring wind whenever they leapt in the river.

62. Here Xu Hun is alluding to the third of a set of three poems by Li Bai entitled "Jinling" 金陵三首, specifically the line: "The mountains resemble Luoyang's greatly"

We might first recall the second line of Liu Yuxi's earlier "Meditation on the Past at Xisai Mountain":

金陵王氣漠然收   the royal aura around Jinling
                          spread out and withdrew

Xu Hun echoes this in his first line, announcing a rhyme other than *ou* in his choice of "gone" (*zhong*) as a contextual synonym for Liu Yuxi's "withdrew" (*shou*):

玉樹歌殘王氣終   The song of jade trees died away,
                          the royal aura was gone[63]

Considering the fact that Jinling again became a capital (of the Eastern Jin) less than half a century later, Liu Yuxi may have been premature in suggesting that the royal aura "withdrew" with the Western Jin conquest of the city, then the Wu capital. Xu Hun, however, begins with the fall of the last Southern Dynasty, the Chen. When he describes the royal aura as "gone," *zhong* 終, it has a finality that invites us to read the "withdrawal" in the parent line as merely temporary. The Last Emperor of Chen's song "On Jade Trees Flowers in the Rear Courtyard" was understood as a sign of the dynasty's impending fall, a counterpart of loss of confidence in the dynasty that left the guard towers empty when the Sui army entered the city.

From fading song, a dissipating aura, and the empty guard towers—the dissolution of the city's last glory on many levels—we move to the present scene of absence in which the trees mark burial sites and the literary but not literal millet marks the site of a former capital. The weather-sign creatures of the third couplet combine in the compound "wind-and-rain," "storm," *fengyu* 風雨, which is sometimes used as a figure representing forces of political disaster but here represents only weather, in that there is no polity left here.

山似洛陽多. Behind both lines, however, stands a famous anecdote from *Shishuo xinyu* (II.31), in which the refugee Western Jin court figures gathered near Jiankang (Jinling), their new capital: "Whenever there was a lovely day, those who had crossed the Yangzi would always invite one another to New Pavilion, where they would sit on the grass, eating and drinking. Among the guests, Zhou Yi sighed: 'The scenery is not all that different, just that the mountains and the rivers are different.' Everyone looked at one another and wept."

63. See note 56.

Finally, we come to a common trope in such poems: the people and the polity are gone, but the landscape remains. In this case, however, the commonplace acquires an extra depth because of the *Shishuo xinyu* allusion, in which the landscape around Jinling still looks much like that of Luoyang, the lost capital in the North.

The Jinling poems offer excellent examples of the web of intertextuality that links poems within a single period and with those belonging to later periods. A good phrase or image is quickly appropriated and re-used. Since there are usually some poems that cannot be dated, we can never be certain who came first. For example, the following poem by Zhang Hu—one of many poems not included in the *Quan Tang shi* that were added with the relatively recent recovery of a Song edition of his poetry—cannot be dated. The poem is of particular interest because it is clearly linked to Xu Hun's well-known poem and to an even more famous poem by Du Mu. Zhang Hu's poem is distinguished by its use of a rhyme different from the *iung* or *ou* rhyme.

張祜, 上元懷古

Zhang Hu, Meditation on the Past at Shangyuan[64]

倚雲宮闕已平蕪	Palace towers that rested in cloud, already a plain of weeds,
東望連天到海隅	gazing east stretching to the heavens all the way to the sea's edge.
文物六朝興廢地	Six Dynasties' finery,[65] a land of rise and fall,
江山萬里帝王都	ten thousand leagues of mountains and rivers, a capital for emperors.
只聞丞相夷三族	One hears only how a Minister had his whole family wiped out,[66]

---

64. Yan Shoucheng 152.

65. "Finery" is an imperfect translation of *wenwu* 文物, which refers to things that represent high culture, particularly ceremonial paraphernalia.

66. Literally, "had his three families wiped out": his father's family, his mother's family, and his wife's family. This usually refers to the fate that befell Li Si, the famous minister of Qin; here it must refer to the Southern Dynasties, perhaps someone like the Eastern Jin dictator Huan Xuan.

不見扁舟泛五湖	one does not see the tiny boat adrift on the five lakes.[67]
遙想永嘉南過日	I imagine the Yongjia Reign far in the past on the day they crossed south,[68]
洛陽風景盡歸吳	and all the scenery of Luoyang went off to Wu.

Whereas Xu Hun begins with the end of the Six Dynasties and continues with a landscape of absence, Zhang Hu begins with a scene of absence and closes by imagining the flight south that announced the beginning of the Southern Dynasties. Nevertheless, both allude to *Shishuo xinyu* in Zhou Yi's 周顗 comment that "the scenery is not different" 風景不殊, but that the "mountains and river are different" 山河之異 ("mountains and river" being not only literal but also a synecdoche for the dynastic territory). The scene of tombs and palaces sunken beneath the soil in Xu Hun's second couplet reappears here in the third line: "Six Dynasties' finery, a land of rise and fall."

Zhang Hu's third line immediately recalls a famous Du Mu poem, usually dated to 838, which uses the same *iung* rhyme as Xu Hun's Jinling poem. Du Mu is writing not in Jinling but in Xuanzhou, another famous site of the Southern Dynasties. Nowadays we consider Du Mu a poet of the first order, Xu Hun a poet of the second order, and Zhang Hu a poet of the third order; but that is not at all their relative prominence in the 830s and 840s. Both Zhang Hu and Xu Hun knew Du Mu, and the latter greatly admired Zhang Hu. Although we cannot know who borrowed from whom, there is no doubt that Du Mu had the talent to make of these poems something more than simply another "meditation on the past."

杜牧, 題宣州開元寺水閣閣下宛溪夾溪居人

Du Mu, On the Water Tower of the Kaiyuan Temple in Xuanzhou: Below the Tower Is Wan Creek, With People Living on Both Sides[69]

六朝文物草連空	Finery of the Six Dynasties, plants stretching to the sky,

---

67. See pp. 555–56.

68. In the Yongjia Reign (307–312) the Western Jin fell to non-Chinese invaders and the dynasty transferred its capital to Jiankang (Tang Jingling, Shangyuan county).

69. 28147; Feng 202.

天澹雲閒今古同	the heavens calm, the clouds at ease, the same in present and past.
鳥去鳥來山色裏	Birds go off, birds come in the colors of the mountain,
人歌人哭水聲中	people sing and people weep in the sound of the waters.
深秋簾幕千家雨	Deep in autumn, curtains, rain on a thousand homes,
落日樓臺一笛風	in the setting sun terrace and tower, a single flute in the wind.
惆悵無因見范蠡	Depressed that I have no way to meet Fan Li—
參差煙樹五湖東	scattered unevenly, misty trees west of the five lakes.

Du Mu effectively covered the first three lines of Zhang Hu's poem in a single line, four characters of which are identical with Zhang Hu's (with the phrases in reverse order). The antithesis between wind and rain in Xu Hun's third couplet reappears with genius in Du Mu's third couplet. Finally, the allusion to Fan Li in the sixth line of Zhang Hu's poem reappears in similar terms—the boat on the five lakes—in the last couplet of Du Mu's poem. Zhang Hu does not see Fan Li's boat. Du Mu looks and sees only trees in the mist—but perhaps it is a mast?

In Li Qunyu we see much of the same material recirculated, again in the *iung* rhyme. Moling is next to Jinling and is used the same way to refer to the site of the Southern Dynasties capital. Li Qunyu uses the same rhyme and many of the same rhyme-words as Xu Hun's and Du Mu's poems.

李群玉, 秣陵懷古
Li Qunyu, Meditation on the Past at Moling[70]

野花黃葉舊吳宮	Wild flowers and yellow leaves, the former palace of Wu,
六代豪華燭散風	power and glory of the Six Dynasties, a candle blown out in the wind.

---

70. 31360; Yang Chunqiu 105.

龍虎勢衰佳氣歇	The power of dragon and tiger waned,[71] the auspicious aura was done,
鳳皇名在故臺空	the name of the phoenix remains, but the ancient terrace is empty.[72]
市朝遷變秋蕪綠	Court and market have shifted, the autumn weeds are green,
墳塚高低落照紅	tombs and mounds high and low, red in the sinking sunshine.
霸業鼎圖人去盡	Overlords' legacy, charts and tripods, those people are departed,[73]
獨來惆悵水雲中	I come alone, sadly brooding, among the waters and clouds.

In place of the "royal aura," *wangqi* 王氣, Li uses "auspicious aura," *jiaqi* 佳氣. In place of Xu Hun's "gone" and Liu Yuxi's "withdrew," Li uses "done," *xie* 歇. For "Six Dynasties" he uses *liudai* 六代 rather than *liu-chao* 六朝. Instead of Xu Hun's "millet growing high and low" 禾黍高低, we have "tombs and mounds high and low" 墳塚高低. (Xu Hun had mentioned the "tombs" in the preceding lines.) Li Qunyu even works in a reference to Li Bai's poem on Phoenix Terrace, cited earlier in this chapter. Still, Xu Hun's poem seems to make its presence felt most strongly in the background: phrases reappear in roughly the same sense.

Xu Hun

英雄一去豪華盡	Once bold heroes departed, the power and glory were ended

Li Qunyu

六代豪華燭散風	power and glory of the Six Dynasties, candles blown out in the wind.

and

霸業鼎圖人去盡	Overlords' legacy, charts and tripods, those people are all departed

---

71. Zhongling, the mountain range to the south of Jinling, was referred to as a "dragon coiling," while the Rock, the citadel to the northwest of the old city, was a "tiger crouching."

72. The reference is to "Phoenix Terrace," on which Li Bai wrote.

73. The "charts and tripods" are the signs of legitimacy, coveted by the king of Chu.

One does not usually associate the Southern Dynasties with "bold heroes," *yingxiong* 英雄. Li Qunyu substitutes a more credible ambition to reconquer China: "Overlords' legacy, charts and tripods." Xu Hun's "bold heroes" of the Southern Dynasties did not, however, disappear from the poetry of Jinling. They reappeared at the end of the ninth century, apparently (and somewhat incongruously) as the emperors, once again with the *iung* rhyme.

韋莊, 上元縣

Wei Zhuang, Shangyuan County[74]

南朝三十六英雄	Thirty-six splendid heroes 　of the Southern Dynasties,[75]
角逐興亡盡此中	struggles for power, rise and fall 　all occurred right here.
有國有家皆是夢	Possessing kingdom, possessing families, 　all was indeed a dream,
爲龍爲虎亦成空	acting as dragon, acting as tiger 　also has turned to nothing.[76]
殘花舊宅悲江令	Last flowers at his old dwelling, 　I grieve for Director Jiang,[77]
落日青山弔謝公	setting sun in green mountains, 　I lament Lord Xie.[78]
止竟霸圖何物在	At last what thing remains 　of their plans for dominance?——
石麟無主臥秋風	a stone unicorn with no master 　recumbent in autumn's wind.[79]

Like Liu Yuxi many decades earlier, Wei Zhuang sums up the Southern Dynasties in an evocative closing image, in this case not an old fortress but a funerary statue in the landscape, with no sense of whose tomb it guards, in the autumn wind of ruin and ending. This was an easy poetic

---

74. 38896; Jiang Congping 江聰平, *Wei Duanji shi jiaozhu* 韋端己詩校注 (Taibei: Taiwan Zhonghua shuju, 1969), 108; Li Yi 李誼, *Wei Zhuang ji jiaozhu* 韋莊集校注 (Chengdu: Sichuan sheng shehui kexueyuan chubanshe, 1986), 190.

75. This probably refers to the emperors of the South. Calling them "heroes" could easily be interpreted ironically.

76. See note 70.

77. The reference is to Jiang Zong 江總, who served as director of the Department of State Affairs under the Last Emperor of Chen.

78. The reference is to the great Jin statesman Xie An 謝安.

79. This refers to a funerary monument.

move: in the seventh line the poet asks what remains and in the eighth line he offers an image. Wei Zhuang performs the move with grace. Another poet from the end of the ninth century tacks the evocative image onto a very different poem, one making the moral judgments that the preceding poems either avoided or implied only indirectly. Here we have the *ou* rhyme.

李山甫, 上元懷古

Li Shanfu, Meditation on the Past at Shangyuan (first of two)[80]

南朝天子愛風流	Southern Dynasties' Emperors doted on panache (*fengliu*),
盡守江山不到頭	as for holding all their rivers and hills they didn't make it (*bu daotou*).
總是戰爭收拾得	By and large through battle and struggle they managed to get it,
卻因歌舞破除休	but then through song and dancing it was ruined and *lost*.
堯行道德終無敵	Yao practiced virtue and morals and never had a rival,
秦把金湯可自由	Qin held a fastness of metal and boiling water, but could it do as it pleased [*ziyou*]?[81]
試問繁華何處有	If you ask of that splendor and glory where to find it now—
雨苔煙草古城秋	rain on moss, misty grass *autumn* in the ancient city.

Finally, at the end of the ninth century, we see the lesson of Jinling returning to the present, as the Tang Dynasty itself was collapsing. Again we have the *ou* rhyme.

崔塗, 金陵懷古

Cui Tu [*jinshi* 888], Meditation on the Past at Jinling[82]

葦聲騷颯水天秋	Sounds of wind rustling through reeds, water and sky turn *autumn*,
吟對金陵古渡頭	I chant facing an ancient *ford* at Jinling.

---

80. 35327.
81. Metal and boiling water were proverbial images for impregnable defenses.
82. 37644; *Wyyh* 308.

千古是非輸蝶夢	The rights and wrongs of a thousand years, belong to the butterfly dream,
一罇風雨屬漁舟	a goblet of wind and rain belong to the fisherman's *boat*.
若無仙分應須老	If you lack the fate of an immortal, you surely must grow old,
幸有青山即合休	luckily there are green mountains, one should *quit* right away.
何必登臨更惆悵	What need to climb and gaze out and feel depressed again—
比來人世只如浮	recently the world of men seems simply all *adrift*.

We might return to the closing lines of Wei Zhuang's and Li Shanfu's Jinling poems.

Wei Zhuang

石麟無主臥秋風	a stone unicorn with no master recumbent in autumn's wind.

Li Shanfu

雨苔煙草古城秋	rain on moss, misty grass autumn in the ancient city.

Earlier we had Liu Yuxi's "Meditation on the Past at Xisai Mountain":

故壘蕭蕭蘆荻秋	winds moan over the ancient fort, and the reeds turn autumn.

The suggestive closing image had long been used in Chinese poetry. In the "meditation on the past" such scenes take on a special weight as scenes of absence. In the particular instances cited above, the scenes include ruins or residual markers of past glory, but this is not always the case. Often those in the past are beneath the soil or the millet grows over ancient sites of splendor. Nature endures and replaces human presence, at the same time reminding us of what is lost. This, of course, became an important part of Chinese landscape iconography.

"Power and glory" may be the designation of absence, but there was a pervasive interest in past pleasures—especially excessive ones. This lies behind Fang Hui's injunction to let the past serve as a warning to the present. The alternative was to be attracted to the very things that should be condemned. One of Xu Hun's most famous poems, composed sometime in the mid-830s, is about the Lingxiao Terrace, built by

Liu Yu, the founder of the Liu-Song Dynasty. Critics were often puzzled because Liu Yu was not known for excessive pleasures and absorption in the beauty of his palace ladies. History does not matter: the poetic trope of vanished sensual excess is so strong that Xu Hun imaginatively fills the ruins with "three thousand singers and dancers."

許渾, 凌歊臺
Xu Hun, Lingxiao Terrace[83]

宋祖功高樂未回	The Song Founder's deeds were great, he had not turned from his revels,[84]
三千歌舞宿層臺	three thousand singers and dancers stayed on the tiered terrace.
湘潭雲盡暮山出	Where the clouds of Xiang's pools ended, the twilight mountains emerged,
巴蜀雪消春水來	when the snows melted in Ba and Shu, spring floods came.
行殿有基荒薺合	Foundations of his leisure palace remain, wild shepherd's purse grows over it;
寢園無主野棠開	no one in charge of his tomb shrine, wild crab apples bloom.
百年便作萬年計	Though in his life span he made plans for ten thousand years,
嵒畔古碑空綠苔	the ancient stele beside the cliff is only covered in green lichens.

To "turn from his revels" is both to return to the capital and the business of government as well as to give up his imagined besottedness. The singers and dancers "stayed," *su* 宿, literally "stayed overnight," suggesting that the revels lasted so long that it was too late to return.

The second couplet is a fairly common type: the "positioning couplet," in which the place of the poem is located by mentioning remote places in different directions, usually in some way linked to the present position by clouds and water. In the third couplet we have the scene of ruins, again with some license since the area around Lingxiao Terrace was not the site of the tomb shrine garden, where the crab apples now

---

83. 28796; Luo 133; Jiang Congping 1.

84. There are serious textual problems with this line. I have selected one among several variants.

bloom. We might read this scene in conjunction with Wen Tingyun's 溫庭筠 poem "The Song of the Embankment Where the Cock Crowed" 雞鳴埭歌, which is about a site in Jinling. The final stanza reads as follows:[85]

芊綿平綠臺城基	A continuous stretch of level green on the Taicheng's foundations,
暖色春容荒古陂	the warm colors of the face of spring run riot on the ancient dike.
寧知玉樹後庭曲	Who would have thought that the song of jade trees in the rear courtyard
留待野棠如雪枝	would last on until the branches of wild crab apples were like snow?

Finally, Xu Hun contrasts the ambition to found a dynasty that would last ten thousand years with the present scene of an old stele covered in lichen. The poet knows—or pretends to know—history; the history inscribed in the landscape, however, is covered over, both by the growth over the ruins and by the lichen over the words of the stele inscription.

No emperor captured the poetic imagination as well as Xuanzong. In the ninth century he was the subject of numerous anecdotes and poems. His reign was close enough in history that writers could often claim some special knowledge of what really happened. In the story of Xuanzong and Lady Yang, love, pleasure, and dynastic splendor were reversed and brought to ruin in a very brief span: the beloved was killed, joy was lost, and the dynasty was destroyed. Mount Li, where Xuanzong had built his winter palace around the hot springs, was a central location in the Xuanzong story. Located near Chang'an, on the frequently traveled road between Luoyang and Chang'an, it was a prominent topographical presence that invited poetry and reflection. It exerted a certain fascination for Late Tang emperors: Jingzong had very much wanted to visit Mount Li but was strenuously dissuaded from doing so by his ministers since it was not an auspicious location.

---

85. 31871.

許渾, 驪山

Xu Hun, Mount Li[86]

聞説先皇醉碧桃	I have heard tell that the former sovereign grew drunk on the sapphire peaches,[87]
日華浮動鬱金袍	the glitter of sunlight drifted and stirred on his saffron robes.
風隨玉輦笙歌迴	Breezes followed the jade palanquin returning from songs to the reed organ,
雲卷珠簾劍佩高	clouds rolled up the beaded curtains, his sword pendants loud.
鳳駕北歸山寂寂	When the phoenix coach returned north, the mountain was gloomy and still;[88]
龍旗西幸水滔滔	when the dragon pennons went westward, waters rolled in flood.
娥眉沒後巡遊少	After those moth brows perished, he toured but rarely,[89]
瓦落宮牆見野蒿	tiles fell from the palace walls revealing the wilderness artemisia.

In the penultimate line I have translated the subject as if it were only Xuanzong, but in the context of the age one may take it as a general statement of emperors: after Lady Yang's death, emperors no longer visit Mount Li. Again we see the evocative closing image, with the trace of ruin (fallen tiles) in a scene of natural growth. Compare this with Zhang Xiaobiao's poem:

章孝標, 古行宮

Zhang Xiaobiao, An Old Imperial Lodge[90]

瓦煙疏冷古行宮	Mist over tiles, sparse and cold, an old imperial lodge,
寂寞朱門反鎖空	in gloomy stillness its vermilion gates now rather lock in empty space.
殘粉水銀流砌下	Traces of powder and liquid mercury flow beneath the stone stairs,

---

86. 28797; Luo Shijin 136; Jiang Congping 3.

87. These are the peaches of the Queen Mother of the West, to whom Yang the Prize Consort was often compared.

88. That is, when Xuanzong returned to Chang'an after his years in Chengdu.

89. Following the death of Yang the Prize Consort.

90. 27027.

墮環秋月落泥中	a dropped ring, the autumn moon,
	falls upon the mud.
鶯傳舊語嬌春日	Orioles pass on what they used to say,
	lending charm to spring days,
花學嚴妝妒曉風	flowers imitate their careful makeup,
	jealous of the breeze at dawn.
天子時清不巡幸	When times are peaceful the Son of Heaven
	makes no grand tours,
只應鸞鳳集梧桐	and I'm sure that only the phoenix
	roosts in the tong tree.

The traces of intertextuality are localized but clear. Here we see it in the seventh line, which recalls Xu Hun's line commenting on imperial tours no longer taken. As the ruin gradually disintegrates into the natural scene, the components of the palace dissolve and disperse: the women's powder and the mercury (used in cosmetics) still flow out in the water. However, gradually nature replaces—in figurative mimicry—the former human presence: the reflection of the moon is a "dropped ring," the orioles repeat palace gossip, and the dawn flowers imitate the makeup of the palace ladies.

After so many meditations on the past in regulated verse in the long line, it is appropriate to consider the crossovers between genres. By the Late Tang poets were reading Du Fu, who bequeathed to his successors many of the poetic images for an abandoned or ruined palace, such as the fallen tiles and the traces of the cosmetics of the palace ladies. We have here a very different genre, namely, old-style verse in the short line.

杜甫, 玉華宮

Du Fu, Yuhua Palace[91]

溪迴松風長	The stream valley turns, wind steady in pines,
蒼鼠竄古瓦	a gray rat scuttles under ancient tiles.
不知何王殿	I know not what prince's palace this was,
遺構絕壁下	abandoned edifice beneath the sheer cliff.
陰房鬼火青	In shadowy chambers ghost-fires are green,
壞道哀湍瀉	mournful rivulets pour over broken roadways.
萬籟眞笙竽	The myriad vents are the true ocarinas,
秋色正蕭灑	autumn colors are at their most brisk and aloof.

---

91. 10561; Qiu 389.

美人爲黃土	Its fair women have become the brown earth,
況乃粉黛假	even more, their artifice of powder and mascara.
當時侍金輿	Waiting on the golden carriage back then,
故物獨石馬	of former things there are only the stone horses.
憂來藉草坐	Cares come, I smooth down the grass and sit,
浩歌淚盈把	sing out loud, tears filling my open hands.
冉冉征途間	Going steadily on in my travels,
誰是長年者	none there is who can extend his years.

We began with the elusive term "tone." The theme here is the same, but the tone is very different. The regulated-verse poets are quietly melancholy; they don't sit on the grass singing with tears streaming down their faces; they don't bring the lesson back to their own mortality. The difference in tone is partly due to purely formal differences between the genres. Another important difference, however, is the way in which images had acquired such a history of associations by the Late Tang that they possessed an aura all their own. Contrast Wei Zhuang's

止竟霸圖何物在	At last what thing remains of their plans for dominance?—
石麟無主臥秋風	a stone unicorn with no master recumbent in autumn's wind.

with Du Fu's

當時侍金輿	Waiting on the golden carriage back then,
故物獨石馬	of former things there are only the stone horses.

Du Fu offers a simple proposition, namely, that only the stone horses survive. Wei Zhuang gestures toward a framed, evocatively "poetic" image that figuratively stands for their plans to reconquer the North and the failure of those plans.

In most of the preceding regulated poems in the long line historical judgment was not an issue. In some places the "meditation on the past" seemed to demand such a judgment. If the Southern Dynasties invoked sympathy tinged with censure and the First Emperor often invoked censure mixed with a certain wonder, some historical situations were unambiguous. King Huai of Chu (ruled 328–299 B.C.) listened to the blandishments of his minion Zheng Xiu and sent the worthy Qu Yuan into exile. Persuaded by the orator Zhang Yi and his courtiers, King Huai rashly attacked Qin, resulting in the loss of both his army and territory. Years later he placed his confidence in a pact with Qin and was taken prisoner at Wu Pass. A few years later he died a captive in Qin. In short, King Huai got what he deserved.

杜牧, 題武關
Du Mu, Wu Pass[92]

碧谿留我武關東	The sapphire creek makes me linger here east of Wu Pass,
一笑懷王跡自窮	I have a laugh at King Huai, how he came to the end of his road.
鄭袖嬌嬈酣似醉	Zheng Xiu was so charming, he was tipsy as if drunk,
屈原顦顇去如蓬	Qu Yuan looked careworn, he left like a tumbleweed.
山牆谷塹依然在	The mountain wall, the valley moat are here as they always were,
弱吐強吞盡已空	what the weak let out the strong swallowed, and now all is gone.
今日聖神家四海	These days one Sage and Divine has the seagirt world as his home,
戍旗長卷夕陽中	garrison banners are ever furled in the light of the setting sun.

The last couplet here is an excellent example of the inertia of a poetic type. As we have seen, there was a strong disposition to end such a poem with a beautiful poetic scene of absence. Wu Pass did not seem to provide such a scene, nor was King Huai of Chu deserving of the nostalgic melancholy implicit in such a scene. The scene is thus shifted to the present age of peace, banners furled in the setting sun. Moreover, in his closing Du Mu is of course rewriting the closing of the poem with which we began this chapter, namely, Liu Yuxi's "Meditation on the Past at Xisai Mountain."

今逢四海爲家日	Now we come upon a time when all the seagirt world is one,[93]
故壘蕭蕭蘆荻秋	winds moan over the ancient fort, and the reeds turn autumn.

---

92. 28232; Feng 265.

93. This refers to the unification of China in the Tang. "Is one" literally means "is his [the emperor's] home/family," being the same term used by Du Mu.

SEVEN

Poets of the Long Line

In this chapter we will consider a group of poets known for their regulated verse in the long line composed from the mid-830s into the 850s. None of these poets belonged to the circle around Jia Dao and Yao He, and most had contact with Du Mu. (Indeed, not a few of Xu Hun's poems were attributed to Du Mu in the appendixes to Du Mu's poems.)[1] The two older poets, Xu Hun and Zhang Hu, also composed a large number of regulated verses in the short line.

Xu Hun 許渾 (ca. 788–ca. 854–60)

Opinion is divided on Xu Hun's poetry.[2] In the tenth century Sun Guangxian 孫光憲 claimed that the general opinion of Xu Hun's contemporaries was that it would have been better if he had never written poetry at all.[3] For Wei Zhuang Xu Hun's poems were more valuable than "ten pecks of pearls."[4] Judging from the number of variants and the unusually large number of known Song editions, Xu Hun's admirers far outnumbered his detractors. As *Tang caizi zhuan* states (probably citing some unknown source): "To this day a great many admire him intensely, and each of them claims that he has gotten hold

---

1. See Wu Qiming 吳企明, *Tangyin zhiyi lu* 唐音質疑錄 (Shanghai: Shanghai guji chubanshe, 1985), 62–66.

2. The many editions of Xu Hun's poems contain differing numbers, though roughly five hundred poems survive.

3. Chen Bohai 2381. The comment is preserved in the sixteenth-century *Tangyin kuijian*.

4. Luo 389.

of the pearl that shines by night from under the jaws of the black dragon."[5]

In his own lifetime Xu Hun experienced little of the adulation that was showered upon Yao He and Jia Dao. Nevertheless, his reputation, like that of Li Shangyin, grew steadily from the end of the ninth century into the Song. Both Li Shangyin and Du Mu were poets whose output was more diverse than that of Xu Hun. Xu Hun wrote only regulated verse, both in the long and short line. Indeed, one could even argue that Xu Hun is the most representative Late Tang poet, writing like many others of the age, yet displaying a singular talent.

Quite apart from their beauty, many of Xu Hun's poems represent that rare pearl snatched from under the black dragon's jaws—in this case a dragon with the epithet *edax rerum*. Xu Hun had a considerable reputation as a calligrapher. As was previously mentioned, 171 of his poems have been preserved in a Song facsimile of the manuscript edition he personally prepared, dated the twenty-fifth of April in the year 850, known as the *Black-silk Border Poems, Wusilan shi* 烏絲欄詩.[6] We have early manuscripts of Bai Juyi's poetry, but Xu Hun represents one of only two cases in which we can match the author's originals against the variation that occurs in manuscript and print culture.[7]

About a decade younger than Jia Dao and Yao He and roughly the same age as Li He, Xu Hun launched a poetic career that extended back into the Yuanhe Reign.[8] He was unsuccessful in his early attempts to

---

5. Fu (1987), vol. 3, 241. The pearl was a traditional figure for something rare and difficult to obtain.

6. The reference is to an elegant writing medium, with black silk at the top and bottom and red-lined columns in between.

7. Since Xu Hun's poems have many variants, we can determine a "correct" reading. This casts doubt concerning poets whose work survived in a unique manuscript or printed edition. As we might expect, the manuscript tradition preserved poems in the shape, more or less, of the originals. The printed text, however, rarely perfectly matches the facsimile. Sometimes the divergences are significant. The greatest amount of variation occurs in the titles. Although we cannot rule out the possibility that the *Wusilan shi* represents the author's revision of poems that may have entered circulation in a different version, we also cannot assume that the received texts we now possess are identical to some "earlier version."

8. Li Lipu estimates that about 40 percent of Xu Hun's poems were composed before he passed the *jinshi* examination in 832. See Li Lipu 李立朴, *Xu Hun yanjiu* 許渾研究 (Guiyang: Guizhou renmin chubanshe, 1994), 121.

pass the *jinshi* examination and instead traveled widely with his family, journeying south to the Xiang region at the end of the Yuanhe, visiting the southeast, and seeking patrons in Sichuan and the northeast. He finally passed the examination in 832. After serving on a mission to the far south, from 837 on he held the post of district defender successively in two counties in Xuanzhou. (Du Mu was also in Xuanzhou at this time.) Thereafter he held a series of mid-level provincial and capital posts.

For the most part, Xu Hun remained outside the poetic circles of the period. He addressed a poem to Bai Juyi, which seems to have gone unanswered. He had a modest acquaintance with Du Mu, who addressed several poems to him. Both he and Du Mu wrote some of their finest poems in the long line in Xuanzhou in 837; the resemblances are obvious. Du Mu has kind words for Xu Hun's poetry, but the boundary between politeness and admiration is often invisible; certainly Du Mu showed nothing like the genuine enthusiasm he evidently felt for Zhang Hu. Xu Hun knew the poet Fang Gan 方干, but there is no evidence of the kind of close poetic interactions we encounter in the Bai Juyi circle or the circle around Yao He and Jia Dao. Falling somewhere between prominence (Jia Dao) and being virtually unknown in poetic circles (Cao Tang), Xu Hun remained on a middle tier.

As with Zhang Hu, we can see in Xu Hun's poetry a compendium of the changing fashions in poetry, from the Yuanhe through the middle of the ninth century. One of Xu Hun's most famous and oft-cited couplets has the distinct flavor of the Yuanhe style.[9]

雨中耕白水   In the rain he plows the white water,
雲外斸青山   beyond the clouds he chops the green hills.

The couplet should indeed have the flavor of the Yuanhe since it is essentially taken from a poem by Meng Jiao.[10] It alters the first hemistich in each line to produce the required tonal balance for regulated verse:

種稻耕白水   To plant rice I plow the white waters,
負薪斫青山   carrying firewood, I chop the green hills.

---

9. 28564; Luo 2; Jiang Congping 197.
10. "Living in Retirement" 退居, 19658; Hua Chenzhi 27.

The general preference for Xu Hun over Meng Jiao from the Song on made these "Xu Hun's" lines, however blatantly derivative.

In Xu Hun's regulated verse in the short line we can see the contemporary fashion for fine couplets, framed by plainer lines that carry the occasional message.

許渾, 早發中巖寺別契直上人

Xu Hun, Setting Out Early from Middle Cliff Temple,
Parting from the Monk Qizhi[11]

蒼蒼松桂陰	Blackish-green, the shade of pine and cassia,
殘月半西岑	the fading moon half on the western crag.
素壁寒燈暗	On the pale wall the cold lamp darkens,
紅爐夜火深	in the red stove, fire deep during night.
廚開山鼠散	The kitchen opens, mountain mice scatter,
鐘盡嶺猿吟	the bell fades, on the ridge gibbons moan.
行役方如此	Thus it is with public missions:
逢師懶話心	meeting Your Reverence, I'm in no mood to talk of Mind.

Xu Hun's message to his host—namely, that he is pressed to be on his way and can't stay to talk—hangs somewhat comically on the beautiful description of dawn and the first stirrings in the temple.

Xu Hun's skill at parallelism both won him admirers and earned him criticism. Fang Hui, often critical of Xu Hun, commented: "Xu Hun's poetic form is quite inferior, and his couplets match too perfectly" 丁卯詩格頗卑, 句太偶.[12] The untranslatable *ge* 格, rendered here as "poetic form," was often seen as the area in which Late Tang poetry generally failed. The problem with *ge* was not in formal issues of versification but rather an elusive sense of stylistic "dignity." Fang Hui usually approves of Jia Dao's couplets and often disapproves of Xu Hun's. The comments above were appended to the following poem, which is exempted from the critique because of one of the parallel couplets.

---

11. 28595; Luo 20; Jiang Congping 209. This poem has also been attributed to the Dali poet Huangfu Ran. Luo, who is cautious about attributions, persuasively argues for Xu Hun's authorship here.

12. Fang Hui 1660.

許渾, 自洛東蘭若夜歸
Xu Hun, Returning by Night from a Meditation
Chamber East of Luoyang[13]

一衲老禪床	In a single cassock, growing old on a Chan bench,
吾生半異鄉	my life, half spent in strange lands.
管弦愁裏醉	Pipes and strings, drunk in melancholy,
書劍夢中忙	book and sword, frantically busy in a dream.
鳥急山初暝	Birds hurry when the mountains first darken,
蟬稀樹正涼	cicadas fewer, the trees now chilly.
又歸何處去	Returning again, where am I going?—
塵路月蒼蒼	a dusty road, the moon blue-gray.

Fang Hui does not specify which of the parallel couplets redeems the poem, but a comparison with the preceding selection in *Yingkui lüsui*—which is also exempted from Fang Hui's general criticism because of one couplet—suggests that Fang Hui means the third couplet. When one has encountered too many cicadas, birds, and darkening mountains, one might prefer instead the striking second couplet, using the low register *mang* 忙, translated as "frantically busy" (diction that would contribute to a judgment of "inferior form").

It may be that the sense of Xu Hun's "inferiority" (*bei* 卑, also "vulgarity") in regulated verse in the short line was due to an energy, intensity, and even a theatricality in a poetic form that had developed an aesthetic of dignity, quietness, and restraint. For those same reasons Xu Hun's regulated verses have proved more durable than those of his more famous contemporaries. The issue here concerns those qualities associated with particular genres of poetry, qualities invited by formal characteristics but not determined by them. What could be perceived as a problem in regulated verse in the short line could be a virtue in regulated verse in the long line. Although Xu Hun wrote regulated verse in both the long and short line throughout his career, from the mid-830s we can see in his work a growing fashion for regulated verse in the long line.[14] Most of his most famous pieces date from this period, including

---

13. 28568; Luo 4; Jiang Congping 225. This poem is also misattributed to Cao Tang (31536).

14. Although at least half of Xu Hun's poems cannot be dated, if we look at the dates assigned by Luo Shijin (allowing that a number of them are tenuous), the preponderance of regulated verses in the long line were written after the mid-830s. It might be noted that Xu Hun has no extant old-style verse.

the "meditations on the past" cited in an earlier chapter. Although some of his regulated verses in the short line were quite well known, later critics often singled out his regulated verse in the long line as his strength.

The long line may have had a different "tone" from the short line, but Xu Hun successfully translated the craft of the couplet into the long line. The following couplet may date from the period before Xu Hun passed the examination.

燈照水螢千點滅	A lamp lights up river fireflies, a thousand spots disappear,
棹驚灘雁一行斜	oars startle the geese by the rapids, a single line aslant.

These are standard images of the regulated couplet in the short line, but they take on a new complexity in the long line, which more commonly has two predicates per line. The single lantern appears on a boat, and a thousand sparkling fireflies disappear (*mie* 滅, as in extinguishing a fire). The reader of couplets knows that a visual line is often matched by an aural line. Indeed the sound of an oar in the water appears to match the lantern; but instead of making the tiny lights of the fireflies disappear, the sound stirs up wild geese, larger bodies of white, flying up and away in a slanting line.

許渾, 留別裴秀才
Xu Hun, Parting from Licentiate Pei[15]

三獻無功玉有瑕	Thrice presented with no success, the jade possessed a flaw,[16]
更攜書劍客天涯	again taking book and sword in hand, a sojourner on the horizon.
孤帆夜別瀟湘雨	Lone sail parting by night, rain on the Xiao and Xiang;
廣陌春期鄠杜花	on broad lanes a meeting in spring, flowers of Hu County and Duling.[17]

---

15. 28828; Luo 165; Jiang Congping 225. Luo takes the subject as Xu Hun himself and thus dates the poem to 824, before Xu Hun passed the examination.

16. The reference is to Bian He's attempt to present an uncut jade to the king of Chu. During the first two attempts, the jade was considered false. This became a standard figure for offering one's talents to the government.

17. Chang'an.

燈照水螢千點滅	A lamp lights up fireflies over waters, a thousand spots disappear,
棹驚灘雁一行斜	oars startle the geese by the rapids, a single line aslant.
關河迢遞秋風急	Rivers and passes stretch far away, the autumn wind blows hard,
望見鄉山不到家	I gaze and see my native hills but never make it home.

The fine couplet is still "framed," but it is framed by an altogether different kind of poetry. Instead of the reserved voice of the craftsmen in the short line, this is a highly charged, even theatrical voice, as the poet, an eternal traveler on the water, now in the strong autumn wind, gazes and sees his native place while simply passing by during his journey. As is often the case in regulated verse in the short line, the beautiful parallel couplet is a snapshot taken on the imagined journey that lies ahead.[18] If the couplet fits the poem thematically, it must be in the image of wild geese taking flight, figures for the traveler.

This issue is, in fact, central to regulated verse in the long line, which in its mid-ninth-century form had an overall directness and momentum that was quite distinct from the more lapidary short line. It played on the tension between fluent spontaneity and fixed form, and its couplets seemed to follow one another naturally.[19] In regulated verse in the short line we often have to ponder the relation between couplets or ignore the framing couplets as uninteresting. With the exception of Li Shangyin, in the characteristic regulated verses in the long line this is rarely true; such poems often fulfill commonplace expectations, but they do so with intensity and panache. The kind of "framed" couplet cited above becomes increasingly rare in Xu Hun's more mature regulated verses in the long line. The beautiful couplet occurs in passing, on the way to some realization, some epiphany, some promise of commitment.

If one visits a monk's quarters, one should praise the latter's commitment to Buddhism, especially when considered against the secular life. We cannot completely differentiate social politeness from poetic trope, realized in hundreds if not thousands of earlier poems. Yet when

18. Or, if the parting occurs in the Xiao-Xiang region, a present scene.

19. This is, of course, a very different use of the form from what we find in the early eighth-century court poets or in Du Fu.

Xu Hun visits the quarters of a Suzhou monk, the old trope takes on the intensity of a personal discovery in the moment.

許渾, 題蘇州虎丘寺僧院
Xu Hun, On a Monk's Quarters in Tiger Hill Temple in Suzhou[20]

暫引寒泉濯遠塵	For the while I draw from a cold spring to wash away dust of far places,
此身多是異鄉人	this body of mine is often a stranger in a strange land.
荊溪夜雨花飛疾	Night rain on Jing Creek, flowers in a hurry to fall;
吳苑秋風月滿頻	autumn wind in the Park of Wu, the moon is often full.
萬里高低門外路	For ten thousand leagues high and low, the road outside the gate;
百年榮辱夢中身	a hundred-year span of glory and shame, a body in a dream.
世間誰似西林客	In all this world who can compare to those who sojourn at Westgrove?[21]
一臥煙霞四十春	once they lie in the mist and clouds, forty springs pass.

The title gives us the social context, which is a Buddhist temple; but the poem does not directly return to that context until the end. He washes away the dust of the road, which is both the figure and the consequence of the life of an official (or an aspirant), continually discovering himself in some new place. Someone who always feels that he is never "at home" implicitly seeks a home, which can be found either in the usual sense or in the fixity of the monks.

The second is the descriptive couplet the form usually demands: spring with falling flowers matches autumn wind; Jingzhou, in the middle reaches of the Yangzi River, matches Wu, which is downstream in Suzhou. The couplet quietly instantiates the passage of time and movement through space, only with the implication of time pressing onward. The third couplet reflects on precisely the questions raised in the second couplet from the perspective of the temple space where the traveler now stands. Outside the gate are the roads by which he came and those by

---

20. 28877; Luo 204; Jiang Congping 97.
21. The reference is to the famous Buddhist temple complex on Lushan.

which he will depart. These roads lead to all corners of the empire. They rise and fall, like the changes in position that send him traveling on those roads, rising and falling in status for a lifetime. These movements are indeed meaningless, illusion and dream. At last he encounters the truth of Buddhism, which is also the required social compliment: it is better to stay in one place, like the monks, and let the years pass.

Although the use of the momentum of the form toward some kind of revelation or understanding is not unique to Xu Hun, he repeatedly launches himself into a swift current of poetry that flows too quickly to allow the fine parallel couplet to be set apart and "framed." Instead, the couplets become integrated into the fluency of the form.

許渾, 滄浪峽
Xu Hun, Canglang Gorge[22]

纓帶流塵髮半霜	Sash and ribbons in sifting dust, half my hair frosty white,
獨尋殘月下滄浪	I went alone seeking last moonlight down through Canglang Gorge.
一聲溪鳥暗雲散	One cry from a bird in the valley, darkening clouds scattered,
萬片野花流水香	from thousands of petals of wildflowers the flowing water smelled sweet.
昔日未知方外樂	In bygone days I did not know joys outside the norms;
暮年初信夢中忙	in my twilight years I first believe that this bustling is in dream.
紅蝦青鯽紫芹脆	Red shrimp, blue carp, purple watercress crisp—
歸去不辭來路長	I will go back, not refusing because the route by which I came is too long.

The momentum of the poem is the counterpart of the waters in Canglang Gorge. The poet begins aging, sullied by the dirt of the social world. He heads off into the darkness in search of moonlight, but the moon is covered by clouds. When a bird cries out and the clouds scatter, we have the illusion of a magical cause and effect (though the causal sequence is actually reversed, with the sudden moonlight making the bird sing out). The question of remote cause reappears in the

---

22. 28817; Luo 154 (who dates the poem to 843); Jiang Congping 34.

matching line of the couplet, in which the waters are scented by petals that have been swept along from far-off places, as in the beautiful closing lines of a poem on the River Fu, associated with the *yuefu* heroine Luofu.[23]

何處野花何處水	Where are the wildflowers, wherefrom the waters,
下峰流出一渠香	down from the peak flowing out in a single channel of fragrance?

The literal "enlightenment" resulting from the appearance of the moon leads to self-reflection by the poet concerning his life, the discovery of the joy of letting go and the conviction that all his frantic busyness (*mang*, here translated as "bustling") has been but a dream. In the final couplet he is carried beyond, to an image of his home, embodied in an idyllic enumeration of local delicacies. This recalls the Jin figure Zhang Han, who quit his office and went home at the onset of the autumn wind and the thought of his local cuisine.

Although much of Xu Hun's poetry used commonplaces, his gift was to make them intensely immediate. The conventionally "poetic" scene was also idyllic. Xu Hun seemed able to step inside and inhabit it. His list of local foods in the poem is inspired by Zhang Han—although Zhang Han remembered the taste of fresh "bream fillets" 鱸膾 (actually sashimi).

許渾, 夜歸驛樓
Xu Hun, Returning at Night to the Post Station[24]

水晚雲秋山不窮	The waters late, the clouds autumnal, mountains without end,
自疑身在畫屏中	it seems to me that my body is in a painted screen.
孤舟移棹一江月	A lone boat, oars moving along through a whole river of moonlight,
高閣卷簾千樹風	in the high tower I roll up the curtains, wind in a thousand trees.
窗下覆棋殘局在	By the window retracing the chess game, the remaining pieces still there,

---

23. 28851; Luo 183; Jiang Congping 69.
24. 28838; Luo 172; Jiang Congping 57.

橘邊沽酒半壜空   beside the orange tree buying ale,
                              the flask, half empty now.
早炊香稻待鱸膾   In the morning I'll cook fragrant rice,
                              but I'll need bream fillet—
南渚未明尋釣翁   before it's dawn at southern isle
                              I seek out an old fisherman.

Zhang Hu 張祜 (ca. 792–ca. 854)

Like Li Shangyin and Wen Tingyun, Xu Hun became an important poet only retrospectively. Zhang Hu,[25] by contrast, was something of a darling both in his own age and in the succeeding generation. Lu Guimeng 陸龜蒙 (d. ca. 881), a prominent poet in the second half of the ninth century, called him "the ultimate talent," *caizi zhi zui* 才子之最. We have described Jia Dao as the perfect embodiment of the "poet." To be considered the ultimate "talent," *caizi*, implies a somewhat different quality, though it does suggest composing poetry. If the "poet" is devoted to his craft—working slowly and taking great pains in revising and choosing his words carefully—the "talent" gives the impression of composing quickly and effortlessly by virtue of his gifts.[26] The "poet," absorbed in his craft, is indifferent to social norms and bumps into high officials on the streets of the capital. The "talent" flouts social norms in a display of freedom from restraint. Li Bai hovers in the background of such talents and, indeed, once visited Zhang Hu in a dream:[27]

問余曰張祜   He asked me: "Zhang Hu,
爾則狂者否   are you a wild man or not?

---

25. The 158 previously unknown poems in the recently recovered Song edition bring Zhang Hu's collection to 468 poems, with a few scattered pieces from other sources. For a survey of the scholarly arguments around Zhang Hu's dates and life, see Du Xiaoqin 588–90.

26. Although the usage is admittedly anachronistic, drawn first from a Song lyric, Wu Xiangzhou offers a good antithesis to the "poet" in the phrase *caizi ciren* 才子詞人, "the talent and writer of lyrics," which he applies to such writers of the period as Zhang Hu. Wu Xiangzhou 吳相洲, *Tangdai geshi yu shige: lun geshi chuanchang zai Tangshi chuangzuozhong de diwei he zuoyong* 唐代歌詩與詩歌: 論歌詩傳唱在唐詩創作中的地位和作用 (Beijing: Beijing daxue chubanshe, 2000), 205–6.

27. Yan Shoucheng 198.

朝來王母宴瑤池　　This morning the Queen Mother
　　　　　　　　　　was feasting at Jasper Pool,

茅君道爾還愛酒　　and Lord Mao said that you
　　　　　　　　　　love to drink ale . . ."

Li Bai goes on to offer Zhang Hu a brief synopsis of his life and informs the latter that his poems are admired, inviting him to visit him at Penglai.

Zhang Hu poetically performed his role of "talent" in a way that made Bai Juyi, the other self-proclaimed "wild man," look tame by comparison. Zhang Hu remained on the margins, seeking and often winning the admiration of famous and powerful men yet ultimately remaining unsuccessful and frustrated. We first encounter him addressing a poem to Han Yu around 810. This was the time when Jia Dao made his first appearance in the capitals and was strenuously promoted by Han Yu and Meng Jiao. No written response to Zhang Hu's poem has been preserved, suggesting that Han Yu did not respond to Zhang Hu with the kind of enthusiasm he felt for Jia Dao. Zhang Hu seems to have addressed the political greats of the age—Li Cheng, Pei Du, Linghu Chu, Li Deyu—as well as senior literary figures like Bai Juyi and Liu Yuxi. A memorial has been preserved in which the great patron Linghu Chu recommended a collection of Zhang Hu's poetry to the emperor. Anecdotal sources relate that the emperor then asked Yuan Zhen for his opinion, whereupon the latter dismissed Zhang Hu's poetry, presumably because of his dislike of Linghu Chu.

According to the most famous anecdote, Zhang Hu went to Hangzhou when Bai Juyi was governor there, seeking a recommendation for the *jinshi* examination in the local levy. Bai Juyi, however, recommended Xu Ning 徐凝 instead. This event was immortalized in a short essay by Pi Rixiu 皮日休 (ca. 834–883), who reluctantly concluded that under the circumstances—men of practical use to the government were being sought—Bai Juyi probably did the right thing.[28] The reliability of "talents" of Zhang Hu's flavor was dubious. At the same time, the essay both confirmed Zhang Hu's fame as a "talent" and contributed to Xu Ning's reputation as a second-rate poet.

---

28. Zhu Bilian suggests that Bai was influenced by the judgment of his close friend Yuan Zhen. Zhu Bilian 朱碧蓮, "Qianshoushi qing wanhuhou—ping Zhang Hu de shi" 千首詩輕萬戶侯—評張祜的詩, *Wenxue yichan zengkan* 16 (1983): 60.

There is an impossibly fine line between the poet who wanders from patron to patron seeking support for the advancement of his career and the poet as itinerant professional. Even in his later years, when all hope of a public career was effectively quashed, Zhang Hu retained the rhetoric of the unrecognized talent seeking a discerning patron.[29] Beneath that necessary fiction, however, we see someone who had crossed over to become a professional, using his reputation as a poet to enhance a patron's prestige. In an anecdote about Wang Zhixing 王智興, the military commissioner stationed in Xuzhou, Zhang Hu presented a poem in praise of Wang. When others in Wang's entourage objected that the poem was sycophantic, Wang replied, "Are you going to then agree if someone says I am a bad man? Master Zhang is a man of letters famous in the world, and a verse is hard to come up with." The anecdote concludes: "Everyone in the world heard it and considered Wang Zhixing to be someone who delighted in virtue."[30] A remarkable homology exists between this anecdote (as well as others concerning poets contributing to the prestige of political patrons) and those about Zhang Hu and Cui Ya 崔涯 celebrating or mocking courtesans, which was said to have increased or ruined their business. The currency by which a poet was paid may have differed in these cases, but the principle of an essentially economic exchange remains the same.

Zhang Hu's collection is filled with traces of repayment for the hospitality various officials, generals, and monks showed him by letting him stay with them a while or offering him a night's lodging. Perhaps more fully than anywhere else, Zhang Hu's poetry shows us what were, in effect, provincial "courts" and their entertainments: we have poems praising skill at polo and the hunt, a poem about a catamite, and numerous poems on the erotically charged "Zhe Branch" 柘枝 dance. This was not poetry involving the finely chosen word and the perfect couplet, which demanded painstaking effort to produce. Much of Zhang Hu's poetry seems quickly composed to patterns that could be and were easily repeated on other occasions.

---

29. See, e.g., "Mooring on the River: Presented to Vice Director Du of Chizhou" 江上旅泊呈池州杜員外 (Yan Shoucheng 138), in which Zhang Hu describes himself as the Warring States retainer Mao Sui to Du Mu's Lord of Mengchang. While seeking a patron, Li Bai had also compared himself to Mao Sui.

30. Wang Zhongyong 1460.

No doubt Zhang Hu once harbored the hope of entering the imperial civil service. At some point he gave in to his self-image as a poet of panache in the manner of Li Bai. This was a poetics of *fengliu* 風流, combining the eccentric, the swordsman, the drinker, and the connoisseur of courtesans. The opposition of the *fengliu* image to punctilious politeness lent credence to the mood of spontaneous enthusiasm, which might otherwise have been construed as sycophancy. It was as a poet of *fengliu* that Zhang Hu presented himself to Du Mu, a poet who sometimes adopted the same persona. Understandably, the two men immediately appreciated one another.

In the following excerpt from Pi Rixiu's essay on Bai Juyi's choice of Xu Ning, he attributes to Zhang Hu a rather conventional course of poetic development, from youthful frivolity to mature seriousness:

During the Yuanhe Reign Zhang Hu wrote poems in the "palace style," and his song had a lush sensuality. The less serious types at that time valued his talent, and he earned praise through the general clamor. When he grew older, he turned his attention to the style of the Jian'an, recited from the records of *yuefu*, and understood the true purpose of an author. In his expressions of criticism and artful resentment he sometimes reaches close to the Six Principles. This is the ultimate thing in using one's talent.[31]

Much of Zhang Hu's poetry is impossible to date. It may be that the few extant pieces in the "palace style" indeed date from his youth, but his later poetry in no way suggests the mature gravity that Pi attributes to it.[32] Rather, we see Zhang Hu as the old eccentric and rake.[33]

Zhang Hu was very much the epigone; throughout his work we see traces of his reading of his Tang predecessors. In earlier chapters we

---

31. Xiao Difei 蕭滌非 and Zheng Qingdu 鄭慶篤, *Pizi wensou* 皮子文藪 (Shanghai: Shanghai guji chubanshe, 1981), 240. This also appears under Lu Guimeng's name in the preface to 34180. Lu Guimeng's version differs in one significant detail: he says "*little* poems in the palace style" 宮體小詩, i.e., quatrains.

32. One rather interesting poem is a versified memorial to the throne entitled "Direct Speech in the Yuanhe" 元和直言詩 (Yan Shoucheng 190). As the title indicates, this is an earlier poem.

33. Zhu Bilian identifies the "palace style" poems with some quatrains on palace ladies, including Zhang's most famous poem, a quatrain in the short line entitled "Palace Lyric" 宮詞. "Palace style" and "palace lyrics" are somewhat different categories. See Zhu Bilian 朱碧蓮, "Qianshoushi qing wanhuhou—ping Zhang Hu de shi" 千首詩輕萬戶侯—評張祜的詩, *Wenxue yichan zengkan* 16 (1983): 61–62.

have seen him redoing poems by poets as diverse as Wang Wei and Li He (see pp. 104–5, 165–66). These are not isolated examples, and Li Bai always hovers in the background of his poetry.

Zhang Hu was a facile poet. This becomes clear when we read his regulated verses in the short line in the context of his contemporaries, who were devoted to the form. Like a heedless archer with a large supply of arrows, he inevitably hit the target now and then. Reading Xu Hun's complete poems, we frequently encounter happy surprises among his unanthologized poems, whereas Zhang Hu is at his best among his anthology pieces. Zhang Hu has several well-known poems about temples, but in his collection we read them in the context of well over a dozen other poems on temples that all belong to a reproducible "type." Consider the following:

張祜, 題潤州金山寺

Zhang Hu, On the Golden Mountain Temple in Runzhou[34]

一宿金山寺	Once I stayed over at Golden Mountain Temple,
超然離世群	passing beyond, I left the world's crowds.
僧歸夜船月	A monk returns: moon on a night boat;
龍出曉堂雲	a dragon emerges: clouds in the morning hall.
樹色中流見	The colors of trees are seen mid-current,
鐘聲兩岸聞	its bell's sound is heard on both shores.
翻思在朝市	Then I think back on life in court and market,
終日醉醺醺	how all day long they are woozy from drink.

Such a poem is perhaps best understood as an advertisement for the temple, composed in exchange for lodging. Zhang Hu mentions Golden Mountain Temple's famous attributes one by one: the moonlight on the Yangzi, its dragon, and the fact that its bell can be heard across the Yangzi. These couplets are framed by the central message that the temple is a fine place to escape the madding crowd.

The discovery of a Song edition of Zhang Hu's poetry, first republished in 1979, substantially altered our understanding of his work and reminded us of what might be missing from works of other poets that originally seemed fairly complete. Only a relatively small group of regulated verses in the long line and almost no longer poems were pre-

---

34. 27357; Yan Shoucheng 47. This popular poem has many variants; I have followed the Song edition reproduced in Yan Shoucheng.

served in the received edition; the Song edition adds more than a hundred pieces, giving us a much fuller image of the *fengliu* poet.

While the long line was clearly Zhang Hu's strength, his regulated verses in the short line show the same facility as his other work. They were not much admired later. *Yingkui lüsui* includes a few of Zhang Hu's regulated verses in the short line but none in the long line. *Tangshi guchui*, an anthology containing regulated verse in the long line, includes only 1 poem (compared to 31 by Xu Hun).

Several poems exchanged with Du Mu will be discussed in a later chapter. Here we will consider a few of Zhang Hu's pieces on the "Zhe Branch" dance to consider both his strengths and weaknesses. The "Zhe Branch" was very popular during this period, with numerous poems by others about this erotically charged dance, which seems to have involved the baring of the dancer's shoulders.

张祜，壽州裴中丞出柘枝

Zhang Hu, Vice Censor-in-Chief Pei of Shouzhou
Puts on the "Zhe Branch"[35]

青娥十五柘枝人	Blue-black brows, age fifteen, "Zhe Branch" performer,
玉鳳雙翹翠帽新	paired wings of a jade phoenix, her azure cap is new.
羅帶卻翻柔紫袖	Her gossamer sash whirls back, purple sleeves supple,
錦靴前踏沒紅茵	brocade boots take a pace ahead and sink in the red plush carpet.
深情記處常低眼	Where deep passions are recalled she always lowers her eyes,
急拍來時旋折身	when the swift clappers come she bends her body sharply.
愁見曲終如夢覺	Sadly I see the piece end as if waking from a dream,
又迷煙水漢江濱	once again lost in the misty waters on the shore of the River Han.[36]

---

35. Yan Shoucheng 142.

36. This may refer to Zheng Jiaofu's meeting with the nymphs of the River Han. After giving him their pendants, they disappeared.

張祜, 金吾李將軍柘枝
Zhang Hu, General Li of the House Guard's "Zhe Branch"[37]

促疊蠻鼉引柘枝	Rapid rolls of southern lizard-skin drums announce the "Zhe Branch,"
卷簷虛帽帶交垂	an empty hat with curling brim, sash ends hang crisscross.
紫羅衫宛蹲身處	Her purple gossamer skirt folds where she crouches down,
紅錦靴柔踏節時	the red brocade boots are supple when she paces to the rhythm.
微動翠娥抛舊態	She faintly moves her azure brows casting off her former pose,
慢遮檀口唱新詞	and languidly covers her sandal-red lips singing out new lyrics.
看看舞罷輕雲起	The dance is just about to end, the light clouds rise,
卻赴襄王夢裏期	and she heads back to a tryst with King Xiang in dream.

張祜, 周員外出雙舞柘枝妓
Zhang Hu, Vice Director Zhou Has a Pair of Entertainers
Put on the "Zhe Branch"[38]

畫鼓拖環錦臂攘	Painted drums are dragged to form a ring, brocade rolled up on arms,
小娥雙換舞衣裳	young maidens in a pair change into their dancing robes.
金絲蹙霧紅衫薄	Golden threads crinkled in fog, their red skirts thin,
銀蔓垂花紫帶長	silver vines dangling flowers, their purple sashes long.
鸞影乍回頭對舉	The simurgh shadows first turn around, heads raised face-to-face,
鳳聲初歇翅齊張	the voice of the phoenix first stops, their wings spread evenly.

---

37. Yan Shoucheng 142. The obviously incorrect readings in Yan Shoucheng are corrected in the *Caidiao ji* version. In the seventh line I have adopted the colloquial *kankan* 看看—attested to as popular Tang poetic usage in Dunhuang lyrics—of *Caidiao ji* rather than the *ke* 客 of the Song edition.

38. Yan Shoucheng 143.

一時折腕招殘拍　At the same moment they bend their wrists
　　　　　　　　to call for the last movement,
斜斂輕身拜玉郎　then draw back their light bodies aslant
　　　　　　　　and bow to the fine gentleman.

Here we see a template that is roughly reproduced in the other poems on the "Zhe Branch." The opening presents us with the girl (or girls) doing the dance, sometimes mentioning the drumming that precedes it. The second couplet provides some combination of cap, skirt, sleeves, sash, and boots—though these items of clothing can spill over into other couplets as well. The third couplet describes sound and movement. The final couplet completes the dance with the erotic fantasies of the viewers or a bow to the host. Bared arms and shoulders and diaphanous fabrics were the order of the day. Lest one suppose that these dances observed the covered-up decorum of later eras, some songs speak of baring shoulders in the "Zhe Branch," and Bai Juyi (in a reference to another dance) clearly states that one could see the woman's skin under the "gossamer," *luo* 羅.[39]

Zhao Gu 趙嘏 *(ca. 806–ca. 850)*

With Zhao Gu[40] we come to a generation younger than Xu Hun and Zhang Hu. After a period of youthful travels, in the early Taihe he joined the entourage of Yuan Zhen, who was military commissioner of Zhedong. When Yuan Zhen's post changed, Zhao Gu entered the service of Shen Chuanshi in Xuanzhou, where he met Du Mu. In 832 he set off for Chang'an to take the *jinshi* examination, which he failed the following year. He appears to have remained in the capital until about 840, trying to make the necessary connections. Thereafter he seems to have wandered a while, returning to Runzhou (modern Zhenjiang), then returning to Chang'an in 843 to take the examination yet again, this time succeeding in 844. In 847, under the new reign of Xuānzong, he was back in the capital and was made district defender of Weinan, near the capital.

---

39. 24072; Zhu 2200.

40. Zhao Gu has about 260 extant poems. A fragment of a separate collection (*Poems Chronologically Arranged, Biannian shi* 編年詩), devoted to historical examples of different ages in human life, has been preserved in the Dunhuang manuscripts. Xu Jun 522–34.

Among poets of this period who belonged to his generation, Zhao Gu's story is fairly typical. However, unlike his contemporaries, who joined the circle around Jia Dao and Yao He, Zhao Gu preferred the long line. Among his poems in the short line is a series of twenty poems entitled *Xixi yan* 昔昔鹽 (understood as 夕夕豔, "Evening After Evening: Prelude"), with each poem taking as its subject a line from a *Xixi yan* by Xue Daoheng 薛道衡 (540–609). There are other cases of ninth-century poets basing a series of poems on lines from an earlier poem—usually dating from the late fifth or sixth century. *Xixi yan* elaborates the ever-popular motif of the woman whose husband is off in the army.

Apart from these twenty pieces, Zhao Gu's surviving poems contain a remarkably small proportion of regulated verses in the short line. We cannot be certain that this heavy emphasis on the long line is not a consequence of the vagaries of transmission of his collected poems, but the disproportionate number is consistent with other poets not in the Jia Dao circle who were writing primarily from the mid-830s on.

It was during his residence in Chang'an in the 830s that Zhao Gu wrote the poem that earned him the nickname (from Du Mu) "Zhao who leans from the tower."

趙嘏, 長安秋望

Zhao Gu, Autumn View from Chang'an[41]

雲物凄清拂曙流	The shapes in the clouds are bleak and clear brushing the dawn-light current,
漢家宮闕動高秋	palace gate-towers of the House of Han stir high autumn.
殘星幾點雁橫塞	Several specks of fading stars, wild geese stretch across the passes,
長笛一聲人倚樓	one note from a long flute, a person leans from the tower.
紫艷半開籬菊靜	Purple voluptuousness half-opened, chrysanthemums serene by the hedge,
紅衣落盡渚蓮愁	their red robes fallen all away, lotuses mourn by isles.

---

41. 30105; Tan Youxue 26. I have followed Tan Youxue's reading of the title and first line.

鱸魚正美不歸去	Just now the bream are at their finest,
	but I do not go back,
空戴南冠學楚囚	in vain I wear my southern cap
	just like the Chu prisoner.[42]

Positioned somewhere between the melancholy of Xu Hun and the panache of Zhang Hu and Du Mu, Zhao Gu provides us with something like the normative Late Tang regulated verse in the long line. The Zhang Han anecdote, ever-popular among southerners, hovers in the background: Zhang Han feels the autumn wind, thinks of the local food of his home (bream), resigns his post, and returns. Zhao Gu has no post to resign, which is perhaps what makes him like the Chu prisoner, stuck in a "foreign" land but never forgetting his home.

The "poem," however, is the early-morning autumn scene of the first six lines, which stirs such longing, beginning with the reflections of clouds set against the poetic solidity of the palace gate towers. The eyes move up to the fading white specks of stars crossed by more substantial white geese, whose inaudible migratory cries are replaced by the note of the flute, and the poet in the tower, who does not go south this autumn. Looking down at the ground, we see the things that remain: the chrysanthemums in their autumn glory and the ruined lotuses.

As we suggested at the beginning of this study, repetition and repeatability are central problems of Late Tang poetry. If we could lose all the other poems with the same images used here, this would be a truly memorable poem. We don't know who first used some of these images. We could search the written record to grant retrospective copyright, but in such cases we usually find that the images evolved gradually, gathering depth and adding fresh configurations. Finally they became worn coinage, rich in aura and very familiar.

Zhao Gu often considers going elsewhere. In Chang'an he thinks of home—if not of Zhang Han's bream, then of Tao Qian's pines and chrysanthemums:

---

42. This refers to an anecdote in the *Zuo zhuan* (Cheng 9), in which the duke of Jin asked who the person in chains wearing a southern-style cap was. He was told it was a Chu prisoner presented by Zheng.

趙嘏, 宿楚國寺有懷
Zhao Gu, Thoughts When Spending the Night at Chuguo Temple[43]

風動衰荷寂寞香	Wind stirs the dying lotuses, fragrant in the lonely stillness,
斷煙殘月共蒼蒼	patches of mist, the waning moon, together are gray-green.
寒生晚寺波搖壁	The cold comes to the evening temple, the waves shake the walls,
紅墮疏林葉滿床	red falls from the half-bare grove, leaves fill my bed.
起雁似驚南浦棹	Wild geese rising seem as if alarmed by the oars at the southern shore,[44]
陰雲欲護北樓霜	shadowy clouds are as if guarding the frost on the northern tower.
江邊松菊荒應盡	My pines and chrysanthemums by the river must be lost now in the weeds:[45]
八月長安夜正長	in Chang'an in the eighth month the nights are truly long.

Perhaps the best way to understand such poetry is not to look for fresh images but rather to read it—as we learn to read regulated verse in the short line—as a play of pattern invited by form. Both in nature and in Tang poetry birds in the water fly up at a sound or the approach of a boat. In the third couplet the rising geese are matched by the dark clouds hovering over the tower, glittering with frost. Quatrains use the same images, albeit usually in closure; they are not part of a parallel pattern but rather are framed as a picture, invested with a special weight because of the silence that follows them. Take the following:

趙嘏, 西江晚泊
Zhao Gu, Mooring in Evening at Westriver[46]

茫茫靄靄失西東	Vast and vague, hazy, I can't tell east from west,
柳浦桑村處處同	willow shores and mulberry hamlets, everywhere the same.

---

43. 30122; Tan Youxue 41. The temple is in Chang'an.

44. The "southern shore" was standard poetic usage for a place of parting.

45. The allusion is to a famous couplet in Tao Qian's *Guiqulai ci*: "The three paths have gone to weeds, but my pines and chrysanthemums survive" 三徑就荒, 松菊猶存.

46. 20262; Tan Youxue 132.

戍鼓一聲帆影盡   A single sound from the guard tower drum,
                                              outlines of sail are gone,
水禽飛起夕陽中   and water birds fly up
                                         in the evening sunshine.

Li Qunyu 李群玉 *(ca. 808/11–ca. 861/62)*

The poets we think of as the most important poets of the 850s are Li
Shangyin and Wen Tingyun (Du Mu passed away in 852); while each
may have had a reputation in certain restricted circles, the patron whose
favors both sought, Linghu Tao, recommended to the throne the
poetry of Li Qunyu,[47] clearly one of the most prominent, perhaps the
most prominent, poet of the day.

   The dates of Li Qunyu's birth and death make him a contemporary of
Li Shangyin (812–858). We know relatively little about his life. He seems
to have met Du Mu in 837, during the latter's second stay in Xuanzhou. It
was probably then that Du Mu dedicated a quatrain to him.

杜牧, 送李群玉赴舉
Du Mu, Seeing Li Qunyu Off as He Sets
Out for the Examination[48]

故人別來面如雪   Since parting from my old friend,
                                        my face is like snow,
一榻拂雲秋影中   my bed brushes the clouds
                                      in autumn light.
玉白花紅三百首   Three hundred poems of jade's white
                                         and the red of flowers—
五陵誰唱與春風   at Wuling who will sing them
                                        for the spring breeze?

In social poems such as this one it is important to note the terms in
which the recipient is represented: Li Qunyu is here presented to us as

---

47. Li Qunyu has approximately 260 poems in a collection that survived independ-
ently, clearly an anthology of an original corpus that was much larger. He has a large
number of quatrains that were not in Hong Mai's *Wanshou Tangren jueju*.

48. 28255; Feng 283. We cannot be sure if Du Mu is implying that he had met Li
Qunyu earlier, although by referring to him as an "old friend" he suggests as much. We
should note that this piece is found among the poems in Du Mu's main collection; that
is, it is a poem he himself preserved, no doubt more to document the social connection
than for the inherent quality of the poem.

a poet, and it was as a poet that Li Qunyu was known in the capital. The very senior Yao He wrote to him, as did young Fang Gan, and in the remains of Li Qunyu's own collection we have a poem addressed to Zhang Hu.

He may have been admired in poetic circles, but his several attempts to take the *jinshi* examination met with no success. We find him at the headquarters of the military commissioner at Changsha in the mid-840s (he was a native of the region), after which he seems to have traveled to Guangdong. His reputation appears to have grown steadily. Probably in 854—no doubt with the encouragement of Linghu Tao—Li Qunyu presented a collection of three hundred of his poems to Xuānzong, along with a memorial of appropriate humility. In addition to the memorial, Xuānzong's oral reply has also been documented: "The poems you presented are extraordinary and of lofty elegance. We have perused them all. At present We have some small brocades and vessels to confer upon you, and it is fitting that you accept them. Considering summer's heat, We hope you have been well these days."[49] Linghu Tao submitted the following recommendation to the throne that Li Qunyu be made an editor in the Institute for the Advancement of Literature: "The preceding songs, products of intense effort (*kuxin* 苦心), are from one whose tracks are screened away amid forested ravines. His fine lines circulate in many mouths; his fair repute is greatly noted in the times. He keeps to the Way and is at ease in his poverty, keeping away from fame and profit."[50] Linghu Tao goes on to recommend the specific position of editor. The request was granted.

As we have seen, the post of editor was an entry-level position that perhaps was somewhat incongruous for a famous poet in his late forties. We can assume that Zhou Pu 周朴 was being intentionally ironic when he began his quatrain lamenting Li Qunyu's death with the lines:[51]

群玉詩名冠李唐　　　The fame of Li Qunyu's poetry
　　　　　　　　　　crowned the whole Tang Dynasty,
投詩換得校書郎　　　he submitted his poems and received
　　　　　　　　　　an editorship in exchange.

---

49. Yang Chunqiu 145.
50. Yang Chunqiu 145.
51. 37232.

We detect a certain loss of faith in the public reward for genius. In any case, in 859 Li Qunyu asked to retire and was granted permission. He went home to the south and died there a few years later.

The "Bibliography" of the *Xin Tang shu* records a collection in three *juan* and a "Later Collection" 後集 in five *juan*. Wan Man believes that the three-*juan* collection is the one presented to the throne, and that the "four *tong*" 通 (common Tang usage for *juan*) mentioned in his memorial is a mistake.[52] Collections of poems for imperial presentation (like Zhang Hu's earlier collection) often consisted of three hundred pieces—the number of poems in the *Shijing*—and we can infer with a fair degree of certainty that the poet who presented such a collection made a careful culling of a larger body of verse, making certain it included nothing that cast his own character in a bad light or would prove offensive to the emperor. We cannot determine if the "poetry collection" mentioned in the "Bibliography" is the same material that was presented to Xuānzong, nor can we ascertain whether the "Later Collection" consisted of poems composed subsequently or was simply a supplement.[53] However, we do know that the current collection, which is based on a Song edition, must be an anthology of Li Qunyu's once more extensive works, drawn from both the "Later Collection" as well as the main collection.

Few poets can charm both contemporary emperors and an exacting community of readers across many centuries. Though he was occasionally admired in later ages, Li Qunyu succeeded in the former but generally failed in the latter. There were good reasons why Li Shangyin became famous while Li Qunyu remained largely forgotten. One reason may have been that poetry had changed in a profound way, demanding more of some circles of readers. In the mid-eighth century almost everyone—from the emperor to singing girls—could enjoy Li Bai's poetry, and the capacity of a broad community to appreciate his works endured in the tradition. Du Fu—as sophisticated a poet as can be imagined—idolized Li Bai. Contemporary taste did not favor Du Fu, but that did not make the latter contemptuous of contemporary taste. By the second quarter of the ninth century we can note a division between Bai

---

52. Wan Man 萬曼, *Tangji xulu* 唐集敘錄 (Beijing: Zhonghua shuju, 1980), 298.

53. Since the current collection includes poems composed after he received his post, it is clearly not identical with the presentation collection (see 31256).

Juyi's popularity among the "commons" and a more elite poetic art that looked on him with contempt. Zhang Hu wisely invoked Li Bai in dream, striving to match his broad appeal. Tough generals might have been pleased with a poem by Zhang Hu, but it is highly unlikely that all of Zhang Hu's generous patrons would have uniformly appreciated Jia Dao's lines, consisting of words chosen with such painful reflection. In any case, Jia Dao never tried to please them.

By the mid-ninth century there were distinct communities of taste, and the forefront of the poetic art had become even more demanding of its readers. We can hardly expect an emperor like Xuānzong to have appreciated the poetry of Li Shangyin or the erudite and witty poetry of Duan Chengshi. Such appreciation depended on groups of highly sophisticated and learned readers, which Li Shangyin may have found in a small circle of his contemporaries and clearly found in tenth-century Chengdu and early-eleventh-century Kaifeng. Li Qunyu was sophisticated enough for a Tang emperor of the mid-ninth century.

Although Li Qunyu has a few very fine poems (for example, the "meditation on the past" at Moling; see p. 206), it is hard to understand his fame. Critics sometimes comment generally on the quality of his old-style verse in the short line, but the only particular poem that received attention is the following:

李群玉, 雨夜呈長官

Li Qunyu, A Rainy Night: Presented to a Senior Official[54]

遠客坐長夜	The traveler from afar sits in the long night,
雨聲孤寺秋	sound of rain, autumn in an ancient temple.
請量東海水	Pray measure the waters of the Eastern Ocean
看取淺深愁	and you will see the depth of my sorrow.
愁窮重如山	Sorrow's straits are as heavy as a mountain,
終日壓人頭	all day long it presses upon me.
朱顏與芳景	My rosy complexion and the fragrant scene
暗赴東波流	go off unseen with the waves flowing east.
鱗翼俟風水	Scales depend on waters, wings on the wind,
青雲方阻修	but now the blue clouds are blocked from me.
孤燈冷素艷	The lone lamp's cold paleness is attractive,
蟲響寒房幽	echoes of insects, these cold chambers
	isolated.

---

54. 31207; Yang Chunqiu 4.

借問陶淵明	I ask Tao Yuanming then
何物號忘憂	what was it he called "care's oblivion"?[55]
無因一酩酊	With no means to get very drunk,
高枕萬情休	all feelings cease in my high pillow.

This can be summarized as follows: I'm very sad; I'm getting older; my career is going nowhere (ll. 9–10); and I don't even have anything to drink. Although in his memorial to the throne Li Qunyu takes pains to point out that he has examples of poetry in all forms, it seems that many poets of the age had virtually forgotten how to write effectively in old-style verse—particularly in the short line.

A few regulated verses in the short line are still readable, but here there is also a general blandness, with none of the brilliant couplets typical of poets of earlier generations. As we might expect in this period, Li Qunyu is better when writing regulated verse in the long line and quatrains.

李群玉, 金塘路中
Li Qunyu, On the Road at Jintang[56]

山川楚越復吳秦	Mountains and river, Chu and Yue, also Wu and Qin,
蓬梗何年是住身	for this stalk of tumbleweed in what year will my body come to rest?
黃葉黃花古城路	Yellow leaves and yellow flowers, road to an ancient city,
秋風秋雨別家人	autumn wind and autumn rain, a person who has left home.
冰霜怯度商於凍	Ice and frost, I dread passing Shangyu freezing,
桂玉愁居帝里貧	jade and cassia,[57] I grieve lodging in the imperial city poor.
十口繫心拋不得	Ten mouths to feed bind my heart, I cannot cast them off,
每回回首即長顰	and every time I turn my head, I immediately give a long frown.

---

55. Ale.

56. 31323; Yang Chunqiu 37.

57. These items represent the wealthy and noble.

To a strict traditional critic of regulated verse in the long line, there is much to object to here, such as the tendency to enumerate, repeated words, and vernacular usage (*paobude* 抛不得; *meihui* 每回). One can scarcely imagine a treatment of this genre more different from Li Qunyu's contemporary Li Shangyin (though Li Shangyin also used lower-register diction in the final couplet). Li Qunyu's diction, syntax, and taxis are often very direct, anticipating one direction in regulated verse in the last part of the century.

Li Qunyu's poetry in the long line often resembles the effortless facility in the form that we see in Zhang Hu, to whom Li Qunyu addressed the following poem. (A presumably original note says that he had not met Zhang Hu personally.)

李群玉, 寄張祜

Li Qunyu, To Zhang Hu[58]

越水吳山任興行	Among Yue's waters and Wu's mountains you go as your whim takes you,
五湖雲月掛高情	the clouds and moon at the Five Lakes capture your lofty mood.
不游都邑稱平子	If not visiting the capital acclaimed as a Zhang Heng,
只向江東作步兵	you are off in the Southland acting like Ruan Ji.
昔歲芳聲到童稚	In years gone by your fine reputation reached us as boys,
老來佳句遍公卿	now aging, your fine lines circulate among all the great lords.
知君氣力波瀾地	I understand that in places where your energy rolls in waves
留取陰何沈范名	you will leave the fame of Yin Keng, He Xun, of a Shen Yue, a Fan Yun.

The allusions are simple: the Eastern Han Zhang Heng represents the poet who receives public acclaim; Ruan Ji represents the recluse poet; the remarkable series of surnames in the last line (expanded to full names in the translation) are all literary men famous around the turn of the sixth century. By the mid-ninth century there was already a continuity of admiration for poets of the first Late Tang generation: Zhang Hu

---

58. 31337; Yang Chunqiu 45.

had been someone Li Qunyu admired as a boy, as Liu Deren had admired Gu Feixiong (see p. 145). This is perhaps the strongest argument for the Late Tang as a period.

As Zhang Hu celebrated dancers and singers—both those privately employed and those belonging to patrons—Li Qunyu could celebrate a patron's favorite singer in an equally fluent manner.

李群玉, 同鄭相幷歌姬小飲戲贈
Li Qunyu, Joining Minister Zheng's "A Small Party with
His Singer": presented whimsically[59]

裙拖六幅湘江水	Her skirt trails six panels of the Xiang River's water,
鬢聳巫山一段雲	her tresses raise a patch of cloud on Wu Mountain.
風格只應天上有	Such a manner should exist only in Heaven,
歌聲豈合世間聞	her song's notes ought not be heard among mortals.
胸前瑞雪燈斜照	On fortunate snows of her chest, the lamp shines aslant,
眼底桃花酒半醺	below her eyes are peach blossoms, half flushed with ale.
不是相如憐賦客	Were not the guest a fun-loving Sima Xiangru,
爭教容易見文君	how could one get so easily to see Zhuo Wenjun?

We may well assume that such a poem was not presented to Xuānzong. Yet a client was sometimes called upon to celebrate the favorite women of friends and patrons.

Du Mu could also write such straightforward regulated verse in the long line, though few would claim that Li Qunyu or Zhang Hu had Du Mu's talent. In certain circumstances, however, this easy style could be used with a genius. Although such poets could no longer write old-style poetry in the long line, they could still write regulated verse in the long line that was just as straightforward.

---

59. 31359; Yang Chunqiu 105. Yang Chunqiu takes this as Zheng Su 鄭肅.

李群玉, 自遣

Li Qunyu, Getting Something off My Chest[60]

翻覆升沈百歲中	Tumbling over and over, rising, sinking within this hundred-year span,
前途一半已成空	the road ahead is only half and has already become nothing.
浮生暫寄夢中夢	A life adrift for a while lodged in a dream within a dream,
世事如聞風裏風	the world's matters, as if hearing a wind inside a wind.
修竹萬竿資閒寂	Ten thousand stalks of tall bamboo provide quiet serenity,
古書千卷要窮通	a thousand scrolls of ancient books, the essentials of success.
一壺濁酒暄和景	A single pot of thick ale, a sunny, balmy scene—
誰會陶然失馬翁	who understands the cheerful old man who has lost his horse?

The "old man who has lost his horse" refers to the famous parable of the "old man of the frontier" who faced the loss of his horse with good cheer under the assumption that it might bring him good fortune. When the horse returned leading a herd of strange horses, he did not rejoice, realizing it might spell bad fortune—as it turned out to be, with several subsequent reversals.

We do not know if this poem (which is included in the primary collection rather than the "Later Collection") was presented to Xuānzong, but it might well have appealed to an emperor who came unexpectedly to the throne as the son of the Yuanhe emperor Xianzong. The new emperor had remained quietly in the background through four reigns of younger men and had seen fortune's odd reversals. The old motif from the *Zhuangzi*, namely, that life is a dream or a dream within a dream, was a consolation for emperors and commoner poets alike in a world that had become increasingly unpredictable.

---

60. 31324; Yang Chunqiu 37.

EIGHT

Du Mu

Different versions of "poetry" were being contested in the Late Tang. Although each version had significant variations, the primary distinction was between poetry as the defining enterprise of one's life (that is, "being a poet") and as an adjunct to a life whose goals lay elsewhere; in other words, poetry as a means of displaying or revealing the self, of participating in the social world, and even of amusing oneself. The person who defined himself as a "poet" might be the devoted craftsman, impoverished by his commitment to the discipline (on the model of a Buddhist monk), or he might be the quasi-professional, traveling from patron to patron and living off his reputation. Such poets often sought public office, but they tended to look on their posts as mere employment, the reward due to their talents, providing the leisure to work on their poetry.

The alternative version of poetry came to so completely dominate later discourse on poetry that its internal distinctions may seem more salient than its deeper opposition to "pure" poets. This was essentially a poetics of personality as socially defined, in which poetry is at best a means to reveal the person and not an end in itself. Du Fu's poetry projects an image of Du Fu deeply engaged in the social and political world, and even as the devoted craftsman he was. Few could claim the same about Jia Dao's poetry, except in the sense that it yields a generic image of the devoted craftsman—one who returns to the poem, the couplet, the line, and the perfectly chosen word. Our distinction is not an ironclad one; rather, it represents two distinct directions in which poets of the period might go.

The poetics of personality contains significant internal distinctions. "Seriousness" meant engagement with public and political life. At the same time, the poetics of personality encompassed various negations of this version of public-minded seriousness. One possibility was withdrawal from society to a private life, what is often termed "reclusion"—though this was a sociable role and was far removed from the "hermits" of the Christian West or even some of the genuinely antisocial recluses of the Six Dynasties. Another negation of public seriousness was sensual self-indulgence. These negations posed no real challenge to seriousness, defined as engagement with public life and the interests of the polity; indeed, they presumed such a definition of seriousness. What neither public seriousness nor its negations could accept was that poetry might itself be "serious," an end in its own right rather than a means of self-expression or entertainment.

Conceiving of the poetics of personality in a broader sense by encompassing its internal oppositions is useful because it allows us to understand how a given poet could easily move among roles that seem outwardly irreconcilable. A poet could present himself both as deeply engaged in political life and as no less deeply resistant to it. Such a poet was Du Mu (803–852).[1]

The discourse of devotion to poetry in its own right had acquired some cachet by Du Mu's time. We have what might, on the surface, seem to be a contradiction to the earlier characterization in Du Mu's "Epistle on Presenting My Poems," a statement of the poet's values that is more direct than almost any other poet's in this period.

I put intense effort [*kuxin* 苦心] into writing poetry, always seeking the highest thing possible. I do not devote myself to intricate beauty [*qili* 綺麗], and I do not venture into the familiar and common [*xisu* 習俗]. I am neither ancient nor modern; I position myself between them. Lacking the talent [for poetry], I merely have the strangeness [*qi* 奇]; when a piece is completed on paper, I often burn it myself.[2]

"Intricate beauty" is often understood as the style of Li He, but the "familiar and common" is clearly associated with Bai Juyi. Li Shangyin's representation of Li He's compositional practice and the values of the craftsmen are present in the background. Du Mu claims to work hard at poetry, and out of such work comes "strangeness." In contrast to Li He, who forgot about his poems once they were finished, Du Mu ac-

---

1. For a survey of the scholarly debate surrounding the date of Du Mu's death, see Du Xiaoqin 611–12.

2. *Fanchuan wenji* 242.

tively burns those that contain imperfections. Such values, articulated against Bai Juyi's pride in casual composition and conservation of flawed poems, seem to have become a widely shared norm.[3]

Of greater interest in the passage, however, are its serial negations, the avoidance of the stylistic extremes associated with the Yuanhe poets. Du Mu is claiming moderation or an intermediate position that differs in spirit from the poet obsessed with his craft, like Li He. This does not really describe Du Mu's actual practice in poetry. He could be all the things he claimed he avoided—offering "intricate beauty," writing in a style marked as "ancient" and in styles marked as "modern." But he truly did "not venture into the familiar and common."

To be known as a poet could be politically useful. In addition to the presentation of his poems, which we have addressed in the passage above, we know of another occasion when, in need of a job and seeking a post on the staff of a military commissioner, Du Mu sent a selection of his poems ahead. Unlike many of the young craftsmen of regulated verse, however, Du Mu did not usually present himself as the "pure" poet. Poetry was for him, as it had been for many before him, the adjunct to a career and an inner life that changed in response to the changes in his career.[4] This is not surprising when we consider his origins, so different from those of most of the poet-craftsmen who gathered around Jia Dao and Yao He. Although he was closely associated with Niu Sengru, Du Mu was precisely the sort of young man Li Deyu had argued was most suited for the responsibilities of public office.

---

3. Note the use of "labor intensely," *kuxin* 苦心, in Linghu Tao's recommendation for Li Qunyu, p. 248.

4, One need not read far in the criticism and scholarship on Du Mu to note a recurrent formulation, which can roughly be paraphrased as follows: "*but* Du Mu was deeply engaged in contemporary political issues." For anyone who reads Du Mu's works in their entirety or even his poetry as a whole, this is patently true. But the formulation reminds us that from the second half of the ninth century on, Du Mu was best known as a melancholy sensualist, one for whom a larger view of change contextualized and diminished the sense of present responsibility. Such a stance of resistance to political engagement and social obligation will always be the more "popular" position, and the poems that celebrate Du Mu in that role were indeed the more popular—based on the evidence of anthologizing, intertextual reference, and critical comment. "Serious" scholars, both pre-modern and modern, quite correctly supplement such poems with Du Mu's considerable output of politically engaged poems and prose.

No other major Tang poet grew up with a family background quite like Du Mu's. In 803, the year of his birth, his grandfather, Du You 杜佑 (735–812), returned to court from his position as military commissioner of Huainan to become a minister. He remained a minister until his death, through the last years of Dezong, the brief reign of Shunzong, and the early Yuanhe reign of Xianzong. Such longevity at the top of the civil bureaucracy was remarkable, particularly across different reigns. Just two years before his return to Chang'an, Du You had completed his massive encyclopedia of knowledge for governing, the *Tongdian* 通典, the fruit of over thirty years of work, and had presented it to the throne. For his leisure time he withdrew to his estate at Red Slope, *Zhupo* 朱坡, in the region south of Chang'an (Chengnan), reputed to have been the finest estate in Chengnan. The estate was in the area long inhabited by the Dus, including another branch of the family that had produced Du Fu. In this region flowed the Fanchuan (Fan River) 樊川, which served as Du Mu's toponym. We can reasonably assume that Du Mu knew the Red Slope estate during his childhood, which possessed an almost magical quality when he subsequently described it in his poetry.

The death of Du Mu's grandfather in 812 seems to have been followed a few years later by the death of his father, who, like Du You himself and other family members, had entered service through the *yin* privilege and rose to mid-level court positions.[5] Unfortunately, Du Mu's father did not rise high enough to pass the *yin* privilege down to his sons. Du Mu and his ill-fated younger brother had to enter the bureaucracy through the *jinshi* examination. Both passed on their first attempt, which may attest to the remarkable resources for learning available to young

---

5. In one letter where he seeks a position Du Mu goes into some detail about his impoverished state in his teens, toward the end of the Yuanhe Reign (*Fanchuan wenji* 244). He claims to have moved constantly, to have eaten wild vegetables, and slept without as much as a candle at night. While it is possible, as Miao Yue suggests, that Du Mu's father Du Congyu, the third of Du You's sons, did not inherit the major portion of the family's wealth, his share must still have been significant; and Du Mu was Du Congyu's eldest son. Du Mu's uncle married the Qiyang Princess and became a favored imperial in-law. To have the uncle living in splendor in Chang'an and the nephew eating wild greens is unlikely. Despite later assumptions that famous poets tell the truth, this account is best understood as the cachet of youthful poverty, particularly impressive when the impoverished youth is from a distinguished clan and has fallen on hard times.

members of the Du family; it also attests to the favoritism toward young men with eminent connections.

Not only was Du Mu the scion of a remarkably eminent family, but he made a name for himself in his early twenties (probably in 826) for his "Poetic Exposition on Apang Palace," *Apang gong fu* 阿房宮賦, which describes the excess and social cost of Qin Shihuang's famous palace. The final lesson was clear and explicit:

滅六國者六國也, 非秦也. 族秦者秦也, 非天下也. 嗟乎! 使六國各愛其人, 則足以拒秦. 使秦復愛六國之人, 則遞三世可至萬世而爲君, 誰得而族滅也? 秦人不暇自哀, 而後人哀之; 後人哀之而不鑑之, 亦使後人而復哀後人也.

Sad indeed! It was the Six Domains themselves and not Qin that destroyed the Six Domains; Qin itself and not the whole world exterminated the house of Qin. Had each of the Six Domains loved its own people, it would have been enough to resist Qin; had Qin loved the people of the Six Domains, then after three generations they might have gone on to be rulers for ten thousand generations. No one could have wiped out the entire ruling house. The people of Qin did not have the chance to lament themselves, yet later people lament them. Yet if later people lament them but do not make them their mirror, then these later people will be lamented by people still later.[6]

The famous conclusion to some degree justifies the common interpretation of the piece as a critique of Jingzong's lavish building projects. Despite Du Mu's apparent disapproval of Bai Juyi's and Yuan Zhen's poetry, it is hard not to see here a move in the poetic exposition that derives from Bai Juyi's and Yuan Zhen's "new *yuefu*": the genre is carried back to its supposed original function, in the end clearly criticizing contemporary social and political problems.

The "Poetic Exposition on Apang Palace" may have been meant as a criticism of Jingzong (though whether before or after his death is uncertain), but it was primarily intended to draw attention to someone who would soon be taking the *jinshi* examination. Circulation of one's writings was the primary means by which an aspirant preparing for the examination attracted sponsors, who would then recommend the former to other highly placed officials, including the examiner. One famous anecdote may be apocryphal, but it does suggest the degree to which success in the examination was in some measure a function of

---

6. *Fanchuan wenji* 2.

sponsors pleading the case for particular individuals. One Wu Wuling, an Erudite in the National University, was so impressed by Du Mu's "Poetic Exposition on Apang Palace" that he told the chief examiner that Du Mu should be the *zhuangyuan* (top graduate). When the examiner informed him that they already had a *zhuangyuan*, Wu said that Du Mu should get the fifth place. When the examiner hesitated, Wu showed him the poetic exposition, following which the examiner agreed.[7]

In 828 Du Mu passed the examination given in Luoyang and then, on May 12, passed a palace examination administered by Wenzong (who, one may recall, was several years younger than Du Mu and had had difficulty obtaining even basic texts of the Classics while still a prince). Following this second examination, Du Mu began a respectable career close to the bottom of the bureaucratic ladder as an editor at the Institute for the Advancement of Literature.

That autumn, after only a few months in office, Du Mu decided to join the entourage of Shen Chuanshi 沈傳師, who had been appointed surveillance commissioner of Xijiang and was headquartered in Hongzhou (Nanchang, in modern Jiangxi). The reasons for this decision are not entirely clear. Shen Chuanshi was an old friend of the family, and service in the entourages of military commissioners and surveillance commissioners was often a good way to acquire patrons. (Du Mu seems to have had no lack of well-placed supporters.) Such provincial staff positions often included a nominal capital post, and Du Mu's nominal post elevated him a step in the bureaucratic hierarchy. It may have been because, after years of making connections and preparing for the examination, he wanted to see a bit of the world, especially the beauties of the southeast. Perhaps he found the work of an editor boring.

Whatever his reasons, Du Mu set off for Hongzhou. After a year there he followed Shen Chuanshi to his new post as surveillance commissioner in Xuanzhou (Xuancheng, in modern Anhui), which was just as scenic as Hongzhou and more famous because it had been under the jurisdiction of the late fifth-century poet Xie Tiao. The precise duties of these posts are often unclear—perhaps drafting documents and going on missions—but the burdens of such offices do not seem to have

---

7. Zhou Xunchu 1225.

been particularly onerous. Feasting and enjoying the local attractions, both human and topographical, seem to have played a large role.

An equally interesting question concerns why some senior provincial officials recruited young men they clearly did not need to perform administrative duties. Perhaps a primary reason was prestige. Power sought visibility in the Tang. Officials assumed their posts flying banners, wearing badges, and deploying various other visible markers of their status. To be surrounded by talented young literary men was also a visible sign of prestige. From a purely practical standpoint, the provinces were boring compared to the social life of the two capitals. Even the beautiful landscapes of some of the circuit headquarters could become routine. If, however, one had an entourage with whom to feast and drink and celebrate the place, it could seem less like an exile. For these senior officials there were two major entertainments: poetry and the "official singing girls," *guanji* 官妓 (or "camp singing girls," *yingji* 營妓, for military offices), who were impressed into service to entertain local officials.

Many of Du Mu's poems are undatable; if we could date such poems, it might affect our understanding of a poet's literary career. Du Mu's earliest securely datable poem was composed during the first years of Wenzong's reign. "What Stirred Me," *Ganhuai* 感懷, is a long old-style poem describing the troubled history of the dynasty and its local armies. It was occasioned by the open defiance of recent court commands by Li Tongjie, one of the virtually autonomous military commissioners in the Northeast. Du Fu's and Han Yu's poetry lies in the background of "What Stirred Me." As in "The Poetic Exposition on Apang Palace," albeit in a different mode, Du Mu here presents himself as the politically engaged poet. Although it is the kind of poem that gave the young poet a certain cachet, it was also the sort of poem few would read and fewer still would remember. "The Poetic Exposition on Apang Palace" possessed a beguiling sense of excess in addition to sharply critical passages that made it the most famous poetic exposition of the Tang and an enduring part of the literary canon. By contrast "What Stirred Me" is now read primarily by those who have already read some poems by Du Mu and wanted to deepen their understanding of the poet.

In Shen Chuanshi's entourage, however, there were occasions for a different kind of composition. One such concerned Zhang Haohao, an "official singing girl" attached to the Hongzhou headquarters. She made her debut there when she was just entering adolescence and so captivated Shen Chuanshi that he took her with him to Xuanzhou. She also attracted the attention of Shen Chuanshi's younger brother Shen Shushi 沈述師, who took her off the official rolls in 832 and made her his personal concubine. Shen Shushi had become a good friend of Du Mu's, and the latter celebrated the singer in her new role as concubine and private entertainer.

杜牧, 贈沈學士張歌人

Du Mu, Presented to Academician Shen's Singer Zhang[8]

拖袖事當年	Trailing sleeves, you serve in the present,
郎敎唱客前	your young man bids you sing for the guests.
斷時輕裂玉	When you break off, it is lightly cracking jade,
收處遠繅煙	as you conclude, strands of mist spun afar.
孤直纚雲定	Lone and upright, constant clouds fixed,
光明滴水圓	luminous, drops of water round.
泥情遲急管	Feeling enmeshed, hurried pipes are slowed,
流恨咽長弦	resentment flows, the long strings moan.
吳苑春風起	Spring breeze rising in gardens of Wu,
河橋酒斾懸	tavern pennons hanging at a river bridge.
憑君更一醉	For your sake I will become drunk again—
家在杜陵邊	my home is there beside Duling.

This is a poem of a fairly common type, in which the poet compliments a host's singer or dancer. In this specific case the opening couplet "broaches the topic," *poti* 破題, with the unusually bald statement that she has been commanded to perform. *Lang* 郎, "the young man," was a term with many associations, including romantic; here it perhaps suggests Shen Shushi's infatuation. In both poetry and prose the ninth century had become an age of love stories, and passionate attachments were in fashion. Displaying one's favorite concubine to friends was a common practice, primarily by having her perform. Friends, in turn, would celebrate her talent and sometimes declare that they were also drawn to her.

The remainder of the poem is taken up with the poetic discourse of performance, with counterparts throughout the poetry of the period. Although Du Mu was later to implicitly concur with a harsh critique of Bai Juyi, he certainly knew the "Ballad of the Pipa" 琵琶行, with its elaborate description of music. Du Mu begins with a couplet mentioning sections ("break off," *duan* 斷, probably refers to the abrupt stops, followed by a pause and continuation), with appropriate metaphors for

---

8. 28113; Feng 166.

their qualities. The third couplet describes the qualities of sound—
though the stillness of clouds often refers to the effect of the music on
the outer world. The dripping of water was a favorite image for sound,
with the visual circles of drops in water playing on the "perfection,"
yuan 圓 ("circularity") of the sounds. The fourth couplet describes the
relation of the singer to the instrumental accompaniment. Finally, the
song seems to evoke pastoral scenes typical of Wu, leading the poet to
think of his own home near Duling, far off in Chang'an. The singer is
complimented for stirring up emotion in the poet to such a degree that
he will drink more, thinking of home.

The poem cited above was probably written not long after Shen
Shushi had sent his midnight messenger asking Du Mu to compose a
preface for the rediscovered poems of Li He. Considering the kind of
poetry Du Mu had been writing and his political prose, his measured
disapproval of Li He was understandable. Du Mu, however, was soon
to become a very different poet.

In 833 Du Mu was sent by Shen Chuanshi on a mission to Yangzhou,
the capital of the Huainan circuit. The new military commissioner of
the circuit was none other than Niu Sengru. Niu had previously served
as minister. Coming under increasing criticism for his handling of an
incident in Sichuan (the jurisdiction of his great enemy Li Deyu), Niu
asked to be relieved of his post. The Huainan circuit was the plum as-
signment. It is fair to say that if one had to be away from the two capi-
tals, Yangzhou was the place to be during the Tang. Located at the
head of the Grand Canal, Yangzhou was the funnel through which all
goods, tribute, and grain moving from the south and Sichuan, as well as
from foreign places, were shipped to Chang'an and Luoyang. Just five
years after Du Mu's arrival, Yangzhou was to host another delegation
from Japan, this one including a monk named Ennin, who was to com-
pose a long and detailed diary concerning his stay in Tang China. Yang-
zhou had been the River Capital 江都 of Sui Yangdi and the site of his
most famous extravagances. It was known as a city of pleasure, both
past and present.[9] Du Mu stayed on with Niu Sengru in Yangzhou, first

---

9. Although Yangzhou experienced major floods in 833 and devastating fires in 834,
we hear nothing about it in Du Mu's poetry. See Li Tingxian 李廷先, *Tangdai Yangzhou
shikao* 唐代揚州史考 (Nanjing: Jiangsu guji chubanshe, 2002), 246.

serving as a local judge (*tuiguan*) and then as his private secretary. This association was to have significant consequences for Du Mu's later career.

Yangzhou seems to have marked a turning point in Du Mu's poetry—or, rather, the beginning of Du Mu's maturation as a poet. Du Mu was to return to Yangzhou briefly in 837 to care for his sick brother, but he seems to have made the most of his first two years in the city under Niu Sengru. The series of three poems simply entitled "Yangzhou" probably date from this period.

杜牧, 揚州三首

Du Mu, Yangzhou[10]

I

煬帝雷塘土	The soil of Yangdi's Thunder-pond,[11]
迷藏有舊樓	the former Palace for hide-and-seek.[12]
誰家唱水調	Who is singing the "River Melody"[13]
明月滿揚州	as the bright moon fills Yangzhou?
駿馬宜閒出	Fitting here that fine steeds go idly forth,
千金好暗投	fine to give away a thousand in gold unseen.[14]
喧闐醉年少	A drunken young man making a row
半脱紫茸裘	half removes his purplish shaggy cape.[15]

---

10. 28137–39; Feng 193.

11. After the Tang took the south, they reburied Yangdi at Thunder-pond, outside Yangzhou.

12. Du Mu is playing on the name of the "Palace for Going Astray," *milou* 迷樓, a pleasure labyrinth constructed for Yangdi. "Hide-and-seek," *micang* 迷藏, was a game played by Xuanzong and Lady Yang, in which both parties were blindfolded and groped for each other.

13. The following note appears in the original text: "After Yangdi finished having the Bian Canal dug, he himself composed the 'River Melody'" 煬帝鑿汴渠成, 自造水調. This line could be understood as a rhetorical question, implying that no one is singing it.

14. Giving away objects of value "in the dark," *an* 暗, often implies arousing suspicion. Zhou Xifu suggests instead that this refers to spending money in the entertainment quarters, in which case we would understand *an* as suggesting "without knowing it," playing on the darkness of night.

15. This gesture is ambiguous. It could suggest the disarray of clothing in drunken revelry or, following the sixth line, it might possibly be sexual in nature. The most likely explanation is that the young man is seeking to pawn his expensive cape for ale.

II

秋風放螢苑	Autumn wind, Park for Releasing Fireflies,[16]
春草鬥雞臺	spring grass, the Cockfighting Terrace.[17]
金絡擎雕去	Golden braid casts an eagle off into flight,[18]
鸞環拾翠來	simurgh rings come, picking up kingfisher feathers.[19]
蜀船紅錦重	Ships from Shu, heavy with red brocade,
越橐水沈堆	Yue sack-wrapping, piled with aloe-wood.[20]
處處皆華表	Wherever you go are stone pillars—
淮王奈卻迴	what can Huainan's Prince do but return?[21]

III

街垂千步柳	Avenues hang with a thousand paces of willows,
霞映兩重城	rose wisps half hide double walls.
天碧臺閣麗	Heavens are sapphire, terrace kiosks lovely,
風涼歌管清	the breeze cool, song and piping clear.
纖腰間長袖	Slim waists in between long sleeves,
玉佩雜繁纓	jade pendants mixed with dense hat ribbons.
柁軸誠為壯	Rudder and axle, truly mighty,[22]
豪華不可名	a domineering splendor that can't be named.

---

16. The reference is to the old Sui imperial park. The name is based on a legend according to which Yangdi ordered all the fireflies for miles around to be caught and then released them together at one time, thereby illuminating the whole landscape.

17. Yangdi visited the old Cockfighting Terrace in Yangzhou and was supposed to have seen an apparition of the Last Ruler of Chen there.

18. That is, someone wearing a gold-braided sash is hawking.

19. Beautiful women, richly adorned.

20. Positioned at the head of the Grand Canal, Yangzhou was the entrepôt for all goods going to Chang'an by water. Brocade and aloes-wood suggest tribute items.

21. This couplet combines two references. First, there is the story of Ding Ling Wei, who became an immortal and returning to his native Liaodong after a thousand years, perched on an inscribed pillar (*huabiao*) and delivered a verse claiming that everything he had known had changed (see Chapter 6, note 31). The Prince of Huainan here is Liu An of the Western Han, who was supposed to have become an immortal.

22. Bao Zhao's "Weed Covered City" 蕪城賦 was understood as describing Yangzhou (Guangling). There Bao Zhao speaks of the city being "ruddered by canals, and axled by hills like Kunlun." The topography of this commercial city reflects its use.

自是荒淫罪   Of course, with his crimes of debauchery
何妨作帝京   nothing stopped him from making it
                                    the capital.[23]

In Chinese poetry it is important to distinguish discourse from behavior—while acknowledging that discursive impressions had social consequences as great as or even greater than actual behavior. Through discourse—sets of images, attitudes, values, and verbal moves—a poet adopted various roles. Such role-playing was part of "real life," but it had many possible relations to real life other than being a direct "reflection" of real life. Poetic role-playing could fulfill routine social expectations, as in praising the singing of a friend's concubine or expressing the utter loss of prospective happiness at a friend's departure. The poet may indeed have enjoyed the performance and felt bad that his friend was leaving; but the persuasive quality of the poem was not dependent on the sincerity or intensity of the poet's true feelings. One mark of such socially expected roles and responses is our recognition that the poet would have been hard put to say the opposite. In other cases roles may be pure play, enjoying the image of oneself created in a poem. At the other end of the spectrum is the role as a consequence of personal conviction or emerging unconsciously from the poet's nature. These are distinctions of convenience, in that there is no clear boundary between play and conviction and it is easy to pass from one stage to another. Moreover, we have no way of determining the actual conviction a poet brought to playing a particular role. There exists the strong yet unwarranted assumption that the more original and successful a poet is in a particular discursive role, the more he "means it" or the truer it is.

At issue here is Du Mu's poetic self-image as a libertine. We have no real evidence that Du Mu had more love affairs with courtesans and drank more heavily than his contemporaries, including those who have left us only a discursively "serious" face. In some of his most effective and memorable poems Du Mu represents himself as a melancholy sensualist, *fengliu* 風流, combining a propensity for love affairs and a sense of panache and indulgence with a sensibility easily moved. Du Mu's *fengliu* behavior is commented on in anecdotal sources and biographical notices. These comments and illustrative anecdotes are more likely

---

23. Yangzhou was Sui Yangdi's beloved "River Capital" 江都, and Yangdi's excesses there were blamed for the fall of the Sui.

adduced from the tone and some claims made in his poetry than from more direct knowledge of his actual behavior.[24] It is also likely that this image of Du Mu almost certainly became part of his reputation during his lifetime. Du Mu clearly enjoyed playing this role, but he equally enjoyed playing the unrecognized military genius and statesman whose policies could restore the empire to its former glory. Du Mu's problem was that more readers were convinced by his poetic role as a sensualist.

The three "Yangzhou" poems are among the earliest we can date in which Du Mu is beginning to sound like the poet who was so beloved. We have been discussing self-representation, yet Du Mu does not speak of himself anywhere in these poems. If, however, we compare these poems to his youthful "Poetic Exposition on Apang Palace," the contrast is striking. Sui Yangdi was an extravagant, "bad" emperor, more a sensualist than the First Emperor of Qin, but he was held equally responsible for the fall of his dynasty. Apart from readers imputing to Du Mu the generally assumed negative judgment of Sui Yangdi, there is nothing in these poems to suggest the kind of moral condemnation that was offered in the poetic exposition. We may interpret the end of the third poem as a condemnation, but it is framed in a most peculiar form.

The first poem begins by invoking the remains of Sui Yangdi in the very earth of his tomb, which is that of Yangzhou. Some pieces of the "Palace for Straying" may have survived (or what were believed to be its remains); but it soon becomes clear that all Yangzhou is a palace for straying. The River Melody is apparently still being sung; the moonlight is still there; and the difference between past and present is nowhere made clear. We see the extravagant young man of wealth and station, a standard poetic figure, going out by night, spending his wealth on wine, women, and song. The "drunken young man making a row" is the very figure of straying, losing oneself, and overspending. We close with an image of the young man half stripped of a costly garment—losing both decorum and capital. Even if he appears somewhat foolish, it is not an image of condemnation but rather of celebrating self-indulgence.

---

24. Consider the story preserved in the *Leishuo* of Du Mu's nocturnal adventures in Yangzhou while being followed by thirty of Niu Sengru's undercover agents, who were ordered to keep him out of trouble. When he was later teased about his behavior, Du Mu is supposed to have professed innocence—until Niu Sengru produced detailed reports of his activities. Zhou Xunchu 1226.

We might here cite the second couplet again:

誰家唱水調   Who is singing the "River Melody"
明月滿揚州   as the bright moon fills Yangzhou?

It is instructive to contrast this with another of Du Mu's most famous poems:

杜牧, 泊秦淮
Du Mu, Mooring on the Qinhuai[25]

煙籠寒水月籠沙   Mist veils the cold waters,
                              moonlight veils the sands,
夜泊秦淮近酒家   by night I moored on the Qinhuai
                              near a tavern.
商女不知亡國恨   The merchant's girl does not understand
                              the pain of ruined kingdoms—
隔江猶唱後庭花   across the river still she sings
                              "Flowers in the Rear Courtyard."

The Qinhuai was a river that flowed through Jinling, the old capital of the Southern Dynasties. We do not know during which of his trips through the area he wrote this poem. "Flowers in the Rear Courtyard" was composed by the Last Ruler of Chen, a sensual song about pleasure. When the moralists among his courtiers heard it, they recognized the "tones of a ruined kingdom" 亡國之音 and knew that the dynasty could not long endure. The speaker in Du Mu's poem plays on his depth of historical understanding, one not shared by the singer. To her it is merely a sensual song celebrating pleasure; to the poet listening across the river it is the memory of a dynasty's ruin—and perhaps a bad sign to have it sung in the present.

The situation here is exactly the same as hearing Sui Yangdi's "River Melody" sung in Yangzhou. In "Yangzhou" the listener is well aware of the historical depth behind this song of pleasure (especially if Du Mu himself added the early note identifying Sui Yangdi as the author). In "Yangzhou," however, there is no moral condemnation; the continuity of the song enhances the nostalgic aura of this city of pleasure.

The seamless continuity of past and present carries over into the second "Yangzhou" poem, which celebrates the sites and pleasures of the city and the quantities of wealth that flow through it. Oddly, that

---

25. 28243; Feng 273.

continuity is invoked in the last couplet, where the numerous inscribed pillars in the city seem to invite the return of the fabled Prince of Huainan, Liu An, as the immortal Ding Ling Wei had returned to his home. Here, however, it seems that the wealth and pleasures of the city would make it a true site of return and recurrence, as opposed to Ding Ling Wei's discovery of change and loss.

In the third poem the poet continues to evoke the pleasures of the city, alluding to Bao Zhao's "Poetic Exposition on the Weed-Covered City." In the Tang the place to which the "weed-covered city" referred was believed to have been Yangzhou. Its geographical position made it a center of commerce, and it grew mighty and overripe, only "in the end to be split like a melon and snapped like a bean" 竟瓜剖而豆分. Perhaps there is an ominous note, then, when Du Mu describes the city as "rudder and axle" of transported wealth. The last couplet is easy to read, but its interpretation is far from clear:

自是荒淫罪	Of course, with his crimes of debauchery
何妨作帝京	nothing stopped him from making it the capital.

The first line clearly refers to Sui Yangdi's excesses and probably suggests that they were due to the person and not the place. The last line may suggest that this was an appropriate capital for such an emperor.

In a pair of poems written at the end of his stay in Yangzhou, ostensibly about parting from a courtesan, we find the characteristic Du Mu *fengliu* persona.

杜牧, 贈別

Du Mu, Presented at Parting[26]

I

娉娉裊裊十三餘	Charming and lithe, just over thirteen,
豆蔻梢頭二月初	the tip of a cardamom branch in the beginning of the second month.
春風十里揚州路	Ten leagues of spring breeze on the roads of Yangzhou,
卷上珠簾總不如	they roll up beaded curtains, and no one is her match.

---

26. 28294–95; Feng 311.

II

多情卻似總無情	Too much feeling may seem instead like no feeling at all,
惟覺罇前笑不成	I realize only that as we drink the laughter will not come.
蠟燭有心還惜別	The wax candle has a heart and still feels bad that we part,
替人垂淚到天明	in place of the person it sheds tears until the day grows bright.

"Ten leagues of spring breeze" became a phase associated with the city ever thereafter. We will not pass judgment on the preference for girls just entering puberty since that was once common in China and much of the rest of the world. She is just over thirteen *sui* (having turned thirteen *sui* on New Year's Day), which means she is probably still twelve, for age is here linked to the spring season, now just entering the second month (which would have begun on March 3 in 835). That focus on the newly blossoming flower is then set within a larger context of "ten leagues" of the entertainment quarter, with curtains being rolled up, women's faces peering out, and the comparative judgment being made that she is the fairest of them all.

The comparative judgment that "you are the fairest of them all" was, as one might imagine, a staple of poems to singing girls; and while it has a universal dimension, it is difficult not to understand it in the context of the male culture of the *jinshi* examination and bureaucracy, with its passion for gradation and comparative judgment.

The psychology of the second poem, clearly on the stated topic of parting, is more interesting and is almost an allegory of metaphor in Chinese poetry. We should first point out that the wick of a candle was its "heart," and that drops of wax were conventionally figured as tears. Tang poets were not generally embarrassed to shed tears; but there was also an aesthetic of repression in which strong feelings spill out in a look or gesture. Here, however, we have a claim of negation: the strongest feeling appears as the absence of feeling. The evidence is in drinking, which should result in smiles and laughter (to purchase a courtesan was to "buy smiles"), but somehow it doesn't work now.

Feeling repressed or blocked returns in the world outside the feeling subject: the candle acts in place of the human beings, shedding tears for them. As an allegory of metaphor, the lesson is that figural expression could and often was understood as a sign of blocked expression (for various reasons, including political troubles). Metaphorical displacement can signal intensification. Yet another poetics is at work here, namely, the metonymic poetics of evidence: from the last line we know that the couple remains there until dawn, presumably the time when they must part.

We might compare Du Mu's explicitly psychological treatment of the inability to speak on parting with Wen Tingyun's more conventionally "poetic" though equally effective treatment of the same situation.[27]

| 別情無處説 | I have no way to speak the feelings at parting: |
| 方寸是星河 | the heart is as far as across the River of Stars. |

Wen Tingyun speaks subjectively about not being able to express his feelings. Du Mu's move is more interesting in that it generalizes the situation as a rule, displacing the immediate awkwardness of the moment on yet another level.

Du Mu clearly enjoyed the *fengliu* persona, but he was also seriously engaged in presenting himself in a very different role, namely, that of the concerned potential statesman. During his years in Yangzhou he was also busy writing political prose, spending much more time at it than at composing the verses we just read. It is ironic that we probably have such prose only because of the verses, which were the later source of Du Mu's fame and one reason for preserving his collected works when the works of so many others were lost.

In the spring of the fateful year of 835 Du Mu, aged thirty-three, was appointed investigating censor (*jiancha yushi* 8a) and left Yangzhou for the capital. Zheng Zhu, a courtier and physician with close ties to the imperial eunuchs, was in power and was generally despised by officialdom. The censor Li Gan 李甘, who was Du Mu's close friend, had openly opposed Zheng. In the seventh month he was banished to Fengzhou, in the far south, where he subsequently died. Perhaps worried about his association with Li Gan, Du Mu claimed he was unable to carry out the burdens of his office and asked to be reassigned. The court granted his request by transferring his post to Luoyang, which was an office without any duties. It turned out to have been a timely move. Either by direct implication in the plot or by casual association with the plotters, many Chang'an officials lost their lives in the bloody

27. 31949; Zeng 69.

purge that followed the Sweet Dew Incident in the eleventh month of that year.

In Luoyang Du Mu again encountered Zhang Haohao, the singer he had praised in Xuanzhou. She was working in a bar, perhaps as a result of having been cast aside by Shen Shushi. For her he wrote a long ballad, mentioned earlier, where he recalled her heyday in Hongzhou and Xuanzhou.

杜牧, 張好好詩
Du Mu, Zhang Haohao[28]

牧大和三年, 佐故吏部沈公江西幕. 好好年十三, 始以善歌來樂籍中. 後一歲,公移鎮宣城, 復置好好於宣城籍中. 後二歲, 爲沈著作述師以雙鬟納之. 後二歲, 於洛陽東城重覩好好, 感舊傷懷, 故題詩贈之.

In the third year of the Taihe Reign [829] I had a position in the Jiangxi headquarters of His Excellency Shen Chuanshi, formerly of the Ministry of Personnel. Haohao was thirteen years of age and had just been registered as a musician for her skill in singing. A year later His Excellency was transferred to the command of Xuancheng, and he also had Haohao listed in the Xuancheng registry. Two years thereafter, Shen Shushi, the editorial director, took her into his household as a "double haircoil" [a personal entertainer]. Two years thereafter I got to see Haohao again in the eastern part of Luoyang. Touched by the past, I felt pain, and thus I wrote this poem for her.

君爲豫章姝	You were a fair maid of Yuzhang,
十三纔有餘	just a little over thirteen.
翠茁鳳生尾	Azure sprouting, phoenix growing a tail;
丹葉蓮含跗	cinnabar leaves, lotus in bud.
高閣倚天半	The high tower rested halfway to Heaven,
章江聯碧虛	the Zhang River joined the sapphire sky.
此地試君唱	In this place they made trial of your singing,
特使華筵鋪	with a splendid feast spread just for you.
主公顧四座	Our host looked around at all the guests,
始訝來踟躕	then marveling how hesitantly you came out.
吳娃起引贊	A Wu damsel commenced the introduction,[29]
低徊映長裾	you held back, half-hidden in long gown folds.

---

28. 28040; Feng 53.

29. In his *Du Mu shixuan* (52) Zhou Xifu interprets this as a Wu maiden introducing Zhang Haohao, which I follow here. Zhu Bilian (39) takes the Wu maiden as Zhang Haohao herself.

雙鬟可高下	Your paired coils just the right height,[30]
繞過青羅襦	barely hanging over the blue gauze jacket.
盼盼乍垂袖	Glancing around, you first let sleeves drop,
一聲雛鳳呼	with a single note the phoenix chick cried out.
繁絃迸關紐	The flurried play of strings burst their ties;
塞管裂圓蘆	the frontier pipes split their round reeds.
眾音不能逐	The many notes could not keep up with you
裊裊穿雲衢	whose sinuous melody pierced clouds' avenues.
主公再三歎	Our host sighed repeatedly
謂言天下殊	declaring you unique in all the world.
贈之天馬錦	He gave you brocade picturing heavenly horses,
副以水犀梳	supplementing it with a walrus tusk comb.
龍沙看秋浪	At Longsha you watched the autumn waves,[31]
明月遊東湖	and in bright moonlight roamed on East Lake.
自此每相見	From this time whenever he saw you,
三日已為疏	just three days seemed like a long separation.
玉質隨月滿	Jade flesh grew fuller with passing months,
艷態逐春舒	your voluptuous figure filled out with the spring.
絳唇漸輕巧	Vermilion lips grew ever more agile and artful,
雲步轉虛徐	cloudlike steps took on ever more dignified grace.
旌旆忽東下	When his pennons and banners went east,[32]
笙歌隨舳艫	your reed-organ songs went with his boats.
霜凋謝樓樹	Frosts scarred the trees of Xie Tiao's Mansion;
沙暖句溪蒲	the sands were warm by Ju Creek's reeds.
身外任塵土	You consigned all beyond you to mere dust,
樽前極歡娛	in drinking you reached pleasure's heights.[33]
飄然集仙客	A visitor, swept along from the Jixian Galleries,[34]
諷賦欺相如	recited fu that put Sima Xiangru to shame.
聘之碧瑤佩	For an engagement gift he gave sapphire pendants,
載以紫雲車	he carried you off in a coach of lavender cloud.
洞閉水聲遠	The grotto was closed, sounds of waters far,

---

30. I follow Zhou Xifu here in his interpretation of *ke gaoxia* 可高下; Zhu Bilian takes this as her kneeling and rising.

31. At Hongzhou.

32. That is, to Xuanzhou.

33. It is unclear whether the subject is Shen Chuanshi or Zhang Haohao.

34. According to Du Mu's note, Shen Shushi, Haohao's subsequent patron, had been a sub-editor, *jiaoli* 校理, in the Jixian Galleries. *Jixian dian* 集仙殿 was an earlier name for the 集賢殿.

月高蟾影孤	the moon was high, its Toad-light, lonely.[35]
爾來未幾歲	Not many years have passed since then,
散盡高陽徒	but Gaoyang companions have all scattered.[36]
洛城重相見	Here in Luoyang I meet you once again,
婷婷爲當壚	as, graceful, you stand at the bar.[37]
怪我苦何事	You marvel at what has caused me such grief
少年垂白鬚	that in youth my beard hangs white.
朋遊今在否	"Are your companions surviving or not?
落拓更能無	can you still be as unrestrained as you were?"[38]
門館慟哭後	After we wept in grief at the lodge's gate,[39]
水雲秋景初	waters and clouds showed autumn's onset.
斜日掛衰柳	The sinking sun hangs in dying willows,
涼風生座隅	and chill winds rise at the edge of my seat.
灑盡滿襟淚	I have shed all the tears that soak my lapels
短歌聊一書	and now write this short song.

The poem leaves certain important things unsaid: we do not know if she was happy to have been taken as a concubine by Shen Shushi, nor do we know what happened between them that led to her ending up as a private entertainer-courtesan in Luoyang. Of course, such things did not need to be mentioned since they would have been known to both Du Mu and Zhang Haohao. This, in turn, reminds us of the degree to which such a poem was indeed "for" Zhang Haohao and not for

---

35. Zhu Bilian 41 interprets this as Zhang Haohao entering an immortal realm, like Liu Chen and Ruan Zhao spending time in the grotto with the goddesses or like Chang E fleeing to the moon. First, we may note that in its ninth-century version, the grotto being "closed" more strongly suggests the attempt of Liu and Ruan to return to the world of the immortals (see pp. 328–29). If the second line is indeed associated with Chang E, she was a figure of lonely solitude, having stolen the elixir of immortality and left her mate. If the line is an allusion to Li He (see p. 179), then it may suggest that she was being taken away from her old master (Shen Chuanshi) by a new one (Shen Shushi).

36. Originally an allusion to Li Yiji 酈食其 and his drinking companions, who included Liu Bang; by the Tang this simply referred to frequent companions at parties.

37. This alludes to Zhuo Wenjun tending bar after having eloped with Sima Xiangru. The implications are unclear, but it may suggest that Haohao has been dismissed from Shen Shushi's household to fend for herself, becoming a public courtesan.

38. This can be taken either as Zhang Haohao's question to Du Mu or as Du Mu's question to Zhang Haohao. The use of *pengyou* 朋遊 suggests the former. *Luotuo* 落拓 can mean either "unrestrained," as translated, or "down and out."

39. The reference is to Du Mu's sense of loss at the death of Shen Chuanshi.

posterity. Instead, the poem concentrates on Zhang Haohao's time with Shen Chuanshi, the elder brother, and on their present grief at his passing.

The pathos of the woman whose first bloom is past, articulated against reminiscences of earlier favor enjoyed, strongly recalls Bai Juyi's famous "Song of the Pipa" 琵琶引 of 816, composed just twenty years earlier.[40] Both formally and rhetorically "Zhang Haohao" is a more "literary" treatment of the theme—though it lacks the complexity of "Song of the Pipa" in weaving the narrative of the woman's youth with an expressive performance on the pipa. Bai Juiyi chose the long line, with rhyming couplets and four-line stanzas. This was the favorite form of long popular song, and "Song of the Pipa" indeed seems to have quickly spread to popular performance venues. Du Mu instead chose a more "literary" medium, namely, the short line with a single rhyme throughout.

The woman of "Song of the Pipa" was not only nameless, but her story was generic—which no doubt enhanced its popularity.

自言本是京城女	She said that she was originally a girl of the capital,
家在蝦蟆陵下住	her home was located at the foot of Frog Mound.
十三學得琵琶成	At thirteen she fully mastered the pipa,
名屬教坊第一部	and her name was listed in the first troupe of the Music Academy.
曲罷曾教善才伏	When a tune was finished, she used to make even the maestro bow down,
妝成每被秋娘妒	her makeup done, she always felt the jealousy of Miss Qiu.
五陵年少爭纏頭	The young men of Five Barrows competed to offer turbans as reward,
一曲紅綃不知數	for a single tune came red silks, more than she could count.
鈿頭雲篦擊節碎	Inlaid pins and mica combs smashed as she strummed the rhythm,
血色羅裙翻酒污	her gossamer skirt the color of blood was stained with overturned ale.

---

40. 22341; Zhu 685.

今年歡笑復明年	The pleasure and laughter of this year, and then of the following year,
秋月春風等閑度	autumn moonlight and spring breeze she passed through without a care.

From a later perspective it is hard not to prefer Bai's "Song of the Pipa," even in this short extract: the energy of the language perfectly evokes her heedless absorption in music and pleasure, getting and spending without counting either gain or loss. We are prepared for the lines that follow the extract, in which, as she matures, her admirers disappear. The heroine of "Song of the Pipa" was indeed a courtesan whose success was measured by the number of clients who admired her—and paid for her services. It is hard not to see her as the double of the poet Bai Juyi (the poem makes that analogy on other grounds): Bai and his friend Yuan Zhen celebrated the widespread popularity of the former's poetry. Such indiscriminate, general popularity later became a charge leveled against Bai's poetry by his detractors.

In this context it becomes easier to comprehend Du Mu's transformation of such a figure in Zhang Haohao. This singer is named and known. She is loved and appreciated by one or two men rather than by all who desire her. Her "success" is measured in terms of depth of feeling, both her own and that of those who admired her, particularly Shen Chuanshi. Loss is viewed not as the passing of her youthful charms but rather as the death of the patron who first admired her. "Elevation" in poetic form and register corresponds to these "higher" values. Although she may now be working in a Luoyang bar, Zhang Haohao is the figure of the loving and beloved concubine rather than the courtesan.

Of less certain date is Du Mu's other famous ballad on "woman's sad fate," "Du Qiuniang" 杜秋娘詩. Miao Yue dates this to 833, the time of his move to Yangzhou, while Fu Xuancong prefers 837. As in the case of the poem to Zhang Haohao, Bai Juyi's "Ballad of the Pipa" lies in the background, though again Du Mu chooses the less popular short line rather than the long line. Compared to "Zhang Haohao," this ballad uses more allusions and a higher register of diction to distance itself even further from the aura of popular poetry. Judging from references to the poem both by Zhang Hu and Li Shangyin, it seems to have been an important part of Du Mu's contemporary fame—though it is far less often commented on by later critics than many of Du Mu's other poems.

While similar themes were not unknown earlier, the discovery of women who had experienced hard times and had fallen in status and celebrity became very popular following the success of Bai Juyi's ballad. Significantly, Du Mu's poem recounted a touching woman's story that intersected with political history. Du Qiuniang had been the concubine of the rebel Li Qi; when Li Qi fell, she was sent into Xianzong's harem and later became a favorite. Under Xianzong's successor she became the governess for one of Muzong's sons, the Prince of Zhang. When the prince was slandered and demoted, she was sent home. She tells her story to Du Mu, who relates it in verse replete with femmes fatales and virtuous women. Just as Bai Juyi saw his own fate in the aging singing girl of "Ballad of the Pipa," so Du Mu sees the fate of scholars in Du Qiu:

女子固不定	Women indeed have no stable fates;
士林亦難期	for scholars too it is hard to predict.

He then launches into a long list of examples of fate's reversals for scholars, at which point we realize that he is not nearly as interested in Du Qiuniang as in the fate of Confucian officials.

In 836, during Du Mu's stay in Luoyang, a much-admired friend named Li Kan 李戡 had died. About a year later Du Mu composed his tomb inscription, which contains a surprising attack on the poetry of Yuan Zhen and Bai Juyi as representing the evils of Yuanhe poetry. The attack is couched in the words of Li Kan, in conjunction with his (now-lost) anthology of Tang poetry. The tomb inscription reads as follows:

Poetry can be set to song, can circulate in bamboo pipes, and can be strummed on silken strings. Women and children all want to recite it. Whether the mores of the dynasty are sound or frivolous, their quality is fanned by poetry, like the swiftness of the wind. It has bothered me that ever since the Yuanhe Reign we have had poems by Bai Juyi and Yuan Zhen whose sensual delicacy has defied the norms. Excepting gentlemen of mature strength and classical decorum, many have been ruined by them. They have circulated among the common people and been inscribed on walls; mothers and fathers teach them to sons and daughters orally; through winter's cold and summer's heat their lascivious phrases and overly familiar words have entered people's flesh and bone and cannot be gotten out. I have no position and cannot use the law to bring this under control.[41]

---

41. *Fanchuan wenji* 137. This passage is commonly viewed as expressing Du Mu's own position since he chose to cite it in the tomb inscription and therefore probably was in basic agreement with Li Kan's antipathy toward this poetry. In the course of the later tradition, Li Kan's judgment, taken as Du Mu's own, led to considerable criticism of

In a modern context Li Kan's acute distress will, of course, be read as moving testimony to the popularity of Bai Juyi's poetry. Here, however, we must exercise the same caution that we observe with Du Mu's image as a sensualist. Li Kan's image of the rampant popularity of such poetry is not simply confirmed in statements by Yuan Zhen and Bai Juyi themselves but may be a product of those same statements.

Beginning in the mid-830s, regulated verse in the long line was increasingly popular, especially in poems describing locales and ancient sites. Du Mu based a pair of Luoyang poems on the fact that the emperor no longer visited, which was a popular Luoyang theme. He also composed a meditation on the past treating the ruins of the old city.

杜牧, 故洛陽城有感

Du Mu, Thoughts Stirred on Old Luoyang[42]

一片宮牆當道危	A stretch of palace wall stands looming on the road,
行人爲爾去遲遲	because of you the traveler goes off slowly.
畢圭苑裏秋風後	In Bigui Park[43] after the autumn wind,
平樂館前斜日時	in front of Pingle Lodge at the moment of setting sun.

Du Mu because of the sensuality of much of his own poetry. See Zha Pingqiu 查屏球, *Tangxue yu Tangshi: Zhong Wan Tang shifeng de yizhong wenhua kaocha* 唐學與唐詩: 中晚唐詩風的一種文化考察 (Beijing: Shangwu yinshuguan, 2000), 278–79. For the scholarly debate over how much this passage represents Du Mu's own viewpoint, see Du Xiaoqin 613–15. It is reasonable to ask what sorts of poetry Li Kan had in mind within Bai Juyi's and Yuan Zhen's diverse output. In "Defining Experience: The 'Poems of Seductive Allure' (*yanshi*) of the Mid-Tang Poet Yuan Zhen (779-831)" (*Journal of the American Oriental Society* 122, no. 1 [Jan.–March 2002], 61–78), Anna Shields points to Yuan Zhen's erotic poetry. I think the target was the long ballads like "Song of the Pipa," which might be described as having "sensual delicacy" 纖豔 yet remained straightforward enough for oral performance and transmission. Li Kan is clearly not referring to the rambling personal poetry of Bai Juyi's old age, which we have discussed earlier (see Chapter 2). It is, however, often useful in the Tang to think of negation as a unifying factor. As different as they were from one another, the famous ballads, the "New *Yuefu*," the carefully crafted but straightforward old-style poems of the Yuanhe, and the willfully rambling poems of Bai's old age were still versions of the "familiar and common" 習俗, defined against equally diverse versions of "elevated" poetic discourse.

42. 28136; Feng 191.

43. Bigui Park was an Eastern Han park.

錮黨豈能留漢鼎	The proscribed faction was not able to preserve the Han tripod;[44]
清談空解識胡兒	metaphysical chat made one merely able to recognize the barbarian.[45]
千燒萬戰坤靈死	A thousand fires, ten thousand battles, the very land died,
慘慘終年鳥雀悲	and mournfully all the year through the sparrows lament.

Du Mu begins with the ruin of what he believes was the Eastern Han palace wall, a reminder of the past that makes the traveler pause in thought. The second couplet is a characteristically Late Tang one, conjuring up two resonant names of Eastern Han sites of which nothing identifiable likely remained in the Tang. They are simply named, set in the dying sunlight and autumn wind, moments of ending. The third couplet offers judgment through allusion. From a time of ending we move back to critical moments in history, when an alternative decision might have made a difference. One such moment occurred before the fall of the Eastern Han, with the massive purge of officialdom that began in 169. Du Mu seems to suggest that had those men remained in office and not been proscribed, they might have been able to save the dynasty. The second moment occurred before the fall of the Western Jin, whose capital was also Luoyang. Here Du Mu suggests the impotence of the contemporary ethos of refined judgment: Although Wang Yan was able to recognize the signs of someone who could destroy the dynasty, he did nothing about it. The seventh line is characteristic of Du Mu at his best, describing a grand vision that makes the general case concrete: Luoyang was the site of many battles and sacked repeatedly, until the land itself (literally the "numen of Earth") died. All that remains is lament, displaced into the chirping sparrows, as the

---

44. The reference is to the association of famous scholars and academy students in the second century whose "faction" enraged the emperor. They were first apprehended and then permanently sent back to their native places. After this the Yellow Turban uprising began. Du Mu's point seems to be that in rusticating all these scholars the Eastern Han court deprived itself of necessary talents, which led to the fall of the dynasty.

45. The reference is to the Jin scholar Wang Yan 王衍, famous for "metaphysical chat," *qingtan*. Shi Le was on a trading venture in Luoyang, and when Wang Yan saw him, he thought him remarkable, commenting that his existence could be catastrophic for the empire. Indeed, Shi Le was a central figure in the fall of the Jin.

sorrow of parting had earlier been displaced into the waxen tears of the candle.

Here we might contrast the following poem by Xu Hun—one of Du Mu's contemporaries and, later, his friend—on the same topic:

許渾, 登故洛陽城

Xu Hun, Climbing the Old Walls of Luoyang[46]

禾黍離離半野蒿	The millet grows lush, half with wild artemisia,
昔人城此豈知勞	they made walls here in olden days, can we realize the effort?[47]
水聲東去市朝變	The sound of the waters goes off east, court and market changed,
山勢北來宮殿高	the mountains' force comes north, palace halls stand tall.
鴉噪暮雲歸古堞	Crows caw among twilight clouds, returning to ancient battlements,
雁迷寒雨下空壕	in the cold rains wild geese lose their way and come down in the empty moats.
可憐緱嶺登仙子	I love the one who became an immortal[48] on Mount Hou's crest,
猶自吹笙醉碧桃	still playing the reed organ himself, getting drunk on sapphire peach brew.

Although this is not Xu Hun at his best, the comparison shows both his strengths and weaknesses. Du Mu's poem presents an overarching vision that gives it structure: beginning with the ruins that tease thought, it moves on to poetically empty scenes of sites that were part of ancient Luoyang's former glory, then on to the moments of decision that led to the city's destruction, and finally to the vision of repeated burnings and battles that decimated a city, which never entirely recovered. Xu Hun's poem moves aimlessly from image to image, at last coming somewhat incongruously to the figure of the immortal Qiao, the prince who rose above it all. Nevertheless, the third couplet evokes the beauty of ruins in a way that is different from anything in Du Mu's poem. Like the fine couplets of the craftsmen of regulated verse in the short line, with

46. 28818; Luo 155; Jiang Congping 35.
47. Or: "they were never rewarded."
48. Wangzi Qiao.

which it shares affinities, it is a kind of beauty that is easily reproduced—and was.

Du Mu's younger brother Du Yi 杜顗 passed the *jinshi* examination in
832. Like Du Mu himself, Du Yi's youthful writings were greatly praised.
When Du Mu was still in Yangzhou, Du Yi had gone off to serve in the
entourage of Li Deyu, the military commissioner of nearby Runzhou
(now Zhenjiang). When Li Deyu was transferred, Du Yi went to Yangzhou, resisting Niu Sengru's invitation to serve out of loyalty to his
former patron. Du Yi suffered from a disease that affected his eyes, and
by 837 he was blind. In response to this family crisis, Du Mu left his
Luoyang post and traveled to Chang'an to ask a famous doctor to treat
his brother. When the pair reached Yangzhou, the doctor concluded
that it was not the eyes themselves but something in the brain. (We
suspect it was a tumor.)

The two brothers were staying in Chanzhi Temple, and it was presumably then that Du Mu wrote one of his most famous poems. The
distance between Chanzhi Temple—on West-of-Bamboo Road to the
northeast of the city—and the lively entertainment quarter seems to
embody the poet's present distance from the Yangzhou he had so enjoyed just a few years earlier.

杜牧, 題揚州禪智寺
Du Mu, On the Chanzhi Temple in Yangzhou[49]

雨過一蟬噪	A rain passes, a single cicada shrills,
飄蕭松桂秋	whistling, pines and cassia turn autumn.
青苔滿階砌	Green mosses fill the steps,
白鳥故遲留	white birds linger there on purpose.
暮靄生深樹	Twilight haze rises in the deep trees,
斜陽下小樓	the setting sun sinks past a small building.
誰知竹西路	Who knows on West-of-Bamboo Road
歌吹是揚州	that Yangzhou is song and piping?[50]

---

49. 28142; Feng 198.

50. The last couplet of this famous poem admits of several interpretations. Here I
have followed a variation on the standard one. The pattern of the seventh line has parallels that suggest the following reading: "who knows of West-of-Bamboo Road [and
Chanzhi Temple]?—/ song and piping, that is Yangzhou," that is, those enjoying the
pleasures of the city know nothing of this quiet temple outside the city.

Du Mu here abruptly begins with a shrill sound intruding into or re-placing the steadier sound of the rain. Although Du Mu's poem is not entirely a regulated verse, it plays at becoming regulated. Although such an opening was not the kind of controlled exposition preferred by the craftsmen of regulated verse, it recalls the opening couplets of some famous eighth-century poems. One is Wang Wei's "Watching the Hunt," cited earlier:[51]

| 風勁角弓鳴 | The wind is strong, the horn-bow sings, |
| 將軍獵渭城 | the general is hunting east of Wei City. |

Another is Li Bai's "Going to See the Daoist Master on Daitian Mountain and Not Finding Him In" 訪戴天山道士不遇:[52]

| 犬吠水聲中 | A dog barks amid the sound of waters, |
| 桃花帶雨濃 | peach blossoms dark, bearing rain. |

The shrill cry of the cicada fades into the sound of the wind blowing through the trees.

Just as the first couplet involves the intrusion of a single sound into an aural ground of continuous sound, so the second couplet sets up a visual ground of green moss with small figures (or figure—perhaps only one white bird) on that ground. This is recognizably a "close" scene, setting up a shift in attention to a relatively "far" scene in the third couplet, one of rising mist and impending darkness. This third couplet effectively closes off the area of the temple, inviting an imaginative shift to the sensual world of Yangzhou beyond that space, a world of noisy sounds that is the very antithesis of the temple's stillness, which draws attention. This final evocation of Yangzhou is, in effect, a "scene of absence," which we have encountered so often in meditations on the past: a poem that begins with sounds ends with distant sounds unheard. Far more than in the earlier Yangzhou poems, a sense of contemplative, often melancholy distance begins to characterize many of Du Mu's poems.

At this point Du Mu's patron was transferred from his Yangzhou command to Luoyang and was replaced by none other than Li Deyu. Du Yi, Du Mu's brother, had earlier served under Li Deyu; but being

---

51. See p. 103.
52. 08680; Qu (1980) 1355.

blind now, there was little he could do. Du Mu was closely identified with Niu Sengru. Armed with a letter and a set of his poems, Du Mu instead sought employment with Cui Dan, the new surveillance commissioner stationed in Xuanzhou, taking his brother to Xuanzhou in late autumn 837.

杜牧, 將赴宣州留題揚州禪智寺

Du Mu, About to Set Off for Xuanzhou, I Leave This
Written on the Chanzhi Temple in Yangzhou[53]

故里溪頭松柏雙	By the creek in my home village a pair of cypress and pine,
來時盡日倚松窗	when I left I spent the whole day leaning at the pine window.
杜陵隋苑已絕國	Duling and the Sui Park[54] are already lands lost to me,
秋晚南遊更渡江	as autumn wanes, I travel south and once more cross the River.

As a young man Du Mu seems to have eagerly set off for the southeast. By this point, however, he was beginning to weary of it.

Some of Du Mu's finest and most famous poems can be dated to this second period in Xuanzhou. The following is a good example:

杜牧, 題宣州開元寺

Du Mu, On the Kaiyuan Temple at Xuanzhou[55]

南朝謝朓樓	Xie Tiao's Tower of the Southern Dynasties,
東吳最深處	the very deepest spot in eastern Wu.
亡國去如鴻	A fallen dynasty, gone off like a swan,
遺寺藏煙塢	the temple left, hidden in a misty vale.
樓飛九十尺	Its tower soars up ninety feet,
廊環四百柱	a porch rings it with four hundred columns.
高高下下中	Between high heights and lowest depths
風繞松桂樹	the breeze winds around pine and cassia.
青苔照朱閣	Green mosses shine by red pavilions,
白鳥兩相語	white birds talk to each other in pairs.

---

53. 28146; Feng 201.

54. Duling was the home region of the Du family, south of Chang'an. The "Sui Park" may refer to Yangzhou, which was Sui Yangdi's capital of Jiangdu.

55. 28058; *Fanchuan shiji zhu* 100. The dating here is based on another poem on the Kaiyuan Temple than can be securely dated to 838.

溪聲入僧夢	The creek's sound enters the dreams of monks,
月色暉粉堵	the moon's color glows on plaster walls.
閱景無旦夕	I view the scenes, whether dawn or evening,
憑欄有今古	leaning on a railing, past and present are here.
留我酒一樽	A cup of ale to make me linger,
前山看春雨	watching spring rain in the mountains ahead.

Although this poem shares elements with the "meditation on the past," it goes far beyond the genre. In addition to being Xie Tiao's "tower," it had also been the site of one of Li Bai's most famous poems, "In Xie Tiao's Tower in Xuanzhou, Holding a Parting Feast for the Collator Shuyun" 宣州謝朓樓餞別校書叔雲, which begins:[56]

棄我去者昨日之日不可留,	The sun of yesterday that left me behind cannot be stayed,
亂我心者今日之日多煩愁	today's sun, throwing my heart into turmoil, brings many cares.
長風萬里送秋雁	A steady wind for thousands of miles sends along autumn's geese,
對此可以酣高樓	facing this scene we may get the entire tower tipsy.

The contemplative tone of Du Mu's poem could not offer a stronger contrast with Li Bai's railing against time's passage and the raucous party in order to seize the moment. The old dynasty departs like a migrating swan, leaving the temple hidden away. Its tower literally "soars up," but it does not fly away. The irony was that such idyllic permanence was an illusion: in less than a decade a new emperor would close virtually all the Buddhist temples.

杜牧, 宣州開元寺南樓
Du Mu, The Southern Tower of the
Kaiyuan Temple in Xuanzhou[57]

小樓纔受一床橫	The small tower can just barely take a single bed stretched across it,
終日看山酒滿傾	all day long I look at the mountains, I tip up full cups of ale.

---

56. 08454; Qu (1980) 1077.
57. 28320; Feng 359.

可惜和風夜來雨	Too bad about the balmy wind
	and last night's rain—
醉中虛度打窗聲	in drunkenness I missed
	its sounds striking the window.[58]

Again we encounter what is, in effect, another scene of absence. We begin to understand that such scenes of absence poetically create worlds that are lost, out of reach, or, in this case, slept through. We have seen how the craftsmen of regulated verse created scenes that were empirically improbable under the circumstances defined by the title or the rest of the poem. The poetic effect of the line was clearly more important than fidelity to experience. The scene of absence was another form of poetic representation that went beyond immediate experience. Only a small leap is required to shift from these two modes of poetic representation to creating scenes that could never happen in real-life experience, scenes that exist only in words.

杜牧, 獨酌
Du Mu, Drinking Alone[59]

長空碧杳杳	The long sky, sapphire, faint and far,
萬古一飛鳥	for all time a single bird in flight.
生前酒伴閑	It used to be my drinking companions were
	at ease,
愁醉閑多少	drinking in sorrow, how much ease is there?
煙深隋家寺	Mist lies deep around temples of the Sui,
殷葉暗相照	blood-red leaves darkly shine.
獨佩一壺游	I roam alone, a jug strung from my waist,
秋毫泰山小	by an autumn hair, Mount Tai is small.

What does "for all time a single bird in flight" actually mean? It may be an impression of timelessness based on seeing a single bird in the vastness of the sky, but there really doesn't have to be a real bird. This is a scene of poetry and not of the real world. It is a way of seeing, like the adjustment of perspective that renders (in Zhuangzi's terms) huge Mount Tai smaller than a filament drifting in the air. That change in perspective, which in Du Mu's world is realized in the work of poetry, transforms the melancholy of drinking alone into a joy.

---

58. Literally, "in drunkenness in vain I passed through the time of its sounds striking the window."

59. 28051; Feng 85.

Late in 838 Du Mu was appointed Rectifier of Omissions of the Left
(7b, under the Chancellery) and Senior Compiler in the History Office.
It is tempting to interpret this appointment in conjunction with Wen-
zong's abortive attempt in the eleventh month to establish Hanlin Aca-
demicians of Poetry. Coming from a distinguished background (Du
Mu's uncle had been married to Xianzong's daughter, the Qiyang prin-
cess) he probably possessed just the right combination of good breed-
ing and poetic talent to suit Wenzong. Right after New Year's (properly
January 19, 839) Du Mu set off for the capital, first settling his younger
brother with his cousin in Jiangzhou.

杜牧, 自宣城赴官上京

Du Mu, Going from Xuanzhou to the
Capital to Take up My Post[60]

蕭灑江湖十過秋	Free and easy on river and lakes ten times I've gone through autumn,
酒杯無日不遲留	not a day went by when a cup of ale did not make me tarry.
謝公城畔溪驚夢	Beside the city of Lord Xie the stream woke me from dream,
蘇小門前柳拂頭	before the gate of Little Su the willows stroked my head.
千里雲山何處好	A thousand leagues of cloudy mountains, what place there is best?—
幾人襟韻一生休	how many men have a temperament that make this enough for a lifetime?
塵冠掛卻知閑事	When this dusty cap is hung away, I will know idleness,
終把蹉跎訪舊游	in the end I will take my wasted chances and visit these former haunts.

It had indeed been ten years since Du Mu gave up his first post and set
off with Shen Chuanshi to Hongzhou. Apart from a brief period in
Chang'an and Luoyang, he had spent those years primarily in Xuan-
zhou and Yangzhou, in the lower Yangzi region. The obvious contrast
in his writing between his public and private personas embodies con-
trary desires, namely, to advance in his career and to enjoy himself.
Here he doubts the value of service, though he cannot resist its lure,

---

60. 28150; Feng 204.

and vows to return in order to satisfy his contrary side. In the parallel "ten years" poem, Du Mu's most famous, the wasted time is the time spent enjoying himself.

杜牧, 遣懷

Du Mu, Getting Things Off My Chest[61]

落魄江南載酒行	Down and out in the Southland I went carrying ale,
楚腰腸斷掌中輕	Chu's slim waists, heartbroken, light in my palm.[62]
十年一覺揚州夢	After ten years I woke at last from my Yangzhou dream,
贏得青樓薄倖名	all I got was a name for careless love in the blue mansions.

Since this poem is included in one of the supplements to Du Mu's collection (*waiji*), which contains numerous spurious attributions, we cannot entirely vouch for its authenticity. Yet the similarities to the opening couplet of the preceding poem are such that we are tempted to both credit it and date it roughly in this period.[63]

The image of Du Mu that endured was that of the pleasure seeker. "Name" or "fame," *ming*, was what one sought in official life; here Du Mu achieves "name," albeit the wrong kind of name and in the wrong quarters.

Du Mu's public career seemed to be back on track after returning to Chang'an. Through his post as Rectifier of Omissions, Du Mu petitioned to have Li Gan posthumously pardoned. In a long old-style poem in the short line entitled "Li Gan" 李甘詩, he tells the story of the rise to power of Li Xun and Zheng Zhu; how Li Gan courageously opposed Zheng Zhu's promotion to minister; how he was exiled and

---

61. 28354; Feng 369.

62. This alludes to the king of Chu's preference for women with slim waists, and to the Han favorite Zhao Feiyan, who was so light that she could dance on the palm. I have retained the ambiguity as to whose heart is broken; most commentators interpret this as the beautiful women breaking the hearts of those who love them, including Du Mu. The actual phrasing of the line leaves the question open, including the possibility that the women are heartbroken because of someone, like Du Mu, who is fickle, a man of "careless love."

63. The poem is included in *Caidiao ji*.

died; and how he intervened to restore Li Gan's good name.[64] The poem does not make exciting reading, but the opening, on Li and Zheng's rise to power, gives one a taste of what follows.

太和八九年	In the eighth and ninth years of the Taihe
訓注極虓虎	Li Xun and Zheng Zhu tiger-howled their loudest.[65]
潛身九地底	From below the earth's lowest levels
轉上青天去	they turned up and rose to the blue heavens.[66]
四海鏡清澄	Encircling seas were a clear, pure mirror,
千官雲片縷	the thousand officers, cloud puffs and threads.
公私各閑暇	Each, in public and private life, was at leisure,
追游日相伍	daily going in bands for excursions.
豈知禍亂根	Who realized that the roots of catastrophe
枝葉潛滋莽	were nurturing hidden leaves and branches?
九年夏四月	In the ninth year, the fourth month, in summer,
天誡若言語	Heaven gave warning as if in words:
烈風駕地震	Fierce winds mounted on earthquakes,
獰雷驅猛雨	brutal thunderclaps drove vicious rain.
夜於正殿階	At night by the stairs of the main palace hall
拔去千年樹	a thousand-year-old tree was torn up.
吾君不省覺	Our lord did not draw the right conclusions,
二凶日威武	these two monsters behaved ever more overbearingly.
操持北斗柄	They grabbed the Northern Dipper's handle
開閉天門路	opened the road to Heaven's gate at will.[67]
森森明庭士	The dense ranks of officers in the bright court,
縮縮循牆鼠	scurried into hiding, mice along a wall.

To open a poem with a date meant that politically serious matters were to follow. Du Fu had begun his "Journey North" and Lu Tong 盧仝, his political allegory "Lunar Eclipse" 月蝕詩 with dates. This was poetry in a very different key from the melancholy *fengliu* image.

In 840, probably after Wenzong's death, Du Mu was promoted a step up to Vice Director of the Catering Bureau (6b), which saw to the

---

64. 28042; Feng 64.

65. Both were the chief architects of the Sweet Dew Incident.

66. Although Li Xun had come from a good background, he had risen from his humble position thanks to the friendship of the eunuch Wang Shoucheng. Zheng Zhu had been a doctor, an occupation despised by the elite.

67. That is, they exercised the power of a minister, controlling access to the throne.

provisions of the palace. Then, in 841, he was transferred to the position of Vice Director of the Board of Review. In late autumn 840, however, Li Deyu had left his Yangzhou command and returned to the capital as minister. In the spring of 842, aged forty, Du Mu was made governor of Huangzhou, also known as Qi'an Commandery (in modern Hubei). Although this was a substantial promotion in the official hierarchy (4a at the lowest level), provincial posts were generally less desirable than a capital post, and some prefectures were more desirable than others. Huangzhou, a small, poor, rural prefecture located on the northern shore of the Yangzi, was not a desirable post, though it was far better than being appointed to the far-flung southern prefectures, which was a form of exile. Huangzhou would become famous again in the Northern Song as the place where Su Shi was exiled—though in a far less exalted office than governor.

Du Mu was clearly dissatisfied with this appointment and seems to have attributed it to the malice of Li Deyu. Although some officials led charmed lives, rising steadily up the ladder of capital posts, it does seem that a term of service as prefectural governor was part of a normal career. It would eventually prove to be the case for Du Mu as well—had he lived longer, he might have risen higher—but for the next six and a half years he was to govern three poor, rural prefectures. For the real needs of the empire, a decent prefectural governor was far more important than most of the prestigious posts in the capital. When Du Mu was at last brought back to the capital in early 849, it was at his earlier level as vice director of a bureau.

In 842 Du Mu was old enough to feel as if his career was a failure and young enough to resent the fact. A number of long poems— "Drinking Alone in the Prefectural Study" 郡齋獨酌 and "In the Snow: Writing What Is on My Mind" 雪中書懷—voice his dissatisfaction in different ways. In the former he knows he is getting older and describes his travels (ll. 1–8):[68]

前年鬢生雪	Last year snow appeared in my sideburns,
今年鬚帶霜	this year my whiskers are touched with frost.
時節序鱗次	Seasons follow in succession like fish scales,

---

68. 28039; Feng 46. For a discussion of this poem, see Michael Fishlen, "Wine, Poetry and History: Du Mu's 'Pouring Alone in the Prefectural Residence.'" *T'oung Pao* 80, nos. 4–5 (1994): 260–97.

古今同雁行	past and present, the same as lines of geese.
甘英窮西海	Gan Ying went all the way to the Western Sea,
四萬到洛陽	forty thousand leagues to reach Luoyang.[69]
東南我所見	The southeast is somewhere I have seen,
北可計幽荒	in the north I can count the wilds of You.

He thinks of the Han explorer Gan Ying and measures his own travels against his: he has indeed seen the "southeast." We have no evidence of his having been in You, in northeast China, so we must take his word for it.

His self-image as someone who is *fengliu* emerges in a passage on the more punctilious officials (ll. 17–20):

促束自繫縛	All harried, they fetter themselves,
儒衣寬且長	in Confucian robes, broad and long.
旗亭雪中過	They pass by a tavern in the snow,
敢問當壚娘	not daring to say hello to the girl at the bar.

Du Mu then turns to two characters he admires: Li Guangyan, one of the great loyalist generals of the late eighth and early ninth centuries, and a village recluse, existing in an idyllic, rustic world, whom Du Mu had met thirteen years earlier. He ends with a flurry of criticism of his own failures while in office in the capital and expresses his desire to serve the empire, restore areas lost to central government control, and make the world prosperous. Finally, he returns to the present moment (ll. 101–8).

孤吟志在此	In my lone chanting are aims like these,
自亦笑荒唐	yet I laugh at my own nonsense.
江郡雨初霽	In this river district the rains are first clearing,
刀好截秋光	scissors could well cut a piece of autumn light.
池邊成獨酌	Beside the pond I pour for myself,
擁鼻菊枝香	the scent of chrysanthemums assails my nose.
醺酣更唱太平曲	Tipsy, I go on to sing a song of an age of peace,
仁聖天子壽無疆	may our kindly and sage Emperor have long life without bounds.

---

69. Gan Ying was a subordinate commander of the frontier general Ban Chao in the Eastern Han. He was dispatched to find the Western Ocean. After his explorations, he returned to the capital at Luoyang.

"In the Snow: Writing What Is On My Mind" is an even more troubled poem. Du Mu begins by praising the emperor and the current government and claiming he has plans that will solve the empire's problems—primarily a way to respond to the Uighur attacks of autumn 848. He concludes by throwing up his hands in despair and imagining what would happen if such plans were presented to the throne (ll. 21–32):[70]

臣實有長策	I truly have an excellent plan:
彼可徐鞭笞	one should chastise them slowly.
如蒙一召議	If I could be summoned to argue my case,
食肉寢其皮	you could eat their flesh and sleep in their pelt.
斯乃廟堂事	"This is indeed a great matter of state,
爾微非爾知	you are low, it is not something you understand."[71]
向來躡等語	In the past speaking beyond one's station
長作陷身機	was ever occasion of personal ruin.
行當臘欲破	Soon, however, the twelfth month will end,
酒齊不可遲	ale-brewing cannot be postponed.
且想春候暖	For the moment I fancy springtime's warmth
甕間傾一卮	and pour a goblet from the jug.

These long, discursive poems recall Du Fu and, especially, Han Yu. The latter's poetry was very much in the background of many of Du Mu's poems. "Ballad of the Heavy Rains" 大雨行 (28059), dating from his second stay in Xuanzhou, is Du Mu rewriting Han Yu. A long poem from Huangzhou giving advice to his nephew (28041) recalls Han Yu writing to his son. These are not the Du Mu poems usually read, but they remind us that for those poets who knew how to make use of it, Tang poetry offered a wide variety of models for treating different topics.

The implied premise of "In the Snow: Writing What Is On My Mind" is that if only court officials would listen to Du Mu's advice, the troubles besetting the empire could be resolved. The political strategist speculates on conclusions and consequences: he is aware of "crisis" in the technical sense, the moment when events can go either way either through conscious decision or chance. When reflecting on the past, such a mind would easily be disposed to counterfactuals, which are relatively rare in Chinese poetry. It was during this period that Du Mu wrote his most famous poem in the tradition based on a counterfactual.

---

70. 28047; Feng 79.

71. Du Mu here rephrases an image from *Zuo zhuan* (Xiang 21).

The two beautiful Qiao sisters were married to Sun Quan, the ruler of Wu, and Zhou Yu, Wu's general and admiral of the Wu river fleet. When Cao Cao planned to cross the Yangzi and invade Wu, Zhou Yu's counterattack with fire-ships depended on the east wind. The east wind did blow that day, resulting in the burning of Cao Cao's fleet. Had it not done so, Cao Cao might have successfully invaded Wu. If he had conquered Wu, he would have claimed the two Qiao sisters. Upon his death, they would then have been confined to Copperbird Terrace, like Cao Cao's other women.

杜牧, 赤壁
Du Mu, Red Cliff[72]

折戟沈沙鐵未銷	Snapped halberd sunk in the sands, the iron not yet rusted away,
自將磨洗認前朝	I take it, wash and polish it, and recognize that former dynasty.
東風不與周郎便	If the east wind had not worked to Zhou Yu's advantage,
銅雀春深鎖二喬	spring's depths around Copperbird Terrace, would have locked in the two Qiao sisters.

Although Du Mu is rarely forthright in revealing his debt to Li He, the latter always reappears in subtle ways in Du Mu's poetry. For example, finding in an ancient artifact the synecdoche of the past takes its inspiration from Li He's "Arrowhead from the Battlefield of Changping" 長平箭頭歌.[73] There the arrowhead evokes the famous battle of Changping, in which Qin destroyed Zhao. When we look at Li He's opening lines, we soon realize that Du Mu has borrowed only the theme and nothing of Li He's distinctive version of the Yuanhe style.

漆灰骨末丹水砂	Char of lacquer, powder of bone, pebble of cinnabar:
凄凄古血生銅花	in the chill gloom the ancient blood blooms flowers in the bronze.
白翎金簳雨中盡	The white feathers and gilt shaft have gone in the rains,
直餘三脊殘狼牙	and all that remains is this three-spined, broken wolf's fang.

---

72. 28239; Feng 271.
73. 20843; Ye (1959) 290.

Du Mu's relative directness and simplicity, however, lead to a no less strange turn of thought as the poet wonders what would have happened if the east wind had not blown that day.

In late autumn 844 Du Mu was transferred eastward to the equally poor prefecture of Chizhou (modern Anhui). The following autumn the poet Zhang Hu traveled from Danyang to visit him. Zhang Hu was about ten years older than Du Mu and had failed to be given an office despite several attempts to recommend him. At this stage in his life he was going from patron to patron, still hopeful of finding a benefactor. Even more than the regulated-verse craftsmen in whose style he sometimes wrote, Zhang Hu was, as we have seen, a quasi-professional poet, repaying with his poetry favors from officials and courtesans alike (and, according to anecdotal sources, poetically insulting courtesans who offended him). It is clear that his purpose in visiting Du Mu was nothing less than to seek his political support—as unlikely a patron as Du Mu might have been.

We don't know whether Zhang Hu or Du Mu first developed the *fengliu* style in regulated verse and quatrains in the long line. There was clearly an affinity between them, though Du Mu rarely shows the theatrical panache of Zhang Hu. This was, however, the aspect of Zhang's poetry that attracted Du Mu. We do not know when Zhang wrote his poem on Yangzhou (Guangling), but Du Mu clearly alludes to it in a poem addressed to Zhang, written in the autumn of 844. We would very much like to be able to date Zhang Hu's poem because the opening couplet is clearly related to Du Mu's poem of 839, cited earlier, as well as to the famous quatrain (see p. 287).

張祜, 到廣陵

Zhang Hu, Reaching Guangling[74]

一年江海恣狂遊	A whole year long on the river and lakes I roamed madly as I pleased,
夜宿倡家曉上樓	I spent my night in brothels, climbed towers in the dawn.
嗜酒幾曾群眾小	Craving drink I never consorted with little men;
爲文多是諷諸侯	in my writing I was usually making satires of great lords.

---

74. Yan Shoucheng 119.

逢人説劍三攘臂	I spoke of swordsmanship with whoever I met, often pulling up my sleeves,[75]
對鏡吟詩一掉頭	facing the mirror I chanted a poem, then turned my head away.
今日更來憔悴意	Today I come here once again, in a dreary mood:
不堪明風滿揚州	I cannot bear how moonlight and breeze are filling all Yangzhou.

To later readers this might seem more like Du Mu than Du Mu himself. It is self-advertising, very much the staged poetry of personality, combining the celebration of pleasure with a sentimental melancholy resulting from returning to the scenes of former pleasure. In the final couplet the poem asserts the melancholy distance from that earlier moment of self-abandon, invoking the standard poetic topic of "moonlight in Yangzhou." Like Du Mu's other poems that follow the same pattern, it derives from a common poetic theme, namely, "Recalling Past Travels," *Yi jiu you* 憶舊遊, in which the poet, either to himself or to a friend, celebrates the insouciant pleasures of the past and the present distance from those pleasures. This is *fengliu* 風流, celebrating the lover, the swordsman, the drinker, and the man of panache and strong sentiment, who is easily moved to tears and melancholy. The traditions of the long line welcome such a manner, which is the very antithesis of the control celebrated by craftsmen of regulated verse in the short line.

Writing to Zhang Hu, Du Mu expresses a similar extravagance of feeling on his part and closes by praising Zhang precisely for his poetic expressions of contempt for the lords of the empire.

杜牧, 登池州九峰樓寄張祜
Du Mu, Climbing Nine Peak Tower of Chizhou: to Zhang Hu[76]

百感衷來不自由	All sorts of stirrings come from within, out of my control,
角聲孤起夕陽樓	the sound of the horn rises alone from a tower in evening sun.
碧山終日思無盡	All the day long in sapphire hills, longing has no end,

---

75. This is a gesture of intense engagement.
76. 28152; Feng 206.

芳草何年恨即休	fragrant plants—when at last will this resentment cease?[77]
睫在眼前長不見	Eyelashes there before one's eyes, but one never sees them,[78]
道非身外更何求	the Way is not outside of one, so what more should one seek?
誰人得似張公子	Who can get to be just like Master Zhang?—
千首詩輕萬戶侯	his thousand poems despising lords of ten thousand households.[79]

Here is Zhang Hu's response:

張祜, 和池州杜員外題九峰樓
Zhang Hu, A Companion Piece to Vice Director Du of
Chizhou's Piece on Nine Peak Tower[80]

秋城高柳啼晚鴉	Autumn city, high walls crying with evening crows,
風簾半鉤清露華	windblown curtains half hooked up, sparkles of clear dew.
九峰叢翠宿危檻	The clustered azure of nine peaks spends the night at this sheer balcony,
一夜孤光懸冷沙	all night long a solitary light hangs on the cold sands.
出岸遠暉帆斷續	Coming forth from the bank in distant glow, sails ceasing then going on,
入溪寒影雁差斜	cold reflections enter the creek, geese flying roughly aslant.

---

77. Commentators generally associate this image with the following passage in "Longing For the Fair One" 思美人: "I regret that I will never reach the ancients, / with whom can I enjoy these fragrant plants?" 惜吾不及古人兮/吾誰與玩此芳草. This and the preceding line are clearly associated with Zhang Hu's isolation, but it may be forcing the issue to closely identify, as Zhou Xifu does, the 芳草 with Zhang Hu and his "failure to meet his time" 不遇時.

78. This image is derived from the following passage in the "Annals of Gou Jian, King of Yue" 越王勾踐世家 in the *Shiji*: 吾不貴其用智之如目, 見毫毛而不見其睫也: "I did not value his cleverness and usefulness, just as the eyes can see a fine hair but cannot see their own eyelashes." The application here is clearly the failure to appreciate Zhang's talents.

79. Though the image had been used previously by Li Bai, Du Mu is here specifically responding to Zhang Hu's line.

80. 27413; Yan Shoucheng 122; the title and text are the version in Yan Shoucheng.

杜陵春日歸應早	To spring days at Duling I'm sure you will soon return,
莫厭青山謝朓家	but weary not of Green Mountain and Xie Tiao's home.

Leaving aside the question of who influenced whom, this was indeed Zhang Hu writing at his best in Du Mu's company. However, even the considerable brilliance of his couplets cannot conceal the conventional template of the occasional poem, which concludes with the reassurance that his host, a provincial official, will soon be recalled to Chang'an.

In Zhang Hu Du Mu saw poetry not as a means for advancement but rather as a means to speak back to those in power. Even if Zhang Hu's poems were much admired in the palace, it did him no good.

杜牧, 酬張祜處士見寄長句四韻

Du Mu, Responding to the Piece of Four Couplets in the Long Line Sent to Me by Zhang Hu, Retired Gentleman[81]

七子論詩誰似公	Considering the poems of the Seven Masters,[82] who can compare with you?
曹劉須在指揮中	Cao Zhi and Liu Zhen are clearly under your command.
薦衡昔日知文舉	Recommending Heng, in olden days we know of Wenju;[83]
乞火無人作蒯通	in asking for fire there is no one to act as Kuai Tong.[84]

---

81. 28260; Feng 286. For Zhang Hu's occasioning poem, see Yan Shoucheng 138.

82. These are the Seven Masters of the Jian'an, one of whom was Liu Zhen.

83. A note in the original text here adds: "Minister Linghu [Chu] once sent in a memorial recommending the retired scholar" 令狐相公曾表薦處士. The comparison is to Kong Rong 孔融 (Wenju) recommending Mi Heng to Cao Cao.

84. The reference is to a story in the "Kuai Tong Biography" in the *Han shu*. Someone suggested that since he was on good terms with Minister Cao, Kuai Tong should recommend two worthy recluses of Qi. Kuai told a story about how, when the family lost some meat, the sister-in-law suspected the wife of stealing it and drove her out of the house. The wife was on good terms with the women of the village and requested their help. The women told her to be at ease. One went to the house asking for fire, saying that dogs had gotten some meat the night before and had killed each other fighting over it; they wanted fire to cook them. Then the wife was immediately called back home. Kuai Tong said he would use the "asking for fire" technique to recommend these recluses to Minister Cao. This seems to refer to Yuan Zhen's intervention to block Linghu Chu's recommendation of Zhang Hu and the failure to circumvent it.

北極樓臺長掛夢	Mansions and terraces of the Pole Star hang ever in your dreams,[85]
西江波浪遠吞空	as the waves of Westriver swallow the sky afar.
可憐故國三千里	Moving, that "Homeland three thousand leagues away,"
虛唱歌辭滿六宮	in vain they sing his lyrics throughout the six palaces.[86]

In early autumn of that same year Wuzong had issued the last of a series of edicts closing down all but a few of the Buddhist temples in the empire and laicizing large numbers of monks and nuns. Du Mu himself had no doubt been required to oversee the disestablishment of the temples in Chizhou. Although Du Mu the public official expressed support for the policy, the poet could not but be troubled by the destruction and social dislocation involved.

杜牧, 池州廢林泉寺
Du Mu, The Abandoned Linquan Temple at Chizhou[87]

廢寺碧溪上	An abandoned temple by the sapphire creek,
頹垣倚亂峰	its fallen walls rest on the tangled peak.
看棲歸樹鳥	I watch roosting birds returning to its trees,
猶想過山鐘	imagining its bell ringing still through the hills.

杜牧, 還俗老僧
Du Mu, On an Old Monk Laicized[88]

雪髮不長寸	His snowy hair has not grown an inch,
秋寒力更微	in autumn's chill his strength grows weaker.
獨尋一徑葉	Alone he goes down a path of leaves
猶挈衲殘衣	still holding the remains of his cassock.
日暮千峰裏	Sunset among a thousand peaks,
不知何處歸	and he does not know where he is going.

In spring of the following year Wuzong was dead and Xuānzong ascended to the throne. Li Deyu was soon out of power and was sent to the far reaches of the empire. In the transfers that generally followed

---

85. That is, the palace.

86. The reference is to one of Zhang Hu's most famous poems entitled "The Lady Meng's Sigh" 孟才人歎一首並序.

87. 28162; Yan Shoucheng 214.

88. 28202; Feng 242.

the enthronement of a new emperor, Du Mu was not recalled but rather sent farther south to yet another poor prefecture in Muzhou (modern Zhejiang). Because one of the three quatrains on the family estate at Red Slope can confidently be dated to Du Mu's term in Muzhou, scholars generally date the others to the same period. If some of Du Mu's poems give us scenes that exist only in poetry, in parts of the Red Slope poems we see that the constructions of memory and poetry disappear into one another. The three quatrains move from the ordinary to the strange.

杜牧, 朱坡絕句三首
Du Mu, Quatrains on Red Slope[89]

I

故國池塘倚御渠	The pools and ponds of my home lie close to the Royal Canal,
江城三詔換魚書	thrice summoned to River cities the "fish letters" changed.[90]
賈生辭賦恨流落	In poetic expositions Jia Yi resented his exile,
祗向長沙住歲餘	but it was only in Changsha he stayed more than a year.[91]

II

煙深苔巷唱樵兒	The mist is deep on the mossy lanes, the wood gatherers sing out,
花落寒輕倦客歸	flowers fall cold and light, the weary traveler returns
藤岸竹洲相掩映	Vine-covered shores, bamboo isles half hide one another,
滿池春雨鷺鶒飛	spring rains covering the pools, the cormorants fly.

---

89. 28115–117; Feng 168.

90. The reference is to his three positions as governor of a prefecture. "Fish letters" refer to his appointment letters.

91. Actually, Jia Yi was in Changsha for a longer time. A note in the original text paraphrases the *Han History*: "After more than a year Wendi thought of Jia Yi" 文帝歲餘思賈生, that is, Jia Yi was upset with one exile, while I am on my third provincial appointment.

III

乳肥春洞生鵝管	Stalactites fatten in spring grottoes producing goose quills,
沼避迴巖勢犬牙	pools avoid the winding cliff, form of dog's teeth.
自笑卷懷頭角縮	I laugh at myself all curled up, the horns on my head withdrawn,
歸盤煙磴恰如蝸	winding back home up misty steps just like a snail.

Like Jia Yi, Du Mu begins "in Changsha," thinking of his home—though this "home" belonged to his childhood. We do not know if Du You's Red Slope estate remained in the possession of the Du family (their urban mansion in Chang'an had been sold in 820). If so, we also do not know the degree to which the grown-up son of Du You's youngest son could still treat it as his "home." In the second quatrain the estate becomes an idyllic scene of poetry and memory to which the poet imagines himself returning. In the strange third quatrain it becomes a cave and a snail shell—though one jagged with stalactites and "dog's teeth" ridges—into which the poet, his own horns withdrawn, can retreat.

The long poem on Red Slope, although not one of Du Mu's better-known works, has a beauty and place in poetic history that deserves some attention. One can trace such densely descriptive poetry back to Du Fu, but perhaps the most significant source is "South of the City" 城南聯句, a linked verse between Han Yu and Meng Jiao composed in 806. From a formal standpoint, this was a new kind of linked verse for the two poets and, insofar as we know, new in the tradition. Rather than composing a couplet or a passage to which another poet would respond, here each poet took turns composing the first line of a couplet, which the other would cap. The element of challenge and response to challenge produced a remarkably dense style containing passages of great beauty.

The pressures of the new form were matched by an occasion that provided a theme that added depth to the form. Meng and Han wrote about an excursion in Chengnan ("South of the City"), a rich agricultural land with great estates (including Red Slope). This was the "Emperor's Domain," the heart of the empire, its sites filled with history. The thickness of the style paralleled the density of this magical place in harvest season. "South of the City" is the itinerant counterpart of Han Yu's highly structured "South Mountains" 南山詩 of the same year.

A few years later (the exact date is uncertain) Li He wrote his "Changgu" 昌谷詩 about the landscape of his own home near Luoyang.[92] Again we have a thick descriptive style that celebrates the mysterious fertility of his own home region. Meng Jiao and Han Yu alternated between scenes of harvest and lush, untended nature. After delving deeply into the natural landscape, in the middle of the poem Li He shifts to the agrarian scene, finally returning to nature on a more intimate scale.

Du Mu had already tried his hand at this style in "On the Pavilion for Enjoying the Waters at Chizhou" 題池州弄水亭.[93] There we find the same kind of dense description of nature, followed by the celebration of a happy agrarian community that recalls Li He's "Changgu." We see this most clearly when we compare Li He's agrarian community at Changgu with Du Mu's Chizhou: Here is Li He writing about Changgu:

珍壤割繡段	Treasured terrain, hacked patches of brocade,
里俗祖風義	village customs revere manners and the right.
鄰凶不相杵	Neighbor's affliction has no pestle pounding,[94]
疫病無邪祀	in times of plague, no dark witchery.
鮐皮識仁惠	Mottled-skinned elders meet with kindness and grace,
丱角知羞恥	while tufted children blush and know shame.
縣省司刑官	The county has reduced officers of punishment,
戶乏詬租吏	households lack clerks cursing them for taxes.

And here is Du Mu writing about Chizhou:

風俗知所尚	Local customs know what to respect:
豪強恥孤侮	the powerful are ashamed to betray and humiliate.
鄰喪不相舂	When a neighbor holds a funeral, they do not hull grain,
公租無詬負	when taxes are gathered, there is no reviling.

---

92. 20809; Ye (1959) 227.

93. 28057; Feng 97.

94. According to the *Classic of Rites,* mortars were not to be used when a neighbor died.

To some degree this is part of a normative idyllic agrarian community, but the parallels in phrasing and topic easily persuade us that Li He's poem is at the back of Du Mu's mind. At the end, however, Du Mu suddenly realized his alienation from this world in which natural beauty and social harmony were combined:

不能自勉去	I cannot force myself to go off,
但愧來何暮	I only feel shame that I have come so late.
故園漢上林	My home gardens are the Shanglin Park of Han;
信美非吾土	though truly beautiful, this is not my land.

However, Red Slope and the Chengnan region surrounding it *was* his land. After Chizhou, in Muzhou, Du Mu could recreate that lost world in poetry.

杜牧, 朱坡

Du Mu, Red Slope[95]

下杜鄉園古	Our home gardens at Xia Du are old,[96]
泉聲繞舍啼	a stream sings out around the house.
靜思長慘切	My calm thoughts are ever sharply saddened,
薄宦與乖睽	that paltry offices keep me apart from it.
北闕千門外	Beyond palace towers and the thousand gates,
南山午谷西	west of Wu Valley on South Mountain,
倚川紅葉嶺	resting by river a ridge of red leaves,
連寺綠楊堤	a bank of green willows, stretching to a temple.
迥野翹霜鶴	In far moors wings up a frosty crane,
激潭舞錦雞	by a pellucid pool dances a brocade pheasant.
濤驚堆萬岫	Billows stir up, heaping ten thousand clefts,
舸急轉千谿	the barge runs swiftly, turning a thousand creeks.
眉點萱芽嫩	Eyebrow spots, xuan sprouts tender,[97]
風條柳幄迷	windblown branches, willow tents make one lose one's way.
岸藤梢虺尾	Vines on shores, dangling adder tails,
沙渚印麖蹄	sandy isles printed with hooves of fawns.
火燎湘桃塢	Fires gleam in dales of Xiang peaches,
波光碧繡畦	waves shine in field-plots of sapphire embroidery.
日痕絪翠巘	Sunbeams string through azure crags,

---

95. 28105; Feng 156.

96. Xia Du was a town just southeast of Chang'an; this area, including Fanchuan, was the Dus' home.

97. The figure of "eyebrow spots" is uncertain.

陂影墮晴霓	reflection on slope, a clear-sky rainbow descends.
蝸壁斕斑蘚	Snail-walls, patterned with lichen,[98]
銀筵豆蔲泥	silver mats, cardamom mud.
洞雲生片段	Clouds from caves are borne in pieces,
苔徑繚高低	mossy paths wind high and low.
偃蹇松公老	Thrusting upward, the pine duke ages,[99]
森嚴竹陣齊	densely dark and stern, bamboo ranks even.
小蓮娃欲語	Small lotus, a maiden about to speak,
幽笋稺相攜	hidden bamboo sprouts, youths hand in hand.
漢館留餘趾	It retains the traces of a Han lodge,
周臺接故蹊	an old path reaches a Zhou platform.
蟠蛟岡隱隱	Coiling kraken, hills shadowed,[100]
斑雉草萋萋	mottled pheasant, plants grow thick and green.
樹老蘿紆組	Trees aged, vines twist in ribbons around,
巖深石啓閨	cliff deep-set, rocks open into chambers.
侵窗紫桂茂	Getting into windows, purple cassia luxuriant,
拂面翠禽棲	brushing the face, kingfishers roost.
有計冠終掛	I have plans at last to hang up my cap,
無才筆漫提	lacking talent, I rashly wield a brush.
自塵何太甚	I have dirtied myself all too much,
休笑觸藩羝	cease to mock the ram, horns caught in the hedge.[101]

The successful snail draws in his "horns," coiling back into its shell. Du Mu is the ram whose horns are caught in the hedge; he therefore cannot withdraw. The only effective withdrawal is into poetry, what the imaginary snail finds when it ascends those misty stairs into the safe, densely vegetative shell.

In autumn 848 Du Mu finally received word of his transfer back to the capital as Vice Director in the Bureau of Merit Titles and was awarded

---

98. Feng Jiwu notes here that in the south people write and draw with snail slime on walls of a room; the slime becomes silver-colored when it dries.

99. Feng Jiwu here cites an anecdote in the *Wu shu* 吳書, quoted in the commentary to the *Wu zhi*. Ding Gu 丁固 dreamed of a pine growing out of his belly. By dividing the character for "pine" into 十八公, "eighteen duke," the dream was interpreted to mean that he would become a duke in eighteen years.

100. The dragon is a creature of the rain, coiled up in its pool. When it flies off, it is accompanied by clouds. Hence the hills are shadowed.

101. This is a standard figure of entanglement in public life; the ram cannot "withdraw."

his old post in the History office. In late autumn he set out, arriving in Chang'an early in 849. Now Du Mu was a known poet, attracting the admiration of younger poets such as Li Shangyin.

李商隱, 杜司勳
Li Shangyin, Du [Mu] of the Bureau of Merit Titles[102]

高樓風雨感斯文	In the high tower wind and rain stir Literature:
短翼差池不及群	short wings fly irregularly not making it to the crowd.
刻意傷春復傷別	In crafting thoughts on the pain of spring as well as parting's pain,
人間惟有杜司勳	in this mortal world there is only Du of the Bureau of Merit Titles.

The implications of the first couplet have been much debated by critics as to whether these lines refer to Li, Du Mu, or both. We do, however, see that Du Mu's poetry is associated with "the pain of spring" and "parting's pain"; that is, with the lighter topics he treated.

Once settled in Chang'an, Du Mu began writing letters asking for a more lucrative provincial appointment, arguing that he had to support a number of dependents, including his brother. He asked to be assigned to Hangzhou, a plum prefecture, but his request was denied. In 850 he was transferred to the post of Vice Director of the Ministry of Personnel and wrote requesting that he be assigned the governorship of Huzhou, a larger prefecture than his earlier posts. This time his request was granted.

杜牧, 將赴吳興登樂遊原一絕
Du Mu, About to Set out for Wuxing,
I Went to Leyou Plain: A Quatrain[103]

清時有味是無能	These untroubled times have appeal, but I lack ability;
閒愛孤雲靜愛僧	idle, I love the solitary cloud; serene, I love monks.

---

102. 29168; *Jijie* 875; Ye (1985) 92; Zhou 172. For a discussion of some problems of interpretation here, see Stephen Owen, "Poetry and Its Historical Ground," in *Chinese Literature: Essays, Articles, Reviews* 12 (December 1990): 107–18.

103. 28131; Feng 185.

欲把一麾江海去	About to take a pennon in hand to go off to the river and lakes,[104]
樂游原上望昭陵	out upon Leyou Plain I gaze on Zhaoling.[105]

Although critics often interpret the poet's gaze on Taizong's tomb as a sign of his despair over the grim political situation of the dynasty, it could just as easily be viewed as reflecting satisfaction at the enduring Tang polity. A local Chinese rebellion against Tibetan domination of a number of border prefectures in the northwest had brought them back under nominal Chinese control—and the recovery of the northwestern prefectures had been one of Du Mu's long-cherished goals. After complaining endlessly about being a prefectural governor—Du Mu seemed incapable of staying in a capital post for long without resigning or asking for a transfer—he now clearly sees that the office has its attractions. He sets off with banners flying and relishing the quiet pleasures of such posts.

Most likely in early 851 Du Mu met the young poet Li Ying in Huzhou and invited him for a drink.

杜牧, 湖南正初招李郢秀才
Du Mu, On New Year's in Hu'nan
Summoning Licentiate Li Ying[106]

行樂及時時已晚	To enjoy oneself one must catch the moment, the moment is already late,
對酒當歌歌不成	facing the ale one should sing, but the song does not come.
千里暮山重疊翠	A thousand leagues of twilight hills, azure in layers and folds,
一溪寒水淺深清	a single creek of cold waters, clear in shallows and deeps.
高人以飲爲忙事	My noble friend takes drinking as a lot of trouble,
浮世除詩盡強名	in this world adrift apart from poems all names are forced on things.

---

104. That is, to become a provincial governor.
105. The tomb of Tang Taizong.
106. 28214; Feng 248.

看著白蘋牙欲吐　　　Just look at the white duckweed
　　　　　　　　　　whose shoots are about to emerge,
雪舟相訪勝閑行　　　to visit me in a boat in the snow
　　　　　　　　　　is better than walking in idleness.[107]

The poem begins straightforwardly enough, with the governor's persuasion to seize the moment. Presumably the song that fails to materialize while drinking is Du Mu's, who lacks a drinking companion. The second couplet describes the scene intended to lure Li Ying to come and is also a demonstration of the poet's art.

The third couplet is the focus of interest in the poem, combining the colloquial *mangshi* 忙事, "a lot of trouble," with an allusion to Laozi, in which the Way is nameless, but he will "force a name on it." Du Mu is making a grand statement about poetry reminiscent of his earlier comments on Li He's poetry, namely, that its qualities were more perfect than their counterparts in the empirical world. In effect, the only "natural," unforced language for the world is poetry. However, we do not know if this is indeed Du Mu's own claim, however playfully made, to persuade Li Ying to come drink or if it is the imputed attitude of Li Ying, who is so absorbed in writing poetry that he won't take the time to enjoy himself.

The closing allusion to Wang Huizhi is no less strange: Wang Huizhi thought of his friend Dai and set off at night in a boat in the snow. But when he reached Dai's gate he turned around and returned home, explaining: "I came on the mood of the moment; the mood is gone, and now I'm going back. Why do I have to see Dai?" This is a most peculiar way to invite a friend for a drink.

In autumn 851 Du Mu was recalled to a capital post as Director of the Bureau of Evaluation (5b) and Drafter. The unfortunate Du Yi died this same year, presumably lightening that part of Du Mu's financial obligations. Du Mu remained in Huzhou long enough to celebrate the harvest before returning to the capital. In 852 he was made Secretariat Drafter. That winter he fell ill and seems to have sensed that the end was near. He composed his own tomb inscription and selected those of his works he wished included in his collected works, the *Fanchuan wenji* 樊川文集. He passed away before the next lunar year, probably at the

---

107. The reference is to the story of Wang Huizhi in the Eastern Jin, who, thinking of his friend on a snowy night, set off in a boat to visit him.

end of 852. The present version of *Fanchuan wenji* was prepared by his nephew, Pei Yanhan 裴延翰.

Burning a substantial portion of one's works or some form of radical culling was common when preparing one's "collected works." Bai Juyi's collection is the unique consequence of a poet who kept almost everything. In the case of Du Mu, his poems were popular—particularly his quatrains—and many of the pieces excluded from *Fanchuan wenji* were later gathered and included as supplements to his collection in the Song. [108] Unfortunately, attributions frequently changed when poems were in general circulation, with the result that the supplementary collections are filled with poems attributed to other poets on better grounds than the attribution to Du Mu. This does not mean that poems without alternative attributions are necessarily by Du Mu—though many of them probably are. What the supplementary collections represent is a "Du Mu" of the Late Tang imagination, a figure who attracted works of a certain type—including many of his most famous quatrains.

Idyll

All Tang poets had their idyllic moments, but Du Mu, perhaps more than any other major poet, was a poet of idyll, a representation of the world as it ought to be.[109] Displaced into a lost past, idyll becomes elegy. We might here recall Du Mu's description of Li He's poetry:

A continuous stream of clouds and mist have not such a manner as his [lit. "are not adequate to make his manner"]; waters stretching off far into the distance have not such a mood as his; all spring's flowering glory has not his gentleness; autumn's bright purity has not his strictness of form; masts driven by the wind and horses in the battle-line have not his daring; tile sarcophagi and tripods with seal-script have not his antiquity; the season's flowers and fair women have not his sensuality; walls run to weeds and ruined palaces, and tomb mounds overgrown with brush, have not his resentment and mournfulness; the leviathan's gaping maw and the leaping sea turtle, the bull demon and the snake god, have not his sense of fantasy and illusion.

---

108. For a discussion of the two supplementary poetry collections, the *Fanchuan waiji* 樊川外集 and the *Fanchuan bieji* 樊川別集, see Wu Qiming 吳企明, *Tangyin zhiyi lu* 唐音質疑錄 (Shanghai: Shanghai guji chubanshe, 1985), 60–74.

109. Here I am using the definition presented in Schiller's *Naive and Sentimental Poetry*.

In a Chinese context this is a description of the idyllic, the poetic world whose qualities are more perfect than the "real" world. In many ways this description better suits Du Mu's mature poetry than Li He's. Du Mu claims a range of possible relations to his poetic idylls: sometimes he is in them; sometimes they existed in the past and are lost (elegy); and sometimes they are a magic space that he can witness but not enter.

This final, marginal relation to an idyllic world is of particular interest because it mirrors the poetic idyll itself: it is "realized" before one but remains out of reach. We can see this in a rustic idyll probably written in 839, when the poet was returning from his second period in Xuanzhou to Chang'an to take up a new post. The biographical occasion is suggestive because the poet had twice abandoned capital posts for the lower Yangzi region, which clearly offered pleasures and satisfactions the capital did not. Now he is answering a summons, tied to a career about which he is ambivalent.

杜牧, 商山麻澗

Du Mu, Hemp Stream at Mount Shang[110]

雲光嵐彩四面合	Light on the clouds, bright colors of haze surround me on all sides,
柔柔垂柳十餘家	the drooping willows pliant, ten or so homes.
雉飛鹿過芳草遠	A pheasant flies, a deer passes by, fragrant grasses stretch far,
牛巷雞塒春日斜	ox lanes and chicken niches as the spring sun sinks.
秀眉老父對樽酒	An old man with bushy eyebrows sits in front of a cup of ale,
蒨袖女兒簪野花	a girl in crimson sleeves puts wildflowers in her hair.
征車自念塵土計	In my journeying carriage I brood on my plans in the dusty world,
惆悵谿邊書細沙	and depressed beside a creek I write in the fine sands.

Although the poem's title sets this little village in imperial geography, the opening couplet locates it elsewhere: the traveler is surrounded by luminous cloud and haze, and the village itself is hidden among willows.

---

110. 28229; Feng 263.

This magical enclosure locates us in a world like those in many Tang tales, a world of immortals and goddesses that blurs into the wondrous agrarian community of Peach Blossom Spring. The presence of skittish deer so close to human habitation is another sign that this is a special place, one far from harm. We pass from wild nature to "ox lanes and chicken niches" (holes in a wall in which chickens nest).

In the farming villages of Tang poetry one rarely encounters children or middle-aged women; as for adult males, as we will see, an oxherd may appear. Most often a poet finds (as here) old men and young maidens, the rustic counterparts of immortals and goddesses. It is a realm of peace and plenty, a world apart.

Although the poet is just passing through, the idyllic vision causes him to reflect on his own life, always going from one place to another. The enigmatic last line links the experience of idyll and writing. Du Mu tells us *that* he writes, not *what* he writes. We only know that writing follows from alienation, a sense of separation and difference from the people in the idyll.

Du Mu's poem bears comparison with a rustic idyll written roughly a century earlier, in which another famous poet observed a farming village: realizing that he could not belong to such a world, he recited a *Shijing* poem rather than write in the sand.

王維, 渭川田家
Wang Wei, Farming Homes by the Wei River[111]

斜光照墟落	The setting light falls on a hamlet,
窮巷牛羊歸	through narrow lanes cattle and sheep return.
野老念牧童	An old rustic, concerned for the herdboy,
倚杖候荊扉	leans on his staff and waits by the ramshackle door.
雉雊麥苗秀	A pheasant cries out, wheat sprouts form ears,
蠶眠桑葉稀	the silkworms sleep, mulberry leaves are few.
田夫荷鋤至	Field hands come, hoes over shoulders,
相見語依依	when they meet, their words are faint.
即此羨閑逸	At such a moment I yearn for freedom and ease,
悵然歌式微	and, downcast, I sing "Hard straits!"[112]

---

111. 05837; Chen Tiemin 561.

112. According to the "Lesser Preface," "Hard Straits" 式微, *Shi* XXXVI, was composed by the liegemen of the Count of Li, who fled to the state of Wei after Li was invaded by barbarians. Because the count was poorly treated in Wei, his liegemen tried to

Though the fundamental exposition is similar, the differences between Wang Wei's and Du Mu's poems in some ways embody the best of the High Tang and the Late Tang. Wang Wei's poem places emphasis on the internal relations between people in the farming community—relations that exclude him—while Du Mu's poem reflects his particular genius in framing the scene: the luminous vapors that surround the place and the unreadable writing that follows. Wang Wei's idyll is very human; it is work and bounty transformed into poetry. Du Mu's idyll is shaped by poetic oppositions (white/red; male/female; old/young; ale/flowers), creating a scene that is idle, timeless, and otherworldly. Nevertheless, both poets come to the edge of a rustic idyll, cannot cross into it, and feel the weight of their public lives.

It seems as if Du Mu had seen that very girl earlier on the same journey, this time near Nanyang and paired with an oxherd rather than an old man. She appears to have been a standard fixture of idyllic poetic villages. In this case, however, rather than experiencing a sense of alienation, Du Mu is welcomed by a rustic host, just as a rustic of antiquity welcomed Confucius's disciple Zilu.

杜牧, 村行

Du Mu, Walking Through a Village[113]

春半南陽西	Mid-spring west of Nanyang
柔桑過村塢	I passed a hamlet with tender mulberries.
娉娉垂柳風	A breeze with willows hanging gracefully,
點點迴塘雨	rain making spots on the winding pool.
蓑唱牧牛兒	In his raincoat, singing, an oxherd,
籬窺蒨裙女	peeking through a hedge, a girl in a crimson skirt.
半濕解征衫	I took off my half-wet traveling clothes,
主人饋雞黍	my host fed me on chicken and millet.[114]

If in the last poem Du Mu experienced Wang Wei's sense of alienation from the rural community, here he enters into the margins of that world. Rain rarely soaks the clothes of Tang poetic travelers as it does ordinary people on the road, but here it is an excuse to pause. The

---

persuade him to return. Wang Wei is obviously less concerned with the full context than with the advice given to return.

113. 28062; Feng 106.

114. *Analects,* vol. 18, 7. This was the food a rustic host fed Zilu, Confucius's disciple, when detaining him for the night.

oxherd is well provided with a raincoat (though we might worry about the girl's crimson skirt). Du Mu's half-wet traveling clothes is not a touch of "realism" but rather a "half" move into the idyllic world, where the poet can enjoy archaic shelter and welcome.

Not all idylls are rustic. One version of idyll, with many precedents, is "recalling past travels," *yi jiu you* 憶舊遊, in which the pleasures of youth are recalled from a weary present. On this same journey from Xuanzhou to the capital Du Mu met Pei Tan, an old friend, providing the perfect occasion to recall and evoke the now lost Xuanzhou of his youth and his more recent experience of Xie Tiao's city.

杜牧, 自宣州赴官入京, 路逢裴坦判官歸宣州, 因題贈
Du Mu, On the Way from Xuanzhou to the Capital to Assume My Post,
I Encountered Administrative Assistant Pei Tan on His Way
Back to Xuanzhou; Thus I Wrote This[115]

敬亭山下百頃竹	At the foot of Jingting Mountain a hundred acres of bamboo,
中有詩人小謝城	there is the city of the poet the younger Xie.[116]
城高跨樓滿金碧	The walls are high, one strides up the tower, gold and sapphire everywhere,
下聽一溪寒水聲	below one listens to the sound of cold water of its single creek.
梅花落徑香繚繞	Plum blossoms fall on the paths fragrantly winding around,
雪白玉瑞花下行	white as snow, jade earrings walking under the flowers.
縈風酒斾掛朱閣	Coiling in breeze tavern streamers hang from vermillion kiosks,
半醉遊人聞弄笙	half-tipsy men out roaming hear reed organs played.
我初到此未三十	When I first came to this place, I was not yet thirty,
頭腦鈒利筋骨輕	my brain was fresh and sharp, my bones and sinews light.
畫堂檀板秋拍碎	Sandalwood castanets in painted halls in autumn clacked to bits,

---

115. 28060; Feng 103.
116. Xie Tiao, the "Younger Xie," had been governor of Xuanzhou.

一引有時聯十觥	and at times in continuous serving, ten drinking horns quaffed in sequence.
老閑腰下丈二組	To grow old, the two yard ribbons hung from the waist left unused,[117]
塵土高懸千載名	but the dirty world meant renown hung high for a thousand years.
重遊鬢白事皆改	Coming there again, my locks were white, and everything had changed,
唯見東流春水平	I saw only, flowing eastward, spring waters level.
對酒不敢起	Facing ale I dared not stir,
逢君還眼明	but meeting you, my eyes were bright again.
雲罍看人捧	I looked at the girl offering the cloud-like flagon,
波臉任他橫	let her cast those glances in waves at others.
一醉六十日	Steadily drunk for sixty days
古來聞阮生	is said of Ruan Ji in olden days.
是非離別際	Only at junctures of judgment and parting
始見醉中情	one sees true feelings in drunkenness.[118]
今日送君話前事	Today in sending you off we chat of what happened before,
高歌引劍還一傾	singing loud, drawing swords, then draining another cup.
江湖酒伴如相問	If drinking companions of the river and lakes should ever ask of me,
終老煙波不計程	I will end up old in the misty waves not reckoning itineraries.

The idyll of pleasure here differs from the rustic idyll above, not just in content but in having been an idyll the poet could fully enter—though only in memory. The poem begins with a timeless Xuanzhou: this is not the Xuanzhou experienced only in youth or now in his more mature years, but the Xuanzhou that "is"—a world of eternal spring, drinking, music, and drunkenness. He came to this Xuanzhou as a young man and believed that he could stay in this world until old age, setting aside all ambition to rise in public life. However, if Xuanzhou

---

117. That is, he would not seek high office, whose badges were strung with ribbons from the waist.

118. This section echoes stories about the Wei eccentric Ruan Ji, famous for his drinking. His neighbor's wife would give him ale; and when he was drunk he would lie by her side, occasioning no suspicion from the husband.

itself seems beyond change, he is not: he left to answer the call of public service. When he returns, Xuanzhou is the same, but he is not. He is still the drinker, but the girl at the bar no longer touches him.

The third occasion for drinking is when he meets Pei Tan on the road. Although this round of drinking seems as passionate as in his youth, here they are no longer in that past world of pleasure but merely reminiscing about it. The poem ends with yet another version of idyll, growing old on the misty rivers and lakes. "Not reckoning itineraries," *bu ji cheng* 不計程, is literally "not reckoning the stages" of a journey: not thinking of how far you will go each day, or where you will stay, to reach some destination.

This elegiac idyll, in which the remembered past is recreated poetically, is the mode most strongly associated with Du Mu.

杜牧, 念昔遊
Du Mu, Thinking on Past Roamings[119]

I

十載飄然繩檢外	Ten years spent swept about beyond ties and norms,
樽前自獻自爲酬	I toasted myself with the goblet, and answered the toast myself.
秋山春雨閑吟處	Autumn hills and rains of spring, places I chanted at leisure,
倚遍江南寺寺樓	I leaned and looked from the upper story of every temple in the Southland.

III

李白題詩水西寺	West of the Water Temple where Li Bai wrote a poem:
古木迴巖樓閣風	ancient trees and winding cliffs, wind in mansion and tower.
半醒半醉游三日	Half-sober and half-drunk I roamed for three days,[120]
紅白花開山雨中	red and white the flowers bloomed in the mountain rain.

---

119. 28082–84; Feng 133.

120. It is not clear whether "half-sober and half-drunk" refers to a continuous state or means "half the time sober and half the time drunk."

In the first poem above we begin to recognize a contemporary trope: recollected wildness. We again quote the opening of Zhang Hu's "Reaching Guangling":

一年江海恣狂遊	A whole year long on the river and lakes I roamed madly as I pleased,
夜宿倡家曉上樓	I spent my night in the brothels, climbed towers in the dawn.

We also have Du Mu's own "ten years" in a "Yangzhou dream" in "Getting Things off My Chest." This is not rustic idyll but rather a *fengliu* idyll of memory. Although the rustic idylls are encountered in the geography of the empire, they do not really belong to it. Similarly, all the temples in the Southland do not provide truly different scenes for the poet gazing from their upper stories. Rather, they give a poetic "traveler" a recurrent vision of the same scene of the Southland.

The third poem begins by recalling a poetic predecessor, namely, Li Bai, another poet of idyll. Du Mu is the poetic latecomer: the poem has already been written. It is worth recalling this poem, which concludes with an invitation to another poet to come and "roam."

李白, 遊水西簡鄭明府
Li Bai, Visiting West-of-the-Water Mountain:
A Note to Magistrate Zheng[121]

天宮水西寺	Heaven's Palace, West-of-the-Water Temple,
雲錦照東郭	cloudlike brocade shines in the eastern suburbs.
清湍鳴迴溪	Clear eddies resound in the winding creeks,
綠竹遶飛閣	green bamboo encircles soaring towers.
涼風日瀟灑	Every day the cool wind is brisk and fresh,
幽客時憩泊	sometimes secluded travelers put up here to rest.
五月思貂裘	In the fifth month one longs for a sable cloak,
謂言秋霜落	thinking that autumn frost is falling.
石蘿引古蔓	Ivy on rocks puts out ancient creepers,
岸筍開新籜	bamboo sprouts on slopes show new skins.
吟翫空復情	Chanting for amusement, an idle mood comes,
相思爾佳作	my thoughts are fixed on your excellent work.
鄭公詩人秀	Zheng is outstanding among poets,
逸韻宏寥廓	his aloof rhymes float in the vastness of space.

---

121. 08547; Qu (1980) 1203.

何當一來遊　　　When will you come and roam with me,
愜我雪山諾　　　to satisfy my vow of the Mountain of Snows?[122]

Du Mu arrives too late and roams through that blossoming space alone, in a world of rain and brightly colored flowers that might seem like a drunken dream even if the poet were not "half-drunk" or "drunk half the time." What sets Du Mu apart, however, is a bounded interval of drunken idyll—whether ten years or, as in the third poem, a mere three days. It is a bounded realm of experience that the poet enters and leaves, measuring the interval in memory.

As in the Red Slope poems, discussed earlier, idyll is the transformative work of poetry, fashioning scenes that never existed in experience and that are so beautiful and alluring they never truly could exist. This was what he had written of Li He's poetry, which so often seemed to haunt the margins of Du Mu's work. In Du Mu, however, this poetic transformation of the world is often connected with ruin and loss. The spring flowers fall and are transformed into a single plane of representation, perhaps brocade worked into images of flowers.

杜牧, 春晚題韋家亭子
Du Mu, Late Spring, Written on the
Pavilion at the Wei Household[123]

擁鼻侵襟花草香　　I hold my nose, it gets into clothes,
　　　　　　　　　　fragrance of plants and flowers,

高臺春去恨茫茫　　from the high terrace spring departs,
　　　　　　　　　　a resentment stretching far.

蔫紅半落平池晚　　The withered red has half-fallen,
　　　　　　　　　　the level pool in evening,

曲渚飄成錦一張　　on winding isles it drifts to form
　　　　　　　　　　a sheet of brocade.

---

122. The monk Wenshu journeyed to the Mountain of Snows in Central Asia, heard the sutras, and then went back to China and entered Nirvana.

123. 28127; Feng 182.

NINE

Daoism

The Case of Cao Tang

Under the rubric "Daoism" we find various bodies of distinct but inter-related lore, which was preserved, studied, and elaborated in Daoist centers during the Tang. This included rituals (including state rituals), a complex pantheon, spells, and technical knowledge to achieve immortality. One body of lore involved accounts of gods and immortals (*shenxian* 神仙), which circulated widely outside Daoist communities. The lore concerning the immortals as well as other lore entered the literary tradition, as practiced by both laymen and adepts.

Claiming descent from Laozi, Li Dan 李聃, the Li imperial house of Tang, had long sponsored its own brand of state Daoism, with particular emperors going further by sponsoring Daoism in general and undertaking a personal quest for longevity. Perhaps the most extreme imperial enthusiast was Wuzong, who not only oversaw the disestablishment of the Buddhist church but also joined a number of his recent forebears as a victim of drugs claiming to foster longevity.

The discourse of the immortals had regularly been used to represent the imperial household in its private entertainments. In the first half of the ninth century this connection between the imperial household and the immortals was reinforced through the voluntary and involuntary removal of princesses and court women to Daoist "nunneries," where some princesses clearly carried on romantic liaisons. Some of the stories concerned erotic encounters between gods and mortals; romantic or erotic attachments in the human world had long been poetically figured in such terms (for example, the interpretation of Cao Zhi's "The Goddess of the Luo" 洛神賦 as the poet's attachment to Empress Zhen). The women were inevitably represented as goddesses, with the men presented either as fellow immortals or as fortunate mortals.[1]

The literary lore of the immortals was thus overdetermined, encompassing actual immortals, the free and easy transcendence of mortal ties, the world of the inner court and the imperial household, and mortal love affairs. Any particular usage of the lore of the immortals might have a clear frame of reference, but in many cases the frames blurred into one another. Here is an example from Li Shangyin.

李商隱, 和韓錄事送宮人入道
Li Shangyin, A Companion Piece with Office Manager Han's
"Seeing Off a Palace Lady Entering a Daoist Nunnery"[2]

星使追還不自由	Messenger stars might overtake and recall, it is not within her own power,[3]
雙童捧上綠瓊輈	a pair of lads lifts and raises green jasper carriage rail.
九枝燈下朝金殿	Beneath the nine-branch lamp she goes to court in the golden palace,
三素雲中侍玉樓	among the three pale-colored clouds she attends in a tower of jade.[4]
鳳女顛狂成久別	The phoenix girl goes mad at long parting come to pass;[5]
月娥孀獨好同遊	the moon maiden lives all alone, fond of companions.[6]
當時若愛韓公子	Had she fallen in love back then with our Master Han,

---

1. In popular lore there was no clear distinction between "gods" or "goddesses" (*shen*) and "immortals" or "transcendents" (*xian*).

2. 29415; for commentaries, see *Jijie* 281 and Ye 363. Some commentators believe Han to be Han Cong 韓琮, a poet known in Li's time. Some determine the date of composition as 838, when Wenzong transferred 480 palace ladies to Buddhist and Daoist establishments in the capital. We could take the "palace lady" of the title as being plural, but the poem is best read using a single case as an example. Of course, the poem might not refer to the events of 838.

3. That is, only by imperial order can she be recalled to the palace.

4. Immortals rode on clouds comprised of the "three pale colors" white, pale purple, and pale yellow.

5. Nongyu, the daughter of the duke of Qin, rode off on a phoenix with her lover, Xiaoshi.

6. Chang E, the goddess of the moon, stole the elixir of immortality and lives alone on the moon.

埋骨成灰恨未休 　　　　　though her bones be buried and her body, ash,
　　　　　　　　　　　　　her bitterness would never have ceased.[7]

Initially the lady's departure from the palace is figured in the common trope of the goddess exiled from Heaven, subject to recall only by "messenger stars" sent by divine authorities. We see her first entering the carriage that will take her away from the palace, then perhaps paying her respects to the emperor before going off to a nunnery. If we possessed the original poem (for which this is a companion piece), the interpretation of the final section might be clearer; but the separation from the palace/Heaven has obviously shifted to the immortal woman's at least speculative separation from a particular mortal lover. Since this is a palace lady, the propriety of the final couplet may be dubious, but it is easy to see how the eroticized world of immortals could slide over into the erotic fantasies of officeholding mortals. Perhaps Han Cong—if it is indeed he—had known her before she entered the palace; we simply do not know. The final line clearly suggests an effective cloistering of this particular nun rather than the potential contact with males that sometimes seems to have occurred in Daoist establishments.

The title here gives us a clear frame of reference, as do poems with titles addressing Daoist adepts, where the discourse of the immortals is rarely eroticized. Li Shangyin's poems with more ambiguous titles using the lore of the immortals have been the source of speculation by commentators for centuries.

Although most poets composed at least a few pieces on Daoist themes or drawing upon Daoist lore when addressing serious practitioners, there are very few poets in our period that we would classify as Daoist poets. Cao Tang 曹唐 (ca. 797–ca. 866) is an exception, even though his Daoism is distinctly literary.[8] A number of poets discussed

---

7. Although Qing commentators proposed various allusions here, *Jijie* is probably correct in interpreting this as—at least on a secondary level—playfully referring to Office Manager Han.

8. It was once generally believed that Cao Tang was a poet who worked primarily in the second half of the ninth century, a contemporary of Luo Yin. More recent scholarship has shown that Cao was active primarily in the period of our study, though he did live long enough to meet Luo Yin. See Fu (1987) vol. 3, 489–96; and Yan Jinxiong 376–77, who draws on the work of Liang Chaoran 梁超然. For a detailed study, in a very different key, of the "Smaller Wandering Immortal Poems" that pays particular

in the present work studied Daoism—most notably Li Shangyin, on whose poetry it left a profound influence. Gu Feixiong, the son of the Daoist Gu Kuang, eventually gave up the secular life and returned to the major Daoist center at Maoshan, from whence he came. The most striking contrast with Cao Tang, however, is Shi Jianwu 施肩吾. After passing the *jinshi* examination in 820, he left Chang'an to spend the rest of his life as a Daoist adept in Hongzhou. We have his poetry but no biographical details beyond that decisive moment. Although his extant poems do touch on Daoist themes more than those of other poets, only a fraction of his works can be called "Daoist."[9]

Cao Tang, by contrast, may have studied Daoism in his youth (like Li Shangyin), but by the early 820s he had given it up for the familiar pattern of examination attempts followed by public service under military commissioners. It is still an open question whether he eventually did succeed in passing the *jinshi* examination; if so, it occurred relatively late in life. He seems to have spent about forty-five years moving between the capital and regional patrons. Whether he returned to his Daoist studies during this period is uncertain. He was not widely known in contemporary poetic circles.[10]

Cao Tang's modest corpus comprises just over 30 occasional poems, all but one of which is regulated verse in the long line.[11] Some of these also treat Daoist themes. Apart from some other purely Daoist poems, Cao Tang's fame rests on almost 100 "Smaller Wandering Immortal Poems" 小遊仙詩, plus 18 out of an original 50 "Larger Wandering

---

attention to Cao Tang's use of Daoist imagery, see Edward H. Schafer, *Mirages on the Sea of Time: The Taoist Poetry of Ts'ao T'ang* (Berkeley: University of California Press, 1985).

9. Shi Jianwu's works were once collected in 10 *juan*; very little survives, and that which does consists primarily of quatrains. Apart from the latter, there are no Daoist poems since those pieces were gathered from early anthologized sources. Hong Mai, however, obviously had access to the complete collection and seems to have copied most or all of the quatrains into his *Tangren wanshou jueju.* (Since Hong Mai preserved virtually all of Cao Tang's extant Daoist quatrains, he bore no prejudice that would have inclined him to exclude Daoist works.) We can therefore probably take the percentage of Daoist poems in the quatrains as roughly representative of the collection as a whole.

10. The poem addressed to Du Mu that is attributed to Cao Tang (35187) is also attributed to Cao Fen 曹汾—probably on better grounds. See Tong Peiji 419, 475.

11. Excluding 35136, which is a misattribution.

Immortal Poems" 大遊仙詩.[12] The former are all quatrains in the long line and the latter are all regulated verses in the long line. This is the largest corpus of such poems in the Tang. We do not know if Cao Tang had a usual "poetry collection"—the earliest notices give his works as surviving in two *juan*. It seems likely that the two sets of "wandering immortal" poems, each set consisting of 400 long lines (each thus comprising a *juan*), originally circulated independently.

We do not know how to interpret Cao Tang's relation to these pieces. For some scholars they represent escapist fancies attendant on a failed civil service career. To Edward Schafer they appear to represent Cao Tang as a committed Daoist. Both interpretations are possible—perhaps simultaneously. Five occasional poems entitled "Winter of the Third Year: The Great Rites" 三年冬大禮五首 (35159–63), composed for a series of Daoist rituals undertaken by Wenzong in the eleventh month of 830, show Cao Tang speaking with evident enthusiasm both for the rites and as an aspirant to public office. Perhaps the best way to approach Cao Tang's relationship to his Daoist poems is to bracket the question of conviction (in contrast to Shi Jianwu, where we have credible evidence of conviction) and to understand Cao's Daoism as a specialized body of learning as well as a discourse.

Critics sometimes mention the "Smaller Wandering Immortal Poems" in conjunction with Wang Jian's 100 "Palace Lyrics" 宮詞, also comprising a cento of quatrains in the long line, which circulated independently. The "Palace Lyrics" were composed around 820 and were very popular.[13] They demonstrate mastery of another "discourse," namely, the world of the Inner Palace. Indeed, they demonstrated it so successfully that gossips wondered how Wang Jian knew so much about this world from which men (apart from eunuchs and the emperor) were excluded. Cao Tang's "Smaller Wandering Immortal Poems" almost certainly postdate Wang Jian's "Palace Lyrics," albeit

---

12. For a discussion of why certain extant regulated verses should be considered as belonging to the series of "Larger Wandering Immortals," see the following: Schafer, *Mirages on the Sea of Time*, p. 32, n. 10 (on a discovery by Stephen Bokenkamp); Fu (1987), vol. 5, 428–29; and Yan Jinxong 379. No one really knows how to construe *you xian* 遊仙, which has been translated as "wandering immortals"; by the ninth century it simply meant a poem about the gods and immortals, as is clear from the "Larger Wandering Immortal Poems," in which there is no spirit journey to Heaven.

13. Fu (1998), vol. 2, 811.

not by very many years. Despite Cao Tang's unknowable intentions, the "Smaller Wandering Immortal Poems" would have been taken as works of the same kind, a cento of quatrains in the long line invoking a body of special knowledge, describing in detail scenes from which most readers of the poems were excluded.[14] Quite beyond the formal resemblance, Cao Tang's quatrains resemble Wang Jian's in many particulars. For example, as Yan Jinxiong notes, Cao Tang pays great attention to the clothing and ornaments of male and female immortals.[15] Details of clothing and ornament play an equally prominent role in Wang Jian's "Palace Lyrics." The world of the immortals is aristocratic and palatial, just as the world of the sublunary palace was conventionally described in terms of the world of immortals (though less directly so in Wang Jian's "Palace Lyrics"). Indeed, it is difficult to read the two centos side by side and not see the close affinity between Cao Tang's poems and those of Wang Jian. Cao Tang's world of the immortals is often described in vignettes describing local activities and gatherings.[16]

XCVIII[17]

絳闕夫人下北方　　　The Lady of the Crimson Tower
　　　　　　　　　　　　descends to the north,
細環清佩響丁當　　　slender rings and clear pendants
　　　　　　　　　　　　echo ding-a-ling.
攀花笑入春風裏　　　Reaching for flowers, smiling she enters
　　　　　　　　　　　　into the breeze of spring,
偷折紅桃寄阮郎　　　stealthily snapping a pink peach blossom
　　　　　　　　　　　　to give to young Ruan.

---

14. The cento of quatrains became widespread only in the last part of the ninth century; we have a number of complete groups, as well as some partial groups, that may once have been full centos. Hu Ceng's "On History" 詠史詩 (35622ff.) extends beyond 100, as does another set of such poems by Zhou Tan 周曇 (40586–778). We have 100 quatrains for the singing girl Bihong 比紅兒詩 (36755–854) by Luo Qiu 羅虯, as well as a set of quatrains in the short line called "Untitled; Traveling by the River" 江行無題 一百首 (39808–907), by Qian Xu. These probably circulated independently as subcollections; see pp. 539–41.

15. Yan Jinxiong 409–10.

16. Compare the scene of gambling in Wang Jian's "Palace Lyrics" (LXXVII) and Cao Tang's "Wandering Immortals" (XCII).

17. 35285.

"Young Ruan" is Ruan Zhao 阮肇, who, with his companion Liu Chen 劉晨, encountered two goddesses on Mount Tiantai, lived with them awhile, and then returned to the mortal world. In the "Larger Wandering Immortal Poems" we will see this story as a narrative frame for lyrics, but here in the "Smaller Wandering Immortal Poems" this character is simply a poetic name for the mortal beloved of a goddess. The women that fill Wang Jian's "Palace Lyrics" are, of course, permitted to long only for the emperor's attention; the transposition to the world of the immortals permits a wider range of longing and flirtation.

As Yan Jinxiong astutely points out, serious Daoism was intent upon eliminating the passions. As we have seen, the popular literary lore of the immortals was intensely eroticized. Although many of the vignettes deal exclusively with male immortals and adepts, the "Smaller Wandering Immortal Poems" are also filled with love affairs, flirtations, women at play, nostalgic memories, and feasting—in striking contrast to the Daoist poems of earlier figures like Wu Yun.[18] Cao Tang's "Smaller Wandering Immortal Poems" clearly do not refer to the world of the Inner Court. Images of ninth-century romance culture and fantasies about palace life have been transferred to the immortal world.

To such vignettes Cao Tang adds the technical vocabulary of Daoism and the immortals' perspective on time, underscoring the difference between the immortal and mortal worlds.

LVI[19]

侍女親擎玉酒巵	The serving girl personally picks up a jade flagon for ale,
滿巵傾酒勸安期	she pours the flagon full of ale and urges Anqi to drink.
等閒相別三千歲	Heedlessly we parted three thousand years ago,
長憶水邊分棗時	but I always recall by the waters the moment we shared eating a date.[20]

The vignette is based on a legend of the immortal Anqi feasting with Lady Taizhen 太眞夫人, transformed here into a serving girl (and thus

---

18. Yan Jinxiong notes (413) the rather striking cases of goddesses referring to themselves as *qie* 妾, "your handmaiden."

19. 35243.

20. *Zao* 棗 was homophonous with 早, "early"; hence, "when we separated too early."

looking more like an incident at a Tang party, with a singing girl encountered in the past).[21] Indeed, in some cases the only thing that separates the immortal from an ordinary human is some celestial "prop," as the shortened colloquial term for a "stage property" becomes a literal "prop" of vermilion clouds.

LIX[22]

風動閒天清桂陰	The breeze stirs the calm heavens, in the clear shade of the cassia,
水精簾箔冷沉沉	curtains made of crystal, cold and sunken away.
西妃少女多春思	The young daughter of the Western Consort is filled with spring passions,
斜倚彤雲盡日吟	and leaning against vermilion clouds, she recites poems all day through.

This scene was a trope taken from contemporary romantic tales. In "Huo Xiaoyu's Story" 霍小玉傳, the mother speaks of Huo Xiaoyu similarly spending the day reciting poems and feeling unfulfilled longing.[23] We meet someone very much like this woman immortal in another poem, though rather than simply reciting poems, she goes on an active—albeit apparently futile—search for her mortal lover.

XXVI[24]

偷來洞口訪劉君	Secretly she came to the grotto's mouth to find Liu Chen,
緩步輕攜玉線裙	stepping slowly, she lightly lifts her skirt with jade threads.
細擘桃花逐流水	Peach blossoms torn into fine bits go off with the flowing water,
更無言語倚彤雲	and saying not a word more, she leans on vermilion clouds.

Many of the "Smaller Wandering Immortal Poems" would "translate" into fine human vignettes and party poems if the span of years

---

21. See Yan Jingxiong 407–8.

22. 35246.

23. "You spend the whole day reciting and fantasizing; how can that compare to meeting him?" 爾終日吟想，何如一見. See Li Shiren 李時人, ed., *Quan Tang Wudai xiaoshuo* 全唐五代小説 (Xi'an: Shaanxi renmin chubanshe, 1998), 728.

24. 25203.

were shortened and the brightness of the celestial nimbus were dimmed a bit. In a mortal poem one would say that in life's "hundred years" (a conventionally hopeful span for mortals) one has rarely had the opportunity to meet some old friend. Anxiously prizing the rare occasion to meet, the particular condition of mere mortals, is directly transferred to immortal spans, where it is oddly incongruous.

LXXXIX[25]

東溟兩度作塵飛	Twice now the Eastern Deeps have turned to blowing dust,
一萬年來會面稀	in the past ten thousand years our chances to meet have been rare.
千樹梨花百壺酒	A thousand trees of pear blossoms, a hundred jugs of ale,
共君論飲莫論詩	let us concern ourselves with drinking and not with poetry.

Often merely through gesture or word Cao Tang humanizes the world of the immortals. The pleasure of the poems is frequently in the tension between the immortal world and the all-too-human one. Master White Stone lived on White Stone Mountain and boiled white stones as his meal.

XV[26]

白石山中自有天	White Stone Mountain has its own heavens,
竹花藤葉隔溪煙	bamboo blossoms and rattan leaves are blocked by the mist on the creek.
朝來洞口圍棋了	With dawn at the mouth of the grotto the go game is done,
賭得青龍直幾錢	he won a green dragon in a wager— how many cash is that worth?

We know that "green dragon" was one of the stages in refining elixir, but whether the immortal has won an elixir or the large and renowned mythical beast in his go game, the poem, after its misty and mysterious setting, still depends on the comic incongruity between the nature of

---

25. 35276.
26. 25202.

such winnings and the unpoetic and very mortal question of how much such a thing is worth.[27]

As fine as many of the "Smaller Wandering Immortal Poems" are, the surviving pieces from the "Larger Wandering Immortal Poems" represent the more significant body of work in the history of Tang poetry. The "Smaller Wandering Immortal Poems" concerns the world of the immortals and presents a rich display of technical lore; the "Larger Wandering Immortal Poems" does involve immortals, but these stories had largely passed into general cultural currency. Essentially the "Larger Wandering Immortals Poems" had transferred the form of the ninth-century history poem to the legends of the immortals (and, of course, insofar as one believes these stories, there is no difference). If we take Li He's famous poem "The Bronze Immortal Taking Leave of Han: Song" 金銅仙人辭漢歌,[28] Wen Tingyun's "Lyrics for the Naval Maneuvers on Lake Kunming" 昆明治水戰詞,[29] or the standard title-form of a common type of poetic exposition in the ninth century that announces some historical or legendary incident,[30] then we have a context for reading the headings or titles from the surviving "Larger Wandering Immortals Poems," such as "Emperor Wu of the Han Awaits the Descent of the Queen Mother of the West" 漢武帝將候西王母下降.[31]

Such title-forms clearly place Cao Tang's poems very much within a contemporary context. What distinguishes Cao Tang is that his titles seem to have been arranged in sets, covering different phases of a known narrative. [32] In the surviving "Larger Wandering Immortal Poems" we have one possibly complete set and several pieces belonging to other sets. Following the above title, we have "Emperor Wu of the Han Feasts the Queen Mother of the West in His Palace" 漢武帝於宮中宴西王母.[33] Next we find a set of five pieces on sequential

---

27. If Cao Tang had meant this as a rhetorical question suggesting "beyond price," he would hardly have used the base term "cash," *qian*.

28. 20703; Ye (1959) 77.

29. 31900; Zeng 32.

30. One could select Li Xian's 李銑 "Sun Wu Teaches Women to Do Battle" 孫武試教婦人戰賦 (QTw 7327) at random from among hundreds of similar examples.

31. 35138.

32. See the discussion in Yan Jinxiong 379.

33. 35139.

phases of the story of Liu Chen and Ruan Zhao meeting goddesses in a grotto.[34] In several cases we see that such poems are not third-person narratives but rather assume the role of a character in a known story, such as "Zhang Shi Sends Another Poem to Du Lanxiang" 張碩重寄杜蘭香 (the first poem has not been preserved).[35] The poem that follows (perhaps in the wrong sequence) is "The Jade Maiden Du Lanxiang Condescends to Marry Zhang Shi" 玉女杜蘭香下嫁於張碩.[36]

Let us look at the set of poems on the story of Liu Chen and Ruan Zhao. We have only the phases of approach and departure; the time Liu and Ruan spend with the goddesses is passed over in silence.

曹唐, 劉晨阮肇遊天台

Cao Tang, Liu Chen and Ruan Zhao Visit Mount Tiantai[37]

樹入天台石路新	The trees stretch into Mount Tiantai, the rocky road is new,
雲和草靜迥無塵	the clouds balmy, the grasses calm, no dust in the distance.
煙霞不省生前事	Among mist and rosy wisps they are unaware of what happened in earlier lives,
水木空疑夢後身	among waters and trees it simply seems they are living in a dream.
往往雞鳴巖下月	Everywhere fowl sing out in the moonlight below the cliff,
時時犬吠洞中春	now and then a dog barks, springtime in a grotto.
不知此地歸何處	Not knowing what place this is where they have come,
須就桃源問主人	they can only go to peach blossom spring and ask the person there.

In the second poem we may have a mismatch between title and text, for by the end of the poem Liu and Ruan haven't actually met the goddesses. It is possible that this set originally consisted of more than the surviving five poems and that this text has the wrong title. Another possibility is that these are not "titles" in the traditional sense but rather "headings," indicating where the text occurs within a prose narrative. For example,

---

34. 35140–44.
35. 35150.
36. 35151.
37. 35140.

the following poem, in which the meeting has not yet occurred, is a verse that prepares us for the meeting that would follow in prose.

曹唐, 劉阮洞中遇仙子
Cao Tang, Liu and Ruan Meet the Immortals in the Grotto[38]

天和樹色靄蒼蒼	The heavens blend with the colors of trees in a blue-gray haze,
霞重嵐深路渺茫	colored wisps in layers, vapors deep, the road fading off into it.
雲竇滿山無鳥雀	Cloudy caves fill the mountains, there are no birds at all,
水聲沿澗有笙簧	sounds of water, along by the torrent the notes of reed organs.
碧沙洞裏乾坤別	Inside a grotto of emerald sands the universe is different;
紅樹枝前日月長	before the branches of red trees days and months last longer.
願得花間有人出	I hope that from among the flowers someone will come out
免令仙犬吠劉郎	to keep the dog of the immortals from barking at young Liu.

If we think of this as part of a narrative, one that may have once had prose, the obvious precedent would be "The Cave of Wandering Immortals" 遊仙窟, dating from the late seventh century, which tells a very similar story in elegant prose with a rich scattering of poems. This piece was preserved in Japan, and (like many things preserved there) offers a unique survival from Tang literature. Although there are indeed works that are truly unique, in most cases where one text survives there were once many. Following this hypothesis, these poems, all preserved in the mid-tenth-century *Caidiao ji*, depend on a virtual narrative that might once have been an actual written narrative. If such a narrative with inserted poems actually existed, we would expect that there were other poems on feasting and flirtation between the goddesses and the young men inside the grotto. (Some of the quatrains would have served this purpose very well.)[39]

---

38. 35141.

39. *Caidiao ji* includes three of the "Smaller Wandering Immortal Poems" (26, 59, and 63), two of which are translated above.

After enjoying the pleasures of life with the two goddesses, Ruan and Liu became homesick. In the next poem we are already at the scene of parting.

曹唐, 仙子送劉阮出洞

Cao Tang, The Immortals See Liu and Ruan
Off as They Leave the Grotto[40]

殷勤相送出天台	With urgent feeling they see them off, leaving Tiantai,
仙境那能卻再來	how to this immortal realm could they come again?
雲液每歸須強飲	The "liquid cloud," whenever you return, you must make yourself drink it;
玉書無事莫頻開	the "jade writings," if you have no problems, don't open them often.[41]
花當洞口應長在	The flowers at the grotto's mouth will surely be always there;
水到人間定不迴	when the waters reach the mortal world, they will certainly not come back.
惆悵溪頭從此別	Downcast here beside the creek, from this point on they part,
碧山明月閉蒼苔	emerald mountains, bright moonlight, covered with green moss.

The scene of discovery of the grotto of the immortals was not a standard topic, but here we have the favorite moments of love poetry: the scene of parting and the scene of the woman (here goddesses) left behind, longing for the absent man.

曹唐, 仙子洞中有懷劉阮

Cao Tang, The Immortals in the Grotto Long for Liu and Ruan[42]

不將清瑟理霓裳	They do not take the clear zither to play "Skirts of Rainbow,"
塵夢那知鶴夢長	how could dreams in the world of dust know how long cranes' dreams last?
洞裏有天春寂寂	The grotto has its own heaven, springtime lonely and still,

---

40. 35142.

41. These are gifts from the goddesses to Liu and Ruan, accompanied by prohibitions. "Liquid cloud" was a drug compounded of mica.

42. 34143.

人間無路月茫茫	no path to the mortal world, moonlight pale and vast.
玉沙瑤草連溪碧	Jade sands and alabaster plants stretch to the emerald creek,
流水桃花滿澗香	peach blossoms in flowing water fill the ravine with scent.
曉露風燈零落盡	Morning dew and windblown lamp are lost and gone,
此生無處訪劉郎	in this lifetime there is no way to visit young Liu.

The second couplet, used in a fabulous account of Cao Tang's death, was his most famous. The Qing critic Huang Ziyun 黃子雲 gave these lines perhaps the highest praise Cao Tang ever received, writing that "the thousand enchantments and hundred charms of Li Shangyin's 'Left Untitled' poems are no match for the ethereal and breathtaking quality of these two lines."[43] It should be added that Huang Ziyun had a strong dislike for Li Shangyin's poetry.

Finally, Liu and Ruan try to find their way back, but all is changed.

曹唐, 劉阮再到天台不復見仙子

Cao Tang, Liu and Ruan Again Come to Mount Tiantai,
But Do Not See the Immortals Again[44]

再到天台訪玉眞	Again they come to Tiantai to visit Jade Purity,[45]
青苔白石已成塵	the green moss and white stones have already turned to dust.
笙歌冥寞閑深洞	Songs and piping dark and still, the deep grotto lies silent,[46]
雲鶴蕭條絕舊鄰	cranes in the clouds in bleakness cut off from former haunts.
草樹總非前度色	The plants and trees in general lack the colors they had last time,
煙霞不似昔年春	mist and rosy vapors do not resemble the spring of that bygone year.

---

43. *Qing shihua* 清詩話 (Shanghai: Shanghai guji chubanshe, 1963), 865.

44. 34144.

45. This was the name of an immortal, here poetically extended to stand for the goddesses.

46. I suspect that *xian* 閑 here is a mistake for *bi* 閉, "closed."

桃花流水依然在 | Peach blossoms and flowing water
    are there as ever,
不見當時勸酒人 | but they do not see from those days
    the women who bade them drink.

These poems use relatively little of the technical vocabulary of Daoism and reflect a loose use of the long line. Moreover, they are made up almost entirely of common compounds that could easily have been understood orally. There is no clear evidence that poems such as these were used in storytelling or with a prose narrative intended to be read out loud. However, if we were to imagine a sophisticated ninth-century verse, perhaps mixed with prose, situated between the earlier "Cave of Wandering Immortals," the roughly contemporary and provincial prosimetric *bianwen* 變文 of Dunhuang, and the twelve songs to *Die lian hua* 蝶戀花 inserted in *Yingying zhuan* 鶯鶯傳 by Zhao Lingzhi 趙令畤 in the Northern Song,[47] we would arrive at something resembling the poems cited above. Even if there were no written prose to accompany these poems, they were clearly composed as poetry in an imagined narrative, with what was probably (in the Tang) a substantial body of material that provided a model of what such poetry should be like.

Many of the other poems we now might include among the "Larger Wandering Immortal Poems" are rather different. A number of phrases in the following poem on Elühua are far less common and thus would be less comprehensible orally; although the component words are common enough, there are a sufficient number of homophones to make a daring phrase like "the sound of flowers idly falling" 花聲閑落 bewildering to the ear. Elühua was a goddess who repeatedly descended to the home of one Yang Quan in the course of a month, claiming that she was also a Yang. She finally gave him a "corpse-releasing" drug (whereby the "dead" person would become an immortal) and then vanished for good. She was clearly a figure of some importance in Daoism because a long verse by her and her story appear at the very beginning of the *Zhengao* 真誥, a central text in the Shangqing Daoist tradition.[48]

---

47. QSc 491.

48. *Daozang* (Beijing: Wenwu chubanshe), vol 20, 491. The *Zhengao* account or some similar version seems to lie behind this version.

In the *Zhengao* version we have a revelation of heavenly secrets, whereas
Cao Tang's version suggests romantic attachment.

曹唐, 萼綠華將歸九疑留別許真人
Cao Tang, Elühua, About to Return to the Nine Doubts Mountains,
Takes Leave of the Realized Person Xu[49]

九點秋煙黛色空	Nine puffs of autumn mist 　　the color of brows gone,[50]
綠華歸思頗無窮	Elühua's longing to return 　　is particularly endless.
每悲馭鶴身難任	Always sad about riding the crane, 　　that it cannot bear his body,[51]
長恨臨霞語未終	ever hating dawn auroras' approach, 　　their talk not yet done.
河影暗吹雲夢月	The river's reflections unseen blow off 　　the moon of Cloud Dream Park,
花聲閑落洞庭風	the sound of flowers idly falling 　　in the wind of Lake Dongting.
藍絲重勒金條脫	With indigo threads and doubly carved 　　her golden bracelet
留與人間許侍中	was left to Palace Attendant Xu 　　of the mortal world.[52]

Although the context involves narratives describing the romantic en-
counters between goddesses and mortals, the situations are mostly the
basic "poetic" moments in a standard love narrative: feasting together,
parting, and romantic longing.

　　When we consider the Elühua poem together with two poems on
the goddess Du Lanxiang, who married the mortal Zhang Shi, we have

---

49. 35147.

50. Although this must refer to Nine Doubts Mountain (the "color of brows" sug-
gests a mountain ridge), the line clearly echoes Li He's "Dream of Heaven" 夢天,
which closes: "Gazing on China from afar: nine puffs of smoke[/mist], / and the whole
depth of the ocean's water trickles into a cup" 遙望齊州九點煙, 一泓海水杯中瀉
(20665); Ye (1959) 28.

51. I have adopted one possible interpretation of this line; perhaps the crane cannot
bear her body or she cannot bear riding the crane.

52. Cao Tang has apparently confused the story of Elühua, who visited the mortal
Yang Quan, with Wang Meilan 王媚蘭, the Lady of Cloudy Forests 雲林夫人, who
visited Xu Mi 許謐. The latter, however, was the patron of Yang.

a roughly contemporary poetic context for a couplet in one of Li Shang-yin's most famous poems:

李商隱, 重過聖女祠

Li Shangyin, Again Stopping by the Goddess's Shrine[53]

白石巖扉碧蘚滋	Door set in cliff of white stone, the sapphire mosses moist,
上清淪謫得歸遲	cast out from the Upper Clarity,[54] permission to return is slow.
一春夢雨常飄瓦	A whole spring of dream rain[55] always gusts over the tiles,
盡日靈風不滿旗	all day long the wind of the gods does not fill the banners.[56]
萼綠華來無定所	Elühua comes at no certain place;
杜蘭香去未移時	Du Lanxiang departs before much time passes.[57]

---

53. 29093; *Jijie* 1330; Ye (1985) 3; Zhou 235. One of the primary questions here concerns the meaning of *shengnü* 聖女. Yao Peiqian insists that there is no such goddess. Feng gives the most common explanation, namely, that it is a cliff in Shanxi that resembles a woman.

54. This is the highest of the three levels of Heaven. Banishment from Heaven because of some (often sexual) misdeed was a common motif. After serving a certain period of time in the mortal world, the deity or immortal would be recalled to Heaven.

55. This recalls the sexual encounter of the Goddess of Wu Mountain and the king of Chu. Although this line is highly ambiguous, mention of the "dream rain" strengthens the possibility that sexual misbehavior was the cause of the goddess's banishment. The line could suggest the goddess's continued sexual adventures in the mortal world, but it is also possible that her tiles keep out spring's "dream rain."

56. This wind marks the arrival and departure of a divinity. The becalmed temple banners may suggest that she receives no visits from the gods.

57. There are two legends associated with Du Lanxiang. The first is that she was discovered at the age of one or two by a fisherman near the Xiang River. As she was entering adolescence, she had become exceptionally beautiful. When "blue lads" 青童 descended from the sky and were about to carry her away, she told the fisherman that she was an immortal who had been banished to the mortal world because of some offense. The second (and probably more germane) story involves her relation to Zhang Shi 張碩. According to one account, she visited him several times in 316, telling him that they were to be married. However, since their ages didn't match, she told him he would have to wait. According to another account, they were eventually married, but Du Lanxiang left as soon as the marriage was consummated (or completed). A little

| 玉郎會此通仙籍 | May the jade lad someday
  enroll her among the immortals,[58] |
| 憶向天階問紫芝 | recalling how on Heaven's Stairs
  she asked of the lavender mushroom.[59] |

This Li Shangyin poem is stylistically much denser than the Cao Tang poems. Despite the fact that it is not provided with a title that links it to a familiar narrative, it is a poem roughly "of the same kind." Let us suppose that the kinds of poems by Cao Tang cited above were not unique but instead represented a particular kind of contemporary lyric treating stories of the immortals in the situations of romance culture (perhaps not unrelated to the interest in Li He, echoes of whose poems crop up often). If we take Cao Tang as a norm, his poems can easily be situated in a known narrative—even in his more complex poem on Elühua.

However, when we look more closely at the Li Shangyin poem, we see the poet using such an assumption of a narrative ground and disrupting it—making the reader uncertain as to what, precisely, is going on. If we consider the poem while ignoring the third couplet, it suddenly becomes transparent. If this is the goddess's shrine, then the goddess lives there. It would be natural for us to take the exile from Heaven as her exile, as Elühua was sent down into the gross mortal world. In the romantic lore of the immortals, having a forbidden lover was a common reason for banishment from Heaven, which seems to be realized in the erotic image of the "dream rain" in the third line and the futile waiting for a god to come (whose arrival would fill the banners with "spirit wind") in the fourth. In the

---

over a year later she appeared to Zhang riding in a carriage. The couple spoke affectionately, but when Zhang tried to mount the carriage, he was thrust off by the maids. It would seem that Li Shangyin is alluding in particular to Du Lanxiang leaving Zhang Shi right after they were married.

58. Jade lads, a category of celestial functionary rather than a name, were in charge of the registry of gods and immortals. The use of *hui* 會 here seems to be "it happened that," or in the future, as an optative or a prediction, "may it happen that," "it will happen that." The future version is roughly equivalent to the English "may a time come when . . . ." *Hui* may be also taken in the sense of "meeting"; that is, "meeting with the jade lad here."

59. We do not know whether the subject of "recalling" is the jade lad or the goddess; the same uncertainty exists regarding the subject of "asked."

final couplet we see her hope to be reenlisted among the ranks of the immortals. (As in the secular Tang world, registration is essential to one's position.)

The couplet concerning Elühua and Du Lanxiang, however, inverts the gender relations and confuses the situation. As we see in the Cao Tang poems on Elühua and Du Lanxiang, both are goddesses who visit mortals and then abandon them. We know that in such situations the mortal lover of the goddess may have once been a divinity himself, though he has been banished from Heaven and no longer remembers his former life there. This motif of the goddess paying brief visits to a mortal lover invites us to change the gender of the person dreaming and waiting in the second couplet and then of the person banished in the first couplet. In this version the feminine pronouns in the last couplet must be replaced by male equivalents. We could even revise the poem presuming first-person subject:

| 白石巖扉碧蘚滋 | Door set in cliff of white stone, the sapphire mosses moist, |
| 上清淪謫得歸遲 | I was cast out from the Upper Clarity, permission to return is slow. |

Here we have the poet waiting for the goddess's unpredictable visits. But then we have that "whole spring of dream rain," implying a duration that does not fit the situation of the poet who is just "stopping by" the shrine.

These are not problems that can be "resolved" by any scenario—the latter being essentially a narrative like those used by Cao Tang. Rather, the poet is giving us something more enigmatic and inconclusive, playing on our hopes for some simple "story" that will make everything clear.

In contrast to these goddesses to whom the aura of an intensely erotic romance culture clings, we might cite a more commonplace poem by Xu Hun, whose site has exactly the same name as in the title of the Li Shangyin poem (though we cannot be certain that it is the same temple). Although the goddess is invisible, her presence imbues the surroundings with mystery and erotic allure. Xu Hun, however, concludes his poem with an injunction not to engage in love affairs, like the goddess of Wu Mountain.

許渾, 題聖女祠
Xu Hun, On the Shrine of the Goddess[60]

停車一卮酒	I stop my carriage, a single cup of ale,
涼葉下陰風	chill leaves descend in a shadowy wind.
龍氣石牀濕	The stone couch wet from dragon vapors,
鳥聲山廟空	mountain temple deserted amid bird cries.
長眉留桂綠	Her long brows remain in the cassia's green,
丹臉寄蓮紅	her red cheeks are left to the red of the lotus.
莫學陽臺畔	Don't act as she did by the Terrace of Light
朝雲暮雨中	in the clouds of dawn and twilight rain.

Throughout the period of our study we find scattered poems that echo the romantic Daoism of Cao Tang and its unique transformation in Li Shangyin. Since the surviving poetry is only the fortunate remains of a much larger world of poetry, mediated by the interests of later ages, such bits and pieces suggest a kind of poetry which we now glimpse only imperfectly.

---

60. 28593; Jiang Congping 208; Luo 19. Most editions read *shennü* 神女 rather than *shengnü* 聖女 in the title, but *shengnü* is the version in the edition from Xu Hun's own manuscript version.

TEN

Li Shangyin

Preliminaries

Over the centuries Li Shangyin has become the pre-eminent figure of Late Tang poetry. Since the mid-seventeenth century, the beginning of the extant commentarial tradition, Li Shangyin has amassed more commentaries than any individual poet except Du Fu.[1] There are probably more book-length studies and articles published on his poetry than all other Late Tang poets combined. Li Shangyin fully deserves his canonical status. However, even more than was the case with Du Fu, his rise to fame was a complex history of changing values. Li Shangyin does not seem to have become prominent as a poet until after his death. We have a few exchange poems addressed to him that were composed during his lifetime, plus laments following his death, but there is little that suggests his poetry was appreciated outside a small circle. We do have a few indications of his posthumous fame as a poet before the turn of the tenth century. One such testimony is found in the 871 preface to the *Songling ji* 松陵集 by Pi Rixiu 皮日休, where he is mentioned together with Wen Tingyun as the "best," *zui* 最, according to contemporary opinion.[2] Another is a striking denunciation by Li Fu 李涪:[3]

---

1. Although a notice exists for a Song commentary (though we do not know if it was complete), a Yuan anthology, and a Ming commentary, these have not survived. See Liu Xuekai 劉學鍇, *Li Shangyin shige yanjiu* 李商隱詩歌研究 (Hefei: Anhui daxue chubanshe, 1998), 113.

2. Liu Xuekai (2001) 3. This is very odd because it is in the context of exchange poetry; apart from one poem by Li Shangyin to Wen Tingyun (29128; *Jijie* 1276; Ye 44) and an uncertain attribution of a poem to Li Shangyin by Wen Tingyun, we have no

近世尚綺靡, 鄙稽古, 商隱詞藻奇麗, 爲一時之最, 所著尺牘篇詠,少年師
之如不及, 無一言經國, 無纖意獎善, 惟逞章句.

Recent times esteem frills and despise reflection on antiquity. The rare beauties
of Li Shangyin's fancy rhetoric are taken as the best [*zui*] of this age, and
young people model their work on his letters and poems as if they worry they
are going to somehow miss out; yet not a single word he wrote contributes to
the state, nor is there even a slender thought that encourages virtue; it is a
mere display of literary craft [*zhangju*].

Li Fu goes on to equate Li Shangyin with a mere craftsman of fine bro-
cade. These are hard words—and, judging from Li's collection as a
whole, quite unfair—yet they do give us some indication of how Li
Shangyin's poetry was regarded in the last part of the ninth century.
The unfairness of Li Fu's judgment may not have simply been the re-
sult of prejudice or blindness; rather, it strongly suggests that Li Fu had
seen only an anthology (*xiaoji*) of Li Shangyin's poetry and not the
complete collection. From this we may further infer the kinds of poems
by Li Shangyin that were in general circulation at the time.

   Despite these and other claims of his being the most famous poet of
the age (clearly not suggesting in Li's own lifetime), Li Shangyin's name
does not figure often in the frequent comments on poetry in the sec-
ond half of the ninth century. We may take Li Fu at his word to the ef-
fect that Li was widely imitated, but if he was, such poems have not
survived in any great quantity. His poetry is moderately well repre-
sented in Wei Zhuang's *Further Mystery* (*Youxuan ji*) from around the
turn of the tenth century, and very well represented (40 poems) in Wei
Hu's 韋縠 *Caidiao ji* 才調集 from the mid-tenth century (though less
well represented than Wen Tingyun or Wei Zhuang). He was given a
biography among the "Biographies of Literary Men" in the *Old Tang
History*, presented to the Later Jin throne in 945. However, he was per-
haps valued more as a stylist of parallel prose than as a poet. His final
rise to prominence as a poet was due to his devoted editor and imitator
Yang Yi 楊億 (974–1020), one of the most distinguished literary figures
at the beginning of the eleventh century.

-----

evidence of exchange between the two. The preface is preserved in *Tangshi jishi*. It is
likely that Li Shangyin and Wen Tingyun were prominent in some restricted circles.

   3. Liu Xuekai (2001) 5. Li Fu, *Kan wu* 刊誤, in Zuo Gui 左圭, *Baichuan xuehai* 百川
學海 (photocopy; Kyoto: Chūbun, 1979), 519.

Yang Yi's surviving account of the history of his edition of Li Shang-yin's poetry not only tells us something about how Li Shangyin's poetry circulated but also tells us much about how Tang poetry in general re-surfaced in the Song.[4] In the Zhidao Reign of Song Taizong (995–97) Yang tells us that he got hold of a copy of Li Shangyin's poetry (that is, an anthology, a *xiaoji*) containing just over 100 poems. Although he was initially quite taken with these, in hindsight they "did not get the deeply engaging quality of his poetry" 未得其詩之深趣. In the Xianping Reign of Zhenzong (998–1003) he describes a general search for surviv-ing Tang poems. Although he does not speak specifically of finding an-other edition or anthology, in the process of searching he enlarged the collection to 282 poems.[5] He had heard that at the end of the Tang there were many editions of Li Shangyin's poetry in the lower Yangzi region, and a friend there gathered more poems, bringing the Li Shang-yin poetry collection to over 400 poems (just over two-thirds the size of the current collection). We might well wish that Yang Yi had told us more about the makeup of the short collection, containing over 100 pieces acquired with apparent ease (he speaks of continuous and strenuous efforts, *zizi* 孜孜, to bring the collection to its second stage). It is tempting to think that the more easily available short collection represented the sorts of poems known to Li Fu and anthologized in *Caidiao ji.*[6]

---

4. The account is cited in Wan Man 萬曼, *Tangji xulu* 唐集敘錄 (Beijing: Zhonghua shuju, 1980), 283–84.

5. Yang Yi's *Xikun chouchang ji* 西崑酬唱集, containing many imitations of Li Shang-yin, was composed between 1005 and 1008. The Li Shangyin poems that were imitated were primarily the erotic poems, the poems on history, and the poems about things.

6. Balancing his comment that Li Shangyin's short collection "did not get the deeply engaging quality of his poetry," Yang Yi later cites and concurs in Qian's [Ruoshui's?] praise of the poem "Jia Yi" (see p. 439). This suggests that "Jia Yi," a poem that offers an unambiguously ethical judgment of history, was added in the final stage of the col-lection's compilation—it was not imitated in the *Xikun chouchang ji*—and that its quali-ties differed from the overall judgment concerning the limitations of the short collec-tion. Another bit of evidence can be found in the 54 Li Shangyin poems that were copied into the *Wenyuan yinghua* in 987: these are almost entirely poems about things, poems on history (dealing with "dissolute" rulers), hermetic poems, and social jeux d'esprit. There is, however, remarkably little overlap with the *Caidiao ji* poems in the same vein.

The eventual transformation of Li Shangyin from a fancy rhetorician to a politically engaged poet of great range seems to have been a function of Yang Yi's painstaking reconstruction of Li Shangyin's collected poems, from the anthology to the substantial corpus four times the size of the anthology (though still considerably shorter than our current edition). There seems little doubt that if the initial anthology had been the only work to survive, our image of the poet would have been very different. Yang Yi's account is also a sobering reminder of how our understanding of many other poets' works has probably been distorted by their preservation only in manuscript anthologies, which were meant to please late ninth- and tenth-century taste. Many Northern Song editors of Tang poets lacked Yang Yi's considerable prominence and cultural influence to undertake and encourage others to help him search for surviving manuscripts of his favorite poet.

Difficulty and Figurative Language

Although some of Li Shangyin's poetry is as straightforward as that of any of his contemporaries, much of his poetry is difficult, and some of it is impenetrably obscure. A smaller yet significant portion of his poetry suggests passionate attachments between men and women. The penumbra of eroticism surrounding his poetry, while never dissipating, has inspired a long series of interpretive countermotions: critics have stressed his stylistic debt to Du Fu; attention has been drawn to his poems of political engagement; and, most important, figurative interpretations have been given to poems that might on the surface seem erotic.

The earliest clear indication of such figurative reading of Li Shangyin's erotic poetry is found in Zhang Jie's 張戒 (*jinshi* 1124) *Suihantang shihua* 歲寒堂詩話, where Zhang is explicitly arguing against general opinion: "People of the age see only that his poems delight in talking about women and do not understand that they [his poems] were a mirror and warning for his age" 世但見其詩喜説婦人, 而不知爲世鑒戒.[7] This is clearly an attempt to rescue Li Shangyin's erotic poetry as one of "seriousness." We should take special note of the age when this comment appears. Zhang Jie's general conclusion follows comments on Li Shangyin's poems that treat imperial excess. Zhang Jie had witnessed

---

7. Liu Xuekai (2001) 37.

the debacle of the fall of the Northern Song, and the consequences of imperial excess were very much a matter of current concern.[8] For the preceding half-century contemporary poetry had been scrutinized for figurative political references; and in a community that expected covert political references, poets certainly engaged in it, offering "a mirror and warning for [their] age." The late Northern Song also saw the politicization of the interpretation of Du Fu as the model poet, who was supposed never for one moment to have turned his attention away from the dynasty and its concerns.

Zhang Jie's injunction to adopt a figurative mode of interpretation for Li Shangyin's poetry gradually grew in scope, culminating in the continuous commentarial tradition that began in the mid-seventeenth century (another age particularly attentive to figurative political reference in poetry). However, it is important for us to recognize that this interpretive practice was a historical phenomenon that grew out of rather particular hermeneutic circumstances. This kind of interpretation did exist in the Tang, but with nothing of the scope, ingenuity, and programmatic application to the larger part of a poet's oeuvre that we find in the mid-Song and Qing.[9]

Although we can see the beginnings of figurative interpretation of Li's poetry in the Southern Song, Li Fu's negative characterization of Li Shangyin as a frivolous rhetorician (one whose work was tinged with eroticism) continued through the Song and into the Yuan. By the time of the commentarial tradition in the mid-seventeenth century, this version of the poet was effectively silenced in favor of Li Shangyin as a "serious" and politically engaged poet. If critics accepted the discourse of eroticism rather than covert political reference, it referred to passionate love affairs rather than rhetorical play or casual erotic role-playing.

---

8. I am grateful to Ron Egan for pointing this out.

9. Li Shanyin himself spoke of figurative composition in "An Epistle Greeting His Excellency of Hedong, Accompanied by Poems" 謝河東公和詩啓: "By fragrant plants I express resentment at the prince; using lovely women I figure the superior man" 爲芳草以怨王孫, 借美人以喻君子. Such a statement must be understood in context, referring, first, specifically to the poems he is sending to Liu Zhongying and, second, as a gesture to justify apparently frivolous topics. See Liu Xuekai 劉學鍇 and Yu Shucheng 余恕誠, *Li Shangyin wen biannian jiaozhu* 李商隱文編年校注 (Beijing: Zhonghua shuju, 2002), 1961–62.

Figurative language (broadly formulated to encompass a wide range
of tropes, including metaphor, metonymy, and synecdoche) and the
larger question of figurative reference for the poem as a whole became
central issues in understanding Li Shangyin's poetry. In the European
tradition figurative language and meaning were essential markers of
"poetry" in the large sense of saying one thing and meaning another. In
the Chinese tradition figurative language and reference were one re-
source rather than a presumed universal, and a high degree of figura-
tion carried specific associations. In the ninth century the most
"poetic" poetry, associated with the Jia Dao tradition of regulated verse,
tended to be nonfigurative on the larger level of reference.[10]

The question of figuration needs to be approached with some tact
because it is an issue that invites essentializing and misunderstanding.
The degree and nature of figuration in Chinese poetry has varied both
historically and by genre. Even in the most straightforward occasional
poem there was a level of figurative language so habitual as to be al-
most invisible. For example, in certain contexts if a poet used the word
"red," *hong* 紅, a reader would know immediately he was referring to
flowers. Poetic language was filled with more "dead metonymies" than
"dead metaphors."

More complex figuration in a ninth-century context had two primary
associations. The first was elevation of register, which we can link to
formal prose ("parallel prose"). This was a mark of learning, and pre-
sumed a community of those who could understand such language
while excluding others. The use of cultural references ("allusions") was
a closely associated phenomenon. In his own day Li Shangyin was
known as a master of such formal prose.

The second common association of figuration was the presumption
of some barrier to direct utterance; this was also a version of figuration
as exclusion. Barriers to direct utterance could occur on various levels.
On the least problematic level there was the obliquity of politeness,
closely related to the community of learning created in formal figura-
tion. To directly seek sponsorship for the purpose of promotion or to
complain that the person had never replied to such a request was as
crass in ninth-century China as it was in many other cultures and eras.

---

10. There were, of course, exceptions. "Poems on things," *yongwu*, for example,
might often figuratively refer to a human situation.

Such circumstances required rituals of politeness, and in ninth-century China figuration was part of such politeness. Sometimes the relation between client and patron was figured as the relation between a woman and a man, seeking favor and pleading neglect. Such gendering of the social hierarchy, however, was not widespread and adhered to certain norms.[11]

Criticism of emperors and high officials also generally required figuration or some form of verbal indirection. The transgression of the "New *Yuefu*" poets in the Yuanhe Reign had been their direct attack on social abuses (to the point of including notes explicitly specifying what they were attacking). The indirectness of figuration generally sanctioned political criticism. As we will see, the problem in this case is that such "indirectness" sometimes meant hiding criticism in what might be taken as innocent, noncritical discourse—what we now call "deniability." We know that such figurative criticism did occur, but in particular cases it is generally impossible to credibly distinguish concealed criticism from poems in which no criticism is implied. When Li Shangyin writes of the Sweet Dew Incident (see pp. 503–4), he is indirect and figurative, but he is in no way ambiguous.

A third and particularly important situation requiring the obliquity of figuration was in passion between men and women. The history here is complicated, and it is impossible to say whether such figurative language was the legacy of a long history of gender figuration in differential power relations between men or grew out of the social taboos in intergender communication.[12] As an elite culture of romance developed in the Mid-Tang—primarily in a male community but also including women—the poetry addressed to women, exchanged between men and women, and performed in song tended to be figurative on some level.[13]

---

11. It has been suggested that erotic figuration was a private mode of expression of problems with a patron or frustration in a career. In a very general way the *Chuci* tradition might sanction that, but in Tang poetry this usually occurs through direct reference to the *Chuci* tradition. To borrow the contemporary poetic discourse of romance for such an end would have few precedents.

12. These issues are discussed extensively by Paul Rouzer, *Articulated Ladies: Gender and the Male Community in Early Chinese Texts* (Cambridge, Mass.: Harvard University Asia Center, 2001).

13. See Owen (1998) 130–48. The striking contrast between some of the Dunhuang songs and the songs of Wen Tingyun is a good marker of the distinction of an elite culture of romance.

The highly figurative language of Daoism was a special case of re-
stricted, figurative discourse, invoking the esoteric knowledge of a par-
ticular elite community. Li Shangyin studied Daoism in his youth, and it
left a strong imprint on some of his work. He often mixes Daoist dis-
course with erotic suggestion (as Cao Tang does). Critics almost never in-
terpret poems as simply Daoist (the later exegetical tradition was also
intensely antagonistic to Daoism and did not take it seriously), except, of
course, for poems that refer to Daoism in an explicitly occasional con-
text, such as poems addressed to Daoist masters. As we have seen, the
two primary frames of figurative reference for Daoist discourse are the
Inner Court and erotic relationships. One line of interpretation manages
to include both possible referents, with the clandestine amours of court
ladies–turned–Daoist nuns. In another sense, however, Daoist discourse
often functions as a metalanguage, its distinctive kind of figuration point-
ing to some referent hidden from common knowledge.

In these situations of figurative language we should again distinguish
between discursive subcommunities, in which repeated figures become
habitual (a code to be learned), and figuration that was original and, in
some way, truly private. A young man from the provincial gentry arriv-
ing in Chang'an and hearing a Wen Tingyun lyric performed in the en-
tertainment quarters for the first time might not have known what to
make of it. Once having grown intimate with the young men who en-
joyed such poetry, he would quickly have learned its habitual discursive
codes.

Suppose, however, that this same young man came across a copy of
Li Shangyin's "The Drug's Transformations" 藥轉 (referring to the
process of refining a drug or elixir) containing the couplet:

長籌未必輸孫皓   In long strips of toilet paper one need not
                              yield to Sun Hao;
香棗何勞問石崇   for fragrant dates, why take the trouble
                              to ask of Shi Chong.

Chang chou 長籌, translated as "long strips of toilet paper," are actually
long bamboo slips used for the same purpose. Our hypothetical young
man would first have needed to know at least one nonstandard refer-
ence. The first allusion is derived from a Buddhist parable included in
the *Fayuan zhulin* 法苑珠林. When Sun Hao was the ruler of Wu during
the Three Kingdoms period, a metal statue of the Buddha was un-
earthed. Not believing in the Buddha, Sun Hao put it in the privy and

used its no-doubt outstretched hand for holding the bamboo slips used for wiping oneself. When the festival for washing Buddha's image took place, Sun Hao urinated on the statue. He soon developed boils, which were especially painful in his private parts. He was given to understand that his affliction was the result of having desecrated the statue of the Buddha. Now a believer, he repented and washed the Buddha's statue with fragrant liquids. Gradually his boils healed.

The allusion in the second line was better known, conflating the opulent bathroom of Shi Chong, famous for his ostentatious display of wealth, with a story about Wang Dun in *Shishuo xinyu* (34/1). When Wang Dun first married the Wuyang Princess in the Western Jin, he entered the bathroom, which contained a lacquer basket filled with dried dates used for stuffing one's nose to keep out the stench. While sitting on the toilet, Wang Dun ate all the dried dates out of ignorance of their purpose, much to the amusement of the bathroom attendants.

Although we can find the references, since we have no idea what Li Shangyin is referring to, we don't even know how to construe the lines. I have taken *shu* 輸 (to "lose" in a competition) transitively as "yield [to Sun Hao]," but we could just as easily take it as "cause [Sun Hao] to yield." Apart from He Zhuo's remarkably terse "This is a poem about going to the toilet," the commentators are wondrously inventive: from a woman knight-errant concealed as a bathroom attendant (Yao Peiqian), to the poet gazing sadly toward his unattainable beloved when going to the toilet (Cheng Mengxing), to the now most favored explanation, a drug-induced abortion (Feng Hao).[14] Modern scholars have produced other interpretations, including a satire on the secret alchemical practices of the decadent elite. Or consider Chen Yongzheng's 陳永正 explanation that the poem concerns compounding drugs in the search for immortality.[15] We here quote the poem in its entirety:

---

14. In discussing Li Shangyin's poems I frequently refer to the premodern commentators. These have been conveniently brought together in *Jijie* and can be found there in conjunction with the individual poems.

15. Chen Yongzheng 陳永正, "'Yao zhuan' shi yu Tangdai liandanshu" 藥轉詩與唐代煉丹術, in Wang Meng 658–60.

李商隱, 藥轉

Li Shangyin, The Drug's Transformations[16]

鬱金堂北畫樓東	North of the saffron hall, west of the painted mansion,
換骨神方上藥通	for the divine technique of changing the bone the supreme drug works.
露氣暗連青桂苑	The dewy vapors unseen reach to the park of green cassia,
風聲偏獵紫蘭叢	wind-sounds everywhere whistle through clumps of purple orchid.[17]
長籌未必輸孫皓	In long strips of toilet paper one need not yield to Sun Hao;
香棗何勞問石崇	for fragrant dates, why take the trouble to ask of Shi Chong?
憶事懷人兼得句	Recalling the event, thinking on the person both have their lines,
翠衾歸臥繡簾中	she/I returned to lie under kingfisher covers within the embroidered curtains.

A closer look at the various interpretations reveals that they are all based upon explanations of the clearest fact in the poem—even though the latter appears in the poem's most unintelligible lines: something in the poem concerns the privy. This was not a standard topic in Tang poetry and had no common poetic associations. Thus, commentators (probably rightly) assumed that this must have been included because of something quite specific. The various interpretations grew up around the attempt to account for the privy: from fantastic tales of female assassins lurking in the privy, to Cheng Mengxing's hopeless longing upon entering, to the privy as the site of the abortion.

Perhaps the most important line in the poem is actually the seventh line, which contains the clearest statement Li Shangyin ever made about poetic reference in such poems. We should consider the line on two levels: first, the claim itself and, second, the significance of the line as a gesture. The line claims that there is a reference to a person and an event in the preceding lines, but only Li Shangyin and perhaps one or two others could possibly know what the event was. This raises the issue of figuration as concealment and exclusion to a whole new level.

---

16. 28183; *Jijie* 1679; Ye 112.

17. *Lie* here seems to be a contracted version of *lielie* 獵獵, describing the sound of the wind.

One might possibly grant that this poem was actually sent to a woman (or man) who possessed the information necessary to contextualize the lines; this woman would have had to be erudite, going beyond the standard range of images in the poetry of romance. Why one would send such a poem is a reasonable question. Why one would keep a copy and circulate it is another valid question.

This brings us to the significance of the seventh line as a discursive function. If the poem were a truly private communication, the seventh line would be pointless, in that the recipient would be the "person" and know the nature of the "event" so obscurely represented. The seventh line seems to presume a readership for whom the line is meaningful information: it affirms what they might guess. Insofar as the line assumes that readers might not know *that* the preceding lines refer to a person and event, it also assumes that readers will not know *what* person and event are referred to. In short, the line gestures to the existence of concealed information that remains concealed.[18] In such theatrical concealment, a presumed need for concealment will restrict the range of possible "events" to those that would need to be concealed. It is, in short, a poetics of the clandestine.

To send the poem to someone in particular would be one thing. To circulate it among male readers who lack the apparently intimate knowledge of the referential circumstance would be something else again. Such an act could only have been done with the full knowledge that ordinary readers would not understand, and that they would suspect that the poem alluded to events that would normally remain concealed. The poem not only implicitly refers to some original circumstance but also explicitly tells the reader in the seventh line that there is such a circumstance involving a particular person. To knowingly circulate such a poem would, in effect, tell readers that there is a secret, but it would not tell them what the secret is. The poem would also imply that the secret was shocking enough or problematic enough to warrant being kept hidden. In short, the act of circulation would invite precisely the form of speculative biographical interpretation of clandestine intent that the poetry received.

---

18. Ron Egan has suggested that if this poem were truly a private communication, such a line might stress the depth of impression on the memory.

In this context a series of difficult but essential questions arise regarding whether all of Li Shangyin's poems were intended for public circulation and, if so, the extent of their public. In the context of Tang circulation, the "public" could mean distinct and widening circles. Exchange poems and occasional poems were often composed for a particular social circumstance, without any expectation that they would find a wider readership. (Li Shen's extensive notes in *Recollecting Past Travels* show how a poet adds clarifying information in anticipation of a general readership—which strangely parallels the gesture in the seventh line of the poem above.) We know from the preface to the "Willow Branch" poems that Li Shangyin's cousin knew the "Yan Terrace" poems—which were both obscure and erotic—by heart. When Li Shangyin's cousin recited the poems to the demimondaine "Willow Branch," the poems passed from a reader with intimate knowledge of the poet to one who did not know the poet at all. The title of a long poem written by Li Shangyin to his friend Xie Fang (which will be discussed shortly) indicates that the latter could recite many of Li Shangyin's poems by heart and could apply them to himself. From this we can deduce that a selection of Li Shangyin's poems was in circulation in his lifetime, but we do not know which poems. The ultimate form of "public" circulation is the poetry collection, in which the poet's works are presented to those who did not necessarily know the poet, including posterity.

Although some part of Li Shangyin's poetry was in circulation in the poet's lifetime, we have no evidence that Li Shangyin himself compiled his poetry collection, either a small selection of his poems or a provisionally complete version of his poetic works.[19] The mid-ninth century was a transitional period, in which some but not all poets compiled their own works for public circulation. Li Shangyin did compile and write prefaces for two collections of his prose works. However, early bibliographies list the poetry collection separately.

Li Shangyin died before fifty. Had he lived longer, he might have turned his attention to his poetry collection. We may indeed owe the preservation of many of his poems to his untimely death; these are exactly the sort of poems that a poet of more mature years and higher

---

19. Here we exclude small sets of poems compiled for presentation to officials. We know that Li Shangyin, like other poets in the period, made such selections.

public position might have expunged from his collected works. We know that Du Mu rigorously "weeded" his collected poems, retaining only about 20 percent. While we cannot rely on a number of attributions in the large supplementary collections of Du Mu's poems, it is clear that many pieces concerned with his private romantic life were excluded (though not all). What we may have in the case of Li Shangyin is an uncritical compilation of his "literary remains" (or "poetic remains") by his heir. Like many Tang collections, this would have evolved into one or more partial collections (*xiaoji* 小集) to suit the taste of readers.

The seventh line of the poem cited above assumes the existence of a "public," albeit a restricted one. Such indications of the "clandestine," however, do raise issues concerning the social consequences of such poems. For example, some clearly allude to the issue of a woman committing adultery (though without any clear context). This does not suggest a casual liaison with a singing girl or maid. The poet might acquire a certain cachet among a restricted circle of close friends if such illicit liaisons were imputed to him. The circulation of such poems in other circles, however, could easily give rise to gossip that would damage his reputation and affect his career. This would not have been a good thing for a man like Li Shangyin, who was dependent on powerful patrons for much of his life and had varying degrees of access to their households.

Once the possibility of concealed referents has been introduced in a poetic oeuvre, it easily comes to haunt other poems that might otherwise be read more straightforwardly. While this generally does not happen with more direct occasional poems, it commonly occurs in subgenres such as "poems on things" (*yongwu*) and "poems on history" (*yongshi*), which have a tradition of figurative reference. Covert erotic references easily cross over into covert political references. The social dynamics of the community that can understand figurative language and figurative reference come into play. To claim that a poem on some past emperor is actually a critique of a contemporary or recent emperor reflects a desire to understand the "real" and "deeper" meaning of the poem. Implicit in such a claim is the suggestion that anyone who believes that the poem is actually about the obvious topic possesses a more shallow understanding. The poet gains distinction by using a historical figure to refer to a contemporary figure, and the reader gains distinction by seeing through the disguise. When lesser poets write about the failures of past rulers, critics are disposed to view such poems as concerning the past emperors described, whereas critics of Li Shangyin often prefer to find a more recent failed emperor lurking behind a historical figure.

Here we are in the unknowable realm of a poet's "intention." Except in datable poems with telltale markers of contemporary reference, we cannot offer even a probable interpretation of such implicit reference. We can, however, outline the possibilities, taking the "poem on history" as an example. Sometimes poets wrote about past figures and were only referring to them, whereas at other times poets wrote about past figures as a way of speaking about contemporary figures. A contemporary reader might take a poem about a past figure as referring to a contemporary figure, whether or not that contemporary reader's assumption was justified. A poet writing about a past figure in a situation in which such a contemporary interpretation might easily have been made would certainly have been aware of that possibility when circulating his poem. In this case the very notion of poetic intention breaks down. Finally, contemporary and recent events might dispose a poet to be interested in analogous cases in the past. All this is meant to suggest that "using the past to talk about the present" is too simple a formulation for a complex, bidirectional relationship. Certainly the emperors who reigned during Li Shangyin's own lifetime were far from perfect and invited analogies with past emperors. Muzong and Wuzong—and perhaps Xianzong as well—died of overdoses of Daoist drugs. Poems about rulers seeking the immortals could thus suggest current or recent rulers. However, that would depend on knowing when such poems were written. If a poem on Han Wudi's passionate quest for immortality were written during the latter part of the reign of Wenzong, it would probably be about Han Wudi (Muzong being far enough in the past to no longer merit satire). If that same poem was still circulating in Wuzong's reign, readers ignorant of the date of its composition might think that the poet's "intention" was to satirize Wuzong's obsession with Daoism.

Poems about birds or flowers may simply be just that—or they may also be figures for the poet or others. Markers of humanity in such poems are often ambiguous: flowers can acquire pathos by being associated with women or, conversely, women can be referred to as flowers.

In short, the dominant late imperial interpretive traditions found particular value in some ultimately human and historically grounded referent for a poem in the poet's life. When modern commentators reject an earlier interpretation based on imputed biographical context, they often say that the poem lacks *shenyi* 深意, "deep meaning" or "deep intent." Even when these commentators are obviously correct in rejecting some of the far-fetched Qing biographical interpretations, the loss of such an interpretation deprives the poem of "seriousness" in the traditional sense of the term—and thus of greater value.[20]

When we encounter this, it is important to bear in mind that there were other competing ideas of "poetry" in the first half of the ninth century: both Li He and Jia Dao were regarded as versions of the pure "poet." These two distinct but related cases presumed that "poetry" was creating a world of words in which biography was secondary—if even relevant. There is no question that some of Li Shangyin's poems do refer to his life and the contemporary scene in precisely the way in which Qing and modern critics found—and still find—satisfying. However, there was an alternative poetics that could compete with the poetics of biographical reference—even in the same poem—and twist it in interesting ways. As we have seen, the poet could play with biographical reference, claiming that it exists yet hiding it in such a way as to produce an altogether different kind of poetry.

Biography

憶事懷人兼得句   Recalling the event, thinking on the person
                               both have their lines

In part because some putative but concealed biographical context is implicit in Li Shangyin's own poetics, the construction of his poetic biography developed a particular urgency ever since the modern exegetical tradition took shape in the mid-seventeenth century. Chinese poems often depend upon a known circumstance—either conventional or hinted at in the title—to construe even the basic meanings of words and the grammar of a line. A defining circumstance whose existence is indicated but whose particulars are concealed creates something of a crisis. The poems seem to beg for a fuller story of the poet's life from

---

20. Wu Diaogong offers a particularly thoughtful approach to these issues. See Wu Diaogong 吳調公, *Li Shangyin yanjiu* 李商隱研究 (Shanghai: Shanghai guji chubanshe, 1982), 97ff.

which particular contextualizing scenarios for poems can be constructed. Much of the extensive exegetical tradition in Li Shangyin's poetry has involved constructing such putative scenarios and circumstances for poems.

Many basic facts surrounding Li Shangyin's life are known, but these do not give us the kind of information that provides a context for poems like "The Drug's Transformations." The collection does include poems with the usual biographical markers—geographical locations, official titles, seasons—that permit precise dating. Critics, however, have often devoted themselves to finding markers in the other poems, both literal and figurative, in order to link them to the biography and give the poem a context. As a result of this process we have fanciful biographies of the inner man, constructed from and, in turn, used to date a much larger corpus of poems. A survey of the widely divergent dating of many such poems inspires distrust in the procedures far beyond doubts about any particular conclusions regarding dating. Those that are wildly improbable, plausible, possible, probable, and verifiably true are all mixed together. The same range of credibility can be found in the circumstances adduced to frame poems.

A "title," *ti* 題, is a context. When we have a title, we know how to interpret parts of the poem or the whole poem, which often remain hopelessly obscure without the contextualizing title. An interpretation often functions much the same way as a title, either supplementing the existing title or supplying a context for a poem classified as "Left Untitled," either literally or effectively (in the case of those poems whose titles are the first two characters of the poem). Because such a contextualizing interpretation makes it possible to understand the poem in a more or less natural way, reading tends to confirm the interpretation, and long familiarity with a certain reading tends to make the interpretation seem self-evident—despite the circularity according to which such understanding may derive only from an interpretation proposed a thousand years after the poem was composed. The inability of such poems to stand on their own without a context contributes to the peculiar conviction regarding particular interpretations which we realize, on reflection, are purely hypothetical. The one thing that saves us from being entirely caught up in this process is the conflict between what seem to different interpreters to be "self-evident" meanings. Rather than making a judgment regarding which version seems "right," we should

return to the indeterminate text to see how it enables the various inter-
pretations attached to it.

Although the poem "Night Rain: Sent North" 夜雨寄北 is not de-
pendent on a full scenario for the most basic level of interpreting the
lines, it is an excellent example of the tenaciousness of a plausible bio-
graphical context once it has become attached to a poem. In most cases
one would take "sent north" at face value (though it is not a common
formulation). However, Li Shangyin's affectionate relations with his
wife and the tenderness of the poem suggested to some commentators
the interpretation of "north" as the northern part of a domestic com-
pound, the "women's quarters"—in other words, that the poem is be-
ing sent to his wife. That this was an early interpretation is attested in
the variant title given in *Wanshou Tangren jueju*: "Night Rain: Sent to My
Wife" 夜雨寄內.

李商隱, 夜雨寄北
Li Shangyin, Night Rain: Sent North[21]

君問歸期未有期	You ask the date for my return; no date is set yet;
巴山夜雨漲秋池	night rain in the hills of Ba floods the autumn pools.
何當共剪西窗燭	When will we together trim the candle by the western window
卻話巴山夜雨時	and discuss these times of the night rain in the hills of Ba?

The reading that makes his wife the recipient is immensely attractive—
especially given its prospective scene of domestic intimacy, in which the
couple's current separation will become something to talk about when
they are together. The poem assumes long-term intimacy. As scholars
delved more deeply into Li Shangyin's biography, however, they real-
ized that his wife had died before his term of service in Sichuan (Ba). In
no small part, I suspect, to preserve the old and satisfying reading of
this famous poem, some scholars proposed an earlier visit—at least to
the easternmost reaches of Ba. Considerable effort was invested in
proving the existence of such a journey, though, as *Jijie* concludes, the

---

21. 29133; *Jijie* 1230; Ye (1985) 50; Zhou 169.

text implies a long stay more consistent with the years Li Shangyin spent in Sichuan following the death of his wife.

The lesson will, I trust, not be lost in the details. Biography, which was supposed to be an independent, external context for reading Li Shangyin's poems, can easily become a construct used to ratify established, attractive, and/or plausible interpretations of poems. The same is often true of historical context.

Li Shangyin's extensive prose works have provided fodder for speculation about his life, as have poems that adequately indicate context. We suspect that he felt hurt and inconvenienced that Linghu Tao sometimes ignored him; his father, Linghu Chu, had been Li Shangyin's enthusiastic patron. We do not, however, know that poems in which a female persona complains of neglect from her man figuratively refer to that circumstance. It is plausible or possible that some poems do, but there is no way of knowing for sure. The fact that such an imputed circumstance makes sense in a poem does not mean that it is true or even probable but merely that it is possible—more credible than, say, a female knight-errant serving as a bathroom attendant, but that is all. Wen Tingyun also wanted Linghu Tao's support, as did others whom we know about, and we can be certain that Linghu Tao was besieged by such petitioners.

One obvious possibility is suggested in a famous passage from one of Li Shangyin's letters, in which he rejected the offer of a well-known entertainer as a concubine following the death of his wife in 851: "Although I have sometimes treated the beguiling maidens of the Southland and the fine singers of Cong Terrace in my compositions, I have in fact had no connection with the gallantry of lovers (*fengliu*)" 至於南國妖姬, 叢臺妙妓, 雖有涉於篇什, 實不接於風流.[22] Irrespective of whether this is or is not a true claim ("in fact," *shi* 實), it has significance in ninth-century poetics. The passage first acknowledges that readers may infer the character of a person from his poems. The passage can and has been understood as justifying figurative interpretation of the erotic poem—a fine example in which the contextualizing prose comment is twisted in order to support an existing tradition of interpretation. The simplest sense of the passage, however, has the poet claim-

22. Zhou 413.

ing that he wrote about the topic without direct personal experience. Clearly Li Shangyin does not feel that this claim of essentially fictive *fengliu* discredits his poems—though we might see this as an attempt to distance himself from a reputation he might have acquired from others reading his poems. This passage, read in conjunction with the seventh line of "The Drug's Transformations," clearly shows how Li Shangyin plays a double game sometimes claiming cryptic reference to personal experience and at other times denying personal experience of such matters. Such claims vary according to the particular circumstances. We cannot know the biographical truth, nor can we take it as "just poetry" without acknowledging at least a pseudobiographical penumbra surrounding the poems and produced by them (which is not the case in much of Li He's poetry or in Wen Tingyun's *yuefu* songs). What we *can* know is how such poetry plays at simultaneously hinting at and concealing private experience. This is the power of such a poetics of the clandestine.

We here offer only a brief sketch of Li Shangyin's relatively short life (811/13–858)—to which we will return in a later chapter, treating the occasional poems that can be dated with some degree of certainty.

In striking contrast to Du Mu, whose grandfather was the most eminent political figure in the empire, Li Shangyin came from a long line of petty officials; there is no clear indication that any ever passed the *jinshi* examination. He claimed distant descent from the imperial house, as was common among gentry surnamed Li, but even members of the imperial family with known lines of descent, like Li He, had grown so numerous that such claims meant very little. With over two centuries of Tang bureaucracy, the number of rising young men who could claim some eminent ancestor was large—and Li Shangyin could not even claim that. He was a true "cold gate," *hanmen* 寒門, an educated young man from a background distinguished neither by wealth nor by social status. His father died by the time he was ten. His mother was a Cui, with at least one highly placed relative, but that hardly constituted the network of family relations needed to get ahead in the Tang. Display of talent was his sole cultural capital. Li Shangyin never did rise very high in office—"cold gate" scholars with only literary skills rarely did in his time. Although his poetry is rich in political opinions on current events, Li Shangyin does not seem to have given serious thought to solutions for the problems besetting the dynasty, in striking contrast to Du Mu.

We would probably never have heard of him without the peculiar institution mentioned at the beginning of this study: the power of military and surveillance commissioners to confer appointment, which was used to assemble groups of talented young men, some of whom might succeed politically and be of future use. Sometime around 829, at the age of eighteen, Li Shangyin attracted the attention of Linghu Chu, a man with a long history as a patron of promising young literary men. As military commissioner of Tianping, Linghu Chu gave young Li Shangyin one of the sinecure positions at his disposal. In 832 Li Shangyin followed Linghu Chu when he was transferred to Hedong as military commissioner. As was appropriate for a "cold gate" scholar, the younger Li Shangyin had originally practiced old-style prose, which was associated with obscure men rising through sheer force of talent. In Linghu Chu's camp parallel prose was the order of the day, and Li Shangyin established himself as a master of the genre under Linghu Chu's direction. The sumptuous rhetoric of formal prose was a class fantasy, one that touched his poetry deeply.

Sponsorship was necessary for success in the *jinshi* examination. Du Mu had many eager sponsors. Li Shangyin would have been largely dependent on the good graces of Linghu Chu if he did indeed take the examinations of 833, when Li Deyu was in power. This was the very time when Li Deyu was telling Wenzong about the evils of factionalism, by which he meant the Niu Sengru faction, with which Linghu Chu was associated. It was not the most propitious moment for someone of Li Shangyin's background to take the examination; if he did so that year, he did not pass. After another unsuccessful attempt in 835, he finally passed it in 837. Sometime during his youth (probably around 835), he spent some time studying at the Daoist centers at Yuyang and Wangwu Mountains.

In 838, after the deaths of Linghu Chu and Cui Rong—the latter being a fairly prominent official and a relation of his mother's—Li Shangyin joined the staff of another military commissioner, Wang Maoyuan, who gave him his daughter in marriage. Since Wang Maoyuan was a member of the Li Deyu faction, while Linghu Chu and his son Linghu Tao were members of Niu Sengru's faction, scholars often suggest that Li Shangyin's failed political career was a result of factional strife. This is a set topic in academic debates on Li Shangyin, with scholars arguing that he belonged to the Niu faction, to the Li Deyu faction, alternatively to both factions, or to neither faction. Li assiduously courted

Linghu Tao, who helped him only sporadically. Linghu Tao's failure to devote himself entirely to Li Shangyin's interests has been seen as pique at Li Shangyin's marriage to Wang Maoyuan's daughter. Li Shangyin himself seems to have felt that his career was being thwarted by political enmity, but that may have been mere vanity and the common delusion of those who felt their position was incommensurate with their talent. The simple fact is that people of Li Shangyin's background rarely got very far in the bureaucracy. Li Shangyin was probably too insignificant politically to be "punished" in consequence of the factional feuds of the age.[23]

In 839 Li Shangyin was appointed as an editor in the Imperial Library, a lowly post, albeit one carrying some prestige. We might recall that this was essentially the same post that Du Mu first received, though the latter was appointed to serve as editor in the Institute for the Advancement of Literature. Li Shangyin was only twenty-seven at the time and was doing very well. (We might here compare Li Qunyu receiving such a post in his late forties.) In contrast to those contemporaries better known as "poets," Li Shangyin excelled in prose (as did young Du Mu). Such a reputation was more valuable for the "literary" posts available to young graduates. Li Shangyin was soon rusticated to the post of district defender—a typical first post for a *jinshi* graduate without powerful connections. This was clearly a demotion, and one can only speculate as to the reasons. There he got in trouble for reversing a legal decision by a superior and was reinstated only when Yao He replaced the superior. After serving his three-year term, in 842 he rejoined Wang Maoyuan. From there he traveled to the capital to take the palace examination. After successfully passing this examination, he was made a proofreader in the Imperial Library. He was clearly back on the "literary track" of an official career. At this point his mother died. Li spent the subsequent mourning period in private life until 845, when he resumed his proofreadership.

---

23. A more plausible—though equally uncertain—explanation for his lackluster career might relate to opinion about his moral character, the result of gossip inspired by his poems. Although the more prominent Du Mu was also the subject of anecdotal gossip, his self-image as projected in his poetry was restricted to fondness for drink and courtesans, unlike Li Shangyin's, which hinted at illicit liaisons that had to be kept secret.

In 847, the first year of Xuānzong's Dazhong Reign, Li Shangyin's younger brother passed the *jinshi* examination. This rather remarkable fact—two "cold gate" brothers both passing the *jinshi* examination—suggests unknown sources of political support. This was the year in which the purge of the Li Deyu faction by the new emperor began. We do not know if Li Shangyin's decision that summer to accompany the military commissioner Zheng Yao to Guilin in the far southwest was related to that purge, but the timing is suggestive. It was during this period that Li Shangyin first edited a volume of his prose.

The following year Zheng Yao was removed from his position. Li Shangyin made his way back to the heartland, remaining a few months at the headquarters of Li Hui, the military commissioner of Hunan, and then returning to Chang'an. Again Li Shangyin was assigned the post of district defender of a county in the capital region. At the end of 849 Li Shangyin again decided to join a military commissioner stationed at Xuzhou, where Lu Hongzheng had command of the sometimes troublesome Wuning Army. He stayed there until the spring of 851, when he returned to the capital to take up the post of erudite at the National University. That summer Li Shangyin's wife died, an experience that greatly affected him. In early autumn he was off again, this time to Sichuan, to serve under the military commissioner Liu Zhongying. In Chengdu he compiled his second collection of parallel prose. When Liu Zhongying returned to Chang'an in 855, Li Shangyin returned with him. Thanks to his recommendation, he was awarded a position in the Salt and Iron Monopoly, for which he may have traveled to the Southland. Finally, in 858 Li Shangyin returned to his home in Zhengzhou, where he died soon thereafter, aged forty-six, according to Chinese reckoning.

Li Shangyin's life was frankly not very interesting. He was never able to stay in one place more than a few years. He moved between posts and changed patrons, producing large quantities of elegant and erudite public prose. Beneath that surface, however, the most talented poet of the Late Tang was producing a substantial body of poetic work that was to become the single most memorable cultural achievement of his era.

ELEVEN

Li Shangyin

The Hermetic Poems

Li Shangyin has a substantial corpus of poetry that was not meant to be "understood" in the usual sense, at least not in public circulation.[1] It gestures toward concealed meaning while simultaneously keeping the latter hidden. Sometimes a general situation is clear beneath the figuration. (In the poem "Yesterday," discussed below, one reads: "we met last night on the fifteenth of the first month, then had to part.") At other times the general situation can be guessed only from fragments, which often cancel each other out. Generations of ingenious commentators have devised scenarios for particular poems and created elaborate stories of love affairs to frame them. Some of these scenarios and romantic biographies are highly unlikely; most can best be judged as merely "not impossible"; some are more plausible than others. When there are divergent scenarios, as there often are, we can say with certainty that only one can be "biographically true"—which is not to suggest that any of them necessarily is so.

In a larger sense, the enterprise of finding the "biographical truth" behind Li Shangyin's poems is not only futile but does not matter. There may have been ordinary human passion behind such poems; there may have been "poetic passion," in which some ordinary human feeling is intensified through the extraordinary poetics Li Shangyin

---

1. The most persuasive contemporary Chinese scholar on Li Shangyin is Dong Naibin, who addresses these same issues in a rather different way, noting how certain images are cultural signs that point in a general direction, whether the reader recognizes figurative intent or not. Dong Naibin 董乃斌, *Li Shangyin de xinling shijie* 李商隱的心靈世界 (Shanghai: Shanghai guji chubanshe, 1992), 44.

developed; there may have been no straightforward human passion at all, only an enchantment with the poetic role of the passionate lover—which is also a passion in its own right. We cannot distinguish among these various compositional possibilities in any given text; we can only observe what the text does.

Reading these poems as a group, it is hard not to be seduced by the idea of some illicit love affair. Indeed, some of these poems make quite explicit allusions to the latter. Certain figures—for example, the blue-bird messenger and the Violet Maid (the goddess of the privy)—are not part of the standard poetic repertoire and recur often, suggesting a private or "in-group" language of equivalences. We can raise the hypothesis, suggested earlier, of the "uncritical editor"—the son, brother, or some other person—who transfers the surviving literary remains to a manuscript of Li Shangyin's "collected poems," heedless of the moral judgments that *might* be made. (Moral judgments were indeed passed on poets.) I am not convinced by this hypothesis, but it remains the only way to avoid a set of problems raised if we assume that such poems were intended for circulation. Who constituted the real or imagined audience of such poems and how would the poet's morals have been judged by contemporary readers? We know that the morals of poets were under scrutiny in this period. A prose tale in which Niu Sengru meets a group of famous historical women and sleeps with Wang Zhaojun was considered so damaging to his reputation that it was attributed to his enemy Li Deyu. In such a historical context one wonders under what circumstances a poet would circulate the following poem:

李商隱,
可歎 Li Shangyin, Pitiable[2]

辛會東城宴未迴　　By fortune gathering in the east of the city,
　　　　　　　　　　　from the party not yet returned,[3]
年華憂共水相催　　worry that the year's flowering
　　　　　　　　　　　will hurry off along with the waters.

---

2. 29298; *Jijie* 1737; Ye (1985) 229.

3. I have taken *xing* 辛 to mean "by [good] fortune," as Wu Qiao 吳喬 does in his paraphrase, but it could also be a gathering on an imperial excursion (*xing*), as Hu Yimei 胡以梅 interprets it; see *Jijie* 1738–39.

梁家宅裏秦宮入	Into the chambers of the Liang household Qin Gong entered;[4]
趙后樓中赤鳳來	in the high mansion of Empress Zhao Red Phoenix came.[5]
冰簟且眠金鏤枕	On an icy sleeping mat she/he rested awhile on the golden engraved pillow,
瓊筵不醉玉交盃	on the jade part mat she/he did not get drunk on the cups crisscrossed with jade.
宓妃愁坐芝田館	Fu Fei sits sadly in her lodge in fields of *zhi*,
用盡陳王八斗才	having used up the Prince of Chen's eight pints of talent.[6]

The commentators, ever solicitous of Li Shangyin's reputation, have a serious problem here; some resemble nothing so much as lawyers trying to make the best case for their client. Cao Zhi, the Prince of Chen, is here the figure of the poet and would normally be understood as referring to Li Shangyin himself. Cao Zhi loves and is beloved by

---

4. The Eastern Han dignitary Liang Ji 梁冀 favored the slave Qin Gong. Upon gaining free access to Liang Ji's house, Qin Gong had an affair with Liang Ji's wife.

5. The Han empress Zhao Feiyan had sexual relations with the palace slave Yan Chifeng (Red Phoenix).

6. The last four lines refer to the story of the early third-century poet Cao Zhi and Empress Zhen. In contrast to the adulterous relations referred to in lines 3–4, Cao Zhi and Empress Zhen were able to meet only after her death, when she reappeared in the avatar of Fu Fei, the goddess of the Luo. Cao Zhi had originally desired Empress Zhen, but she was given instead to Cao Zhi's elder brother, Cao Pi, later Emperor Wen of the Wei. After Empress Zhen was slandered and put to death, Cao Zhi visited court and Cao Pi showed him Empress Zhen's golden engraved pillow. When Cao Zhi involuntarily began to weep, Cao Pi realized the depth of his brother's feelings and gave the pillow to him. On his way back to his fief, Cao Zhi stopped by the Luo River, in fields of *zhi*, a kind of fungus that was believed to bestow immortality. There he again encountered Lady Zhen in the person of Fu Fei, the goddess of the Luo River, and wrote his poetic exposition "The Goddess of the Luo" 洛神賦. According to Li Shan's commentary to the poetic exposition, Fu Fei / Lady Zhen was supposed to have recognized the pillow, saying that first she had shared it with Cao Pi, but that now she would share it with him. In line 8 the Prince of Chen is Cao Zhi. To the poet Xie Lingyun was attributed the comment that if there was a bushel (*dan* 石 = ten "pints," *dou* 斗) of talent in the world, Cao Zhi got eight pints, Xie himself got one pint, and everyone else divided up the last pint. Apparently Cao Zhi expended all his talent in composing "The Goddess of the Luo."

Empress Zhen, the wife of his brother, appearing in the guise of Fu Fei, the Goddess of the Luo River. The second couplet, however, makes unmistakable reference to how slaves had illicit sexual relations with the wives of their masters, betraying their trust. The argument that Li Shangyin is satirizing some illicit affair *in contrast to* the chaste passion between Cao Zhi and Empress Zhen (implicitly contrasting someone else's situation with his own case) is not impossible, although it is the most generous reading. A more suspicious reader would easily interpret the second line as a desire to make the most of youth, leading quite naturally to the illicit affair indicated in the second couplet, with the conclusion of the poem being the aftermath of the affair. Our advocate-commentators would have pointed out to the suspicious reader that Li Shangyin would surely not have compared himself to despicable figures like Qin Gong and Red Phoenix; but those commentators appeared on the scene eight centuries after the suspicious readers we have imagined. Indeed, contemporary readers might have known Li He's "Qin Gong" 秦宮詩, in which Li He presents a highly romanticized portrait of the adulterous slave that concludes with the following stanza:[7]

皇天厄運猶曾裂	Glorious Heaven's fate was in peril, once it even split open,
秦宮一生花底活	Qin Gong spent a whole lifetime surviving under the flowers.[8]
鸞箆奪得不還人	He snatched away her simurgh comb and would not return it,
醉睡氍毹滿堂月	he slept drunkenly on plush carpets with moonlight filling the hall.

Again, the generous reader could take Li He's poem on Qin Gong as subtle satire; such a reader, determined to find satire, scrutinizes the text for subtle clues that reveal satirical intent and scorns the naïveté of the reader who might view the poem as a celebration of adulterous romance. And yet Qin Gong the slave may not have cared that "glorious Heaven's fate was in peril." There may have been circles in which the image of adulterous romance had some cachet. Conversely, other

---

7. 20801; Ye (1959) 212.

8. Compare this with the last couplet of Li Shangyin's "Twisting River Park," pp. 436–37.

circles might have considered such an attitude to be scandalous and unworthy of a gentleman.

Throughout his life Li Shangyin was politically ambitious and dependent on powerful patrons to advance his career. If a poem such as "Pitiable" had come to the attention of any patron to whose household women Li Shangyin had had any access, one can imagine the consequences. Li Shangyin might well have protested that he wasn't referring to himself or anyone, that the poem was a mere jeu d'esprit, but this would have counted for very little. Such a poem would have inspired gossip. The poet might have claimed that it referred to wickedness in the households of the aristocracy. However, any straightforward reading of the first lines would suggest that the poet himself wanted to make the most of his youth, which would naturally include sexual adventures. An innocent reading of the poem is possible, but human nature does not prefer the innocent reading.

We are left with the following possibilities: someone else composed this poem under Li Shangyin's name to harm him (exceedingly unlikely); the poem was preserved in the poet's papers with no intent that it ever be made public; the original social context of the poem made it clear he was referring to someone other than himself (though such a context could easily be forgotten in the circulation of the poem); the poet was so enamored of his image as a poet in a culture of romance that he circulated the poem within a small circle, oblivious of the social consequences if the poem went beyond that circle. We do not know which, if any, of these possibilities is true, but it remains a problem in any historical and biographical reading, one that cannot be resolved by mere commentarial goodwill.

More contextualization is clearly necessary here. We know that in the ninth century men with power might display their concubines or household entertainers to guests, who might respond flirtatiously, as Li Shangyin himself sometimes did. (Apparently this was the polite response.) One such poem has the following note appended to the original text: "I was serving in Guilin, and Mr. Zheng of my former office brought out his household performer; he then ordered me to write a poem on Gaotang" 予爲桂州從事，故府鄭公出家妓，令賦高唐詩. The poem requested is erotic in tone, Zheng no doubt being proud of the charms of his singer. Li Shangyin gives him good-natured teasing.

李商隱, 席上作
Li Shangyin, Composed at a Party[9]

淡雲輕雨拂高唐	Pale cloud and light rain brush Gaotang,
玉殿秋來夜正長	autumn comes to the jade halls, the nights grow longer.
料得也應憐宋玉	I suspect she surely must have loved Song Yu,
一生惟事楚襄王	but all her life she only served King Xiang of Chu.

Here is an alternative version:

淡煙微雨恣高唐	Pale mist and gentle rain run wild at Gaotang,
一曲清塵遶畫梁	one song, and the pure dust circles the painted rafters.
料得也應憐宋玉	I suspect she surely must have loved Song Yu,
只應無奈楚襄王	it's just that she must have had no choice about King Xiang of Chu.

Li Shangyin is here clearly suggesting that Zheng's performer would prefer himself, the poet figured as Song Yu. However, while teasing Zheng, he nevertheless reaffirms that the singer serves only Zheng (King Xiang)—even if out of necessity rather than choice.

What we find in "Pitiable" is thus an interesting case. The public circulation of a poem that might be taken as suggesting illicit relations with a woman belonging to one's patron could have been a very serious problem. At the same time, at least in some venues one could celebrate a woman who longed for illicit relations with someone outside her household. As Li Shangyin wrote in "Sentiments of the Women's Quarters" 閨情:[10]

紅露花房白蜜脾	Flower buds with red dew, white nectar for honey,
黃蜂紫蝶兩參差	yellow bee, purple butterfly, both flitting about.

---

9. 29226; *Jijie* 643; Ye (1985) 160.
10. 29306; *Jijie* 1839; Ye(1985) 237.

春窗一覺風流夢　　By the spring window she wakes
　　　　　　　　　　　from a dream of passion,
卻是同袍不得知　　but he who shares the long gown with her
　　　　　　　　　　　cannot know.[11]

If this were semipublic discourse, as suggested in the original note to "Composed at a Party," such poetry would have been presented before women and become part of a shared discourse of romance. Here we encounter the vexed question of behavior and representations. It is hardly surprising that wives, concubines, and indentured entertainers might fancy men other than their "masters." Ninth-century poetry added a certain cachet and legitimacy to the simple fact. Although China never developed a romance culture of tacitly accepted adultery, as was the case in medieval Provence and Japan, at several moments in history it came close to celebrating illicit love.

In addition to erotic interpretations of such poems, there is a long tradition of commentators who take obvious eroticism as figurative, either as the poet expressing his desire for his patron's "favor"[12] and complaining of neglect or as satirical, aimed at emperors or those in power. Such commentators always select certain poems for such interpretations and ignore others as purely erotic. The principle seems to be that if a figurative interpretation can be made that is not too absurd, it must be true.

The Li Sao tradition indeed sanctioned one of lower status assuming a feminine voice when seeking "favor" from someone of higher status. However, any survey of contemporary usage will immediately reveal

---

11. The one "who shares the long gown" was, among other things, a term for one's spouse. (The association with friendship does not work in a poem with this title.) It is possible (though unlikely) that the man is the dreamer and the woman is ignorant of his dream. A poem with this title, however, would generally lead to the assumption that the woman is the topic from the beginning—hence the woman as dreamer. The most reasonable alternative possibility (which would change our interpretation) is that he "who shares the long gown" is a husband who is far away, thereby missing the opportunity of her stirred desire. *Jijie* prefers the late Ming variant *tongqin* 同衾, he "who shares the quilt," which would dispel ambiguity. There is no doubt that the associations of the first couplet are sexual, though the poem is ambiguous as to whether the couplet refers to the content of the dream figuratively or describes the scene outside the "spring window."

12. "Favor," *en* 恩, when compounded as *enqing* 恩情 or *en'ai* 恩愛, refers to a man's continuing love for a woman.

that Tang poets did not generally do this in the considerable corpus of poems overtly addressed to patrons. On some occasions the poet who seeks a patron's attention might figure himself as an abandoned woman, and some poems about abandoned women have been interpreted as figurative; but such poets-as-women are usually plaintive and alone in their longing. Less commonly, a poet might speak as a new bride (see p. 132). However, no poet appealed to a patron with scenes hinting at sexual intimacy, secrecy, and blocked passion on both sides. To present such a poem to a patron would, quite frankly, have been bizarre. The poems that are explicitly addressed to a patron like Linghu Tao sometimes show Li Shangyin's density and figurative language, but they do not speak of a lingering scent in the bed from which the beloved has departed. That is, Li Shangyin's poems intended for patrons sometimes share elements with the hermetic, erotic poems—such as the imagery of gods and immortals—but to interpret many of the erotic poems as referring to his relations with a patron reflects an attempt to grant them respectable "seriousness."[13]

"Heyang"

Rather than trying to judge some particular frame of reference—be it erotic or political—and construct a scenario for a particular poem, the best way to approach Li Shangyin's hermetic poetry is to examine in detail *how* such a poem simultaneously gestures toward a concealed

---

13. It often seems that critics have become so accustomed to the closed world of interpretation of Li Shangyin's poems that they do not think of poems outside the corpus. Tang social poetry was governed by contemporary proprieties of discourse, and no situation required the proper tone as much as that of addressing a superior from whom one wanted a favor. Such poems often included figurative elements, and there are poems without explicit markers of address to patrons that have Tang traditions of figurative reference to patrons. The kind of quasi-erotic Li Shangyin poems that are often interpreted figuratively as referring to a patron represent an unprecedented reconfiguration of Li Sao tropes; in a Tang social context this would have been considered "off." One could imagine the erotic and the political converging in a homoerotic relationship with Linghu Tao, but I suspect commentators who prefer the figurative interpretation for its respectability would not like such a reading. We can, of course, view the poems simply as expressive vehicles for the poet's disappointment, with no intention that they ever reach the eyes of patrons, but the intense, usually clandestine eroticism would still be very strange.

referent and blocks easy coherence. That is, we should look at the poem as a process of meaning-formation, bracketing the question of some ultimate experiential referent. Here we may consider "Heyang," one of Li Shangyin's most obscure poems, which has generally been read in the context of a presumed love affair.

Li He was clearly a major influence in the formation of this style, and we know that Li Shangyin became acquainted with Li He's poetry in his youth. A period in his life spent studying Daoism seems to have had an equally profound influence on his imagery. Finally, as Qian Zhongshu has argued, the techniques of parallel prose are very much in evidence. None of these influences, however, can explain what Li Shangyin did with these various formative elements.

李商隱, 河陽詩

Li Shangyin, Heyang[14]

黃河搖溶天上來	The Yellow River heaves churning, coming down from Heaven,
玉樓影近中天臺	the reflections of jade mansions near the Terrace That Strikes Heaven.
龍頭瀉酒客壽杯	Dragon heads spill forth the ale, the guests offer toasts,
主人淺笑紅玫瑰	the hostess lightly smiles a red carnelian.
梓澤東來七十里	Coming from Catalpa Marsh to the east, seventy leagues,
長溝複壍埋雲子	long channels and double moats bury the child of cloud.
可惜秋眸一臠光	Alas for those sweet morsels, the glint of autumn eye pupils,
漢陵走馬黃塵起	from a galloping horse at Hanling the brown dust rose.
南浦老魚腥古涎	At Southbank the aged fish reek with ancient slime,
真珠密字芙蓉篇	pearls, the secret words written, the poem, a lotus-bloom.
湘中寄到夢不到	Sent all the way to the Xiang region, dreams reach not so far,

---

14. 29648; *Jijie* 1643; Ye (1985) 619; Zhou 81.

衰容自去抛涼天　　　the wasted visage goes off by itself,
　　　　　　　　　　　　leaving cool skies behind.

憶得蛟絲裁小樟　　　I recall the merman silk
　　　　　　　　　　　　being cut on the small table,

蛺蝶飛迴木棉薄　　　butterflies turning in flight,
　　　　　　　　　　　　kapok fibers thin.

綠繡笙囊不見人　　　Green embroidered pouch for the pipes,
　　　　　　　　　　　　the person is not seen,

一口紅霞夜深嚼　　　a mouthful of red tendrils of mist
　　　　　　　　　　　　chewed deep in the night.

幽蘭泣露新香死　　　The hidden orchid sheds tears of dew,
　　　　　　　　　　　　its recent fragrance dies,

畫圖淺縹松溪水　　　the picture, pale celadon green,
　　　　　　　　　　　　waters of Song Creek.

楚絲微覺竹枝高　　　From Chu silk one faintly notices
　　　　　　　　　　　　the Bamboo Branch songs loud,

半曲新詞寫縣紙　　　new lyrics for half a song
　　　　　　　　　　　　written out on cotton paper.

巴陵夜市紅守宮　　　In Baling at night they market
　　　　　　　　　　　　red poultice, "Chamber-Guard,"

後房點臂斑斑紅　　　in the back rooms it dots the arm,
　　　　　　　　　　　　streak on streak of red.

堤南渴雁自飛久　　　South of the embankment the thirsty goose
　　　　　　　　　　　　long has flown on its own,

蘆花一夜吹西風　　　reed flowers all night long
　　　　　　　　　　　　blown by the west wind.

曉簾串斷蜻蜓翼　　　The morning curtain pierces and breaks
　　　　　　　　　　　　wings of the dragonfly,

羅屏但有空青色　　　the gossamer screen has only
　　　　　　　　　　　　the bare color green.

玉灣不釣三千年　　　The jade bay is unfished
　　　　　　　　　　　　for three thousand years,

蓮房暗被蛟龍惜　　　unseen in darkness the lotus pod
　　　　　　　　　　　　wins the pity of dragons.

濕銀注鏡井口平　　　Damp silver pours in the mirror,
　　　　　　　　　　　　flat mouth of a well,

鸞釵映月寒錚錚　　　simurgh hairpins glint in moonlight,
　　　　　　　　　　　　cold and clinking.

不知桂樹在何處　　　I know not of the cassia tree,
　　　　　　　　　　　　where it may be found,

仙人不下雙金莖	the immortals do not come down from the paired metal columns.
百尺相風插重屋	A hundred feet up the weather vane set on a tiered roof,
側近嫣紅伴柔綠	close beside the vivid red companion to frail green.
百勞不識對月郎	The shrike does not recognize facing the Moon Lad,
湘竹千條爲一束	a thousand stalks of Xiang bamboo make one bundle.

Little is to be gained by citing all the biographical theories of critics regarding Li Shangyin's hermetic poems, so we will here provide only a brief overview. Zhu Heling and a number of critics that followed him interpreted the poem as a lament for the death of his wife. Heyang was the place where Wang Maoyuan, Li Shangyin's father-in-law, was military commissioner (but only between the fourth and ninth months of 843). Zhu understands the first stanza as describing the marriage. The second stanza invokes the beautiful girls there and the sadness of their dispersal, including the death of his wife. Each of the subsequent stanzas offers slightly different inflections of loss and loneliness. Yao Peiqian accepts the premise that this is a poem lamenting his wife, but he sees each stanza as a retrospective survey of different phases of the poet's past life. Qu Fu also identifies the title as Wang Maoyuan's headquarters, but he makes the lost beloved not the poet's wife but some woman in Wang Maoyuan's establishment with whom Li Shangyin had had a clandestine affair. Cheng Mengxing accepts the title as referring to Wang Maoyuan's command, but he places the time of composition at a time when Li Shangyin was with Liu Zhongying in Sichuan. According to Cheng, one part of the poem represents a lament for his wife, while the other deals with Li's refusal of the entertainer Zhang Yixian to be his concubine (the topic of his "Epistle to the Duke of Hedong" 上河東公啓). Thus, for Zhu Heling the lines beginning "Damp silver pours in the mirror" concern the poet looking at the objects of his late wife, while for Cheng Mengxing they represent Zhang Yixian (the singer offered to Li as a concubine) putting on her makeup.

We note here that the earliest commentators made the identical assumption, namely, the association of Heyang with Wang Maoyuan, but subsequently differed with regard to particulars. Not until Feng Hao's commentary (1763; revised 1801) was it pointed out that Li Shangyin's marriage did not occur when Wang Maoyuan was military commissioner at Heyang. Noting the similarities between this and other poems, Feng went on to argue that such writing was not appropriate for a wife. Based on his note concerning the title, Feng Hao clearly understands "Heyang" not as Wang Maoyuan's headquarters but rather a poetic place, its most famous precedent occurring in Jiang Yan's "Poetic Exposition on Parting" 別賦:

又若君居淄右, 妾家河陽, 同瓊佩之晨照, 共金爐之夕香.

And then again suppose you are dwelling in Ziyou,
and I, the woman, at home in Heyang;
together we had the morning sunshine on our alabaster pendants,
we shared the evening incense from the golden brazier.

For Feng Hao the poem has nothing to do with the poet's wife. Rather, it concerns a clandestine love affair, in which the beloved was later taken away by someone else, finally going south to the Xiang River region. In the sixth stanza ("South of the embankment the thirsty goose") the poet travels south to where the woman was taken, only to find her gone.

Modern commentators tend to offer some variation on Feng Hao's scenario. In *Li Shangyin shige jijie* Liu Xuekai and Jin Shucheng adopt the notion of a woman with whom he had an affair in Heyang, later taken south as a concubine and dead by the time Li Shangyin goes south and tries to find her. Zhou Zhenfu also modifies the Feng Hao interpretation, understanding the poem as a sequel to the "Yan Terrace" poems (see pp. 180–82) and thus explicable in relation to Zhou's interpretation of the situation in those poems. We are on very shaky ground here, for Zhou assumes that if something was mentioned in one poem, it need not be mentioned in others. Zhou's major revision is based on the assumption that Li Shangyin himself never went south to the Xiao-Xiang region. Li Shangyin is therefore expressing sympathy for the woman, who was carried off against her will. One of the Qing commentators had offered a partly political interpretation of the poem, but lest Feng Hao's interpretation seem to be guiding a modern consensus, we note the recent critic Ye Congqi's interpretation of the poem as a lament for Wang Maoyuan.[15]

---

15. See also Zheng Zaiying (302–3) for another version of the standard interpretation.

It is useful to think of the interpretive procedures here in conjunction with how more ordinary poems are read. Most poems involve a conventional situation with a variable set of virtual possibilities derived from prior reading experience. Since Chinese poetic language lacks tense, pronominal markers, and explicit subordination, readers were sensitive to other markers by which to "locate" a line or couplet within the range of virtual possibilities. For example, in a parting poem occurring in the afternoon or evening there may be a couplet representing a river scene in the morning. Readers know that such a scene is what the traveler will see the next day or in the course of his journey even though the perceiver and the tense are not marked.

Such a reading practice is contingent on a circumscribed and habitual range of variation around conventional situations. "Heyang" has no such conventional situation behind it. The Qing and modern commentators are using the usual procedures to construct a nonstandard contextual scenario so that the lines will make sense and cohere. Our own interpretive practice will be restricted to what the community of readers could share, namely, the procedures. We will not carry that further to the conclusions individual readers might reach but that would not necessarily be shared by an interpretive community. That is, we will observe how the text creates small coherences and points to some underlying scenario while simultaneously denying us access to it. The poem, in short, enacts the clandestine. The moment we "decode" it, we have lost it.

Poems with place names as titles usually invoked shared lore about the place. Heyang was not such a place. There was, however, one important precedent for a poem on Heyang, a "Heyang Song" by none other than Li He. Though it is short, it is one of Li He's most enigmatic pieces:

李賀, 河陽歌

Li He, Song of Heyang[16]

染羅衣	Dyeing gossamer,
秋藍難著色	autumn indigo is a color hard to set.
不是無心人	I am not someone without a heart,
爲作臺邛客	acting as a sojourner in Taiqiong.[17]

---

16. 20792; Ye (1959) 201.

17. Since "Taiqiong" makes no sense, commentators generally prefer the emendation Linqiong 臨邛, which refers to Sima Xiangru, who served there.

花燒中潬城	Flowers burn Zhongdan City,[18]
顏郎身已老	Gentleman Yan has now grown old.[19]
惜許兩少年	I regret allowing a pair of youths
抽心似春草	to make my heart sprout like a plant in spring.
今日見銀牌	Today I saw the silver badge,[20]
今夜鳴玉讌	tonight a feast with ringing jades.
牛頭高一尺	Oxhead a whole foot high,[21]
隔坐應相見	I'll surely see her on the other side of the table.
月從東方來	The moon comes out from the east,
酒從東方轉	the ale comes around from the east.
舮船飫口紅	Beakers, the moist mouth red,
蜜炬千枝爛	a thousand branches of wax tapers glittering.

I will not even venture an interpretation of the more obscure parts of this poem; but if we assume that Li Shangyin knew it, as is likely, there is one apparent common thread: a night feast with the poet seeing someone he desires.

Heyang was on the Yellow River, so that the Yellow River in the first line of Li Shangyin's poem evokes a modicum of geographical precision. This initial gesture to place, however, is soon lost in an undefined private space, only to re-emerge several stanzas later in southern China, far from Heyang.

黃河搖溶天上來	The Yellow River heaves churning, coming down from Heaven,
玉樓影近中天臺	the reflections of jade mansions near the Terrace That Strikes Heaven.
龍頭瀉酒客壽杯	Dragon heads spill forth the ale, the guests offer toasts,

---

18. In the Heyang area.

19. This probably refers to Yan Si, who was an elderly court "gentleman" (a post for young men). Emperor Wu asked him why he was in this post, and Yan Si replied that in the reign of Emperor Wen, the emperor liked men with talents for civil government, whereas he, Yan Si, favored the martial arts. In the subsequent reign of Emperor Cheng, the emperor liked good-looking men, while he was ugly. Finally, Emperor Wu favored young men, while he had grown old.

20. Official singing girls had to wear a silver badge inscribed with their names.

21. This is usually understood as a drinking vessel.

主人淺笑紅玫瑰   the hostess lightly smiles
                                   a red carnelian.

The first stanza is a feast scene, beginning with an obvious rework-
ing of the famous opening line of Li Bai's "Bring in the Ale" 將進酒:
"Have you not seen how the Yellow River's waters come down from
Heaven" 君不見黃河之水天上來. The third line recalls an even more
fantastic feast as the "dragon heads [spouts of servers] spill forth ale," a
phrase from Li He's poem "The King of Qin Drinks" 秦王飲酒. Both
earlier feast poems celebrate drunken absorption in the moment, as
does the end of Li He's "Song of Heyang." Like Li He's excessive king
of Qin, King Mu of Zhou aspired to immortality and built the legen-
dary "Terrace That Strikes Heaven."

Given that the title may suggest a personal experience underlying the
poem, the extremely artful construction of the first stanza, which is eas-
ily recognizable, suggests careful poetic construction that becomes far
less perspicuous in the stanzas that follow. The first stanza moves from
a large scope through increasingly smaller scale, until it comes at last to
a single point of attention. The stanza moves from "Heaven" on the
horizon, following the Yellow River to Heyang, where motion is ar-
rested by the reflection of buildings that seem to rise back to Heaven.
We next move into the building to feasting within, ale pouring forth
like the river on a smaller scale, coming at last to the red lips of a
woman, which may also "spill forth" in words or song (perhaps recall-
ing "the moist mouth red" at the end of Li He's song).[22] However, in
contrast to the extravagance of the feast, this is only a "light smile,"
suggesting a reserve of feeling within.

梓澤東來七十里   Coming from Catalpa Marsh to the east,
                                   seventy leagues,
長溝複塹埋雲子   long channels and double moats
                                   bury "child of cloud."
可惜秋眸一臠光   Alas for those sweet morsels,
                                   the glint of autumn eye pupils,
漢陵走馬黃塵起   from a galloping horse at Hanling
                                   the brown dust rose.

---

22. In the translation I have followed Feng Hao in taking *zhuren* as "hostess," the
woman in question; but this also might be the "host," faintly smiling at the woman's
red lips.

The relative clarity of the first stanza is immediately lost in the second. Catalpa Marsh in Heyang was another name for Golden Valley, the park of the fabulously wealthy Shi Chong, who lived during the fourth century. This spot lay northeast of Luoyang, with its "long channels and double moats," near which was Hanling, the site of the Eastern Han imperial tombs. Commentators have offered up various interpretations of "child of cloud," but it was properly a small grain of white rock used in alchemy or flecks of mica. Ji Yun, always seeking some pragmatic basis for images, points out that mica was used in ancient burials. Commentators differ over whether the "burial" is literal or figurative, with one or more beautiful women seized by powerful men in Luoyang.

Each stanza of "Heyang" has a separate rhyme and exists as a formally distinct unit. If one were to extract this stanza as a separate quatrain and entitle it "Green Pearl," it would present no serious difficulty to any commentator. Green Pearl was the favorite concubine of Shi Chong, whose estate was located at Catalpa Marsh. A powerful Jin figure demanded that Shi Chong give up Green Pearl and sent men (perhaps riders at Hanling) to seize her. When they arrived, Shi Chong was feasting with her. At this point Green Pearl drank a toast to Shi Chong and committed suicide by throwing herself from the high terrace. If, furthermore, Li Shangyin's poem was indeed about "Heyang," the story of Shi Chong and Green Pearl would be one of the tales that defined the place. Such an obvious reading of the poem cannot be sustained in the stanzas that follow, which seem to refer to a more private experience. Nevertheless, this would be the only reasonable reading if the poem ended here.

南浦老魚腥古涎	At Southbank the aged fish reek with ancient slime,
眞珠密字芙蓉篇	pearls, the secret words written, the poem, a lotus bloom.
湘中寄到夢不到	Sent all the way to the Xiang region, dreams reach not so far,
衰容自去抛涼天	the wasted visage goes off by itself, leaving cool skies behind.

In the third stanza we leave the relatively precise geography of Heyang and Luoyang and move farther south to modern Hunan, the Xiang River region and Lake Dongting. (Baling, mentioned later in the poem, is Yueyang, located on the shores of Lake Dongting.) The commentators are quick to take all the hints the poet has left in standard poetic associations and exercise their powers of fabulation.

Southbank, Nanpu 南浦, was a standard poetic figure for a place of parting, and associated with the south. Since there is a "sending," the fish suggests a letter, either as a carp-shaped letter case or poetically in a fish's belly. We have a poem, presumably part of the message, sent by Li Shangyin (or another person) to someone in the Xiang region. We know nothing of the contents except that the "secret words written" 密字 (or "densely spaced words") indicates a clandestine communication. Whether the secrecy is in the fact of communication or in the mode of writing is uncertain, but such attractive secrecy suggests illicit desire. As a mode of writing, it would also characterize the present poem. Finally, we have a "wasted [or aging] visage" leaving a place of "cool skies [or weather]." It is uncertain whether the "wasted visage" is Li's own (presumably from longing) or the woman's (an element of aging suggested in "autumn eye-pupils"). If this is a woman, "aging" might mean as early as the mid-twenties. Here one should recall that popular entertainers were often taken as private concubines of gentry or wives of commoners. We saw in Du Mu's two long ballads something of the early-ninth-century fascination with the pathos of women past their adolescent prime. There is no question that here Li Shangyin is playing with elements that hint at a narrative. This stanza provides the core of the Feng Hao scenario of the woman carried off to the Xiang region. As with the "Green Pearl" interpretation of the preceding stanza, it is a narrative that is hard to carry through the following stanzas without resorting to excessive ingenuity.

With the other components of the stanza, a fish may indeed suggest a letter, but what are we to make of the fact that "aged fish reek with ancient slime?" This is Li Shangyin again showing his debt to Li He. It is in Li He's "Ballad of Li Ping's Harp" 李憑箜篌引 that "aged fish leap from waves and gaunt dragons dance" 老魚跳波瘦蛟舞. And his "Lyrics for the Whisk Dance" 拂舞歌辭 closes with: "warped scales and unbending shells are slick with reeking slime" 邪鱗頑甲滑腥涎. Commentators are quick to identify the "fish" with a letter, but they ignore its more unpleasant aspects. Perhaps this malodorous medium contrasts with the "pearls" and "lotus" within, the latter rising out of the muck to show its pure beauty. Or perhaps the imagery is motivated by a desire for poetic effect, however derivative, rather than a hidden referent, which in turn should invite the reader to wonder how much else here is presented for the same reason.

憶得蛟絲裁小榡	I recall the merman silk being cut on the small table,
蛺蝶飛迴木棉薄	butterflies turning in flight, kapok fibers thin.
綠繡笙囊不見人	Green embroidered pouch for the pipes, the person is not seen,
一口紅霞夜深嚼	a mouthful of red tendrils of mist chewed deep in the night.

The fourth stanza begins with an explicit scene of recollection (*yide* 憶得) of the woman doing needlework. Presumably the butterflies, figures for lovers, were in the embroidery. Commentators generally want the third line to refer to the woman's possessions remaining after she is gone, but we must leave open the possibility that the pouch is personified as not seeing the woman; that is, she is no longer performing but doing needlework.

A line with green begs for a matching line with red, closing the stanza with one of the strangest images in the poem, coming back in memory again to her mouth, this time not her red lips but chewing "red tendrils of mist." The earlier commentators cite Daoist texts, where rose clouds, "red tendrils of mist," are the diet of immortals. Precisely how this would fit into the intimate boudoir scene is less clear. *Li Shangyin shige jijie* offers the closest parallel I know, which is found at the end of Li Yu's lyric "A Bushel of Pearls" 一斛珠:[23]

繡床斜憑嬌無那	She leans aslant on the embroidered bed, utterly charming,
爛嚼紅茸	and chewing thoroughly the red fibers,
笑向檀郎唾	laughing she spits them out at her true love.

Zhou Zhenfu agrees that in the Li Shangyin stanza the image must refer to red embroidery threads (though he suggests chewing betel nut as a secondary possibility). The problem is that while the Li Yu lyric does offer a very suggestive parallel, the woman there is clearly not embroidering—she is far too drunk. She has been singing, drinking, and stick-

---

23. Kong Fanjin 孔范今, ed., *Quan Tang Wudai ci shizhu* 全唐五代詞釋注 (Xi'an: Shaanxi renmin chubanshe, 1998), 780.

ing her tongue out at her beloved to tease him. The erotic suggestion in the Li Yu lines works less well for "red tendrils of mist."

Although we cannot comfortably explain this image, we might here take a step back and observe that this strongly suggests a domestic scene for which the poet claims personal memory. It is no wonder, then, that some commentators took the poem as referring to his wife. In contrast, the secrecy of communication in the preceding stanza argues strongly against the woman in question being his wife. Assuming that some experience is being referred to, what might this have been? It is no passing sexual experience with a singing girl or demimondaine, as we might have guessed from the opening stanza. Although the secrecy of their communication and the use of "chamber-guard" a few stanzas later suggests that any relation between him and this woman would be "adulterous" (or however one properly describes relations with another person's concubine), this scene of embroidery suggests a quiet domesticity in an established household. In short, Li Shangyin is using established poetic codes to point to situations that are, however, in conflict. This forces ingenious commentators to devise ever more complex narrative scenarios.

It is presumably the suggested shift from the accessibility to the inaccessibility of the woman that led Feng Hao and later commentators to suggest that at some point the woman was taken into someone's household. Prior to that we might postulate how a young member of the elite in effect lives with a demimondaine for a certain term (perhaps renting lodging in her house, as was proposed in the tale "Li Wa") and then moves on, compelled by financial exigency or posting.

We can play with biographical scenarios to account for such problems, but at some point we should realize that in the process we are moving imaginary players across the map of China—and redefining their relationships—in order to produce a set of scenes and moments that run a gamut of tender moments in the Chinese romantic repertoire. Is this a single narrative or a repertoire? We have "observing the beloved at a feast," "the secret communication," "the surviving objects that remind the poet of the beloved," "the remembered scene of domestic pleasure late at night," and later "the poet visits the site where the beloved used to be and feels her absence." Only the truly anomalous images—such as the streaks of red "chamber-guard" on her limbs as a sign of potentially adulterous behavior—suggest a biographical level underlying the conventional one.

幽蘭泣露新香死	The hidden orchid sheds tears of dew, its recent fragrance dies,
畫圖淺縹松溪水	the picture, pale celadon green, waters of Song Creek.
楚絲微覺竹枝高	From Chu silk one faintly notices the Bamboo Branch songs loud,
半曲新詞寫縣紙	new lyrics for half a song written out on cotton paper.

In this stanza Zhou Zhenfu is impressed by the woman's artistic skills: not only can she do embroidery, but she can also paint and write song lyrics. (Indeed, the anonymous beloved here begins to resemble the famous late Ming courtesans.) Since we have no idea who did the painting and do not know whether the poet or the beloved is writing song lyrics, interpretive scenarios and imputed agents are clearly moving from the plausible to the fanciful. Commentators agree that this is a painting of an orchid that is pale green, like Song Creek. If we want the poetic situation "the lover looks at things left behind by the beloved," we have a problem in the third line, in which the "Chu silk" must refer to zither strings. I have translated *gao* 高 as "loud" (popular songs like the "Bamboo Branch" type were associated with loudness), but it could also mean "lofty," in which case the poet would have a vague sense of the noble sentiments behind the popular songs being sung.

巴陵夜市紅守宮	In Baling at night they market red poultice, "Chamber-Guard,"
後房點臂斑斑紅	in the back rooms it dots the arm, streak on streak of red.
堤南渴雁自飛久	South of the embankment the thirsty goose long has flown on its own,
蘆花一夜吹西風	reed flowers all night long blown by the west wind.

From the quiet domesticity of the "I recall" stanza we come to another stanza suggesting not simply a clandestine relationship but concern about an adulterous affair. "Chamber-guard" was the name given to a poultice supposedly made by feeding cinnabar to a gecko and then grinding the creature up. The poultice was applied in spots on the limbs of the women of the household. It was supposed to leave a mark that was indelible, unless the woman was unfaithful, in which case the mark would disappear. The "streaks" 斑斑 may suggest an intense anxiety about adultery. The latter recalls the earlier letter containing "secret words." Clearly the poet (or male protagonist) is not the person guarding the woman. The fact that the marks are red suggests that the woman has remained faithful despite suspicions to the contrary.

The poem keeps returning to those small spaces of red: first the woman's lips, then the mouth filled with "red tendrils of mist," and finally the streaks of red "chamber-guard" on the woman's limbs, streaks that would not be visible to most eyes. This redness to which the poem draws attention always hints at intimacy—in the lips, the unreadable chewing of red tendrils of mist late into the night, the red streaks watched to guard against sexual misbehavior.

In contrast to the guarded enclosure of the woman in the back rooms, we have the transit of the single wild goose, migrating southward in autumn, marked by reed flowers and the west wind. Its direction would be toward Baling and the Xiang River region, where the woman seems to be located; and its "thirst," *ke* 渴, would be associated with the urgency of desire (as in the Buddhist term *ke'ai* 渴愛, "thirsty desire"). Feng Hao identifies the wild goose with the poet himself, though he takes the line that follows as suggesting that when the poet arrives, the woman is gone, as if blown away by the west wind; the former is marginally plausible and the latter excessive. Although Li Shangyin may indeed have visited the region in autumn of 848 (he probably came in summer), he was traveling north.

曉簾串斷蜻蜓翼	The morning curtain pierces and breaks wings of the dragonfly,
羅屏但有空青色	the gossamer screen has only the bare color green.
玉灣不釣三千年	The jade bay is unfished for three thousand years,
蓮房暗被蛟龍惜	unseen in darkness the lotus pod wins the pity of dragons.

Commentators have generally interpreted this stanza as describing the scene of the deserted chamber after the woman has gone. Although absence is a possible association of the second line of the stanza and perhaps an attempt to pun on "lotus pod" as "chamber of the beloved," such an interpretation is merely an extension of the scenario constructed earlier. The images are suggestive, beautiful, and truly in-comprehensible, with none of the conventionally coded images of stan-zas like the second. We cannot read even the simplest level of reference into a line like: "The morning curtain pierces and breaks [or "com-pletely pierces"] wings of the dragonfly." We have translucent surfaces, picked up in the "gossamer screen" and perhaps made opaque in the "jade bay." The bay, in turn, may have lotus pods on the surface and dragons underneath. That is, there are suggestive internal relations within the stanza that also link it to the following stanza, but they elude the kind of repressed narrative with which the poet was playing earlier.

濕銀注鏡井口平	Damp silver pours in the mirror, flat mouth of a well,
鸞釵映月寒錚錚	the simurgh hairpins glint in moonlight, cold and clinking.
不知桂樹在何處	I know not of the cassia tree, where it may be found,
仙人不下雙金莖	the immortal does not come down from the paired metal columns.

In the penultimate stanza, the "damp silver" is explained by com-mentators as the light from the mirror, which is further compared to the mouth of a well (or perhaps the mouth of a well is compared to a mirror). Some want the hairpins to be objects left behind, but the fact that they are "clinking" suggests that they are being worn, which im-plies the woman's presence. The cassia tree is found on the moon, where Chang E fled after obtaining the elixir of immortality. The final line of the stanza refers to the bronze immortal of Emperor Wu, hold-ing a pan to catch the dew from which the elixir of immortality can be made (though Zhou Zhenfu prefers to identify the reference as "gold stem flowers" 金莖花). The surface of the water in the preceding stanza can be associated, in turn, with a mirror, a well, and the moon. Li He compared the dew pan of the bronze immortal to the moon. As-sociations crisscross everywhere but do not cohere. The grand finale, moreover, gives us nothing with which to tie the pieces together.

百尺相風插重屋	A hundred feet up the weather vane set on a tiered roof,
側近嫣紅伴柔綠	close beside the vivid red companion to frail green.

百勞不識對月郎　　　The shrike does not recognize
　　　　　　　　　　　　facing the Moon Lad,
湘竹千條爲一束　　　a thousand stalks of Xiang bamboo
　　　　　　　　　　　　make one bundle.

Seasonal images were one of the most consistent markers in Tang poetry. The biographical critics—who would have the poet visiting the dwelling of the beloved in the Xiang region during autumn—are here faced with a scene of late spring, which ends when the shrike cries out. The bamboo of the Xiang region were said to have been speckled by the tears of the Xiang River goddesses, the wives of Shun, lamenting his death. The commentators take the Moon Lad as Li himself and the last line as referring to how many tears he has shed—though the shrike might "not recognize the lad facing the moon," an alternative reading of the line that might pick up Chang E's flight to immortality in the moon in the preceding stanza.

As the commentators attempt to explain the final stanzas, we see their interpretations becoming more general and forced. They clearly feel that they "got" the story early on and can only explain the rest in terms of vague references to the poet's unhappiness.

We have subtitled this chapter "The Hermetic Poems," a term that was chosen advisedly. It is a poetry that promises to disclose a secret code that will unlock its mystery yet willfully frustrates the interpreter. We must at least entertain the possibility that Li Shangyin is here engaging in poetic action rather than encoding meaning. He sets up difficult but intelligible situations involving some form of passionate or conjugal relation between a man and a woman. Such coded language used in a relatively easily interpretable way can be seen in the song lyrics and many of the *yuefu* of Wen Tingyun. In Li Shangyin's hermetic poems those situations do not, however, cohere in the usual sense. At a certain point in the poem the margin of intelligibility is removed, leaving us with a series of images with complex interrelations but no easy ground of coherence. Another way of saying this is that in the course of the poem, the poet plays with interpretive habits, drawing the reader to the margin of making sense and then pushing him or her over the edge. The poem enacts a process of confusion, which the poet will often tell us is the "blur" or confusion of passion and memory.

Perhaps in "Heyang" the poet went too far; it was never one of his most popular poems. Other poems, no less difficult but usually shorter, caught his readers' imaginations. Interpreters offered various explanations, but readers were clearly captivated by that fragile margin between making sense and eluding understanding.

"Walls of Sapphire"

In Li Shangyin's collection there are about thirteen poems that come to us with the title *wuti* 無題, "without a title." Since Chinese poems generally have titles that provide essential information for understanding a poem, I translate *wuti* as "Left Untitled," to suggest that the refusal to provide a title is a significant act.[24] Such a title already points to information concealed and establishes the mystery that is central to Li Shangyin's poetics in this mode. There is a larger body of poems, including "Walls of Sapphire" and "Brocade Zither" (discussed below), in which the title is simply the first two characters of the first line; many of these poems are of the same type as the "Left Untitled" poems.

It is far from certain that Li Shangyin himself assigned such "titles" (including "Left Untitled"). As we suggested earlier, we have no evidence that Li Shangyin compiled an edition of his own poems. These two different conventions of giving titles to poems of roughly the same kind may reflect differing editorial decisions in various manuscript versions concerning how to handle poem texts that simply lacked titles. It would have been easy to circulate and preserve a single poem on a piece of note paper (*jian* 箋) without a title. When preparing a manuscript with many poems, however, a title, written in a separate column, was a necessary convention used to separate one poem from another.[25] As we have seen, Yang Yi drew upon different manuscript sources in compiling his edition. It is not impossible that such differences in titling

---

24. This is based on the possible but highly uncertain assumption that the designation *wuti* was Li Shangyin's own.

25. Li Shangyin's collected poems have no overall organization. Bai Juyi's later poems were clearly organized chronologically, and we see loose chronological sequences in some other ninth-century collections. The disorganization of the collection is consistent with (but does not prove) a posthumous editor working with poems written on note papers.

represent different ways in which scribes in distinct manuscript lineages handled poems without titles.

Since the hermetic poems involve a problematic relation to an imagined community of readers (as opposed to some potential singular recipient who can immediately decipher obscure references), the history of their reception is of particular interest. Unfortunately, we have no indication of contemporary responses to such poems, and the one poem by Li Shangyin that addresses the reading of his poetry, however interesting, does not necessarily refer to the hermetic poems.[26] The earliest indication of interest in such poems dates from the turn of the tenth century and the mid-tenth century, when the cultural world of the mid-ninth century had basically been destroyed. Wei Zhuang's *Youxuan ji* (turn of the tenth century) includes a few poems, and Wei Hu's mid-tenth-century *Caidiao ji* includes such a substantial selection (40 poems) that he clearly considered Li Shangyin an important poet. The *Youxuan ji* and *Caidiao ji* have two poems in common: one is a clever, inconsequential quatrain for a singer and the other is one of the finest of Li Shangyin's hermetic poems, "Walls of Sapphire." The poem anthologized by both is the first of a set of three (*Caidiao ji* gives all three); and while the modern reader may feel that the poem should be considered in the context of the set, that was probably not an issue for the ninth- and tenth-century reader.

In his hermetic poems Li Shangyin often has recourse to the discourse of legendary immortals, esoteric knowledge, and Daoism, just as often contrasting it to the mortal world. Daoism was a religion based on a select community, unified by the understanding of a special discourse and defined against a larger community of the uninitiated. There is a profound homology between this religious structure of understanding and Li Shangyin's poetics. This is not to say that Li Shangyin is a "Daoist poet," but rather that Li Shangyin's poetic imagination was formally homologous to Daoist knowledge, discursively separating the initiate from the uninitiated.

---

26. See pp. 492–95.

李商隱, 碧城
Li Shangyin, Walls of Sapphire[27]

I

碧城十二曲闌干	Walls of sapphire, railings in twelve bends,[28]
犀辟塵埃玉辟寒	narwhale tusk wards off the dust, jade wards off the cold.[29]
閬苑有書多附鶴	In Lang Park there are letters, often sent by crane;[30]
女牀無樹不棲鸞	on Maidensbed Mountain no tree without perching simurghs.[31]
星沈海底當窗見	Stars sinking to the sea's bottom are at its windows seen,
雨過河源隔座看	rain passing the Yellow River's source is watched across from one's seat.[32]

---

27. 29242–44; *Jijie* 1660; Ye (1985) 174; Zhou 245.

28. The *Taiping yulan* speaks of the deity Primal Heavenly Majesty 元始天尊 as living in a city "walled with sapphire cloud" 碧霞爲城. It is unlikely that any particular deity is intended in Li Shangyin's poem, but this is clearly a dwelling in Heaven.

29. The *xi* 犀 here is a sea creature of the south whose horn was supposed to repel dust. It was used in women's hairpins and combs. Although there are legends of "fire jade," jade is generally thought of as warm.

30. Lang Park was a dwelling of the immortals. Zhou Zhenfu suggests an alternative possibility, noting the park constructed by two early Tang princes who were governing Langzhou (though his attempt to link that with the Daoist nunneries constructed by Tang princesses is forced). Cheng Mengxing cites a poem by Lu Lun (14678): "I blame the crane, crossing the sea bearing a letter, for being too slow" 渡海傳書怪鶴遲. In tales of immortals, cranes often bear messages. Ye, however, insists that these are books rather than letters and cites a story in the *Jincheng ji* in which a man raised six cranes, which, after three years of tending, could read. When the man wanted a book, he would send a crane to fetch it.

31. In the *Shanhai jing* Maidensbed Mountain is given as the home of the "simurgh," the *luan* phoenix. Hu Yimei points out the obvious play on the name here. Most commentators take this as roosting in pairs, hence romantic assignations, but Hu Yimei appeals to the old story of the simurgh longing for its mate to suggest that these birds are alone.

32. As I have translated the line, it assumes a heavenly perspective. Qian Liangze, however, interprets it as meaning when one star sinks beneath the sea, another is seen at the window. Feng Hao sees this as the Three Immortal Isles lying beneath the sea, so that this vision is possible. Zhou sees the mention of the "River's source" as referring to the story of the "third month raft," where the sea joins the River of Stars and flows back down to earth again. According to the original version of that story, the River of

| 若是曉珠明又定 | If only morning's pearl would be bright and also still,[33] |
| 一生長對水精盤 | I would spend my whole life facing the bowl of crystal.[34] |

Rather than trying to "decode" the poem or show how the associations of various lines guide (and often thwart) the decoding process, let us

---

Stars brings one back to the Yangzi rather than to the Yellow River. However, in his "Autumn Thoughts," *Qiuxing bashou*, Du Fu links the legend with Zhang Qian, who was sent to discover the source of the Yellow River. Many commentators identify the rain here with the "clouds and rain" of sexual encounter. Qian Liangze, following an interpretation that sees the series as referring to Xuanzong and Yang Guifei, interprets it as the arrival of Lady Yang following the death of Wu Huifei. Zhou Zhenfu offers a very different interpretation, suggesting "the evidence of indulgence in union by night and separation by day." His version reads: "When the stars sink to the sea's bottom, he appears at the window, / when the rain [nighttime sex] passes the River's source, he/she watches [the other] from the other side of the table."

33. Commentators generally take "morning's pearl" as the sun. Zhu Heling associated it with a miraculous pearl in the *Feiyan waizhuan* 飛燕外傳, but Feng Hao rightly dismisses that notion. *Jijie* cites the opinion of Chen Yixin that these are dewdrops.

34. *Pan* 盤, translated as "bowl," is often rendered "plate." We should, however, never think of a flat plate but rather something with sloping sides. "Pan" is often a good rendering, though in English we never think of pans as transparent. Zhu Heling cites the *Taizhen waizhuan* 太真外傳 for the famous story of Zhao Feiyan, whose body was so light that Han Chengdi feared she would be carried off by the wind. He therefore had a crystal bowl made, to be held up by palace women when she danced. Presumably Zhao Feiyan would dance under it, protected from the wind yet visible to the emperor. Feng Hao rejects this and cites another story of Dong Yan 董偃 and a crystal bowl used for holding ice, which he ultimately rejects. Since Dong Yan was the favorite of a Han princess, interpreting the allusion in this fashion supports the line of interpretation that views the set in reference to Tang aristocratic women setting themselves up in private Daoist establishments. Ye, seeing the set as a satire against Wuzong, takes this as the bowl in which Wuzong kept his elixirs. Yao Peiqian identifies the crystal bowl with the moon, which is followed by a number of modern commentators. I agree with Zhu Heling. To see the crystal bowl as the moon makes very little sense in this context. Zhao Feiyan's crystal bowl is by far the most famous, and the image of watching a performer for a lifetime is echoed in the penultimate line of "Autumn" in the *Yantai sishi* 燕臺四時: "Singing lips a whole lifetime watched holding back tears" 歌唇一世銜雨看. Qian Liangze, following the Xuanzong interpretation, associates Zhao Feiyan with Wu Huifei; thus, if time had stopped, he *would have* spent his whole life watching Zhao Feiyan dancing. Feng Hao's interpretation is completely distinct, seeing the "crystal bowl" as a figure for the woman's [Daoist nun] chastity: if it were always daytime, then she would be always chaste.

consider the poem on a simpler and more fundamental level. The first six lines are all, in some way, descriptive of what there is, what is seen. The last two lines form a conditional sentence that makes a rather extravagant claim on the part of the speaker. Fixity is one of the conditions of the protasis (line 7), and fixity would be the state achieved in the apodosis (line 8). Whatever the earlier lines "mean," they draw heavily on the imagery of immortals and an unchanging world. The final image of imagined stasis is a peculiar one: the speaker would spend a whole lifetime (a mortal's lifetime) facing and gazing at a crystal bowl. The crystal bowl is open to various interpretations, but as an object it recapitulates the situation of a speaker: one can see through but not go through. In the stasis of the gaze the speaker can neither leave nor approach. If "morning's pearl" in the penultimate line is the sun, then the proposed condition is one of time stopping in eternal light. It is also an impossible condition that implicitly reminds us that we inhabit a world of ongoing time.

If the final couplet implies a mortal perspective, albeit one that aspires to the stasis of immortals, the third couplet is not simply the world of the immortals but the perspective of immortals. If the "windows" and "seat" are in the same hypothetical "place," then we have a height that suggests impossible perspectives: Heaven or, perhaps, the heights of the Kunlun Mountains. The palace of the immortals in the Kunlun Mountains is protected from the mortal world, with its contaminating dust and the cold of seasonal change and the waning year. We never see the immortals—only passing cranes bearing communications whose contents are illegible. As with the image of the crystal bowl, we can behold it at a certain distance, but we can never get inside that world.

It is problematic to read too many texts metapoetically, yet the poem recalls Du Mu's description of Li He's poetry in the preface, which we know Li Shangyin read and admired: Li He's poetic worlds were more real and perfect than those we experience in the world. Whatever the possible topical referents in the sublunary world (if any) in Li Shangyin's poem, it is unlikely that the anthologists Wei Zhuang and Wei Hu were interested in them. This was a visionary world, represented in poetry and animated by the final couplet that positions the mortal in relation to such a world. In the mid-ninth century Li Shangyin's poetic imagination may have been a "class fantasy," a seemingly timeless world beyond reach, the woman he would stare at for a lifetime through a crystal bowl. Perhaps by the tenth century it had become a "period fantasy," a vanished splendor of the Tang.

II

對影聞聲已可憐	Facing her outline, hearing her voice, already lovable,
玉池荷葉正田田	the lotus leaves on Jade Pool, just now spreading.[35]
不逢簫史休迴首	Unless meeting Xiaoshi, she will not turn her head;[36]
莫見洪崖又拍肩	she never sees Hongyai and again claps him on the shoulder.[37]
紫鳳放嬌銜楚珮	The lavender phoenix shows its charm, holding Chu pendants in its beak;[38]
赤鱗狂舞撥湘絃	crimson scales dance madly, to the strumming of Xiang strings.[39]

---

35. He Zhuo cites Wang Jinzhu's 王金珠 version of the *Huanwen ge* 歡聞歌 (a Southern *yuefu* type): "Sensual, the girl of the golden tower, / her heart is like the lotus on Jade Pool" 豔豔金樓女, 心如玉池蓮 (Lu Qinli 2127). *Tiantian* 田田 describes the quality of lotus leaves. Qian Liangze, the most ardent exponent of the Xuanzong interpretation, takes this as referring to Xuanzong granting Yang Guifei the privilege of a bath in the hot springs at Huaqing Palace.

36. The implied subject is Nongyu 弄玉, the daughter of the duke of Qin, who flew off to Heaven with her lover Xiaoshi.

37. Hongya was an immortal. The line echoes Guo Pu's *Youxian shi* 遊仙詩: "To the right I clap Hongya on the shoulder" 右拍洪涯肩. Hu Yimei sees this couplet as the beloved affirming that she will not be intimate with others. Qian Liangze takes Xiaoshi as referring to the Prince of Shou and Hongya to An Lushan. A basic division here is between those who take the relation between the hemistiches in line 3 as above and those who take the relation as conditional.

38. Feng takes the second hemistich as a reference to Zheng Jiaofu meeting the two nymphs of the Han River, who undid their waist pendants and gave them to him as a sign of their love. Zhou interprets this and the following line as the Daoist priests, who are the lovers of aristocratic nuns, capering for them. The pendants they hold are supposed to be the love gifts from the nuns.

39. This is often taken as a reference to Hu Ba 瓠巴, whose zither playing brought the fish up to listen. As Zhu Heling notes, the more immediate source is Jiang Yan's "Poetic Exposition on Parting" 別賦, in particular the line: "It caused to jut up the crimson scales of the fish from the abyss" 挈淵魚之赤鱗. The *Yuanyou* in the *Chuci* speaks of "making the Xiang spirits play the zither" 使湘靈鼓瑟兮.

鄂君悵望舟中夜   The Lord of E looks in despair
                                    to that night in the boat;[40]
繡被焚香獨自眠   embroidered blanket and burning incense,
                                    he sleeps all alone.

One reason to read the closing image of the first poem as Zhao Fei-
yan dancing under (or on) a bowl of crystal is the opening line of this
poem, which, with the repetition of "facing," seems to carry on the im-
age. Following this, however, we encounter a series of allusions without
the markers that position the speaker, which we do have in the first and
final poem.

In reading Li Shangyin's most difficult poems, it is often best to be-
gin at the end. Let us assume (suspending our doubts) that there is no
gender issue in the allusion in the final couplet (that is, the beloved is
the beloved regardless of gender). In these poems so filled with "fac-
ing," "looking," "seeing," and "gazing," the poem ends in solitude,
"gazing" to a scene and moment in the past. It is not difficult to see
how such a retrospective gaze is the double of gazing through the
crystal bowl: one can see, but one cannot reach. If the crystal bowl
in the first poem was transparent, here we have an opaque blanket,
under which once lay the handsome young Yue boatman favored by
the Lord of E.

The third couplet seems to be a scene of presence. If, however, the
association of the "Chu pendants" with the nymphs of the Han River is
correct, it is a presence that immediately slips away. (The two nymphs
of the Han undid their pendants and gave them to Zheng Jiaofu, only
to disappear when he turned his head.) Such elusiveness follows an-
other statement of lost or rejected companionship (with the immortal
Hongya) and a claim of singularity of affection. Nongyu, the daughter
of the duke of Qin, became Xiaoshi's wife. Here she will notice only
Xiaoshi.

The poem cannot be "deciphered" and probably was not intended
to be. It begins and ends with an image of looking. If we carry the

---

40. The Lord of E was the brother of the king of Chu. While boating, the young
boatman of Yue sang him a love song, and the lord embraced him and covered him
with an embroidered coverlet. Qian Liangze takes this as referring to Xuanzong follow-
ing the loss of Lady Yang. Zhou sees this as the despair of the aristocratic nuns, who
are thinking of aristocratic lovers (as opposed to their Daoist priests).

"facing" of the preceding poem over to this poem, it is a gaze that implies a distance that cannot be crossed.

III

七夕來時先有期	When she came on the Seventh Eve, the date had been set before,[41]
洞房簾箔至今垂	the curtains of the inner chamber hang down to this day.
玉輪顧兔初生魄	The gazing hare in the jade orb when the moon's dark first appears,[42]
鐵網珊瑚未有枝	the coral in the iron net had no branches yet.[43]
檢與神方教駐景	Inspecting the divine technique, make the daylight halt,
收將鳳紙寫相思	gathering up the phoenix paper, write out longing.[44]
武皇內傳分明在	The "Secret History of Emperor Wu" survives for all to see—[45]
莫道人間總不知	don't say that in the mortal world it is not generally known.

---

41. Zhu Heling interprets this line as a reference to a story in the *Han Wudi neizhuan*, in which the jade maiden Wangzi Deng appeared to Wudi and announced that on the double seventh the Queen Mother of the West would visit him. Feng Hao prefers the meeting of the Oxherd and Weaver Woman on the Seventh Eve. *Jijie* follows Feng. Qian Liangze sees this as referring to the vow between Xuanzong and Yang Guifei on the Seventh Eve. As Ye points out, this does not accord with the phrasing of the line.

42. The first appearance of the dark of the moon would be after the fifteenth of the month. Cheng Mengxing and others take this as a reference to the woman being pregnant, "dark [of the moon]," *po* 魄, also being a "soul."

43. Iron nets were supposedly used to gather coral. According to Cheng Mengxing, this means the pregnant woman has not delivered. "Having no branches" is also "as yet having no limbs," perhaps referring to an early-term fetus.

44. *Jijie* suggests that these lines involve the technique used for inducing an abortion. Feng notes that "phoenix paper" was used in the palace and also in Daoist prayers. Feng paraphrases this as a wish that the beauty of youth stay and that passion not wane.

45. Hu Zhenheng here cites his son, mentioning a poem by Liu Yuxi that makes reference to Han Wudi stopping by the residence of Princess Guantao and calling her lover Dong Yan the "Mistress's Old Man" 主人翁. In Liu Yuxi's case this is used as a figure for the Tang emperor stopping by the residence of Princess Jiuxian and asking about the Daoist priest who was her lover.

We do not have a "referent," nor do we even have a narrative that could be mapped on some recorded or imagined referent. We have fragments that might form part of a narrative, which, in turn, might have a referent. We have a solitary figure "gazing" toward a moment in the past; we may have a figure who would like to gaze at the beloved through crystal. Here we have a prearranged past meeting behind curtains in the inner chamber. We will not ask whether that meeting was with the Queen Mother of the West (Xiwangmu), the Weaver Woman, or a Tang princess. We know it is past because those curtains "hang down to this day." Assuming that the beginning of the second poem picked up at the end of the first poem, we can here see a recapitulation of the end of the second poem (recalling the absence of the beloved under the embroidered blanket in the second poem). The imagery and theatrical secrecy all point to a sexual meeting.

Before considering the cryptic middle couplets, we will turn again to the final couplet, in which the poet, for all his poetic indirectness, says that something is "generally known." This is closely related to the discursive move at the end of "The Drug's Transformations": here the poet gestures toward a specific referent and even claims that everyone knows. It is no wonder that Qing and modern commentators have combed the historical record to discover what might be so "generally known." They can, alas, never know if this "generally known" matter refers to Emperor Wu of the Han, Xuanzong, some emperor or personage of Li Shangyin's day, or to something else altogether. We can read the "Secret History of Emperor Wu" and still not know what Li Shangyin claimed was so clear. Rather, we must take this claim of public knowledge as somehow belied by the cryptic lines.

Perhaps the middle lines refer to an abortion—as some commentators have suggested—and if this is the case, the pregnancy was certainly the result of the meeting referred to in the opening lines. We will never know.

The three "Walls of Sapphire" poems occupy an important place among Li Shangyin's hermetic poems, and the interpretations offered up to explain them are quite diverse. The oldest, by the late Ming critic Hu Zhenheng 胡震亨, sees them as referring to Tang princesses setting themselves up outside the palace as Daoist "nuns" in private religious foundations, thereby making possible romantic affairs. Variations on this interpretation are followed by Cheng Mengxing, Feng Hao, and others, including *Jijie* and Zhou Zhenfu. Another line of interpretation, begun by Zhu Heling, sees them as erotic poems involving phases of union and loss. Zhu Yizun was the first to view them as referring to the love between Xuanzong and Lady Yang. To give some sense of the elasticity of interpretation, Qian Liangze sees the three poems as following the course of Xuanzong's romance with Lady Yang in life, while Lu Kunceng interprets it all as occurring after Lady Yang's death and apotheosis, in which the Daoist wizard is seeking Lady Yang in Heaven. Xu Dehong represents yet another line of interpretation, in which the three poems are understood as offering images of Li Shangyin's depression over the failure of his political career. Yao Peiqian sees the situation somewhat differently as expressing Li Shangyin's alienation from the ruler and desire to serve the state. Ye dismisses both the "Daoist nun" interpretation and the Xuanzong interpretation, instead seeing the set as a satire against Wuzong. This divergence of opinion among so many learned commentators should remind us that they are asking the question in such a way that the possible answers cannot command any modern community of assent, nor can we imagine a broad community of assent to any such interpretation even in the mid-ninth century. We can reach a level of "understanding" only by posing different kinds of questions.

Endings

Much of the appeal of Li Shangyin's hermetic regulated poems lies in the strong contrast between the density and difficulty of the inner couplets and the relative directness of the closure, often marked by an urgency of address or some emotional coloring (*xu* 虛). Although a difference in tone between the parallel inner couplets and the final couplet was normative for regulated verse, being a consequence of the form, it was nevertheless susceptible to significant variations. In discussing Late Tang regulated verse in the short line, we commented on how the formal difference between the parallel middle couplets and the final couplet was often exaggerated in the Late Tang to produce a framing effect: carefully crafted "poetic" couplets are set in a discursive, sometimes almost vernacular frame. Although Li Shangyin never slips into this somewhat crude variation on formal structure, in many of the hermetic regulated verses he does play on the stylistic difference of the final couplet. We are first presented with a series of suggestive, formally perfect,

obscure lines, followed by a concluding couplet that is gestural, filled
with particles, and relatively straightforward. The poet passes judgment,
sums up, or exhorts, often with an intensity that animates what is con-
cealed in the preceding couplets.

武皇内傳分明在   The "Secret History of Emperor Wu"
                          survives for all to see—
莫道人間總不知   don't say that in the mortal world
                          it is not generally known.

As was noted earlier, although the closing couplet of the third "Walls of
Sapphire" poem poses its own problems of interpretation, on one level
it is very clear. The claim of common knowledge and the implicit claim
that this is important knowledge make the inner couplets something
more than difficult ornamental rhetoric.

    Often the final couplet contains a "message" that few would have
had difficulty understanding.

人間桑海朝朝變   Mulberry fields and seas in the mortal world
                          change place every morning—
莫遣佳期更後期   do not make our sweet date of union
                          postponed for a later date.

In other words, things are always changing, so don't postpone the date
on which we agreed to meet. If, however, we look at the poem to
which this conclusion is appended, we see a peculiarly mysterious con-
text for the clear message.

李商隱, 一片

Li Shangyin, A Swathe Of[46]

一片非煙隔九枝   A swathe of not mist
                          blocks the nine-branched candelabra,[47]
蓬巒仙仗儼雲旗   on Penglai's ridge the immortal guards
                          have cloud-banners in array.[48]

---

46. 29272; *Jijie* 1984; Ye (1985) 205; Zhou 259.

47. Commentators generally associate "not mist," *fei yan* 非煙, with auspicious
clouds. The "nine-branched candelabra" is literally a "nine-branch," *jiuzhi* 九枝. The *ge*
隔 here is ambiguous and can just as easily be translated: "A swathe of not mist lies on
the other side of (i.e., is blocked by) the nine-branched candelabra."

48. Penglai was the isle of the immortals in the Eastern Ocean. Worlds of the im-
mortals were conventionally associated with the imperial court, and guards were more

天泉水暖龍吟細	In Heaven's Spring the waters are warm, the dragon intones faintly,[49]
露畹春多鳳舞遲	on dewy acres spring is full, the phoenix's dance slowed.[50]
榆莢散來星斗轉	Elm pods come scattering, the Dipper turns in the stars,[51]
桂華尋去月輪移	go off to seek cassia blossoms, the moon's orb shifts on.[52]
人間桑海朝朝變	Mulberry fields and seas in the mortal world change place every morning—[53]
莫遣佳期更後期	do not make our sweet date of union postponed for a later date.

One could spend much time discussing the first six lines of this poem, yet all the mystery comes at last to the explicit injunction at the end: don't postpone the date on which we agreed to meet. This "message" is not the poem, but it remains the final word that contextualizes the difficult lines. The ending gives us a way to try to read the poem that the title does not; in some ways it serves the contextualizing function of a title.

Li Shangyin's endings often address someone or seem to share a personal confidence with the reader, creating an intimacy that is in many ways the counterpart of the sense of a secret truth in the obscurity of the inner couplets. Sometimes the poem is not difficult, but the closing lends it the same sense of intimacy.

---

commonly associated with the court. "Cloud banners" may be either real banners decorated with clouds or clouds resembling banners.

49. Feng Hao cites "Heaven's Spring" in Jin Luoyang, with a pair of bronze dragons feeding it with water from the imperial moat. The "intoning," *yin* 吟, of the dragon could be the water pouring in, a dragon in the pool, or an imperial poem.

50. "Slowed," *chi* 遲, can either mean that the dance continues on or is "slow in coming" (i.e., delayed). It might also mean that the dance movements are slow.

51. Elm trees were supposed to grow in the heavens.

52. A cassia tree grew on the moon. The relevance of the reference is uncertain, but "picking the cassia" also meant passing the examination.

53. *Sanghai* 桑海, literally "mulberry [groves] and oceans," was a shortened version of the notion that mulberry groves would someday become oceans and vice versa, that is, there would be major changes in the world.

李商隱, 無題
Li Shangyin, Left Untitled[54]

相見時難別亦難	Having a time to meet is hard, 　　parting too is hard,[55]
東風無力百花殘	the east wind lacks strength, 　　all the flowers fade.[56]
春蠶到死絲方盡	When spring's silkworm meets death, 　　then will its threads run out;[57]
蠟炬成灰淚始乾	when the wax taper turns to ash, 　　only then its tears will dry.[58]
曉鏡但愁雲鬢改	In the mirror at dawn grieving only 　　how cloudlike tresses change,[59]
夜吟應覺月光寒	chanting by night, surely feeling 　　moonlight's cold.
蓬山此去無多路	From this point on the road is not long 　　to Penglai Mountain—
青鳥殷勤爲探看	bluebird, do your best 　　to spy it out for me![60]

Although the closing addresses the bluebird, it suddenly changes the tone from hopeless longing to hopeful urgency. Although it doesn't really follow from the immediately preceding lines—it does follow from the first line—it seems to.

No other poem by Li Shangyin captured critical attention so early and consistently as "Brocade Zither." Though it hardly represents the full scope of the poet's work, it has become the touchstone for Li Shangyin's poetry and has served as the catalyst for interest in his poetry. Apart from the Xikun imitations, the earliest comment on the poem, found in Liu Bin's 劉攽 *Zhongshan shihua* 中山詩話, is paradigmatic: "No one understands what it means; some people claim that it [Brocade Zither] was the name of a servant girl in Linghu Chu's house-

---

54. 29241; *Jijie* 1461; Ye (1985) 173; Zhou 198.

55. This line plays on the *Yan'ge xing* 燕歌行 of Cao Pi: "How easily the day of parting comes, the day of meeting hard" 別日何易會日難.

56. The east wind is the spring wind.

57. Li Shangyin is here punning on *si* 絲 "threads" and *si* 思 "longing."

58. "Tears" was the conventional metaphor for the wax drippings of a candle.

59. "Cloudlike tresses" are conventionally associated with women. The "change" is a turning white.

60. The bluebird was the messenger of the Queen Mother of the West.

hold."[61] We should note the exegetical process: difficulty in understanding led to postulating a biographical context (an affair with his patron's servant), which provided the ultimate referent, explained the title, and suggested a reason why the poem was hard to understand (the relationship was clandestine). The "servant girl" explanation was dropped relatively early. The range of later interpretations has been summarized by James Liu in English and in many Chinese sources.[62] None of these explanations is ultimately persuasive, though the theory that it is the "preface" to his poetry collection and refers to his poetry has the merit of being capacious enough to encompass the various associations. Most interpretations of the hermetic poems contain at least one line that has to be played down or ingeniously explained in order to make the interpretation fit. In "Brocade Zither," for example, the interpretation that understands the poem as a lament for his wife is attractive, but the allusion to Emperor Wang of Shu, who gave up his throne in remorse for having committed adultery with the wife of a minister, is definitely a sticking point. Perhaps in this case the cuckoo weeping tears of blood is only a figure of misery, but that is not how the allusion is used elsewhere.

李商隱, 錦瑟
Li Shangyin, Brocade Zither[63]

錦瑟無端五十絃	It just happens that the brocade zither has fifty strings,[64]
一絃一柱思華年	each string, each peg turns thoughts to the flowering years.

---

61. Liu Xuekai 劉學鍇, *Huipingben Li Shangyin shi* 匯評本李商隱詩 (Shanghai: Shanghai shehui kexueyuan chubanshe, 2002), 244.

62. James Liu 51–57. "Brocade Zither" is perhaps unique in Tang poetry in having occasioned so many articles that primarily summarize earlier interpretations. A particularly good one that is also more recent than James Liu's study is found in Zhang Mingfei 張明非, "Li Shangyin Wuti shi yanjiu zongshu" 李商隱無題詩研究綜述, in Wang Meng 771–80.

63. 29092; *Jijie* 1420; Ye(1985) 1; Zhou 1.

64. The reference here is to the story of how the Sunü 素女 played a *se* zither of fifty strings for the Yellow Emperor, who found the music so sad that he broke it into two zithers, each containing twenty-five strings. *Wuduan* 無端 generally means "for no reason." Wang Ying proposes the sense of *wuxin* 無心, "without feeling" (*Shi ci qu yuci lishi* 245).

莊生曉夢迷蝴蝶	Zhuang Zhou's morning dream, lost in a butterfly,[65]
望帝春心託杜鵑	Emperor Wang's spring heart, lodged in a cuckoo.[66]
滄海月明珠有淚	When the moon grows bright on the gray sea, there are tears in pearl;[67]
藍田日暖玉生煙	when the sun warms Indigo Fields the jade gives off a mist.[68]
此情可待成追憶	One should wait until these feelings become remembrance,[69]
只是當時已惘然	it's just that at the moment I was already in a daze.[70]

Poems like "Brocade Zither" are a gift of form. The middle lines, objects of intense critical scrutiny, would become virtually invisible in a long *pailü* of fifty couplets. They are animated by their frame. Although here and in a handful of the most famous such poems, the opening couplet is as effective as the final couplet, the final couplet is the best place to begin to reflect on the poem.[71]

---

65. The reference here is to Zhuangzi's famous "butterfly dream," recounted in *Qiwu lun* 齊物論.

66. Emperor Wang of Shu sent Bieling 鼈靈 to work on flood control. During the latter's absence he began a liaison with his wife. Feeling ashamed, he then gave his kingdom to Bieling. According to one legend, following his death Emperor Wang was transformed into a cuckoo, which always sings sadly and weeps tears of blood.

67. According to one legend, pearls were the tears of mermen. Another legend had it that pearls grow and shrink with the phases of the moon.

68. Sikong Tu quoted the late eighth-century poet Dai Shulun as saying that "the scene a poet creates is as when the sun is warm on Indigo Fields [Lantian, southeast of Chang'an], and the jade produces mist: you can gaze at it, but you cannot place it before your eyes."

69. *Jijie* interprets *kedai* 可待 as a rhetorical question: "How can one wait?"

70. *Jijie* interprets *zhishi* 只是 as "right then."

71. Wu Benxing offered the interesting suggestion that one might consider the poem as consisting of two quatrains, one consisting of the first and last couplets and one made up of the middle couplets. The notion of the middle couplets forming an independent quatrain obviously does not work, but to take the first and last couplets as a quatrain is often very effective, a relatively lucid "container" for the middle couplets. See Wang Meng 774. Wang Meng makes a similar point in "Hundun de xinling chang—tan Li Shangyin Wuti shi de jiegou" 混沌的心靈場—談李商隱無題詩的結構. *Wenxue yichan*, no. 3 (1995); rpt. in Wang Meng 676–90.

The final couplet of "Brocade Zither" possesses its own kinds of uncertainties resulting from the numerous particles that impart "discursive quality," *yuqi* 語氣, to an utterance. In the seventh line *ke* 可 can mean "might" or an implied "should," as I have taken it to mean. It can be interrogative—"could one wait?"—but it can have other qualities as well. *Dangshi* 當時, "at the moment," usually implies the past, though it might mean the present. The poem would take on a rather different tone were we to translate the last line as follows: "it's just that at the moment I am already in a daze." *Zhishi* 只是, "it's just that," sometimes has the sense of "right now." In short, this closing personal comment that seems so direct opens up a variety of possibilities, each of which would change the meaning, sometimes significantly so. In most cases such discursive lines are very straightforward because we understand the context in which they are made. This, however, is a statement in a daze. The one "clear" thing in this daze is that the couplet creates an interval between "at the time" (then or now) and a relative future when the feelings of the past will or might become "remembrance." The voice seems to be speaking from some intermediate stage in that interval (unless we take the last line as present).

The lines also seem to suggest some similarity between "remembrance," *zhuiyi* 追憶, and the daze, perhaps in the sense that both involve the element of blurring.[72] As we move backward to the sixth line, we have a further context for the motif of blurring, the scene of mist rising at Indigo Fields (Lantian). If Li Shangyin knew and had in mind the quotation from Dai Shulun cited by Sikong Tu, this was a figure for poetic representation. What Dai Shulun described as a "scene," *jing* 景 (*shijia zhi jing* 詩家之景, "the scene a poet creates"), is picked up in the next line as "these feelings," "mood," *qing* 情. The basic terms of later poetics are already here, one moving into the other.

There is a poetics implicit here, crossing easily from poetic representation to memory to immediate feeling. It is a poetics of blurriness,

---

72. A good example of "in a daze," *wangran* 惘然, used in recollection is found in Bai Juyi, "Pei Five" 裴五 (22558; Zhu 894). Li Shangyin's commentators and modern lexicography often interpret *wangran* as a blur or confusion, shifting from the subject's mental state, a "daze" out of distress, to an uncertainty and blurring of mental representations. This is probably due to the context here; indeed, *Hanyu dacidian* cites this line as the first use of *wangran* in this sense.

in which obscurity of representation corresponds to the daze of immediacy—whether such "immediacy" is that of present passion or intense memory. Such a poetics well describes many of Li Shangyin's most famous poems. As mist detaches objects from a coherent ground and makes them appear blurred and isolated, this poetics detaches scenes in lines from a ground, whether it be a representational spatial ground or a narrative ground. They become fragments, set adrift, which imply a whole and draw their intensity from the implied whole. In the end, Li Shangyin's claim is that such a "blur" is how they were experienced immediately. The poem reproduces the state of mind it describes.

If we turn back to the first couplet, the beginning of the frame, we begin to see how the poem functions. We cannot know what the "brocade zither" represents. We can, however, describe how it is represented. The poet counts the strings and seems to suggest precise correspondences (just as he suggested an exact correspondence between an event and an elusive poetic image in "The Drug's Transformations"). Next we notice that he tells us that such exactitude "has no reason," "just happens [to be so]," *wuduan* 無端. In music the capacity to evoke feeling derives from each string and the position of each peg; but in music the sounds of the individual strings work together and blur into a whole. Most of all, the opening couplet establishes the distance of remembrance that is invoked again in the final couplet.

The scenes of the middle couplets must be figures for the memories invoked, just as music poems often describe a series of scenes the music evokes. Both lines of the second couplet are scenes of metamorphosis. Although the butterfly of Zhuang Zhou's dream is not erotic, the butterflies of Tang poetry were, especially in conjunction with *mi* 迷, "to be lost in," "go astray." The figure of Emperor Wang as a cuckoo suggests sexual transgression and regret. Considering the direct references to adultery and the language of secrecy in many of Li Shangyin's poems, we cannot dismiss this aspect of the image of Emperor Wang. Reading the lines of the couplet in parallel, as we normally do, we have oppositions of straying and repentance, happiness and pain.

One who drinks wine in dream may weep in the dawn. One who weeps in dream may go off on a hunt with the coming of dawn. But while they are still dreaming, they know not that they dream. In their dreams they may even read the meaning of dreams within dreams. But only after waking do they know it was a dream.

The transition to the third couplet, the "turn," is beautifully handled. To mention Emperor Wang as cuckoo immediately evokes the cuckoo's "tears of blood." The repressed tears appear in the third couplet in a different guise, presenting a double etiology of pearls as the tears of mermen and appearing in oysters with the full moon, the symbolic doubles of the moon. The opposition between "ocean" and "fields" suggests cosmic changes. Pearls were also a common image for beautiful lines of poetry (as well as notes of music). Taken together, the lines of the third couplet suggest distance and another kind of transformation, namely, that of experience into poetry.

We do not know who placed "Brocade Zither" as the first poem in Li Shangyin's works; its fame may partly be due to its placement there. The poem deserves its fame. Those who interpret the poem as Li Shangyin's preface to the poetry collection may be going too far, but the poem does seem to address the relation between experience and poetry in a memorable and unique way.

Titles

The Qing and modern commentators have long recognized that poems whose titles are the first two characters of the text are basically of the same kind as the "left untitled" poems. Compare the following two poems, the title of the first being its first two characters, "Yesterday," and the second, a famous "Left Untitled," beginning with "Last Night."

李商隱, 昨日
Li Shangyin, Yesterday[73]

昨日紫姑神去也	Yesterday the goddess the Violet Maid left.
今朝青鳥使來賒	this morning the bluebird messenger delays to come.
未容言語還分散	No chance for words to be spoken, we divided again,
少得團圓足怨嗟	rarely reaching union/fullness supplies reproachful sighs.
二八月輪蟾影破	On the sixteenth in the moon's orb the Toad's outline is broken,

---

73. 29460; *Jijie* 1759; Ye (1985) 398; Zhou 257.

十三絃柱雁行斜   the thirteen string pegs
                                are a line of geese aslant.
平明鐘後更何事   After the bell of daybreak,
                                what further occurred?—
笑倚牆邊梅樹花   smiling she rested against
                                plum blossoms by the wall.

The Violet Maid was the Goddess of the Privy, originally a concubine
mistreated by the primary wife and assigned the chore of cleaning the
privy. Some accounts claim she simply died there. One account speci-
fies that she was murdered there by a jealous first wife on the fifteenth
day (full moon) of the first month, which became her festival. The
bluebird was the messenger of the Queen Mother of the West, an-
nouncing the goddess's impending visit to Emperor Wu of the Han.
What do these two allusions have to do with one another? We do not
know, but we find them together again in the opening lines of one of
the longer poems entitled "The Goddess's Chapel" 聖女祠.[74]

杳靄逢仙跡   A far blur of haze, I found an immortal's traces,
蒼茫滯客途   in a vast expanse the traveler's course delayed.
何年歸碧落   What year did she return to the Biluo heavens?
此路向皇都   this road goes toward the royal capital.
消息期青雀   For news, one expects the bluebird messenger,
逢迎異紫姑   a reception differing from that of Violet Maid.

Quite possibly we have here a private set of identifications—though in
"Yesterday" it may simply be a way of saying that "yesterday" was the
fifteenth of the first month.

The middle couplets play on union and separation, playing on the
word *tuanyuan* 團圓, referring both to the union of those parted and the
fullness of the moon (the fifteenth). The lovers appear to have been
together on the fifteenth but were unable to speak—hence the sighs of
reproach or disappointment. On the sixteenth fullness and union are
broken. The thirteen pegs belong to the zither (*zheng* 箏), and the asso-
ciation with a line of wild geese may suggest travel or the character
"one" 一, suggesting solitude.

We assume that the last couplet refers to the woman—though how
he would know this and why she was smiling remain enigmatic. The

---

74. 29417; *Jijie* 1683; Ye (1985) 365; Zhou 49.

one thing we know is that with plum blossoms this meeting was indeed on the fifteenth of the first month, the anniversary of the murder of the Violet Maid.

The following poem, one of Li Shangyin' most famous, is "Left Untitled"; but the similarities with "Yesterday," *zuori* 昨日, are such that we would not be surprised were it entitled "Last Night," *zuoye* 昨夜.

李商隱, 無題

Li Shangyin, Left Untitled[75]

昨夜星辰昨夜風	Last night's stars, last night's wind,
畫樓西畔桂堂東	the western side of the painted mansion, east of the cassia hall.
身無彩鳳雙飛翼	For bodies, no wings in paired flight of the parti-colored phoenix;
心有靈犀一點通	for hearts, one point running through the magic rhino horn.[76]
隔座送鉤春酒暖	The hook passed across the table, the springtime ale warm,[77]
分曹射覆蠟燈紅	divided in teams, guessing what was covered, the waxen lamp shone red.[78]
嗟余聽鼓應官去	Alas that I heed the drumbeat and go off to my official duties,
走馬蘭臺類轉蓬	galloping my horse to Orchid Terrace, the likes of a rolling tumbleweed.[79]

---

75. 29202; *Jijie* 389; Ye (1985) 136; Zhou 94. For a longer discussion, see Stephen Owen, "The Difficulty of Pleasure," *Extreme orient/extreme occident* 20 (1998): 24–26.

76. The *tongxi* 通犀 is the central core of rhino horn. The play here is on the mutual communication of hearts 兩心相通.

77. "Hiding the hook," *cang gou* 藏鉤, was a drinking game. According to Zhou, teams seated across from one another would pass a hook concealed in the hand back and forth, and the opposing team had to guess where the hook was. Presumably the spring ale was the drinking forfeit.

78. This game is referred to in the biography of Dongfang Shuo. Some object would be hidden under a cup, and the participants would have to guess what it was. Feng and several other commentators interpret this as Li watching a group of women play rather than participating himself.

79. Some editions have *duan* 斷 instead of *zhuan* 轉. The Orchid Terrace was a name for the imperial library. The same term has been used for the Censorate. Feng Hao insists that here it refers to the library. This would date the poem to 842, when Li

Commentators here differ as to whether this is simply an erotic poem or figures the poet's relation to prince or patron under the guise of the erotic. There is, however, general agreement that on one level the poem is erotic. It should be pointed out that commentators like Feng Hao and Ji Yun, often strongly disposed to finding figurative references, take this as Li watching a party of house concubines or of singing girls.

There can be no doubt that this is a more considerable poem than "Yesterday," with the tension of the lovers being together but unable to communicate. Like "Yesterday," the situation is not difficult to understand, but it appeals to private knowledge shared with another person, from which the reader is excluded, except by his power of inference. The form of the two poems is strikingly similar, which strongly suggests that the "Left Untitled" poems and those whose titles are the first two characters are merely distinct titling conventions for poems that are essentially of the same kind.[80]

The issue of titles is a significant one. There are poems in the collection that could easily have been included among the "left untitled," but that have occasional titles that contextualize the reading and often dispel the mystery that gives poems "left untitled" much of their force. Consider the following as "Left Untitled" or "In the Grotto":

洞中屐響省分攜	Clogs' echoes in the grotto, infer the parting of ways;
不是花迷客自迷	it is not that flowers lead him astray, the traveler strays on his own.
珠樹重行憐翡翠	Pearl trees' layered lines, feel for the kingfisher,
玉樓雙舞羨鵾雞	in the jade mansion dancing in pairs envy the storks.
蘭迴舊蕊緣屏綠	The orchid brings back its former buds along the green screen,
椒綴新香和壁泥	the pepper compounds a fresh scent mixed with the plaster walls.

---

was a Proofreader in the library. Compare the similar ending of 29392 (*Jijie* 401; Ye [1985] 339).

80. Although "Brocade Zither" is often treated as a significant title, it is another example of titling a poem based on the first two characters.

唱盡陽關無限疊　　　　Sing "Yang Pass" all the way to the end,
　　　　　　　　　　　　　　countless stanzas,
半杯松葉凍頗黎　　　　a half cup of pine needles
　　　　　　　　　　　　　　in frozen lapis lazuli.

The vagueness of the translation here attempts (very imperfectly) to re-
produce the indeterminacy produced in the poetic language when there
is no circumstantial context. In this form we have a wonderfully myste-
rious and obscure poem. Unfortunately, however, the poem was not
"left untitled."

李商隱, 飲席戲贈同舍
Li Shangyin, At a Drinking Party, Playfully Given to a Colleague[81]

洞中屧響省分攜　　　　Clogs' echoes in the bedroom
　　　　　　　　　　　　　　lets me infer that you are parting,[82]
不是花迷客自迷　　　　it is not that the "flowers" led you astray,
　　　　　　　　　　　　　　you led yourself astray.
珠樹重行憐翡翠　　　　In the multiple lines by the pearl trees
　　　　　　　　　　　　　　you fancied the kingfisher,
玉樓雙舞羨鶺鴒　　　　in paired dancing in the jade mansion
　　　　　　　　　　　　　　you envied the storks.
蘭迴舊蕊緣屏綠　　　　The orchid brings back its former buds
　　　　　　　　　　　　　　through the green screen,
椒綴新香和壁泥　　　　the pepper compounds a fresh scent
　　　　　　　　　　　　　　mixed with the plaster walls.
唱盡陽關無限疊　　　　She sings "Yang Pass" all the way to the end,
　　　　　　　　　　　　　　countless stanzas—
半杯松葉凍頗黎　　　　a half cup of pine needles
　　　　　　　　　　　　　　in frozen lapis lazuli.[83]

We know the poem describes a drinking party and is meant for a col-
league. *Dong* 洞, first translated literally as "grotto," can be a poetic refer-
ence to the bedroom; now we know that it is indeed the bedroom, where
his colleague is taking leave of a courtesan. We know who is parting and
who the "guest" or "client" is. (Without this context the *ke* 客, translated

----

81. 29138; *Jijie* 1304; Ye 54.

82. "Bedroom" is "grotto" in the first translation, suggesting the dwelling of immor-
tals, and by extension, courtesans.

83. Pine needles were added to ale. The lapis lazuli (or glass) is the material used to
fashion the ale cup.

contextually as "you," could easily be a poetic "traveler" or "sojourner.") Without the occasional title, the second line becomes a beautiful general statement; with the title it is mere teasing. The middle couplets, hopelessly obscure if this were "Left Untitled," clearly refer to the courtesans and their quarters. (Indeed, the third line seems to suggest that his colleague chose his girl, the "kingfisher," from several rows of available women.) As "Left Untitled" we would read the last couplet in much the same way, but the expressly playful tone changes the quality of the closing image of a half-finished cup of ale. When provided with an occasional context, the poem becomes remarkably trivialized. The best "Left Untitled" poems are better than the above, yet we must recognize that part of their beauty derives from an absence of a circumstantial frame that lends the poem both mystery and indeterminacy. Moreover, many words, such as *dong* ("grotto") or *ke* ("traveler"), are forced to serve a more specific reference ("bedroom," "client") by such a circumstantial context. Another example of how a title can restrict and thus change the meaning of a poem that could easily be "Left Untitled" is "A Companion Piece with Office Manager Han's 'Seeing a Palace Lady Entering a Daoist Nunnery,'" discussed earlier (see pp. 316–17).[84] Such poems lend a degree of credibility to the kind of scenarios that commentators have constructed around Li Shangyin's hermetic poems—although it is credibility only in kind and not in particulars. The occasional title is the counterpart of the interpretive scenario—though in the cases above the scenarios are social *jeux d'esprit* rather than passionate attachments or political satires. Were we to construct a title of the form "A Playful Companion Piece for . . ." for the famous "Left Untitled" ("Last night's stars"), discussed above, the poem would be changed rather dramatically, with a "you" as the subject throughout and a teasing tone. If the absence of titles in the "Left Untitled" poems were indeed an instance of mere editorial accident—poems preserved on pieces of note paper without notation of occasion—then we would possibly have a great body of poetry emerging out of historical misunderstanding.[85]

---

84. See also 29357–58 (*Jijie* 174; Ye [1985] 289; Zhou 37). We would read these very differently if they were "Left Untitled" rather than "Companion Pieces for a Friend's 'Sent Playfully'" 和友人戲贈.

85. Modern scholars prefer to view the "Left Untitled" poems as a kind of poetry rather than an editorial response to poems without titles. Thus, we have examples like 29216 (*Jijie* 26; Ye [1985] 151), in which a poem originally joined with another piece as

While this might well be true in some cases, we can see from other poems that do have occasional titles that Li Shangyin did indeed employ a poetics of mystery purposefully. One excellent example is "Again Stopping By the Goddess's Shrine," discussed earlier (see pp. 331–33).

In some cases we find specifics that lend a degree of credibility to some of the figurative interpretations.

李商隱, 中元作

Li Shangyin, Written on Zhongyuan (7.15)[86]

絳節飄颻宮國來	Crimson standards flapping, they came to the palace,[87]
中元朝拜上清迴	paying dawn court respects on zhongyuan, they return to the Upper Clarity.
羊權雖得金條脫	Although Yang Quan got a golden bracelet,[88]
溫嶠終虛玉鏡臺	Wen Qiao's jade mirror stand was ultimately in vain.[89]
曾省驚眠聞雨過	I once startled awake from sleep, hearing the rain's passage,[90]

"Left Untitled" is disjoined by Ye and *Jijie* and renamed "Title Lost" 失題 because it is thematically incongruous with the image of the "Left Untitled" poems.

86. 29366. See the following commentaries: *Jijie* 1706; Ye (1985) 304; Zhou 84. The fifteenth day of the seventh month (Zhongyuan) was the Ullambana Festival 盂蘭盆, for feeding the hungry ghosts. There were ceremonies in the city as well as in the palace.

87. This is the reading and interpretation followed by *Jijie*. Despite the troubled usage of *gongguo* 宮國, it reads better with the next line. *Jijie* interprets this as palace women who have become Daoist nuns returning to the palace for the festival. Zhou Zhenfu reads the variant *kong guo* 空國: "[they come] emptying the capital."

88. The reference is to the story of the goddess Elühua (see pp. 329–30), who left a bracelet, a *tiaotuo* 條脫, as a gift when she visited Yang Quan. The *tiaotuo* (variously written) is mentioned as a love-gift in Po Qin's "Plighting Troth" 定情詩.

89. *Shishuo xinyu* (XXVII.9) tells how Wen Qiao, an important statesman of the Eastern Jin, was given the task of finding a husband for the daughter of a distant relation. Wen took a fancy to the girl himself. He claimed to have found a prospective husband and gave a jade mirror stand as surety. Later it turned out that he himself was the groom.

90. This seems to refer to the sexual encounter with the goddess of Wu Mountain.

不知迷路爲花開	I strayed from the road unawares because of flowers blooming.[91]
有娀未抵瀛洲遠	The You-Song is not so far away as Yingzhou,
青雀如何鴆鳥媒	how can the Bluebird be the venom-owl matchmaker? [92]

We have one clear occasional reference—a visit to the palace for the Ullambana Festival—and one general thematic reference—a promised liaison that did not come to fruition. The last couplet alludes to a passage in the Li Sao:

覽相觀於四極兮	I let my gaze sweep over all the world's ends,
周流乎天余乃下	I roamed throughout sky, then I came down.
望瑤臺之偃蹇兮	I viewed the surging crest of a terrace of onyx,
見有娀之佚女	there saw a rare woman, the You-Song's daughter.
吾令鴆爲媒兮	I bade the venom-owl make match between us,
鴆告余以不好	and the venom-owl told me she was not fair.
雄鳩之鳴逝兮	Early summer's dove-cock went away singing,
余猶惡其佻巧	and I still loathe its petty wiles.

The standard figurative interpretation of the Li Sao passage has Qu Yuan seeking a worthy prince who will appreciate his merit and take him as his minister. The "venom-owl" represents the bad matchmaker who ruins the chance of such a meeting. Indeed, in the Tang the patron who would introduce an aspirant to those in power was treated as a matchmaker. This led some early interpreters, such as Hu Yimei, to interpret the poem as referring to the poet's hopes for a position and their frustration by some ill-intentioned intermediary.

Later commentators generally rejected this interpretation because it failed to account for the specificity of the first couplet, which refers to a visit to court on the occasion of the Ullambana Festival. This was, moreover, an Inner Court ceremony, so the participants would be women with court connections. Combined with the reference to the

---

91. Perhaps to match the reference to the goddess of Wu Mountain in the preceding line, this is taken to refer to Liu Chen and Ruan Zhao meeting the two goddesses on Mount Tiantai (see pp. 325–29).

92. Yingzhou was one of the isles of the immortals in the Eastern Ocean. Presumably the Bluebird messenger could reach such a distant place (see p. 392). For the daughter of the You-Song and the venom-owl, see later discussion.

Daoist heaven, the Upper Clarity, commentators make the reasonable inference that these were court women turned Daoist nuns who were visiting the court on this occasion.

This circumstance, combined with the failed love match, yields one of the favorite interpretive scenarios: Li Shangyin's love for a court lady turned Daoist nun. *Jijie* has Li Shangyin seeing her returning from the court ceremony and recalling their past relationship. The second stanza clearly suggests that although at one point both had agreed to be lovers (the goddess gives a bracelet; the man gives a jade mirror stand), the woman did not keep her promise. The third couplet suggests that they did have a sexual liaison, but that it passed fleetingly and could not be recovered. In the final couplet the poet seems to blame some intermediary for the failure of the relationship. Earlier we have seen the Bluebird leading the way to Penglai. Yingzhou was its companion isle of immortals, but in this poem the beloved is not that far away.

In this case the evidence of the poem makes such an interpretation not only plausible but probable on some level, though refinements to the scenario—such as *Jijie*'s explanation that the poet sees the woman returning from the ceremony and recalls the past—remain merely plausible. The phrase "probable on some level" refers only to the general scenario: we assume that Li Shangyin himself is the implied male in the relationship, but it could easily be someone else (in which case the subject of the third couplet would be "he" or "you"). Here we might recall "A Companion Piece with Office Manager Han's 'Seeing off a Palace Lady Entering a Daoist Nunnery'" (see pp. 316–17). Another question is whether such an interpretation (a love affair with a Daoist nun) can be generalized and applied to poems using similar images, such as the "Left Untitled" ("Having a time to meet is hard"), discussed above, or the version ("That you would come was empty words") to be discussed below. Very similar imagery, however, is used in social jeux d'esprit. The best we can say is that there is a discourse of love in Li Shangyin's poetry that is sometimes grounded in circumstance by the title or by the text itself, but that this discourse moves among many possible circumstances and, as seems to be the case in "Yan Terrace," may be purely poetic play at the language of romance.

Some of the hermetic poems seem quite private and have an intensity that cannot easily be dissipated by a speculative occasional circumstance, whether an exegetical scenario or an imagined title. A number of commentators have taken the following poem as referring to Linghu Tao. As we argued earlier, any survey of contemporary poems addressed to patrons (of which there are many) leads to the conclusion that if Li Shangyin had sent this to Linghu Tao, the poem would have sounded very strange indeed. When seeking favors from a patron, the last thing a poet wanted was to sound strange.

李商隱, 無題四首
Li Shangyin, Left Untitled (first of four)[93]

來是空言去絕蹤	That you would come was empty words, you left without a trace, [94]
月斜樓上五更鐘	the moon slants down past the upper storey, the fifth watch bell.
夢爲遠別啼難喚	Dreamed of a distant parting, crying couldn't summon,[95]
書被催成墨未濃	a letter was hastily finished, ink only half thickened.
蠟照半籠金翡翠	Light from wax candle half encloses golden kingfishers;[96]
麝熏微度繡芙蓉	aroma of musk faintly crosses embroidered lotuses.[97]

---

93. 29205–8; *Jijie* 1467; Ye (1985) 139; Zhou 200.

94. Wang Biqiang interprets the first four lines as a dream scene, with the waking from dream occurring only in the latter half. Chen Yongzheng attempts to resolve the problem posed by the first line by suggesting that once she left, she did not come again.

95. Early editions have *huan* 換 rather than *huan* 喚. This sensible emendation is universally accepted.

96. The golden kingfishers are probably embroidered on the bed curtains. In one of his *Pusa man* Wen Tingyun refers to gilded paintings on gauze: "painted gauze, golden kingfishers" 畫羅金翡翠. Without giving any reason, Ye argues that this is a golden kingfisher painted on a glass lamp.

97. There is some disagreement as to whether the embroidered lotuses are on the bedding or the bed curtains. The use of "crosses," *du* 度, suggests the bed curtains, as in the couplet of Xiao Gang's "Unclassified" 雜詠 (Lu Qinli 1970): "The gauze bed curtains are not the sea's waters, / but how can one tell before crossing?" 羅帷非海水, 那得度前知. Chen Yongzheng suggests that musk was used to scent bedding as well as clothes, implying that this is a mark of status rather than gender, an interpretation requiring further research.

劉郎已恨蓬山遠	Young Liu already hated how far
	Penglai Mountain was,[98]
更隔蓬山一萬重	on the other side of Penglai Mountain
	are ten thousand ridges more.

This famous poem is a perfect example of the equipoise of urgency and concealment that animates the best of Li Shangyin's poems. The discursive situation, moreover, is beautifully recapitulated in this poem about words, writing, and significant traces that are hard to read. The apparent straightforwardness of the opening is deceptive: we do not know if the person actually did not come, came only in dream, or did indeed come physically (her departure making it seem as if she had not come at all). Each of the possibilities is partially confirmed in one of the lines that follow. The uncertainties presented to the reader re-enact the uncertainties of the speaker.

In the second line we find the speaker awake during the last part of night, suggesting that he spent the night waiting. The second couplet, however, begins with a meeting in dream, seen only in its aftermath, with the beloved fleeting away and the speaker unable to call the beloved back. We are, of course, uncertain if the speaker was asleep and this was a real dream or if there was a real parting that now seems like a dream. (If the beloved had said she would come, it would have been rather ungallant to fall asleep.) Next we have a letter, desperate words written in urgency. The ink was ground too quickly in the speaker's haste, so the written words are pale, as if fading. Again, we cannot read the words, only their urgency. This is in many ways the allegory of such poems: we cannot read the message itself, only the fact that it is terribly important.

---

98. "Young Liu" may refer to Liu Chen 劉晨, who, together with Ruan Zhao 阮肇, met two goddesses while picking herbs in the Tiantai Mountains. Staying there for what seemed only a half year, when they left they discovered that seven generations had passed in the human world. This was a standard poetic figure for a love affair. In Li He the phrase "Young Liu" is used for Han Wudi, whose futile quest for immortality would correspond to seeking Penglai, one of the three isles of the immortals in the Eastern Ocean (though Feng Hao, interpreting the poem as intended to win the favor of Linghu Tao, takes it as a reference to the Hanlin Academy). With few exceptions, pre-modern commentators generally accepted Han Wudi as the referent, but *Jijie* adds the Liu Chen reference.

In the third couplet the "eyes" of the poem turn to the bed where the lovers did or did not meet in body or in dream. We try to "read" the bed. We know that candles were placed inside the bed curtains, but we don't know whether this candle shines inside or outside the curtain. Only half the bed space is lit; the other half is in shadow, out of sight. The musk is something else. It may be true that this is not necessarily the mark of the beloved having been present, but its placement in the poem is highly suggestive, to the point that we wonder whether the beloved really was here and that this is some remaining trace.

Just as we are blocked from knowledge throughout the course of the poem, so the poem ends, first with a simple but vast distance, then finding ten thousand more blocking folds of mountains beyond. In the early twentieth century Wang Guowei was to describe a certain kind of song lyric as *ge* 隔, "blocked" or "on the other side of." Many of the lyrics in this category draw on the tradition of Li Shangyin's poetry. Both the beloved and the situation to which the poem refers are out of sight and reach, beyond countless folds of mountains. Yet as we stand and look, we believe that the beloved and the poem's "meaning" can indeed be found there beyond those mountains.

It is a poetry of barriers and partially legible traces or uncertainties. The themes of these poems always return in the poetics of the poems. The poet does poetically what he says, and the reader is drawn into the poet's intensity, his uncertainty, and his inability to reach or hold onto what is sought.

李商隱, 正月崇讓宅
Li Shangyin, First Month at Chongrang House[99]

密鎖重關掩綠苔	Locked up tight, barred gate on gate, cased in green moss,
廊深閣迥此徘徊	hallways deep within, tower remote, here I pace back and forth.
先知風起月含暈	I know beforehand the wind will rise, a halo around the moon;
尚自露寒花未開	and still the dew is too cold, the flowers have not yet bloomed.

---

99. 29574; *Jijie* 1354; Ye (1985) 504.

蝙拂簾旌終展轉	A bat brushes the curtain sash,
	I end up tossing and turning,
鼠翻窗網小驚猜	a mouse overturns the window screen,
	somewhat startled, wondering.
背燈獨共餘香語	I snuff the lamp and all alone
	talk with the lingering scent,
不覺猶歌起夜來	still singing unaware
	"Rise and Come by Night."

This is a singularly beautiful poem that begins with locked gates, layer upon layer, like the folds of mountains beyond Penglai. The gates are covered in moss, never opened. Where the poet is standing is often important in Chinese poetry, but it is not clear here. The "halls deep within, tower remote" seem to lie beyond those locked gates, but when the poet says "here I pace back and forth," we don't know if he has magically been transported inside or is pacing back and forth in front of the blocked gates. Chongrang House was the residence of Wang Maoyuan, where Li Shangyin should have had some access.

In Li Shangyin's poetry there is a close relationship between omnipresent blockage and reading traces or evidence. *Tong* 通, to "get through," is also to "understand." He reads the weather signs and the signs in the flowers, all pointing to the future. He seems still to be outside, blocked and pacing in the cold of the first month. But in the third couplet, the "turn" in regulated verse, he is suddenly inside, in bed, still trying to interpret signs—the movement of the curtain sash, the window screen overturned—possible signs of the beloved coming, but signs that deceive. The poem began with a barrier that could not be crossed and now the poet is clearly looking for evidence.

The poet puts out the lamp, and in the most remarkable moment in the poem "all alone he talks with the lingering scent." In this poem of such blockage, where did the scent come from that is now "lingering"? The reader knows someone was there, a woman. We don't know how long ago. Here we have a poet who talks to traces. He speaks in solitude to metonymies, which stand for the absent beloved.

At last he becomes aware of what he did unawares, breaking into song, one whose title comes at last to a textual problem. The song or song words in the original version are *ye qilai* 夜起來, "night rise come," which is changed in the exegetical tradition to the phrase with precedent *qi ye lai* 起夜來, "rise night come."[100] We don't know why Li Shangyin began singing unawares—though we know that if he sang these words or this song without realizing it, it was very important. The words can be parsed in various ways in their different arrangements, but perhaps in this case alone we should simply read the individual words: "by night, rise up, come." These are the words for someone at night listening for sounds that might signal someone's approach and someone who talks to a fading scent from someone who seems to have once come to his bedroom by night.

It is useful to read these poems—with the poet in a bedroom, trying to read the signs and traces—alongside the following quatrain, in which the beloved's possible visit does not seem to be in question. The poem evokes the same aura of mystery without suggesting a scenario against which to read the mystery. The traces are mere accident, meaning nothing.

李商隱, 夜半

Li Shangyin, Midnight[101]

三更三點萬家眠	Third fifth of the third watch, thousands of homes asleep,
露欲爲霜月墮煙	the dew is ready to turn to frost, the moon is shedding mist.
鬥鼠上床蝙蝠出	Quarreling mice climb onto my bed, the bats come out,
玉琴時動倚窗絃	on the jade zither at times there stir strings by the window.

The hermetic poems of Li Shangyin ultimately cannot easily be contained in any simple exegetical structure. It is true that he uses the same language for very trivial occasional pieces as well as for poems that seem to be much more personal. Sometimes we cannot tell the difference beyond accidents of titling; but in other cases we can. In the best poems the recurrent thematic concerns are inseparable from the unique form of presentation: the poet who claims to be in a daze writes in a

---

100. Both versions occur elsewhere.
101. 29255; *Jijie* 1973; Ye (1985) 189.

daze; the poet who cannot "get through" writes a poetry that tries to "get through" to us but cannot because of layers of blockage—mountains in folds, barred gates, textual obscurities. While many other things are gifts of form or the accidents of history, this poetry is the gift of a unique mind.

TWELVE

Li Shangyin

The History Poems

李商隱, 詠史
Li Shangyin, On History[1]

歷覽前賢國與家	I have read of all former worthies, of their families and domains,
成由勤儉破由奢	success came from earnestness and restraint, ruin came from excess.[2]
何須琥珀方爲枕	What need must it be amber before one can have a pillow?[3]
豈得珍珠始是車	why should one have to have pearls in order to have a carriage?[4]

---

1. 29200; *Jijie* 347; Ye (1985) 134; Zhou 102.

2. *Han Feizi, Shi guo* 十過: You Yu 由余 was sent on a diplomatic mission to Qin, where Duke Mu asked why rulers gained or lost their domains. You Yu replied: "They always gain it by restraint and lose it by excess" 常以儉得之, 以奢失之.

3. There are several amber pillows mentioned in the historical record. Zhou Zhenfu and Ye cite the most famous example of the amber pillow included in the gifts to Zhao Feiyan when she became empress. This best fits the context. *Jijie* prefers an allusion to another amber pillow presented as a tribute gift to Song Wudi. On his campaign north, Wudi learned that amber could heal wounds made by weapons and ordered that the pillow be broken up and distributed to his generals. *Jijie* clearly interprets the line as an example of frugality and restraint.

4. *Shi ji, Tian Jingzhong Wan shijia* 田敬仲完世家: King Wei of Qi met the king of Liang, who boasted that although his domain was small, he had huge pearls to adorn the princely carriages. King Wei of Qi responded that his treasures were of a different sort and began enumerating his advisers, whose "light shone a thousand leagues."

運去不逢青海馬	Fate's cycle wanes, one does not find Kokonor horses,[5]
力窮難拔蜀山蛇	strength runs out, one cannot pull up the snake in Shu's mountains.[6]
幾人曾預南薰曲	How many men could ever anticipate the song of the aromatic south wind?—[7]
終古蒼梧哭翠華	at Cangwu for eternity they weep for the kingfisher bunting.[8]

In many ways "On History" represents the sober ideal of the "poem on history," *yongshi shi* 詠史詩. From the experience of reading such poems one should derive finely phrased lessons, distilled from the poet's own reading, about the successes and failures of rulers. The lesson is repetitive and stated baldly in the second line: earnestness and restraint bring success, while excess brings ruin. Although Li Shangyin does mention several positive examples here, he as well as most poets prefer to comment on excess and attendant ruin. In some cases Li Shangyin does precisely what he is supposed to do, offering examples and passing judgments without ambivalence. The problem is that excess, described sumptuously and with a certain investment of poetic interest, tends to have the diametrically opposite effect from the one putatively intended. This fact had long been understood in the Chinese tradition—at least as far back as the late Western Han writer Yang Xiong, who commented on Emperor Wu's court poet Sima Xiangru's

---

5. *Sui shu, Xiyu zhuan* 西域傳: At the onset of winter the Tuyuhun people of Kokonor place a mare on an island in Kokonor to "get the dragon seed." The resulting colt is called a Kokonor Dapple. Ye thinks this reference is incorrect and takes the line as referring to the "horses of heaven" of Han Wudi's reign, which ceased to be sent to China when Han fortunes declined. Although Kokonor is not mentioned specifically, it is representative of this horse-producing region.

6. The reference here is to the story, found in several sources, of how the king of Qin promised five beautiful maidens in marriage to the king of Shu. The latter sent five strong men to fetch the women. In the mountains they came upon a huge snake, which disappeared into a hole. When the five men joined forces to pull it out, the mountain collapsed and the way between Qin and Shu was opened up.

7. The "South Wind" was the name of a song played on a zither by Shun: "The aroma of the south wind / can release my people from their woes" 南風之薰兮, 可以解吾民之慍兮.

8. Shun was buried at Cangwu. The "kingfisher bunting" refers to banners in the royal regalia.

work: rather than "criticizing," *feng* 諷, it "encourages," *quan* 勸, the very behavior it was meant to prevent. For the reader resistant to historical homily, irony becomes invisible; for the reader looking for moral lessons, irony can always be found. As we have said, although some poems do pass unambiguous historical judgments, many on beguiling historical excess are willing to satisfy both kinds of reader—or the ambivalence of a single reader.[9]

Even though the poem above describes no beguiling excess, the poet goes awry in confronting one of the central problems for ethical judgment on history. From the moral determinism of the second line, the third couplet shifts to a motif that looks very much like inevitable decline: once fate runs out, strength is exhausted. From this point the poem moves to irrevocable loss: Shun, the very embodiment of good government, can never return.

Zhuge Liang—the favorite historical figure of Du Fu, the worthy minister of the Shu-Han kingdom who tried to do his best at the wrong moment in history—reappears in Li Shangyin's poems. We may consider him beside Jiang Zong, the poet-minister of the Last Ruler of Chen, representing excess, laxness, and ineptitude. The kingdoms of both ministers fell; it seems to have made no difference that one was the best and the other the worst of political advisers. "Fate's cycles" had run out. Like Sima Qian in the famous "Biography of Bo Yi and Shu Qi," Li Shangyin affirms the moral order of history but he knows history too well to believe that such a moral order actually works.

Li Shangyin certainly knew Du Mu's famous "Poetic Exposition on Apang Palace," which became famous when he was a child. Du Mu passed a simple judgment: the lords of the "Six Kingdoms" of the Warring States brought ruin upon themselves through their own excess. Their conqueror, Qin, brought ruin on itself in turn through its own excess, embodied in Apang Palace. The moral historian's judgment could not be clearer. Consider Li Shangyin's quatrain on the Qin capital at Xianyang.

---

9. In arguing that Li Shangyin often presents too beguiling an image of what he criticizes, I differ from virtually all Chinese critics, who find such poems unambiguously critical. See, e.g., Liu Xuekai 劉學鍇, *Li Shangyin shige yanjiu* 李商隱詩歌研究 (Hefei: Anhui daxue chubanshe, 1998), 4–10.

李商隱, 咸陽
Li Shangyin, Xianyang[10]

咸陽宮闕鬱嵯峨	The palace towers of Xianyang 　　swelled up looming,
六國樓臺艷綺羅	the Six Kingdoms' mansions and terraces 　　were gorgeous with filigree gauze.[11]
自是當時天帝醉	Obvious that in those days 　　the Lord of Heaven was drunk—
不關秦地有山河	it had nothing to do with the fact that Qin 　　had such rivers and hills.[12]

Li Shangyin's historical imagination noticed the palaces of those same lords of the Six Kingdoms re-established in the Qin capital at Xianyang. If, as Du Mu suggested, Heaven was punishing the Six Kingdoms for their excess, it was a peculiar punishment, with simulacra of those very excesses transferred to Xianyang itself. The Lord of Heaven is supposed to keep an eye on behavior down below on earth and mete out rewards and punishments. The Lord of Heaven seems to have been on the mark in punishing excess, but his system of rewards was inexplicable. The only explanation is that the Lord of Heaven was drunk—the supreme moral agency guilty of precisely the kind of excess that loses kingdoms on earth. The final line forces commentators to understand "rivers and hills" in the less usual sense, though one attested to in Jia Yi's famous essay entitled "On the Excesses of Qin" 過秦論. Here the "rivers and hills" represent both the territory of the Qin kingdom and its topographical advantage, which made it possible to attack others while withstanding all attacks against itself. In short, Li Shangyin ends by rejecting an amoral analysis of Qin's empirical advantages and affirms the moral order of history, with the qualification that the divine agency in charge of moral enforcement was not on duty.

　　Not only is the Lord of Heaven not on duty, but the poet as historical moralist—the duty proclaimed in "On History"—often seems to be

---

10. 29126; *Jijie* 1536; Ye (1985) 42; Zhou 267.

11. Whenever the First Emperor destroyed one of the domains, he had a copy of its palace built near Xianyang and filled it with the beautiful women and treasures of the defeated feudal lord.

12. This may refer to Qin's essential reliance on its natural defenses to protect and extend itself.

indecisive. We have here a poetic version of the "subtle words" 微言 of Confucius, the model for all moral historians. Confucius's judgments in the *Spring and Autumn Annals* were supposed to have been made obliquely, through subtle choices of phrasing, but they were subsequently made all too explicit by Han and later exegetes. The problem is that when the poet plays this game, we are often uncertain as to the moral judgment.

The following poem deals with the fall of the Southern Qi, one of the "bad" Southern Dynasties.

李商隱, 齊宮詞

Li Shangyin, Qi Palace Lyrics[13]

永壽兵來夜不扃	When soldiers came to Yongshou Palace, that night it was unbarred;[14]
金蓮無復印中庭	never again would golden lotuses imprint the mid-courtyard.[15]
梁臺歌管三更罷	Song and piping on Liang Terrace ceased at the third watch,[16]
猶自風搖九子鈴	and still the wind was shaking the jiuzi bells.[17]

Directly or indirectly, the closing of a historical quatrain often contains the "point." Assuming that "Liang Terrace" does refer to the Liang dynasty, we can easily read the "judgment" of the poem in two contradictory ways: either the Liang continued the excesses of the Qi, or it learned to stop its revelry at the third watch (midnight), with the

---

13. 29277; *Jijie* 1378; Ye (1985) 209; Zhou 254.

14. Yongshou Palace was one of the three palace buildings that Qi Feidi had erected for Consort Pan 潘妃. When Xiao Yan, the founder of the Liang, attempted to overthrow the Qi, two traitors left the palace gates open for the troops to enter the palace compound. The rebels caught Feidi in Hande Palace. *Jijie* suggests that Li Shangyin changed Hande to Yongshou Palace in order to evoke associations with Consort Pan. The phrasing of the line suggests that the palace was left unlocked rather than the gates being opened by traitors, implying heedlessness.

15. During the reign of Feidi, lotuses were made of gold and put in the ground. Feidi had Consort Pan walk on them.

16. The palace compound of Jiankang was known as the Taicheng 臺城, the "Terrace City." Thus "Liang Terrace" here is taken as the Liang palace.

17. The *jiuzi* bells were removed from a Buddhist temple for Consort Pan. *Jijie* suggests that this and the third line show that the Liang continued the excesses of the Qi.

continuing ringing of the *jiuzi* bells, picking up from the music, as a warning against excess that the Liang heeded. (Truly excessive revelry usually continues until dawn.) Reading the commentaries, we find that scholars often differ as to whether a particular passage contains praise or blame. The Liang developed a bad reputation during its last few years. However, with the exception of this period, the dynasty was under Liang Wudi, one of the longest reigning emperors in Chinese history and anything but an indulgent sensualist. We earlier suggested that many of Li Shangyin's hermetic poems point to a specific referent while simultaneously hiding it. In the same way, the historical poems often point to moral judgment while leaving that judgment ambiguous. As we will see, when Li Shangyin is not ambiguous, he is often ambivalent.

Li Shangyin's favorite historical topics were also the favorites of the age—in historical songs, in "poems on history," and in "meditations on the past" (*huaigu* 懷古). These were usually moments of seductive excess—albeit of different kinds and in different flavors. For example, there is the doomed sensuality of the Southern Dynasties and Sui and, earlier, of the Warring States kingdoms of Wu and Chu; the extravagance of Emperor Wu of the Han in his quest for the immortals and love of Lady Li, or the story of Xuanzong and Lady Yang the Noble Consort. Li Shangyin also wrote on other, less common topics. He very much shared in the contemporary historical imagination, seen in poetic expositions (*fu*) on historical topics, "meditations on the past," and Wen Tingyun's *yuefu*.

To those who knew the standard histories virtually by heart, Li Shangyin wove together perfectly phrased moments into a reconfiguration of a historical whole. The places and the names were rich in associations. To modern readers, Chinese as well as Western, such allusive depth is transformed into footnotes, which provide some context for educated Chinese readers but remain fragments of an unknown whole for most Western readers.

The Last Ruler of Chen

Let us try to frame the pieces of one such poem simply called "The Southern Dynasties." Though the title is general, the poem focuses attention on the last dynasty, the Chen, and the Last Ruler of Chen.

李商隱, 南朝
Li Shangyin, The Southern Dynasties[18]

玄武湖中玉漏催	On Xuanwu Lake the dripping of the jade water clock hurried on,
雞鳴埭口繡襦迴	at the mouth of Cockcrow Locks embroidered jackets return.
誰言瓊樹朝朝見	Who claims that the "alabaster trees," seen every morning at dawn,
不及金蓮步步來	were no match for the golden lotuses that came with every step?
敵國軍營漂木柹	From the camp of the enemy army chips of wood came drifting,
前朝神廟鎖煙煤	the spirit temples of former reigns locked in soot from smoke.
滿宮學士皆顏色	The "scholars" that filled the palace were all fair of face,
江令當年只費才	in those years Director Jiang only wasted his talents.

If you go to modern Nanjing (Jiankang), destroyed and rebuilt many times, Xuanwu Lake is still very much in evidence. Now a city park, it was the site of imperial excursions in the Southern Dynasties. Connecting the lake with the Qinhuai River were the Cockcrow Locks, so named because Emperor Wu of the Southern Qi, who lived about a half century before the Chen, would make excursions to Langye, setting out from the imperial city before dawn and only reaching these locks as the cock was crowing. Wen Tingyun began his own poem "The Song of Cockcrow Locks" 雞鳴埭歌 with the following stanzas:[19]

南朝天子射雉時	When the Southern Dynasties Emperor went off to shoot pheasants,
銀河耿耿星參差	the Silver River was sparkling, its stars unevenly strewn.
銅壺漏斷夢初覺	The dripping ceased from the jug of bronze, it was then they first woke from dream,

---

18. 29120; *Jijie* 1372; Ye (1985) 34; Zhou 282.
19. 31871; Zeng 1.

寶馬塵高人未知	from jeweled horses the dust rose high, and others never knew.
魚躍蓮東蕩宮沼	The fish leapt east of the lotuses, making waves on palace pools,
濛濛御柳懸棲鳥	in the hazy imperial willows hung roosting birds.
紅妝萬戶鏡中春	Rouge in ten thousand windows, spring within a mirror,
碧樹一聲天下曉	a single sound through sapphire trees and all the world turned dawn.

This is the dawn scene. Li Shangyin begins by playing on the implicit "setting out" in Cockcrow Locks with an evening scene of time passing and a sense of the inevitable return.

玄武湖中玉漏催	On Xuanwu Lake the dripping of the water clock hurried on,
雞鳴埭口繡襦迴	at the mouth of Cockcrow Locks embroidered jackets return.

The steady drip of the water clock of course seems to "hurry" only subjectively, but it hurries those who listen.

   The second couplet turns to the beautiful consorts who were the objects of so much imperial attention, an absorption that in the minds of later historians and moralists led to the downfall of the southern polity. The "alabaster trees" were the image of the imperial favorites of the Last Ruler of Chen, Zhang the Noble Consort 張貴妃 (Zhang Lihua) and Kong the Noble Mate 孔貴嬪. The *History of the South* cites a couplet attributed to the Last Ruler.[20]

璧月夜夜滿	Jade-disk moon, every night full,
瓊樹朝朝新	alabaster trees, every morning new.

The couplet is associated with "On Jade Trees Flowers in the Rear Courtyard," *Yushu houting hua* 玉樹後庭花, the sensual song that seemed to historically savvy officials to carry "the tones of a fallen kingdom," *wangguo zhi yin* 亡國之音, which foretold the imminent fall

---

20. Lu Qinli 2511.

of the dynasty. We might note that "alabaster trees" is an elegant varia-
tion on "[white] jade tree" in the title of the song. The jade-disk moon
and alabaster trees are clearly figures for the beautiful consorts. The
claim of their unchanging presence, like precious stones, contrasts with
a real world in which both moon and trees are constantly changing—
the world of passing time and the water clock.

The "alabaster trees," the lovely consorts of Chen, are, in Li Shang-
yin's second couplet, compared to Consort Pan 潘妃 of Feidi (or the
Count of Donghun 東昏侯), the last real ruler of the Qi Dynasty. Ac-
cording to legend, Feidi had golden lotuses fashioned and laid out on
the ground. Then he had Consort Pan walk upon them, exclaiming:
"Lotus flowers appear with her every step!"

誰言瓊樹朝朝見	Who claims that the "alabaster trees," seen every morning at dawn,
不及金蓮步步來	were no match for the golden lotuses that came with every step?

The rhetoric is habitual: "Who claims X is no match for Y?" was simply
a way of saying that X and Y were alike. This was the image of the late
Southern Dynasties, an enclosed, artificial world for the sensual plea-
sure of its emperors, heedless of the forces that were gathering and that
would eventually destroy them. In the background is the dripping of
the water clock, approaching darkness that sends the excursionists hur-
rying home. The claim of the unchanging is shadowed by time.

敵國軍營漂木柹	From the camp of the enemy army chips of wood came drifting,
前朝神廟鎖煙煤	the spirit temples of former reigns locked in soot from smoke.

In later poetics the third couplet was known as the "turn," *zhuan* 轉,
and the poem does indeed turn. Upstream from Jiankang and the
pleasure excursions of the Chen court, the Sui was assembling a great
battle fleet that would eventually sail downriver and destroy the city.
The woodchips from shipbuilding could be seen floating in the Yangzi
River.

Two interpretations of soot in the ancestral temples have been sug-
gested. The first attributes it to the Last Ruler's failure to show proper
respect for his ancestors. The alternative interpretation, originally sug-
gested by Zhu Heling, sees it as the traces of a great fire in Jiankang

that started in a pagoda the Last Ruler was having built, which was taken as a sign of Heaven's displeasure.

滿宮學士皆顏色	The scholars that filled the palace were all fair of face,
江令當年只費才	in those years Director Jiang only wasted his talents.

Here we should note a variant, preferred in *Jijie*: some texts read *lian* 蓮 rather than *yan* 顏—"all the color of lotus"—which is a smoother reading. In either case, this seems to refer to the "women scholars" of the Last Ruler, who participated in court functions and composed poems with the male favorites. It is important to remind ourselves that noblewomen of the Southern Dynasties were often learned and wrote poetry, a phenomenon that troubled Confucian moralists (though this was true in the first part of the Tang as well), and that court women commonly appeared in public from Empress Wu's reign through that of Xuanzong.

Finally we come to the man who should have been responsible for guiding the emperor on the proper path: Jiang Zong 江總, who was both director of the Imperial Secretariat and a favorite literary courtier. Indeed, Jiang Zong no doubt held his high office because of his talents in poetry and prose.

The final days of the Chen was a topic to which Li Shangyin repeatedly returned.

李商隱, 陳後宮
Li Shangyin, The Rear Palace of the Chen[21]

玄武開新苑	A new park opened by Xuanwu Lake,
龍舟讌幸頻	the dragon boat often goes there to feast.
渚蓮參法駕	Lotus by isles join in the Prescribed Escort,
沙鳥犯鉤陳	sand birds trespass the Gouchen Constellation.
壽獻金莖露	Toasts present the bronze column's dew,
歌翻玉樹塵	songs send flying the dust of "Jade Trees."
夜來江令醉	At night Director Jiang is drunk;
別詔宿臨春	special edict has him stay over at Linchun.

---

21. 29509; *Jijie* 7; Ye (1985) 443.

We begin again with an imperial excursion on Xuanwu Lake. The "Prescribed Escort," *fajia* 法駕, was the minimal level of attendants and guards properly accompanying the emperor on his excursions. The line probably suggests the informality of such occasions, the emperor going out without the proper escort. The lotuses, commonly understood as figures for women, are mirrors of his female companions. The Gouchen Constellation was the counterpart of the rear palace, containing the emperor's private quarters and harem. Entrance was strictly forbidden, yet birds from the shores fly in, perhaps suggesting the mixing of courtiers and court ladies in the preceding poem. The "bronze column" held the bronze immortal erected by Emperor Wu of the Han, with a pan to catch sweet dew for an elixir of immortality. We have seen "Jade Trees" in the preceding poems. The "dust" is probably in the palace rafters, shaken loose when a song is beautifully sung. Linchun Palace was erected by the Last Ruler as his personal residence.

Li Shangyin returned to the Chen in another poem as well:

李商隱, 陳後宮
Li Shangyin, The Rear Palace of Chen[22]

茂苑城如畫	Park in Full Flower, the city like a painting,[23]
閶門瓦欲流	Heaven's Gate's tiles are ready to flow.[24]
還依水光殿	He goes back to rest at Water Light Hall,
更起月華樓	then next ascends Moonshine Tower.
侵夜鸞開鏡	At nightfall simurgh mirrors are brought out.[25]

---

22. 29134; *Jijie* II; Ye (1985) 50.

23. This refers to the parks inside the Taicheng 臺城, the palace compound at Jiankang, which included parks. Li may have had in mind the phrase used as a name, "Park in Full Flower," Maoyuan, in the "Poetic Exposition on the Capital of Wu" 吳都賦 by Zuo Si; here, however, the Taicheng parks are clearly meant.

24. "Heaven's Gate," *changmen* 閶門 or *changhemen* 閶闔門, was the title given to the main gate of the Taicheng. That the tiles are "ready to flow" suggests not only their glossy sheen but also disintegration, one of the most common terms for which was "come apart as tiles."

25. This conventional modifier for fine mirrors is based on an old story claiming that a silent *luan* phoenix ("simurgh") broke out in song upon seeing its reflection in a mirror. The implication here is that the palace ladies are beginning their makeup early.

迎冬雉獻裘	greeting winter, a pheasant-feather cape is presented.[26]
從臣皆半醉	Attendant officials are all half-drunk,
天子正無愁	the Son of Heaven is indeed without sorrow.[27]

While "The Southern Dynasties" has generally been interpreted as passing judgment on the Southern Dynasties and the Chen, both poems entitled "The Rear Palace of Chen" have often been interpreted figuratively as covert criticism of the adolescent Jingzong, who was noted for his excesses. A number of modern editions—including the most thorough commentary, *Li Shangyin shige jijie*—arrange the poems in putative chronological order, with the result that such interpretations can take on an unwarranted persuasiveness for the uncritical reader.[28] To understand why the two versions of "The Rear Palace of Chen" are read as veiled criticism of a Tang ruler while "The Southern Dynasties" is not reveals little about the ninth century but much about early modern and contemporary traditionalist modes of reading. The dis-tinction seems to be that while the two "rear palace" poems con-cern a single historical moment, "The Southern Dynasties" places the Chen moment in a larger context covering the late Southern Dynasties as a whole—significantly including wood chips floating past Jiankang as an ominous sign prefiguring dynastic fall. The second of the "rear palace" poems, moreover, describes the Last Ruler of Chen in terms proper to the Last Ruler of the Northern Qi, thus making him less a

---

26. This echoes a story of Cheng Ju 程據, who presented the Jin emperor with a cape ingeniously woven with feathers from the head of a pheasant. Because it was considered ostentatious and violated canonical rules, it was publicly burned in front of the palace. In this case no burning is mentioned and the transgressive cape is apparently accepted.

27. This was said of the last Northern Qi emperor, who was fond of a type of music called "without sorrow" 無愁, which he would sing while accompanying himself on the pipa, with hundred of his attendants joining in. As a result, he was referred to by the general populace as "The Emperor Without Sorrow" 無愁天子.

28. In other words, the assumption that the poem was written in Li Shangyin's mid-teens can make the application to Jingzong persuasive. The poems, however, were dated to Li Shangyin's teens because of the editors' decision that they were satires on Jingzong.

particular historical figure and more a type that can be figuratively transferred.[29]

Li Shangyin's vision of excess and the breakdown of boundaries—between the sexes and between levels of hierarchy—was quite satisfying. In Chinese moral tracts this was often linked to images of liquefaction or "dissolution." The characters of such a world continue their revels, ignorant of or paying no heed to the doom that is about to descend on them. In most of the history poems we observe such an absorption in the moment and loss of a larger perspective: we know the irony of the "Son of Heaven Without Sorrow." "Sorrow," *chou* 愁, can also mean "worries" or "anxieties." The reader, existing outside the historical moment, knows that this Son of Heaven should be very worried indeed.

History poems like the ones given above are valuable foils against which to read some of Li Shangyin's most famous hermetic poems. In the latter poems we are placed inside such a world, with the speaker enacting or claiming just such complete absorption. Here we lack the distance of history and foreknowledge of consequences that frame the history poems. Such a margin between distance and absorption is permeable, with the speaker always on the edge of falling into and out of heedless absorption. In this context we can return to the last couplet of Li Shangyin's most famous poem, "Brocade Zither" 錦瑟:

此情可待成追憶	One should wait until these feelings became remembrance,
只是當時已惘然	it's just that at the moment I was already in a daze.

Wangran 惘然, "in a daze," is the blur or loss of clarity about things and the relationship between them. This is the blur of complete absorption.

The poet as historical moralist often stands just outside but close to the edge of such absorption. In two of Li Shangyin's finest historical quatrains, he perhaps ventures too close to the edge. The Southern Dynasties was a favorite poetic topic in the first half of the ninth century, but Li Shangyin was also drawn to the fate of the Last Ruler of the

---

29. Such a distinction fails to hold in the ninth century. Du Mu's "Poetic Exposition on Apang Palace" includes both historical sweep and dynastic fall yet was almost certainly read in reference to Jingzong.

Northern Qi (ruled 565–76), the "Son of Heaven Without Sorrow," and his passion for Feng the Pure Consort 馮淑妃, named Xiaolian 小憐 or "Little Love," who was first introduced as a poetic topic by Li He. The Last Ruler of the Northern Qi was off on a hunt with Little Love when the rival Northern Zhou invaded his kingdom. During the course of the morning, dispatch riders kept coming, bringing word of the urgency of the crisis; but a minister objected that the emperor was enjoying himself and should not be bothered with minor border skirmishes. That evening a courier brought news that the city of Pingyang had fallen, and the emperor was at last informed. The emperor was about to return to the capital when Little Love suggested that they hunt one more round. A few months later the Northern Zhou army captured the capital of Jinyang.

李商隱, 北齊二首
Li Shangyin, The Northern Qi[30]

I

一笑相傾國便亡	One smile toppled it, the kingdom then was lost,
何勞荊棘始堪傷	why bother about thorns and brambles and only then feel pain?[31]
小憐玉體橫陳夜	On the night that Little Love's white body lay stretched before him,
已報周師入晉陽	we already had the news that the Zhou army had entered Jinyang.[32]

30. 29117–18; *Jijie* 539; Ye (1985) 32; Zhou 297.

31. In the *Wu Yue chunqiu* Wu Zixu warned the king of Wu that unless he was heeded, brambles would end up growing on the palaces of Wu.

32. It is uncertain whether Li Shangyin made the same mistake here that he obviously made in the second poem. Jinyang was the capital, which did eventually fall to the Western Zhou. Pingyang was the city that fell while the Northern Qi emperor was on his hunt. Since the first couplet predicts the fall of the dynasty, there is no problem in reading Jinyang—though the claim would be poetically daring. If Pingyang is meant, the last line is literally rather than figuratively true, marking the beginning of a process that will bring the dynasty down.

II

巧笑知堪敵萬機   I know that an artful smile is the match
                                      for he of myriad devices,[33]
傾城最在著戎衣   a city-toppling beauty is best
                                      when wearing a soldier's armor.
晉陽已陷休迴顧   Jinyang has already fallen,
                                      don't look back—[34]
更請君王獵一圍   she begs her lord and ruler
                                      to hunt another round.

The first poem presents the outsider's perspective, the point of view of the moralist historian who can read consequences. Here we may have "metalepsis," an effect known through a remote cause: a woman's naked body prefigures the Western Zhou army entering the capital and thorns growing in the ruins. The poem, in fact, is about precisely such a power of prediction, evidence of a mechanism of destroying the polity driven by necessity—without the possibility of choice or accident disrupting the sequence of events. In order to achieve this certainty of prediction, however, the historian must reveal to us what should normally be hidden from view: he transports us into the emperor's inner chambers. We have to come to the very edge of that body's power to understand it.

In the second poem the woman reappears clothed, albeit in armor, the antagonist in a contest of power, with the quasi-military enterprise of the hunt as the figure for that contest. Her weapons are beguiling words that force one to choose between pleasure and duty. What gives the woman's siren song its power is the knowledge we have gained from the first poem: it is indeed too late; there is no point in looking back now; one might as well hunt another round.

There is no question that on some level these poems are minatory, which is how all Chinese commentators have taken them (although there is no basis to see them as directed at a particular Tang emperor, such as Wuzong, as *Jijie* suggests). The problem here is that a moralist

---

33. "He of myriad devices" 萬幾 or 萬機, is a kenning for the emperor, who deals with such matters on a daily basis.

34. While Jinyang may be appropriate in the first poem, with its omen of the fall of the capital, I agree with Zhou Zhenfu that Jinyang in the second poem must be a mistake for Pingyang, the city that actually fell to Zhou forces on the day of the hunt.

poet, effectively representing the danger, lets the reader feel the power of the lure. In both attraction and the call for judgment Li Shangyin's version of Little Love is markedly different from the pathos of Li He's version, which apparently presents her in hiding after the fall of the Northern Qi.[35]

As the poet straddling that margin, Li Shangyin can sometimes offer the proper criticism, but we should remember that he, too, is subject to the lure of absorption. King Xiang of Chu dreams of the visit of the goddess, but his obsession with that dream ennobles him and separates him from the mere pleasures of lesser men.

李商隱, 過楚宮

Li Shangyin, Passing the Chu Palace[36]

巫峽迢迢舊楚宮	Far off in the Wu Gorges, a former palace of Chu,
至今雲雨暗丹楓	even today the clouds and rain darken the red maples.
微生盡戀人間樂	Small lives all yearn for joy in the mortal world,
只有襄王憶夢中	but only King Xiang thinks back to what happened in dream.

Only those rulers driven by their passions, blind to the doom that shadows their absorption, become the subject of legend and poetry. Often they long to cross the boundary that separates mortals from gods, to be outside of time through absorption or to "go beyond," to reach Heaven or cross the seas to the isles of the immortals. The "bad" rulers who are infatuated lovers and those who yearn for the secrets of immortality are two aspects of the same passion.

The figure of Sui Yangdi is like that of the Last Ruler of Chen, only with a slightly different flavor. Instead of simple self-abandon to sensuality, Sui Yangdi represents a certain mad extravagance. The other motif is travel, or "going too far." Although the Southern Dynasty emperors are represented as going off on excursions, they generally fail by enclosure. Yangdi leaves his capital in Chang'an to travel, especially to his beloved and fatal Jiangdu (Yangzhou).

---

35. 20784; Ye (1959) 190.
36. 29409; *Jijie* 781; Ye (1985) 357.

李商隱, 隋宮
Li Shangyin, The Sui Palace[37]

紫泉宮殿鎖煙霞	Lavender Spring's palace halls shut in mists and rose clouds,[38]
欲取蕪城作帝家	he wished to take City of Weeds to be an emperor's home.[39]
玉璽不緣歸日角	Had the jade seal not, by consequence, gone to the sun-knobs,[40]
錦帆應是到天崖	I am sure those brocade sails would have reached the horizon.[41]
于今腐草無螢火	Even today the rotting plants are bare of fireflies,[42]
終古垂楊有暮鴉	yet forever the weeping willows will have their twilight crows.[43]

---

37. 29190; *Jijie* 1395; Ye (1985) 121; Zhou 285.

38. "Lavender Springs," properly Lavender Abyss 紫淵 (according to Zhu, the alteration is intended to avoid the taboo against using Tang Gaozu's name), is used in the *Shanglin fu* to represent the area north of Chang'an. Here it is used to represent the palaces in Chang'an. According to Zhou, "shut in mists and rose clouds" suggests the palace's abandonment.

39. According to then-current interpretations, Bao Zhao's "Poetic Exposition on the City of Weeds" 蕪城賦 was written when Bao was serving the Liu-Song prince of Linhai. The prince was considering rebellion at Guangling, the former capital of Liu Pi, the Han prince of Wu, who had rebelled against the Han emperor and had been crushed. Bao Zhao's description of the city in all its splendor and then in ruins was meant to serve as a warning for the prince of Linhai. Guangling later became Yangzhou, which Sui Yangdi made his "River Capital" 江都.

40. "Sun knobs" were protuberances on the forehead that were supposed to mark the physiognomy of an emperor. Li Yuan, later Tang Gaozu, was observed to have such marks before he rose in rebellion against Sui Yangdi. The *xi* 璽 was the imperial jade seal, in this case marking legitimacy.

41. The use of palace brocade for sails was one of the legendary signs of Yangdi's extravagance.

42. According to the *Sui History*, "At the end of the Daye Reign, brigands had risen all over the empire; at Jinghua Palace the emperor [Yangdi] commanded that fireflies be found and brought to him, which were several bushelsworth; by night he went traveling in the mountains and released them, and they lit up the mountains and valleys."

43. Yangdi ordered the Sui Canal constructed, which linked the Huai and Yellow Rivers. Willows were planted along the embankments to protect against erosion. This project, of great economic importance, was understood as having been undertaken for the purpose of Yangdi's pleasure excursions. To travel up the canal to Daliang, Yangdi

地下若逢陳後主　　　If under the earth he happens to meet
　　　　　　　　　　　　the last ruler of Chen,

豈宜重問後庭花　　　it would not be right again to ask
　　　　　　　　　　　　for "Flowers in the Rear Court."[44]

Li Shangyin begins "The Sui Palace" with Yangdi leaving the palace in Chang'an and heading for Jiangdu. Yangdi did not "return" *gui* 歸, the term here translated as "gone to" in reference to the royal seal, "returning" to where it rightfully belonged, to the founder of the Tang and Chang'an. The "return" of the jade seal to Chang'an blocks a continuing outward motion. We have another counterfactual that is no less visionary but less precise than Du Mu's famous speculation on the fate of the Qiao sisters, namely, brocade sails heading off over the horizon.[45]

From that blocked motion toward "going too far," we turn to the present, in which we see the consequences of two of Yangdi's grand projects. The first, involving the fanciful capture and release of all the fireflies in the region for one glorious moment of brightness, has left the area without fireflies. The other project is no less excessive, albeit different in nature, namely, the Grand Canal. Li Shangyin cannot have been unaware—particularly in his lifetime—that this was the salvation of his own dynasty, enabling the rich southeastern prefectures to supply regular tax revenues to the capital. The willows planted along the Grand Canal might seem poetically decorative from one perspective, but Li Shangyin must have known that their purpose was practical and that without them the banks would have soon collapsed. In a poem entirely about self-destructive excess, this allusion to the Grand Canal hints at the ambivalence toward the extreme use of imperial power. The exercise of such power at certain moments in history can effect changes that have a lasting beneficial influence on the empire.

---

was supposed to have ordered the construction of five hundred boats, the imperial boat having been fitted with sails of palace brocade.

44. According to legend, during his years of dissipation at Jiangdu, Yangdi once had a vision that he met Chen Shubao, the Last Ruler of the Chen Dynasty. The Last Ruler was with several dozen dancing girls, one of whom caught Yangdi's eye. The Last Ruler said that she was [Zhang] Lihua 張麗華, the famous beauty who had been his favorite. After Yangdi and the Last Ruler grew merry from drinking, Yangdi asked Lihua to dance the infamous "On Jade Trees Flowers in the Rear Courtyard" 玉樹後庭花.

45. See p. 292.

Finally, we come to what separates Sui Yangdi from the emperors of the Southern Dynasties: the figure of conscious repetition. Just as King Xiang of Chu is bound in memory to an image of the goddess of Wu Mountain, so Yangdi is bound to an image transmitted in poetry and song: the Southland, embodied in the Last Ruler's famous song, sung by none other than Zhang Lihua. In "The Southern Dynasties" we saw the Last Ruler of Chen's obsession with his consort both as competition with and continuation of the obsession of the last Southern Qi emperor. Sui Yangdi, however, represents a figure that is more complicated. He is an emperor not continuing but imitating; he comes from somewhere else and wants to reproduce the Southern Dynasties. His consorts are not as famous. The celebrated story is the dream in which he meets the Last Ruler of Chen and Zhang Lihua performs for him the song that had become the mark of dynastic ruin. Excess is no longer innocent: it has become the object of desire in its own right. The last couplet of the poem invokes choice. The voice of wonder at Yangdi's excess returns to the voice of the good minister and observer offering judgment: "it would not be right." There is a speculative moment of decision, and Sui Yangdi makes the wrong decision.

The Southland and Southern culture were seen as dangerous. Northerners like Du Mu and Li Shangyin clearly felt this (and Du Mu had tasted its pleasures). It was already a trope in the ninth century, a geography for conflicting desires. To "go south" was to give up social constraints and goals. The Last Ruler of Chen was a Southerner; his doom was in his environment. Yangdi chose the South, and in doing so he chose dynastic destruction. Unlike Jiang Zong, the Last Ruler's minister and drinking companion, Yangdi's officials objected, but Yangdi did not listen.

Palace brocade was a tribute offering from Sichuan (Shu). From a practical standpoint it was useless. It was "valued" in a recognizably economic sense, a valuable commodity defined both by labor value and scarcity. It was used as imperial currency: rulers used it to pay and reward the services of officers both military and civil. In the legends of Yangdi, however, it is capital profligately consumed and wasted: sewn into sails for the imperial flotilla or made into mudguards for land travel.

李商隱, 隋宮
Li Shangyin, The Sui Palace[46]

乘興南遊不戒嚴	On a whim he traveled south, without preparing the way,
九重誰省諫書函	in the nine-layered palace who took to heart the boxes with written criticisms?[47]
春風舉國裁宮錦	In the spring breeze all the lands were cutting palace brocade:
半作障泥半作帆	half was made into mudguards, and half was made into sails.[48]

One of the most interesting phrases in this poem is the loaded "on a whim," *chengxing* 乘興, a phrase always associated with the Eastern Jin Wang Huizhi and his decision, one snowy night, to pay a visit to his friend Dai Kui, sailing off in a boat, then turning back before meeting his friend with the phrase: "I came on a whim; the whim is past, and now I'm going home—why should I have to see Dai?" The recurrence of this figure of Jin eccentricity in an emperor reminds us of the difference, precisely the transgression of the imperial role. Wang Huizhi sets off "on a whim" but returns, whereas Sui Yangdi does not. When an emperor travels, there must be a formal "preparing the way"; the emperor is trying to act like an ordinary human being, and that is not allowed because of the nature of his power. His "whim" sets "all the lands" to work to provision his journey. The imitation Jin eccentric, invested with imperial power, destabilizes the polity.

The failure of all these rulers—Emperor Wu of the Han, the Last Rulers of Chen or the Northern Qi, Sui Yangdi, or King Xiang of Chu—lies in desires that can never be satiated.

---

46. 29218; *Jijie* 1392; Ye (1985) 153; Zhou 284.

47. When Sui Yangdi decided to leave Chang'an for Jiangdu (Yangzhou, designated as Yangdi's southern capital), several officials remonstrated and were executed. *Jieyan* 戒嚴, translated as "preparing the way," involved the preparation and precautions taken when an emperor traveled. *Jijie* suggests that this implies Yangdi's confidence in the peace and security of his empire. Yangdi traveled to Jiangdu three times. On the last occasion rebellion was breaking out everywhere. He was assassinated in Jiangdu.

48. These allusions come from the legends of Sui Yangdi's extravagance, making lavish use of the tribute brocade designated for palace use. Mudguards were used on saddles to protect clothing.

李商隱, 楚宮
Li Shangyin, The Chu Palace[49]

十二峰前落照微	In front of the twelve peaks[50] the setting sunlight is faint,
高唐宮暗坐迷歸	the palace at Gaotang darkens, he now cannot find the way back.
朝雲暮雨長相接	Dawn's clouds and twilight rain always follow one on another,
猶自君王恨見稀	but still the ruler resents that he sees her too rarely.

The sexual "clouds and rain" of the goddess are continuous, but for King Xiang of Chu it is still not enough.

Another such figure is the great Emperor Wu of the Han, in whom the passionate quest for immortality is combined with his passion for Lady Li. The desire is so strong that he is beyond disillusion. Again we stand with the poet on the margin: we accept that the quest is futile, yet we also know that without such an excess of desire, Emperor Wu would become uninteresting.

李商隱, 漢宮
Li Shangyin, The Han Palace[51]

通靈夜醮達清晨	The night jiao service at Tongling Terrace lasted until clear dawn;[52]
承露盤晞甲帳春	the pan to catch the dew was dry, the primary screen showed the spring.[53]

---

49. 29355; *Jijie* 784; Ye (1985) 287. This poem is sometimes linked to another poem (29356) that has nothing to do with the topic.

50. The "twelve peaks" refer to Mount Wu.

51. 29284; *Jijie* 557; Ye (1985) 215.

52. Han Wudi erected a Tongling (Communicating with the Gods) Terrace in Ganquan Palace. It is unclear whether *tongling* is here the proper name of the place or simply means "[a night *jiao* service] to communicate with the gods." The *jiao* 醮 was a Daoist ritual.

53. Han Wudi erected a statue of a bronze immortal holding a pan to catch the sweet dew falling from Heaven, which was to be used in an elixir of immortality. The "primary screen," *jiazhang* 甲帳, was a screened enclosure, composed of pearls and precious stones, used to contain gods and spirits when they were summoned. The point of the line seems to be that these attempts to draw on Heaven's power or to summon the spirits do not work.

王母不來方朔去	The Queen Mother would not come,
	Dongfang Shuo went away,[54]
更須重見李夫人	yet still he insisted on once again
	seeing Lady Li.[55]

Although the last line refers to the séance in which the wizard Young Old Man summoned up Lady Li's ghost, it also echoes the famous story in the *Han History* in which Lady Li is on her deathbed. Emperor Wu pleads with her to let him see her face just one more time, but she keeps her face hidden beneath the covers.

Xuanzong

The final great example of excessive imperial passion was, of course, Xuanzong and Lady Yang, a favorite topic in poetry, poetic exposition, and prose narrative in the first half on the ninth century. The motifs associated with other excessive emperors are again present, albeit with a distinct sympathy. Two of the most famous poems concern Mawei, the post station where the imperial guard demanded Lady Yang's death.

李商隱, 馬嵬
Li Shangyin, Mawei[56]

I

冀馬燕犀動地來	Horses of Ji, armor of Yan
	came shaking the earth;[57]
自埋紅粉自成灰	in due course her pink powder was buried,
	in due course she turned to ash.[58]

---

54. Han Wudi was said to have been visited by the goddess Queen Mother of the West; in this poem she does not make an appearance. Dongfang Shuo was a courtier of Han Wudi and was supposed to have been an immortal banished to earth.

55. Lady Li was Han Wudi's favorite. When she died young, the emperor was disconsolate and arranged a séance with a wizard who claimed that he could bring back her spirit. A figure that looked like Lady Li appeared in a curtained enclosure and then disappeared. The *Han History* account of this incident clearly suggests that it was a fraud.

56. 29296–97; *Jijie* 307; Ye (1985) 226; Zhou 263.

57. *Yan xi* 燕犀 literally means "Yan rhino [hide]," metonymy for armor. Yan and Ji were in the Northeast, the command of the rebel An Lushan.

58. The reference is to the mandated suicide of Lady Yang.

君王若道能傾國	If the lord and ruler had understood 　　that she could indeed topple kingdoms,[59]
玉輦何由過馬嵬	how would it have come to pass 　　that the Jade Palanquin passed Mawei?

II

海外徒聞更九州	In vain we hear that beyond the sea 　　is another domain of nine lands,[60]
他生未卜此生休	ere fortunes were told for the life to come, 　　this life was over.[61]
空聞虎旅鳴宵柝	She heard only the Tiger Troop 　　sound watch rattles by night;
無復雞人報曉籌	never again would the Rooster Man 　　announce that marker of dawn.[62]
此日六軍同駐馬	On this day the sixfold army 　　stopped their horses in unison;[63]
當時七夕笑牽牛	back then on the Seventh Eve 　　they had mocked the Oxherd.[64]

---

59. "Topple kingdoms," *qingguo* 傾國, is a literalization of a standard kenning for a beautiful woman, "[one who can] topple a kingdom."

60. China comprised "nine lands"; what lay beyond China was a world of immortals that was also thought to consist of "nine lands," or islands. According to the evolving legend, Yang Yuhuan, Lady Yang, was supposed to have been an immortal.

61. This seems to refer to the vow made by Xuanzong and Lady Yang, namely, that they would remain husband and wife in their lives to come.

62. The "Tiger Troop" is the imperial guard. The "Rooster Man" announces dawn in the palace. *Jijie* agrees with Feng Hao that this refers to the scene at Mawei. This is appropriate since the guard would be present, while the Rooster Man would not. The subject must be Yang Yuhuan, who never returned to the palace.

63. The "sixfold army" was the term for a complete imperial army. Such an army was not present with Xuanzong at Mawei. They halted because they refused to go on unless Yang Yuhuan was executed.

64. The reference is to the famous scene of the Seventh Eve when Xuanzong and Yang Yuhuan looked at the Oxherd and Weaver Woman constellations and made their vow to be husband and wife in future generations. In his study of poetic usage entitled *Shiciqu yuci huishi* 詩詞曲語辭匯釋, Zhang Xiang 張相 interprets the *xiao* 笑 as suggesting envy. In doing so he seems to be taking *dangshi* 當時 ("back then") as referring to the situation at Mawei. I prefer a more common interpretation of *xiao* as "laugh at" or "mock," ironically evoking that time on the Seventh Eve, before the Rebellion, when Xuanzong and Yang Yuhuan could believe that their ability to be together daily was far

如何四紀爲天子　　　　How can it be that, having been Son of Heaven
　　　　　　　　　　　　　for four decades,

不及盧家有莫愁　　　　he was not so lucky as the Lu household,
　　　　　　　　　　　　　which had Mourn-No-More?[65]

The two *zi* 自 in the second line of the first poem—"naturally" or, as translated, "in due course"—recall the historian's judgment on Little Love of the Northern Qi in the first quatrain: these consequences follow inevitably from imperial passion. Here, however, Li Shangyin makes the issue of decision explicit: *if* Xuanzong had understood the consequences, this would not have happened. This is a supposition that Li Shangyin did not bring up for other doomed emperors in the more distant past—perhaps because Xuanzong was closer in time and more human, as we see at the end of the second poem.[66]

Xuanzong did not possess the passion for excess that characterized the other rulers we have discussed. He wanted only what the lowliest of his subjects might have, but this desire was denied an emperor. Li Shangyin begins the second poem by dismissing the poetic myths that had grown up around Xuanzong, which were given general currency in Bai Juyi's famous "Song of Lasting Pain" 長恨歌. In this version's fullest elaboration, the mortal suffering of the lovers was mitigated by the fact that both Xuanzong and Yang Yuhuan were immortals, destined to suffer a season of mortal life. For Li Shangyin this is a story told "in vain"; the simple fact remains that they did not get to live out this life. All that was familiar came at last to Lady Yang's death at Mawei Station.

We return to Xuanzong's failure to understand. Xuanzong and Yang Yuhuan had mocked the Oxherd and Weaver Woman because those lovers in Heaven were permitted to meet only once a year, albeit for eternity. To be emperor is, however, closer to the restrictions of immortals than to the ordinary Lu household. Even the emperor's great power—ruling well and peacefully for four decades—did not allow him

---

superior to the union of the Oxherd and Weaver Woman, who could meet only once a year.

65. Here Li Shangyin refers to one version of the Mourn-No-More story, in which she was married into the Lu household. That is, commoners could live out their natural span with their spouses, while an emperor could not keep his own beloved.

66. Li does come close to such a speculative choice at the end of "The Sui Palace," which we discussed above.

to live a normal life. Here the name "Mourn-No-More," usually seen as ironic, becomes the simple literal name for the happiness of married life.

The motif of the yearly meeting of the Oxherd and Weaver Woman as opposed to the impossibility of ever meeting again returns in a Seventh Eve poem. The poem is generally interpreted as referring to the death of the poet's own wife, which is plausible, but it can also serve as a gloss on the sixth line of the poem cited above.

李商隱, 七夕

Li Shangyin, The Seventh Eve[67]

鸞扇斜分鳳幄開	The simurgh fans divide slanting, the phoenix curtain opens,
星橋橫過鵲飛迴	she passes over the bridge in the stars, the magpies fly turning back.
爭將世上無期別	How can parting in this mortal world with no hope of meeting
換得年年一度來	be exchanged for this one crossing that happens year after year?

Mortals may laugh at the Oxherd and Weaver Woman, but for those immortal stars there is never the irrevocable parting caused by death.

The following poem, one of Li Shangyin's most famous, is variously interpreted as referring either to the Sweet Dew Incident or to Xuanzong and Lady Yang. The third line seems to demand that we take it as a poem about the latter. Rather than a true "poem on history," this is closer to a "meditation on the past," with the poet at the site, speaking in the present about the past.

李商隱, 曲江

Li Shangyin, Twisting River Park[68]

望斷平時翠輦過	I gaze as far as I can to where in days before the azure palanquin passed,
空聞子夜鬼悲歌	and hear nothing more than Ziye songs sadly sung by a ghost.[69]

---

67. 29294; *Jijie* 1201; Ye (1985) 224.
68. 29584; *Jijie* 132; Ye (1985) 513; Zhou 100.
69. There is disagreement among the commentators regarding whether *ziye* 子夜 refers to the Jin singer, to whom is attributed a collection of quatrain songs, or "midnight." *Jijie* agrees with Ji Yun that *ziye* means "midnight" here, but this is far from

金輿不返傾城色	The golden coach did not bring back the city-toppling charms,[70]
玉殿猶分下苑波	the jade-white halls still divide the waves in the Lower Park.[71]
死憶華亭聞唳鶴	Dying, recalled Huating, hearing the cranes cry out,[72]
老憂王室泣銅駝	aging, worried about the royal house, weeping over the bronze camels.[73]
天荒地變心雖折	Heaven and Earth turn to wilderness, and though the heart breaks,
若比傷春意未多	if compared to the pain of spring, it didn't matter much.

The poet begins with a scene of absence, looking out at Chang'an's Twisting River Park and imagining the imperial palanquin. Since emperors in Li Shangyin's lifetime frequently visited the park, we have here a long-lost emperor. The second line is the subject of much debate, but if we interpret it in light of the above, we have a ghost singing love songs of an ordinary commoner. Combining that with the azure palanquin, we have the motif of an emperor and the love of an ordinary person, which perfectly matches the version of Xuanzong and Yang the Noble Consort presented in the second "Mawei."

The golden coach bearing the emperor did return; the beloved Lady Yang (who scandalously rode with the emperor) did not. As is often the case in "meditations on the past," we have a couplet contrasting what is absent with what survives.

---

usual Tang usage. Daoyuan, the earliest commentator (mid-seventeenth century), cites a passage in the *Jin History* in which, in the late fourth century, a ghost sang Ziye songs in the home of the Prince of Langye.

70. That is, of a femme fatale.

71. Since the streams of Twisting River Park connected with the imperial moat, *Jijie* reads this line as follows: "The jade-white halls [of the palace] still share the waves of the Lower Park."

72. When the Jin writer Lu Ji was traduced and about to be executed, he wrote a letter containing the line: "Will I never again hear the cranes cry out by Huating?"

73. Suo Jing of the Jin knew that the dynasty was about to collapse and addressed the bronze camels before the Luoyang palace gates: "A time will come when I see you among thorns and brambles."

The third couplet alludes to Jin figures Lu Ji and Suo Jing. Although there is usually strict gender segregation of allusion, the contrast between one dying (indeed, going to execution) and another growing old so perfectly fits the case of Lady Yang and Xuanzong that it is hard not to see them as the implied subjects of the parallel line.

The final couplet is as ambiguous as it is beautiful. It recapitulates Li Shangyin's version of the love between Xuanzong and Yang the Noble Consort: there is imperial responsibility toward Heaven and Earth and there is ordinary mortal feeling for what is close at hand, whether it be a shared sentimental sadness at spring passing or the aging and bereft Xuanzong feeling the loss of Lady Yang. Whether we read the comparison as straight or ironic depends on where we stand and where we assume the poet stands. If we adopt the stance of the poet-moralist, we read the last lines while shaking our heads: "[for him] it didn't matter much." Yet obvious sympathy for the couple invites the more radical reading, in which that private feeling, set in the balance with the whole world, somehow was truly more important. If we were to interrogate the poet, he would surely back away from that space he has opened. Yet he enters that space freely in many of his other poems that lack the competing claim of imperial responsibility.

Critique and Admiration

To end the discussion of Li Shangyin's history poems here would do him an injustice. Once he moves away from the theme of imperial excess and passion, his poems frequently offer up judgments that are clear—albeit often made no less implicitly than his more ambivalent poems. Representing Xuanzong and Lady Yang, he can offer sympathy and judgment simultaneously, but he also remembers that Xuanzong took Lady Yang from his son, the Prince of Shou. He imagines a party at Dragon Pool in Xingqing Palace, with the princes in attendance and Xuanzong playing the *jie* drum, as he loved to do. Lady Yang is the unstated presence.

李商隱, 龍池
Li Shangyin, Dragon Pool[74]

龍池賜酒敞雲屏   At Dragon Pool His Majesty offers ale,
         the mica screens are spread,

---

74. 29410; *Jijie* 1514; Ye (1985) 358; Zhou 259.

羯鼓聲高眾樂停	the sound of the jie drum is loud, all the musicians stop.
夜半讌歸宮漏永	At midnight returning from the feast the palace water clocks drip long,
薛王沈醉壽王醒	the Prince of Xue is reeling drunk, the Prince of Shou is sober.

It is remarkable how little the last line says—and needs to say. We can imagine anger and humiliation, magnified by the prince's forced attendance at a party where his father is enjoying himself immensely, playing his *jie* drum. Lady Yang, his own former court lady, would also be there. The prince's feelings, which would have to be masked in court life, are also masked in the poem, condensed into the simple final hemistich: "the Prince of Shou is sober."

The following famous quatrain on the Han statesman Jia Yi is very much the moral historian's quatrain: it retells a moment from the histories in such a way that a judgment is clear. The *Shiji* "Biography of Jia Yi" simply tells us that when he was recalled from exile, Han Wendi summoned him for a midnight interview, in which Wendi asked him to explain the essentials of the spirit world. Jia Yi gave a full account that pleased the emperor. The poet and reader also know that Jia Yi had grand plans for political reform.

李商隱, 賈生
Li Shangyin, Jia Yi[75]

宣室求賢訪逐臣	The Reception Chamber sought worthies, had the banished official visit,
賈生才調更無倫	Master Jia's talent and temperament were beyond all compare.
可憐夜半虛前席	Too bad that at midnight it was in vain he came forward on the mat—
不問蒼生問鬼神	he was not asked about the people, he was asked about ghosts and spirits.

In a sense this quatrain "sums up" Jia Yi's fate and deserves its place in the cultural repertoire. Like "Dragon Pool" the judgment, though clear, is left implicit.

---

75. 29489; *Jijie* 1518; Ye (1985) 428; Zhou 142.

Li's less famous quatrain on Wang Zhaojun begins in the same spirit of retelling a famous story, but it closes with a line that is suggestive yet far from clear. Wang Zhaojun was a beautiful Han palace lady who, because of her poverty, was unable to bribe the court painter Mao Yanshou. As a result, Mao painted her as ugly. Looking at only portraits, Han Yuandi decided to marry her off to Huhanye, the ruler of the Xiongnu, discovering his error only when she was ready to depart. Her tomb in the steppes was supposed to be always green.

李商隱, 王昭君
Li Shangyin, Wang Zhaojun[76]

毛延壽畫欲通神	Mao Yanshou's painting would convey the spirit,
忍爲黃金不顧人	because of gold he was ruthless, did not care about the person.
馬上琵琶行萬里	On horseback her pipa went ten thousand leagues,
漢宮長有隔生春	for the Han palace there was always spring appearing after her life.[77]

The final line is characteristic of Li Shangyin in that it is highly suggestive and eludes definitive interpretation. In a quatrain in this style, its role is one of summation. Although commentators have wished to link it to her evergreen tomb, the poem specifies: "in the Han palace." *Ge sheng chun* 隔生春 ("spring appearing after her life") is literally "spring separated by / from beyond life." It is a phrase that hangs at the edge of making sense, and can be interpreted in various ways.

In 851 Li Shangyin went to Sichuan, where Du Fu had sojourned almost a century earlier. It is hard to say when Li Shangyin's interest in Du Fu was first kindled; we can already hear echoes in earlier poems. In the west, however, he remembered Du Fu and the latter's admiration for Zhuge Liang, the failed minister of Shu-Han during the Three Kingdoms. In Chengdu Li Shangyin wrote a poem about the ancient cypress of the Zhuge Liang Shrine, though it met with far less success than Du Fu's famous poem. The best known of Li Shang-

---

76. 29499; *Jijie* 1528; Ye (1985) 435.

77. This line is obscure, though commentators generally agree that it refers to Wang Zhaojun's tomb, Green Mound, in the steppes.

yin's Zhuge Liang poems, emulating Du Fu's thick style with Li Shangyin's mannered twist, was a poem on Choubi Post Station, where Zhuge Liang had halted the Shu-Han army to draw up his plans against Cao Cao.

李商隱, 籌筆驛
Li Shangyin, Choubi Station[78]

猿鳥猶疑畏簡書	Gibbons and birds still seem "awed by the documents,"[79]
風雲長爲護儲胥	windblown clouds ever guard the wooden stockade for him.[80]
徒令上將揮神筆	The great general was brought to wield his divine brush in vain;[81]
終見降王走傳車	in the end one saw his surrendered ruler speed away in a post coach.[82]
管樂有才眞不忝	Guan Zhong and Yue Yi had talent, truly no shame in comparison,[83]

---

78. 29192; *Jijie* 1318; Ye (1985) 124; Zhou 217. Choubi (Planning Brush) Station was located in Tang Mianzhou 綿州, in modern Sichuan.

79. The earliest editions read *yu* 魚 for *yuan* 猿. Commentators have consistently preferred the variant, though early citations confirm the reading *yu*. "Awed by the documents" alluded to "Sending Forth the Chariots," *Chuche* 出車, in the Lesser Odes. "Of course we think on going home, / but we are awed by the documents" 豈不懷歸, 畏此簡書. This is traditionally taken to refer to the commands that forbade desertion. Here it refers to Zhuge Liang's military orders.

80. The *chuxu* 儲胥 is either the stockade itself or the defensive rim of stakes driven in the ground outside the stockade.

81. The reference is to Zhuge Liang's strategies.

82. The reference is to Liu Chan 劉禪, the second and last of the Shu-Han rulers, who had himself bound and then went out and surrendered to the invading Wei general Deng Ai 鄧艾. From there Liu Chan and his family were sent to the Wei capital at Luoyang.

83. Guan Zhong 管仲 was the minister who made Duke Huan of Qi overlord. Yue Yi 樂毅 was the famous strategist employed by King Zhao of Yan against Qi. That is, Zhuge Liang's talents were such that they were comparable to those of Guan Zhong and Yue Yi. The line echoes a passage in Zhuge Liang's biography in the *Record of Shu* 蜀志 in which he was supposed to have compared himself to Guan Zhong and Yue Yi. Most dismissed the comparison, with the exception of a few friends who knew his worth.

關張無命欲何如	if Guan Yu and Zhang Fei were not to survive, what could he do?[84]
他年錦里經祠廟	In another year I passed his shrine in Brocade Town,[85]
梁父吟成恨有餘	when his Liangfu Song was done, it was replete with resentment.[86]

"Choubi Station" is essentially a "meditation on the past" rather than a pure poem about history. It begins with Li Shangyin's favorite variation on the scene of absence: a past splendor is gone, but the present natural world seems figuratively marked by the past. Thus, the landscape around Yangzhou (Sui Yangdi's Jiangdu) is still empty of fireflies. If the gibbons and birds are wary of people, it is a lingering awe at the strictness of Zhuge Liang's command. If the place is in a wilderness with clouds blowing through it, those clouds are still guarding his encampment, which remains a hazy presence in the scene.

To Chinese poets heroic history often centered on a scene of writing or command—plans, orders, commemorations—rather than active battles. The warriors and generals, like Guan Yu and Zhang Fei, who would dominate popular traditions were mere instruments of the planner-writer. Li Shangyin is, however, aware that if those instruments failed or were killed, all the wisdom and cultural force invested in the brush was wasted. Despite having a minister equal to the ancient exemplars Guan Zhong of Qi and Yue Yi of Yan, the Shu-Han kingdom collapsed soon after the death of the First Ruler Liu Bei, and his son Liu Chan was forced to surrender to Cao Cao.

---

84. Guan Yu 關羽 and Zhang Fei 張飛 were the two most talented generals of the Shu-Han kingdom. Both were killed earlier in battle.

85. Chengdu.

86. The *yuefu* "Liangfu Song" (梁父吟 or 梁甫吟) was traditionally attributed to Zhuge Liang. The *Record of Shu* 蜀志 credits Zhuge Liang with a fondness for the "Liangfu Song" while he was still living a private life. The song was originally a type of dirge, and probably there were other lyrics in addition to the anonymous early lyric that has been preserved. *Jijie* makes the improbable suggestion that the last line here refers to Li Shangyin's own poem "The Old Cypress at the Shrine of the Martial Count [Zhuge Liang]" 武侯廟古柏 (29195). Thus, commentators would read the last line: "When *my* Liangfu Song was done . . . ."

We come at last to the "Liangfu Song." The surviving version, believed in the Tang to have been by Zhuge Liang, celebrates the power of the clever minister over the military hero. The song refers to a story in the *Yanzi chunqiu* in which Yanzi plotted with Duke Jing of Qi to get rid of the three strongmen. Yanzi came up with a scheme whereby the three were given two peaches and told that they were to decide among themselves who was the most worthy and hence the most deserving of the peaches. Each boasted his own merits, and when Guyezi boasted about his, the others were so ashamed by the fact that they had made claims on the peaches that they killed themselves. Witnessing this, Guyezi too felt ashamed and killed himself.[87]

步出齊東門	I walked out of the east gate of Qi,
遙望蕩陰里	and gazed on Dangyin Village afar.
里中有三墳	In the village there were three tomb mounds,
纍纍正相似	heaped high and looking just alike.
問是誰家墓	I asked: Whose graves are these?—
田疆古冶子	Tian [Kai]jiang's and Guyezi's.
力能排南山	Might that could push South Mountain aside,
文能絕地紀	writings that could break the earthlines.
一朝被讒言	In one morning they suffered slander,
二桃殺三士	and two peaches killed three warriors.
誰能為此謀	Who could make such a plan as this?—
國相齊晏子	The domain's minister, Yanzi of Qi.

If this song is "replete with resentment," it is because in this case the clever adviser, Zhuge Liang, still failed.

Li Shangyin's finest tribute to Du Fu occurs in a poem virtually unprecedented in the tradition, the major exception being a poem by Li He, presented as the poem the sixth-century poet Yu Jianwu "should have written" when coming out of hiding after the fall of the Liang (see p. 176). Li Shangyin writes in the same spirit as Du Fu in Chengdu.

---

87. Lu Qinli (1983) 281.

李商隱, 杜工部蜀中離席

Li Shangyin, Du Fu at a Parting Banquet in Shu[88]

人生何處不離群	Where in this life do we not become separated from others?—[89]
世路干戈惜暫分	warfare on the world's paths makes us begrudge even brief division.
雪嶺未歸天外使	Snow Ridge has not yet seen the return of the envoys beyond the horizon,[90]
松州猶駐殿前軍	Songzhou still has a palace army halted there.[91]
座中醉客延醒客	Those drunk at the party invite to drink those who are still sober,
江上晴雲雜雨雲	the sunlit clouds over the river are mixed with rain clouds.
美酒成都堪送老	Chengdu, with its fine ale, can go with me on to old age—
當壚仍是卓文君	at its bars still there are Zhuo Wenjuns.[92]

---

88. 29189; *Jijie* 1169; Ye (1985) 119; Zhou 222. Though Li Shangyin does imitate Du Fu's style, this is not a formal "imitation" 擬 but rather the construction of a fictional occasion. Du Fu is here referred to by the title Gongbu, of the Board of Works, a titular position he held thanks to his service on the staff of Yan Wu, the military governor. Cheng Mengxing advocates the variant *bi* 辟 for *Du*, thus making the title refer to Li himself as having been "appointed" to a position on the Board of Works. Most commentators reject this. Ye points out that *bi* would be the wrong term for such an appointment.

89. The loose usage of *hechu* 何處 in Tang poetic diction extends this to "when?" "under what circumstances?"

90. The reference is to the two envoys sent to the Tibetans in 763 and detained there. Snow Mountain was in Songzhou in Sichuan, roughly marking the border between the Chinese and Tibetans.

91. Western frontier commands sought registration as palace armies because the pay and provision were better. Songzhou was one of the most important western commands on the Tibetan frontier. As Zhou Zhenfu and others have pointed out, even though the historical specifics in the second couplet belong to Du Fu's age, they echoed the troubles in the west of Li Shangyin's day.

92. The reference is to the celebrated beauty who married the poet Sima Xiangru and kept a bar with him in Chengdu.

Three poets in Chengdu are united across a millennium: we have Li Shangyin writing as Du Fu, who at last becomes the Han writer Sima Xiangru. In both Du Fu's and Li Shangyin's time Chengdu was in close proximity to a troubled frontier; when parting occurs, reunion is uncertain. In a very different key, Li Shangyin's impulse toward absorption in the pleasures of the moment returns, now in the traditional guise of the persuasion to pleasure at the feast. For the Last Ruler of the Northern Qi we were given Little Love's naked body as the image that absorbed him. Here in his closing words the poet invokes Zhuo Wenjun, decently clothed but no less alluring. Going forth into the world is dangerous. Chengdu's fine ale and beauties like Zhuo Wenjun can hold one in place "on to old age."

We may recall that the difference between Sui Yangdi and the Last Ruler of Chen was Yangdi's desire to emulate the image of the former, embodied in legend and, most of all, in a famous song. Li Shangyin was clearly no less beguiled by those images of the past, even when he tried to maintain himself at a distance, offering the judgment of the moral historian. With Tang poets and writers he can cross that barrier of fascination and stand in their shoes. In the poem above he perfectly captures the tone of Du Fu's poetry, as he does for Han Yu's poetry in his famous tribute to him, celebrating the power of writing.

In the middle of the second decade of the ninth century Xianzong had decided to reassert imperial authority over the Huaixi circuit, which had been autonomous for over half a century. Imperial forces had bungled the operation and Chief Minister Wu Yuanheng was assassinated by operatives from another autonomous circuit that did not want imperial forces to succeed. Pei Du, Han Yu's patron, then took Wu Yuanheng's place as chief minister, pressed the war efforts, and even visited the front to coordinate Tang forces. At last victory was achieved. Han Yu was called upon to compose the stele inscription celebrating the victory and, as might be expected, gave pride of place to the achievements of his patron, Pei Du. Others at court, however, felt that Pei Du's achievements were exaggerated. The stele was pulled down, the inscription effaced, and another was put in its place. The Huaixi inscription remained one of Han Yu's most famous works. The point was not lost on Li Shangyin that a text and its tangible inscription were different things.

李商隱, 韓碑

Li Shangyin, Han Yu's Stele[93]

元和天子神武姿	The Yuanhe Son of Heaven of divine and warlike mien,
彼何人哉軒與羲	what sort of man was he?— like the Yellow Emperor or Fu Xi.
誓將上雪列聖恥	He vowed that he would wipe away the shame of successive sovereigns,
坐法宮中朝四夷	he sat in the Hall of Justice, barbarians all around came to court.
淮西有賊五十載	Huaixi had been in brigands' hands for fifty years,
封狼生貙貙生羆	a great wolf spawned a wildcat, the wildcat spawned a bear.[94]
不據山河據平地	They did not occupy mountain or river, they occupied level land,
長戈利矛日可麾	with long pike and sharp spear they could direct the sun.[95]
帝得聖相相曰度	The Emperor found a sagely minister, the minister was called Du,[96]
賊斫不死神扶持	brigands smote him, he did not die— he was supported by the gods.[97]
腰懸相印作都統	From his waist hung the Minister's seal, he served as Campaign Commander,[98]
陰風慘澹天王旗	a shadowy aura blew ominously from the Great King's banners.
愬武古通作牙爪	Li Su, Han Gongwu, Li Daogu, and Li Wentong served as the teeth and claws,[99]

---

93. 29148; *Jijie* 828; Ye (1985) 64; Zhou 120.

94. The Huaixi circuit had been in the hands of strong generals since the Dali Reign.

95. The reference is to a story in the *Huainanzi* in which the lord of Luyang was doing battle with Han Gou. He was so absorbed in the fighting that when the sun was setting, he wielded his pike and directed the sun to return to a higher position in the sky.

96. Pei Du.

97. The reference is to an assassination attempt on Pei Du in the capital.

98. The commander in the field was Han Hong.

99. These were subordinate commanders.

儀曹外郎載筆隨	the Vice Director of the Ministry of Rites went along bearing his brush.[100]
行軍司馬智且勇	The adjutant of the expedition was canny and was bold,[101]
十四萬眾猶虎貔	a host of four hundred thousand like tigers and panthers.
入蔡縛賊獻太廟	They entered Cai, bound up the brigands, presented them to the Ancestral Temple,
功無與讓恩不訾	for deeds that yielded to none imperial grace was beyond measure.
帝曰汝度功第一	The Emperor spake: "You, Du, your deeds are the highest;
汝從事愈宜爲辭	it is fitting that your attendant Yu write of this."
愈拜稽首蹈且舞	Han Yu bowed and kowtowed, he skipped and danced:[102]
金石刻畫臣能爲	"To carve and mark on metal or stone is something your subject can do;[103]
古者世稱大手筆	in ancient ages they spoke of this as writing of great importance;
此事不繫於職司	matters such as this are not tied to the usual office functions;
當仁自古有不讓	in kindly tasks since ancient times there is no deferring."[104]
言訖屢頷天子頤	These words concluded, the Son of Heaven often nodded his chin.
公退齋戒坐小閤	Han Yu withdrew and fasted, seated in a small chamber,
濡染大筆何淋漓	soaking his great brush in ink, how the words flowed!

---

100. The reference is to Li Zongmin, who served as Pei Du's secretary.

101. The reference is to Han Yu.

102. "Skipping and dancing" was the proper sign of pleasure at an imperial order.

103. Takahashi Kazumi takes this as a rhetorical question, implying that this is something the emperor should do.

104. This echoes *Analects* XV.35: "In kindly tasks one does not yield even to one's teacher" 當仁不讓於師.

點竄堯典舜典字
He expanded and shortened passages
    from the Canons of Yu and Shun,[105]

塗改清廟生民詩
he varied and altered Poems,
    "Pure Temple," "Giving Birth to the Folk."

文成破體書在紙
The text finished, it broke the usual forms,
    he wrote it out on paper,

清晨再拜鋪丹墀
on a clear morning he repeatedly bowed,
    unrolling it in the Cinnabar Courtyard.

表曰臣愈昧死上
The memorial said: "Your subject Yu,
    heedless of risk of death,

詠神聖功書之碑
has sung of deeds of divine sageliness
    and written a stele inscription."

碑高三丈字如斗
The stele was three yards high,
    the characters like tadpoles,

負以靈鼇蟠以螭
born on the back of a sacred tortoise,
    with dragons coiled around.

句奇語重喻者少
The lines were strange, the diction weighty,
    there were few who got the sense,

讒之天子言其私
they maligned him to the Son of Heaven,
    saying he was biased.

長繩百尺拽碑倒
With a long rope of a hundred feet
    they pulled the stele down;

龘砂大石相磨治
with coarse grit and large rocks
    they ground it away.

公之斯文若元氣
His text that represents this Culture
    is like the Primal Essence:

先時已入人肝脾
well before this it had already
    entered people's innards.

湯盤孔鼎有述作
Tang's basin and Kong's tripod
    had their inscriptions;[106]

今無其器存其辭
we no longer have the vessels today,
    but their words have been preserved.

---

105. These are sections of the *Shujing*.

106. Tang's basin belonged to the Shang founder. Although its inscription was preserved, the vessel itself was lost. There is debate over "Kong's tripod," but it probably refers to the tripod of Zheng Kaofu, inscribed in the Zhou.

嗚呼聖皇及聖相	Alas for that Sage Ruler
	and his sagely Minister:
相與烜赫流淳熙	together they were glorious,
	with a pure and radiant legacy.
公之斯文不示後	If his text that represents this Culture
	is not shown to posterity,
曷與三五相攀追	how can we attempt to reach
	the Three God-kings and Five Emperors?
願書萬本誦萬遍	I wish to make ten thousand copies
	and recite it ten thousand times,
口角流沫右手胝	saliva dripping from mouth's corners,
	my right hand calloused.
傳之七十有二代	Pass it on for generations,
	seventy and two,
以爲封禪玉檢明堂基	to use it in the Feng and Shan rites, jade tablets,
	and the foundation of a Hall of Light.

Although this poem is not one that welcomes translation, it has achieved a secure place in the canon of Tang poetry. The resonant archaism in the Tang long line is a formal continuity that matches the continuity of values from the remote cultural past to Li Shangyin's recent past in Han Yu's prose. It shows a faith in the power of words, slipping away from the effaced inscription and "entering people's innards." This is the positive counterpart of Du Mu's friend Li Kan's anxiety about Bai Juyi's and Yuan Zhen's poetic words possessing infectious toxicity, entering people's flesh and bones. The unique text of a stele inscription becomes the continually reproduced text, "in ten thousand copies," a fantasy of preservation and public circulation that brings us to the very edge of print culture, whose great early printing projects were undertaken precisely with this motive in mind. This new vision of "publicity" differed profoundly from the Tang carving of the Confucian Classics on stone, initiated through a proposal by Zheng Tan in 837. As poetry had left the court, the culture-bearing "writing of great importance," *dashoubi* 大手筆, was specifically not instantiated in the court-sanctioned stone inscription but rather in the "text" that could be infinitely reproduced.

Han Yu was still writing in the context of the state. In "Han Yu's Stele" the state effaces the text, but the text has escaped the state's control. In effect, the Tang state has lost the real monument of cultural authority, which through eternal reproduction returns at the end as the basis for an ideal state in the "Feng and Shan rites" and in the "Hall of Light."

The figure of Han Yu composing his "new" text by culling words from past texts is perhaps the double of Li Shangyin writing as Han Yu. This is a style Li Shangyin uses nowhere else. Within the stylistic reproduction it is the figure of textual reproduction and dissemination, reciting and copying: "saliva dripping from mouth's corners, my right hand calloused."

It may seem difficult to reconcile this image of Li Shangyin with the poet of the hermetic pieces, staring a lifetime at the singer's lips or the dancer under bowl of crystal, the poet in a daze of passion or memory. Yet everywhere he seeks repetition or a focus on something singular, an absorption that organizes his poetic world around it. When he looked into history, he found himself with emperors who were obsessed, focused on a woman or an image. In Han Yu it is the single text, constantly repeated and copied.

THIRTEEN

Li Shangyin

"Poems on Things"

"Poems on things," *yongwu* 詠物, formed an important subgenre in the poetic tradition. "Things" here comprise a limited range of artifacts and things in nature, a range represented in the early encyclopedias, *leishu* 類書. Some things were "poetic," while others were not. Mirrors were poetic; brick molds and bricks, basic artifacts of Chinese civilization, were not. Cicadas were poetic; earthworms were not. Certain trees, aromatic herbs, and flowering plants were poetic and noticed; others were poetically invisible.

Each of the common "things" of poetry came with its own lore, allusions, associations, and history of prior use. Some histories of lore and use were long, while others were short. Those differing histories exercised a profound influence on the ninth-century poem. The associations of a particular poetic "thing" suggested the style and even the poetic genre in which the thing was best represented.

The cicada, believed to feed only on dew, was a figure of purity and austerity. It had been used in a famous prison poem by Luo Binwang in the seventh century as a figure for the poet himself.[1] The gaudy peony, which became all the rage in the eighth century, became a poetic topic only around the end of the eighth century. Two poetic expositions on the peony dating from the first half of the ninth century, one by Shu Yuanyu 舒元輿 and another by Li Deyu, both proudly proclaim that no one had written poetic expositions on the subject. The peony was a

---

1. 04190; Chen Xijin 陳熙晉, *Luo Linhai ji jianzhu* 駱臨海集箋注 (Shanghai: Shanghai guji chubanshe, 1985), 159.

flashy, feminized flower and demanded a style very different from that appropriate for writing on the cicada. It is also not surprising that Li Shangyin chose regulated verse in the short line for his cicada poem. He wrote a number of poems on peonies, but the famous ones are written in the long line.[2]

李商隱, 蟬
Li Shangyin, Cicada[3]

本以高難飽	By high-minded nature not eating its fill,
徒勞恨費聲	wasted effort, voice spent in resentment.
五更疏欲斷	Before dawn cries sparse, almost ceasing,
一樹碧無情	a whole emerald tree doesn't care.
薄宦梗猶泛	I, low official, a bough still adrift,[4]
故園蕪已平	weeds already cover my garden at home.[5]
煩君最相警	You have kindly warned me most strongly:
我亦舉家清	I and all my family are pure like you.[6]

Commentators always point out that the first couplet is particularly ambiguous as to whether it refers to the cicada or to Li Shangyin himself (though in such a poem the "thing" of the title will normally be presumed to be the subject). The ninth-century reader would, however, already be disposed to take the cicada as the poet's double. The older tradition of the cicada as poet, represented by the Luo Binwang poem, was supplemented by the conventional ninth-century comparison of the recitation of poetry to a cicada's cries. The cicada's cries were precisely *kuyin*, the "bitter chanting" that became "painstaking composition." Li Shangyin's poem, however, is a far cry from the regulated-verse craft. Although it borrows the restraint associated with the form, it is an integral exposition rather than a container for fine couplets.

---

2. It should, however, be noted that Li Shangyin's poem directly echoes a cicada poem by Lu Sidao 盧思道 (535–586), written in irregular lines, entitled "On Listening to Cicadas Sing" 聽鳴蟬篇. See Zhu Shangshu 祝尚書, *Lu Sidao ji jiaozhu* 盧思道集校注 (Chengdu: Ba Shu shushe, 2001), 39.

3. 29109; *Jijie* 1027; Ye (1985) 24; Zhou 177.

4. The reference is to an imaginary dialogue in the *Zhanguo ce* and *Shuo yuan* in which an earthen statue addressed a figurine carved from a peach bough, telling it that when the rains fell, it would be swept away by the river.

5. This recalls Tao Qian's concern prior to deciding to give up his office and return home.

6. This is interpreted as being like the cicada in never eating its fill.

The poet's song is a wasted expense of voice. Hearing his cicada-double is a warning, in the context of remembering Tao Qian's garden and the possibility that he, too, can quit and return home. Although that was not a realistic possibility, it perhaps provided some consolation.

To juxtapose Li Shangyin's famous "Cicada" poem with the most famous of his poems on peonies is a striking reminder of the nature of his talent. Li Shangyin does not have a single "characteristic" style. Rather, he writes in many styles and is original in many of them. Here the sumptuous descriptive style, containing an allusion in almost every line, is a counterpart and tribute to the famously gaudy flower.

李商隱, 牡丹
Li Shangyin, Peonies[7]

錦幃初卷衛夫人	Brocade curtains just rolled up, the Lady of Wei;[8]
繡被猶堆越鄂君	embroidered blankets still piled in heaps, Lord E of Yue.[9]
垂手亂翻雕玉佩	Dangling hands send flying wildly pendants of carved jade;
折腰爭舞鬱金裙	bending waists compete to set dancing saffron skirts.[10]
石家蠟燭何曾剪	Wax candles of Shi Chong's home, never once trimmed;[11]
荀令香爐可待熏	incense burner of Director Xun, aroma to anticipate.[12]

---

7. 29260; *Jijie* 1548; Ye (1985) 193; Zhou 15.

8. When the Lady of Wei had Confucius come to meet her, she took her proper position behind a brocade curtain. Confucius faced north toward the curtain and kowtowed, and she bowed behind the curtain. This same person, called Nanzi, had an affair with a prince of Song.

9. The *Shuo yuan* relates how Lord E of Yue was out boating, during which his boatman sang a romantic song. Lord E embraced him and covered him with an embroidered blanket.

10. "Dangling hands," *chuishou* 垂手, was both a gesture in dance and the name of a dance. "Bending waists," *zheyao* 折腰, was also a conventional description of a kind of dance with bows. *Jijie* suggests that this passage describes the flowers waving in the breeze.

11. As an example of the famous Shi Chong's extravagance, the *Shishuo xinyu* notes that he used wax candles in place of kindling.

12. According to a comment in the *Xiangyang ji* 襄陽記, whenever Xun Yu 荀彧 visited someone's home, the spot where he sat would remain fragrant for three days.

我是夢中傳采筆   I am he to whom in dream
                                     was given the brush of many colors[13]
欲書花片寄朝雲   and wish to write on the flower petals
                                     to send to "clouds of dawn."[14]

Li Shangyin opens with images of exposure and concealment, pre-
sumably corresponding to peonies that are open and those that are still
closed. The flowers are not only erotic but illicitly erotic: Nanzi, the
Lady of Wei, might have met Confucius behind a curtain, as some
commentaries remind us, but here the curtain is rolled up, exposing this
woman, notorious for her adulterous affair with a nobleman of Song.
Lord E of Yue's beautiful boatman under heaps of blankets was the
tradition's most famous figure of male beauty and homoerotic desire.

The second couplet gives us the movements of dance, probably cor-
responding to the peonies swaying in the breeze. (Peonies have overly
large flowers and do bend heavily when they blossom.) The dance is
anything but a stately one: it is seems like a frenzied expense of energy,
picked up in Shi Chong's lavish use of candles, the red peonies always
"burning" and never needing "trimming" to hold their flame ("trim-
ming" the wick of a candle playing on "cutting" the flowers). Even
though Magistrate Xun did not expend himself in giving off aroma,
here he is represented as an incense burner, burning up inside, produc-
ing the rich aroma of the peonies. The peonies are figures of sensual
display, but it is a display that consumes itself quickly. The third couplet,
matching color with scent, also recapitulates the figures of female and
male beauty in the first couplet, along with the images of expo-
sure (flame of the candle) and covering (smoldering incense within an
incense burner).

The last couplet is, if not a misuse, then a very troubled use of allu-
sion. In Jiang Yan's dream, the poet Guo Pu did not bestow his brush
of many colors but rather took it back (though one could read *chuan* 傳
as "passed back"). Zhou Zhenfu here has Li Shangyin recalling Linghu
Chu's instruction in parallel prose and wanting to send the poem to

---

13. The reference here is to the story of the poet Jiang Yan, who once dreamed that
Guo Pu appeared to him and asked him to return his "brush of many colors." When
Jiang Yan awoke, his poetic talent had deserted him.

14. In the *Gaotang fu* the "clouds of dawn" were the morning form of the goddess of
Wu Mountain.

him. The relationship between Guo Pu and Jiang Yan would indeed have been a fine figure for Li Shangyin's relationship to his mentor and patron. However, only the tradition of Li Shangyin scholarship might suggest that a young poet would refer to his aging and highly distinguished patron as the goddess of Wu Mountain.

What we have is an inspiration of limited duration—the brush cannot be kept. Moreover, it would appear that this dreamy inspiration comes from the peonies themselves, whose frail petals will be used as the medium of the text. The goddess of Wu Mountain ("clouds of dawn") also visits in dream and stays only a short while. The natural way to take it would be as Li Shangyin's "beloved," whether real or imagined.

To offer a period comparison, consider a poem by Han Yu, probably dating from the second decade of the ninth century. The peonies are typically beautiful women, but the light wit of the Yuanhe poet focuses on relationships rather than pure display.

韓愈, 戲題牡丹

Han Yu, Playfully on the Topic of Peonies[15]

幸自同開俱隱約	By good fortune they opened together, all in a blur,
何須相倚鬪輕盈	why must they rest on each other in contest of light charms?
陵晨並作新妝面	At the break of dawn they all have newly made up faces,
對客偏含不語情	facing visitors they show special reserve, passions unspoken.
雙燕無機還拂掠	No designs on them, a pair of swallows again brushes past them,
游蜂多思正經營	but roaming bees are full of longing and now busy at them.
長年是事皆拋盡	For an older person all such concerns have been entirely left behind,
今日欄邊暫眼明	but today beside my fence my eyes sparkle for a moment.

The passions of these peonies are held back—*han* 含, "reserve"—because, like peach and plum, they do not speak. They are adorned to

15. 18033; Qian Zhonglian 943.

attract attention, but they are shy. The paired swallows, content with each other, are indifferent; only the bees are hard at work. The peonies do attract the attention of the poet, but they do not induce a state of dreaminess. Rather, they put a spark in an old man, chuckling at himself, for just a little while.

Although Li Shangyin's "Peonies" is unique, the comparison with Han Yu's poem captures one essential change between the Mid-Tang and Late Tang. Although irony and wit were hardly universal in the Mid-Tang, they nevertheless were an important dimension in Mid-Tang poetry, a sophisticated bemusement with oneself that we see so often in the poetry of Han Yu and Bai Juyi. "Playful" poems continued to be written by Late Tang poets. As we will see when discussing Wen Tingyun and Duan Chengshi, there were many "teasing poems," *chao* 嘲, and jeux d'esprit. Han Yu's lightness of tone, however, playing on simultaneous engagement and disengagement, became much less common.

When there is irony in Li Shangyin, it is sharper. The associations of the peony were fixed, but they could be treated very differently from Li's earlier poem.

李商隱, 牡丹

Li Shangyin, Peonies[16]

壓逕復緣溝	Pressing on paths and lining moats,
當牐又映樓	at windows and half hiding mansions.
終銷一國破	They are at last worth a state's ruin,[17]
不啻萬金求	not to be had for mere thousands in silver.
鸞鳳戲三島	Phoenixes sporting upon the Three Isles,
神仙居十洲	immortals who live on the Ten Continents.[18]
應憐護草淡	I'm sure they pity the day lily's pallor—
卻得號忘憂	but it does get called "care's oblivion."

Peonies were indeed quite popular in the eighth and ninth centuries; and Li Shangyin is here clearly playing on the contrast between their ubiquitous presence and the commonplaces of their rare value. The peonies are seductively beautiful women, the sort that can destroy the polity; but perhaps such beauties are as common as the peonies. These

---

16. 29267; *Jijie* 1554; Ye (1985) 200.

17. The peonies are here represented as beautiful women who "make kingdoms fall," *qingguo* 傾國.

18. These are the isles of the immortals in the Western Ocean.

"phoenixes" and "immortals," who create their own ambience, are, of course, only short-lived flowers. Their sense of superiority in pitying the day lily is ironically reversed by the poet's comment in the final line.

The sumptuous peony of the first poem and the somewhat stranger peony of the second poem become the peony as an object of pathos in a pair of poems, written when Li Shangyin was serving with Wang Maoyuan, about peonies ruined by a rainstorm.

李商隱, 回中牡丹為雨所敗二首
Li Shangyin, Peonies Ruined by Rain in Huizhong[19]

I

下苑他年未可追	Those of Lower Park from other years are now beyond recall,[20]
西州今日忽相期	but today in this western district all at once we meet.
水亭暮雨寒猶在	Twilight rain on a river pavilion, a chill that still remains,
羅薦春香暖不知	gossamer mat and spring incense, but no warmth is discerned.
舞蝶殷勤收落蕊	Dancing butterflies do their utmost to gather the fallen stamens,
有人惆悵臥遙帷	there is someone sick at heart lying in far-off bed curtains.
章臺街裏芳菲伴	Of your fragrant companions on the Zhang Terrace roads[21]
且問宮腰損幾枝	I wonder how many sprays of those palace-girl waists were ruined.

II

浪笑榴花不及春	Rashly mocked was the pomegranate for missing out on spring,[22]
先期零落更愁人	but these, destroyed before their time, sadden me still more.

---

19. 29674–75; *Jijie* 270; Ye (1985) 693; Zhou 91. Huizhong was located in Anding.

20. The Lower Park was part of the Twisting River Park in Chang'an.

21. The willows.

22. The Sui official Kong Shaoan joined the Tang founder too late to win a top position. At a banquet he responded to the set topic "Pomegranate" with the couplet: "Only because they were late to come, / they missed spring in their blooming" 祇爲來時晚, 花開不及春.

玉盤迸淚傷心數	Tears scattered on plates of jade frequently pain the heart,
錦瑟驚弦破夢頻	the brocade zither's strings twang often shattering dream.
萬里重陰非舊圃	Thousands of leagues of layered shadow, not the garden of old,
一年生意屬流塵	the life of the whole year goes off with the flowing dust.[23]
前溪舞罷君迴顧	When the dance "Creek Ahead" is done, you will look back[24]
併覺今朝粉態新	realizing all their powdered charms were fresh only this morning.

Sadness at the falling of flowers was already a favorite motif in Tang poetry, which is here carried to a mannered excess that is the counterpart of the excessive rhetorical elaboration in the first peony poem. This aspect of Li Shangyin's poetry (which by no means characterizes all his poetry) to some degree deserves James J. Y. Liu's characterization of Li Shangyin's poetry as "baroque." In contrast to the aesthetics of restraint in the regulated verse masters of the 820s and 830s, these two poems, written around 838, foreground their excess. The undatable first poem on "Peonies" is playfully artificial in its excess. These two poems go to excess in mannered sensibility. They are cousin to the excessive emperors in the history poems and of the passionately excessive speakers in the hermetic poems.

As the cicada is the poet's double, so the peonies are figured as women, and vice versa. The capacity to play such poetic roles of emotional engagement in describing "things" depends on a permeable boundary between the human and nonhuman. The opposite, then, of such a relation are those things that resist meaning, that are simply themselves. We do find this—though rarely in poems specifically about "things."

---

23. Broken flower petals were called "fragrant dust."

24. This was a Southern *yuefu* with the lines: "The flowers fall and go off with the current, / when will you see them return on the current?" 花落隨流去, 何見逐流還.

李商隱, 日射
Li Shangyin, The Sun Shoots[25]

日射紗窗風撼扉	The sun shoots into meshed windows, wind shakes the door,
香羅掩手春事違	scented gossamer hides hands, spring's matters gone awry.[26]
迴廊四合掩寂寞	The winding arcade on all sides, hiding a stillness:
碧鸚鵡對紅薔薇	an emerald green parrot faces the red roses.

If "Peonies Ruined by Rain" represents the pathos of a supremely in-terpretable natural phenomenon, "The Sun Shoots" brings us to some-thing unreadable—or, rather, readable in its form rather than in a weight of associations.

We begin with penetration and assault on enclosure: light and breeze (*fengguang* 風光, spring weather) are breaking into barriers that define an enclosure. Next we see hands wrapped in gossamer, followed by the peculiar comment in this context: "spring's matters gone awry." The gossamer hiding hands implies a woman (and a chill getting in), so that "spring matters gone awry" hints at some romantic difficulty behind the unspringlike chill. Next we have a covered walkway that seems to encircle an inner courtyard. The poem moves us through frames and barriers that enclose to a final point of melancholy stillness, namely, a parrot facing the roses. The parrot is a common "thing" of poetry, as-sociated with women, repeating their gossip so that one has to hold one's tongue around the bird. The "thing" here, however, has become unreadable, part of a pattern of colors. It notices neither us nor the woman of the second line. The bird's "facing" seems intentional, yet it is an intention we cannot understand.

If the bird's act of "facing" seems intentional, it is perhaps because we recall another poem, written by Du Mu around 842, which arrives at a very similar ending that also uses the verb "face," *dui* 對, in the fourth position of the last line. Here the facing is clearly intentional, refusing to notice the human being who watches.

---

25. 29273; *Jijie* 1836; Ye 206; Zhou 251.

26. 拭 is a late variant for 掩 and has been accepted by *Jijie* and Zhou in order to avoid redundancy.

杜牧, 齊安郡後池絕句
Du Mu, The Rear Pool of the Commandery
Offices at Qi'an: A Quatrain[27]

菱透浮萍綠錦池
    Water-caltrops pierce floating duckweed,
        a pool of green brocade,

夏鶯千囀弄薔薇
    summer orioles trill a thousand times,
        enjoying the roses.

盡日無人看微雨
    All day long no one else around
        I watch the light rain,

鴛鴦相對浴紅衣
    a mandarin duck couple face each other
        bathing their robes of red.

We cannot know for certain if Li Shangyin knew Du Mu's poem, but based on the date and the relative prominence of the two poets, it is more likely that Li Shangyin knew the Du Mu poem than the other way around.

When Is a Willow a Willow?

Those moments when the "things" of the world can escape the consuming poetic domain of human feelings and meanings are rare and peculiarly enigmatic. The more common question in Li Shangyin's poetry and that of other poets is where the center of gravity lies. Is the poet using human associations to invest things with meaning and value, or is he using things to figuratively refer to something specifically human? This is essentially the same question we posed in the history poems. Is the poem about a past ruler indeed about that past ruler or is it a figurative reference to a current or recent Tang ruler? As in the history poems, in "poems on things" we know that both possibilities occur. Usually, however, we cannot decide which is the case.

Willow trees present us with a fine example of the problem. It is always worth keeping in mind the fact that real willows were everywhere: their utility in water management (they grow quickly and retain the soil on banks) in a culture concerned with water management guaranteed their common presence in the empirically visible Tang world. They were also overdetermined by human meanings. The two most prominent frames of reference could be but were not essentially related. First,

27. 28158; Feng 211.

willows played a role in parting because of the phonological similarity between *liu* 柳, "willow," and *liu* 留, "stay." As a result of this phonological accident, the branches of many botanically correct willows were conventionally snapped at parting as a gesture inviting the traveler to stay. Second, "willow" was a common figurative reference to professional singers and courtesans. We know of one girl to whom Li Shangyin was attracted who went by the name "Willow Branch," Liuzhi 柳枝 (though we do not know if she called herself that or was called thus by Li Shangyin), and the term was also a popular song type. A *ke* 客 is both a "traveler" and a "client" (figured as "guest"). For a courtesan, when a *ke* "snapped a willow branch," it had a somewhat different sense than when a group of male friends "snapped willow branches" when seeing a friend off on a journey (*ke*). But since the *ke* as "client" would also soon be on his way, these discrete senses easily became commingled. Thus, we have the following Dunhuang song, perhaps dating from the ninth century but quite possibly later:[28]

莫攀我	Don't grab hold of me,
攀我太心偏	grabbing me, the heart too carried away.
我是曲江臨池柳	I am a pond-side willow of Twisting River,
者人折了那人攀	this guy breaks me, that guy grabs.
恩愛一時間	Their love lasts only a moment.

Here we obviously have a woman speaking "as a willow," with the ultimate referent being the woman. This song is not about a tree.

Most of Li Shangyin's willow poems are feminine, though we may remain uncertain whether the poems are about trees or women. A minority are not clearly marked as feminine and have often been interpreted as referring to Li Shangyin himself. In Li Shangyin's more sophisticated poetry it is best to think of the boundary between the literal and figurative as being highly unstable.

The history of willow poems is not as continuous as one might expect. There was a minor tradition of poetic expositions on the willow in the third century, but in that genre it largely disappeared as a distinct "topic" through the Tang, with the exception of a set topic on the willows by the western palace gate. Although in poetry it was sometimes a

---

28. Kong Fanjin 孔范今, ed., *Quan Tang Wudai ci shizhu* 全唐五代詞釋注 (Xi'an: Shanxi renmin chubanshe, 1998), 1333.

topic in the sixth and seventh centuries, it was not particularly common in the eighth century. (Willows were nevertheless ubiquitous as images within poems.) In the first part of the ninth century, however, it became very popular as a poem "topic," *ti* 題.

The revival of willow poetry and its association with a beloved woman probably occurred in the late eighth century with the popular "Tale of Miss Liu (Willow)," *Liushi zhuan* 柳氏傳. In addition to being a tree, *liu* (Liu) was also a common surname—and in the title of this tale it is only her surname. The tale tells how the poet Han Hong 韓翃 lost his beloved Miss Liu and finally recovered her. Such a surname invited playing on its literal sense, which we find in a famous poem attributed to Han Hong in the tale:[29]

章臺柳	Zhang Terrace willow,
章臺柳	Zhang Terrace willow,
顏色青青今在否	Do you still have your complexion so green?
縱使長條似舊垂	Even if your long fronds hang as they used to,
也應攀折他人手	I'm sure that you've been grabbed and snapped by another.

Since snapping willows at parting was already a well-established poetic custom, we here see the "snapping" of the woman-willow in an extended sense. This well-known song probably contributed to the sense of the term that appears in the Dunhuang song.

Chinese commentators have wanted Li Shangyin's willow poems to be figurative—probably because the poem gains cultural value through such an interpretation, *shenyi* 深意, "deeper meaning." Zhou Zhenfu has taken the nineteen willow poems in Li Shangyin's collection and identified twelve of them as "erotic" (*yanqing* 艷情); the remaining seven are either figurative for Li Shangyin himself or are seen as referring to his patron Liu [Willow] Zhongying 柳仲郢 (or his son).[30] Only in one case—explicitly describing the experience of seeing a willow—is an ordinary willow tree admitted into the poem—although it immediately makes Li Shangyin reflect on himself. One wonders if all the willow poems by Li Shangyin's contemporaries should also be interpreted as figurative. One suspects that for other poets, from whom "deeper

---

29. Chen Wanghe 陳王和, *Han Hong shiji jiaozhu* 韓翃詩集校注 (Taibei: Wenshizhe chubanshe, 1973), 440.

30. Zhou 189–92, 273–76.

meaning" is less demanded, a willow could sometimes be simply a poetic topic, perhaps conjoined with actually seeing a willow. Although there can be no doubt that some of Li Shangyin's willow poems are figurative, it is Li Shangyin's aura of seriousness, acquired in the commentarial tradition, that presses so many of these poems to be interpreted figuratively.

Before turning to Li Shangyin's willow poems, we might look at the willows of some older poets and contemporaries. Poets did not comment on the actual historical importance of willows except incidentally, noting their presence on embankments and along canals. Poetic willows were noted for their white "flowers," their leaves (like brows), their long fronds hanging down to the ground or water, and the pufflike floss (*xu* 絮) that carries the seedpods in the wind. The first growth of willows was often poetically described as a "mist." The full growth of the leaves in late spring was a sign of the season's impending end. Poets never notice the trunk, bark, or roots. Willows had other common associations unrelated to courtesans and parting. They were associated with the poet Tao Qian, who represented himself in the figure of "Master Five Willows," and with "Thinwillow" 細柳 camp, near Chang'an, where the Han general Zhou Yafu quartered his army to defend the capital against a Xiongnu threat.

The following two quatrains by Li Shen represent the plainer style of willow poem:

李紳, 柳二首
Li Shen, Willows[31]

I

陶令門前冒接籬	Before the gate of Magistrate Tao they snared his jieli cap,[32]
亞夫營裏拂朱旗	within the camp of Zhou Yafu they brushed the crimson banners.
人事推移無舊物	Human affairs shift and change, nothing is familiar,
年年春至綠垂絲	but every year when spring arrives their strands of green hang down.

---

31. 25690–91; Wang Xuanbo 149.
32. The *jieli* cap was the mark of an eccentric and a recluse.

II

千條垂柳拂金絲	A thousand fronds of drooping willows brush golden strands,
日暖牽風葉學眉	in sunlight's warmth pulled by wind the leaves imitate brows.
愁見花飛狂不定	I'm saddened to see the flowers fly loose, wild and unsettled,
還同輕薄五陵兒	it's much the same as heedless wastrels, the lads of Wuling.[33]

No one, I think, would insist upon a figurative reading of these quatrains. Li Shen touches on some of the standard associations of the topic (Tao Qian's "Five Willows"; General Zhou Yafu's camp; the leaves like brows). In the first quatrain there is a nice, if conventional, contrast between the mutability of human affairs and the regularity of nature. In the second quatrain the conventional gendering of the willow as a dissolute young women (female gendering is implicit in the second line) becomes masculine in the figure of the young aristocratic wastrels of Wuling. As usual, Li Shen is competent and unexciting.

Although Du Mu wrote a few poems on willows—most of them quatrains—the following regulated verse in the long line captures the popular style of the age:

杜牧, 柳長句
Du Mu, Willows (in the long line)[34]

日落水流西復東	The sun sinks, the waters flow from west to east,
春光不盡柳何窮	springtime light unending, willows without limit.
巫娥廟裏低含雨	In the temple of Wu Mountain's maiden, they hang low, heavy with rain,
宋玉宅前斜帶風	before the lodgings of Song Yu they slant, catching the wind.
莫將榆莢共爭翠	Take not the example of elm pods to compare in azure green,
深感杏花相映紅	deeply moving how apricot flowers juxtapose them with red.

---

33. Wuling was an area near Chang'an associated with the rich and wealthy.
34. 28189; Feng 235.

| 灞上漢南千萬樹 | Beside the Ba and in Hannan
millions and millions of trees, |
| 幾人遊宦別離中 | and how many officials on travels
are in the process of parting? |

These are clearly the willows of parting rather than feminized willows. We encounter a geography that probably places the poet in Hannan, on his way back to the capital ("beside the Ba"). The poem begins with an impossibly vast scene of setting sunlight and expanses of late spring willows. By her shrine Wu Mountain's goddess, who is the sexual "clouds and rain," has willows that are wet and heavy. Song Yu, who composed poetic expositions on the goddess and on the wind, is given windblown willows. Old texts and stories survive in the imagined scene of the present. The third couplet is an example of standard poetic rhetoric, where the green of the willows is praised through comparison and contrast. Finally, the poet's vision encompasses all the willows and the officials, sent back and forth to posts and missions, parting.

In the last comparative case we have the willows of Wen Tingyun, which are even more sensual than Li Shangyin's willows, lightly touching the body, fragile and feminized.

温庭筠, 題柳

Wen Tingyun, On Willows[35]

楊柳千條拂面絲	A thousand willow fronds, strands brushing the face,
綠煙金穗不勝吹	green mist, golden tassels that cannot bear the breeze.
香隨靜婉歌塵起	A scent rises with song-stirred dust from Zhang Jingwan;[36]
影伴嬌饒舞袖垂	shadows hang matching the dancing sleeves of Dong Jiaorao.[37]
羌管一聲何處曲	In a single note from the Qiang pipes a melody from where?[38]
流鶯百囀最高枝	a hundred trills of fluent orioles in the very highest branches.

---

35. 31992; Zeng 93.

36. Zhang Jingwan was a famous Liang singer.

37. Dong Jiaorao was a figure in a song attributed to the Eastern Han; here it is simply the type of a beautiful dancer.

38. The reference seems to be to the old *yuefu* "Breaking Willow," *Zhe yangliu* 折楊柳.

| 千門九陌花如雪 | At the thousand gates and on the nine lanes
    their flowers like snow,[39] |
| 飛過宮牆兩自知 | they fly across the palace walls
    and both sides know. |

None of these poets are using willows for any particularly "deep" (figurative) significance. They are performing a popular contemporary poetic topic, adjusting it to their whim of the moment and perhaps to a specific situation. An immediate or prior experience of empirical willows may be in the backs of their minds, but that experience is immediately translated into the poetic "willow," with a rich accumulation of associations and lore. Tang poets learned to write on topics, some of which were occasions and some poetic "things." They could adjust both to the circumstances of the moment, which are now unknowable. Sometimes they would choose a "thing" to write about something else; such cases are truly figurative poems. Sometimes we are given a context in the title, preface, or details of the texts that tells us a poem is figurative; in some cases we can guess that it may be so, but we don't know for certain. However, in a number of cases in Li Shangyin's poetry, so heavily invested with figurative import by the critical tradition, we have every reason to suspect that Li Shangyin is simply writing on a conventional topic.

李商隱, 柳

Li Shangyin, Willows[40]

動春何限葉	Unending leaves stir spring into motion,
撼曉幾多枝	so many branches rock the morning.
解有相思否	Does it grasp that there is loving-longing?—
應無不舞時	I'm sure the dancing never stops.
絮飛藏皓蝶	Floss flies, hiding snow-white butterflies,
帶弱露黃鸝	supple fronds expose yellow orioles.
傾國宜通體	A kingdom-toppling beauty should be so from head to toe—
誰來獨賞眉	who comes to appreciate brows alone?[41]

---

39. The "thousand gates" refers to the imperial palace. The "nine lanes" are the streets of the capital.

40. 29124; *Jijie* 1558; Ye (1985) 40; Zhou 273.

41. Willow leaves were conventionally compared to brows.

Feng Hao interprets this as a poem written for "Willow Branch" (Liuzhi), the girl with whom Li Shangyin almost had an affair in Luo-yang before she was taken by another man. (We know these facts from Li Shangyin's own account, though "Willow Branch" was made to play a large role in the speculative narratives of the poet's private life that were invented to contextualize his hermetic poetry.) *Jijie* finds the tone too light for the imagined passions involved in the "Willow Branch" story and thinks the willow in this poem is a representative figure for a singing girl. Indeed, *Jijie* explains the last couplet as Li Shangyin teasing the girl because she casts seductive glances.

If other poems celebrate the willow, this poem is about the willow in motion. As in many such poems, the text is situated indeterminately be-tween one willow, many willows, and willows as a general category. The willow, moving in an unmentioned breeze, is a space of motion, stirring the world around it—in a striking phrase, it "rocks" [or 'shakes'] the morning." This is clearly the feminized willow, a perpetual dancer, with the motions that recall the instigation of desire ("stirring spring") but oblivious to desire.

The white puffs of floss blowing in the breeze hide white butterflies, a commonplace figure for young men seeking women. The fronds, also moving, at times reveal the orioles, a figure for singers. The willow is both a figure for the dancer and a space within which the play of sing-ers and their lovers is re-created.

By the end we arrive at the willow as type—the "kingdom-toppling beauty." Every couplet has treated the pervasiveness of the willow: "unending leaves"; "so many branches"; dancing that "never stops"; and the echo of the game of attraction in the miniaturized image of butterflies and orioles within the moving space of the willow. In other words, the poem has set up the unusual criterion—"throughout the body," *tongti* 通體; "from head to toe"—for a superlative beauty. The leaves of the first line return at the end in their common feminized metaphor of "brows."

It is hard to think of this poem as more than play on a popular po-etic topic, but the last line—the witty "comment"—returns us to the is-sue of figuration in a way that touches on Li Shangyin's poetics. *Tongti*, "throughout the body," is also "throughout the form of the poem." We doubt that Li Shangyin is intentionally talking about his poetry here, but he is comparing figuration that is partial and thus marked as such (leaves like women's brows) to a pervasive figuration in which the female performer and the willow "blur" into one another. It is a poetics of disorientation. The leaves no longer simply "imitate brows," as Li Shen would have it. Rather, the entire willow becomes the body of the dancer.

The following version of "Willows" has been much admired in the critical tradition and is usually interpreted as Li Shangyin writing about his beloved.

李商隱, 贈柳
Li Shangyin, To Willow[42]

章臺從掩映	Let them half hide Zhang Terrace,[43]
郢路更參差	beyond that, scattered on the road of Ying.[44]
見說風流極	It's said they are the height of amorousness,[45]
來當婀娜時	now I meet the moment of their litheness.
橋迴行欲斷	The bridge turns, passage was almost cut off,
堤遠意相隨	the levee runs far, their thoughts go with me.[46]
忍放花如雪	How can they let flowers like snow so bloom,
青樓撲酒旗	hitting wine-banners of the blue mansions?[47]

The use of "to" or "presented to," *zeng* 贈, in the title implicitly anthropomorphizes the willow, inviting the traditional interpretation as a particular person. By translating the willow as plural, however, we are reminded that whatever "willow" might represent in Li Shangyin's mind, the willows here are those remembered in Chang'an and encountered around Jiangling. These are again the feminized willows, the willows of Zhang Terrace. Feminine they may be, but the allusion to their *fengliu* ("amorousness" or "gallantry") has a strong tinge of homoerotic

---

42. 29141; *Jijie* 1563; Ye 57; Zhou 76.

43. The Zhang Terrace Road, which lay to the southwest in Han Chang'an, was associated with courtesans, referred to in the Tang as "willows." See the Han Hong poem above.

44. Ying, the capital of the ancient state of Chu, is here used as a substitute for Jiangling.

45. This line alludes to a story about Qi Wudi, who admired the young Zhang Xu. Later, when willows were sent from Sichuan, the emperor had them planted by Linghe Palace and sighed at their "amorousness," "gallantry" and "panache" (*fengliu* 風流), which he said reminded him of how Zhang Xu used to look.

46. Or "my thoughts went with them." *Yi* 意 here suggests "loving thoughts." The willows, lining the embankment, seem to stay with him.

47. The "blue mansions" are the brothels.

attraction in the allusion. Just as the second line affirms their presence in the immediate scene juxtaposed against a scene of memory (already a poetic "Zhang Terrace"), so the fourth line confirms the truth of the opinion given in an old text.

The third couplet has been particularly admired. Turning onto the bridge, the poet meets a curtain of willow fronds that seem to block his passage. As he moves alongside the levee into the distance, a continuous line of willow trees "goes with him," as if filled with feeling for him. This claim of personal engagement with him is belied by the final couplet, where the willows bloom, like their feminine counterpart, among the bars and brothels. These are, after all, the professionally amorous "Zhang Terrace" willows.

Oddly enough, in the course of the poem we discover that we have come again to the counterpart of figuration in a particular referent. We have the categorical willow—or the categorical singing girl who is the willow's counterpart—set against the claim of particular feeling for the poet. They are professionally and categorically the "ultimate *fengliu*." They do not bloom for him alone, whether through botanical indifference or professional necessity. Erotics and poetics are intertwined in a most peculiar way.

One of the most interesting aspects of Li Shangyin's poetry is how often it returns in some way to the metapoetic, where experiences of the world and the work of poetry are often related. The particular and the categorical is not only a general issue in Tang poetry but a specific issue in the interpretation of Li Shangyin's *yongwu*, as well as an issue in a romance culture, where fashionable passion was usually invested in singing girls. The "things" of poetry were also overdetermined: willows were both a figure of courtesans and a figurative marker of parting, used in rituals of parting, which most often involved men parting from men. It was inevitable that these two frames of reference would overlap and create semantic dissonance. When the female singer in the Dunhuang song complains of men "breaking" twigs from her, the common marker of parting has slipped over into the courtesan-as-willow domain, with the gesture of parting signaling cruel abandonment (as it was not in the verses attributed to Han Hong). In Li Shangyin's poetry we also see these two frames of reference coming into conflict, with the poet judiciously dividing the willows in half, each part intended to serve in different frames of reference.

李商隱, 離亭賦得折楊柳二首

Li Shangyin, At the Parting Pavilion: On the topic
'Breaking the Willow Branch'[48]

I

暫憑樽酒送無憀	For the while I depend on my cup of ale to send off my ennui,
莫損愁眉與細腰	do not ruin these sad brows and slender waists.
人世死前惟有別	But in this mortal world, before death, there is only parting—
春風爭擬惜長條	the spring breeze would surely not begrudge us these long branches.

II

含煙惹霧每依依	Filled with mist and enticing fog, ever a blur of longing,[49]
萬緒千條拂落暉	ten thousand fronds, a thousand branches brush the sunset glow.
爲報行人休盡折	Tell the traveler for me not to break them all—
半留相送半迎歸	half should go to seeing him off, a half should welcome his return.

The "logic" of this poem is inextricably bound up with the issue of poetic reference, the fact that "willows" have two distinct frames of reference. We might presume a "parting pavilion" provided with both botanical willows and figurative ones in the person of singers brought to entertain those parting. Li Shangyin begins the first quatrain with the feminized willow: "sad brows and slender waists." He protests against their being broken as a sign of parting. The beautiful third line gives us the human gravity of parting. It is always worthwhile—as a modern individual accustomed to mobility and equipped with a remarkable technology of communication—to recall the difference between that

---

48. 29314–15; *Jijie* 1568; Ye (1985) 244; Zhou 265.

49. *Yiyi* 依依 was used in the *Shijing* to describe willows and became the attribute of the tree. Qian Zhongshu argues that the *yiyi* carries the sense of "yearning," which the compound certainly suggested later on (see Zhou 77). It does seem likely that in the Tang the *Shijing* sense was conflated with "yearning."

age and our own. Usually leaving behind their homes and all that was familiar, the Tang bureaucratic elite were constantly on the move, with the new ties they formed constantly being broken.

The final line of the first poem appeals to the "long branches" of the willow as some consolation for this pain that should not be begrudged. These are, of course, the branches broken by those parting, but they must also be the figurative "willows," the singers that give some pleasure to the feast.

The second poem similarly opens with the feminized willow, *yiyi* 依依, now describing both the quality of the willows in full leaf that see the traveler off (as in the *Shijing*) and the quality of "yearning" that is part of the singer's performance. Such "yearning" is both the gendered, erotic longing of the romance tradition and the homosocial yearning of friends for friends.

The conclusion of the second quatrain literally cuts in half what had been poetically fused together—a division oddly echoed in the song title ("Breaking Willow"). Let half of the willow branches be put to use in the frame of reference of parting, broken and ruined to signify loss. Let the other half be the singers, singing songs of yearning (*yiyi*), the desire for reunion shared by male friends. Those willows should be left alone to rejoice when the traveler returns.

This constitutes an economy of reference that could be accomplished in a parallel couplet matching the feminized willow with the parting willow, as in the second couplet of the following regulated verse, of which Zhu Yizun (or Qian Liangze, according to Feng Hao) observed that in its "ease and light steadiness it doesn't seem like Li Shangyin's style" 平易輕穩, 不似義山手筆:

李商隱, 柳
Li Shangyin, Willows[50]

江南江北雪初消	South of the river, north of the river the snow begins to melt,
漠漠輕黃惹嫩條	spreading widely a light yellow teases out tender twigs.

---

50. 29590; *Jijie* 1561; Ye (1985) 521.

灞岸已攀行客手	On the Ba's shores already snapped 　　by the hands of travelers,
楚宮先騁舞姬腰	at the Chu palace early displayed 　　in waists of dancing maidens.
清明帶雨臨官道	Rain-soaked on the Clear and Bright Festival 　　they look over the official road,
晚日含風拂野橋	late in the day filled with wind 　　they brush a bridge in the wilds.
如線如絲正牽恨	Like threads, like strands of silk 　　they now pull forth resentment,
王孫歸路一何遙	how far it is, the road 　　that the prince must follow home!

Li Shangyin begins by troping on the opening line of a famous Du Fu poem, "A Guest Comes" 客至. The melting of the snows will, of course, bring spring floods. Thus, a poet with a thatched hut located at the bend of the river might write, as Du Fu does: "South of my cottage, north of my cottage, spring waters everywhere" 舍南舍北皆春水. Li Shangyin's eyes are drawn, however, to the yellowish green of the emerging willows. Again these are categorical willows, described in early spring and then in the third month on the Clear and Bright Festival, finally seeing spring off, spring leaving (gui 歸) or the prince "going home." They are situated along the Yangzi River but stretch from Sichuan (Ba) downstream to Chu. They are, as we have previously observed, both the feminized willows and the willows of parting.

Ultimately we usually cannot tell if we have a poem performing the poetic topic, perhaps occasioned by an experience of the tree, or one in which willows are the mere figure of something human. We can always invent an interpretation that adds to their value by making their referent human ("deeper meaning"). In this sense the exegete resembles nothing so much as the artisan who adds value by processing raw material into some shape that is admired.

Willows are associated with spring and are poetically most visible during that season. I have never come across a Chinese poem about a willow tree in winter—though the trees were still there. Autumn is the outer limit of visibility of the poetic willow. Its appearance in autumn can be occasion for poetic surprise, recalling its spring manifestation and wondering why it is still here in the wrong season.

李商隱, 柳
Li Shangyin, Willow[51]

曾逐東風拂舞筵	Once you moved with the spring breeze brushing the dancers' mats
樂遊春苑斷腸天	in a spring park on Yueyou Plain, in weather that breaks the heart.
如何肯到清秋日	How was it you were willing to come to these clear autumn days
已帶斜陽又帶蟬	already bearing the setting sunlight, also bearing cicadas?

Willows present a special problem in figurative reading because of the weight of their associations. As a topic the "lamp" presents no such issue. The following poem was included in *Caidiao ji* and was probably precisely the kind of piece Li Fu had in mind when he denounced Li Shangyin as nothing more than a craftsman of fine brocade. In this version we have a series of situations in which the lamp is present, culminating in a moment during which the fading lamplight shines on a beautiful woman as the bed curtains are lowered. This is a common rhetorical pattern for "poems on things," running the gamut of variations and leading up to one culminating moment, a pattern we will see in "Tears" below. The Qing and modern commentarial tradition, however, interpret the "lamp" as a figure for Li Shangyin himself, or for his situation. This can be sustained, more or less, up to the erotic closure, which requires considerable exegetical ingenuity to explain. It is remotely conceivable that Li might compare himself to the famous beauty "Mourn-No-More" upon receiving a guest in order to suggest that the guest's presence cheered him. However, the final scene of a man and a woman getting into bed together is too much. In *Jijie* Liu Xuekai and Yu Shucheng outdo themselves, associating "dropping the bed curtain" 下幃 with "leaving headquarters" 罷幕 at Guilin, presumably on the grounds that "headquarters," *mu* 幕, is literally a "tent" or "cloth hanging," poetically replaced by a "bed curtain," *wei* 幃. In

---

51. 29233; *Jijie* 1258; Ye (1985) 166; Zhou 189. Zhou Zhenfu, picking up on the fact that they were heartbreaking even in spring, takes these as a figural reference for Li Shangyin himself, first in the lowly position of proofreader in the Imperial Library and later returning to the same position.

many ways we can see an exegetical tradition that is still defending Li Shangyin against Li Fu's charges, namely, that such a poem might simply offer the pleasure of beautiful lines.

李商隱, 燈
Li Shangyin, Lamp[52]

皎潔終無倦	Of gleaming purity, never tiring,
煎熬亦自求	it even seeks itself to burn away.
花時隨酒遠	When flowers bloom, it goes far with the ale;
雨夜背窗休	on rainy nights it ends, snuffed at the window.
冷暗黃茅驛	Cold and dark, a station among yellow rushes,
暄明紫桂樓	warm and bright, a mansion of purple cassia.
錦囊名畫揜	Famous paintings enclosed in brocade bags,
玉局敗碁收	defeated pieces gathered from jade chessboard.
何處無佳夢	Why is there no wonderful dream?—
誰人不隱憂	who does not lie awake with brooding cares?
影隨簾押轉	Its shadows turn with the curtain weights,
光信簟文流	its light entrusted to the flow of mat patterns.
客自勝潘岳	My guest is finer than Pan Yue[53]
儂今定莫愁	I now am Mourn-no-More indeed.
固應留半焰	Indeed, one should keep a half-faded flame
迴照下幃羞	to turn shining on shyness as bed curtains drop.

Comparison and Competition

Although our evidence begins about a century after Li Shangyin's death, it is interesting to note which "poems on things" attracted early notice. The *Caidiao ji* of Wei Hu seems to represent the sophisticated coterie taste of Chengdu in the mid-tenth century. The Li Shangyin poems imitated by Yang Yi and his circle between 1005 and 1008 in the *Xikun chouchang ji* 西崑酬唱集 represent a very different but no less sophisticated coterie and cultural milieu in Kaifeng. The former anthology and the latter imitations share one Li Shangyin "poem on things" in common, a poem that might not otherwise attract the attention of a modern reader.

---

52. 29309; *Jijie* 739; Ye (1985) 240; Zhou 150.
53. Pan Yue was known for his good looks.

李商隱, 淚
Li Shangyin, Tears[54]

永巷長年怨綺羅	Long years in Everlasting Lane,[55] resentment in figured gossamer,
離情終日思風波	daylong feelings of separation, longing in wind and waves.
湘江竹上痕無限	On the bamboo of the River Xiang, their stains without limit,[56]
峴首碑前灑幾多	before the stele atop Mount Xian how many have been shed?[57]
人去紫臺秋入塞	A person left Lavender Terrace, entered the frontier in fall,[58]
兵殘楚帳夜聞歌	the last of the battle, in a Chu tent, one heard a song by night.[59]
朝來灞水橋邊問	But if at dawn you ask those beside the bridge that crosses the Ba,
未抵青袍送玉珂	none of these equal a blue gown[60] sending off jade bridle pendants.

A great many "tears" were shed in Tang poetry, but before Li Shangyin the tears themselves were never a topic either for poetry or for poetic exposition. Each of the seven occasions for tears that comprise the poem was a fairly common situation referred to in poetry. Part of the poem's appeal was perhaps not only the novelty of the topic but the way in which the latter created a commonalty between circumstances— particularly the historical ones—that would otherwise have seemed incommensurate. "Tears" comes at last to a present parting, and the form

---

54. 29411; *Jijie* 1636; Ye (1985) 359; Zhou 155.

55. This was where Han palace ladies who were out of favor lived.

56. These are the bamboo supposedly stained by the tears of the Xiang goddesses, weeping for their husband Shun.

57. The "Stele for Shedding Tears" was on Mount Xian, near Xiangyang. It was dedicated to the good Jin governor Yang Hu, in whose remembrance visitors would shed tears.

58. The reference is to the Han palace lady Wang Zhaojun, who was sent to marry the ruler of the Xiongnu.

59. Xiang Yu, hearing Chu songs all around him at Gaixia, realized that he had finally lost out to Liu Bang.

60. A blue gown, which is supposed to identify a "student," is here either an official or a *jinshi* candidate.

of the poem recalls nothing so much as the poetic exposition "Parting," *Bie fu* 別賦, by Jiang Yan 江淹 (444–505), which is included in *Wen xuan*.[61] The poetic exposition, however, provides the amplitude to elaborate a series of exemplary cases. Li Shangyin's regulated verse in the long line allows no such scope; each circumstance is framed in a nicely phrased single line.

On a superficial level, one can build a poem through a series of allusions, "Tears" in this case resembling "Peonies," discussed earlier. "Peonies," however, is far more complex, metaphorically describing different aspects of the flower in something like a process. The latter, we might add, was neither anthologized in *Caidiao ji* nor imitated in *Xikun chouchang ji*. It is fair to pose an unanswerable question: What was the appeal of "Tears"?

Setting aside the apparently general case in the second line, the most striking feature of this poem lies in taking the most famous and resonant instances of tears shed throughout history and legend and not only placing them on the same level as a common situation in the Tang but comparing them and finding those famous earlier cases not as compelling as the present scene of parting. Li Shangyin frames this artfully: "if you ask." The judgment is delivered not by the poet but by those experiencing parting. The grounds for such a comparative judgment are determined by the fact that the quotidian parting in the present is rendered in the same high metonymic language as the ancient cases. Closer reflection on the comparison, however, shows how skewed it is. Having a friend leave Chang'an may indeed be sad, but it doesn't really compare with Xiang Yu having come to the very edge of taking imperial power and then failing to achieve it, being defeated in battle, and about to lose his beloved Fair Yu, his favorite horse, and his life. Li Shangyin is here close to suggesting that those grand tragic moments in the cultural past cannot compare to what is felt here and now; in other words, the immediacy of personal experience trumps historical knowledge—a striking claim for a poet of allusion.

A certain display of rhetoric as such, closely allied to poetic expositions and parallel prose, dominates many of the "poems on things" even more so than in Li Shangyin's other poetry. One facet of such a stylized

---

61. It also resembles another of Jiang Yan's poetic expositions, "Hard Feelings," *Hen fu* 恨賦.

display of rhetoric is judging cases and making comparative evaluations, as in "Tears." When the poet does not offer judgment (hence a judgment undecided), the precondition of judgment is often poetically represented as a competition, often conjoined with personification.

In many though not all of Li Shangyin's "poems on things" a rhetoric of personification is foregrounded. To another poet the beauty of moonlit frost in late autumn might be an integral scene. Li Shangyin takes the components apart and transforms them into a contest of display on the part of their respective goddesses.

李商隱, 霜月

Li Shangyin, Frost and Moon[62]

初聞征雁已無蟬	The migrating geese are first heard now, the cicadas are already gone,
百尺樓南水接天	south of the hundred-foot tower waters stretch to the sky.
青女素娥俱耐冷	The Blue Woman and Pale Maid, both put up with the cold:[63]
月中霜裏鬪嬋娟	in moonlight and in frost they hold a contest of beauty and grace.

We have here a canonical text. While such personification is normative in pre-Romantic European poetry, it is far less so in the Chinese tradition. The first line is a commonplace trope, locating the moment between two well-known seasonal markers. Such predictability is precisely what is undone in the rhetorical competition of the second couplet, where we have a contest (using the strong *dou* 鬪 rather than the common *zheng* 爭) whose outcome is not judged. The second line gives us the vista, the scene as integral, which the second couplet splits apart.

We suppose it is the poet himself who "puts up with the cold," *naileng* 耐冷, to enjoy the scene. When that is transferred to the two goddesses (not otherwise known to be sensitive to the cold), the meaning changes. The goddesses endure the cold in order to win the contest, to outdo the other in display. This is very much a Tang cultural world of display and relative status achieved through display. Only the poet, a Chinese Paris, is there to judge the competition, and he wisely does not judge.

---

62. 29099; *Jijie* 1629; Ye (1985) 11; Zhou 231.

63. The Blue Woman is the goddess in charge of the frost. The Pale Maid is Chang E, the moon goddess.

In the case of a poet whose poetry has too often been read politically, one hesitates to offer a political reading of one of his apparently least political poems. Yet in some fundamental way the poetic act here seems to formally reproduce the ninth-century polity. For the eighth-century poet the moonlight on the frost would have been an integral, as both society and the polity should be. The ninth-century poet splits that integral into competing agencies struggling for dominance. We know that without the moonlight the frost would be invisible, and without the frost the moonlight would be less dazzling. The beauty of the scene is due to the fact that both elements are dependent on one another. Only a rhetoric of competition for dominance divides them. I am not suggesting that Li Shangyin intended this poem as an allegory of the polity, but rather that this poetic rhetoric is a way of thinking about the world that is profoundly homologous with the polity of Li Shangyin's age.

If this suggestion seems excessive, we might compare the following poem, which *was* interpreted politically, as referring to the military commissioners or court factions. Although there is a classical precedent, suggested by Feng Hao, in the image of "bound cocks," *lianji* 連難, found in the "Qin ce" of the *Zhanguo ce*—where the feudal lords are compared to cocks tied together and unable to share a single roost— that does not quite fit the poem, in which an integral natural phenomenon (the cock crowing at dawn) becomes a contest between opposing parties.

李商隱, 賦得難
Li Shangyin, On the Cock[64]

稻梁猶足活諸雛	The grain is still enough to keep its many chicks alive,
妒敵專場好自娛	yet in spiting foes and ruling the field it happily finds delight.
可要五更驚曉夢	Would it willingly at the fifth watch awake from its morning dream?—
不辭風雪爲陽烏	but it does not avoid the frost and snow because of the sun-crow.[65]

---

64. 29249; *Jijie* 429; Ye 184.

65. The sun was supposed to have a three-legged crow in it; here it is the morning sun. The sun was often a figure for the emperor. If we read the poem figuratively from that perspective, this can be taken as a willingness to serve—in Qu Fu's terms

When another bird—in this case the sun-crow—appears on the scene, the rooster rises from its comfortable rest to crow and proclaim its mastery of its own territory. This, too, may be a pure act of poetic play, like "Frost and Moon." The question is not whether the poet intended the poem to refer to a contemporary political situation. Rather, it is a way of thinking about the world, competing and always comparing, or wondering which is better and better off. If we understand such competition as a passion—the hypertrophy of comparative Tang ranking and status—the apparently odd moves in some poems become explicable.

李商隱, 石榴
Li Shangyin, Pomegranate[66]

榴枝婀娜榴實繁	Pomegranate branches pliant and swaying, pomegranate fruits thick,
榴膜輕明榴子鮮	pomegranate tissue light and bright, pomegranate seeds fresh.
可羨瑤池碧桃樹	Yet enviable is the sapphire peach tree by Alabaster Pool,
碧桃紅頰一千年	the sapphire peaches get rosy cheeks once every thousand years.

There may or may not be figurative correspondences in such poems, but we can more confidently observe recurring patterns of competition or comparative judgment. The ordinary mortal fruit is luscious, but to be the famous immortal peach of the Queen Mother of the West is better. One can read through minor poems by Li Shangyin and see a range of variations on this pattern, which remains constant below the surface. The motif of competition can be done not with two different things but with the same thing, the second couplet declaring that the "thing" would be better off in another situation.

"showing one's utmost loyalty to the court" 盡忠朝廷. The second line, however, clearly suggests that the sun-crow is a competitor to be challenged.

66. 29136; *Jijie* 1596; Ye (1985) 53. Ye suggests that this refers to a passage in the *Nanshi*, in which Liu Quan 劉悛, while governor of Yizhou (Ba), sent Liang Wudi bamboo from the region, which Wudi greatly enjoyed. Ye takes this as referring to Li Shangyin's own wish to be brought back to the capital.

李商隱, 巴江柳
Li Shangyin, The Willows of the Ba River[67]

巴江可惜柳	Too bad about the willows by the Ba River,
柳色綠侵江	the willows' green gets into the river.
好向金鸞殿	Better to be by Golden Simurgh Hall,[68]
移陰入綺窗	shade transplanted, entering tracery windows.

"Simurgh Hall," the palace, is the poetic equivalent of the world of the immortals, like the Queen Mother of the West with her famous peaches. One can also write the same poem in which the judgment favors the first term of the comparison, the transient and fragile thing. The tree hibiscus may bloom only for a day, but its moment is cherished. The comparative term is found in those palace ladies who keep "blooming" but whose time of beauty passes unnoticed.

李商隱, 槿花
Li Shangyin, Hibiscus[69]

風露淒淒秋景繁	The wind and dew are dreary and chill, it is full in the autumn scene,
可憐榮落在朝昏	to be pitied, how it flowers and falls between dawn and dusk.
未央宮裏三千女	Inside Weiyang Palace are three thousand women
但保紅顏莫保恩	who keep only rosy complexions but do not keep favor.

These judgments are accompanied by terms that place either the speaker of the poem or the thing itself in a position that is better or worse off: the recurring terms are *kexi* 可惜 ("too bad"; "to be regretted"), *kexian* 可羨 ("enviable), *kelian* 可憐 ("to be pitied"; occasionally "lovable"). Such judgments of comparative status can go either way. Recall how the peonies earlier "pitied" (*kelian*) the day lily, only to have the poet reverse their judgment.

---

67. 29125; *Jijie* 1256; Ye (1985) 41.
68. That is, the palace.
69. 29463; *Jijie* 1604; Ye (1985) 400.

Fragility and Transience

The first term in the comparative pattern described above is often the fragile, transient thing. Lamenting the fall of spring flowers was such a common poetic motif that it lacks any distinction, but Li Shangyin seems to have had a particular fascination with delicate things and their ruin. This sensibility often seems mannered, but it is hard not to see this as the counterpart or double of his images of permanence and fixity—as in the poetic vision of attention focused for a whole lifetime on some object of desire (for example, the singer's lips in "Yan Terrace: Autumn"; the crystal bowl in "Walls of Sapphire"; or Little Love's naked body in "Northern Qi"). These two terms—the fragile versus the immortal/imperial—are, of course, the terms of comparative judgment in the quatrains above.

The following pair of poems was among those by Li Shangyin imitated in the *Xikun chouchang ji*. If fragile things in particular held Li Shangyin's interest, then nothing was as fragile as the tree hibiscus (*jinhua*), which blooms for only a single day.

李商隱, 槿花二首
Li Shangyin, Hibiscus[70]

I

燕體傷風力	Swallow's body, by wind's force harmed,[71]
雞香積露文	chicken-tongue, piled with dew patterns.[72]
殷鮮一相雜	Its maroon fresh, all mixed together,
啼笑兩難分	hard to tell weeping from smiling.
月裏寧無姊	Certainly it has a sister in the moon,
雲中亦有君	in the clouds there is also its lord.[73]
三清與仙島	From Three Pure Realms and immortal isles
何事亦離群	for what reason does it live apart?[74]

---

70. 29165–66; *Jijie* 1598; Ye (1985) 89.

71. The reference is to the Han consort Zhao Feiyan ("Flying Swallow"), who was so light that the wind could almost blow her away.

72. "Chicken tongue" is a poetic reference to cloves.

73. The reference is to the "Lord in the Clouds," one of the deities in the "Nine Songs" of the *Chuci*.

74. The "Three Pure Realms" are the Daoist heavens. The point of these lines is that the hibiscus's flowers, which last only a day, are from the world of the immortals.

II

珠館薰燃久	Scented blazing in crimson lodges lasts,[75]
玉房梳掃餘	jade chambers after combing and brushing.[76]
燒蘭纔作燭	Orchid oil burning, acts as a candle,
襞錦不成書	brocade split, but never becoming writing.[77]
本以亭亭遠	By nature it is distantly remote,
翻嫌脈脈疏	but it hates yearning estrangement.
迴頭問殘照	I turn my head and ask the last shining,
殘照更空虛	the last shining grows ever more empty.

The "smiling" of the first poem is associated with blossoming. The dew is the "weeping" of the flower that is destroyed as soon as it appears. What we see here in the first poem, however, is the mechanism of comparison in the quatrains above (half the poem devoted to the frail mortal, half to the immortal) reproduced in a new context and argument. The hibiscus, the most transient of flowers, becomes the immortal creature destined to "live apart [from its kind]" if only for a day.

The second poem of the pair is stranger still. We suspect, for example, that the red hibiscus is the "scented blazing" and the "orchid oil burning." The "lasts [long]," *jiu* 久, is nice because the fiery flower, though consuming itself, does last longer than other more literal flames—though it does not really "last long." By the end of the day the flower is gone, and the poet "asks" the fading sunlight (implying "asks about it" in some general way, such as where the flower has gone or why this should be). The question is given in waning light that is "empty" of the flower and is itself "empty."

In the following poem the commentators are abuzz with speculative referents for the bees, from lascivious women to Li Shangyin's colleagues at the headquarters of some military commissioner.

---

75. I follow Feng Hao, who here suggests that 珠 and 朱 are interchangeable and that this refers to Daoist temples.

76. The reference is to women's chambers. "Brushing" refers to painting the eyebrows.

77. The reference is to the palindrome woven into brocade.

李商隱, 蜂
Li Shangyin, Bees[78]

小苑華池爛熳通
To the small park and flowery pool
    they come through in wild disorder,

後門前檻思無窮
at the rear gate and front railing
    their longing is endless.

宓妃腰細纔勝露
Fu Fei's waist so thin
    it can barely take the dew;[79]

趙后身輕欲倚風
Empress Zhao's body so light,
    it will almost go with the breeze.[80]

紅壁寂寥崖蜜盡
The red cliff is still and forlorn,
    the "slope honey" is gone,[81]

碧簾迢遞霧巢空
the sapphire curtains are remote,
    their foggy hives are deserted.[82]

青陵粉蝶休離恨
Let Qingling's powdery butterflies
    cease their pain at separation:[83]

長定相逢二月中
it is certain you will always meet
    in the second month of spring.

The usual gendering of bees as men who go chasing after women ("flowers") is reversed here, with the bees as famous beauties. They first appear streaming into the flower garden and are then described in their fragility. Suddenly, in the third couplet, they are gone and the hives are empty. "Bees and butterflies" were commonly paired. In the closing couplet we have the remaining butterflies, apparently feeling

---

78. 29247; *Jijie* 1030; Ye (1985) 181.

79. Fu Fei was the goddess of the Luo River. One would normally associate the narrow waists specifically with wasps; the latter are here subsumed under the general category "bees."

80. Han Chengdi's empress, Zhao Feiyan, was famous for the lightness of her body, recounted in anecdotes where she was in danger of being blown away.

81. "Slope honey" was an especially prized variety of green honey.

82. This seems to refer to bee-keeping.

83. The reference is to the story of Han Ping 韓憑, whose beautiful wife was taken by King Kang of Song, who then built Qingling Terrace. Han Feng committed suicide, and his wife threw herself off the terrace and died. King Kang, in a fit of anger, had them buried separately. According to the most common legend, trees grew from the tombs and entwined their branches. However, another tradition associated the lovers with large butterflies. Dong Naibin argues that the butterflies are female, while bees are male, a figure for the poet himself. See Dong Naibin 董乃斌, *Li Shangyin de xinling shijie* 李商隱的心靈世界 (Shanghai: Shanghai guji chubanshe, 1992), 31–37.

the "pain of separation" at the disappearance of the bees, with the reassurance that the two will meet again in spring.

The poems on things constitute an unusually large part of Li Shangyin's poetry and share many of the same issues of figurative reference with the hermetic poems as well as those on history. Although some of the more overtly political poems treated in the next chapter have achieved prominence in the Li Shangyin canon, early selections, imitations, and references to his poetry are largely confined to poems in the three groupings discussed above, along with lighter social poems that draw on these discourses.

FOURTEEN

Li Shangyin

The Poems on Occasion

Poetics

李商隱, 樂遊原
Li Shangyin, Yueyou Plain[1]

向晚意不適	I felt dissatisfied late in the day,
驅車登古原	I galloped my coach to the ancient plain.
夕陽無限好	The evening sun was limitlessly fine,
只是近黃昏	it was just that it was drawing toward dusk.

Success in the short-line quatrain was difficult to achieve, and poets who attempted it often stood in the shadow of Wang Wei. Li Shangyin here created something distinctive. The rhythm of moods in the poem is perfect: a restless sense of unease, resolved in riding out of Chang'an to Yueyou Plain and discovering the beauty of the setting sunlight, a beauty immediately qualified by the poet's awareness of the coming darkness. He does not say directly that the last sunlight is beautiful because it will be so brief; "it's just that," *zhishi* 只是, suggests a sudden awareness of limits in what is literally supposed to be "limitless."

Li Shangyin did not, of course, know that he was a Late Tang poet. Like other poets of his age, he was fascinated with the last phases of historical periods, which may suggest a general sense of "lateness," but he certainly did not anticipate the catastrophes that would befall his dynasty a few decades after his death. His last moment of glorious light

---

1. 29116; *Jijie* 1942; Ye (1985) 31.

before nightfall was unwittingly portentous; yet it is impossible for later readers not to hear such a resonance in the poem. In Li Shangyin's moment, however, such a vision was yet another variation on his fascination with speculative images of permanence and with the fragile and the transient.

The poet of "Yueyou Plain" was the same poet who wrote the impenetrable "Heyang," discussed earlier (see pp. 364–79), and wrote in a variety of other styles as well. Such diversity represents one side of contested values in ninth-century poetry. Was the "true poet" distinguished by his range or by the intensity of his focus? The first clear articulation of poetic greatness achieved through diversity and range was in Yuan Zhen's funeral inscription for Du Fu.[2] We saw the echo of that Mid-Tang value in Liu Yuxi's preface to the poetry of Lingche (see p. 91), where Lingche's poetry is praised as superior to other poet-monks because of his range and their limitation.

In his "Epistle Presented to the Vice Minister of Rites, His Excellency of Julu" 獻侍郎鉅鹿公啓, written in 847, Li Shangyin does offer a broader judgment on Tang poetry, one favoring breadth:[3]

> Since the founding of our dynasty, this Way [of poetry] has flourished greatly. Yet all have fallen into some one-sided artfulness [*pianqiao* 偏巧], and few have talents that combine all things. Those who rest their heads on stones and rinse their mouths in the current tend to prefer dried-up and quiet lines; those who have clung to scales and wings [rising high in office] are foremost in pieces of excessive opulence. Among those who advocate Li Bai and Du Fu, resentment and satire occupy the greater part, while imitators of Shen Quanqi and Song Zhiwen go to extremes of frivolous delicacy.

Although this passage is, in part, driven by rhetoric and established commonplaces, the general referents would be clear in a contemporary context. The "advocates of Li Bai and Du Fu" would certainly be Yuan Zhen and Bai Juyi, remembered for their "New *Yuefu*" in a mid-ninth-century context; Han Yu might also be included. The "imitators of Shen Quanqi and Song Zhiwen" would be the regulated-verse craftsmen.

---

2. *Yuan Zhen ji* 元稹集 (Beijing: Zhonghua shuju, 1982), 600–601.

3. "Epistle Presented to the Vice Minister of Rites, His Excellency of Julu" 獻侍郎 鉅鹿公啓, in Liu Xuekai 劉學鍇 and Yu Shucheng 余恕誠, *Li Shangyin wen biannian jiaozhu* 李商隱文編年校注 (Beijing: Zhonghua shuju, 2002), 1188–89.

Although this is Li Shangyin presenting a "proper" public face to a high official, the conviction that a poet should do many different things is instantiated in his work.

Such large issues tend to appear in antithetical pairs. Poetic focus, "one-sided artfulness," was no less a value in the age. In the Mid-Tang as well we find poets like Meng Jiao and Li He, whose poems bear the indelible trace of each poet's personality. These two poets were admired then and later in the ninth century for an intensity of poetic focus that both defined their work and simultaneously limited it. Although Meng Jiao and Li He were poets of "personality" realized in a single style, it was an easy transition to poets like Jia Dao, who lacked a strong personality but who focused on craftsmanship that was largely realized in a single genre and a single "kind" of poem. Certainly the craftsmen of Late Tang regulated verse made that association, finding in Meng Jiao (who almost never wrote regulated verse) a forerunner of their devotion to craft.

The interest in a poet representing some "one-sided artfulness," some single identifiable style, not only manifested itself in the self-image of poets themselves and their work but also played an important role in the formation of popular anthologies of a poet's work—and even in the eventual editing of "complete works" from surviving manuscripts in the Northern Song. This also seems to have governed the selections of Li Shangyin's poetry that were in general circulation for a century and a half following his death. This was the same Li Shangyin who had been denounced by Li Fu and whose poems were represented in *Caidiao ji* and *Wenyuan yinghua*. We owe our much broader image of Li Shangyin to the good editor Yang Yi. We might, however, contrast a comment made by Song Minqiu 宋敏求 in putting together the diverse assortment of manuscripts of Meng Jiao's poetry: "I took out duplicates and those pieces that were not like his style" 摘去重複, 若體製不類者.[4] This tells us that if Meng Jiao had experimented with different styles and if they had survived in the manuscript tradition, the Northern Song editor would have removed them on the grounds that they were "not like his style." Indeed, the surviving collection of Meng Jiao's poetry is remarkably stylistically consistent (to the point of including poems by later poets in Meng Jiao's style).

---

4. Hua Chenzhi 694. The phrasing is peculiar.

This question of broad range versus poetic focus is obviously the counterpart of another issue we addressed earlier: Was poetry merely one aspect of a full life, an adjunct of both public and private concerns, or was it an almost religious vocation or profession requiring complete devotion to attain perfection?

Here we will offer up another poem by Li Shangyin. In the summer of 851 Li Shangyin's wife died. He was clearly disconsolate. He was thirty-nine. His career was going nowhere. That autumn he set off for Sichuan to enter the service of another military commissioner. He left his beloved son A'gun with relatives in Chang'an. Later a certain Yang Chou arrived from Chang'an. Yang had seen A'gun there and brought news of how the boy was doing. Li Shangyin was delighted.

李商隱, 楊本勝説於長安見小男阿衮

Li Shangyin, Yang Bensheng (Chou) Tells Me How
He Saw My Infant Son, A'gun, in Chang'an[5]

聞君來日下	I hear that, coming from the capital,
見我最嬌兒	you saw my dearest son.
漸大啼應數	Older now, I'm sure he cries on several counts,[6]
長貧學恐遲	always poor, I worry his studies will be delayed.
寄人龍種瘦	Left with others, dragon-spawn grows thin,[7]
失母鳳雛癡	losing his mother, the phoenix-chick is foolish.
語罷休邊角	We finish talking, the frontier bugles cease,
青燈兩鬢絲	in green lamp-fire, both side locks silken white.

If one reads Late Tang poetry other than that by Li Shangyin, poems like this are very rare. One will certainly not find its like among the poems of Jia Dao and his circle. The model of Du Fu, who often wrote about his family, is obvious here, yet it is not the version of Du Fu that leads to limited "resentment and satire." Nor was the model of Du Fu confined to cases where Li Shangyin wrote affectionately about his family. Like Du Fu, Li Shangyin responded to a wide range of life experiences, including voicing his opinions about current political events. We should make clear here that in pointing to the "model of Du Fu"

---

5. 29176; *Jijie* 1214; Ye (1985) 104; Zhou 213.

6. Feng Hao explains this as A'gun crying not only for his father but now also for his mother. One could also simply take *shuo* 數 to mean that he cries "often."

7. The term "dragon-spawn" suggests that Li Shangyin claimed remote ties to the imperial family.

we are not referring to the influence of Du Fu's poetic style(s)—though that influence is clear in many cases. Rather, the model of Du Fu was an image of what a poet "should be" in a larger sense. That model had been carried on in the works of two Mid-Tang poets who, in Li Shangyin's time, loomed very large in the recent history of poetry, namely, Han Yu and Bai Juyi—even if Bai was a problematic model.

We earlier mentioned that Li Shangyin did not belong to the circles of poets prominent in the 830s to 850s. In many ways this poet, who has come to define the Late Tang, did not belong to the Late Tang—or at best he had only a partial investment in the poetry of his own age (though that investment probably was responsible for the preservation of his poetry). Poets like Jia Dao or Xu Hun wrote in a primarily contemporary context that viewed "poetry" very differently. Li Shangyin situated himself in the larger tradition, rich in references to the cultural past, going beyond patrons, friends, and a solitary life to express political criticism and discuss domestic cares. Although it seemed to most later readers that such a range was indeed "grander," it is important to bear in mind that at this point the Chinese tradition had not yet fully decided that Du Fu's version of the poet was the greater one, confirmed by his two very different poetic descendents, Han and Bai. Du Fu was widely admired in the Late Tang without being influential in a general sense. The poetics of single-minded focused craft contested the values embodied in Du Fu's poetry (though one aspect of Du Fu's work was focused craft). In the poem to A'gun there are no fine couplets; and if one were presenting a small anthology of poems to the emperor (as Zhang Hu and Li Qunyu did), such a poem would have no place. It is most unlikely that Li Shangyin himself included this poem, written while serving with Liu Zhongying in Sichuan, in the collection of poems he presented to Liu.[8]

Our evidence is very limited, but when we look at the Li Shangyin poems anthologized in Wei Zhuang's *Further Mystery* and in Wei Hu's *Caidiao ji* (an extensive selection), the poems included in *Wenyuan yinghua*, and the poems imitated in Yang Yi's *Xikun chouchang ji*, they are

---

8. "An Epistle Greeting His Excellency of Hedong, Accompanied by Poems" 謝河東公和詩啓, in Liu Xuekai 劉學鍇 and Yu Shucheng 余恕誠, *Li Shangyin wen biannian jiaozhu* 李商隱文編年校注, 1961–62.

almost entirely restricted to the kinds of poems represented in the preceding three chapters or convivial pieces. This suggests something of the narrowness of late ninth- and tenth-century taste. Such taste governed the production of anthologies of a poet's work, the form in which poetry most often circulated. Were it not for the fortuitous discovery of a more complete version of the collection in the southeast, this would surely have been the only Li Shangyin we know. Yang Yi seems to have had more catholic tastes than the tenth-century norm; but only in the generation after Ouyang Xiu in the eleventh century was Du Fu's poetry generally accepted as the model for the highest values in poetry. If the greatest interest in Li Shangyin remained the hermitic poems, the poems on history, and the poems on things, Li's poems on culturally and historically "serious" topics also began to attract interest. In the seventeenth century the conditions were ripe for the widespread revival of interest in his poetry. Li Shangyin emerged as very much a poet in the Du Fu tradition.

It is hard to know how Li Shangyin saw himself in relation to the poetry of his time. Far more than most of his contemporaries, he was clearly a devoted reader of earlier Tang poetry and, like Du Fu, composed a series of quatrains that touch on poetry. Although not addressing contemporary poets directly, his quatrain on the masters of the Early Tang may suggest his opinion of the contemporary poets of craft.

李商隱, 漫成五章
Li Shangyin, Five Offhand Compositions[9]

I

沈宋裁辭矜變律	Shen and Song crafted phrases[10] boasting of changing the rules;
王楊落筆得良朋	Wang and Yang set brushes to paper and found good friends.[11]

---

9. 29538; *Jijie* 912; Ye (1985) 468; Zhou 160.

10. Shen Quanqi 沈佺期 (656–ca. 716) and Song Zhiwen 宋之問 (656–712) are credited with the perfection of the rules of regulated verse.

11. Wang Bo 王勃 (ca. 648–ca. 684) and Yang Jiong 楊炯 (650–ca. 693) are two of the "Four Talents of the Early Tang" 初唐四傑. The other two, Lu Zhaolin and Luo Binwang, are the "good friends."

當時自謂宗師妙　　Back then they considered themselves
　　　　　　　　　　　to have the finesse of masters,
今日惟觀對屬能　　but today we observe only
　　　　　　　　　　　a skill in parallelism.[12]

Such "skill in parallelism" is set against Li Bai and Du Fu in the quatrain that follows, who "both got all the fine points of pattern of the Three Endowments and myriad images" 三才萬象共端倪. The "Three Endowments" are Heaven, Earth, and mankind. The contrast between the restricted ability in parallelism and a larger vision of poetry could not be clearer.

Li Shangyin knew quite well what a "poet" was supposed to be in his age. He only occasionally speaks of "painstaking composition," but clearly he did not take pride in an image of easy spontaneity, as Bai Juyi did. The following poem makes a nice contrast with the anecdotes about Jia Dao wandering about, oblivious to his surroundings, struggling to find the right words for a couplet. Li Shangyin had been at a party, but the right words for a poem for the occasion didn't come to him. On the way back the scene and the right lines suddenly presented themselves, albeit out of the social context in which they were needed. The poem that emerged, however, was not the one that originally should have been written but one about the experience of composition itself.

李商隱, 江亭散席循柳路吟歸官舍

Li Shangyin, After a Party Broke up at the River Pavilion,
I Made My Way Back to the Official Residence
Along a Willow-lined Road Chanting[13]

春詠敢輕裁　　Would I dare carelessly craft a spring poem?—
銜辭入半杯　　I held back my lines halfway into my cup.
已遭江映柳　　I have come upon willows reflected in the river,
更被雪藏梅　　and next plums hidden by snow.
寡和眞徒爾　　With few to write with me, it is truly in vain;
殷憂動即來　　deep cares often come right away.
從詩得何報　　What recompense do I get from my poems?—
惟感二毛催　　I sense only gray hair coming more quickly.

---

12. *Neng* 能, translated as "skill," is "ability," "to be good at something"; it is definitely on the moderate side of hyperbolic descriptions of excellence. It seems to have something of the contemptuous tone in English when someone is described as "able."

13. 29110; *Jijie* 1247; Ye 25.

In contrast to the poet who must struggle for the right words (Jia Dao), Li Shangyin's poem comes to him immediately. Yet there is, at the same time, a commitment to a fineness of poetic expression that excludes the poem that can come spontaneously at any time (Bai Juyi). This is a variation on the new sense of the "poet" in the Late Tang. It excludes the casual and realizes that the art brings no "recompense." It is not, however, the poetry of the craftsman of fine couplets.

The importance of the following poem in terms of Li Shangyin's sense of poetry was first noticed by Zhou Zhenfu.[14]

李商隱, 謝先輩防記念拙詩甚多異日偶有此寄
Li Shangyin, Xie Fang, of a Senior Examination Class,
Could Recite Many of My Poems from Memory.
On another day I happened to send him this.[15]

曉用雲添句	At dawn I add lines with clouds,[16]
寒將雪命篇	in the cold I take snow as a poem's topic.
良辰多自感	On fine days often moved on my own—
作者豈皆然	but how can writers be always thus?[17]
熟寢初同鶴	Sleeping soundly, I'm first like the crane;[18]
含嘶欲并蟬	shrill cries held back, I almost match the cicada.[19]
題時長不展	When I write, it never rolls forth freely,
得處定應偏	when I get something, it must be singular.

---

14. See Robert Ashmore, "Hearing Things: Performance and Lyric Imagination in Chinese Literature of the Early Ninth Century" (Ph.D. diss., Harvard University, 1997), 93–106. Ashmore provides an extensive and thoughtful reading of the poem, parts of which I agree with. The various Chinese commentaries also offer thoughtful and sometimes extensive discussions of this difficult poem.

15. 29295; *Jijie* 1487; Ye (1985) 225; Zhou 261. *Jinian* 記念 normally means "commemorate," but the context here strongly suggests the translation given.

16. Or "add clouds to lines."

17. The line literally means, "As for writers, how can they be thus in all cases?" We cannot tell if the line is as translated above or: "How can all writers be thus?"

18. Zhou Zhenfu cites a bit of crane lore from the *Chuxue ji* to the effect that the crane cries out at midnight. Zhou speculates that Li means that he will be sleeping soundly, then suddenly wake and compose, like the crane crying out. *Jijie* notes how often the image of the sleeping crane is used in Tang poetry; although it cites the lore about the crane crying out, it seems to accept that the crane is indeed sleeping.

19. Zhou Zhenfu associates this with longing for someone, the person missing in the following line, to whom he sends the poem as a message. In addition to Li Shangyin's poem "Cicada" (29109), one should also note that the cry of the cicada was strongly associated with *kuyin* 苦吟, "bitter chanting" or "taking pains in poetry."

南浦無窮樹	The endless trees of South Shore,[20]
西樓不住煙	or unsteady mists by the western hall.
改成人寂寂	Revisions complete, I'm left silent and alone,[21]
寄與路綿綿	I send it on the road stretching far.
星勢寒垂地	Stars tending to hang toward earth in the cold,
河聲曉上天	or River's sound, rising to Heaven at dawn.[22]
夫君自有恨	If you have some bitterness all your own,
聊借此中傳	you may convey it through these lines.[23]

We know that Li Shangyin is saying something about his poetry here, but, since many of the lines are open to widely varying interpretations, it is not clear precisely what he is saying. As we have understood the third and fourth lines, Li Shangyin begins with cases of immediate experience that might be the occasion for a poem but then points out that not all poems can be written from such spontaneous stirrings (echoing his problem at the party in the preceding poem). We cannot be sure what to make of the line on sleeping soundly since it stands between immediate experience (ll. 3–4) and slow composition (ll. 7–8), which is a version of *kuyin* and the poetics of spending time.[24] As mentioned in the note, the cries of the cicada (l. 6) are strongly associated with "painstaking composition," and these cries are *han* 含, "held back," or "kept in reserve." The crucial phrase is *ti shi* 題時, translated

---

20. This is the standard site of a parting and a reference to parting poems.

21. I have taken 人 as referring to Li himself, but it could refer to others, suggesting that he finishes his revision late at night when others are all silent. For a parallel situation with this and the following line, see Meng Jiao, "Song of Sending a Letter Home" 歸信吟 (19597).

22. *Jijie* suggests that this is the scene after he finishes revising his composition, citing Li He's "I chant poems all night long, and the east turns white" 吟詩一夜東方白. The couplet, however, is itself so consciously "poetic" that it seems hard to take it as the extra-poetic world in which composition occurs.

23. That is, Xie Fang can express his own feelings by reciting Li Shangyin's poems.

24. We might here recall the advice in the treatise on composition attributed to Wang Changling in *Bunkyō hifuron*: "After a journey by boat, you should sleep peacefully right away; when you have slept enough, you can be certain that many clear scenes of mountains and rivers will fill your feelings, which will merge to generate inspiration; you should block out all practical worries and give yourself over entirely to feelings and inspiration" 舟行之後, 即須安眠. 眠足之後, 固多清景, 江山滿懷, 合而生興, 須屏絕事務, 專任情興. Wang Liqi 王利器, ed., *Wenjing mifulun jiaozhu* 文鏡秘府論校注 (Beijing: Zhongguo shehuike chubanshe, 1983), 306.

imperfectly as "when I write." This can either mean "when I write on it"—that is, the spontaneous experience mentioned in the third line—or "when I write on a topic," as when one is required to produce a poem at a party. Here we have one of those moments when Li Shangyin clearly claims for himself *kuyin*, "painstaking composition." We see that it is associated with producing something that is *pian* 偏, the "singular" or "one-sided," suggesting a lack of balance or moderation ("extreme" might be an appropriate translation). This is, however, the same term Li Shangyin used in the earlier quotation, where he condemned "one-sided artfulness."[25]

When we compare this poem with the earlier passage from the "Epistle Presented to the Vice Minister of Rites, His Excellency of Julu," we cannot escape a contradiction in values. The "one-sided" or "extreme" was condemned earlier; here it seems to be an implicit value. The contradiction arises in part from the different situations of discourse: a statement of one's poetic values in formal prose to a patron puts the poet in a position very different from writing to a poetry-loving friend. The contradiction, however, remains a potent one. We can see it in Li Shangyin's poetry collection, which not only contains the broadest range of styles and themes of any Late Tang poet but which also contains a core of poems that are perhaps more "one-sided" or "extreme" than any other Late Tang poet. This is precisely the contradiction in contemporary poetic values we discussed earlier. The poet's capacity to sustain both sides of that contradiction is perhaps the basis of Li Shangyin's remarkable longevity in the tradition.

We do not know exactly how to take the two scenes of the fifth couplet, but they seem to be the kinds of lines Li Shangyin produces in this type of composition, namely, dreamy and evocative.[26] Revision is appropriate in "painstaking composition." While we cannot be sure whether he revises when others are silent or feels melancholy isolation following revision, we note that the poem is immediately sent off to "someone" who is far away. This is in keeping with the topic, for Xie

---

25. Although *pian* can have a pejorative sense, the most common ninth-century poetic usage of the term as an adverb meaning "particularly" (e.g., *pianhao* 偏好, "particularly good") remained neutral.

26. Recall the cases of Yao He (pp. 120–21) and Yong Tao (pp. 143–44), discussed earlier, in which a couplet on poetic composition is followed by a finely crafted couplet that suggests the kinds of poetic lines composed.

Fang knows many of his poems. Here we might recall the motif in the biography of Li He, where the poet pays no further attention to a poem when it is completed, and the poems are removed by friends. The penultimate couplet is interesting in bringing back the "dawn" (*xiao* 曉) and "cold" (*han* 寒) of the opening couplet in lines that are indeed distinctly *pian*, "singular," "one-sided," "extreme." If those immediate experiences signal the beginning of the poetic process described in the poem, the penultimate couplet seems to be the poetic "end" of the process.

From this process emerges the remarkable final couplet. *Zi* 自, translated in the next-to-last line as "all your own," is the same word translated in the third line as "on my own." We thus have a situation in which the poet's "own" experience goes through the process of composition, perfected in a poem that is immediately sent away. Now Xie Fang, a receiver and admirer of Li Shangyin's poems, can convey "his own" feelings through Li Shangyin's lines.

If our interpretation is correct, this is a most remarkable poem—the only case I have seen in which the experience of the reader is situated in the context of a poetics of the poet's own personal experience. Xie Fang as reader does not try to decode Li Shangyin's experience (though such an understanding of poetry did exist in the Tang). Rather, Li Shangyin's experience, transmuted through a process of poetic composition, becomes the medium through which others can convey their experiences.

Du Fu never talked about the process of poetic composition to such an extent—nor had anyone else (except Li Shangyin himself writing about Li He). The poem belongs to an age when composition was an issue inextricably linked to the recent question of what poetry "is." Although Li Shangyin's admiration for Du Fu and Li Bai is clear—as is his scorn for the Early Tang poets—the conception of his own poetics lies somewhere between Du Fu and the new poetic values of the Late Tang. The one possible poetic value that he clearly rejects is the careless spontaneity of Bai Juyi.

Poems in the Context of Li Shangyin's Life

Having discussed several groups of poems that are mostly undatable, it is useful to turn to those poems that can be securely dated. Were we to restrict ourselves only to such poems, Li Shangyin would be remembered as a very different kind of poet. The very conditions that make a poem datable often restrict the scope of the poetry being dated.[27]

Although scholars have attributed a number of poems to Li Shangyin's youth, only a handful can be securely dated before 837, when the poet passed the *jinshi* examination in his mid-twenties. This is not unusual. Apart from Li He, whose work was restricted to juvenilia, we often have few datable surviving poems from before a poet's full maturity. One reason may be that older poets rejected the poetry of their youth. Another reason may simply relate to the question of what makes a poem datable: our capacity to date works depends heavily on references to known figures and a poet's presence in certain locations at certain times—possibilities that tend to occur either after passing the *jinshi* examination or upon entering mature networks of poetry exchange.

The poems that we can confidently date to Li Shangyin's youth are suggestive. We have already discussed the "Yan Terrace" poems, showing the influence of Li He. There are several poems composed around the death in 834 of Cui Rong 崔戎, a patron and perhaps a maternal relation. One of these, studded with allusions and requiring painstaking reading in translation, was actually quite remarkable for its time, with a seriousness and "thickness" that one might expect of a young master of parallel prose.[28]

Perhaps the earliest securely datable poem, from roughly 830, has suggestive similarities to some of the hermetic poems, though here in a transparent social pleasantry.

---

27. A comparison of different chronological arrangements of Li Shangyin's poetry and a weighing of competing arguments for dating particular poems should inspire considerable agnosticism. Not only must we exclude a large number of poems whose dates are based on pure conjecture regarding the poem's referent or circumstance, but on closer examination many of the poems with specific reference to persons and places become uncertain.

28. "Passing By the Former Dwelling of Cui Yanhai [Rong] and Talking About Former Times with the *Xiucai* Cui Ming; then sent to my former colleagues, the three officers Du [Sheng], Zhao [Xi], and Li [Pan]" 過故崔兗海宅與崔明秀才話舊, 因寄舊僚杜趙李三掾 (29581); *Jijie* 67; Ye (1985) 510; Zhou 21.

李商隱, 天平公座中呈令狐令公

Li Shangyin, At a Public Banquet of the Tianping Military
Region, Presented to Linghu Chu, Director of the
Department of State Affairs[29]

罷執霓旌上醮壇	Done holding the rainbow banner and ascending the jiao altar,
慢妝嬌樹水晶盤	a charming tree in light makeup, with a crystal bowl.[30]
更深欲訴蛾眉斂	The hour grows late, about to protest, her moth brows knit;
衣薄臨醒玉艷寒	her clothes thin, as she sobers, luscious jade-flesh feels cold.
白足禪僧思敗道	The white-footed Chan monk longs to break his vows;[31]
青袍御史擬休官	the green-robed censor considers quitting his post.
雖然同是將軍客	Even though I am, like them, a guest of the General,
不敢公然子細看	I do not dare openly look at her carefully.

Here we see the "bowl of crystal" from the end of the first "Walls of
Sapphire." Again we have a poem in which the host displays one of
his women, with the male guests complimenting him by revealing
their attraction. Li Shangyin, still in his teens, modestly averts his eyes
while playfully foregrounding the effect of the woman's charms on the
other guests. Li Shangyin's hermetic poems touching on love affairs
have been attributed to various periods in his life, either interpreted

---

29. 29600; *Jijie* 42; Ye (1985) 531; Zhou 14. The following note is included with the
title: "Cai Jing was then present at the party; Jing had once been a monk, hence the fifth
line" 時蔡京在座, 京曾爲僧徒, 固有第五句.

30. Since the second line clearly refers to a beautiful woman, the first line probably
does as well. *Jijie* understands the couplet as referring to a woman in Linghu Chu's
household who was previously a Daoist nun. The *jiao* was a Daoist ceremony. Zhou
Zhenfu prefers to view this woman as still a Daoist nun, perhaps brought to the gather-
ing for a ritual. *Jijie*'s explanation seems preferable because the following lines suggest
that she is attending at the banquet.

31. The reference is to an anecdote about the monk Huishi in the *Wei shu*: Although
he walked in the dust and dirt, his feet remained pure white, by which he came to be
called the "white-footed reverend."

figuratively or as referring to real passions. It is no less likely that many of them were written in his twenties, under the first flush of Li He's influence and carried away by real or imagined romantic passions. Such a suggestion admittedly has the aura of a stereotype; but there are few securely datable poems from Li Shangyin's poetic maturity that provide us analogues, as we find in some of the early poems.[32]

This brings us back to willow poems, specifically the poems to "Willow Branch," the young woman of Luoyang who was drawn to Li Shangyin's "Yan Terrace" poems and tried to arrange a meeting. Li Shangyin conveniently had to leave town. When he later heard that she had been taken as a concubine by some powerful person, he had occasion to express poetic loss at a safe distance. Such safe distance from romantic entanglements also enabled a peculiar publicity of passion: Li Shangyin asked his cousin Rangshan to write these poems (literally "to put them in ink") where she used to live (因寓詩以墨其故處). It is hard to know exactly what was intended—perhaps graffiti on the outer wall of Willow Branch's home. What is clear, however, is the highly public nature of the act: in no way are these poems simply intended "for" Willow Branch herself. Here we have a rare indication of "publication" and potential readership, as well as the status that might accrue from such publicity. We must assume the existence of a community of young men and women of Luoyang who would read and transmit these poems, and who were already familiar with the "story" of Li Shangyin and Willow Branch.[33] The interesting question is why Li Shangyin adds the preface, whose only purpose is make the context clear to those who do not belong to that local Luoyang community. The quatrains in the short line

---

32. One might also note "Playfully Sent: Companion Pieces for a Friend" 和友人戲贈二首 (29357–58; *Jijie* 174; Ye [1985] 289ff; Zhou 37) and "After Those Two Poems, Again Playfully Sent to Licentiate Ren" 題二首後重有戲贈任秀才 (29359; *Jijie* 181; Ye [1985] 291), which contain interesting analogies with the hermetic poems. *Jijie* dates these to 838 based on criteria that are better than attempts to date many poems but not entirely secure.

33. Although I do not advocate such an interpretation, one might take these poems as Li Shangyin's attempt to regain his lost dignity. In the preface Willow Branch says she wants to meet him on a certain date, but Li leaves Luoyang early, offering the most peculiar excuse, namely, that a friend took his luggage away as a prank. We might here recall the teasing Zhang endures in *Yingying zhuan* when he refuses to take part in the pleasures his friends are enjoying.

evoke the *yuefu* of the Southern Dynasties, frequently concerned with love affairs, only here with a sophisticated Tang twist.

李商隱, 柳枝五首
Li Shangyin, Willow Branch[34]

I

花房與蜜脾	Flower calyx and honeycomb,
蜂雄蛺蝶雌	the bee male, the butterfly a girl.
同時不同類	Together at the same moment, not of the same kind,
那復更相思	how can they go on longing?

We clearly see Li Shangyin's capacity for romantic fantasy here. The most striking line is the third: the lovers meet, but they are "not of the same kind," *bu tong lei* 不同類. What seems to be essentially class difference is here figured as species difference.[35] The last line is ambiguous. It could simply be Li Shangyin himself who is asking: "Why do I go on longing?" The question could also be rhetorical ("Of course we don't keep on longing for one another / I don't keep longing for her."). It would remain for the young people of Luoyang to decide how to take it—though they would surely prefer a reading in which Li Shangyin is still longing for her.

II

本是丁香樹	She was in essence the cloves tree,
春條結始生	on springtime branches, knots first form.[36]
玉作彈碁局	Of jade was made the "marbles" board,[37]
中心亦不平	its very center was not level.[38]

---

34. 29628–32; *Jijie* 99; Ye (1985) 565; Zhou 70. On the preface, see Stephen Owen, "What Did Liuzhi Hear? The 'Yan Terrace Poems' and the Culture of Romance," *T'ang Studies* 13 (1995): 81–118.

35. *Jijie* specifically rejects the class issue (106), and by doing so acknowledges that it does come to mind. *Jijie*, however, does allow such species difference between Willow Branch and the "eastern grandee" who took her. See also Wu Tiaogong 吳調公, *Li Shangyin yanjiu* 李商隱研究 (Shanghai: Shanghai guji chubanshe, 1982), 109.

36. "Knots," *jie* 結, are the cloves and a "compact" between lovers.

37. *Tanqi* 彈棋, freely translated as "marbles" (or, better, "tiddledywinks") was a game in which the players used counters to knock aside the other player's counter. The center of the board had a raised depression to catch the counters.

38. A pun that can also be translated: "The heart within was not at ease."

This is a punning quatrain in the manner of Southern Dynasties popular *yuefu*. The first line of a couplet describes something in the external world, while the second line amplifies it with a pun that applies to the lovers.

III

嘉瓜引蔓長	The finest melons grow long vines,
碧玉冰寒漿	sapphire, the icy cold juice.[39]
東陵雖五色	Though they show five colors at Dongling,[40]
不忍值牙香	one cannot bear the fragrance when it meets the teeth.

This quatrain is understood as referring to Willow Branch being taken off by a powerful patron, perhaps because of the opening couplet in "Sapphire's Song" from the Southern Dynasties:

碧玉小家女	Sapphire was a girl of a humble family
來嫁汝南王	who married the Prince of Ru'nan.

Commentators like to see the implied subject of the final line as Willow Branch herself, still in love with Li Shangyin and distressed at being taken and enjoyed by another. However, it can just as likely refer to Li Shangyin's own distress.

IV

柳枝井上蟠	Willow branch coiling above the well,
蓮葉浦中乾	lotus leaves drying up on the shore.[41]
錦鱗與繡羽	Scales of brocade and embroidered feathers
水陸有傷殘	suffer harm on both water and land.

The willow branch is, of course, the girl's name, while the "lotus," *Lian* 蓮, was a venerable pun on "love," *Lian* 憐. This can also be understood as Willow Branch's unhappiness at being taken away, though it is far from clear. If the fish ("scales") and bird ("feathers") represent the poet and Willow Branch, both are damaged.

---

39. "Sapphire," *biyu* 碧玉, plays on a *yuefu* heroine's name and a song that begins: "When Sapphire 'broke the melon'" 碧玉破瓜時. "Breaking the melon" was a standard term for turning sixteen, based on the character for "melon," which, divided, becomes two "eights," *ba* 八.

40. The reference is to the Qin Count of Dongling, who, following the fall of Qin, grew melons outside Green Gate in Chang'an.

41. Zhu Yizun comments that neither is planted in the right place.

V

畫屏繡步障	Painted screen, embroidered room divider
物物自成雙	there every creature forms a pair.
如何湖上望	How is it gazing on the lake
只是見鴛鴦	that we only see the mandarin ducks?

In many ways the final poem of the set is most remarkable in its contrast between interior representations and the outside world. In the interior world of representations "every creature forms a pair," but on the outside one sees such pairing only in mandarin ducks, standard figures of permanently mated couples. Should we recall the first poem in which Li claimed they were "not of the same kind"? Perhaps not, but it is a peculiar, uneasy echo. Zhou Zhenfu takes this as simply not seeing Willow Branch when he gazes across the lake, but the opposition seems to be between a general pairing in representation and pairing restricted to mandarin ducks in the world.[42]

Even among these relatively early poems Li Shangyin's work showed great diversity. In addition to the playful banter at Linghu Chu's party, the perfervid eroticism of "Yan Terrace," and the Southern *yuefu* manner of "Willow Branch," we can see him adopting a grand theatrical style, without allusion, in the following quatrain dating from 833–34:

李商隱, 夕陽樓
Li Shangyin, Tower in Evening Sunlight[43]

花明柳暗繞天愁	Flowers bright, willows hiding,
	a sadness encircling Heaven,

---

42. A love affair has also been imputed between Li Shangyin and a Daoist nun named Song of the Huayang nunnery in Chang'an. The evidence for this is based on two poems, "Presented to the Immortal Song of the Huanyang Lodge; Also Sent to Master Liu of the Pure Metropolis" 贈華陽宋眞人兼寄清都劉先生 (29354; *Jijie* 1913; Ye [1985] 284) and "On a Moonlit Night, Again Sent to Sisters Song of Huayang Lodge" 月夜重寄宋華陽姊妹 (29472; *Jijie* 1920; Ye [1985] 409). It is possible to interpret the second of these as Li's poetic expression of a desire to see one or both of the sisters, though such an interpretation is by no means inevitable. Moreover, even if he is suggesting a wish to be able to see her, we have no idea of the degree of seriousness implied.

43. 29364; *Jijie* 77; Ye (1985) 303. The following early note is appended to this poem: "In Yingyang. This was written in the days when the current Vice Director Xiao of Suining, a supportive friend, was governing Yingyang" 在榮陽. 是所知送寧蕭侍郎牧榮陽日作者.

上盡重城更上樓 I have climbed all the layers of walls,
         now I go on to climb the tower.
欲問孤鴻向何處 I wanted to ask where
         the lone swan is heading,
不知身世自悠悠 not realizing that self and world too
         just go on and on.

The poet is here clearly figuring himself as the lone swan. Part of the effect of the poem depends on the expression *youyou* 悠悠, translated lamely as "go on and on." When applied to the visible world, it usually refers to things in the sky, such as the heavens themselves, clouds, or, as here, a lone swan. *Youyou* implies both space and time, something that keeps going on and goes off into infinite distances. This works visually with the swan and figuratively with "self" and "world." We might add that although this is a quatrain in the long line, it is yet another example of climbing a tower, with the familiar rhyme words in the *ou* rhyme.

The indirectness and figuration of Li Shangyin's poetic language differed in kind and degree according to distinct venues and discursive communities (allowing that the same individuals might belong to different groups). Although no one could "understand" a series of poems like "Yan Terrace" in the conventional sense, someone like Willow Branch could hear the poems, be moved by them, and generally know "what to make of them" despite their obscurity. Within a community where love poetry circulated, the compounds used in "Yan Terrace" would probably have been comprehensible orally. By contrast, Willow Branch would most likely not have been able to make sense of any line in the following poem, nor could it have been understood without a written text. The poem is the first in a set of two (with a third added later) written in response to the Sweet Dew Incident, which occurred during the winter of 835. The poet's note reads: "I was stirred by something in 835; the poem was completed in 836" 乙卯年有感, 丙辰年詩成. Although this could be considered a dangerous topic, no one seems to have gotten in trouble for such poetic responses, couched as they are in a thick and allusive language. In contrast to some later eras, those in power in the Tang did not seek out evidence of literary disaffection (though an effective "ballad" in language popular enough to be orally repeated might have been a different matter). Despite the courage later critics ascribed to Li Shangyin for "speaking out," we have no indication that the poem ever circulated. If it did, its reception would have demanded a highly literate community.

李商隱, 有感二首
Li Shangyin, Stirred by Something (two poems)[44]

I

九服歸元化	Nine Reaches obey Primal Transformation,[45]
三靈叶睿圖	the Three Lights accord with astute plans.[46]
如何本初輩	How was it then that Benchu's ilk[47]
自取屈氂誅	brought Quli's punishment on themselves?[48]
有甚當車泣	Worse than "weeping by the carriage,"[49]
因勞下殿趨	thus came duress to scurry from the palace.[50]
何成奏雲物	Did this amount to a report on cloud aura?—[51]
直是滅萑苻	they simply wiped out those in the rushes.[52]

---

44. 29360-61; *Jijie* 108; Ye (1985) 292; Zhou 23.

45. The entire empire ("Nine Reaches" refers to the nine levels of distance from the capital and the empire's center in the ruler) turns in its collective heart to the emperor's capacity to civilize and transform the people through his virtue.

46. The sun, moon, and stars ("Three Lights" and hence the signs in the heavens, representing the will of Heaven) show their agreement. That is, Heaven might support the overthrow of the eunuchs.

47. Benchu was the courtesy name of Yuan Shao 袁紹 in the Eastern Han. Yuan Shao marched his troops into the palace and slaughtered the court eunuchs, effectively ending their power.

48. Quli refers to Liu Quli, who held the post of minister in 91 B.C. A eunuch accused him of witchcraft, specifically of having placed a curse on Han Wudi in order to set the Prince of Changyi on the throne. As a result, he was executed. The implication is that the Tang plotters who planned the attack against the eunuchs were incompetent in drawing up their plans.

49. The reference is to an anecdote in the *Han shu* in which Han Wendi had the eunuch Zhao Tan ride together with him in the imperial carriage. Yuan Ang prostrated himself and asked how the emperor could ride together with "one left over from the knife." Zhao Tan then dismounted from the carriage and wept.

50. The reference is to a prophetic verse in the early sixth century: "When Mars enters the Southern Dipper, / the Son of Heaven will run down from the palace." This seems to criticize the plotter Li Xun for wanting to kill all the eunuchs, thus driving them to seize the emperor.

51. The reference is to the report of the "sweet dew," which served as a sign for the coup.

52. A passage on the twenty-eighth year of Duke Zhao in the *Zuo zhuan* tells of a band of kidnappers who would carry their victims off to a marsh of rushes and were

證逮符書密	From testimony, arrests: documents, secret;
辭連性命俱	words implicated others: the lives of both lost.[53]
竟緣尊漢相	Ultimately from reverence for Han's Minister[54]
不早辨胡雛	they did not early discern the barbarian whelp.[55]
鬼籙分朝部	Ghost Registers took a portion of court ranks,
軍烽照上都	army beacon fires shone in the capital.
敢云堪慟哭	Dare I speak what brings pained weeping?—
未免怨洪爐	I cannot help resenting the Great Forge.[56]

Although we earlier discussed the Sweet Dew Incident in general terms, some further specifics are required here. Wang Ya, one of the plotters, confessed under torture that if the plot had been successful, Zheng Zhu, an architect of the plot together with Li Xun, was to be put on the throne in Wenzong's stead. This became the "line" of the victorious eunuchs, justifying the brutality of the purge; Wenzong at least pretended to believe it. While he is here reasonably clear in his opposition to the eunuchs, Li Shangyin also seems to accept this interpretation of the incident, according to which a coup against the eunuchs was also covertly a coup directed at the Tang imperial house.

As we suggested at the beginning of this chapter, Li Shangyin could work in many forms. "Yueyou Plain" is a narrative, albeit an elementary one. The "Yan Terrace" poems derive much of their force by indexing a narrative or scenario that we can never find or be certain of (what we referred to earlier as the poetics of the clandestine). "Stirred by Something," by contrast, is held together by reference to a known narrative

---

wiped out by the military forces of Zheng. It is uncertain whether this refers to the plotters, as translated here, or to the eunuchs, in which case we would translate "one should simply."

53. That is, both the informer and the person informed on paid with their lives.

54. The reference is to the large and imposing Han minister Wang Shang. In this context it refers to Li Xun, one of the plotters.

55. The reference is to an incident recorded in the *Jin shu* in which Wang Yan saw a young barbarian ("barbarian whelp" is literally "barbarian chick") and thought he looked unusual and would lead to troubles for the empire. This turned out to be Shi Le, who in fact later overthrew the Jin. Commentators generally take this as referring to Zheng Zhu, one of the plotters and the person who was to be put on the throne, according to Wang Ya's forced confession. Li Shangyin seems to blame Zheng, though it is uncertain whether this is because he partially believed the accusations or because he thought the plot was ineptly conceived.

56. The reference is to the universe or the cosmic order.

and transforming moments in that narrative into finely crafted and cryptic lines. Sometimes we are not certain as to what part of the narrative of the Sweet Dew Incident particular lines refer, or we are uncertain of the poet's judgment, but knowledge of the concrete historical event is necessary to read the poem. Such indirect reference to an underlying scenario is the model for the hermetic poems, one the latter constantly frustrate.

It was at the beginning of 838, while on his way back to Chang'an, that Li Shangyin witnessed the devastation of the northwestern agricultural region near the capital. In "Coming to the Western Suburbs" 行次西郊作一百韻, a mammoth piece consisting of two hundred lines in the tradition of Du Fu, Li Shangyin places an account of the devastation of the area and of the fortunes of the dynasty in the mouths of the local peasants. (The humble interlocutor was common in such poems.) Here is the first part of the poem:[57]

蛇年建丑月	In the Year of the Snake, the twelfth month,
我自梁還秦	I was returning from Liang to Qin.
南下大散嶺	To the south I came down from Dasan's ridge,
北濟渭之濱	northward I crossed the banks of the Wei.
草木半舒坼	half the plants were putting out shoots,
不類冰雪晨	not at all like a morning of frost and snow.
又若夏苦熱	Yet like summer's bitter heat as well,
燋卷無芳津	scorched and curled, with no sweet moisture.
高田長檞櫪	In the upper fields grew pin and chestnut oak,
下田長荊榛	in the lower fields grew scrub and briars.
農具棄道傍	Farm tools were left by the roadside,
飢牛死空墩	a starved ox lay dead on a bare mound.
依依過村落	In a daze I passed through a village,
十室無一存	not one home in ten had survived.
存者皆面啼	Those left all turned away weeping,[58]
無衣可迎賓	having no proper clothes to welcome a guest.

The peasants tell the sad story of the dynasty, so often retold in poetry, from early prosperity through the An Lushan Rebellion, on to the mounting troubles of the dynasty and the burden on the peasants. For

---

57. 29657; *Jijie* 232; Ye (1985) 661; Zhou 51.

58. Several Qing critics prefer the variant *bei* 背 to *jie* 皆. *Jijie* argues that turning one's back may be implicit in *mian* 面.

these peasants the last straw was the Sweet Dew Incident, as the Palace Army turned to destroy Zheng Zhu, the chief instigator of the plot, who was military commissioner in Fengxiang. With the appearance of fifteen thousand palace troops requiring provisions and quartering, the villagers simply fled for the hills. The years that followed were no better. The grim humor in the following passage assumes knowledge of the role of the post station chief, who was in charge of capturing bandits. Unfortunately, this station chief had been killed by the military commissioner at Fengxiang.

盜賊亭午起	Bandits rise up at midday.
問誰多窮民	Who are they?—mostly poor folk.
節使殺亭吏	The commissioner killed the station chief,
捕之恐無因	so I fear that there's no way to arrest them.
咫尺不相見	We can't see each other a foot away,
旱久多黃塵	there is so much dust from the long drought.
官健腰佩弓	Soldiers with bows slung at their waists
自言爲官巡	say they are on an official patrol;
常恐值荒迥	but we always fear when they come to the wilds,
此輩還射人	their type will just shoot the people.

Although descriptions like this are often classified as "realism," there is undoubtedly a measure of peasant hyperbole of complaint compounded by poetic hyperbole. Beneath the hyperbole, however, there is probably an equal measure of truth. Such truths are also local—there is little historical evidence to make us doubt contemporary rustic idylls of Chengnan, "South of the City," on the other side of Chang'an—but the aggregation of such "truths" of local devastation posed serious problems for the dynasty.

If we simply knew only the hermetic poems and the poems on things, Li Shangyin might be considered a poet like Wen Tingyun. However, after he had passed the *jinshi* exam and matured, we find increasing numbers of poems commenting on contemporary politics. This was poetic "seriousness" according to one definition within the tradition. Li Shangyin shares such "seriousness" with Du Mu. This quality played a major role in the elevation of both to canonical status.

By later standards Li Shangyin's poetic "letters to the editor" were usually "politically correct" in that they represented the anti-foreign, anti-military sentiments of lower officialdom. They are, however, often naïve in the context of contemporary political realities. One can only sympathize with Wenzong and his advisers, trying to hold together a fragile polity with the diminished resources at hand. One such resource was the reservoir of imperial princesses, who could be used to strengthen uncertain loyalties. In 837 the Shou'an Princess was married off to Wang Yuankui, the military commissioner of the Chengde Army, stationed in modern Hebei. This was one of the most troubled areas in the empire. Wang Tingzou, Wang Yuankui's Uighur father, had openly defied imperial authority. The Chengde Army was nominally a Tang army, and Wang Yuankui held an imperial appointment. In the fifth line Li Shangyin pointedly compares the wedding to a "marriage pact," *heqin* 和親, a venerable tool of Chinese foreign policy, marrying Chinese princesses to foreign rulers to produce heirs that would be blood relations (often "nephews") of the imperial house.

李商隱, 壽安公主出降
Li Shangyin, The Shou'an Princess Gets Married[59]

嫣水聞貞媛	He heard of a virginal damsel by Gui's waters,[60]
常山索銳師	from Mount Chang crack troops fetched her.[61]
昔憂迷帝力	Earlier worried he might fall afoul of the Emperor's power,[62]
今分送王姬	his present lot is to be sent a royal Ji.[63]
事等和強虜	The event equals a marriage pact with powerful nomads,
恩殊睦本枝	Imperial Grace is greater than favor shown to his own line.
四郊多壘在	On the meadows around the capital many forts remain,[64]
此禮恐無時	I fear that these rites are untimely.

---

59. 29363; *Jijie* 194; Ye (1985) 301; Zhou 44.

60. The Gui River, in Shanxi, was where Yao married his two daughters to Shun. The subject here is Wang Yuankui. Any implied comparison of a Uighur warlord to sage-king Shun is meant to be ironic.

61. Chang Mountain in modern Hebei was the headquarters of the Chengde Army.

62. This seems to refer to Wang Yuankui's father, Wang Tingzou.

63. The Ji was the Zhou ruling house. Here it stands for Wenzong's daughter, the Shou'an Princess.

64. The reference is to a passage in the *QuLi* 曲禮 of the *Liji*: "Many forts on the meadows around the capital are the shame of ministers and grand masters" 四郊多壘, 此卿大夫之辱也.

Although a poem like this is hard to present either gracefully or effectively in English, it is the work of a master ironist. Indeed, this is one of those few Tang poems in which satirical irony attains the level of sarcasm. The poem begins with the resonantly archaic scene of sage-king Yao's daughters being given to his successor, Shun, shifting suddenly to a wedding party composed of tough northeastern troops. A daughter of the royal house of Zhou (Tang) is a reward for dubious loyalty. Someone who is supposed to be a Tang general is treated like a foreign potentate. At the end the poet passes the rich, archaic judgment "untimely" in resonantly classical phrases. Li Shangyin's indignation, however, does not resolve the question of a practical alternative for dealing with Wang Yuankui and the Chengde Army.

In 838, after passing the *jinshi* examination the preceding year, twenty-six-year-old Li Shangyin was off to the headquarters of Wang Maoyuan, military commissioner of Jingyuan and soon to become his father-in-law. This was all that remained of the Tang "northwest," not very far from the capital. It was during this period that Li Shangyin wrote "The Wall Tower of Anding" (see p. 207) and "Peonies Ruined by Rain in Huizhong" (see pp. 457–58). The range of this poet, still only in his mid-twenties, was not only remarkable but unparalleled in the Late Tang. Even the versatile Du Mu could not claim to have worked with distinction in so many different styles. Li Shangyin's range is particularly impressive because we can date so few poems to this period with any degree of certainty.

Around 844 and 845 the poet was staying in Yongle County while observing the period of mourning for his mother. The poet of clandestine passion and political ire here adopts the poetic role of rustic gardener.

李商隱, 永樂縣所居一草一木無非自栽今春悉已芳茂因書即事一章
Li Shangyin, Where I Am Living in Yongle County, There Is Not a Tree or
Plant That Was Not Planted by Me Personally. This spring they are all
flowering and flourishing. Thereupon I wrote this piece to describe it.[65]

| 手種悲陳事 | Planting things, I grieved at things past, |
| 心期翫物華 | the heart anticipated enjoying the season's splendor. |

---

65. 29558; *Jijie* 497; Ye (1985) 489.

柳飛彭澤雪	Willows now send the snow of Pengze flying,[66]
桃散武陵霞	peach trees scatter rose clouds of Wuling.[67]
枳嫩棲鸞葉	Bramble tender, leaves for simurghs to perch,
桐香待鳳花	tung tree fragrant, flowers waiting the phoenix.
綏藤縈弱蔓	My vine-sash is wound with pliant creepers,
袍草展新芽	my grass-colored gown unfolds new sprouts.
學植功雖倍	In studying planting, though the deed is doubled,[68]
成蹊跡尚賒	the traces are still far from a path forming.[69]
芳年誰共翫	Who will share the enjoyment of the year's sweetness?—
終老召平瓜	I will grow old at last by Shao Ping's melons.

One almost forgets that the poet is in his early thirties rather than the mellow old gentleman that the poem suggests. Li Shangyin's propensity to high poetic rhetoric does not leave him entirely, but this is a quieter poem, different from earlier works. The opening couplet must be set in the past, and the anticipation of spring's "splendor" (*hua* 華, "flowering," "floweriness") is realized not only in the vegetation but in the poetic rhetoric that survives it. This is "studying planting," which is also the horticulture of literary study that produces its own "flowers." The garden, like the poet's skill, will grow—though the speculative consequences diverge. One "end" of the process is the mature fruit tree, whose annual flowering attracts throngs of admirers who form a path beneath. The alternative "end" is given in the conclusion, namely, the fruit that follows flowering, the Count of Dongling's fine melons, which also attract crowds—though in a different key.

Dating poems is always problematic, but the following famous quatrain by Li Shangyin to his patron Linghu Tao probably dates from roughly the same period.

---

66. Pengze refers to Tao Qian, known as "Master Five Willows." The "snow" is the willow floss.

67. Peach Blossom Spring was located in Wuling. The "rose clouds" are the peach blossoms.

68. "Studying planting" plays on "the planting of study," i.e., its accumulation.

69. Paths forming beneath peach and plum were proverbial for those things that attract others by their good qualities. Li is here saying that his trees are not yet mature enough to draw crowds (or that his own accomplishments are still inadequate to attract attention).

李商隱, 寄令狐郎中
Li Shangyin, To Secretary Linghu Tao[70]

嵩雲秦樹久離居	Long dwelling apart, I by Mount Song's clouds, 　　you by Qin's trees,
雙鯉迢迢一紙書	a paired carp case came far 　　with a letter in one page,
休問梁園舊賓客	Ask not of him who was once a guest 　　in the Liang Park:
茂陵秋雨病相如	the autumn rain at Maoling, 　　Sima Xiangru sick.[71]

Scholars of Li Shangyin's poetry generally feel that Linghu Tao should have done more to support Li's career.[72] Scenarios are created in which Linghu Tao was displeased because of Li Shangyin's marriage to the daughter of Wang Maoyuan, who belonged to the opposing court faction. There is no evidence that factional animosities descended as low as Li Shangyin's level. Recall that Du Mu was closely associated with Niu Sengru while his brother served Li Deyu. Li Shangyin's petitions for patronage were standard practice. From the other angle, Linghu Tao seems to have been much sought after as a prospective patron. Linghu Tao, Linghu Chu's son, must have known Li Shangyin when he was a young client of his father's ("a guest in the Liang Park"); and he obviously kept in touch with Li. The situation described in the poem is clear: Linghu Chu has sent a letter asking after Li, with the poem being his response. The reader of the preceding poem is justified in wondering where the happy gardener is, willing to grow old raising melons like the Count of Dongling. Instead we find Li Shangyin in the role of Sima Xiangru, the most famous of Han literary men, wasting away sick and ignored. We presume Linghu Tao's letter asked, in an appropriately rhetorical way, "How are you doing?" "Ask not," replies the poet, supplying the missing information in a highly resonant image. The poet may have felt—indeed, almost certainly did feel—very different when he wrote these two poems, separated as they are by at least a season

---

70. 29160; *Jijie* 529; Ye (1985) 85; Zhou 127.

71. Li Shangyin is comparing himself to Sima Xiangru, a former client of the Prince of Liang who in his later years lived near what later became Maoling.

72. Li Shangyin himself felt the same and complained, even contrasting Linghu Tao's indifference with the generosity of his father; see 29594 (*Jijie* 935; Ye [1985] 524; Zhou 158).

and perhaps as much as a few years. The more interesting question, however, concerns the relation between the poet and poetic role-playing—allowing that such role-playing can be deployed, as here, for useful, persuasive ends. Li Shangyin was very much a poet who could not only adopt a role but inhabit it fully and persuasively. His position is neither "sincere" nor "insincere," residing in the capacity to envision himself fully in the poetic image he creates of himself. He finds himself in many roles, from the thirty-two-year-old aging gardener, content in his rustic life, to the sick and dying poetic genius who is ignored by the court. In each case it is more than an "allusion": in these poems he temporarily inhabits these resonant figures of the past.

In 846 and 847 Li Shangyin went off to the headquarters at Guilin. Like many poets before him finding themselves in the southern reaches of the empire, he wrote of the strangeness of the place.

李商隱, 桂林
Li Shangyin, Guilin[73]

城窄山將壓	Walls narrow, mountains press upon them,
江寬地共浮	the river broad, the earth floats with it.
東南通絶域	Southeast it leads to the farthest regions,
西北有高樓	to the northwest there is a high tower.
神護青楓岸	Gods protect shores with green maples,
龍移白石湫	a dragon moves to White Stone Tarn.
殊鄉竟何禱	In this strange land what do they pray for?—
簫鼓不曾休	the pipes and drums never cease.

李商隱, 桂林路中作
Li Shangyin, Written on the Guilin Road[74]

地暖無秋色	The place is warm, no autumn colors,
江晴有暮暉	the river in clear weather, with sunset glow.
空餘蟬嘒嘒	Nothing remains but the shrilling of cicadas,
猶向客依依	still facing the traveler with longing.
村小犬相護	The village small, a dog protects it,
沙平僧獨歸	the sands level, a monk returns alone.
欲成西北望	I want to fulfill my northwest gazing
又見鷓鴣飛	and once again I see the partridges flying.[75]

---

73. 29132; *Jijie* 621; Ye (1985) 49.
74. 29210; *Jijie* 672; Ye (1985) 145.
75. According to folklore, the partridge always flies south.

In this relatively plain style, without allusions, we can see the legacy of
the craftsmen of regulated verse in the short line. Indeed, the third
couplet of "Written on the Guilin Road" could disappear invisibly into
a poem by Jia Dao. The plain style is particularly effective in "Guilin,"
which describes the mysterious and barbarian southwest, haunted by
local gods, with its continuous music from local religious ceremonies.

This is not the place to engage the dating problems surrounding Li
Shangyin's poems for Liu Fen 劉蕡, renowned for an incident in 828 in
which Liu responded all too forthrightly to a palace examination ques-
tion—denouncing the eunuchs, questioning the means by which Wen-
zong acquired the throne, and describing the empire as being in dire
straits and on the verge of collapse. Needless to say, Liu Fen did not
pass. One scholar who did pass, Li He 李郃, offered to exchange his
place with Liu Fen. (We should note that Du Mu was another who
passed the same examination.) Yielding to widespread sympathy on the
part of officialdom, Liu Fen was merely exiled to Liuzhou in the far
south (where Liu Zongyuan had been posted earlier). Li Shangyin's
famous poem to Liu Fen has been dated between 841 and 848. In the
end it really does not matter. The Liu Fen poem provides a good con-
trast with the relatively straightforward Guilin poems cited above. The
style here is thick, allusive, and strongly reminiscent of Du Fu, where
the physical world becomes the figurative embodiment of the Confu-
cian polity.

李商隱, 贈劉司户蕡

Li Shangyin, To Liu Fen, Revenue Manager[76]

江風揚浪動雲根	Winds on the river raise waves, they stir the "roots of cloud,"[77]
重碇危檣白日昏	piled mooring stones, looming mast, the bright sun darkens.
已斷燕鴻初起勢	They have already blocked the force of the swan of Yan's first rising,[78]

---

76. 29112; *Jijie* 701; Ye (1985) 27; Zhou 107.

77. "Roots of cloud" was a conventional metaphor for mountain stone. The figure
of storm is suggestive of political troubles.

78. The reference is to Liu Fen being thwarted by the court eunuchs. As *Jijie* points
out, the common qualification of swans as being from Yan here takes on additional
force in that Liu Fen was a native of the northeast. The subject here is apparently the

更驚騷客後歸魂	and further startled the later returning Sao poet's soul.[79]
漢廷急詔誰先入	To the Han court's urgent summons, who was first to enter?—[80]
楚路高歌自欲翻	singing loud on the roads of Chu, you want to compose on your own.[81]
萬里相逢歡復泣	We meet after thousands of leagues, rejoice and then weep,[82]
鳳巢西隔九重門	to the west the phoenix's nest is blocked by nine layers of gates.[83]

The "swan of Yan" at last becomes a phoenix, in this poem rich in Confucian imagery, a figure for the virtuous person exiled and unappreciated. Liu Fen is Qu Yuan and Jia Yi—and perhaps even Jieyu, the madman who sings of the fallen virtue of the times.

Li Shangyin could use the short line to similar purpose, as in two of his famous laments in that form on the occasion of Liu Fen's death, the first of which we quote here.

---

wind, though it could also be taken impersonally: "Already blocked, the force of first rising . . . ."

79. The reference is to Liu Fen's return from exile in Liuzhou in the south. The comparison is to Qu Yuan and the "Summons to the Soul," which was purportedly written to bring Qu Yuan back from exile.

80. The reference is to Jia Yi, who was summoned to an audience with Han Wendi after his recall from exile. The implication is that Liu Fen was not similarly summoned.

81. Many commentators associate this with Jieyu 接輿, the "madman of Chu," who sang of the phoenix to Confucius and "how greatly virtue has declined." *Jijie*, however, takes this as continuing the motif of Qu Yuan, introduced in line 4. *Fan* 翻, here understood as composing a song, could also mean "fly," suggesting that either the poet or his songs have taken flight.

82. I interpret the "thousands of leagues" as representing the distance Liu Fen has traveled in returning from exile in Liuzhou. However, those who take the poem as having been written when Li Shangyin supposedly met Liu Fen in the south will read this line as the two men meeting "thousands of leagues" from the capital.

83. The phoenix, which roosted in the Yellow Emperor's palace, would be a highly auspicious sign. The "nine layers of gates" are those of the palace. The point here seems to be that the phoenix, Liu Fen, cannot reach his nest because it is too far removed within the palace, i.e., he is blocked by his enemies at court.

李商隱, 哭劉司戶二首
Li Shangyin, Lamenting Revenue Manager Liu Fen[84]

I

離居星歲易	Dwelling apart, the star-signs changed,[85]
失望死生分	hope lost, the living divided from the dead.
酒甕凝餘桂	The last cinnamon dries in the ale jug,
書籤冷舊芸	old rue grows cold on the bookslips.
江風吹雁急	River winds keen, blowing wild geese,
山木帶蟬曛	mountain trees' sunset glow, bearing cicadas.
一叫千迴首	I shout once, my head turns a thousand times,
天高不爲聞	but Heaven is high and will not hear me.

The second of these poems is more allusive, but the tightness of the short line gives the poem a different quality.

We may contrast another lament for Liu Fen in the long line.

李商隱, 哭劉蕡
Li Shangyin, Lament for Liu Fen[86]

上帝深宮閉九闈	The High God's deep-set palace, the ninefold gates are closed,
巫咸不下問銜冤	Shaman Xian does not come down to ask of grievances.[87]

---

84. 29113–14; *Jijie* 962; Ye (1985) 28; Zhou 117.

85. Literally the "year star," Jupiter. In other words, time passed.

86. 29167; *Jijie* 954; Ye (1985) 91; Zhou 116.

87. The reference here is apparently to the Li Sao, in which Shaman Xian descends from Heaven and Qu Yuan tells him of his plight. But there is clearly also a reference to the fragmentary preface to "Calling Back the Soul," in which the High God sends a Shaman Yang 巫陽 to call back a soul of someone dead or dying, traditionally understood as a figurative reference to Qu Yuan wandering distraught in exile. Zhu Heling thinks—quite reasonably—that Li Shangyin actually meant "Shaman Yang." He Zhuo, agreeing that Shaman Yang is intended, offers some earlier allusions that help account for why Li chose Shaman Xian here. Taking "Calling Back the Soul" into account places the responsibility for the shaman's failure to descend on the High God (easily associated with the emperor) and introduces the element of death—since Liu Fen is dead. Ye Congqi favors the Li Sao allusion. It seems best to take the lines as a conflation of the two—or simply that Li Shangyin forgot which shaman was involved in "Calling Back the Soul."

黄陵別後春濤隔　　After parting from you at Huangling,
　　　　　　　　　　we were separated by spring waves.[88]

溢浦書來秋雨翻　　the letter came from Penpu
　　　　　　　　　　as autumn rains were spilling.[89]

只有安仁能作誄　　There is only Anren who is skilled
　　　　　　　　　　at writing eulogies;[90]

何曾宋玉解招魂　　when did Song Yu ever truly know
　　　　　　　　　　how to call back a soul?[91]

平生風義兼師友　　In your character all your life
　　　　　　　　　　you were both teacher and friend,

不敢同君哭寢門　　but I dare not think myself your equal
　　　　　　　　　　and weep at the inner chamber door.[92]

It was probably during his journey back from Guilin that Li Shang-yin stopped off at the headquarters in Tanzhou, the old Changsha in modern Hunan and the site of Jia Yi's famous exile.

李商隱, 潭州
Li Shangyin, Tanzhou[93]

潭州官舍暮樓空　　Tanzhou's official residence,
　　　　　　　　　　at twilight the tower deserted,

今古無端入望中　　past and present inexplicably
　　　　　　　　　　come into my gaze.

---

88. Huangling is He Zhuo's emendation for Guangling 廣陵, which appears in the oldest text. The basis for the emendation, given by Cheng Mengxing, is another poem lamenting Liu Fen, in which he speaks of parting from him at Huangling (in Hunan, near the mouth of the Xiang).

89. Presumably this is a letter bringing news of Liu Fen's death.

90. Anren was the courtesy name of the Jin writer Pan Yue 潘岳, famous for his mastery of funerary genres.

91. Song Yu was supposed to have written "Calling Back the Soul," *Zhaohun* 招魂, for Qu Yuan, but the ritual was understood as calling back the soul (consciousness) to a body either dead or unconscious.

92. According to the rituals for mourning prescribed by Confucius in the *Tangong* 檀弓 chapter of the *Liji*, a student was allowed to mourn for his teacher in the inner chamber, while a friend was supposed to mourn outside the door to the inner chamber. Li here seems to be saying that his proper position is that of student and that he should therefore be permitted to mourn in the inner chamber.

93. 29111; *Jijie* 750; Ye (1985) 25; Zhou 109.

湘淚淺深滋竹色	Xiang River tears soak the bamboo's colors, both shallow and deep,[94]
楚歌重疊怨蘭叢	Chu songs repeatedly express resentment though clumps of orchid.[95]
陶公戰艦空灘雨	Lord Tao Kan's war galleys: rain on the empty rapids;[96]
賈傅承塵破廟風	Jia Yi the Tutor's dust canopy: wind in a broken-down temple.[97]
目斷故園人不至	My eyes gaze off to my home gardens, no one comes,
松醪一醉與誰同	with whom can I share getting drunk on this pine-flavored brew?[98]

Li Shangyin's reading of Du Fu is still evident, but "Tanzhou" is much more closely related to the Late Tang regulated verse in the long line. Recall the closing of Du Mu's poem of 842 with which we began our study:

可憐赤壁爭雄渡	I am moved how at Red Cliff, the crossing where heroes contended,
唯有蓑翁坐釣魚	there is only an old man in a raincoat, sitting and fishing.

---

94. This refers to the mottled bamboo of the Xiang region, whose patterns were supposedly caused by the tears shed by the widows of Shun.

95. This is a general reference to Qu Yuan and perhaps explicitly to the "Nine Songs." Feng Hao takes this as "expressing resentment at orchid clumps," understanding the orchid as Zilan 子蘭, the Chu vizier who slandered Qu Yuan. Although this would work well with yuan 怨, "to express resentment," in most cases the "orchid" (thoroughwort) is a figure of virtue and beauty, which Qu Yuan associates with himself.

96. Tao Kan 陶侃 was the Jin governor of Jiangxia 江夏, known for turning transport boats into warships to resist the depredations of Chen Hui, sent by his brother Chen Min to harass Wuchang. After his initial success, Tao moved on to take Changsha, the district in which Tanzhou was located.

97. This refers to Jia Yi's exile in Changsha. According to the *Xijing zaji* account of Jia's composition of his "Poetic Exposition on the Owl," the owl was supposed to have perched on Jia's "dust canopy," a covering erected to keep off the dust and, in particular, droppings from the rafters. According to the commentary to the *Shuijing* 水經, the temple to Tao Kan, located west of the official residence in Xiangzhou 湘州 (Tanzhou), was supposed to have originally been Jia Yi's dwelling. Elsewhere (*Huanyu ji* 寰宇記) this same place is described as a temple to Jia Yi.

98. Pine sap and pine needles were evidently used in producing an ale that, *Jijie* suggests, was a well-known local product of Tanzhou.

Du Mu evoked a past scene and then superimposed a present scene on it. Learning from Du Fu's "line construction" (*jufa* 句法), Li Shangyin accomplishes the same kind of scene more economically about five years after Du Mu's lines. The poet tells us that "past and present inexplicably come into my gaze":

陶公戰艦空灘雨	Lord Tao Kan's war galleys: rain on the empty rapids;
賈傅承塵破廟風	Jia Yi the Tutor's dust canopy: wind in a broken-down temple.

Looking out into the rain, the poet sees the galleys of Tao Kan as ghostly presences from the past disappearing in the rain. In Jia Yi's shrine he imagines the canopy where the famous owl perched and delivered its great sermon in verse on change, instantiated in the present as the wind blows through the broken-down temple.

Back in the capital in 849, Li addressed several poems to Du Mu, who was employed in the Bureau of Honorifics (see also p. 303).

李商隱, 贈司勳杜十三員外
Li Shangyin, Presented to Du Mu, Vice Director
of the Bureau of Honorifics[99]

杜牧司勳字牧之	Du Mu, of the Bureau of Honorifics, courtesy name Muzhi,
清秋一首杜秋詩	in clear autumn a single poem on Du, Autumn Lass.[100]
前身應是梁江總	In a former life I'm sure he was Jiang Zong of the Liang,
名總還曾是總持	whose name was Zong and also called Zongchi.[101]
心鐵已從干鏌利	Your iron heart is already as sharp as Ganjiang and Moya,[102]
鬢絲休歎雪霜垂	cease to sigh how the silk at your temples hangs as frost and snow.

---

99. 29596; *Jijie* 878; Ye (1985) 527; Zhou 173.

100. One of Du Mu's most famous poems was "Du Autumn Lass (Qiuniang)" 杜秋娘 (see pp. 276–77).

101. Jiang Zong's name Zong was a component of his courtesy name (*zi*) Zongchi, just as Du Mu's courtesy name was Muzhi.

102. The reference is to famous swords of antiquity.

漢江遠弔西江水   From the River Han you have gone far
                       to lament by the waters of Westriver,
羊祜韋丹盡有碑   and now Yang Hu and Wei Dan
                       both have stele inscriptions.[103]

There no doubt that this poem is intended to praise Du Mu, but it is a peculiar poem of praise. It was common to praise someone by comparing this person with some earlier figure with the same surname—in this case Du Yu. The comparison of Du Mu's inscription to Du Yu's famous inscription is gracefully complimentary. However, to make a comparison on the basis of the fact that name and courtesy name share a word in common and have the same pattern was novel and clever. Jiang Zong, the person to whom Li compares Du Mu, was a poet of dubious repute and was sometimes portrayed in a highly unfavorable light by Li himself in other poems (see pp. 418, 421). Li Shangyin does specify Jiang Zong "of the Liang," but few would forget Jiang Zong's career as the carousing and irresponsible minister of the Last Ruler of Chen. Li Shangyin is enjoying the play of repetitions: two "autumns" (*qiu* 秋), two Dus in the text and a third (Du Yu) implied at the end; Jiang 江 both as a surname and as "river" in the seventh line. In this general spirit of repetitions, Jiang Zong was an ingenious parallel in the relation between name and courtesy name, but it may have been an unfortunate choice. We do not know how Du Mu reacted to Li Shangyin's poem since we have no poem written in response.[104] It was not a friendship that blossomed.

After leaving Chang'an to spend about a year in Xuzhou at the headquarters of Lu Hongzhi, Li Shangyin returned in 851 to take a post in Chang'an. That summer his wife died. Early that same autumn, just before setting off for Sichuan, he composed the following poem:

---

103. Xuanzong 宣宗 had been attempting to determine the merit of lower-grade officials during the Yuanhe Reign and was told of Wei Dan of Jiangxi, whom people young and old still remembered in their songs. Du Mu was commissioned to write his stele inscription, as another Du (Du Yu) had done for Yang Hu on Xiang Mountain by the River Han.

104. In the selection of his poems that constitute the main body of his poetry collection, made a few years later (in 852), Du Mu preserved the verses that showed his connection with the well-known poets of the day, such as Zhang Hu and Li Qunyu.

李商隱, 辛未七夕

Li Shangyin, The Seventh Eve in the Year *Xinwei* (851)[105]

恐是仙家好別離	I suspect that the immortals 　　must like their separation,
故教迢遞作佳期	on purpose making their happy unions 　　to be so far apart.
由來碧落銀河畔	It is always in the celestial vault 　　by the silvery river of stars,
可要金風玉露時	and awaits the season 　　of metal wind and jade dew.[106]
清漏漸移相望久	Clear water clock drips gradually on, 　　they gaze at each other long;
微雲未接過來遲	the faint clouds have not yet joined, 　　they are late to cross over.
豈能無意酬烏鵲	How can it be that they do not intend 　　to repay the magpies[107]
惟與蜘蛛乞巧絲	and only provide spiders to 　　imprecations for craft of thread?[108]

Li Shangyin begins his poem with an unusual speculation. The "immortals," who seem to like separation, must be the Oxherd and Weaver Woman themselves. Just as the lovers wait, so the poet—and the poem—wait, deferring the crossing first with a "time and place" couplet and then with the dripping of the water clock as they gaze in anticipation (or he gazes long at the heavens in anticipation). He watches for the clouds in the Milky Way that will cover the crossing, but no clouds appear and they are late to cross over. The growing intensity of deferred desire generates in the poet's thoughts proportional gratitude for those—here the magpies—that help them fulfill their desire.

---

105. 29251; *Jijie* 1058; Ye (1985) 185; Zhou 187.

106. "Celestial vault" is *biluo* 碧落, a Daoist term for the heavens. Metal was the element associated with autumn; hence "metal wind" is the autumn wind. Likewise, "jade dew" is associated with autumn. Sometimes this is viewed as a question: "Why must they wait?"

107. The magpies were supposed to form a bridge so that the lovers could cross.

108. On the Seventh Eve women seeking greater skill in needlework traditionally placed fruits and melons in the courtyard, and if a spider made a web on the fruit, then their prayer would be granted. The Weaver Woman provides spiders for the women praying for skill in needlework but apparently neglects the magpies, who perform a substantial service for her.

Perhaps due to accidents of what can be securely dated, most of the datable poems that most closely resemble the undatable hermetic poems come from the 830s, when Li Shangyin was in his late teens and twenties. Among the later poems, we come close in a few poems on the death of his wife in 851.[109]

李商隱, 房中曲

Li Shangyin, Music for Private Apartments[110]

薔薇泣幽素	Roses weep hidden white,
翠帶花錢小	on azure sashes, blossom-coins small.
嬌郎癡若雲	My dear lad is foolish as cloud,
抱日西簾曉	embracing the sun, west curtain's dawn.[111]
枕是龍宮石	The pillow is a dragon palace stone
割得秋波色	cut into colors of autumn waves.[112]
玉簟失柔膚	The jade mat has lost the supple flesh,
但見蒙羅碧	I see only the covering of gossamer emerald.
憶得前年春	I recall spring last year,
未語含悲辛	she didn't speak, her bitter pain withheld.
歸來已不見	By the time I returned she was gone,
錦瑟長於人	the brocade zither lasted longer than her.
今日澗底松	Today, a pine in the stream valley,
明日山頭蘗	tomorrow, the bitter bo oak on the hill.
愁到天地翻	I will sorrow until Heaven and Earth turn over,
相看不相識	we will look at each other and not recognize each other.

Although this is, on the whole, more direct than many of the hermetic poems, some of the denser lines recall them, as does the passionate closing couplet.

Li Shangyin's decision to go off to Sichuan seems to have been in no small measure a consequence of grief at his wife's death. His close

---

109. Many poems have been interpreted as concerning the death of his wife. Here I am referring solely to those poems that are unmistakably about her death.

110. 29468; *Jijie* 1034; Ye (1985) 405.

111. These lines have received numerous explanations. *Jijie* champions the notion that the child's folly is his failure to feel grief at the loss of his mother and his desire to continue sleeping, embracing his pillow when the sun is already high. James Liu prefers the boy embracing his father. Ye wants this to be Li Shangyin's wife, though he doesn't account for the masculine gender of *lang* 郎.

112. The "waves" suggest a woman's glances.

friend Han Zhan (the poet Han Wo's father), who had married the sister of Li Shangyin's wife, saw him off. Li Shangyin here reflects on their different turns of fortune.

李商隱, 赴職梓潼留別畏之員外同年

Li Shangyin, Going to My Post at Zitong, Detained on
Parting by Vice Director Weizhi[113]

佳兆聯翩遇鳳凰	Lucky predictions: in succession 　　we met our phoenixes,[114]
雕文羽帳紫金牀	feathered curtains, wrought with patterns, 　　beds of purple and gold.
桂花香處同高第	When the cassia blossoms were fragrant, 　　we both ranked high in the examination,[115]
柿葉翻時獨悼亡	but when the persimmon leaves spread, 　　I alone mourned a wife's death.[116]
烏鵲失棲常不定	The magpie loses its roosting place, 　　it grows ever unsettled;
鴛鴦何事自相將	how is it that the mandarin duck couple 　　go along together?[117]
京華庸蜀三千里	The capital and Yong-Shu 　　are three thousand leagues apart,[118]
送到咸陽見夕陽	you send me off to Xianyang 　　where we see the evening sun.

Mourning can occur grandly, as above, or it can also be triggered by a small immediate circumstance, such as crossing the snow of Dasan

---

113. 29209; *Jijie* IIII; Ye (1985) 143; Zhou 205. Li Shangyin was on his way to take a post with Liu Zhongying 柳仲郢, the military commissioner of Dongchuan, in modern Sichuan. Weizhi was Li's friend Han Zhan 韓瞻.

114. The meeting of phoenixes refers to a marriage (*Zuo zhuan*, Zhuang 22). Both Li and Han were married to daughters of Wang Maoyuan 王茂元.

115. "Plucking the cassia" was a standard phrase for passing the *jinshi* examination. Both Li and Han passed the same year; hence the reference to Han as *tongnian* 同年 in the title.

116. The reference is to an anecdote about Liu Xiao 劉歊 in the *Nan shi* 南史. In the spring before Liu died, someone planted a persimmon tree in Liu's courtyard. Liu predicted that he would not live to see it bear fruit. That autumn he died. This refers to the death of Li's wife.

117. That is, Han Zhan gets to stay with his wife.

118. Yong-Shu is Sichuan, where Li is headed.

Pass and realizing that one's clothes are not heavy enough. For clothes a man depended on the women in the family—especially one's wife.

李商隱, 悼傷後赴東蜀辟至散關遇雪
Li Shangyin, After Mourning the Loss of My Wife, I Go to Take
Up an Appointment in Eastern Shu and Encounter
Snow When Reaching Dasan Pass[119]

劍外從軍遠	Far beyond Jian'ge I will serve with the army,
無家與寄衣	there is no one at home to send me clothes.
散關三尺雪	The three feet of snow in Dasan Pass
迴夢舊鴛機	sends dreams back to the old mandarin
	duck loom.

Ji Yun, so often critical of Li Shangyin's less well known poems, approves this quatrain for being reminiscent of the High Tang.

In Sichuan Li Shangyin's engagement with Du Fu became even more apparent.[120] Du Fu, of course, had resided in Chengdu, with an appointment dependent on the patronage of the regional governor, as Li Shangyin's appointment was. Earlier we discussed a poem dating from this period—almost unique in the Chinese poetic tradition—in which Li Shangyin wrote "as" Du Fu (see p. 444). Li's identification with Du Fu went even further. Li had earlier expressed his opinions on current events, as in the poem on the Shou'an Princess. Here, however, we have the poet offering general political advice in a style strongly reminiscent of Du Fu. Like Du Fu a century earlier, Li Shangyin was a political nonentity. His sense of the dignity and responsibility of the poet's role was his alone. Du Mu also offered poetic political advice, but it was often qualified by the recognition that he would not be heeded (see p. 261). Li Shangyin spoke with an authority that was dependent on that of his great poetic predecessor, without addressing the question of whether he would be heeded.

Sichuan was heavily militarized and had a long history of separatist movements, most recently in the rebellion of Liu Pi 劉闢 during Xian-

---

119. 29115; *Jijie* 1115; Ye (1985) 30.

120. Du Fu does, however, appear earlier in his poetry. In a banqueting poem that is probably earlier, Du Fu even seems to have been given to Li as an assigned topic for imitation; see 29608 (*Jijie* 1956; Ye [1985] 539).

zong's reign. Li Shangyin warns any and all who might consider rebelling against imperial authority.

李商隱, 井絡

Li Shangyin, The Well Rope[121]

井絡天彭一掌中	The Well Rope, Tianpeng Mountain all in a single palm,
漫誇天設劍為峰	they rashly boasted that Heaven set swords to serve as peaks.[122]
陣圖東聚煙江石	East the "Formations Diagram" clusters south of the misty river,[123]
邊柝西懸雪嶺松	west frontier clappers resound[124] in pines of Snow Mountain's clefts.
堪嘆故君成杜宇	Meriting sighs, that olden king turned into a cuckoo,[125]
可能先主是眞龍	is it really possible the First Ruler was indeed a true dragon?[126]
將來爲報姦雄輩	Be sure to inform the type of men who are wickedly aggressive[127]
莫向金牛訪舊蹤	they had better not visit the former site at Golden Oxen Gorge.[128]

When Liu Zhongying ended his term at the headquarters in Zizhou (Sichuan), Li Shangyin returned with him to Chang'an and left the following farewell to those who stayed in Zizhou:

---

121. 29482; *Jijie* 1177; Ye (1985) 419; Zhou 320. The "Well Rope" was a constellation that corresponded to the Min Mountain region in Sichuan.

122. The reference is to Big Sword and Small Sword Mountains in the region.

123. This is a set of dolmens that tradition ascribed to Zhuge Liang, the minister of the Shu-Han Kingdom, understood as a military diagram for the conquest of Wu.

124. The clappers signal the presence of troops.

125. Wangdi, an ancient ruler of Shu, who yielded the throne after an illicit liaison with the wife of one of his ministers.

126. The reference is to Liu Bei, who founded the Shu-Han Kingdom.

127. This term was applied to Cao Cao. *Jijie* takes this as the frontier commanders.

128. The reference is to a story recounting that the king of Qin had five stone oxen made, after which he let it be known in the Shu Kingdom that these were golden oxen. Shu sent five heroes to get them, thus opening the route between Qin and Shu and preparing for the Qin conquest of Shu. This is a variant version of the story mentioned on p. 413. Here Li Shangyin is clearly warning against separatist moves in the west: the road from Chang'an to Shu is open.

李商隱, 梓州罷吟寄同舍

Li Shangyin, Ending My Poems in Zizhou:
To my colleagues[129]

不揀花朝與雪朝	Not choosy whether dawns of flowers or dawns of snow,
五年從事霍嫖姚	five years I spent in the service of "Fleet" Huo Qubing.[130]
君緣接坐交珠履	You, when sitting next to me, crossed pearled shoes,
我爲分行近翠翹	I, when in separate rows, drew near to kingfisher feathers.[131]
楚雨含情皆有託	"Chu's rain" has sentiments in reserve, always expressed indirectly,[132]
漳濱多病竟無憀	very sick on the Zhang's shore, in the end none to rely on.[133]
長吟遠下燕臺去	Chanting long, far away I descend Yan Terrace and go off,[134]
惟有衣香染未銷	only the scent that permeates my clothes has not faded.

There are ways to read this poem so as to reconcile it with Li Shangyin's famous statement, expressed in a letter to Liu Zhongying, that although his poems may have touched on romantic attachments, he did not actually engage in this type of behavior. Such readings (for example, Zhou Zhenfu's) are counterintuitive, taking the prose statement as definitive and the poem as ambiguous and open to other interpretations.

It is unwise to engage in speculations about Li Shangyin's love life—despite his numerous poetic invitations for us to do so. Still, the first two couplets here do seem to suggest continuous rounds of parties and carousing. The fifth line does seem to gesture toward love affairs, to

---

129. 29456; *Jijie* 1309; Ye (1985) 394; Zhou 227.

130. Liu Zhongying is here figured as the famous Han commander Huo Qubing.

131. Commentators take this couplet as a *huwen* 互文, in which both predicates apply to both subjects. Pearled shoes refer to fine guests, while kingfisher feathers is a metonymy for courtesans.

132. "Chu's rain" refers to sexual encounters.

133. The Jian'an poet Lu Zhen long lay sick by the River Zhang.

134. Yan Terrace here refers to the famous Terrace of Gold of King Zhao of Yan, where he received scholars from many regions.

feelings greater than could be expressed straightforwardly, and to indirect expression. The term for "indirect expression," *tuo* 託 (literally "to entrust [to something else]"), is the term used for figurative expression in Chinese poetics. The Qing commentator He Zhuo and several others take the "indirect expression" as referring to Li's political feelings expressed *through* the sentiments of love rather than the sentiments of love expressed figuratively. According to such an interpretation, this line has been the major internal support for the interpretation of the hermetic poems in political terms. Such a reading of the line, however, is only one among several possible readings. It is no less likely, as we suggested above, that Li Shangyin is here referring to the figurative expression of love affairs. Moreover, *Jijie* takes the line as referring to his colleague(s) rather than to Li himself—and consequently to actual love affairs rather than love affairs as the figurative expression of political sentiments. According to the *Jijie* interpretation, only in the sixth line does Li turn to his own case. Another—perhaps the most obvious—interpretation is to read the *jing* 竟, "in the end," strongly: for five years I expressed my passions figuratively, and now, in the end, I am the poet who is sick and without anyone to rely on.

One way to interpret the final couplet is suggested in a note: Yan Terrace is King Zhao of Yan's Terrace of Gold, here a figure for Liu Zhongying's generosity as a patron. As he leaves, the scent, the lingering trace of Liu Zhongying's grace, remains upon him. "Yan Terrace" is, of course, also the title of the intensely erotic poems Li Shangyin wrote as a youth; the term clearly had a special meaning for him. With Yan Terrace viewed in this sense, the lingering scent takes on a very different association. Here we should recall the last couplet of "Yan Terrace: Autumn" (see pp. 180–81):

歌脣一世銜雨看	Singing lips for a whole lifetime watched, holding back rain,
可惜馨香手中故	a pity that the fragrance grows old upon the hand.

Perhaps he doesn't actually spend his lifetime watching those singing lips. In the end, perhaps he must leave "Yan Terrace."

長吟遠下燕臺去	Chanting long, far away I descend Yan Terrace and go off,
惟有衣香染未銷	only the scent that permeates my clothes has not faded.

The lines may not be related. If they are, the pairing of the couplets can be interpreted in many ways. Nevertheless, set side by side, these two couplets—one dating from the early 830s and the other from 855—suggest a private "mythology," a network of terms with a special meaning for the poet that endured in his work, perhaps taking on radically different meanings in different contexts. Perhaps the continuity is the term "Yan Terrace" itself, suggesting an erotic meaning at one point and a tribute to patronage at another. Readers of Li Shangyin soon come to recognize these recurrent images—the "brocade zither" or the "Purple Maid"—realizing that their force in his poetry cannot be fully explained either by immediate context or by tradition. They seem to be his private images.

Only a handful of poems can be securely dated to Li Shangyin's last years, between his return from Sichuan in 855 and his death in 858. Perhaps these were prolific years for his poetry; we cannot tell. Figuratively, if not literally, we can take the last lines of "Ending My Poems in Zizhou" as Li's farewell to poetry.

In the end, Li Shangyin remains an elusive poet whose varied style and obscurity make it impossible to tie him to one dominant concern—whether it be a personal beloved, his own political career, or the fate of the dynasty. That very elusiveness ensured his survival, as changing communities over the century read his poetry carefully and always found that which they were seeking.

FIFTEEN

Wen Tingyun

The Hanshang tijin ji: Poets at Play

In 855, three years after the death of Du Mu and a few years before the death of Li Shangyin, a scandal erupted involving the *jinshi* examination. The topic set for the poetic exposition had leaked out before the examination and an exam candidate had hired a master of the form to write the required composition in advance. The master in question was the poet and prose stylist Wen Tingyun. We do not know if his ensuing disgrace was the immediate cause, but a year or two later Wen set off for Xiangyang, the headquarters of the military commissioner Xu Shang 徐商. There he found himself in congenial company, in the person of Duan Chengshi 段成式 (d. 863), best remembered for his anecdotal collection *Youyang zazu* 酉陽雜俎. Also in Xu Shang's entourage were the poets Wei Chan 韋蟾 and Yuan Yao 元繇.[1] During this period in Xiangyang Wen Tingyun's brother Wen Tinghao 溫庭皓 also joined the group for a while.

Duan Chengshi compiled works composed by this group between roughly 857 and Xu Shang's transfer in 859 in the *Hanshang tijin ji* 漢上題襟集 ("Writing Our Bosom Thoughts by the Han River"). This collection may have survived as late as the Qing, but pieces that clearly belonged to it have been preserved in various sources.[2] Among these is a

---

1. Yuan Yao is given in poem titles and throughout the tradition as the more famous poet Zhou Yao 周繇. For a discussion of the confusion and an argument that this is Yuan Yao, see Tao Min's analysis in Fu (1987), vol. 5, 439–41.

2. See Fu (1987), vol. 5, 439–40. Jia Jinhua has collected the pieces that she believes once belonged to it; see Jia Jinhua 賈晉華, *Tangdai jihui zongji yu shirenqun yanjiu* 唐代集會總集與詩人群研究 (Beijing: Beijing daxue chubanshe, 2001), 438–56.

poem by Duan Chengshi on a very unusual topic. The occasion was a challenge from Wen Tingyun to employ words that were not part of standard poetic vocabulary.[3]

At a night banquet at Guangfeng Pavilion some singing girls got into a drunken brawl. Wen Tingyun said, "If one were to describe this, you ought to put 'throttled necks' in parallel with 'scratched faces.'" Duan Chengshi then uttered:

捽胡雲彩落	Throttled necks, cloud-glitter tresses fall,
痕面月痕消	scratched faces, the moon-marks fade.[4]

He went on:

擲屨仙鳧起	Tossed slippers, immortal mallards rising,
撏衣蝴蝶飄	ripped clothing, butterflies aflutter.
羞中含薄怒	In embarrassment they hold back mild rage,
顰裏帶餘嬌	in their frowns they bring abundant charm.
醉後猶攘臂	When drunk they still have rolled-up sleeves,
歸時更折腰	withdrawing, they bend their waists still more.[5]
狂夫自纓絕	Wild fellows laugh until hat ribbons break—
眉勢倩誰描	who now can they get to paint their brows?

The poetic language describing beautiful women performers is transferred to scratching, ripping each other's clothes, and throwing shoes. Wei Chan contributed a verse with outrageous allusions rather than mere description:

爭揮鈎弋手	Struggling they swing Lady Gouyi's hands,[6]
競聳踏搖身	they compete to keep bodies of the "Stamping Song" woman erect.[7]

---

3. Wang Zhongyong 1556; Yuan Feng 7.

4. The reference is to one of various cosmetic patterns with which women decorated their faces.

5. "Bending the waist" was both a dance movement and a bow to the host. Yuan Feng suggests their waists are bent because they are aching from the fight.

6. Lady Gouyi was a consort of Han Wudi and the mother of Zhaodi. She was so named because sickness had left one of her hands paralyzed in a hook-like shape. That image is suggested here.

7. The reference is to the story describing the origins of a kind of song called the "Stamping Song." An ill-tempered husband used to regularly beat up his wife, who was good at singing and vented her grievances in this song. The implication here is that these women look as though they were beaten up.

| 傷煩詎關舞 | Wounded cheeks have nothing to do with a dance, |
| 捧心非效嚬 | hands clasped to heart are not imitating Xi Shi's frown.[8] |

Wen Tingyun's offering in the set of responses seems the least daring:[9]

吳國初成陣	The Wu kingdom first forms its ranks,
王家欲解圍	the royal house wants to lift the siege.
拂巾雙雉叫	Waving kerchiefs, two pheasants cry out,
翻瓦兩鴛飛	knocking over tiles, a pair of mandarin duck hens fly.

We suspect that Wen's first couplet plays on the names or place of origin of the singing girls. Wu could be a surname as well as a place of origin, and the "royal house," *wangjia* 王家, might refer to a singer named Wang ("she of the Wang family"). The last line refers to a dream of Cao Pi's in which tiles that had fallen from the palace roof turned into a pair of mandarin ducks, an omen portending a sudden death in the harem.

Such comic poetry had long been part of the Chinese tradition, though it was preserved with increasing frequency in the ninth century. Sometimes, as here, its humor arose from the disparity between elevated poetic erudition and a low topic. The men laugh and are entertained at this outbreak of feminine violence, reminding us of the tensions among singing girls lying just below the surface of the stylized charm of their performances.[10] It is poetry trying to contain something that lies outside the stylized domain of poetry.

The *Hanshang tijin ji* displays great delight in the play of rhetoric and learning, elaborating simple topics (which might earlier have been treated by means of a pair of allusions) to the edge of irony, while not

---

8. The beauty Xi Shi had a bad heart that caused her to clasp her hands to her heart and frown, which increased her charm. Her ugly-looking neighbor tried to imitate her but only looked uglier.

9. 32199; Zeng 210. Reading 陣 for 陳.

10. Yuan Feng implies that this is a mock combat; he is perhaps unable to believe that an actual fight could really happen. We should recall that "official singers," *guanji*, were usually girls taken from families of condemned criminals. While we can be certain that many decent families were victims of Tang law, it did not overlook the roughest elements of society.

necessarily crossing that edge, as happens in the poems cited above. Such poetry was closely allied to parallel prose. Parallel prose, however, never breaks away from its high register, while this poetry often mixes the elevated and erudite with the crude and vernacular (as in the verbs of "scratching" and "ripping" in Duan's poem cited above).

A nice pairing of parallel prose letter and poem occurs when Wen Tingyun asks for some note-paper from Duan Chengshi. In his reply Duan demonstrates his knowledge of the lore of fine paper (the kind of information one would find in an encyclopedia entry under "paper").

段成式, 寄溫飛卿箋紙
Duan Chengshi, Sending Note-paper to Wen Tingyun[11]

One day I was graced with a little piece of paper of nine inches from Feiqing [Wen Tingyun], with two lines in his own hand, in which he asked of me ten strips of colored paper to transcribe drafts of his short poems. I possess several packets of note-paper of various kinds and am often selecting out pieces to give to others, while enjoying their bright and light quality, so different from the "hemp" and the "glossy."[12] I am embarrassed by what the senior Yu received, which came to four hundred sheets; but I would never reach Wang Xizhi's excess in handing over all his ninety thousand pieces.[13] Thus I realize that upon these flat-pounded emerald chessboards you will recompose lyrics of love's torment; on these red fibers in squares you will continue to imitate songs of longing. Indeed, one should make "mulberry root" the basis, and use "rattan corners" for the wrapper; one need not value the ancient crudeness of Count Cai;[14] one should be particularly tolerant of Huan Xuan's new style.[15] It is not just that one prizes either the square or rectangular when the ink is dashing on; one especially wants the "angled pattern" paper when freely plying the brush. It is to be regretted that I have none of the color of duck eggs or shapes like horse livers, suited to copy out palindromes or to write on torn brocade. When I was in Nine Rivers I decided to produce some "cloud indigo" paper;

---

11. 32212; Yuan Feng 15.

12. The reference is to two varieties of Chengdu paper.

13. The first allusion is a slightly misremembered reference to Yu Yu 虞預, who was secretary to Yu Chen 庾琛, the governor of Kuaiji in the Eastern Jin, who wrote a memorial asking for four hundred sheets of paper from the treasury. The second allusion is to the calligrapher Wang Xizhi, who gave away his entire stock of ninety thousand sheets when Lord Xie asked for some paper.

14. The reference is to Cai Lun, the legendary inventor of paper in the Eastern Han.

15. Huan Xuan, who overthrew the Eastern Jin, was credited with the invention of several new kinds of paper.

lacking the technique of Zuo Bo[16] and utterly without the achievement of Zhang Yong,[17] I send you a portion of fifty sheets along with a quatrain, which may, in your leisure, serve as temporary antidote for your needs.

三十六鱗充使時	When thirty-six scales serve as your messenger,[18]
數番猶得裹相思	several exchanges can still enclose love-longing.
待將袍袄重抄了	Soon you will have these paoao robes to copy them all out again,[19]
盡寫襄陽播搦詞	and write out the lyrics of Xiangyang's "Bonuo" songs.[20]

Such a quatrain is not memorable in the annals of Tang poetry, but it provides us with some insight into the discursive culture of high rhetoric and its putative link to a semi-secret love life. This is a possible context for reading Wen's song lyrics—though they themselves do not play on concealed meaning—and for understanding the reception of Li Shangyin's poetry, which, as we have seen, does play on concealed meaning.

As Duan's letter presents his request, Wen Tingyun does not say that he wants to copy out love poems but rather only wants to write down "little poems," *shaoshi* 少詩 (presumably *xiaoshi* 小詩). Wen Tingyun already had a reputation as a lover, which becomes the context for understanding such a simple request. We know that fine note-paper was indeed used in sending love poems, but the context here demands further clarification. This fine paper is not to be used to write poems to send to his imagined beloved but rather to recopy them—presumably for the purpose of circulation among his friends.

There is every reason to be highly suspicious of the numerous later anecdotes in which Wen Tingyun is portrayed as a rake. In the Duan Chengshi poems, however, we have perhaps our unique piece of contemporary testimony.

---

16. Zuo Bo was an Eastern Han master of *bafen* script and of paper manufacture.

17. Zhang Yong was a Liu-Song calligrapher who made his own paper.

18. Thirty-six scales is a carp, hence a kenning for a letter, conventionally sent in a fish-shaped container.

19. *Paoao* robes are ritual clothes, here standing for the fine paper.

20. In some texts the proposed lyrics are given as "Juezhe" 掘柘 rather than "Bonuo." Since we do have "Quzhe" lyrics by Wen, this is probably an emendation.

段成式，嘲飛卿七首
Duan Chengshi, Teasing Feiqing[21]

I

曾見當壚一個人	Once I saw a certain person standing at the bar,
入時裝束好腰身	dressed in the current fashion, well-proportioned body.
少年花蒂多芳思	A youth, a flower stem full of tender longings
只向詩中寫取眞	whose perfect portrait is painted only in his poems.[22]

II

醉袂幾侵魚子纈	His drunken sleeves sometimes encroach on the fish ornamental tie,[23]
飄纓長冑鳳皇釵	his fluttering hat ribbons always get tangled in phoenix hairpins.
知君欲作閑情賦	I know that you are going to write a fu on "Calming the Passions":
應願將身作錦鞋	I'm sure you want to turn yourself into a brocade shoe.[24]

III

翠蝶密偎金叉首	Azure butterfly cuddling close to the golden hairpin tip,[25]
青蟲危泊玉釵梁	green beetle carapace moors perilously on the jade hairpin stem.
愁生半額不開靨	Melancholy grows over half her forehead, her dimples do not show,

---

21. 32226–332; Yuan Feng 29.

22. I have taken the "youth" as referring to the woman (as it rarely is). It could be a young man, but the subsequent poems clearly refer to a woman.

23. A *xie* 纈 is described as patterned fabric, but it seems to be some sort of ornamental tied pattern. Here it clearly belongs to a woman.

24. This plays on Tao Yuanming's "Calming the Passions," in which the poet imagines various transformations to get close to the body of the beloved. Yuan Feng cites Wen's "Fu on the Brocade Shoe" 錦鞋賦, with the line: "it wants to twine itself around the fragrant toes."

25. 叉 here is probably a mistake for 釵.

只爲多情團扇郎	all because of her passionate "round-fan" lover.[26]

IV

柳煙梅雪隱青樓	A mist of willows, snow of plums hides the green mansion,
殘日黃鸝語未休	in fading sunlight the orioles chatter without stopping,
見說自能裁袙腹	It is said that she is able to cut out a belly wrapper,
不知誰更著帩頭	I don't know who will anymore show his headband.[27]

V

愁機懶織同心苣	At her sad loom too lazy to weave lover's knot pattern,[28]
悶繡先描連理枝	depressed in embroidery she first depicts branches twined together.
多少風流詞句裏	From among all those lines of love poems,
愁中空詠蚤環詩	in melancholy she simply sings the poem on the "louse ring."[29]

We have quoted here the first five of seven quatrains. Thousand-year-old wit does not survive well in translation. Although the quatrain in the long line has a witty, discursive element, the in-group references, both decipherable and indecipherable, recall Li Shangyin. In the final poem the woman—presumably a singing girl—at last wins her lover. Although we will probably never know what her skill in cutting a "belly wrapper" suggests, Wen Tingyun's response is of some interest:

---

26. This echoes an old *yuefu* story in which Wang Min of the Jin gave his sister-in-law's maid a round fan. The sister-in-law beat the maid. Wang Min stopped her, and on command the maid sang a "round-fan" song. Here it simply means the girl's lover.

27. This is an obscure verse. The last line refers to the beauty of Luofu in *Moshang sang*, a beauty such that young men would take off their hats and show their headbands. What this has to do with the woman's "belly wrapper" in the preceding line is unclear. Perhaps it is to conceal her pregnancy.

28. No one really understands the *ju* 苣 here, except that it is based on a line from *Yutai xinyong* and refers to some brocade pattern suggesting union of lovers.

29. The poet is here punning on "come back soon," *zao huan* 早還.

溫庭筠, 答段柯古見嘲
Wen Tingyun, Answering Duan Chengshi's Teasing[30]

彩翰殊翁金繚繞	Bright plumage, rare gorge-feathers, wound about with gold,
一千二百逃飛鳥	one thousand two hundred birds fled the world in flight.[31]
尾生橋下未爲癡	Master Wei below the bridge was not acting like a fool:[32]
暮雨朝雲世間少	twilight rain, the clouds of dawn are rare in this mortal world.

The opening lines evoke the legendary case of the number of women who were lovers of the Yellow Emperor, but their apotheosis seems to have permanently diminished the possibility of meeting such women in the mortal world. Among mortals passionate devotion is not a foolish thing precisely because sexual encounters (or those of a quality that match the king of Chu's meeting with the goddess of Wu Mountain) are rare. The sexual "clouds and rain" is cleverly linked to the rising flood that eventually drowns Master Wei. The poem is indeed a jeu d'esprit, but the latter can often be revealing. It we take the statement seriously, it complicates the conventional image of Wen as a rake (in contrast to Du Mu, who does indeed sometimes play the rake). Wen Tingyun's answer has a place in the Tang culture of romance. This is not to suggest that he loved a single woman all his life but rather that he believed both in a depth of attachment and the rarity of mutual passion. This more perfectly matches the values in his poetry than the anecdotes of Wen as a rake.[33]

We are far closer here to Li Shangyin's poetry of passionate attachment than to the craftsmen of regulated verse in the short line, or even

---

30. 32175; Zeng 203.

31. The reference is to the twelve hundred women who achieved immortality because the Yellow Emperor had intercourse with them.

32. The reference is to the story in the *Zhuangzi* in which Master Wei agreed to meet a girl under a bridge. The girl didn't show up. Although the stream waters were rising, Wei remained in place and drowned.

33. It would, of course, be possible to take the opening couplet as boasting of the number of his own lovers and the second couplet as teasing Duan Chengshi: "But for a Master Wei staying under the bridge is not actually foolish, / For him twilight rains, the clouds of dawn are few in the mortal world."

to the *fengliu* regulated verse in the long line of the mid-840s. Those fashions still lived on. The poetic heirs of Jia Dao and Yao He were still prolific, and poets like Liu Cang 劉滄 had made the regulated verse in the long line a specialty. Wen Tingyun himself wrote with distinction in both forms. It is perhaps a mistake to see in this group of poets active in the provinces—none of whom had particularly distinguished themselves in the world of poetry—signs of changes in taste in the second half of the 850s; but through Li Shangyin and, to a lesser degree, Wen Tingyun this sumptuous, allusive style would come to virtually define the Late Tang. The anecdotes say that "Wen and Li were famous in the age," but such claims always beg the questions "when?" and "for whom?" Li Shangyin was clearly not one of the more famous poets during his lifetime, and by the second half of the 850s Wen Tingyun seems to have gained far more notoriety for his behavior than for his poetry. Neither Wen nor Li is often mentioned in the rather large body of comment on poetry in the second half of the ninth century. Perhaps Zhang Wei's 張爲 *Shiren zhuke tu* 詩人主客圖 dating from the end of the century is incomplete, but neither Wen nor Li appear in its extensive list of poets, primarily drawn from the late eighth and ninth centuries. It is perhaps best to understand the phenomenon of "Wen and Li" as reflecting the taste of a certain group, probably established in the 850s, and continuing among a minority—even "underground" popularity—into the tenth century, when this poetry ultimately found a community that fully appreciated it.

We do have some standard displays of gorgeous description that were probably included in the *Hanshang tijin ji*, particularly the three sets of poems on the local custom of burning the vegetation on nearby mountains during the Lantern Festival, with a prose preface by Duan Chengshi.[34] It is clear, however, that the collection contained a great deal of shared poetic play, including many teasing poems, *chao* 嘲, like the poems cited above—often with replies. Although teasing was not absent in exchanges in the Bai Juyi group, this collection, with topics such as brawling singing girls, seems to have preserved a peculiar kind of sophisticated poetic play.

---

34. These have been collected in Jia Jinhua, *Tangdai jihui zongji yu shirenqun yanjiu*, 442–43.

Biography and Reputation

Almost a century of painstaking scholarship has determined that Wen Tingyun, the third major figure of Late Tang poetry after Li Shangyin and Du Mu, was born between 798 and 824.[35] Many dates between those two extremes have been proposed and strongly advocated. Such variance of opinion, which spreads the possible dates for Wen's birth across more than a quarter of a century, calls into question the utility of attempts at biographical precision in the absence of clear and unambiguous testimony. Unlike many of the most famous mid-ninth-century poets, Wen Tingyun is given short biographies in both the *Old Tang History* and the *New Tang History*. However, as Fu Xuancong notes, these "biographies" are a patchwork of anecdotal sources, with the few shreds of biographical fact sandwiched between gossip and good stories. Wen's perceived importance in the history of the song lyric (*ci*) has invited intense scrutiny of his life by scholars. Instead of arriving at reassuring certainties, however, both the degree of attention involved and the resulting variable conclusions force us to question the usual procedures of biographical research and make us wonder about the conclusions drawn in the biographies of less well studied poets.[36]

A partial consensus places Wen's birth around 801, which would make the poet at least fifty-seven according to Chinese reckoning in those Duan Chengshi poems teasing Wen about his amorous adventures. If Wen were then fifty-seven, we would expect some reference to his age in the poems, and yet there is none. If we suppose that Wen was born later, a 200-line *pailü* explicitly dated to 840 makes 824 the latest imaginable date for Wen's birth. On the most basic level, if we think in terms of generations, we really don't know to which generation Wen Tingyun belongs.

We can, however, establish a few things with certainty. We know that he took but did not pass the *jinshi* examination. As was mentioned

---

35. For the various dating proposals, see Fu (1987), vol. 3, 444–45. See also Zhang Yanjin 1104–5.

36. A case in point involves the number of men surnamed Li who served as "Vice Director" of the Department of State Affairs across a span of two decades. A poem addressed to "Vice Director Li" has been used to date Wen's birth—but there are many other candidates. When Wen writes to "Drafter Du" 杜舍人, does that mean he knew Du Mu?

earlier, we can date one poem securely to 840. He may have been a companion of Wenzong's Crown Prince Zhuangke in the late 830s, but the inferences here are less certain. We are reasonably certain that he was involved in the examination scandal of 855. We can also place him in Xiangyang between 857 and 859. We know that he held a post as district defender and that he served as instructor in the Directorate of Education. Although we know he traveled widely, the dates assigned to some travels are far from certain. Fu Xuancong places his death around 866. We do not, however, know when he was writing the poetry for which he is now best known, namely, the song lyrics and the *yuefu*.

Apart from these few facts—none of which are enough to constitute a "biography"—everything else involves escapades, anecdotal material that may or may not have some basis in fact, but within which fact is beyond recovery. Such a preponderance of anecdotes leads us to believe that Wen Tingyun was indeed a bit of a rake—though anecdotes feed on previous anecdotes, and a rake's reputation often far exceeds his actual experiences. Perhaps he did indeed have his teeth knocked out by the night watchman after a night of carousing. Far more significant than the truth may be his inclusion in the "Biographies of Men of Letters" in the *Old Tang History*, presented to the Later Jin throne in 945. In hindsight, the succeeding century considered him the representative of one imagined version of the mid-ninth-century "poet," while many other less sensational poets were overlooked.

In literary history it is important to slow down and look at decades, quarter-centuries, and half-centuries in varying locales and groups. More often than not, this simply reveals insignificant shifts in reputation based on partial evidence. However, there are also crucial moments in which texts are diminished or foregrounded and reputations are made or lost—often for reasons that are grounded in the specificities of a particular historical moment. In the late ninth and tenth centuries, at the very edge of print culture and the new literary scholarship of the early eleventh century, manuscripts that were often copied had a better chance of survival. Du Mu was indeed fairly prominent in the mid-ninth century and remained so. There is little indication that Wen Tingyun and Li Shangyin were particularly prominent in the 840s and 850s. As was mentioned earlier, somewhat later (871) Pi Rixiu referred to Wen in conjunction with Li Shangyin as being the "best," *zui* 最, in the age (see p. 335), but this is a single reference in an age when other poets were far more celebrated. What seems likely is that Wen Tingyun and Li Shangyin were admired in certain circles and that the conjunction of "Wen and Li" gradually became more established over the course of the latter part of the ninth century.

Apart from his friends in Xiangyang, the only people in the community of poets with whom he had certain contact were Li Shangyin and the rather obscure Li Yuan 李遠. He wrote a companion piece to a poem by Zhao Gu, but we don't know whether he knew Zhao Gu or was "matching from afar." Li Shangyin has a poem addressed to Wen, and a poem under Wen's name to Li Shangyin was preserved in *Wenyuan yinghua*, but it is not in his regular collection.[37] In short, Wen's general isolation from contemporary poetic communities is nothing short of remarkable.

Wen Tingyun emerges to documented prominence in the tenth century in Chengdu, where a very special regional culture had arisen. That sophisticated elite culture of the two Shu kingdoms of Sichuan has given us not only the first anthology of song lyrics in irregular lines (*ci*), the *Huajian ji* 花間集, but it also produced the largest extant anthology of Tang poetry before the Song, the *Caidiao ji* 才調集, in which Wen Tingyun was the second most fully represented poet. (He is also very well represented in the *Huajian ji.*) As we noted earlier, Li Shangyin was also well represented in that anthology, though not as extensively as Wen. The Tang poet with the largest number of poems in *Caidiao ji* is Wei Zhuang 韋莊 (836–910), who emigrated to Chengdu in 901 and became a foundational figure in Shu culture of the Five Dynasties. Wei Zhuang's much smaller anthology of Tang poetry, *Further Mystery* 又玄集, also represents Wen Tingyun on the same level as Du Mu.

What this suggests is that as Wen Tingyun's anecdotal reputation as a rake grew toward the end of the ninth century (perhaps combined with a body of his lyrics in singers' repertoires), his poetry acquired greater cachet, particularly among the sophisticated elite of Chengdu, who appreciated sensual poetry. (The particular selections in the *Caidiao ji* as well as the lyrics in *Huajian ji* attest to this.) Chengdu was also one of the most important centers of early printing and was spared the devastation that occurred in many areas in the Five Dynasties. Poetry

---

37. The companion piece to Du Mu's "Huaqing Palace" has been shown to be by Zhang Hu.

popular there consequently had a particular advantage in terms of survival.

Although Wen's poetry collection survived, apart from a few famous regulated verses it did not attract particular attention in the Song. The compilers of *Wenyuan yinghua* had some version of Wen Tingyun's collection and there were copies of different collections or versions of collections in imperial and private libraries. With the exception of the famous regulated verses and couplets, it was a poetry without impact, in striking contrast to the growing prominence of Li Shangyin. It was Wen's position in the song lyric tradition that brought attention back to (and perhaps ensured the preservation of) his poetry collection.

The Collection

In the case of Wen Tingyun's collection, we are faced with the complex question of how Tang poetry circulated before the major scholarly projects of the eleventh century, in which so many Tang literary collections were put together in the basic form we now have them. Forms of circulation have significant consequences for preservation, and a systematically skewed pattern of preservation can, in turn, have consequences for our image and understanding of both individual poets and the period as a whole. In the case of Li Shangyin, we have seen that the most widely available early short versions of the collection seem to have focused on the hermetic poems, the poems on history, the poems on things, and social jeux d'esprit. We would now have a very different image of Li Shangyin had it not been for Yang Yi's exceptional devotion to gathering all his works, which was particularly effective thanks to his extensive network of friends and his social and political prominence.

Although complete poetry collections of individual poets were sometimes in circulation, Tang poetry seems to have circulated primarily in smaller anthologies of a poet's work.[38] From the early ninth century we begin to see subcollections—in effect, books of poetry devoted to a particular type or on a particular topic—circulating in an author's lifetime.[39]

---

38. For a detailed study of the circulation of poetry in the Tang, see Christopher Nugent, *The Circulation of Poetry in Tang Dynasty China* (Ann Arbor, Mich.: UMI, 2004).

39. We can find isolated examples of this before the ninth century, but nothing comparable to the scale of subcollections in the ninth century.

One example involves collections of exchange poems, which first appeared in the last part of the eighth century but grew in size and frequency in the ninth century. The poets of "new *yuefu*" 新樂府 circulated these works as small collections, which were included in Yuan Zhen's and Bai Juyi's "collected works." Anna Shields has published an important article in which she discusses Yuan Zhen's *Yanshi* 艷詩, which eventually circulated independently and are not included in the current version of Yuan's "collected works" (whether through deliberate omission or loss of parts of the collection).[40] As was mentioned earlier, Wang Jian's "Palace Lyrics" circulated independently, as did Cao Tang's "Smaller Wandering Immortal Poems" in all likelihood. Here we see two phenomena that should be considered together: first, the independent circulation of poems of a particular kind in a subcollection; and, second, the intervention of authors or early (i.e., Tang) editors of poetry collections, who selected only part of a poet's complete oeuvre to serve as the "poetry collection." The publication of poetry in the ninth and tenth centuries had certain characteristics that distinguish it from earlier—and sometimes later—practice: earlier collections comprised the entire "literary remains"; eleventh-century and later editing practice also gives us the entire "literary remains" (making a generic exclusion of song lyrics, *ci*).[41] In the ninth century, however, a "poetry collection," *shiji* 詩集, seems to have been a narrower bibliographical genre that might often exclude material of specialized collections. Anyone who has worked extensively with Late Tang poetry has seen traces of this, both in bibliography and what has survived. We have the surviving works of poets that are made up almost entirely of occasional poems (sometimes with a few very tame *yuefu*). We have the surviving works of other poets that are entirely or largely devoted to a single topic or represent one type of poetry. We have seen this phenomenon

---

40. See Anna M. Shields, "Defining Experience: The 'Poems of Seductive Allure' (*yanshi*) of the Mid-Tang Poet Yuan Zhen (779–831)," *Journal of the American Oriental Society* 122, no. 1 (Jan.–March 2002): 61–78. Li Kuo 李廓, who was mentioned earlier as a poet of the Jia Dao circle and as someone who probably met with approval in Wenzong's proposal for Academicians of Poetry, survives primarily in poems about young rakes and those on *yuefu* topics. The explanation is that he survives because he was anthologized in *Caidiao ji*.

41. We do, however, also see some subcollections circulating in the Song and author-edited collections that omit things.

earlier in Li Shen's *Recalling Past Travels*, and there are many other examples one could cite. Zhao Gu has a collection distinct from his "poetry collection," called *Biannian shi* 編年詩, with a poem on each of the hundred years of human life, with examples drawn primarily from history.[42] Hu Ceng 胡曾 has a collection of quatrains exclusively devoted to historical topics and organized chronologically. Wanting to show only his most sternly Confucian face, young Pi Rixiu compiled the *Pizi wensou* 皮子文藪, including both prose and poetry; the preservation of his later work in more standard occasional forms depends primarily on the pieces written with Lu Guimeng, included in Lu's *Songling ji* 松陵集. Toward the end of the ninth century we have a collection of sensual verses called *Xianglian ji* 香奩集, attributed to Han Wo 韓偓 (844–after 914) and circulated independently of Han Wo's regular poetry collection, which consisted of occasional poems in a very different tone.[43] In the cases of Pi Rixiu and Han Wo, if we had only one of the venues in which their poems were preserved, it would give a very skewed and incomplete image of the poet.

It is essential to bear in mind that the issue here is one of different manuscripts that survived into the Song, some of which were partially copied into Song compilations while others of which entered the lineage of print culture in their entirety. Some manuscripts were "poetry collections" (sometimes large, but often *xiaoji*), while others were specialized collections. In the case of Cao Tang, the scattered remnants of his occasional poems have been re-collected from early anthology sources. However, the "Smaller Wandering Immortal Poems" 小遊仙詩 contains only a few pieces in early anthology sources, suggesting that it was preserved separately, to be copied into *Wanshou Tangren jueju*.

This brings us to the case of Wen Tingyun, where perhaps bibliographical accident gives us a suggestive image of how different manuscript sources may have contributed to the gradual formation of a poet's "complete works." Our current version of Wen's poetry collection is in nine *juan*, of which the first seven were "original," with two added later. The first two *juan* consist of Wen Tingyun's remarkable

---

42. The preface and ages 1 to 28 have been preserved in the Dunhuang manuscripts. See Xu Jun 522–34.

43. Han Wo's authorship has been contested, but this suggests why such collections circulated separately.

yuefu in the manner of Li He. The next five *juan* begin with a few more rather conservative *yuefu* but are for the most part conventional occasional poems that are remarkably similar to other "poetry collections" of the era. As Paul Rouzer has noted, this is the side of Wen Tingyun that is typical of the various kinds of poetry common in the middle of the century. The two supplementary *juan* (8–9) include poems attributed to Wen from other sources. Significantly, in the ninth *juan* we find the strange and witty exchange pieces taken from the *Hanshang tijin ji*. These are stylistically distinct from the poems preserved in the "main" collection and were clearly not included when it was compiled. Here we have clear evidence of the segregation of poetry according to type.[44] Since the *Hanshang tijin ji* was widely known and readily available, we can see that the compiler of the "original" poetry collection was not trying to include all of Wen's poetry. (The exclusion of the song lyrics from the collection is discussed below.)

Turning to the early bibliographical notices, we note that Wen Tingyun has an unusual number of works listed under his name in the "Bibliography" of the *New Tang History*: a *Wolan ji* 握蘭集 in three *juan*, a *Jinquan ji* 金荃集 in ten *juan*; a *shiji* 詩集 ("poetry collection") in five *juan*; and a *Hannan zhen gao* 漢南眞稿 in ten *juan*. In the "Bibliography" these works are listed among complete literary works (that is, including prose as well as poetry) rather than among poetry collections. This indicates that at least one of these collections consisted of Wen's prose or included prose. The question arises as to what these different titles represent. Considering Wen's fame as a parallel prose stylist and composer of poetic expositions, we would expect a substantial prose collection. It is unclear, however, which title would contain his prose. The title of *Hannan zhen gao* refers to his period in Xiangyang; this may have been restricted to works composed during his residence in Xiangyang, or it may simply mark where he was living when he compiled the collection. The *Jinquan ji* is mentioned in the preface to the *Huajian ji* as a collection of song lyrics. We discuss below the problematic relation between this collection and Wen Tingyun's extant song lyrics (*ci*).

---

44. Even if Wen Tingyun or his literary executor did not include the poems from the *Hanshang tijin ji* on the grounds that they had already been included in that collection, it is highly unlikely that Wen did not write other poems in that playful, witty style. In other words, there is an aesthetic ideology that governed the initial formation of the "poetry collection."

As was noted earlier, in the current version of Wen's poetry (that is, the seven *juan* of the "original" version) there are exactly five *juan* of conventional poetry, which precisely corresponds to the five *juan* "poetry collection" *shiji* 詩集 in the "Bibliography." We are left with two *juan* of *yuefu* songs and a title of a collection, the *Wolan ji* 握蘭集 in three *juan*.[45] It is not unreasonable to assume that the *yuefu* songs originally circulated in a separate manuscript and were added to the beginning of the "poetry collection" in the Song, when the generic structure of poetry collections assumed a normative form, according to which *yuefu* and stanzaic songs, regardless of mode or subject matter, would be placed at or toward the beginning of a collection.

There are other reasons to suspect that the *yuefu* and stanzaic songs in Li He's style circulated independently. Although a number of these are included in *Caidiao ji*, none are included in the immense *Wenyuan yinghua* compiled at the end of the tenth century. Since *Wenyuan yinghua* did include *yuefu* and songs by Li He himself, the probable explanation for the absence of such pieces by Wen Tingyun is that the compilers in the capital did not have access to Wen's *yuefu*—though a copy did exist in Chengdu.

If Wen's *yuefu* had been included in *Wenyuan yinghua*, they would not have been in the "poetry" section. *Wenyuan yinghua* diverges from its *Wen xuan* model by creating a category of "songs," *gexing* 歌行, distinct from "poetry," *shi* 詩. These are generally not "old *yuefu*" but rather new songs to Tang titles. In this relatively early period, the mature generic system, in which "songs" and *yuefu* are always treated as a subset of the general category "poetry," had not yet ossified.[46]

Although we have no way of knowing with certainty if Wen Tingyun's *yuefu* songs did indeed circulate independently of his "poetry collection," we do know that his song lyrics in irregular meters did so, as did his clever exchange poems composed in Xiangyang. Certainly not all the *yuefu* songs are "sensual." There are also songs on history from

---

45. *Wolan*, literally "clutching the orchid," has strong *Chuci* associations. Recall that Du Mu filiated Li He's poetry to the *Chuci* tradition. Although grammatically different in form—the two titles should not be read as exactly parallel—the *quan* 荃 of *Jinquan ji* also has *Chuci* associations and, indeed, is used in parallel with *lan*, "orchid" (thoroughwort) in the *Li Sao*.

46. We see this in the "Bibliography" of the *New Tang History*, where the collections of Liu Yanshi 劉言史 and Zhang Bi 張碧 are given as their "songs."

which moral lessons could be drawn. The segregation, if it ever existed, could simply have been according to "type." However, even the history poems have a daring and allure that are outside the scope of the usual occasional poems and the blander *yuefu* that seem to have been part of the "poetry collection."

The case of Wen Tingyun, together with many other supporting hints elsewhere in ninth-century poetry, raises the following possibility that is admittedly speculative but of considerable significance. The proliferation of subcollections facilitated poetic experimentation in diverse directions. The poet who planned to edit his own collection could maintain a certain degree of control over how he would be represented to posterity by excluding certain kinds of material. The Wen Tingyun of the first two *juan* of *yuefu* or the poems from the *Hanshang tijin ji* is unimaginable based solely on the graceful, conservative verse of the five-*juan* "poetry collection."

At the same time, the incipient segregation of poetic production into conservative "poetry collections" and less conservative subcollections may have skewed our understanding of the poetry of the period. The survival of manuscripts into the Song was a function of popularity and accident. Sometimes particular subcollections have survived, while the poet's more normative work has been lost except for chance survivals in anthologies. In other cases we see only the normative "poetry collection" and wonder what else the poet might have written "on the side." Although we are limited by the poetic corpus that survives, we can at least see how the vagaries of survival may have shaped what we know.

The Chen Palace

While the majority of the poems in the core five *juan* of Wen Tingyun's "poetry collection" treat standard occasions of social poetry, some share themes with the *yuefu* songs. (We find a scattering of such poems in the poetry collections of other poets as well.) A good example is found in the dawn excursions, together with his palace ladies, of the Last Ruler of Chen. We previously discussed Li Shangyin's version of this same historical scene, citing the opening stanzas of Wen Tingyun's poem "The Song of Cockcrow Locks" (see pp. 418–19), which is the first poem in the collection. Here we return to Wen Tingyun's song in its entirety and compare it with a treatment in regulated verse in the short line from the core *juan* that probably represent the "poetry collection."

温庭筠, 雞鳴埭歌
Wen Ting-yun, The Song of Cockcrow Locks[47]

南朝天子射雉時	When the Southern Dynasties Emperor went off to shoot pheasants,
銀河耿耿星參差	the Silver River was sparkling, its stars unevenly strewn.
銅壺漏斷夢初覺	The dripping ceased from the jug of bronze,[48] it was then they first woke from dream,
寶馬塵高人未知	from jeweled horses the dust rose high, and others never knew.
魚躍蓮東蕩宮沼	The fish leapt east of the lotuses, making waves on palace pools,[49]
濛濛御柳懸棲鳥	in the hazy imperial willows hung roosting birds.
紅妝萬户鏡中春	Rouge in ten thousand windows,[50] spring within a mirror,
碧樹一聲天下曉	a single sound through sapphire trees and all the world turned dawn.
盤踞勢窮三百年	Its force, crouching and coiling,[51] after three centuries gone;
朱方殺氣成愁煙	the southland's atmosphere of killing became melancholy mist.[52]

---

47. 31871; Zeng 1. This spot, outside the Southern Dynasties capital of Jiankang, was so named because Emperor Wu of the Southern Qi would often set out early, accompanied by his court ladies, to hunt pheasants on Mount Zhong. Just as he was passing this embankment, the cock would crow, announcing the arrival of dawn.

48. The reference is to the water clock.

49. The reference is to an old *yuefu* entitled 江南 "Jiangnan," which was the region of Jiankang.

50. The "ten thousand windows" (or "doors") was a conventional synecdoche for the imperial palace.

51. The famous Shu minister Zhuge Liang described Jiankang (then Jianye, the capital of the enemy state of Wu) in terms of two of its prominent topographical features: Mount Zhong was a "dragon coiling" and the fortress hill known as The Rock was a "tiger crouching."

52. The "southland" is literally the "red direction." The "atmosphere of killing" represents the martial vigor of the Southland, which had deteriorated over the three centuries of rule by the Southern Dynasties.

彗星拂地浪連海	Comets brushed the earth,[53] 　　waves stretched across the seas,
戰鼓渡江塵漲天	drums of battle crossed the Yangzi, 　　dust flooded the heavens.
繡龍畫雉填宮井	Embroidered dragon and painted phoenix 　　stuffed the palace well,[54]
野火風驅燒九鼎	Wildfires, driven by winds, 　　burned the Nine Tripods.[55]
殿巢江燕砌生蒿	Its palaces offered nests for river swallows, 　　the stone steps grew with weeds,
十二金人霜炯炯	upon the twelve statues of bronze 　　the frost was sparking.[56]
芊綿平綠臺城基	A continuous stretch of level green 　　on the Taicheng's foundations,[57]
暖色春容荒古陂	the warm colors of the face of spring 　　run riot on the ancient dike.
寧知玉樹後庭曲	Who would have thought that the song 　　of jade trees in the rear courtyard
留待野棠如雪枝	would last on until the branches 　　of crabapples were like snow?[58]

---

53. Comets were a sign of military troubles and, in particular, of barbarian incursions. The reference may be to Hou Jing, whose rebellion overthrew the Liang Dynasty; but the following lines clearly refer to the Sui conquest of the south.

54. The "embroidered dragon" refers to the robes of the emperor, while the painted phoenix refers to the empress's robe. When Sui troops entered Jiankang, the Last Ruler of the Chen hid in the palace well with his two favorite concubines.

55. The ancient Nine Tripods are here a figure for the continued blessing of Heaven to rule, a blessing that the Chen lost.

56. After unifying China, the First Emperor melted all the captured weapons and cast them into twelve large statues that stood in front of the Qin place in Xianyang.

57. The Taicheng was the palace compound of Jiankang, now overgrown with vegetation.

58. The Last Ruler of the Chen was famous for his song "On Jade Tree Flowers in the Rear Courtyard," whose sensual preoccupation was understood as a sign that his dynasty would not endure. In the ruins of the Taicheng palace compound of Jiankang, the crabapples continue to produce such blossoms.

温庭筠, 陳宮詞
Wen Tingyun, Chen Palace Lyrics[59]

雞鳴人草草	The cock crows, people bustling,
香輦出宮花	scented palanquins emerge from palace flowers.
伎語細腰轉	Singers talk, slender waists turn,
馬嘶金面斜	horses whinny, golden foreheads aslant.
早鶯隨綵仗	Early orioles follow pikes' bright bunting,
驚雉避凝笳	startled pheasants flee the long notes of oboes.
淅瀝湘風外	Beyond the whishing wind from the Xiang,
紅輪映曙霞	red wheels half hidden in morning rose cloud.

On the surface the comparison between these two versions might be other than what one would expect. The song tells the story of the exhaustion of the Chen and its fall, with the natural scene enduring, as in so many "meditations on the past." The regulated verse has the imperial entourage disappearing off into the clouds, without any hint of the doom that hangs over them. By comparison, Li Shangyin's versions seem to imply judgment. This is only the surface comparison, however, and its inversion tells us much about the weight of poetic form. For all its interest in simply "picturing" the scene, the regulated verse is stiff. As in ordinary occasional poems, pattern triumphs over "content." The poem can almost serve as a touchstone of how regulated parallelism can efface the particular associations of its components. The female entertainers are not seductive but rather festively chattering, a sound that is playfully set against the whinnying of the horses. Their turning waists are not part of a dance but rather the parallel of the slanting horses' foreheads. Parallelism integrates all particulars into a balanced whole. Some birds follow, while others flee (recalling that in the song this is a pheasant hunt): sound matches color. At last the whole noisy, brightly colored entourage is swallowed up in colored clouds.

In the *yuefu* song the doom that hangs over the Chen intensifies its allure, its heedless pleasure. In the regulated verse we at least have women's waists and chatter, whereas in the song the women are represented only by the color of makeup reflected in a mirror and robes in the well. In place of the single scene of the regulated verse, placed onstage and then covered over by colored clouds, we have a series of

---

59. 31948; Zeng 68.

moments in which the sensual scenes acquire pathos through imminent loss.

If the Last Ruler of Chen's excursions are formalized and displaced in the regulated verse, we might press one stage further, in which the Last Ruler returns in an occasional poem, not in person but somehow embodied in what was apparently an architectural representation on a screen.

溫庭筠, 和友人溪居別業

Wen Tingyun, A Companion Piece for a Friend's "Villa Lodging by a Stream"[60]

積潤初銷碧草新	Gathered moisture begins to evaporate, the emerald grasses fresh,
鳳陽晴日帶雕輪	sun in clear sky, phoenix-light, lines finely wrought wheels.
絲飄弱柳平橋晚	Floss tosses on pliant willows, the level bridge late in day,
雪點寒梅小院春	snow dots the wintry plums, spring in the small garden.
屏上樓臺陳後主	Terrace and tower upon the screen, the Last Ruler of Chen;
鏡中金翠李夫人	gold and kingfisher in a mirror, Lady Li of the Han.
花房露透紅珠落	To the flower calyx the dew gets through, beads of red fall,
峽蝶雙雙護粉塵	and butterflies in their pairs guard the fragrant dust.

In this characteristically idyllic representation of what must be a friend's villa, we see a strange transfer of imperial pleasures to the pleasures of the villa in representations on flat surfaces. The first flat surface, the painted screen, apparently contains a scene of palaces, which Wen takes as those of the Last Ruler. The parallel flat surface of representation is a mirror, in which Lady Li appears, bringing sensual figures of the past into the present—perhaps in the form of the friend's beautiful favorite. From the reappearance of Lady Li we move to the closely focused scene of the seventh line, whose images have distinctly sexual overtones.

---

60. 31988; Zeng 91. Several variants of the title exist, none of them satisfying.

Li He's Legacy

Li Shangyin's poetry already showed the influence of reading Li He in the first half of the 830s. We do not know when Wen Tingyun wrote his two *juan* of *yuefu* songs.[61] Wen, however, was a very different reader of Li He. Li Shangyin absorbed the "lesson of Li He" and pressed it further than Li He ever had. In doing so, he pushed beyond the poetics of "art"—which is how Li Shangyin himself had described Li He's work—into a poetics of putative biographical reference. At some point poetic "difficulty" can suggest concealment. In this respect Wen Tingyun was more conservative. Few would choose to read his *yuefu* as cryptic references to his private life (in part because of the nature of the titles Wen chose, which appealed to a *yuefu* tradition), though the general aura of sensuality clung to Wen's reputation like dirty clothes. Wen Tingyun also pressed his model, albeit in other directions.

We may have Wen Tingyun's *yuefu* tribute to Li He thanks to particular accidents of valuation and transmission, but Wen's *yuefu* remain among the most striking and distinctive poems of the Late Tang. Paul Rouzer has roughly divided them into sections on traditions of "palace poetry" (shading over into poetry on immortals) and pieces on historical figures. Du Mu had commented on Li He's pleasure in finding and poetically rendering hitherto unnoticed moments in history—as well as more common ones. Wen Tingyun also picks out small moments in the *yuefu* tradition and legend. Both the scenes of women and the historical pieces are unified by a common style: fragmentary images or "montage," to use Rouzer's term. The fractured images of regulated verse and quatrains, bound to habitual parallel structures and habits of exposition, acquired an entirely different effect when translated into longer song forms.

As was mentioned earlier, Li He actually has relatively few erotic poems credited to him, but the particular sensuality of his poetry somehow strongly suggested eroticism to Li Shangyin and Wen Tingyun,

---

61. If, as Fu Xuancong argues, Wen Tingyun was born around 801, he would have been older than Li Shangyin and his *yuefu* could well have been contemporary with Li Shangyin's early work. It cannot be proven, but I suspect Wen was younger than Li Shangyin and that his *yuefu* were composed around the middle of the ninth century.

who were among his Late Tang readers. If we set a Li He banquet song beside one by Wen Tingyun, we can see that Wen has captured the intensity but has eroticized it far beyond Li He.

李賀, 將進酒

Li He, Bring in the Wine[62]

琉璃鐘	In goblets of lapis lazuli,
琥珀濃	an amber dark and strong,
小槽酒滴眞珠紅	from small casks the wine dribbles forth 　　in pearls of red.
烹龍炮鳳玉脂泣	Stewing dragon, roasting phoenix 　　weep tears of jade fat;[63]
羅幬繡幕圍香風	mesh curtains and broidered arrases 　　enclose aromatic breeze.
吹龍笛	Blow dragon fifes,
擊鼉鼓	strike lizard-skin drums,
皓齒歌	gleaming teeth sing,
細腰舞	frail waists dance.
況是青春日將暮	Now most of all in green spring, 　　with the sun about to set,
桃花亂落如紅雨	and a tumult of peach blossoms falling, 　　like a rain of red.
勸君終日酩酊醉	I urge you to spend this whole day through 　　reeling drunk,
酒不到劉伶墳上土	for wine will never reach the soil 　　on the grave of Liu Ling.[64]

Li He, writing against Li Bai's *yuefu* with the same title, includes the women dancers only as a necessary part of the feast: pleasure is desperate and shadowed by mortality. When Li He writes about women, as in "Pearl, the Fair Maid of Luoyang" 洛姝眞珠, the eroticism is much dreamier. Wen Tingyun scales erotic frenzy into the limits of the night: personal mortality is no longer an issue.

---

62. 20854; Ye (1959) 303.

63. Most commentators stress that the weeping is the sound of the fat crackling, though the visual image of beads of fat oozing out would seem to be more appropriate.

64. Liu Ling was a third-century eccentric who was known as a great drinker.

溫庭筠, 夜宴謠
Wen Tingyun, Song of the Night Banquet[65]

長釵墜髮雙蜻蜓	Long hairpins, trailing tresses, 　　paired dragonflies,
碧盡山斜開畫屏	sapphire ends, hills slant, 　　a painted screen spread open.
虬須公子五侯客	Lordlings with bushy whiskers, 　　retainers of the Five Counts,
一飲千鐘如建瓴	a thousand flagons drunk steadily 　　like rainspouts.
鶯咽姹唱圓無節	Lasses with nightingale throats sing 　　to perfection with no rhythm beaten,
眉斂湘煙袖回雪	brows draw in Xiang River mist, 　　their sleeves swirl snow.
清夜恩情四座同	Tender passions in the clear night 　　shared by all the guests,
莫令溝水東西別	let the moat waters never part, 　　turning east or west.
亭亭蠟淚香珠殘	Candles straight and tall whose tears 　　are fragrant pearls fading,
暗露曉風羅幕寒	unseen dew, the morning wind, 　　gossamer hangings cold.
飄搖戟帶儼相次	Wind-tossed sashes from halberds 　　ordered in strict lines,
二十四枝龍畫竿	twenty-four bills, 　　the dragon-painted staffs.[66]
裂管縈弦共繰曲	Screeching pipes, strings quickly strummed 　　join in an orchestral song,
芳樽細浪傾春釀	tiny waves in the sweet-smelling cups 　　drain the spring brew.
高樓客散杏花多	From high upstairs the guests scatter, 　　apricot flowers abound,
脈脈新蟾如瞪目	and the yearning of the new toad-moon 　　is like a staring eye.

---

65. 31873; Zeng 4; Rouzer 82. See also Paul Rouzer's discussion of the poem after the translation.

66. Wen Tingyun is here describing the scene of the guards at dawn court.

In the first stanza we have the two essential groups of participants in the scene: the dancers defined by their hair and ornaments and the young aristocrats drinking. In the second line we have a painted screen, interposing itself formally between the women and men. In the second stanza, the scene of song, we have the singers as natural and merging into nature. The *wujie* 無節, the song performed "without rhythmic beat," is also "without scruple," or "without a level of restraint," the very definition of social immorality. The women singers perform nature and become nature, and the "tender passions," *enqing* 恩情, are specifically the emotions of the men toward the women. The desire never to part—echoing the voice of the woman in *Baitou yin* 白頭吟—is hard to locate specifically in either party and must be shared by both the men and the women. Here we have the makings of a failed desire for union, to become permanently attached.

The candles, of course, shed their waxen tears in foreknowledge of imminent parting, and the touch of the morning wind anticipates the end of the party. The images of the imperial guard in the second half of the third stanza may seem out of sequence, but young men like these might well be guardsmen, required to set off for their morning duties. At the beginning of the last stanza we are back at the feast—specifically the crescendo of the music and end of the feast—as the revelers drain their cups.

Passion in the performance was part of the performance. The men go their ways, and presumably the female performers go to bed. Assuming we are voyeurs, we are left with one of the strangest moments of voyeurism in the tradition: the new moon as a great eye, still staring on the emptied scene with yearning.

The "Typical" Late Tang Poet

We can never know if *juan* three through seven in Wen Tingyun's current collection made up the "poetry collection" listed in the "Bibliography" of the *New Tang History*; but to think of that segment of his poetic works as the "poetry collection" situates his work comfortably with other "poetry collections" of the period. It begins with some *yuefu* and old-style poems, then moves to regulated verse in the long line.[67] As a

---

67. The third *juan* has a few songs in the long line, but these are not stanzaic.

standard "poetry collection," it contains excellent work. However, in contrast to the stanzaic *yuefu* songs of the first two *juan*, it is not surprising poetry.

The following *yuefu* on the knight-errant from the "poetry collection" displays some of vividness and dramatic fragmentation of the stanzaic songs, but it remains a familiar type of poem, with many parallels in other poets.

溫庭筠, 俠客行

Wen Tingyun, Ballad of the Man at Arms[68]

欲出鴻都門	About to go out Hongdu Gate
陰雲蔽城闕	shadowy clouds cover the wall towers.
寶劍黯如水	His precious sword is dark as water,
微紅濕餘血	faint red, wet with remaining blood.
白馬夜頻嘶	His white horse often whinnies by night,
三更霸陵雪	the third watch, the snow of Baling.

A killing has occurred—presumably righteous revenge or righting some wrong. The compression of the verse is effective: a scene of setting out (Luoyang), an image of the sword with evidence of the killing, and a final scene of whinnying at midnight in the snow, with Baling (near Chang'an) indicating where the assassin went. By way of contrast, from the first two *juan* we cite the first stanza of "Song for the God Count Jiang" 蔣侯神歌, the guardian deity of Mount Zhong overlooking the Southern Dynasties capital at Jinling.[69]

楚神鐵馬金鳴珂	The Chu god's armored horse, its golden bangles ringing,
夜動蛟潭生素波	by night stirred in the kraken tarn producing pale waves.
商風刮水報西帝	Autumn wind scraped the waters, announcing the Western Emperor,
廟前古樹蟠白蛇	round the ancient tree before the shrine a white serpent coiled.

This is clearly a different kind of poetry altogether, not only on the level of poetic daring but also in the scenario that makes the poem cohere. The "Ballad of the Man at Arms" may be a *yuefu*, but its fragments

---

68. 31939; Zeng 63.
69. 31895; Zeng 25.

are held together by an elementary narrative conventionally associated with men at arms (sometimes translated as "knights-errant," master swordsmen who do daring deeds of righteous violence). Although it may be difficult to see, the stanza from "Song for the God Count Jiang" coheres through reference to a specific text by Li He entitled "Song for the Sword of the Proofreader in the Spring Precinct" 春坊正字劍子歌.[70] This is an imaginative though not impossibly difficult description of a sword.

先輩匣中三尺水	In this box of my elder are three feet of water
曾入吳潭斬龍子	that once entered a tarn in Wu to slay dragon-spawn.
隙月斜明刮露寒	Slanting brightness, moonlight through crack, scraped the dew cold,
練帶平鋪吹不起	sash of satin spread out flat, blown on but not rising.

We have "tarn," *tan* 潭, in the fourth position of the second line, followed in the next line by the striking use of "scraping," *gua* 刮, water or dew. The moonlight through a crack is a figure for the sword, as the "autumn wind" (literally "*shang* wind") is also the "metal wind." The Li He subtext lets us know what Count Jiang is doing in the dragon tarn in Wen Tingyun's poem: "producing pale waves" is the visible evidence that he is slaying a dragon below. The second two lines of Wen Tingyun's stanza pick up a later section of the same Li He poem. The god of the West (the "Western Emperor" or "White Emperor") is also a white serpent. Han Gaozu once slew the white serpent. At the end of Li He's poem the sword is lifted:

提出西方白帝驚	Raise it in the west, the White Emperor will be alarmed,
嗷嗷鬼母秋郊哭	his wraith-mother wailing weeps on autumn moors.

In short, the remarkable juxtapositions in Wen Tingyun's stanza are unified only through their reference to the Li He source text.

In the mid-ninth century there was something of a vogue for regulated verses on temples of popular religion, with their resident tutelary

---

70. 20659; Ye (1959) 20.

deities and dragons. Such poems would often evoke the mystery and power of the deity. They bear a relation to the stanza on Count Jiang cited above that is very similar to the relation between the regulated verse on the Last Ruler of Chen and the stanzaic song discussed earlier.

溫庭筠, 題蕭山廟
Wen Tingyun, On the Shrine on Mount Xiao[71]

故道木陰濃	Shade of trees heavy on the old road,
荒祠山影東	rundown shrine east of the hill's shadow.
杉松一庭雨	Fir and pine, a whole courtyard of rain,
幡蓋滿堂風	pennon and canopy, wind fills the hall.
客奠晚沙濕	Evening sands wet from libations of visitors,
馬嘶春廟空	a horse whinnies, the spring temple deserted.
夜深雷電歇	Deep in night thunder and lightning ceased,
龍入古潭中	and the dragon entered the ancient tarn.

The "Ballad of the Man at Arms" and "On the Shrine on Mount Xiao" are exceptions in the "poetry collection." Most poems are occasional and echo the work of more famous contemporaries both in tone and phrasing.

溫庭筠, 利州南渡
Wen Tingyun, The South Crossing at Lizhou[72]

澹然空水對斜暉	Still and empty waters face the sinking glow of the sun,
曲島蒼茫接翠微	a vast expanse of winding isles touching the azure haze.
波上馬嘶看棹去	A horse whinnies over the waves, I watch the oars depart,
柳邊人歇待船歸	beside the willows people are gone, I await the boat's return;
數叢沙草群鷗散	Several clumps of plants in the sand, a flock of gulls scatters,
萬頃江田一鷺飛	over ten thousand acres of River fields a single egret flies.

---

71. 32088; Zeng 159.
72. 31968; Zeng 80.

| 誰解乘舟尋范蠡 | Who is able to take a boat
    and seek out Fan Li?— |
| 五湖煙水獨忘機 | in misty waters on the Five Lakes
    alone free of motive. |

This is a fine example of the mid-ninth-century regulated verse in the long line. The move in contemporary poetry that is easiest to recognize is the "Fan Li" ending, in which the poet thinks of the ancient minister of Yue sailing off to become a recluse after encompassing the destruction of Wu. We have already cited two earlier examples by Zhang Hu and Du Mu (see pp. 213–15), but we could easily add another:

杜牧, 西江懷古

Du Mu, Thoughts on the Past in Westriver[73]

上吞巴漢控瀟湘	Upriver it swallows the Ba-Han region, it draws in the Xiao and Xiang,
怒似連山淨鏡光	in rage it is like linked mountains, when clear, a mirror's light.
魏帝縫囊真戲劇	The Wei Emperor's sewn bags were truly mere sport,[74]
符堅投棰更荒唐	Fu Jian's claim about tossing down his whip was even more outrageous.[75]
千秋釣艇歌明月	For a thousand autumns a fishing skiff, singing in bright moonlight,
萬里沙鷗弄夕陽	for ten thousand leagues the sand gulls play in the evening light.
范蠡清塵何寂寞	How silent the pure dust of Fan Li has become,
好風唯屬往來商	the fine breeze belongs only to merchants going back and forth.

Du Mu's is, of course, a very different poem, contrasting the might of the Yangzi with the peaceful river scene at the end. Wen Tingyun gives us only the idyllic scene, though Du Mu's gulls are still there in the evening sunshine. Du Mu may have contributed the model for Wen's "ten thousand . . . a single . . ." line:

---

73. 28143; Feng 199.

74. Wu heard a rumor that Cao Cao had ordered his troops to fill bags with sand and dump them into the Yangzi in order to block it up so that his army could cross.

75. While planning to invade the Eastern Jin, the Northern warlord Fu Jian claimed that he could cross the Yangzi as easily as throwing down his whip.

| 萬頃江田一鷺飛 | over ten thousand acres of River fields
  a single egret flies. |

The second line of Du Mu's "Drinking Alone" has something very similar, but the "ten thousand" (*wan* 萬) is "all time," *wangu* 萬古.[76]

| 長空碧杳杳 | The long sky, sapphire, faint and far, |
| 萬古一飛鳥 | for all time, a single bird in flight. |

These are all modest similarities rather than direct echoing. We may simply have an instance here of the poet recycling images and patterns that were widely shared. Du Mu's sand gulls "play in the evening light," *nong xiyang* 弄夕陽, at the end of a long line, while at "South Lake" 南湖 Wen Tingyun observes something similar:[77]

| 野船著岸偎春草 | A rustic's boat is pulled up on the shore,
  hugging the spring plants, |
| 水鳥帶波飛夕陽 | water birds line the waves
  and fly in the evening light. |

Wen Tingyun's handling of regulated verse in the long line and his preference for it suggest the poetic fashion of the late 830s, which continued throughout the 840s and into the 850s. As Rouzer notes, he also had a talent for regulated verse in the short line and the craft of the couplet. A regulated verse in the short line entitled "Traveling Early at Mount Shang" 商山早行, which is discussed extensively by Rouzer, is probably his most famous single poem.[78] His couplets, moreover, often appeared in later lists of exemplary couplets, *jutu* 句圖. The following does not explicitly declare itself to be an example of the old motif of "visiting the recluse and not finding him in," but it strongly suggests that motif in never representing Mr. Lu and in the trail that leads off into the clouds.

溫庭筠, 題盧處士居
Wen Tingyun, On the Recluse Lu's Dwelling[79]

| 西溪問樵客 | At west creek I asked the woodsman, |
| 遙識主人家 | and from afar I knew where your home was. |

---

76. 28051; Feng 85.
77. 31974; Zeng 83.
78. 32076; Zeng 155; Rouzer 18.
79. 32059; Zeng 150. Or: 處士盧岵山居.

古樹老連石   Ancient trees, stretching to rock as they age,
急泉清露沙   swift stream, so clear it shows the sands.
千峰隨雨暗   A thousand peaks darken with the rain,
一徑入雲斜   a single trail slants into clouds.
日莫鳥飛散   At twilight the birds scatter in flight,
滿山蕎麥花   and buckwheat flowers fill the mountains.

For all his talent as a lyricist and writer of stanzaic *yuefu*, it must be said
that Wen Tingyun understood the strengths of each form in which he
worked. In regulated verse in the short line he knew how to play with
pattern (for example, the twisting roots of ancient trees set in parallel
with the course of the swift stream); balance near and far, light and dark;
and constrict and extend vision. He knew how to surprise within the
limits of the craft. Consider the closing of the following dawn poem:[80]

林外晨光動   Beyond the forests dawn's rays stir,
山昏鳥滿天   mountains darken with birds filling the skies.

Dawn's light, just streaming in, is suddenly darkened by flocks of birds
taking flight.

   For whatever reason, Li Shangyin's collection entered circulation
with a significant number of poems that at least gestured toward love
affairs that were more personal than Du Mu's self-representation as a
"careless lover" in the entertainment quarters. Duan Chengshi's poems
to Wen Tingyun suggest a similar passion for a particular woman—or
women. In the "poetry collection" (as opposed to the song lyrics, the
stanzaic *yuefu*, and the material from *Hanshang tijin ji*) we find a few
pieces that suggest such attachments, though with little of the mystery
of Li Shangyin or the sensuality of Wen's own *yuefu*. The first is pre-
sented under a title only slightly less evasive than the "Left Untitled" of
Li Shangyin's collection.

温庭筠, 偶遊
Wen Tingyun, Chance Roaming[81]

曲巷斜臨一水間   A winding lane slants, looking over
                                              a stream of water,
小門終日不開關   a small gate all the day long
                                              never unbarred.

---

80. 32075; Zeng 155.
81. 31997; Zeng 95.

紅珠斗帳櫻桃熟	A small tent with red pearls,
	cherries ripe,
金尾屏風孔雀閒	screen with a golden tail,
	the phoenix at ease.
雲髻幾迷芳草蝶	A cloudlike coif almost leads astray
	butterflies in fragrant plants,
額黃無限夕陽山	forehead's yellow dot without limit
	hills in evening sunshine.
與君便是鴛鴦侶	"Since you and I, sir,
	are mandarin duck companions,
休向人間覓往還	cease your attempts to go back and forth
	in the mortal world."

This sounds like anything but a "chance roaming." The poem leads us through a city to a compound, and then to a "tent" (*zhang* 帳, sometimes a single panel of hanging fabric, sometimes an enclosure, though often without a top), evidently in the garden. The third couplet introduces a woman who issues a command to the man in the final couplet. If there was a "chance roaming," it would have to be the kind of venture that the woman is forbidding.

Although such poems are few in the "poetry collection," love, like an ancient site, becomes acceptably "poetic" in being lost and leaving only traces.

温庭筠, 懷真珠亭
Wen Tingyun, The Pavilion of Harboring a Pearl[82]

珠箔金鉤對彩橋	Beaded curtains and golden hooks
	face a brightly colored bridge,
昔年於此見嬌饒	it was right here in bygone years
	I met Jiaorao.
香燈悵望飛瓊鬢	By fragrant lantern sadly gazing,
	Feiqiong's tresses,
涼月殷勤碧玉簫	pleading in the cool moonlight,
	Sapphire's flute.
屏倚故窗山六扇	The screen lies against the old window,
	mountains in six panels,
柳垂寒砌露千條	willows hang down to cold pavements,
	a thousand branches of dew.

---

82. 32011; Zeng 102.

| 壞牆經雨蒼苔徧 | The broken walls have passed through rain, green moss grows everywhere, |
| 拾得當時舊翠翹 | and I pick up from those days an old kingfisher plume. |

The deserted place where he had been with an old lover evokes memories, like the scenes of absence in the "meditation on the past." Like Du Mu finding an old halberd near the site of Red Cliff, Wen Tingyun finally picks up a kingfisher feather of olden times.

The Song Lyrics

While the witty social poems from the *Hanshang tijin ji* and perhaps the *yuefu* were eventually incorporated into Wen Tingyun's "poetry collection" by Song editors, a corpus of about 70 allometric (*changduanju* 長短句) lyrics to known melodies were excluded from the poetry collection in its basic, pre-modern form. These verses were excluded because, from a Song point of view, they belonged to a genre, "song lyric" (*ci* 詞), that was considered distinct from "poetry." If the ninth and early tenth centuries had many kinds of subcollections, "song lyric" alone continued to circulate in subcollections in the Song. Such increasingly habitual relegation of song lyrics to subcollections was the bibliographical basis of conceiving the "song lyric" as a distinct genre.

If the song lyric became a distinct genre in the Song Dynasty, the question still remains as to how the lyrics of Wen Tingyun would have been conceived in the mid- and late ninth century. A great deal of attention has been devoted to Wen Tingyun's song lyrics because they stand (or have been placed) at the beginning of the history of song lyric. In many ways this is anachronistic, with scholars seeking the origins of a distinct genre that did not exist until much later.

These lyrics have almost all been preserved in the Chengdu anthology of song lyrics (*ci*), the *Huajian ji* 花間集 (preface 940).[83] Together with a handful of lyrics by Huangfu Song 皇甫松, Wen Tingyun's is the only substantial corpus of song lyrics dating from before the very end of the ninth century. Moreover, the preface to the *Huajian ji*

---

83. For a study of this anthology and early song lyrics in general, see Anna Shields, *Crafting a Collection: The Cultural Contexts and Poetic Practice of the* Huajian ji 花間集 *(Collection from Among the Flowers)* (Cambridge, Mass.: Harvard University Asia Center, 2006).

mentions the *Jinquan ji*, the ten-*juan* subcollection that may have been the source for Wen's song lyrics in the anthology.

We can provide several possible explanations for the sources of Wen's song lyrics and the implications, though we cannot adjudicate which explanation is the case or even most likely.

First, it is possible that the *Jinquan ji* was composed entirely of allometric song lyrics, which would have meant a corpus of around five hundred lyrics.[84] This would imply that a sense of allometric song lyric as a form distinct from other kinds of isometric song material already existed in the mid-ninth century. Although it would be anachronistic to think of this as a full-fledged genre, it would represent a distinct type of poetry appropriate for a subcollection.

Second, it is possible that the *Jinquan ji* contained many kinds of poetry considered outside the range of a mid-ninth-century "poetry collection." Ouyang Jiong, the editor of *Huajian ji*, selected the pieces that matched the contemporary interest in allometric song lyric.[85] In this case the categorical distinctness of the form would be a product of the tenth century.

Third, it is possible that the material in *Jinquan ji* was isometric, perhaps in the form that Ren Bantang calls *shengshi* 聲詩 (isometric verse to song lyric titles that later appeared as allometric). The isometric material would have been transformed by singers to suit the musical fashions of Chengdu in the tenth century and transcribed as allometric verse in *Huajian ji*. This would suggest a divergence between performance practice and transcription practice in the ninth century.

Fourth, in the preface to the *Huajian ji* Wen's *Jinquan ji* is placed in parallel to Li Bai's *Qingping yue* 清平樂, isometric quatrains that are not included in *Huajian ji*. It is possible that the *Jinquan ji* likewise contained isometric lyrics for singing, and that the allometric lyrics in the anthology came from a different source—perhaps the repertoire of singers. In this case the attribution of the lyrics to Wen Tingyun would be open to question.

---

84. There was great variation in the number of poems included in a manuscript *juan*. Northern Song bibliographical notices suggest anywhere from 25 to about 70 poems of roughly the same length per *juan*.

85. The closest parallel would be the inclusion of two lyrics to the tune *Huanxi sha* 浣溪沙 is the *Xianglian ji* 香奩集, a subcollection of erotic verse circulating separately from the regular poetry collection of the late ninth-century poet Han Wo 韓偓.

The third possibility deserves further comment. In the ninth century we encounter a fair number of isometric lyrics to tunes that were musically allometric, a fact we can infer from later occurrences. This strongly suggests that in these cases transcriptional practice and performance practice were not identical. In other words, a skilled performer could take isometric lyrics and recast them as a allometric song, or a literary man might transcribe allometric song as isometric. Although these are complicated issues that fall beyond the scope of this study, it is important to note that what is at stake in the early history of song lyric, *ci* 詞, is the possibility that written allometric lyrics represent a new transcriptional practice for allometric song rather than the emergence of a new "genre."

We will here simply observe what is known. We know from the Dunhuang manuscripts that allometric transcription probably existed in the northwestern frontier region on a semipopular level in the ninth century. There was elite allometric transcription of song in Chengdu, which was also in western China, in the first half of the tenth century. There was allometric transcription of song in the Southern Tang kingdom beginning in the mid-tenth century. From this very limited evidence it seems that allometric song transcription, not generally practiced in elite circles in the ninth century (with the possible exception of Wen Tingyun), became increasingly widespread in the tenth century.

Although in the tradition of critical writing on song lyric Wen Tingyun is most commonly compared and contrasted with Wei Zhuang, in the context of the present study we should stress that Wei Zhuang was probably writing about a half century after Wen Tingyun—and, at the very earliest, writing in a subsequent generation when the Tang world was collapsing. We should therefore think of Wen Tingyun's song lyrics in the context of mid-ninth-century poetry.

On one level Wen Tingyun's song lyrics are a veritable compendium of scenes from ninth-century romance culture, mostly representing the woman in various stages of longing for her beloved. Although Li Shangyin often wrote from the perspective of the male lover, he also wrote from the woman's perspective, with some poems marked as *dai* 代, "composed in the person of." Wen Tingyun's song lyrics subtly alternate between voyeurism and *dai*, "composed in the person of" the woman lover as type. In this context it is important to bear in mind that these lyrics were composed to be performed by a female singer, either in actuality or in one's imagination.

On another level we have the profound poetic differences that follow from genre and form. Earlier we saw how different the treatments of a Chen palace scene were in regulated verse and in *yuefu* in the Li He manner. Allometric song lyric changed the way in which the commonplace scenes of romance appeared in language. Those differences between isometric poetry and allometric song are striking examples of how shared material can become essentially different through differences of poetic form. The short lines of the song lyrics popular in this period (all "short songs," *xiaoling* 小令) pressed the paratactic, juxtaposing style of much mid-ninth-century poetry even further.

Because song lyric is generally studied in blissful generic isolation, attention is usually focused on the subtle differences among individual lyricists, often separated by several decades or even half a century.[86] Assuming a broader view reminds us of the degree to which the genre appropriated the mid-ninth-century poetic discourse of romance. Although the latter was refined over the next two centuries—with new things added, particularly motifs from popular poetry—in many ways the song lyric embalmed this discourse.

溫庭筠, 更漏子

Wen Tingyun, to "Genglouzi" (1)

柳絲長	Willow fronds long,
春雨細	spring rain fine,
花外漏聲迢遞	beyond flowers the water clock's sound in the distance.
驚塞雁	Startling the geese from the frontier,
起城烏	making crows on the city wall rise,
畫屏金鷓鴣	a painted screen with golden partridges.
香霧薄	Fragrant fog thin,
透簾幕	getting through curtains and drapes,
惆悵謝家池閣	depressing, the pool pavilion at the Xie home.
紅燭背	Red candle snuffed out,

---

86. Wen Tingyun's lyrics and the relation of early song lyric to Late Tang poetry are discussed in Shields, *Crafting a Collection*.

繡簾垂   embroidered curtains hang,
夢長君不知   the dream lasts long, but you do not know.

The reader (or listener) knows that the fine willow fronds may be fig-
ured as rain, so we do not know if this is a real or a figurative rain. The
sound of the water clock indicates that it is still dark, though the geese
and crows rising mark the transition to dawn. Suddenly we have a
nominal line that moves us inside the house to painted birds: "a painted
screen with golden partridges." The short, independent predicates of
the allometric tune pattern invite such sudden juxtapositions, which are
an effective gift of form. Critics of Wen Tingyun often comment on
the interplay between animate nature and its static representations of
nature in interiors. However, this poetic move belongs to the era. We
need only recall the fifth of Li Shangyin's "Willow Branch" poems:

畫屏繡步障   Painted screen, embroidered room divider,
物物自成雙   there every creature forms a pair.
如何湖上望   How is it gazing on the lake
只是見鴛鴦   that we only see the mandarin ducks?

Wen Tingyun uses the form for a sudden shift to an interior with
painted representations. Li Shangyin, working with the quatrain, makes
a less striking shift from interior representations to their counterparts
(or general absence thereof) in the outer world. Nevertheless, the terms
of opposition are established.

The "fragrant fog" (a borrowing from Du Fu) would immediately be
associated with a woman's hair, but the image shifts with the following
line into a real fog that gets into interiors, turning attention outward
again to the garden scene, which is "depressing"—the only term of
emotion in this lyric. The "Xie home" probably refers to "Miss Xie," a
generic name for the beloved demimondaine in Wen's lyrics and in the
poetry of romance. The reader, trained to notice seasonal markers, time
of day, and the position of the speaker, is situated somewhere between
inside and outside, late night and dawn.

Looking in again, we see the "red candle snuffed out." If the woman
had gone to bed early the night before, it would mean nothing to re-
mark on this. In such songs and poems, however, we are used to the
woman staying awake through the night. We thus take the snuffed can-
dle as indicating that the woman has recently gone to bed. The curtains
now "hanging [down]" may suggest an earlier position in which she
lifted them and looked out—to the scene earlier in the lyric.

At last we have a single line of address to a "you." Although less intense than the concluding acts of address in Li Shangyin's hermetic poems, it is nevertheless reminiscent of them. As in Li Shangyin's "Left Untitled," the poet moves from description to engage the reader. Since Wen Tingyun's song lyrics so often represent the woman longing for her absent beloved, we are tempted to take the "you" as the distant lover. However, we do have the following precedent (cited in an earlier chapter) for a man being ignorant of a woman's dreams:

李商隱, 閨情

Li Shangyin, Sentiments of the Women's Quarters[87]

紅露花房白蜜脾	Flower buds with red dew, white nectar for honey,
黃蜂紫蝶兩參差	yellow bee, purple butterfly, both flitting about.
春窗一覺風流夢	By the spring window she wakes from a dream of passion,
卻是同袍不得知	but he who shares the long gown with her cannot know.

Here it may be the man sleeping by her side who cannot know her dreams—which are dreams of another—or perhaps the distant beloved who doesn't know her dreams. We have the same moment—the closing invocation of the male who cannot know the woman's dreams—in Wen Tingyun's lyric. Is this the male nearby or the distant male? Either possibility could be realized in performance by a look, a stress, or a pause in the singing.

Wen Tingyun's song lyrics marked the beginning of the history of a genre that had not yet come into being. Rather than reading them in the context of their future, it would be best to read them in the context of poetry, both contemporary and dating from the recent past. Although it is true that the new form wrought a transformation on this contemporary poetic "material," in this new form many elements of mid-ninth-century poetry lived on into the succeeding centuries.

---

87. 29306; *Jijie* 1839; Ye (1985) 237.

Conclusion

With the deaths of Du Mu, Li Shangyin, and Wen Tingyun, an era had ended. Nevertheless, the "Late Tang" was far from over. Depending on how one chooses to define it, it would continue for at least another half century after 860—and perhaps even a century and a half beyond that. The range of poetic possibilities opened up in our thirty-five-year span, however, by and large set the limits for the rest of the Late Tang. There were excellent poets and memorable poems written afterward, but there were no more strong poetic personalities to leave a lasting mark on the poetry of the next millennium. Pi Rixiu and Lu Guimeng, who began working at the end of the period covered in this study, are partial exceptions, but they were never commanding presences in the later view of Tang poetry on the level of Du, Li, and Wen, or even of Jia Dao and Xu Hun. Yu Xuanji's small corpus of poetry makes her one of the two most striking women poets of the dynasty, but hers is a strong personality working within a shared style. Sikong Tu was important, but he is remembered primarily as a critic (in large measure for a work that may well be a Ming forgery). Han Wo is remembered for his erotic vignettes, but he was perhaps the most talented follower of Du Fu in the period. Du Xunhe enjoyed a revival of interest in the mid-twentieth century for his vernacularization of poetry. Wei Zhuang, who lived on to become a grand old man of letters in the Former Shu Kingdom, was considered important in the early history of the song lyric, and in poetry known for his narrative on Huang Chao's sack of Chang'an entitled "Ballad of the Lady of Qin" 秦婦吟, many versions of which were recovered in the Dunhuang manuscripts. Leaving aside the question of whether or not the judgment of history was fair, despite the fact that there were many other worthy poets active in this period, none achieved the stature of the central figures in the first phase of the Late Tang.

However we choose to label this period spanning the mid-820s to 860, the poetry produced had a lasting impact extending down through the history of Chinese classical poetry. Despite the fact that this period often met with disapproval in accounts of the history of Tang poetry, its major poets remained prominent. Although Bai Juyi belongs more to the Mid-Tang, his work was a large presence, albeit often a negative one during this period. He represented one possibility for classical poetry that would ever remain in the background, continually resurfacing among poets who by instinct and their historical moment reacted against the poetic "high style." Bai Juyi played received poetic form against vernacular utterance that resisted the form. Classical poetry could indeed sound almost like someone talking, the "familiar and common" that Du Mu rejected. Resistance to that possibility helped inspire many variations on poetic density or formal dignity.

For Bai Juyi poetic "form" simply meant line length, rhyme, and proper balance of tones, along with a lucidly linear exposition. As he wrote of the monk Daozong's Buddhist didactic verse, within those minimal restrictions of form poetry can move freely and escape the impression of the "written word" (*wenzi*). For Jia Dao and the poets of his circle "form" meant something very different: it was a controlled style that marked artfulness and its difference from natural language, set within a stylized pattern of exposition. Their contribution to the Chinese poetic tradition was no less significant than Bai Juyi's. There had been earlier poets who excelled in craft, but Jia Dao and his group associated excellence in poetic craft with the expenditure of time and effort. They did not often speak of "talent," that inborn gift that effortlessly bends the rules. Rather, theirs was a poetry that called for passionate devotion—and there is a fine line between passionate devotion and simple hard work. In effect, they offered a model for poetic excellence that could be learned, an aesthetic social mobility by means of which marginal figures could, through their own efforts, surpass those who had grown up in a community of elite poetic practice or those who claimed to compose spontaneously as a result of sheer talent. It is not surprising that so many poets in the Jia Dao group came from minor gentry, with little or no history of participation in the central government bureaucracy. It should also come as no surprise that their poetry became so important in later poetic pedagogy and served as a model for the urban poets of the Southern Song who worked outside or on the margin of the government bureaucracy.

Du Mu, by contrast, has the charm of downward social mobility, with all the learning and fluency that resulted from growing up in one of the most distinguished families of the age. He was deeply engaged in the problems of the empire and was often a politically committed poet—even though he was never entirely taken seriously. One strain of poetic criticism in the late imperial period—more fully developed when Chinese literature became academic in the twentieth century—always reminds readers of Du Mu's seriousness. Such reminders are a sign that this was not the version of Du Mu that readers first knew and loved. That popular Du Mu was the poet of the quatrain and a body of melancholy *fengliu* poetry celebrating the pleasures of the world, often tinged with nostalgia. This was the Du Mu alluded to in later poetry and song lyric and represented in drama. His was not a significant poetics, unlike that of Bai Juyi or Jia Dao; but it was an immensely seductive sensibility with an appeal that has persisted down to the present. Du Mu was in many ways the belated double of Li Bai, a poet of panache, but one who turned retrospective and elegiac.

Since Li Shangyin was by far the most complex of the Late Tang poets, his legacy was equally so. On the simplest level, echoes of his poetry became common in erotic poetry, particularly in song lyric. But his poetics of concealed reference continued to tease the tradition, blurring the distinction between public engagement and private passion. Although his style was often imitated, beyond that the figural reading of his work encouraged a tendency—already present in the tradition—to discover political seriousness behind ostensibly private themes. The exegetical tradition on Li Shangyin's poetry, which began in earnest in the mid-seventeenth century, was something quite distinct from the exegesis of other poets. There were disagreements over the interpretation of other poets, but nowhere was radical disagreement as pervasive as it was in the interpretation of Li Shangyin's poetry—which continues to the present. Even some of the earliest comments on Li Shangyin's poetry in the Song already show the capacity of his work to generate conflicting interpretations. In this respect Li Shangyin represented a new kind of poetry, one that could be interpreted but never finally understood. In the centuries to come Chinese poetry would back away from and return to this margin of figural difficulty many times.

The ninth century was also the final and most fully developed phase of manuscript culture in China. Although manuscript transmission of texts would continue to play an important role in Chinese literature until the late Qing, from the end of the tenth century onward the printed book assumed an increasingly dominant role in literary dissemination. At the very beginning of the period of our study, in 824, Yuan Zhen added a famous note to his "Preface to Bai Juyi's *Changqing Collection*" 白氏長慶集序, apparently indicating that his and Bai Juyi's poems were being printed and sold in Yangzhou and Yuezhou.[1] If this interpretation of the passage is correct, it would not suggest books of poetry but most likely broadside sheets similar to Buddhist devotional printing during the era. This ninth-century interest in literary reproduction and dissemination, which we discussed in relation to Bai Juyi and to Li Shangyin's "Han Yu's Stele," culminated in the late second or third decade of the tenth century when Tanyu 曇域, the disciple of the poet-monk Guanxiu 貫休, posthumously printed the poetry collection of his master in Chengdu. In the course of the following century and a half manuscript reproduction would become increasingly restricted to rare scholarly texts and the private circulation of works during a poet's lifetime.

At the end of the tenth and the beginning of the eleventh centuries, a new kind of literary scholar emerged, who tried to gather together and reconcile the scattered remains of the Tang manuscript tradition that had survived the fires and destruction of the end of the Tang and the Five Dynasties. It is not surprising that the works of ninth- and early tenth-century writers were the best preserved. Although their editorial work underwent subsequent losses, changes, and recoveries, we can still find some of the traces of that textual world. Behind those traces we glimpse a new figure: the person who defines himself as a "poet," who works at his art, and who seeks to control the product of that art: not just poems but a book of poetry.

---

1. *Yuan Zhen ji* (Beijing: Zhonghua shuju, 1982), 555.

Reference Matter

Works Cited

Short References for Works Commonly Cited

Chen Bohai   Chen Bohai 陳伯海, ed. *Tangshi huiping* 唐詩彙評. 3 vols. Hangzhou: Zhejiang jiaoyu chubanshe, 1995.

Chen Tiemin   Chen Tiemin 陳鐵民. *Wang Wei ji jiaozhu* 王維集校注. Beijing: Zhonghua shuju, 1997.

Du Xiaoqin   Du Xiaoqin 杜曉勤. *Sui Tang Wudai wenxue yanjiu* 隋唐五代文學研究. 2 vols. Beijing: Beijing chubanshe, 2001.

Fanchuan wenji   Du Mu 杜牧. *Fanchuan wenji* 樊川文集. Shanghai: Shanghai guji chubanshe, 1978.

Fang Hui   Li Qingjia 李慶甲, ed. *Yinkui lüsui huiping* 瀛奎律髓彙評. 3 vols. Shanghai: Shanghai guji chubanshe, 1986.

Feng   Feng Jiwu 馮集梧. *Fanchuan shi jizhu* 樊川詩集注. Shanghai: Shanghai guji chubanshe, 1978.

Fu (1987)   Fu Xuancong 傅璇琮, ed. *Tang caizi zhuan jiaojian* 唐才子傳校箋. 4 + 1 vols. Beijing: Zhonghua shuju, 1987–90.

Fu (1996)   Fu Xuancong 傅璇琮, ed. *Tangren xuan Tangshi xinbian* 唐人選唐詩新編. Xi'an: Shaanxi renmin chubanshe, 1996.

Fu (1998)   Fu Xuancong 傅璇琮, ed. *Tang Wudai wenxue biannian shi* 唐五代文學編年史. 4 vols. Shenyang: Liaohai chubanshe, 1998.

Hua Chenzhi   Hua Chenzhi 華忱之. *Meng Jiao shiji jiaozhu* 孟郊詩集校注. With notes by Yu Xuecai 喻學才. Beijing: Renmin wenxue chubanshe, 1995.

James Liu   Liu, James J. Y. *The Poetry of Li Shangyin*. Chicago: University of Chicago Press, 1969.

Jiang   Jiang Weisong 蔣維崧 et al. *Liu Yuxi shiji biannian jianzhu* 劉禹錫詩集編年箋注. Ji'nan: Shandong daxue chubanshe, 1997.

Jiang Congping	Jiang Congping 江聰平. *Xu Hun shi jiaozhu* 許渾詩校注. Taibei: Taiwan Zhonghua shuju, 1973.
Jijie	Liu Xuekai 劉學鍇 and Yu Shucheng 余恕誠. *Li Shangyin shige jijie* 李商隱詩歌集解. 5 vols. Beijing: Zhonghua shuju, 1988.
Jiu Tang shu	*Jiu Tangshu* 舊唐書. Beijing: Zhonghua shuju, 1975.
Li Dongsheng	Li Dongsheng 李冬生. *Zhang Ji ji zhu* 張籍集注. Hefei: Huangshan shushe, 1988.
Li Jiayan	Li Jiayan 李嘉言. *Changjiang ji xinjiao* 長江集新校. Shanghai: Shanghai guji, 1983.
Liu Xuekai (2001)	Liu Xuekai 劉學鍇, et al. *Li Shangyin ziliao huibian* 李商隱資料彙編. 2 vols. Beijing: Zhonghua shuju, 2001.
Liu Yan	Liu Yan 劉衍. *Yao He shiji jiaokao* 姚合詩集校考. Changsha: Yuelin shushe, 1997.
Lu Qinli	Lu Qinli 逯欽立. *Xian-Qin Han Wei Jin Nanbeichao shi*. Beijing: Zhonghua shuju, 1983.
Luo	Luo Shijin 羅時進. *Dingmao ji jianzheng* 丁卯集箋證. Nanchang: Jiangxi renmin chubanshe, 1998.
Owen (1998)	Owen, Stephen. *The End of the Chinese "Middle Ages": Essays in Mid-Tang Literary Culture*. Stanford: Stanford University Press, 1998.
Qi	Qi Wenbang 齊文榜. *Jia Dao ji jiaozhu* 賈島集校注. Beijing: Renmin wenxue chubanshe, 2001.
Qian Zhonglian	Qian Zhonglian 錢仲聯. *Han Changli shi xinian jishi* 韓昌黎詩系年集釋. Shanghai: Shanghai guji chubanshe, 1984.
Qiu	Qiu Zhaoao 仇兆鰲. *Du shi xiangzhu* 杜詩詳注. Beijing: Zhonghua shuju, 1973.
QSc	Tang Guizhang 唐圭璋. *Quan Song ci* 全宋詞. Beijing: Zhonghua shuju, 1965.
QTw	*Quan Tang wen* 全唐文. Rpt. Beijing: Zhonghua shuju, 1983.
Qu (1980)	Qu Tuiyuan 瞿蛻園 and Zhu Jincheng 朱金城. *Li Bai ji jiaozhu* 李白集校注. Shanghai: Shanghai guji chubanshe, 1980.
Qu (1989)	Qu Tuiyuan 瞿蛻園. *Liu Yuxi ji jianzheng* 劉禹錫集箋證. Shanghai: Shanghai guji chubanshe, 1989.
Rouzer	Rouzer, Paul. *Writing Another's Dream: The Poetry of Wen Tingyun*. Stanford: Stanford University Press, 1993.
Tan Youxue	Tan Youxue 譚優學. *Zhao Gu shi zhu* 趙嘏詩注. Shanghai: Shanghai guji chubanshe, 1985.

Tang yulin	Wang Dang 王讜. *Tang yulin jiaozheng* 唐語林校證. Beijing: Zhonghua shuju, 1987.
Tang zhiyan	Wang Dingbao 王定保. *Tang zhiyan* 唐摭言. Shanghai: Zhonghua shuju, 1959.
Tong Peiji	Tong Peiji 佟培基. *Quan Tang shi chongchu wushou kao* 全唐詩重出誤收考. Xi'an: Shaanxi renmin, 1996.
Wang Guo'an	Wang Guo'an 王國安. *Liu Zongyuan shi jianshi* 柳宗元詩箋釋. Shanghai: Shanghai guji chubanshe, 1993.
Wang Meng	Wang Meng 王蒙 and Liu Xuekai 劉學鍇, ed. *Li Shangyin yanjiu lunji 1949–1997* 李商隱研究論集 1949–1997. Guilin: Guangxi shifan daxue chubanshe, 1998.
Wang Xuanbo	Wang Xuanbo 王旋伯. *Li Shen shi zhu* 李紳詩注. Shanghai: Shanghai guji chubanshe, 1985.
Wang Zhongyong	Wang Zhongyong 王仲鏞. *Tangshi jishi jiaojian* 唐詩紀事校箋. Chengdu: Ba Shu shudian, 1989.
Wyyh	*Wenyuan yinghua* 文苑英華. Beijing: Zhonghua shuju, 1966.
Xin Tang shu	*Xin Tangshu* 新唐書. Beijing: Zhonghua shuju, 1975.
Xu Jun	Xu Jun 徐俊. *Dunhuang shiji canjuan jikao* 敦煌詩集殘卷輯考. Beijing: Zhonghua shuju, 2000.
Yan Jinxiong	Yan Jinxiong 顏進雄. *Tangdai youxian shi yanjiu* 唐代遊仙詩研究. Taibei: Wenjin chubanshe, 1996.
Yan Shoucheng	Yan Shoucheng 嚴壽澂. *Zhang Hu shiji* 張祜詩集. Nanchang: Jiangxi renmin chubanshe, 1983.
Yang Chunqiu	Yang Chunqiu 羊春秋. *Li Qunyu shiji* 李群玉詩集. Changsha: Yuelu, 1987.
Yang Jun	Yang Jun 楊軍 and Ge Chunyuan 戈春源. *Ma Dai shi zhu* 馬戴詩注. Shanghai: Shanghai guji chubanshe, 1987.
Ye (1959)	Ye Congqi 葉葱奇. *Li He shi ji* 李賀詩集. Beijing: Renmin wenxue, 1959.
Ye (1985)	Ye Congqi 葉葱奇. *Li Shangyin shiji shuzhu* 李商隱詩集疏注. Beijing: Renmin wenxue chubanshe, 1985.
Yuan Feng	Yuan Feng 元鋒 and Yan Zhao 煙照. *Duan Chengshi shiwen jizhu* 段成式詩文輯注. Ji'nan: Ji'nan chubanshe, 1994.
Zeng	Zeng Yi 曾益. *Wen Feiqing shiji jianzhu* 溫飛卿詩集箋注. Shanghai: Shanghai guji chubanshe, 1980. Supplements by Gu Yuxian 顧予咸 (jinshi 1647) and Gu Sili 顧嗣立 (jinshi 1712); Gu Sili's version, building on his father's draft, was first published in 1697.
Zhang Yanjin	Zhang Yanjin 張燕瑾 and Lü Weifen 呂薇芬. *Ershishiji Zhongguo wenxue yanjiu: Sui Tang Wudai wenxue yanjiu*

二十世紀中國文學研究: 隋唐五代文學研究. 2 vols. Beijing: Beijing chubanshe, 2001.

Zheng Zaiying   Zheng Zaiying 鄭在瀛. *Li Shangyin shiji jinzhu* 李商隱詩集今注. Wuhan: Wuhan daxue chubanshe, 2001.

Zhou   Zhou Zhenfu 周振甫. *Li Shangyin xuan ji* 李商隱選集. Shanghai: Shanghai guji chubanshe, 1986.

Zhou Xiaotian   Zhou Xiaotian 周嘯天 and Zhang Xiaomin 張效民. *Yong Tao shi zhu* 雍陶詩注. Shanghai: Shanghai guji, 1988.

Zhou Xunchu   Zhou Xunchu 周勛初, ed. *Tangren yishi huibian* 唐人軼事彙編. 4 vols. Shanghai: Shanghai guji chubanshe, 1994.

Zhu   Zhu Jincheng 朱金城. *Bo Juyi ji jianjiao* 白居易集箋校. 6 vols. Shanghai: Shanghai guji, 1988.

Zhu Bilian   Zhu Bilian 朱碧蓮. *Du Mu xuanji* 杜牧選集. Shanghai: Shanghai guji chubanshe, 1995.

Zizhi tongjian   Sima Guang 司馬光. *Zizhi tongjian* 資治通鑑. Beijing: Zhonghua shuju, 1995.

Other Works Cited

Ashmore, Robert. "Hearing Things: Performance and Lyric Imagination in Chinese Literature of the Early Ninth Century." Ph.D. diss., Harvard University, 1997.

Cao Zhongfu 曹中孚. *Wan Tang shiren Du Mu* 晚唐詩人杜牧. Xi'an: Shaanxi renmin chubanshe, 1985.

Cen Zhongmian 岑仲勉. *Tangren hangdi lu* 唐人行第錄. Shanghai: Zhonghua shuju, 1962.

Chen Wanghe 陳王和. *Han Hong shiji jiaozhu* 韓翃詩集校注. Taibei: Wenshizhe chubanshe, 1973.

Chen Xijin 陳熙晉. *Luo Linhai ji jianzhu* 駱臨海集箋注. Shanghai: Shanghai guji chubanshe, 1985.

Chen Yingluan 陳應鸞. *Suihantang shihua jiaojian* 歲寒堂詩話校箋. Chengdu: Ba Shu shushe, 2000.

Chen Youqin 陳友琴. *Bai Juyi shi pingshu huibian* 白居易詩評述匯編. Beijing: Kexue chubanshe, 1958.

Chen Zijian 陳子建. "Du Mu 'Li Changji geshi xu' 'li' yibian" 杜牧李長吉歌詩序理義辯, *Shehui kexue yanjiu* 1988, no. 6.

De Woskin, Kenneth, and J. I. Crump. *In Search of the Supernatural: The Written Record*. Stanford: Stanford University Press, 1996.

Dong Naibin 董乃斌. *Li Shangyin de xinling shijie* 李商隱的心靈世界. Shanghai: Shanghai guji chubanshe, 1992.

Du You 杜佑. *Tong dian* 通典. Beijing: Zhonghua shuju, 1988.

Dudbridge, Glen. *The Lost Books of Medieval China*. London: British Library, 2000.

Fishlen, Michael. "Wine, Poetry and History: Du Mu's 'Pouring Alone in the Prefectural Residence.'" *T'oung Pao* 80 (1994) Fasc. 4–5: 260–97.

Fu Xuancong 傅璇琮, Zhang Chenshi 張忱石, and Xu Yimin 許逸民. *Tang Wudai renwu zhuanji ziliao zonghe suoyin* 唐五代人物傳記資料綜合索引. Beijing: Zhonghua shuju, 1982.

Guo Shaoyu 郭紹虞. *Canglang shihua jiaoshi* 滄浪詩話校釋. Beijing, 1961.

He Lintian 何林天. *Chongding xinjiao Wang Zi'an ji* 重訂新校王子安集. Taiyuan: Shanxi renmin chubanshe, 1990.

Hiraoka Takeo 平崗武夫, Ichihara Kōkichi 市原亨吉, and Imai Kiyoshi 今井清. *Tōdai no shihen* 唐代の詩篇. Tang Civilization Reference Series 11–12. Kyoto: Institute for Humanistic Studies, 1964–65.

Hu Kexian 胡可先. *Du Mu yanjiu conggao* 杜牧研究叢稿. Beijing: Renmin wenxue chubanshe, 1993.

Hu Wentao 胡問濤 and Luo Qin 羅琴. *Wang Changling ji biannian jiaozhu* 王昌齡集編年校注. Chengdu: Ba Shu shushe, 2000.

Hu Yinglin 胡應麟. *Shi sou* 詩籔. Shanghai: Shanghai guji chubanshe, 1979.

Hu Zhonghang 胡中行. "Luelun Jia Dao zai Tangshi fazhanzhong de diwei" 略論賈島在唐詩發展中的地位. *Fudan xuebao* 1983, no. 3.

Hu Zi 胡仔. *Tiaoxi yuyin conghua* 苕溪漁隱叢話. Beijing: Renmin wenxue chubanshe, 1962.

Jia Jinhua 賈晉華. *Tangdai jihui zongji yu shirenqun yanjiu* 唐代集會總集與詩人群研究. Beijing: Beijing daxue chubanshe, 2001.

Jiang Congping 江聰平. *Wei Duanji shi jiaozhu* 韋端己詩校注. Taibei: Taiwan Zhonghua shuju, 1969.

Kong Fanjin 孔范今, ed. *Quan Tang Wudai ci shizhu* 全唐五代詞釋注. 3 vols. Xi'an: Shaanxi renmin chubanshe, 1998.

Kubin, Wolfgang. *Das lyrische Werk des Tu Mu*. Wiesbaden, 1976.

Kung Wei-kai. *Tu Mu (803–852): His Life and Poetry*. San Francisco: Chinese Materials Center, 1990.

Li Guosheng 李國勝. *Wang Changling shi jiaozhu* 王昌齡詩校注. Taibei: Wenshizhe chubanshe, 1973.

Li Lipu 李立朴. *Xu Hun yanjiu* 許渾研究. Guiyang: Guizhou renmin chubanshe, 1994.

Li Shiren 李時人, ed. *Quan Tang Wudai xiaoshuo* 全唐五代小説. Xi'an: Shaanxi renmin chubanshe, 1998.

Li Tingxian 李廷先. *Tangdai Yangzhou shikao* 唐代揚州史考. Yangzhou: Jiangsu guji chubanshe, 1992, 2002.

Li Yi 李誼. *Wei Zhuang ji jiaozhu* 韋莊集校注. Chengdu: Sichuan sheng shehui kexueyuan chubanshe, 1986.

Li Yunyi 李雲逸. *Wang Changling shizhu* 王昌齡詩注. Shanghai: Shanghai guji chubanshe, 1984.

Liang Chaoran 梁超然. "Wan Tang shiren Cao Tang ji qi shige" 晚唐詩人曹唐及其詩歌. *Tangdai wenxue* 1 (1981).

Liao Meiyun 廖美雲. *Tangji yanjiu* 唐伎研究. Taibei: Xuesheng shuju, 1995.

Liu Xuekai 劉學鍇. *Huipingben Li Shangyin shi* 匯評本李商隱詩. Shanghai: Shanghai shehui kexueyuan chubanshe, 2002.

———. *Li Shangyin shige yanjiu* 李商隱詩歌研究. Hefei: Anhui daxue chubanshe, 1998.

Liu Xuekai 劉學鍇 and Yu Shucheng 余恕誠. *Li Shangyin wen biannian jiaozhu* 李商隱文編年校注. 5 vols. Beijing: Zhonghua shuju, 2002.

Mao Lei 毛蕾. *Tangdai Hanlin xueshi* 唐代翰林學士. Beijing: Shehui kexue wenxian chubanshe, 2000.

Miao Yue 繆鉞. *Du Mu zhuan* 杜牧傳. Shijiazhuang: Hebei jiaoyu chubanshe, 1999.

Nugent, Christopher. "The Circulation of Poetry in Tang Dynasty China." Ph.D. diss., Harvard University, 2004. Ann Arbor: UMI, 2004.

Ono Katsutoshi 小野勝年. *Nittō guhō junrei kōki no kenkyū* 入唐求法巡禮行記の研究. Tokyo: Suzuki Research Foundation, 1969. Ennin's diary.

Ouyang Xiu 歐陽修. *Liuyi shihua* 六一詩話. Edited by Zheng Wen 鄭文. Beijing: Renmin wenxue chubanshe, 1983.

Owen, Stephen. "The Difficulty of Pleasure," *Extreme orient / extreme occident* 20 (1998).

———. "Poetry and Its Historical Ground." *Chinese Literature: Essays, Articles, Reviews* (December, 1990): 107–18.

———. "Spending Time on Poetry: The Poetics of Taking Pains." In Olga Lomová, ed., *Recarving the Dragon: Understanding Chinese Poetics*. Prague: Charles University in Prague, 2003.

———. "What Did Liuzhi Hear? The 'Yan Terrace Poems' and the Culture of Romance." *T'ang Studies* 13 (1995): 81–118.

Piliére, Marie-Christine Verniau. "Du Mu: comment rendre justice à l'homme et à l'oeuvre?" *Études Chinoises* 6, no. 2 (Fall 1987): 47–71.

Qing shihua 清詩話. Shanghai: Shanghai guji chubanshe, 1963.

Reischauer, Edwin O. *Ennin's Travels in T'ang China*. New York: Roland Press, 1955.

Ren Bantang 任半塘. *Tang sheng shi* 唐聲詩. Shanghai: Shanghai guji chubanshe, 1982.

Ren Haitian 任海天. *Wan Tang shifeng* 晚唐詩風. Harbin: Heilongjiang jiaoyu chubanshe, 1998.

Rouzer, Paul. *Articulated Ladies: Gender and the Male Community in Early Chinese Texts*. Cambridge: Harvard University Asia Center, 2001.

Schafer, Edward H. *Mirages on the Sea of Time: The Taoist Poetry of Ts'ao T'ang.* Berkeley, 1985.

Shang Wei. "The Prisoner and the Creator: The Self-Image of the Poet in Han Yu and Meng Chiao." *CLEAR* 16 (December 1994): 19–40.

Shields, Anna M. *Crafting a Collection: The Cultural Contexts and Poetic Practice of the Huajian ji* 花間集 *(Collection from Among the Flowers).* Cambridge, Mass.: Harvard University Asia Center, 2006.

———. "Defining Experience: The 'Poems of Seductive Allure' (*yanshi*) of the Mid-Tang Poet Yuan Zhen (779–831)." *Journal of the American Oriental Society* 122, no. 1 (Jan.–March 2002): 61–78.

Tan Youxue 譚優學. "Xu Hun xingnian kao" 許渾行年考. *Tangdai wenxue luncong* 8 (1986): 78–113.

Tian Gengyu 田耕宇. *Tangyin yuyun: wan Tang shi yanjiu* 唐音餘韻: 晚唐詩研究. Chengdu: Ba Shu shushe, 2001.

Wan Jingjun 萬競君. *Cui Hao shi zhu* 崔顥詩注. Shanghai: Shanghai guji chubanshe, 1982.

Wan Man 萬曼. *Tangji xulu* 唐集敘錄. Beijing: Zhonghua shuju, 1980.

Wang Liqi 王利器, ed. *Wenjing mifulun jiaozhu* 文鏡秘府論校注. Beijing: Zhongguo shehuike chubanshe, 1983.

Wang Meng 王蒙. "Hundun de xinling chang—tan Li Shangyin Wuti shi de jiegou" 混沌的心靈場—談李商隱無題詩的結構. *Wenxue yichan* 1995, no. 3.

Wang Xiping 王西平 and Gao Yunguang 高雲光. *Du Mu shimei tansuo* 杜牧詩美探索. Xi'an: Shaanxi renmin chubanshe, 1993.

Wang Ying 王鍈. *Shi ci qu yuci lishi* 詩詞曲語辭例釋. Beijing: Zhonghua shuju, 1986.

Wei Qingzhi 魏慶之. *Shiren yuxie* 詩人玉屑. Shanghai, 1958.

Weng Fanggang 翁方綱. *Shizhou shihua* 石州詩話. Beijing: Renmin wenxue chuanshe, 1981.

Wu Diaogong 吳調公. *Li Shangyin yanjiu* 李商隱研究. Shanghai: Shanghai guji chubanshe, 1982.

Wu Qiming 吳企明. *Tangyin zhiyi lu* 唐音質疑錄. Shanghai: Shanghai guji chubanshe, 1985.

Wu Xiangzhou 吳相洲. *Tangdai geshi yu shige: lun geshi chuanchang zai Tangshi chuangzuozhong de diwei he zuoyong* 唐代歌詩與詩歌: 論歌詩傳唱在唐詩創作中的地位和作用. Beijing: Beijing daxue chubanshe, 2000.

Wu Zaiqing 吳在慶. *Du Mu lun'gao* 杜牧論稿. Fujian: Xiamen daxue chubanshe, 1991.

Xiao Difei 蕭滌非 and Zheng Qingdu 鄭慶篤. *Pizi wensou* 皮子文藪. Shanghai: Shanghai guji chubanshe, 1981.

Xu Peng 徐鵬. *Meng Haoran ji jiaozhu* 孟浩然集校注. Beijing: Renmin wenxue chubanshe, 1989.

Xu Zong 許總. *Tangshi tipailun* 唐詩體派論. Taibei: Wenjin chubanshe, 1994.

Yang, Xiaoshan. *Metamorphosis of the Private Sphere: Gardens and Objects in Tang-Song Poetry.* Cambridge: Harvard University Asia Center, 2003.

Yin Zhanhua 尹佔華. *Lüfu lungao* 律賦論稿. Chengdu: Ba Shushushe, 2001.

Yu Xianhao 郁賢皓. *Li Bai xuanji* 李白選集. Shanghai: Shanghai guji, 1990.

Yuan Zhen ji 元稹集. Beijing: Zhonghua shuju, 1982.

Zha Pingqiu 查屏球. *Tangxue yu Tangshi: Zhong Wan Tang shifeng de yizhong wenhua kaocha* 唐學與唐詩: 中晚唐詩風的一種文化考察. Beijing: Shangwu yinshuguan, 2000.

Zhan Ying 詹鍈. *Li Bai quanji jiaozhu huishi jiping* 李白全集校注彙釋集評. Tianjin: Baihua wenyi chubanshe, 1996.

Zhang Hongsheng 張宏生. "Yao Jia shipai de jienei liubian he jiewai yuxiang" 姚賈詩派的界內流變和界外餘響. *Wenxue pinglun* 1995, no. 2.

Zhou Xifu 周錫韋/复. *Du Mu shixuan* 杜牧詩選. Hong Kong: Sanlian shuju, 1980.

Zhou Yigan 周義敢. *Zhang Ji shizhu* 張繼詩注. Shanghai: Shanghai guji chubanshe, 1987.

Zhou Zuzhuan 周祖譔. *Sui Tang Wudai wenlun xuan* 隋唐五代文論選. Beijing: Renmin wenxue chubanshe, 1990.

Zhu Bilian 朱碧蓮. *Du Mu xuanji* 杜牧選集. Shanghai: Shanghai guji chubanshe, 1995.

———. "Qianshoushi qing wanhuhou—ping Zhang Hu de shi" 千首詩輕萬戶侯—評張祜的詩. *Wenxue yichan zengkan* 16 (1983): 59–72.

Zhu Jincheng 朱金城. *Bo Juyi nianpu* 白居易年譜. Shanghai: Shanghai guji chubanshe, 1982.

Zhu Shangshu 祝尚書. *Lu Sidao ji jiaozhu* 盧思道集校注. Chengdu: Ba Shu shushe, 2001.

Zuo Gui 左圭. *Baichuan xuehai* 百川學海. Photorpt. Kyoto: Chūbun, 1979.

Index

Harvard East Asian Monographs
(*out-of-print)

Harvard East Asian Monographs

48. Paul Richard Bohr, *Famine and the Missionary: Timothy Richard as Relief Administrator and Advocate of National Reform*

49. Endymion Wilkinson, *The History of Imperial China: A Research Guide*

50. Britten Dean, *China and Great Britain: The Diplomacy of Commercial Relations, 1860–1864*

51. Ellsworth C. Carlson, *The Foochow Missionaries, 1847–1880*

52. Yeh-chien Wang, *An Estimate of the Land-Tax Collection in China, 1753 and 1908*

53. Richard M. Pfeffer, *Understanding Business Contracts in China, 1949–1963*

*54. Han-sheng Chuan and Richard Kraus, *Mid-Ching Rice Markets and Trade: An Essay in Price History*

55. Ranbir Vohra, *Lao She and the Chinese Revolution*

56. Liang-lin Hsiao, *China's Foreign Trade Statistics, 1864–1949*

*57. Lee-hsia Hsu Ting, *Government Control of the Press in Modern China, 1900–1949*

*58. Edward W. Wagner, *The Literati Purges: Political Conflict in Early Yi Korea*

*59. Joungwon A. Kim, *Divided Korea: The Politics of Development, 1945–1972*

60. Noriko Kamachi, John K. Fairbank, and Chūzō Ichiko, *Japanese Studies of Modern China Since 1953: A Bibliographical Guide to Historical and Social-Science Research on the Nineteenth and Twentieth Centuries, Supplementary Volume for 1953–1969*

61. Donald A. Gibbs and Yun-chen Li, *A Bibliography of Studies and Translations of Modern Chinese Literature, 1918–1942*

62. Robert H. Silin, *Leadership and Values: The Organization of Large-Scale Taiwanese Enterprises*

63. David Pong, *A Critical Guide to the Kwangtung Provincial Archives Deposited at the Public Record Office of London*

*64. Fred W. Drake, *China Charts the World: Hsu Chi-yü and His Geography of 1848*

*65. William A. Brown and Urgrunge Onon, translators and annotators, *History of the Mongolian People's Republic*

66. Edward L. Farmer, *Early Ming Government: The Evolution of Dual Capitals*

*67. Ralph C. Croizier, *Koxinga and Chinese Nationalism: History, Myth, and the Hero*

*68. William J. Tyler, tr., *The Psychological World of Natsume Sōseki,* by Doi Takeo

69. Eric Widmer, *The Russian Ecclesiastical Mission in Peking During the Eighteenth Century*

*70. Charlton M. Lewis, *Prologue to the Chinese Revolution: The Transformation of Ideas and Institutions in Hunan Province, 1891–1907*

71. Preston Torbert, *The Ching Imperial Household Department: A Study of Its Organization and Principal Functions, 1662–1796*

72. Paul A. Cohen and John E. Schrecker, eds., *Reform in Nineteenth-Century China*

73. Jon Sigurdson, *Rural Industrialism in China*

74. Kang Chao, *The Development of Cotton Textile Production in China*

203. Robert S. Ross and Jiang Changbin, eds., *Re-examining the Cold War: U.S.-China Diplomacy, 1954–1973*

204. Guanhua Wang, *In Search of Justice: The 1905–1906 Chinese Anti-American Boycott*

205. David Schaberg, *A Patterned Past: Form and Thought in Early Chinese Historiography*

206. Christine Yano, *Tears of Longing: Nostalgia and the Nation in Japanese Popular Song*

207. Milena Doležebvá-Velingerová and Oldřich Král, with Graham Sanders, eds., *The Appropriation of Cultural Capital: China's May Fourth Project*

208. Robert N. Huey, *The Making of 'Shinkokinshū'*

209. Lee Butler, *Emperor and Aristocracy in Japan, 1467–1680: Resilience and Renewal*

210. Suzanne Ogden, *Inklings of Democracy in China*

211. Kenneth J. Ruoff, *The People's Emperor: Democracy and the Japanese Monarchy, 1945–1995*

212. Haun Saussy, *Great Walls of Discourse and Other Adventures in Cultural China*

213. Aviad E. Raz, *Emotions at Work: Normative Control, Organizations, and Culture in Japan and America*

214. Rebecca E. Karl and Peter Zarrow, eds., *Rethinking the 1898 Reform Period: Political and Cultural Change in Late Qing China*

215. Kevin O'Rourke, *The Book of Korean Shijo*

216. Ezra F. Vogel, ed., *The Golden Age of the U.S.-China-Japan Triangle, 1972–1989*

217. Thomas A Wilson, ed., *On Sacred Grounds: Culture, Society, Politics, and the Formation of the Cult of Confucius*

218. Donald S. Sutton, *Steps of Perfection: Exorcistic Performers and Chinese Religion in Twentieth-Century Taiwan*

219. Daqing Yang, *Technology of Empire: Telecommunications and Japanese Expansionism, 1895–1945*

220. Qianshen Bai, *Fu Shan's World: The Transformation of Chinese Calligraphy in the Seventeenth Century*

221. Paul Jakov Smith and Richard von Glahn, eds., *The Song-Yuan-Ming Transition in Chinese History*

222. Rania Huntington, *Alien Kind: Foxes and Late Imperial Chinese Narrative*

223. Jordan Sand, *House and Home in Modern Japan: Architecture, Domestic Space, and Bourgeois Culture, 1880–1930*

224. Karl Gerth, *China Made: Consumer Culture and the Creation of the Nation*

225. Xiaoshan Yang, *Metamorphosis of the Private Sphere: Gardens and Objects in Tang-Song Poetry*

226. Barbara Mittler, *A Newspaper for China? Power, Identity, and Change in Shanghai's News Media, 1872–1912*

227. Joyce A. Madancy, *The Troublesome Legacy of Commissioner Lin: The Opium Trade and Opium Suppression in Fujian Province, 1820s to 1920s*